The prolific writer Boris Sokolov – author of biographies of Georgii Zhukov and others – returns with a new book on Rodion Yakovlevich Malinovskii (1898-1967): a Marshal of the Soviet Union and former Defence Minister, who like so many of those who made their name during the Great Patriotic War, joined the czarist army at the outbreak of the First World War. Unlike the others, however, his service took him to France as a member of the Russian Legion – a move designed to show Russia's support for its French ally in the struggle against the Germans on the Western Front. Despite the Bolshevik coup and Soviet Russia's withdrawal from the war, Malinovskii elected to remain in France and serve with the French Army until the Armistice – after which he made his way back to Russia, where he joined the Red Army in the waning days of the Civil War. The young Malinovskii chose to remain in the army and rose steadily through its ranks. He was later sent to Spain as a military advisor to the Spanish Republic during that country's Civil War. This fortuitous posting not only allowed Malinovskii to gain valuable combat experience, but also kept him out of the country at a time when Stalin's military purge was gutting the armed forces. However, it is Malinovskii's service during the Great Patriotic War that constitutes the heart of this book. Sokolov traces his subject's rise from corps to army commander, and finally to the command of various fronts. During 1943-1944 the forces under Malinovskii's command played a major role in expelling the Germans from the Donets Basin, Southern Ukraine, Romania, Hungary, Austria and Czechoslovakia. Following the defeat of Germany, Malinovskii was assigned to command the main front in the brief war against Japan and remained as Commander-in-Chief of Soviet forces in the Far East for several years. He was summoned back to Moscow as Deputy Defence Minister and later took an active part in the removal of his boss, Georgii Zhukov, whom he replaced in 1957. It was under his decade-long tenure that the Soviet Armed Forces made the transition to a truly modern force – and changed the country's status from that of a regional power to superpower.

MARSHAL MALINOVSKII: HERO OF THE SOVIET UNION

Architect of the Modern Soviet Army

Boris Sokolov

Translated and Edited by Richard W. Harrison

Helion & Company

Published in cooperation with the Association of the United States Army

Helion & Company Limited
26 Willow Road
Solihull
West Midlands
B91 1UE
England
Tel. 0121 705 3393
Fax 0121 711 4075
Email: info@helion.co.uk
Website: www.helion.co.uk
Twitter: @helionbooks
Visit our blog http://blog.helion.co.uk/

Published by Helion & Company 2017, in cooperation with the Association of the United States Army 2017
Designed and typeset by Mach 3 Solutions Ltd (www.mach3solutions.co.uk)
Cover designed by Paul Hewitt, Battlefield Design (www.battlefield-design.co.uk)
Printed by Short Run Press, Exeter, Devon

Text © Boris Sokolov 2017. Translation by Richard W. Harrison © the Association of the United States Army 2017.
Photographs
Maps drawn by George Anderson © Helion & Company Limited 2017.

ISBN 978-1-910777-83-1

British Library Cataloguing-in-Publication Data.
A catalogue record for this book is available from the British Library.

For details of other military history titles published by Helion & Company Limited contact the above address, or visit our website: http://www.helion.co.uk.

We always welcome receiving book proposals from prospective authors.

Contents

List of Photographs

List of Maps

Translator's Note

The book contains a number of terms that may not be readily understandable to the casual reader in military history. Therefore, I have adopted a number of conventions designed to ease this task. For example, a *front* is a Soviet wartime military organization roughly corresponding to an American army group. Throughout the narrative the reader will encounter such names as the Second Ukrainian Front. To avoid confusion with the more commonly understood meaning of the term front (i.e., the front line); italics will be used to denote an unnamed *front*. Similar German formations (i.e., Army Group South) are also spelled out in full.

I have chosen to designate Russian/Soviet armies using the shortened form (i.e., 46th Army). German and satellite armies, on the other hand, are spelled out in full (i.e., German Sixth Army, Hungarian Third Army). In the same vein, Soviet corps are designated by Arabic numerals (75th Rifle Corps), while German units are denoted by Roman numerals (e.g., IX SS Army Corps). Smaller units (divisions, brigades, etc.) on both sides are denoted by Arabic numerals only (110th Guards Rifle Division, 76th Infantry Division, etc.).

Given the large number of units involved in the operation, I have adopted certain other conventions in order to better distinguish them. For example, Soviet armored units are called tank corps, brigades, etc., while the corresponding German and satellite units are denoted by the popular term *panzer*. Likewise, Soviet infantry units are designated by the term rifle, while the corresponding German and satellite units are simply referred to as infantry.

The work subscribes to no particular transliteration scheme, because no entirely satisfactory one exists. I have adopted a mixed system that uses the Latin letters ya and yu to denote their Cyrillic counterparts, as opposed to the ia and iu employed by the Library of Congress, which tends to distort proper pronunciation. Conversely, I have retained the Library of Congress's ii ending (i.e., Malinovskii), as opposed to the commonly-used y ending. I have also retained the apostrophe to denote the Cyrillic soft sign.

The author also refers to a number of people and events in Russian-Soviet history that may not be familiar to the non-specialist reader. In such cases, these terms are explained in greater detail in editor's notes. The author also left a number of asides throughout the text, which are designated by parentheses, with his initials, B.S., at the end.

Introduction

Rodion Yakovlevich Malinovskii has not been very fortunate in the way of biographies and post-humous fame. Today he is much less known to the broad public than Stalin's marshals of the first rank—Zhukov, Rokossovskii, Konev, and Vasilevskii. Nonetheless, during the Soviet period Malinovskii was minister of defense for almost ten years, serving only less time at this post than Voroshilov. However, it was precisely during his tenure that the Soviet army acquired that modern look that it maintained until the very end in 1991. One can probably say that of all the military establishment's leaders it was precisely Malinovskii who made the greatest contribution to the building of the Soviet armed forces during the postwar period. Rodion Yakovlevich also enjoyed glorious victories in the Great Patriotic War, although he also knew painful defeats, the most well known of which was his forces' abandonment of Rostov-on-Don and Novocherkassk in July 1942, which brought about Stalin's menacing Order No. 227. But absolutely all of the Soviet generals and marshals suffered defeats. After all, among Malinovskii's victories was the Iasi—Kishinev operation, the first successful encirclement and elimination of a major enemy group of forces since Stalingrad, the number of which exceeded 200,000 men. Soviet forces did not carry out a more successful encirclement operation than the Iasi—Kishinev "Cannae"[1] during the Great Patriotic War. However, this victory remained in the shadows over recent decades, in as much as the "main" marshals of victory—Zhukov, Rokossovskii and Konev did not take part in its preparation or conduct. However, Marshal Malinovskii had no less important victories to his credit. In December 1942 the 2nd Guards Army, under his command, launched a decisive attack against the enemy's Kotel'nikovo group of forces and thus excluded the possibility of the encircled German Sixth Army's breakthrough out of Stalingrad. During the brief Soviet-Japanese War Rodion Yakovlevich commanded the Trans-Baikal Front, which thanks to its unique passage over the Great Khingan Range launched a decisive attack against the Kwantung Army.

However, all of Malinovskii's achievements during the last decades have remained in the shadow of the developing cult in society of Marshal Zhukov, who has become the chief marshal of victory. Without a doubt, Georgii Konstantinovich's contribution to victory, in his capacity as a *Stavka* representative and *front* commander, in charge of the most numerous Soviet groups of forces, is more than substantial. However, the losses which Soviet forces under his command suffered were the greatest, in comparison to those that the troops suffered under the command of other marshals, and the correlation of losses of Zhukov's forces with German losses is the least favorable for the Red Army. In this regard, one can say that Malinovskii was lucky. For a significant part of the war, the *fronts* under his command fought against the armies of Germany's allies—Romania and Hungary—which were significantly inferior to the Wehrmacht as regards combat capability. Thus the correlation of losses was more favorable for Malinovskii's forces compared to those Soviet *front*s which had to fight exclusively against the Germans. It is also worth noting that, in any case, in his memoirs Khrushchev rated Malinovskii as a commander, at least higher than Konev,

---

1   Editor's note. The Battle of Cannae was fought on 2 August 216 BC in southeastern Italy during the Second Punic War between Rome and Carthage. At Cannae the Carthaginian forces under Hannibal defeated the Romans with a double envelopment. This has come to be seen as the apotheosis of the encirclement battle.

although at that moment it was unlikely that he had warm feelings for Rodion Yakovlevich. After all, Malinovskii played an important role in overthrowing "dear Nikita Sergeevich."

All of Malinovskii's life looks like a real adventure novel. There is the mystery of his birth, for no one knew who his father was. Then there is his three-year sojourn in France as part of the Russian Expeditionary Corps during the First World War. Here Russian brigades fought against the Germans as part of the French army. Malinovskii was the only one of the Soviet marshals who had experience on the Western Front during the First World War, where the concentration of forces, particularly in artillery, on both sides was several times greater than on the Eastern Front. And then there were the years in Spain and participation in the civil war on the side of the Spanish Republicans. Rodion Yakovlevich was the only one of the Soviet marshals who could more or less fluently express himself in two languages—French and Spanish. He became famous for victories in the Great Patriotic and Soviet-Japanese wars. Following the war, Malinovskii played an active role in removing Marshal Zhukov from the post of minister of defense and Nikita Sergeevich Khrushchev from the post of first secretary of the Central Committee of the CPSU[2] and head of the Council of Ministers. Rodion Yakovlevich was the first of the postwar ministers of defense to carry out a true restructuring of the Soviet armed forces, emphasizing missile and nuclear weapons and the development of modern detection and guidance equipment.

As the journalist Yevgenii Zhirnov rightly wrote, "Marshal Malinovskii always stood out among Soviet military leaders; chiefly for his real, and not feigned, concern for the soldiers and level of operational planning."

Naturally, Malinovskii was a member of the CPSU (otherwise, he could not be a marshal), and in his public addresses he often spoke about the importance of party-political work among the troops, studiously citing the classics of Marxism-Leninism, the addresses of party leaders, and the decisions of party congresses, etc. However, deep down the marshal always remained a Russian and Ukrainian patriot and the greatest love of his life was the army. Despite the fact that Malinovskii luckily avoided any repressions, many circumstances of his biography gave rise to suspicions among the security organs. We have his lengthy stays overseas—in France and Spain—plus his ability to speak two foreign languages. Soviet leaders, not without reason, feared that the experience of life in Western Europe would not incline him to sympathize with the USSR. Malinovskii and Rokossovskii were the only Soviet marshals of that time who never swore and who never laid a hand on their subordinates (although several times Rodion Yakovlevich had to hint to his equals or superiors in rank and position that he might resort to force if he were insulted). This also aroused a certain wariness in high places, although both marshals enjoyed the unstinting love of their subordinates. As is known, Stalin encouraged his generals to "punch out" their subordinates, in order to rouse them to carry out the assigned task at any cost. Generals and marshals who didn't curse and fight aroused his definite suspicions as carriers of "moral holdovers" from the past. The circumstances under which Malinovskii joined the Red Army (did he serve with the Whites?) also seemed suspicious. And following two extraordinary incidents during the Great Patriotic War—when his adjutant crossed the front line without leave, and later, at the end of the year, when the Germans had already been encircled around Stalingrad, Larin, a member of the 2nd Guards Army's military council and longtime friend and comrade in arms of Malinovskii, unexpectedly committed suicide. After this, according to Khrushchev, Stalin ordered him to keep an eye on Malinovskii, although a month later Nikita Sergeevich testified to Rodion Yakovlevich's reliability and Stalin appointed him commander of the Southern Front. Subsequently, to judge by events, faith in Malinovskii was restored. Otherwise, Stalin would not have promoted him to marshal and would not have awarded him the title of Hero of the Soviet Union. He probably also

---

2   Editor's note. CPSU stands for Communist Party of the Soviet Union.

knew about Malinovskii's tense relations with Zhukov and this suited Stalin during the period of Zhukov's disfavor. Never the less, he preferred, just in case, to keep Malinovskii in the Far East, far from Moscow.

Rodion Yakovlevich Malinovskii was a brave man, did not hide from bullets and shells, and was wounded three times (the last time as *front* commander). He was not guilty, as opposed to many commanders, of appropriating captured property. Malinovskii maintained an amazing modesty up to his death, never exaggerated his services and preferred to remain in the shadows, even when he rightfully deserved glory.

I want to express my most sincere thanks to Natal'ya Rodionovna Malinovskaya, without whose help this book could not have appeared in its present form.

1

Just who was his Father?

Rodion Yakovlevich wrote the following in his personnel form in 1948: "I was born in Odessa on 23 November (New Style) 1898. My mother, Varvara Nikolaevna Malinovskaya was not married and I was listed as 'illegitimate' in the birth registry. I don't know who my father was. My independent working life began in the spring of 1911. I started work as a farm laborer at Shenderov farm, for the landlord Yaroshinskii." This would seem to be the whole truth. According to a certificate issued by the Odessa Oblast' State Archives on 10 March 2000, "in the registry book of the Nikolaevskaya Church at the Botanical Gardens in the city of Odessa for 1898, there is registration no. 138 for 22 November 1898 of the birth of Rodion Malinovskii on 10 November (Old Style) 1898." By the way, this was Saint Rodion's day, in whose honor the newborn was named.

There is a dash in the certificate where the father's name should be, while the mother is listed as a "peasant woman, Varvara Nikolaevna Malinovskaya, from the Podol'ya Province, Bratslavskii County, Shpikovskaya District, a maiden and Orthodox Christian." If we refer to the text of the registry book itself, we learn that the godparents at the christening were Aleksandr Prusakov, a lower middle class man from Kolpino, in Saint Petersburg Province, and Ludovica Bozelli, a hereditary noblewoman.

Strictly speaking, if we count by the new style, according to the Gregorian calendar, then Rodion Yakovlevich was born on 22 November, and not 23 November. But such was the custom that he, like many others born in the nineteenth century, preferred to observe their birthday according to the Julian calendar; that is, on 23 November, New Style.

V. Golubovich, one of Malinovskii's biographers, supposing that Malinovskii became a farm laborer in 1911, maintained: "Two years of hard farm labor taught him a lot." To be sure, the biographer added that farm labor did not keep Rodion from getting hold of and reading quite serious books, such as a calendar issued on the anniversary of the Fatherland War of 1812, or Lev Tolstoi's novel *War and Peace*. And as we will see further on, two years of farm work were only a forced fantasy of Rodion Yakovlevich, who had to hide certain facts about his early life in official forms.

This is what is known about the relatives of Malinovskii's mother. Her grandfather, the marshal's great grandfather, Anton, or Antonii Malinovskii, had at a minimum two sons and a daughter and lived at one time in Zhmerinka. Rodion Yakovlevich's grandfather, Nikolai Antonovich (or Antonievich) Malinovskii, died in 1902. He worked at one time as a warden; that is, as an assistant to the overseer, who made the rounds of wooded or other lands, in order to protect them. It is possible that Nikolai Antonovich was later promoted to overseer. One should add that a warden, as someone who directly levied fines for damages to the landlord's crops, was for the peasants one of the most hated categories of the rural population. Nikolai Antonovich served in the village of Voroshilovka, Tyvrovskii District, Podol'ya Province, not far from Gnivan' station along the Southwestern Railroad.

Rodion's uncle, Vasilii Antonovich Malinovskii, ended up in hard labor in Siberia for some sort of crime, from which he returned with a wife, by whom he had a daughter.

Another uncle, Yakov Nikolaevich Malinovskii, worked as a technical supervisor of the buildings at Birzula station, on the Southwestern Railroad, up until 1913. He was married to Jadwiga

Kazimirovna, the daughter of an engineer. Yakov Nikolaevich's wife was a Pole. This may indicate the Polish descent of the Malinovskii family. I should note that the former Polish nobility in the western Russian provinces often occupied the positions of overseers, forestry officers, or wardens. As we know, the czarist government sought in various ways to reduce the numbers of the Polish gentry and often did not confirm the nobility of those members of the gentry who no longer owned serfs.

Natal'ya Nikolaevna Malinovskaya, Rodion's favorite aunt, never married. She first worked as a medical orderly in an orphanage, and then as a sorter in a Kiev shoe factory. She had a son, Yevgenii Georgievich Malinovskii, who worked as a borer in an arsenal in Kiev. In Kiev they lived at 11 Kirov Street, apt. 11. As Rodion Yakovlevich's daughter, Natal'ya recalled: "Unfortunately, aunt Natasha died together with her son Zhenya in Kiev (during the German occupation, B.S.). Papa made a special trip there and the neighbors told him the sad story. He loved her very much and was very upset."

Yet another aunt, Lidiya Nikolaevna, whose husband's last name was Nagotchuk, lived in the town of Nemirov, Bratslavskii District, Podol'ya Province.

Another aunt, Yelena Nikolaevna, was married to Mikhail Aleksandrovich Danilov, a weight inspector at the Odessa freight station. In Odessa they lived at 69 Pioneer Street. Their children were Aleksandr, Vadim and Melan'ya. Aleksandr worked as a metal worker in the Odessa Mechanical Factory, and Vadim worked there as an engineer. Melan'ya's husband, Yasinskii, was also a worker at this factory. Vadim Danilov's family lived in Odessa in the 1870s at 7 Shevchenko Prospekt, apt. 72.

So, who was the marshal's father? It seems as though there was never the less one conscious inaccuracy in the personnel form. It seems that Rodion Yakovlevich never the less knew his father's name and profession.

In 1954, in anticipation of the latest elections to the USSR Supreme Soviet, in which Marshal Malinovskii was running from the Khabarovsk Territory, Nikolai Mikhailovich Shvernik, the chairman of the Central Electoral Commission, received a denunciatory letter from the marshal's first wife, Larisa Nikolaevna Malinovskaya, whom he had divorced in 1946. She was living in Irkutsk, where she had become acquainted with Rodion Yakovlevich in the beginning of the 1920s. The journalist Yevgenii Zhirnov published this denunciation in magazine *Vlast'* on 8 May 2006 and we will quote it according to the text in the publication. We should note right off that L.N. Malinovskaya's letter had no effect on the course of the elections, as no one thought to remove the marshal's candidacy. On 14 March Rodion Yakovlevich was, as was the custom, unanimously elected a deputy. However, one cannot exclude the possibility that the country's leadership received the letter after the elections.

Larisa Nikolaevna wrote:

> There will soon take place in our country elections to the Supreme Soviet and the Soviet of Nationalities of the Soviet Union. The best of the best comrades will be put forward as candidates for deputy. The workers do not always personally know the recommended candidate and acquaint themselves with his biography, which is printed in the newspapers. I don't know who writes these biographies and where they get their information; but as regards one biography, I want to say a little something.
>
> During the last elections Rodion Yakovlevich Malinovskii, Marshal of the Soviet Union, was recommended as a candidate for the Soviet of Nationalities. I only read his biography much later, as I am far away from him… The biography incorrectly informed the workers. It's likely that Malinovskii's candidacy will be recommended for these elections as well, and I would like to make some corrections beforehand to the biographical details.
>
> Since when did Malinovskii become a farm laborer and the son of a farm labor woman?

Here we will interrupt and say that Malinovskii, as opposed to other marshals, wrote almost no memoirs, except for individual articles for collections. On the other hand, he wrote about his youth and participation in the First World War in the novel *Soldiers of Russia*, which was posthumously published in 1969. The novel features the autobiographical hero Ivan Grin'ko. His father was supposedly a land surveyor, with whom his mother, Varvara Nikolaevna, ran away from her parents to Odessa:

> But their happiness proved short-lived. A real tragedy befell them: his crazed brother attacked the land surveyor with a knife. He inflicted several deep wounds. The land surveyor died. This was when she was already near her time. A son was born—Vanyusha. He was considered illegitimate and the young mother knew that mockery and contempt awaited him in the future. She had to return in shame to her parents in Voroshilovka. The parents were beside themselves when she ran off with the land surveyor, but then reconciled themselves to the fact and forgave their unhappy wayward daughter—a name which they had long given to girls in Ukraine who begat children without a father—and fell in love with their grandson. However, she was unfortunate with her parents: her mother died, followed a year later by her father. He worked for a landowner as a warden. She had to move in with her sister Yelena, who, having married a weight inspector, lived at Kalinovka station.

Malinovskii did not bother to change the name of the mother in the novel. As was written in *Soldiers of Russia*, Varvara Nikolaevna found work in the kitchen of a hospital, which was supported by Countess Geiden: "The countess visited the hospital several times and would drop in without fail on Varvara Nikolaevna in the kitchen. Vanyusha's mother evidently appealed to her by her tidiness and good nature. These visits concluded with her taking Varvara Nikolaevna on as a cook at her estate." However, from the subsequent narrative it becomes clear that Malinovskii's mother was a housekeeper at the estate and cooked only when the head chef went on a drinking spree.

In the denunciation a completely different version of Rodion Yakovlevich's origins was given.

> R.Ya. Malinovskii was born in Odessa. His father, the Latvian Yakov Burgon' (I don't swear to the accuracy of the surname), was the chief of the gendarme administration for Odessa,. R.Ya. carries the name of his grandfather, who for his entire life was an overseer on landlords' estates in Ukraine…
>
> When the father of R.Ya. was dying, his mother, Varvara Nikolaevna, taking advantage of the father's patronage, became a housekeeper for the neighboring landlord, Count Geiden (Vinnitsa Province). R.Ya. was raised there together with the count's sons and even wore the same suits as they did, while on the estate they considered him the count's third son.

The episode with the suits is mentioned in Malinovskii's novel. It is clear that Larisa Nikolaevna could have obtained all of this information, as well as the information about his father, only from her husband. It seems as though she had never been in Odessa. And if she had wanted to invent something about the father—a gendarme colonel or chief of police, then she would probably have given his exact name, and not from hearsay or memory. It is this circumstance that supports the idea that the mysterious Yakov Burgon' (who he was, we'll reveal later) really was the father of the future marshal.

Problems began for the young Rodion when his mother married for a second time. This is what Larisa Nikolaevna wrote about that in her denunciation: "The mother, Varvara Nikolaevna, being still young, married the landlord's young floor polisher, S. Zalesnyi, who had completed his military service. The neighbors considered this marriage madness: to have a position and marry a floor polisher, and to be ten years older than him. R.Ya. shared this opinion. Varvara Nikolaevna moved to her house in the village."

In his personnel form, written on 3 January 1946, Malinovskii offered the most dramatic take on his hard youth:

> In 1910 my mother married a footman, who was working for the same landlady (Geiden, B.S.). For this reason, the enraged landlady fired my mother and the footman—Sergei Isanurovich ZALESNYI (we should note that the name Isanur, which means "bright" in Arabic, is not a Christian name, but a Muslim one and is widespread in the Northern Caucasus, where Sergei's father likely came from, B.S.) and they moved to the neighboring village of Klishchev, where ZALESNYI was from. I finished the village school in this village in 1911.
>
> ZALESNYI was very poor and had less than an acre of land and no cows or a horse, and worked as a joiner, and played the violin at all the village revels and weddings. His mother was an old woman who went around begging, and I often accompanied her, protecting her from dogs.
>
> There were scenes in the family because of our poverty, and I was driven out of the house in 1911, and from that moment I began my independent working life.
>
> From the spring of 1911 through the autumn of 1913 I worked as a farm laborer (as a child and a teenager) at landlord Yaroshinskii's Shenderevo farm in the same Tyvrovskii County, Vinnitsa Oblast'.

V.S. Golubovich writes about Varvara Nikolaevna's marriage that in 1910 she married and settled in the village of Klishchev, in Podol'ya Province, where her husband lived. "However, Rodion did not have it easy here and he had bad relations with his stepfather. There were constant arguments in the family because of their material shortages and due to the stepson's recalcitrance, etc." The stepson was undoubtedly recalcitrant, but not so much the material shortages. In all probability Varvara Nikolaevna had managed to save up a decent amount of savings, by local standards, from her service with Count Geiden, which had attracted her spouse. And Nikolai Antonovich probably left her some sort of inheritance. It's quite possible that Rodion's father, to judge from everything, loaned his mistress sufficient money for a non-impoverished existence.

Malinovskii's statement that the landlady was incensed at the marriage between the cook and footman appears strange. Such marriages were a common affair and, as a rule, did not arouse the masters' anger.

Rodion Yakovlevich's assertion that Zalesnyi had less than an acre of land stands out. It really was impossible to carry out any kind of real farming on such a small patch of land and it would only be good for a kitchen garden. Thus one can understand why Zalesnyi went to work as a footman. However, why he picked a woman much older than himself for his wife and, if one is to believe Rodion Yakovlevich, just as poor, is a mystery. And if the first wife did not lie in her denunciation, then this was purely a marriage of convenience. A well-to-do housemaid took as her husband a poor footman, significantly younger than her, but attracted by her wealth. Then the grandmother, begging for alms and accompanied by her grandson Rodion, is simply an artistic fiction. It is more likely that Varvara and her husband had a well-to-do life as rentiers from the interest on their money. Their problems began after the October Revolution of 1917, when the Bolsheviks nationalized the banks and they lost their savings. At that point Sergei and Varvara really did become poor and it is not excluded that after 1917 Zalesnyi really did work as a joiner and played the violin, in order to support himself.

As we shall see, the conflict with the stepfather most likely occurred not in 1911, but in 1913, and its reason was in no way due to poverty, but because the stepfather was only a bit older than his stepson and Rodion did not want to treat him as a stepfather.

This story was also reflected in the novel *Soldiers of Russia*, only the stepfather's name here is not Zalesnyi, but Lesnoi, and he, the count's footman, "was only ten years older than Vanyusha and just as much younger than her." According to Larisa Nikolaevna, "since he could not immediately come to terms with his young stepfather and desiring to study in the officer training school, R.Ya. ran away from home and really did herd cows during the summer, in order to earn money for the trip to Odessa." It seems that the future marshal was drawn to military service even then. In his novel Malinovskii also wrote about Vanya Grin'ko's desire to enroll in officer training school, but instead of this Count Geiden suggested the medical orderly school, which the novel's hero turned down.

Natal'ya, the marshal's daughter, recalled:

> In his last year I asked him "What did you want to be?" I had heard earlier that he didn't want to be a soldier: "It's unnatural to want to be a soldier. One should not wish for war. It's understandable when a man wants to become a scientist, an artist or a doctor—they create things." As to the question of what to be, papa then replied: "A forester." I think that was the truth, although not for his whole life, but during his final year. He would have replied otherwise as a young man, all the more so as his ambition was exacerbated by the bitter memory of humiliations experienced in childhood. If forestry had become his work, he would have devoted himself to studying the life of the taiga with the same zeal and fervor with which he studied ancient strategists.

The novel also contains the episode with the medical orderly school. It follows right after the count's suggestion to Vanyusha to enroll in an agricultural academy:

> "I won't go to any kind of agricultural academy, and will only go to a military school," snapped Vanyusha, unexpectedly for everyone.
>
> Varvara Nikolaevna was frightened of his impudence:
>
> "What's the matter, have you lost your mind?"
>
> "It's nothing mama, I haven't lost my mind," continued Vanyusha in the same tone, "but I won't go to an agricultural academy."
>
> The insult inflicted by Dorik welled up inside him.
>
> The count smiled in a puzzled manner. Dorik haughtily looked at Vanyusha and, turning to his father, said:
>
> "Papa," he said, with the accent French style, on the last syllable, "doesn't he want you to appoint him to the officer training school?"
>
> "But I can't appoint him to the officer training school," the count said, as if not noticing Dorik's obvious derision, "although in Zhmerinka there's a military orderly school, where they accept boys. You may approach this school, Varvara Nikolaevna, and I'll write the authorities to have him accepted," the count concluded graciously.
>
> "I most humbly thank your grace," said Varvara Nikolaevna, happy that the incident was over and that everything had worked out.
>
> "Good bye,Varvara Nikolaevna," the count said. "I wish your son success," and he added with a smile: "See what a strong and muscular boy he is. And he wants to be a soldier, that's commendable," and the count clapped Vanyusha on the shoulder.
>
> Varvara Nikolaevna and Vanyusha walked away from the manor house along the garden path, together with Herr Otto. The German did not miss the opportunity to reprove Vanyusha for his impudence toward his grace, but never the less agreed that Dorik really had become overly proud, having become a cadet, and it wasn't surprising that this had cut Vanyusha

to the quick and offended him. He tried to calm Varvara Nikolaevna and then, unnoticed, returned to the conversation with the count:

"It's a shame Vanyusha doesn't want to enter the agricultural academy: to be an agronomist, or even a horticulturalist, is the most wonderful profession in the world."

"I still won't go there," repeated Vanyusha.

But Herr Otto did not back off:

"You know, Vanya, the military profession is a difficult and bad one. All a military man's skill consists of killing people."

"That's good," thought Vanyusha to himself, "I would have killed Dorik with pleasure."

It seems to me that this scene reflects a real conversation, in which they suggested the medical orderly school or an agricultural academy to the young Rodion, instead of officer training school; only this conversation was not with Count Geiden, but with whom, we shall see later.

In the novel there appears the hero's colorful uncle, Vasilii Antonovich:

Varvara Nikolaevna's and Vanyusha's trip to Zhmerinka coincided with the completely unexpected appearance there of Vasilii Antonovich Grin'ko, the late grandfather's long forgotten brother. It transpired that he had been in hard labor somewhere in the Far East and, having served out his sentence, had gotten rich on deliveries to the Russian army in the fighting with the Japanese. He had arrived in Zhmerinka as a rich man. He brought a young and pretty wife, with Gypsy features, whom he had stolen from some Vladivostok big shot. She had two children by the big shot and a young daughter, about whom everybody made a great fuss, by Vasilii Grin'ko.

Grandfather Vasilii bought a house and began to live in high style, bestowing expensive presents on all his kinfolk. To be sure, Varvara Nikolaevna didn't get much: she hurriedly left for Klishchev, without having decided to enroll Vanyusha in the medical orderly school. It was necessary to sign a contract to enroll her son for nine years of study, after which he was obliged to serve for four years, only after which he would have the opportunity to retire from military service or remain in the service with the rank of sergeant.

It should be added that this had no attraction for Vanyusha.

Varvara Nikolaevna departed and Vanyusha remained, together with aunt Natasha and with grandfather Vasya, as they called Vasilii Antonovich. Aunt Natasha worked as a cook and Vanyusha carried water, chopped firewood and ran errands to wherever he was sent. Feasts were arranged in the house almost every day, so there was enough work to go around. When there were no guests, they would invite Vanyusha to eat with them. Once some children his age gathered and were dancing to a gramophone. Grandfather Vasya's older daughter invited Vanyusha to dance. He accepted the invitation with delight, but began to dance Klishchev style, tripping along and tracing various figures with his feet. Suddenly the girl became flustered and jumped away from Vanyusha:

"Mama," she screamed, "he's jumping like a goat; can you really dance this way? He doesn't know how to dance."

Vanyusha was struck dumb; he blushed and lowered his eyes. Yes, the other boys and girls danced smoothly, carefully carrying out each step. This was surely no "Klishchev" school.

This incident put Vanyusha off dancing forever.

Grandfather Vasilii was an outwardly healthy and strong man of about 50 years, but as early as Siberia he had come down with a prolonged illness: he suffered from back pain and his lower back often hurt. When the pain became unbearable he would make Vanyusha rub his back with liquid ammonia. Vanyusha tried as hard as he could, while his grandfather would groan with pleasure and would continue to shout:

"Harder, Vanya, squeeze harder!"

And Vanya would rub and rub until his grandfather's back was dry, although his hands hurt a lot. Grandfather Vasilii was happy. Vanya would return from the bedroom to the kitchen and, although sweating profusely, also in a good mood.

However, before long the happy life in grandfather Vasilii's house came to an end. He began to host fewer banquets and no longer showered his relatives with presents. He had a falling out with them. Those who had extolled him not long ago began to revile him and even played dirty tricks on him: someone would break the windows in the home or used his front porch as a toilet.

Dissension broke out in grandfather Vasilii's family as well. The big shot whose, wife he had stolen, found out that the "young folks" were in Zhmerinka and began to demand the return of his spouse. She, to judge from everything, began to lean toward going back. Once grandfather Vasilii began to beat his devoted wife amidst the children's' crying and screaming; he grabbed her by the hair and her hairdo fell apart and gold coins scattered on the floor. This was clear proof that she really was getting ready to run back to her old husband, and the argument became even more exacerbated.

Aunt Natasha, upon consulting with Vanyusha in the kitchen, also decided to leave grandfather while the getting was good.

The finale to this entire tale was Vasilii Antonovich Grin'ko's departure from Zhmerinka, which was as unexpected as his appearance. He left no trace behind. People said that he only told one distant relative his address and made him swear not to tell anyone.

Vasilii Antonovich was a real person. Malinovskii wrote about him in his personnel report in 1938. This is what he wrote there about all his relatives.

My mother and her husband Zalesnyi, as well as her children by Zalesnyi: Nina, Aleksandr, Vera, and Anna Zalesnyi—lived very poorly before the revolution: the three Zalesnyi brothers had two acres of land, never had a horse and my mother acquired a cow only with my help, and since 1931 they've lived on a collective farm in this same village of Klishchev, Tyvrovskii County, Vinnitsa Oblast'. My mother's husband, Sergei Zalesnyi, died in 1937 and my mother now lives alone, and I help her regularly.

Auntie Yelena died long ago and her husband Mikhail Danilov now lives with his children in Odessa, at 69 Pioneer Street; his daughter married Yasinskii, a worker from the Odessa Mechanical Factory, and his sons work at the same factory—one as a metal worker and the other as an engineer. My second aunt, Lidiya, married Nagotchuk as early as 1910 in the village of Rogozino (ten kilometers from Klishchev) and now lives in the town of Nemirov, while her husband is serving somewhere; I have no contact with her.

My third auntie, Natal'ya Nikolaevna Malinovskaya did not get married, although she had a child out of wedlock; she worked as an orderly in an orphanage in Kiev, where she now lives at 11 Kirov Street, apt. 11. My auntie now works as a sorter in a shoe factory in Kiev and her son, Yevgenii Georgievich Malinovskii (he fell off the stove in childhood and is now a hunchback) works as a borer in an arsenal in Kiev. He's a Stakhanovite[1] and by the first congress of Stakhanovites he had set a record for labor productivity, having fulfilled his work

---

1   Editor's note. This term comes from Aleksei Grigor'evich Stakhanov (1906-77), a coal miner who reportedly mined a record amount of coal in a single shift in 1935. This feat was widely trumpeted by Soviet propaganda and served as the stimulus for the entire "Stakahnovite," or "shock worker" movement in various industries. The original claims for Stakhanov's feat have since been discredited.

norm by 1,200 percent, and he was written up in *Izvestiya*.[2] I maintain contact with them and sometimes visit them, and they me, because this aunt paid attention to me and helped me, and now I help her. My uncle, Yakov Nikolaevich Malinovskii, was a building supervisor at Birzula station, on the Southwestern Railroad. I saw him in passing in Odessa in 1913 and since then have had no contact with him and don't know where they live now and only know that he stopped working at Birzula station in 1913. My uncle, Nikolai Malinovskii, worked as a steward for a landlord in the small town of Voroshilovka (seven kilometers from Gnivan' station on the Southwestern Railroad) and died in 1902. His brother, Vasilii Malinovskii, was sentenced to hard labor during the Japanese War and even earlier, although I don't know what for; he came to Zhmerinka in 1913 and left that same year, although I don't know where.

What is noteworthy is that in the novel Vasilii Antonovich was getting rich on military deliveries during the Russo-Japanese War, while in the personnel report he is serving hard labor at the same time. It seems to me that what was communicated in the personnel report was never the less closer to the truth. It seems to me that Vasilii Antonovich was given some qualities of yet another relative of Rodion Yakovlevich, about whom he did not want to talk at all.

Before she even found out about the Chernigov—Mariupol' track in her father's biography (we will speak of this track later), Natal'ya Rodionovna Malinovskaya wrote:

> Grandmother worked for a few years as a cook in the district hospital before working for the countess, so the work of doctors and nurses became a common sight for my father (who was five years old at the time) and which he could have learned. It's not for nothing that somewhat later the doctor suggested to the young cook that he enroll her son in a medical orderly school, but she couldn't decide on this, as her son was still very young and it was a contract for 15 years!
>
> The amazing surgeon, Vitalii Petrovich Pichuev, in recalling the long conversations with papa (they became acquainted in 1960, when mama was undergoing surgery), spoke about the lively interest that surprised him in papa each time they talked about medical work, new diagnostic methods and new medical equipment. And each time papa would speak to him with particular warmth about the doctor from the district hospital—the first person who aroused in him unconditional respect. Moreover, my father told Vitalii Petrovich that as early as after the civil war, when speaking about further study, he requested his commander to write him a recommendation for the Military-Medical Academy, but received a decisive rebuff. "There's nothing for you to do there! You're a born commander!" So, if papa had become a doctor that would have been understandable and natural, and even achievable, while literature always remained for him an unachievable dream, a *terra incognita*, a pie in the sky.

As concerns her father's interest in medicine, I think Natal'ya Rodionovna is absolutely right. However, as we will see later, he was tied to those circumstances in his life about which he didn't mention in his service report.

Larisa Malinovskaya maintained that upon arriving in Odessa Rodion got a job as a steward and was "supported by a merchant's young wife." There's also an analogous episode in the novel, only there Vanya works in a store, while the landlady of the apartment where he lives, the wife of a captain who was away at sea, is not indifferent to him.

---

2   Editor's note. *Izvestiya* was founded in 1917 as the newspaper of the Petrograd Soviet of Workers' Deputies and afterwards became the official organ of the Soviet government. The newspaper has been in private hands since 1992.

Anna Ivanovna quietly walked up to Vanyusha and began to admire his handwriting. She bent down so low that the boy felt her breath on his neck and he instinctively turned his face toward her. Anna Ivanovna looked directly into his eyes with a long and languorous stare and, taking his head in her warm hands, pressed it to her soft breast. Then Anna Ivanovna powerfully and juicily kissed Vanyusha's lips. It was as if the kiss burned Vanyusha and he felt his heart begin to pound in his chest. A quarter-hour later he was already walking along Shtiglits Street toward the cathedral, shaken and crushed by all that had happened. He had the feeling that he had done something terrible.

Larisa Nikolaevna undoubtedly heard this story from her husband as well. Only it seems that she made up the part about being supported by the merchant's young wife. After all, Rodion was then 15 or 16 years old and it's possible that the affair with the merchant's wife was purely platonic.

Further on, in order to further compromise her former spouse; Larisa Nikolaevna reported that Malinovskii supposedly received his first officer's rank in the czarist army (more on this in the next chapter). She also covered his relatives' unfavorable social origins: "His aunt on his mother's side—Lidiya—was a lady-in-waiting at court and during the Soviet years married a big kulak[3] and lived in an individual holding in Vinnitsa Province. His uncle on his mother's side (which his service biography refers to as a farm laborer, although he had his own transportation and servants) ran away overseas."

Love for the merchant's wife was evidently not compromising. More serious was the accusation that Malinovskii knew that his father was an important gendarme chief and, to judge by his position, no less than a colonel. In Stalin's[4] time this was called hiding one's social origins and threatened the most serious consequences, all the way to execution. Once a man hides who his real father was, it means that he can't be trusted. One of the reasons behind the death of Colonel General Grigorii Mikhailovich Shtern,[5] who was executed in October 1941, was that he hid his unfavorable social origins (he called himself a doctor's son, when his father was actually quite a well-to-do worker in a credit firm), about which he was forced to admit in a penitential letter to Voroshilov.[6] He was rehabilitated in 1954, at exactly the same time when the denunciation of Malinovskii was written. Obviously, to deliver such a denunciation before 1946, when they were divorced, would be for Larisa Nikolaevna tantamount to sawing off the branch she was sitting on. But why did she

---

3   Editor's note. A kulak ("fist") was the pejorative term for a well-to-do peasant in the Russian countryside. The term was taken up by the Soviet government during the collectivization campaign of the early 1930s, when many who refused to join the new collective farms were branded as kulaks and exiled or killed.

4   Editor's note. Iosif Vissarionovich Stalin (Dzhugashvili) (1879-1953) joined the Russian Social Democratic Worker's Party as a young man and soon aligned himself with the Bolshevik faction under V.I. Lenin. Following the Bolshevik coup, Stalin was appointed people's commissar for nationalities and was a political commissar during the civil war. In 1922 Stalin was appointed general secretary of the party and used this position to increase his power and eliminate his rivals. During the Great Patriotic War he was simultaneously general secretary of the Communist Party, chairman of the Council of People's Commissars, people's commissar of defense, supreme commander-in-chief, and chairman of the State Defense Committee. Following Stalin's death, his successors denounced him as a mass murderer.

5   Editor's note. Grigorii Mikhailovich Shtern (1900-41) joined the Red Army in 1919 and fought in the civil war. During the interwar period he served as a military adviser in Spain and commanded armies in the Far East and Finland and was briefly commander of the Far Eastern Front. Shtern was appointed chief of National Air Defense in 1941, but was arrested shortly afterward and shot.

6   Editor's note. Kliment Yefremovich Voroshilov (1881-1969) joined the Bolshevik faction early on and served as a commander and commissar with various units during the civil war. He served as defense commissar during 1925-40 and is chiefly responsible for the Red Army's lack of preparedness for the German invasion in 1941. Following a brief and unsuccessful period of command during the war, he was relegated to ceremonial positions for the rest of his life.

wait eight whole years after the divorce? Did she really feel sorry for her former husband and was scared that they would execute him? I think the reason lies elsewhere. It was precisely in 1954 that Varvara Nikolaevna, who was born in 1879, passed away. It's clear that with the marshal's mother still alive, to write that his father was a high-ranking gendarme officer would simply be risky, whether or not that corresponded to the truth. It's not likely that Varvara Nikolaevna would have confirmed the version about the gendarme chief, but would have thought up some kind of parent for Rodion Yakovlevich with a worker-peasant background. Then they could have accused Larisa Nikolaevna of slander, with all the consequences flowing from that (especially if at that moment Stalin had no need to get rid of Malinovskii). After all, Varvara Nikolaevna was very proud that her son was a marshal and would not have compromised him.

So, who exactly was the marshal's father? According to the information in the *Kherson Provincial 1901 Yearbook* (Odessa, I should remind you, was only a district city in Odessa Province, although, according to the 1897 census, it was the fourth largest city in the Russian Empire, with 404,000 residents, surpassed only by Saint Petersburg with 1,265,000, Moscow with 1,039,000, and Warsaw with 629,000), the chief of the Odessa gendarme administration was Colonel Vladimir Aleksandrovich Bezsonov. There also existed the police administration in Odessa. Colonel Viktor Yakovlevich Shemanin headed this. As we can see, the surname of Burgon' has nothing in common with these two surnames. It's impossible to confuse them, even if one wanted to. However, according to the information from the same *Provincial Yearbook*, the chief of the Odessa city police was "acting chief of police Yakim Ivanovich Bunin, an infantry officer seconded to the city's mayor." Now the surname Bunin is obviously consonant with the surname of Burgon', particularly considering that Larisa Nikolaevna most likely stressed the first syllable. Taking into account the fact that, as we shall see further on, everyone in Odessa called Yakim Ivanovich Bunin Yakov Ivanovich, thus changing the rare name of Yakim (from Joachim) to the more common Yakov, then the Odessa chief of police becomes a realistic candidate to be the marshal's father. This is all the more so, as we shall see, Bunin was called Yakov Ivanovich in all official documents.

Yakim (Yakov) Ivanovich Bunin, Marshal Malinovskii's presumed father, really had an amazing biography. He belonged to the famous Bunin noble family, which gave to the world a great writer and laureate of the Nobel Prize—Ivan Alekseevich Bunin.[7] According to legend, the founder of the clan is considered to be the Polish nobleman Semyon (Simon) Bunkievskii (Bunkovskii), who left for Russia at the end of the XV century from Lithuania to serve the Grand Duke of Moscow, Vasilii the Dark.[8] Ivan Alekseevich, in a letter to A.N. Sal'nikov,[9] dated 2 March 1901, spoke of his origins "from Semyon Bunkovskii, who left Poland in the XV century." However, the author here somewhat modernized the past. At the end of the XV century Poland did not border on the Muscovite state, but rather Lithuania, and it was precisely Lithuanian noblemen who often travelled to serve the Muscovite grand dukes. Bunin was thinking in terms of the Rzeczpospolita— the unified Polish-Lithuanian state, which arose in the second half of the XV century and which people usually referred to as Poland. Thus the Bunin clan was of Lithuanian descent. In the USSR they always outrageously confused Lithuania and Latvia, and it is therefore possible then

---

7   Editor's note. Ivan Alekseevich Bunin (1870-1953) was a Russian writer whose career spanned the pre-revolutionary and Soviet periods. He lived as an exile after 1920 and continued to write and was awarded the Nobel Prize for literature in 1933. Bunin died in Paris.

8   Editor's note. Vasilii Vasil'evich II ("*Temnyi*") (1415-1462) was intermittently the grand duke of Moscow from 1425 until his death. A struggle for power broke out early in his reign and he was captured by his enemies and blinded and was thus afterwards referred to as "the Dark." He regained his throne permanently in 1447 and ruled until his death. Vasilii's son was Ivan III ("the Great").

9   Editor's note. Alesandr Nikolaevich Sal'nikov (1851-1909) was a Russian writer and literary critic.

why Larisa Malinovskaya called Rodion Yakovlevich's father a Latvian. We should also note that Simon Bunkovskii's great grandson, Aleksandr Lavrent'evich, died in 1552 while taking Kazan'.

At the end of the XIX century among the representatives of this clan was "Yak. Iv. Bunin, Odessa, Tambov Province, Borisoglebsk District. He is a colonel and a nobleman with the right to vote." This is undoubtedly Yakim Ivanovich.

Researchers into Bunin's work, particularly Irina Il'inichna Petrova, believe that that "Yakov Ivanovich Bunin (born 1837), who took part in the defense of Sevastopol' as a cadet and who distinguished himself in the battle for the third bastion on the day of the final attack," served as the prototype of the main protagonist's uncle, Colonel Nikolai Sergeevich, in the novel *Arsen'ev's Life*. "He was a colonel during I. Bunin's youth and in 1902, upon his retirement, he was awarded the rank of Major General." Bunin is actually called Yakov Ivanovich in the album *The Defenders of Sevastopol'*. The name Yakov probably appealed to him more than Yakim. This is what is written in the biographical information included in the album: "In 1855 Yakov Ivanovich Bunin was a cadet in the Kamchatka Jaeger Regiment. He was in Sevastopol' from 23 June through 27 August. He suffered a head concussion. He was awarded the rank of ensign for distinction in the fighting for the third bastion on 27 August. He was born in 1837. In 1902 he was a retired major general." His photograph was displayed here.

Leonid Somov, another researcher, disagreed with I.I. Petrova:

Proceeding from the realities of the novel *Arsen'ev's Life*, the uncle was called Nikolai Sergeevich. Was he really a hero of the siege of Sevastopol'? It's doubtful. As a result of a very thorough archive search, I managed to establish that there was a defender of Sevastopol', a cadet from the Kamchatka Jaeger Regiment, Yakov Ivanovich Bunin, born in 1837, who was promoted to the rank of ensign for bravery demonstrated on 27 August 1855 on the third bastion. By the way, he successfully survived the campaign and died in 1902, with the rank of a retired major general. Thus in Bunin's autobiographical novella there are certain facts that one should regard as artistic inventions…

If one believes L. Somov, then it turns out that Yakim Ivanovich Bunin died in 1902, the same year that Rodion's grandfather, Nikolai Antonovich. He probably was retired when he was already seriously ill and did not survive long at the rank of major general. In principle, one cannot exclude the possibility that he was killed by his insane brother, as Vanya Grin'ko's father perished in the novel *Soldiers of Russia*. The fact that Ya.I. Bunin retired in 1901 or in the beginning of 1902 cannot be doubted. According to the information contained in the *All Odessa* guidebooks, in 1901 he was still listed as police chief, while a N.S. Golovin is already listed at this post in 1902. He is listed as acting police chief in the guidebook, which was passed by the censors on 18 February 1902.

Of course, Yakim Ivanovich Bunin could not have perished on Malakhov mound in 1855, insofar as he died in Odessa, or possibly at his estate, in 1902. In the same way, Yakim Ivanovich could not be a colonel at Sevastopol'. All of this is undoubtedly literary license, although probably based upon the writer's knowledge of Yakim Ivanovich's biography. However, it's possible that there was a kinship between Yakim Ivanovich Bunin and Ivan Alekseevich Bunin, although most likely far more removed than between uncle and nephew. The author lived in Odessa during the final years of Yakim Ivanovich's life and, in theory, could have met with the police chief, and it was precisely police chief Bunin who on 21 December 1898 presented material gathered by the police on Ivan Alekseevich in connection with the author's still-born appointment as editor of the Odessa newspaper *The Southern Review*. It was noted in the police materials that there was nothing reprehensible in I.A. Bunin's past. To be sure, there is nothing about a meeting between the author and the chief of police in either letters or memoirs. So, the idea that Bunin's father supposedly took part in the defense of Sevastopol' and met Lev Tolstoi on the famous fourth bastion, which he frequently mentions in his *The Liberation of Tolstoi*, is pure fantasy. The only representative of the Bunin clan (if you count all of them as descendents of Semyon Bunikievskii) who took part in the defense of Sevastopol' was Yakim (Yakov) Ivanovich. Aleksei Nikolaevich actually did leave for the war together with his brother Nikolai, with the militia. Only the 47th, 48th and 49th detachments of the Kursk militia were in time to take part in the last fighting for the city. The commander of the 42nd detachment of the Kursk militia, which did not take part in the fighting, was a Major Bunin, although he had not relation to the author's family. Nikolai Nikolaevich and Aleksei Nikolaevich Bunin left for the Crimean War as part of the 65th Yelets Militia Detachment from Orel Province, which was stationed at Bakhchisarai, on the north side of Sevastopol' and thus took no part in the fighting for Sevastopol', or in any fighting at all. The detachments from the Orel militia arrived in the Crimea only in October and November 1855, already after the fall of Sevastopol'. Of the 40,730 militiamen from the Kursk, Orel, Kaluga, and Tula militias that arrived in the Crimea in October-November 1855, only 21,347 remained on duty by the beginning of March 1856. Only about 500 militiamen died in the fighting, although tens of thousands died from epidemics. On the whole, the escapade with the militia simply proved to be harmful. Tens of thousands of men, untrained for camp life and deprived of the necessary medical assistance, perished without ever having fought. And if they had fought, it's likely that they would have perished without having caused any harm to the enemy, because they had not been trained as soldiers.

If the author's father, Aleksei Nikolaevich, took part in the defense of Sevastopol', then they would probably have placed him in one of the albums featuring the heroes of Sevastopol', which were very popular in Russia at the end of the XIX and beginning of the XX centuries. After all, Aleksei Nikolaevich died on 6 December 1906, at the age of 82 years, having outlived Yakim Ivanovich by four years. If he had taken part in the defense of Sevastopol', then he would have been one of the most long-lived surviving defenders of the city. So, Ivan Alekseevich was not telling the truth when he sought to convince his readers that he believed his father's stories about his participation in the defense of Sevastopol'. However, it's possible that the author himself probably wanted to make a hero of the defense of Sevastopol' out of his father. In Ivan Alekseevich's words: "My father (who in his youth participated, like Tolstoi, in the defense of Sevastopol') would tell me: 'I knew him a little. I met him during the Sevastopol' campaign." It's most likely that Aleksei Nikolaevich told the God's truth here. He really did meet Tolstoi in the Crimea; only it was only after the conclusion of the defense of Sevastopol', either on the northern side of the city, or in Bakhchisarai. It's quite possible that Lev Nikolaevich, according to Bunin's account in *The Liberation of Tolstoi*, really did say to him during their first meeting in Moscow: "Bunin? Did I meet your father in the Crimea?..." At the same time, he could have had in mind either Nikolai Alekseevich or Yakim Ivanovich.

Yakim Ivanovich's biography contains much that is interesting, aside from the defense of Sevastopol'. In 1882 he was appointed police chief in Odessa, where he served for 20 years, almost up to his time of death. In Odessa they joked when the former Police Street, which during Soviet times was called Rosa Luxemburg Street, was renamed Ivan Bunin Street under the independent Ukrainian regime, that it would have been more correct to have named it in honor of another Bunin, the police chief, insofar as the city police headquarters had been located on this street. It should be noted that in Ya.I. Bunin's time the police chief's office was located at 38 Preobrazhenskaya Street, which crosses Police Street. It's apropos to note that the fire observation tower was located here.

Yakim Ivanovich is famous for the fact that neither before nor after him did anyone so long occupy the post of chief of the city police, which in Soviet and post-Soviet times was called the militia. He forbade Jews; that is, people of the Hebrew faith, to serve in the city police. Strictly speaking, such a ban existed throughout the Russian Empire, although in Odessa, a good third of the population of which consisted of Jews, it was not observed in practice. Many Jewish policemen operated quite successfully. However, ten days following his accession to this post (he arrived in Odessa on 2 June), Colonel Bunin ordered "the removal of all policemen of Jewish nationality from service and not to accept Jews into the police in the future."

At the end of the XIX and the beginning of the XX centuries, Odessa was one of the criminal capitals of Russia. Legends were told of many famous criminals linked to Odessa. People told about how when they were sending Son'ka Golden Hands from Odessa to hard labor on Sakhalin Island, the mayor and police chief came to see her off. She managed to cut off Colonel Bunin's gold watch, although she immediately returned it to her victim. In another version, Son'ka stole the watch of the mayor, P. Zelenyi.

His personal file, which is stored in the Russian Federation State Archives (GARF, fond 102, D-1, opis' 4. 1884, delo 117), reveals the life of the Odessa police chief Yakov Ivanovich Bunin. The most complete account is contained in the "Service Record of the Police Chief, Army Infantry Colonel Yakov Ivanovich Bunin," which was begun on 12 February 1889. I should note that in all service records Bunin is always called Yakov Ivanovich, although in the Odessa address book he is listed as Yakim Ivanovich. It's difficult to say for sure which was his Christian name, Yakov or Yakim.

Yakov Ivanovich came from hereditary nobles from Tambov Province and had estates, which he acquired himself, one of 759 acres in Tambov Province and one of 57 acres in the Lipetsk District.

Bunin was educated in the Tambov provincial high school and, having passed out of the seventh class, "passed the required examination for an appointment to military service in an officer training school." He began his service on 23 June 1855 as a non-commissioned officer with the Kamchatka Jaeger (from 17 April 1856, Infantry) Regiment. He served with the regiment in the Crimean War and during the defense of Sevastopol'.

The service record notes that in 1855 Bunin "was concussed by a shock wave from a bomb in the right half of his head, and was deafened in his right ear, accompanied by a loud noise in his head and pain in the right side of his head and in his right ear. Following this concussion, he was employed first in the Sevastopol' military hospital, and then carried out duties in his regiment."

On 29 September Bunin was promoted to cadet for distinction and to ensign on 12 November 1855.

On 5 November 1856 Bunin was appointed to perform the duties of the regimental duty officer, and on 23 October 1858 he was promoted to second lieutenant. On 31 October 1858 Bunin became a battalion adjutant and on 2 June 1861 was promoted to lieutenant. He was transferred on 6 March 1863 to the Belyov Infantry Regiment, where on 26 November he was appointed a battalion adjutant. On 22 January 1864 Bunin was promoted to staff captain and on that same day was made regimental adjutant.

On 21 February 1865 Bunin was "released to visit the Lipetsk mineral waters to treat the illness resulting from a concussion." On 14 June 1865 he became a captain, and on 7 September a company commander. In the beginning of 1866, "due to vision needs resulting from a concussion," Yakov Ivanovich was authorized to wear glasses.

On 11 March 1866 Bunin turned over his company and was seconded to the headquarters of the Tambov provincial military chief as a member of the clerical accounting commission. He was appointed a parade brevet major or parade adjutant. As noted in his service record, in carrying out these duties, Bunin was very zealous and knowledgeable of his clerical duties and thus, although he has not completed his probationary period, to judge by his displayed abilities, if he should wish to continue serving, he would completely deserve the post offered to him." However, without completing the probationary period for parade major Bunin "was discharged from the service due to a head concussion, with the rank of major, with his uniform and a pension equal to one-third of his salary, 103 rubles and 95 kopecks."

Before long, following his retirement, Yakov Ivanovich's police career began. At the suggestion of the governor of Tambov Province, State Councilor Nikolai Martynovich Garting, on 18 November 1867 Bunin was appointed deputy to the Lipetsk district police chief. On 4 August 1869 he was transferred to the same post in the Kirsanov district. For some reason, this transfer was not to Yakov Ivanovich's liking and on 22 September 1869 he retired "at his own request," but as early as 25 November 1869 was once again hired and appointed assistant to the police chief of the Borisoglebsk District. On 1 December 1871 Bunin began performing the duties of the Spassk district police chief.

On 10 April Bunin was appointed chief of the Borisoglebsk district, and on 3 May 1874 he received "sincere thanks for the excellent efficiency which he exhibited during the trip and stay in the town of Borisoglebsk of His Highness, Grand Duke Nikolai Nikolaevich Senior." On 15 August he was appointed a member of the Borisoglebsk Training Council from the Ministry of Internal Affairs.

On 8 February 1875 Bunin once again retired "in connection with his election as a member of the Borisoglebsk district office for peasant affairs." He returned to government service on 15 June 1876, when he was appointed director of the Borisoglebsk prison department. On 26 January 1878, having served a three-year term, Bunin left the office for peasant affairs, having failed to express a desire to run for another term, and on 26 January 1878 he left the Borisoglebsk Training Council due to illness.

On 28 December 1878 Bunin was appointed the Berdichev district chief of police in Kiev Province. From the point of view of bribes, this was a much more lucrative position than similar positions in the Tambov Province's districts. Berdichev was located within the Pale of Settlement and its numerous Jewish population, which was engaged in trading and manufacturing was a source of police extortion, because the police closed their eyes to the violation of the various restrictive rules imposed on Jews. On 6 January 1881 Yakov Ivanovich became an honorary member of the Kiev provincial trusteeship for orphanages. This may indirectly indicate that he had sufficient funds to donate to orphanages. Later, in Odessa, he was the permanent chairman of the executive committee of the Odessa Society for the Care of the Poor's orphanage and thanks to his efforts the orphanage significantly broadened its activities and embraced the care of more than 300 poor and homeless every day.

Bunin's career really took off in 1882. On 13 March 1882 he retired once again, having been chosen as the Uman' District leader of the gentry and chairman of the Uman'—Zvenigorod Congress of Arbitrators. It's quite possible that this was only a bureaucratic move, insofar as early as May 6 1882 Bunin became the police chief of Odessa. It's not excluded that the question of his appointment had been decided as early as March and they made him leader of the gentry so as not to appoint him the police chief of Odessa from among the Berdichev chiefs of police, which would have indicate a huge gap in the level of positions.

In May 1884 the rank of major was abolished and Bunin was immediately promoted to lieutenant colonel, although as a civilian civil servant he was not entitled to this. He also received his next two ranks outside the rules. He received only thanks and awards and not a single reprimand.

In his service record of 12 February 1889 there is a notation that Bunin was married to the daughter of Major Peremezhko-Galich, Aleksandra Aleksandrovna. The Peremezhko-Galichs were a Ukrainian noble family from Chernigov Province. The father of Bunin's wife, Aleksandr Yefimovich Peremezhko-Galich, was forced in 1849 to sell his estate in the village of Fedot'evo, Spasskii District, to his brother Pavel. He had probably gone bankrupt. In his service record there is a notation that Bunin

has a daughter Mariya, born on 2 March 1872, a son Aleksei, born on 28 January 1874, a daughter Nadezhda, born on 20 January 1875, a son Aleksandr, born on 22 April 1876, and a son Boris, born on 20 January 1878, of which the daughter Mariya is in an institute in Odessa, sons Aleksei and Boris are in the Poltav officer training school, son Aleksandr is in the Richelieu high school, and daughter Nadezhda is in the Mariinskaya girl's high school. The wife and children are Orthodox Christians.

It's of interest that in an earlier service record of October 1884 another son, Ivan, born on 27 January 1871, is mentioned, and it was noted that "… the wife and children are with him, except for the eldest, Ivan, who is studying in the Kiev military high school." However, Ivan Bunin is not in an earlier service record of 15 May 1882, although Bunin's remaining children are present. It is possible that this record contains only those children who were living with Bunin. However, in none of the later service records from 1887 and 1889, is there any mention of Ivan Bunin, although they list children no longer living with the parents. One can assume that Ivan Bunin either died between 1884 and 1887, or that his father lost contact with him for some reason.

Judging by the first son's date of birth, one may assume that Bunin got married either in 1869 or 1870.

On 23 January 1887 Count Ivan Davydovich Delyanov, the minister of education, informed the police department that

> Odessa chief of police, Yakov Bunin, has always rendered and is rendering very efficacious support to the university and academy inspectorate in keeping track of the students beyond the walls of academic institutions and that thanks to his skill and efficiency, the activity of the inspectorate for internal supervision has been significantly eased, because Bunin's orders and instructions to his subordinates in the police, in cases of the latter coming into contact with students, have always been distinguished by a correct, and humane formulation of the question, from the point of view of instruction… Colonel Bunin's activity has always facilitated forestalling and preventing misunderstandings and evasions of mandatory rules of behavior by the students beyond the walls of academic institutions.

On 23 April 1888 an anonymous denunciation was made against Bunin. Here is its text.

> Top secret.

> I request your confidence.
> What a horrible position have the capital police, and particularly the Odessa police, been placed in. Where's the security? Where's the truth? As a result of the disgusting bribe taking, claims and desires, the police have been degraded in everyone's eyes, while a lack of order and oppression run higher and further. Can a good chief of police, serving like Bunin under the protection of a highly-placed person, have accumulated a fortune of 500,000 rubles in such a short time, except by extortion; where are the designated funds? Where are the office funds? Where's the leftover money for outfitting the police? Where are all the other funds of the Odessa police?—in the pockets of Bunin and his secretary Sorochan, a very refined bribe taker. These are two uncontrolled despots, friends and extortionists. Mayor Zelenoi and his ruler Dmitrenko are both fine and very noble people, but are not capable of penetrating into these refined schemes and fraudulent schemes of the police. One should look closely at how the poor scribes labor in the precincts for 25 rubles a month, while the law states that you can't torment the workers; but these unfortunates are tormented, engaged day and night with inordinate labor, while the police bigwigs buy estates for themselves under the guise of piety and high-ranking patronage, using money appropriated by the city and treasury.

In whose hands are the protection of the Fatherland and our great sovereign?—in the hands of the police, and in this case the low-level police bureaucrats have the greatest importance. The closer they stand to the matter of tracking down and destroying socialists and subversives, then they can only be of service. However, instead of appointing the most honest, noble and dignified people to these low-level bureaucratic positions, anyone may be hired in Odessa as the result of patronage and various shady types serve as precinct supervisors, such as tailors, shoemakers, tradesmen, and hobos, who are always proving their relationship or nobility, or some kind of rank, then honest lower-level sergeants subordinated to them—people with a name, and not bums, then it is no wonder that policemen often beat up precinct supervisors and say: "What kind of 'your honor' are you, you're a bum, and I'm a faithful servant of my sovereign." Besides this, when some kind of mercenary person or tradesman, who has gotten on the good side of the police chief or his secretary through some present, and his son, who has been expelled from an academic institution, full of socialism, an outright enemy of the Fatherland, serves as a precinct supervisor and is responsible for security, here the procuresses—those who maintain houses of ill repute, pay off the precinct supervisors. A young man, "Ropol," recently came to see me. A foreigner, who knows Russian well; probably an escaped criminal from Russia, returned with false documents and worked for a procuress at the snack bar, where he performed his bordello work well, and endeared himself to the procuress and cost her 700 rubles in bribes. He was accepted as a Russian subject and now serves as a precinct supervisor and is guarding the Fatherland? Under what guise is he protecting and developing evil? And the poor, retired bureaucrats and officers perish and go about begging for a job; but they don't have patronage and have no money to buy their offices, and they lack the kind of conscience that enables them to purchase a state position for money, or through special patronage, for each honest and noble civil servant with an honest chief makes his own patronage. One noble supervisor killed himself and his family, having been unable to find justice, and they wrote it up to drunkenness and delirium tremens, and he could not go against his convictions and conscience and give money to a corrupt police officer. They began to squeeze him out. He went to explain the matter to the higher authorities, but they sent him packing and he lost his mind to injustice and killed all his family and himself; and there are a lot of such cases.

And these Yid slimy deals continue successfully in the Odessa police; Bunin's secretary, Sorochan, is married to a Yid and baptized his grown Yid kids; for the sake of a joke, of course, and these Yid kids run the whole show, walk around and sniff out all the slimy deals, take good care of their business and in every way help their stepfather and his boss; that is, Sorochan and Bunin, and eliminate any misunderstandings in the way of bribes, etc. While receiving the salary of police bureaucrats, they offer protection to the Yids not only for their affairs, but even offer them civil positions in the police. For example, I needed a certificate, so I sent my overseer to the police with a request. They told him that the precinct supervisor would come and carry out an inquest. Suddenly, a few days later this little Yid appears at my place with a briefcase. "Are you count …?" I: "What can I do for you?" "I came to carry out the inquest." "Are you really the supervisor?" "No, I'm the clerk, and Shvaikevich is the supervisor.' "He's probably some fugitive Pole?" "I don't know who he is." "Who are you?" "I'm a Jew and I studied in high school." I gave him a ruble and he carried out the inquest. At another time I needed a certificate to go abroad. I went to the Kherson precinct in Odessa myself and a little Yid, who took a ruble from me, issued me a certificate there. I was quite kind to him in order to find out about the secretary's patronage for the Yids and the Yid stepsons and found out the details of everything. He told me their Yid names and surnames, but I remembered. These are the hands the police are in, and these types will take a ruble and will carry out any kind of inquests for anyone—for the most obvious criminal with the most obviously forged documents, and will do what they want, as long as there's money in it. This is why, despite all our strictness, socialists and subversives are growing, etc. The entire evil of the Fatherland is being covered up.

By the way, as if there's no one to work. My doors never shut due to people asking for help, be it a retired officer or retired civil servant. These people are perishing of want because they don't have a position, but why? Because they cannot be handled like simple hobos or Yids and I fully sympathize with these deserving and honest workers and help them. I tried to help some of them out, but all of them avoided trying to get a job through the police and, not believing this, I asked personally, and the chief of police replied that "In general, we don't take civil servants or officers," which shook me up and forced me to peer into the depths of the police hierarchy and find out why they are afraid to take on honest and deserving people for the job. Everything is based on the Poles in the municipal boards and city offices in Odessa. I also sent unfortunates there with a request to take them on, but alas! They were turned down because they weren't Poles, while the chief of one of the office's liked the handwriting of one person I sent, so they said they would take him on. "You're not a Pole, but convert to Catholicism for form's sake. Call yourself a Pole, bring proof from a priest that you're a Pole, prepare for communion, and then we'll hire you." I think that police positions should be occupied by civil servants and officers, especially the position of precinct supervisors, on which depend the police's most important activities in every regard, as they stand close to the matter, and in any event they are superior to other hobos. Of course, I am not able to describe everything, even these things. One gives his footman 200 rubles. He took them to the secretary, followed by two words of recommendation from his master, and he's a precinct supervisor. I've seen it all and heard it all—counts, generals and criminals and swindlers, etc. Who carries out inquests—people who have not earned and who are not worthy of the slightest trust, the most degraded, who do not value their honor and have no honor to value. This situation should be changed. Please accept my assurances as a full-blooded descendant of Russia.

On 23 May 1888 this anonymous letter was forwarded from the Ministry of Internal Affairs to the mayor of Odessa. The Odessa authorities took Bunin under their protection. On 3 August the mayor, Rear Admiral Pavel Alekseevich Zelenoi reported to the police department about the investigation conducted.

As a result of the memorandum No. 3323 of 23 May of this year, I have the honor to report that the Odessa chief of police Bunin has shown himself in his irreproachable and strict performance of his duties in the course of nearly seven years, as well as in his previous service career, in the best light. Bunin has often faced the necessity of firing civil servants under his command, as well as refusing to hire many people seeking a job, and in this manner Bunin has aroused irritation against himself and, as a consequence, denunciations, which are widely practiced in Odessa. Despite the fact that anonymous denunciations are not followed through on, on the basis of existing laws, a thorough-going investigation was carried out on the basis of such denunciations, on the order of the Odessa Governor General and Bunin himself, which support the complete legality of all of Bunin's activities. The present denunciation is, in all likelihood, a means of personal revenge by some fired police civil servant and contains the most unfounded accusations. A strict account, under my control, is kept of all monies at the disposal of the Odessa chief of police. The assignment and firing of all service personnel is also carried out with my knowledge and permission.

As regards the police secretary Sorochan, who was appointed by my predecessor (Ivan Ivanovich Sorochan was a veteran of the Odessa police organs). As early as 1866 he is listed in the *Kherson Province Address Book* as a department head of the legal section of the Odessa city government, with the rank of a provincial secretary XII class, B.S.), police chief Bunin often expressed a lack of faith in his moral qualities, but taking into account his service experience acquired in the position of court investigator for the old institutions and of precinct police officer, which he earlier occupied in Odessa and, not having any factual basis for accusing him of abuses in office, did not raise the question of his dismissal. The attached denunciation is being returned with this report.

Here one must say that Zelenoi was probably right that Bunin was in no way linked to embezzlement, in the same way that the author of the anonymous letter was in no way a count, but rather a fired petty police bureaucrat. A count would hardly have written an anonymous letter with so many orthographic mistakes. A police chief would have more than enough money from business. If one believes the anonymous denouncer, then by the end of his life Bunin should have been a millionaire. This was indeed the case, as we will see later on, and his older daughter had a considerable fortune before 1917. If one believes the same denouncer, the position of a precinct supervisor (a precinct inspector in modern terms) cost from 200 to 700 rubles, probably depending on the area of the city and the personality of the one who recommended him. As the third largest city in the Russian Empire (not counting the Kingdom of Poland) and a major port and trading center, it offered rich sources of graft for policemen and mayors. I should note that in Bunin's time three mayors succeeded each other (Pavel Kosagovskii, Pavel Zelenoi and Count Pavel Shuvalov). As concerns the struggle against Jewish domination in the Odessa police, only a week after taking office Yakov Ivanovich issued a decree to remove all Jews from the Odessa police. However, obviously, there was no hindrance to hiring them as clerks. Undoubtedly, as we will see later, the all-powerful Ober-Procurator of the Holy Synod, Konstantin Pobedonostsev,[10] was the police chief's high-ranking patron. One encounters the assertion that supposedly "Yakov Bunin was given a Turkish order for the detention of a Turkish criminal and that his uncle was the Ober-Procurator of the Holy Synod himself, Konstantin Pobedonostsev." More than likely, Yakov Ivanovich received an order not for the detention of a Turkish criminal, but for the warm reception shown some Turkish official. It is not yet possible to establish the degree of Bunin's kinship with Pobedonostsev. In any event, such patronage explains a lot regarding Bunin's career leap in the beginning of the 1880s, when Pobedonostsev was the most influential man in the empire and that his promotion was outside the rules.

It's interesting that Bunin felt no respect for army generals, although he remained in the modest rank of lieutenant colonel. Testimony to this is the letter from the chief of the Main Staff, General Nikolai Nikolaevich Obruchev, in the name of the war minister, to the minister of internal affairs and member of the Privy Council Ivan Nikolaevich Durnovo, on 19 June 1890:

> Dear Sir, Ivan Nikolaevich.
> The commander of the Odessa Military District drew up a petition to bestow upon the police chief of the city of Odessa, Lieutenant Colonel Bunin, the corresponding civil rank and the above-mentioned staff officer expressed a complete lack of understanding of the relations that should exist between him and senior army ranks and in eliminating his harmful influence on the young officers.

---

10   Editor's note. Konstantin Petrovich Pobedonostsev (1827-1907) joined the Russian civil service at an early age and quickly rose through the ranks. He later became a noted university professor and was appointed tutor to the future emperor Aleksandr III and influenced the latter's deeply reactionary views. In 1880 he was appointed chief procurator of the Holy Synod, or head of the Orthodox Church in Russia. Pobedonostsev lost influence under Nicholas II and retired following the 1905 revolution.

General Roop (commander of the Odessa Military District and Odessa Governor General Khristofor Khristoforovich Roop, B.S.) offered the following from a number of incidents establishing this conviction:

1) The Greek queen, having arrived in Odessa, changed her route and, instead of leaving Odessa at eight in the morning, delayed it until eight in the evening. Lieutenant Colonel Bunin did not inform the military leadership of this and thus deprived it of presenting itself to her Majesty. On the basis of article 9 of the "Rules on Mutual Relations between Civil and Military Authorities," the police chiefs of towns where the military district commander resides, are obligated to present reports on arriving personages, much less of royalty;

2) In January his Majesty's adjutant, Prince Shakhovskoi, was sent to represent his Imperial Sovereign at the funeral of General Radetskii (General Fedor Fedorovich Radetskii was a member of the State Council, B.S.). Due to the extraordinary situation concerning the funeral, the prince demanded to see the police chief, and the latter presented himself only after the passage of considerable time, while at the same time putting forth the most insufficient excuses.

3) Lieutenant Colonel Bunin allows himself to take on a familiar tone in addressing senior personages and generals, with whom he is not in the least close, which naturally arouses dissatisfaction among these people. Aside from this, he does not always offer the established salute to senior army officers.

I have the honor of reporting this to the discretion of your Excellency.
I ask you accept my sincere esteem and respect.

However, mayor Zelenoi decisively rose up to defend his police chief. On 21 July 1890 he wrote the director of the Police Department P.N. Durnovo:

Dear Sir, Petr Nikolaevich.
Apropos of the incidents communicated in letter no. 4241 of the past 26 June, by General Roop as evidence of the supposed complete lack of understanding by the chief of the Odessa police, Lieutenant Colonel Bunin, of the relations that should exist between him and senior army officers, I have the honor to report to your Excellency the following information in my possession.

1) As regards the arrival of her royal majesty, the queen of Greece, in Odessa. Having received on 14 March of this year a report from an agent of the Ministry of Foreign Affairs in Odessa that the queen would arrive in Odessa on the steamship *Sfaktoriya*, on Sunday 18 March, on that same day I reported this information (no. 2902) to the commander of the Odessa Military District. Independent of this, in accordance with a telegram from our emissary in Athens of 15 March, I informed General Roop (no. 2989) that the queen requested that the Odessa authorities refrain from organizing an official meeting. On the eve of the queen's visit, I was visited by Count Gendrikov, the chief of protocol, who had arrived from Petersburg to meet and accompany her royal majesty, and who told me in passing that he had spoken to General Roop regarding the queen's arrival and departure and that the general was not going to meet the queen, due to the desire expressed by her not to have an official meeting. At 7:50 on the morning of 18 March, the yacht *Sfaktoriya* entered the quarantine port and at ten o'clock her highness deigned to meet me and my wife, who had brought a bouquet of flowers. She also met the acting mayor, who carried bread and salt, Gendarme General Tsugalovskii, the port captain, the

Greek consul and his wife, Count Gendrikov, the chief of police, members of the Greek Philanthropic Society, and others. Neither the military district commander nor the corps commander was present at the meeting.

During the breakfast, to which I was invited, Count Gendrikov told the queen that having been warned about the hour of her majesty's arrival the evening before, General Roop asked to convey his apologies that he could not appear to greet the queen, because he was afraid to violate the wish expressed by her majesty in this regard. Her highness replied to this that "I thought that he was not in Odessa." Then at 6:30 in the evening, at the queen's invitation, which had been conveyed by Hofmarshal Messali, Roop appeared on the steamship at the general table, as if justifying himself against the queen's rebuke that had probably been communicated to him and then first told Count Gendrikov and then her majesty that he had not been informed of her arrival, as a result of which he had been deprived of the opportunity to meet her.

The departure of the queen of the Hellenes had been fixed, according to a previously compiled schedule, known to General Roop from Count Gendrikov, at eight o'clock that same evening by special train and there was no change in this regard. However, as we were breaking up following the departure of the royal train, General Roop, having declined the order by the policemen there to bring up his carriage, walked over to it himself and, completely unexpectedly for those present, expressed his dissatisfaction that my carriage supposedly was standing at a more honorable place than his and shouted to my driver: "Get back, you twit!" Unfortunately, the matter did not end there. Soon I began to hear rumors that the military district commander, while accusing police chief Bunin of insufficient deference, was determined to appeal to the war minister about reassigning this officer a corresponding civilian rank.

In view of all the rumors aroused by the military district commander's dissatisfaction with Lieutenant Colonel Bunin, all of these details, which remain in my memory, have been laid out here by me to clearly show you that there was no such incident, as reported by General Roop, that the Greek queen, having arrived in Odessa, supposedly changed her route and instead of leaving Odessa a 8:00 in the morning, delayed it until 8:00 in the evening, and that the military leadership was not deprived of the opportunity to be presented to her majesty, as can be seen from the copies of the previously-cited messages attached to this letter. Finally, even if some kind of change had taken place in the queen's arrival and departure, then the Odessa chief of police would not have informed the commander of the military district, but rather the gendarme railroad police or the port captain, as the train was located in the area of the port territory entrusted to him.

The accusation against the Odessa chief of police that when General Count Shakhovskoi, who had been commandeered by the sovereign emperor to be present at the funeral of General Radetskii, demanded that Lieutenant Coloenl Bunin appear before him in connection with some special need regarding the funeral, the latter supposedly allowed himself to appear only after some time had passed and offering the most misplaced excuses, is not supported by the facts. Because the death of General Radetskii took place while I was in Petersburg, in order to establish this fact I entered into confidential correspondence with the commander of the 11th Army Corps (General Prince Aleksei Ivanovich Shakhovskoi, B.S.) which, as can be seen from the attached copy of his letter no. 12 to me, informed me that while in Odessa to be present at General Radetskii's funeral he had never felt the need to approach the chief of police, which is why there was no case of Lieutenant Colonel Bunin's failing to appear before his highness.

However, independent of the issues raised in your letter, the man who performed the duties of the mayor of Odessa during my absence informed me upon my return to Odessa that complete order was maintained during the burial ceremony and that the chief of police, for his part, reported that he met his excellency upon the latter's arrival in Odessa and also accompanied him during his departure. At the railroad station the prince, in the presence of the commander of the military district, and while saying farewell to those accompanying him, praised Lieutenant Colonel Bunin as a tireless police chief and thanked him twice for the order at the funeral.

3) As regards the charge that Lieutenant Colonel Bunin supposedly allows himself to adopt a familiar tone in addressing senior personnel and generals with whom he is by no means closely acquainted, and that he does not even always salute senior army officers, this accusation seems too broad. Quite the opposite, having closely followed the activity of this officer over the course of more than five years of joint service in Odessa, I always had to give him credit for his ability to carry himself with the necessary deference toward his seniors and sufficient fastidiousness in his selection of acquaintances. Everybody in Odessa knows what kind of favor Lieutenant Colonel Bunin enjoys on the part of the corps commander and the division chief, not only because he not only always avoids grounds for any kind of clashes with the military chiefs, but in those cases in which for whatever reason they do arise between officers and the police, he immediately tries to eliminate the misunderstanding. Thus the absence of references to individual cases in which Lieutenant Colonel Bunin supposedly allowed himself to be disrespectful to senior generals, as ascribed to him by General Roop, and thus depriving me of the opportunity to present any kind of explanations in this regard, gives this declaration the air of untruth.

In view of what has been expressed here, one must reach the conclusion that assigning the Odessa chief of police, Lieutenant Colonel Bunin, the corresponding civil rank can in no way be supported by the reasons given here and presented by the commander of the Odessa Military District in his request on this matter.

While not touching on the moral aspect of this matter, which, I cannot hide, created a depressing impression on me, I must state that the question of assigning Lieutenant Colonel Bunin a civilian rank is very closely linked to the cancellation of military prerogatives in Odessa, namely that the individual occupying the post of chief of police in this town should have a military rank. Aside from those considerations, which were frequently expressed by the former governor general of Odessa as to the necessity of the Odessa police chief retaining a military rank, now with the elimination of position of the commandant of Odessa, this circumstance acquires enormous importance. The police chief's frequent run-ins with the great number of military personnel here are resolved only because the police chief has a military rank; stripping him of this would be the same as depersonalizing him in the eyes of the officers, particularly the young ones, and would create extremely undesirable conditions for the matter of preserving social order and calm. As a result, I consider it my duty to most zealously request that your Excellency inform the minister not to assign a civilian rank to Lieutenant Colonel Bunin, all the more so that it would be a completely undeserved reprimand for him.

I humbly beseech your Excellency to accept my complete regard and devotion.

Your humble servant.

Insofar as all the documents mentioned by Zelenoi are in Bunin's file, one can assume that the version laid out by the mayor corresponds to reality and that Roop distorted the facts. However, there also can be no doubt that Bunin had bad relations with the commander of the Odessa Military District, although this did not affect his career.

On 30 August 1893 Bunin was finally given the long-sought rank of colonel and, as usual, "outside the rules." He had been repeatedly put forth for this rank, but here the agreement of the war ministry was required and the latter objected on the pretext that not a single lieutenant colonel who had been promoted with him to this rank at this time and on military, and not the civil service, had yet to achieve the rank of colonel for longevity in service, and not for exceptional work. However, Pobedonostsev's patronage overcame this obstacle as well.

In recalling his conflict with the generals, on 22 November 1895 Bunin was attached to the Ministry of Internal Affairs and "commandeered to be at the disposal of the mayor of Odessa for carrying out duties at the same position."

Yakov Ivanovich Bunin had the following Russian orders: the Order of Saint Vladimir, third and fourth classes, the Order of Saint Anna, second class, the Order of Saint Stanislav, second and third classes, two rings with the imperial monogram, silver medals for the defense of Sevastopol and in memory of the reign of Emperor Aleksandr III, and a bronze one for service in the Crimean War of 1855-56. Besides this, he had been awarded with the following foreign orders: the commander's cross of the Greek Order of the Savior (the Greek queen had not forgotten him), the Persian Order of the Lion and the Sun, second class, the Turkish Order of Medzhidie, third class, an Italian officer's cross of the Order of the Crown, the Bukhara Order of the Rising Star, second class and gold (this had been awarded during the trip by the Emir of Bukhara across Russia in 1893), the Abyssinian Order of Solomon's Sword, second class, and the Bulgarian Order of Saint Aleksandr, third class. This was due to the presence of numerous foreign consulates in Odessa. Besides this, foreign monarchs often visited Odessa during their visits to Russia.

In 1898, as in the previous year, the police chief did not take a vacation, although before this and subsequently he regularly took one. This may be connected to his affair with Varvara Malinovskaya.

Bunin began to be ill often. On 1 June 1899 he submitted a request to take sick leave in Russia and abroad and to award him a 500 ruble allowance for treatment. Permission was granted, but an allowance was not assigned, due to the absence of funds in the treasury.

A document was drawn up on Bunin, in connection with his request, where it was written:

> Colonel Bunin, the acting chief of police of Odessa, has been on government service for 41 ½ years, of which more than 27 years have been in police positions, with 17 years in the present capacity.
>
> He receives the following per year:
>
>> A salary of 1,500 rubles, a meal allowance of 1,500 rubles, a housing allowance of 1,000 rubles, a travel allowance of 1,000 rubles, and a wound pension of 103 rubles and 95 kopecks. In all, 5,103 rubles and 95 kopecks.
>
> Bunin has a wife and five children, between 21 and 27 years old.
> In view of the significant compensation, the request by the mayor of Odessa for a treatment allowance for Colonel Bunin was turned down in April 1900.

Evidently Yakov Ivanovich's poor health forced him to think about retiring. However, his efforts to secure a pension dragged on. In February 1901, in connection with his forthcoming retirement, a new and more detailed document on Bunin was drawn up in the mayor's office.

> Colonel Bunin, attached to the Ministry of Internal Affairs and acting chief of the Odessa police (sixth class), 63 years old (this means that Yakov Ivanovich was most likely born in 1837, B.S.), has served more than 43 years, including 18 years in his last post; he has a right to a full pension, III rank, second degree, of 428 rubles and 85 kopecks per year; an augmented

pension may be requested according to the rules established by the Council of Ministers, in the amount of two-thirds of the maintenance cost for his position, meaning a salary of 1,500 rubles, a meal allowance of 1,500 rubles (a housing allowance of 1,000 rubles and a travel allowance of 1,000 rubles, which are authorized for this position, are not counted), for an amount of 2,000 rubles per year; he receives a pension for having being wounded of 103 rubles and 95 kopecks per year; the right to payroll deductions from his military salary can be determined only through communication with the war ministry chancellery.

He is married and has grown children and has an estate of 759 acres in Borisoglebsk District, Tambov Province.

Bunin, in accordance with the regulations of the Awards Committee, was awarded from on high on 30 August 1893 the rank of colonel, outside the rules. Thus in view of the comment to article 40, Book 8 of the Code of Military Decrees, published in 1889, those promoted to the rank of colonel while serving in a civilian department are not promoted to the rank of major general upon retirement, but may be reclassified at the corresponding civil rank according to the rules existing for civilian ranks. Bunin may not be reclassified as a major general upon his retirement.

The chiefs of police in Saint Petersburg (V class), Dubel't-Kraon, Ritter, Biron, and Yesipov solicited an augmented pension of 3,000 rubles each for more than 35 years of service, as an exception for these individuals and not to be imitated by others, and because in view of the class (VI) of the position occupied by Colonel Bunin and his family and property situation, can hardly count on a pension exceeding 2,500 rubles, even if he petitions as a special case, if he has not acquired the right to a military payroll deduction.

I should note that in 1901 a colonel and a state councilor could count on a maximum pension from the payroll deduction fund account of 860 rubles, while a general and a full state councilor could count on 1,290 rubles.

However, Bunin proved to be quite the petitioner.

The director of the Department of Police, Sergei Erastovich Zvolyanskii, informed the director of the department of general affairs, V.F. Trepov, on 24 January 1902:

Dear Sir, Vladimir Fedorovich

The Ober-Procurator of the Holy Synod, State Secretary Pobedonostsev, approached the deputy minister, Prince Svyatopolk-Mirskii, with a petition to render assistance in favorably resolving the appeal by the mayor of Odessa to promote the police chief of Odessa, Colonel Bunin, to the rank of major general and awarding him an augmented pension.

For his part, Prince Svyatopolk-Mirskii recognizes the petition raised by Colonel Count Shuvalov to be fully worthy of approval.

Keeping in mind the fact that the petition by the mayor about Colonel Bunin, as someone employed by the Ministry of Internal Affairs, arrived at the department of general affairs, I consider it my duty to communicate this information to your Excellency for your approval.

Please accept, your Excellency, my assurances of respect and devotion.

The petition by Pobedonostsev, who was evidently Bunin's patron, had its effect. On 17 February 1902 a notice was published in *The Russian Invalid* that in accordance with an imperial decree to the war ministry of 16 February, "the acting chief of the Odessa police, serving with the Ministry of Internal Affairs, Colonel Bunin, has been promoted to major general and retired from the service with a uniform and a pension."

On 2 March a grateful Yakov Ivanovich telegraphed the colleague of the minister of internal affairs, Prince Petr Dmitrievich Svyatopolk-Mirskii the following: "I express my sincere thanks for your assistance in the matter of my promotion. I venture to once again most humbly request your Excellency not to turn down my request to assign me an augmented pension. I request that you honor me with your reply.

"Major General Bunin."

To judge by the note left on the paper regarding the assignment of a pension to Bunin, which arrived in the department of general affairs on 4 March 1902, it was decided to define the size of the pension at 3,500 rubles. However, Yakov Ivanovich did not have long to be a general and to receive an augmented pension. In accordance with a communication by the Sevastopol' journalist Leonid Somov in the newspaper *The Glory of Sevastopol'* of 16 June 2009, Yakov Ivanovich Bunin, who was born in 1837, died in 1902.

The final document in Bunin's file is dated 18 March 1908. This was an accompanying letter that

> The department of Police is passing this petition on to the department of general affairs from the grown and incurably ill daughter of the former chief of the Odessa police, Major General Bunin, the maiden Mariya Bunina, to assign her an augmented pension with a single attachment, as the pension assigned to the above-named civil servant, who was last attached to the Ministry of Internal Affairs, was assigned by the department of general affairs.

Despite her incurable disease, Mariya Yakovlevna lived 90 years on this earth. This is what her nephew—the artist Kirill Borisovich Ivanov, probably the son of her younger sister Nadezhda reports:

> Mariya Yakovlevna Bunina was born in March 1872 at the estate of Ternovoe near Lipetsk. She was the daughter of a general, a graduate of the institute of noble maidens in Odessa, she underwent many privations. In her younger years, when she dreamed of an artistic career in Moscow, "papa would give out only enough money for a single pastry, and I thought, when should I eat it, in the morning or evening?" (Yakov Ivanovich was evidently kind of cheap and did not show off his wealth, B.S.). After the death of her father she became the full-fledged mistress of the Bunins' estate near Tambov, which was named Khludnevka. She inherited some stocks from her husband's mother before the revolution and doubled its value by playing the stock market.
>
> The establishment of Soviet power in Odessa in 1920 overturned her entire life: she was kicked out of her five-room apartment, which belonged to her, and instead, they gave her two rooms on different floors. All of her movable and non-movable property was lost, including her bank deposits. Nonetheless, M. Bunina, who had a broad nature, connived to acquire six grown adopted children and for an entire year fed a family of refugees who had escaped from Kiev to Odessa. They promised to pay for everything from hidden diamonds until she was finally reduced to selling the cross worn next to her skin.
>
> In 1922 Bunina's adopted daughter married a professor Filatov, an optician, who later became an academic. Mariya Yakovlevna became the manager of the Filatovs' home. During the NEP[11] years not everyone had it good, but Mariya Yakovlevna had sufficient food supplies so that each hungry person could get a plate of borshcht in her home.

---

11   Editor's note. The NEP (*Novaya Ekonomicheskaya Politika*), or the New Economic Policy, was adopted by the Bolsheviks in 1921, following the rigors of the "War Communism" of 1917-21. This policy of "state capitalism" relaxed some of the controls the state had placed on the economy. The NEP was succeeded by Stalin's forced industrialization and collectivization policies in 1928-29, under the heading of the five-year plans.

In 1931 Malya, which is what they called Filatov's young wife, left the professor, who was 30 years older than her and took up with a handsome harp player, who was six years younger than her. All of the abandoned husband's anger was directed at his mother-in-law, whom he literally drove out of the house. To top of the disaster, they arrested Mariya Yakovlevna during the time of the so-called "search for valuables." Having spent a few nights and days with the GPU[12] without sleep, standing in a jail cell filled to bursting with people, she turned over everything she had—ten czarist-era gold five-ruble pieces—in exchange for the freedom she received after a month in prison.

Nothing could reconcile her to Soviet power which, in her opinion, was defended only by "robbers and scoundrels"…

In 1935 they once again arrested Mariya Yakovlevna and her sister, Nadezhda Yakovlevna. Fortunately, both sisters were released, having spent about three months in prison. Fortunately, they did not touch either of them anymore. Mariya Yakovlevna survived the Great Patriotic War and passed away in 1962, in her ninetieth year.

In all likelihood, her nephew got something confused regarding Mariya Yakovlevna's first husband, who supposedly left her a rich inheritance. She was still a maiden in 1908 at the age of 36 and, to judge by everything else, retained the surname of Bunina, and thus did not get married before the revolution. Most likely, the inheritance, in the form of real estate and bank deposits and stocks came her way not through relatives of a first husband, but from her father, the chief of police, or her mother, who could have outlived her husband by several years. However, everything turned to ashes in 1917.

Since Colonel Bunin served 20 years at his last posting and was awarded the rank of general upon retiring, it means that he suited the provincial and capital leadership. On the other hand, he was not implicated in taking bribes and, according to the *All Odessa* guidebook from 1899; he had not acquired any property in Odessa. However, in such cases property was written up in other people's names. And in this same guidebook, on page 197, among the dachas located along the road from the train station to Skakovoe Field, the dacha of an S. Malinovskii is listed as no. 28. It's worth noting that it was located not far from the Botanical Gardens, in the church within which Rodion Malinovskii was christened. Thus it cannot be excluded that the dacha belonged to one of Varvara Nikolaevna's relatives. If this is true, then the marshal's first wife was right when she maintained that his mother's family was by no means poor.

Practically all of the police in the Russian Empire existed on bribes and without them did not even have the funds to carry out their professional activities (for example, police chancelleries were sometimes supported by bribes). The size of the bribes varied, depending upon the wealth of the region. One cannot be in doubt that Malinovskii's father, being the chief of police in the unofficial capital of south Russia, could simply not but take bribes in his position. Prince S.D. Urusov, who was appointed the governor of the neighboring province of Bessarabia in 1903, recalled:

Once with the assistance of one of the members of the prosecutor's office, who knew the area well, I tried to ascertain the approximate amount of the extractions carried out by the police across the province. It came out to significantly more than one million rubles per year (that is; at a minimum one-sixth of the overall volume of the province's industrial production). In

12   Editor's note. The GPU (*Gosudarstvennoe Politicheskoe Upravlenie*), or State Political Directorate was the name of the political police in Soviet Russia during 1922-23. It succeeded the "Cheka" ("Extraordinary Commission") and was succeeded by the Unified State Political Directorate (OGPU). The GPU was headed by F.E. Dzerzhinskii.

order to somewhat rehabilitate the Bessarabian police in the eyes of naïve people who may at some point read these lines, I will mention that the Petersburg police, according to the most thorough inquest by an expert in these matters, who served in the city government, receive up to six million rubles per year in extorted money alone; that is, which are not paid out for violation of the laws or bureaucratic abuses, but simply due to the fact that there exist inhabitants—home owners, shopkeepers, tavern owners, and manufacturers, etc. Extractions for violation of the laws in the interests of those who give them are not counted here, due to the impossibility of accounting for them… The bribe among the Bessarabian police, with minor exceptions, plays a major role. It's not difficult to be convinced of this, when one sees how the head policemen travel around in fours in spring carriages, travel first class by train, acquire homes and plots of ground and lose hundreds, and sometimes thousands, playing cards.

However, at the same time, Ya.I. Bunin, to judge by everything, knew moderation and kept control of the level of crime in Odessa which, contrary to widespread opinion, by the end of the nineteenth and beginning of the twentieth centuries, was by no means the highest among the cities of the Russian Empire and was significantly behind the capitals.[13] In 1912 the number sentenced by general and arbitration courts was 253 per 100,000 in Kherson Province, while this figure reached 307 in Estlandia.[14] To be sure, compared to several neighboring provinces, Kherson Province, thanks to Odessa, was confidently in the lead. In Kursk province the number of condemned per 100,000 inhabitants was only 45, 145 in Podol'ya province, and 73 in Bessarabia.

It's worthy of note that in October 1916 the leadership of the Odessa police launched a notorious case, during the course of which it came to light that the previous leadership; that is, Ya.I. Bunin's successors, had carried out a large-scale financial operation, offered protection to local business and covered the delivery of contraband articles to the Central Powers,[15] including gold.

The 1954 denunciation had no consequences for Marshal Malinovskii. According to a KGB eavesdropping tape, in 1963 the disgraced marshal Zhukov[16] told his wife the following about the "Malinovskii affair":

As is known, at that time his old wife wrote a very troubling letter and I was entrusted with carrying out an investigation and I recalled him from the Far East and investigated the matter. This material was forwarded to defense minister Bulganin.[17] Where these materials are, I don't know. What was communicated? The fact that Malinovskii, instead of returning to the motherland, remained in France in the Moroccan units, in which he supposedly enlisted

---

13   Editor's note. The mention of two capitals refers to Russia's traditional capital of Moscow, before the seat of government was moved to St. Petersburg in 1713. The Bolsheviks moved the capital back to Moscow in 1918.
14   Editor's note. Estlandia ("Estland," in German) was the pre-revolutionary name of modern Estonia.
15   Editor's note. This refers to the wartime alliance of Germany, Austia-Hungary, Bulgaria, and Turkey.
16   Editor's note. Georgii Konstantinovich Zhukov (1896-1974) was drafted into the imperial army in 1915 and joined the Red Army in 1918. In 1939 he defeated a major Japanese incursion in Mongolia. During the Great Patriotic War he served as chief of the General Staff and commanded several *fronts*. In 1942 he was appointed deputy supreme commander-in-chief, directly under Stalin. Following the war, he was relegated to several minor posts. After Stalin's death he served as defense minister and was a member of the Communist Party Presidium. Nikita Khrushchev removed Zhukov from all his posts in 1957 and he lived as a "non-person" until Khrushchev's own ouster in 1964.
17   Editor's note. Nikolai Aleksandrovich Bulganin (1895-1975) joined the Bolsheviks in 1917 and served for several years in the Cheka. He later became a manager and served as deputy chairman of the Council of People's Commissars and minister of the armed forces under Stalin, and in 1955 he became chairman of the Council of Ministers. Bulganin was implicated in the plot to overthrow Nikita Khrushchev in 1957 and was stripped of all his positions the following year.

to serve before 1920. And then, when we had already routed Kolchak,[18] for some reason he crossed Kolchak's front line through the Far East and joined the Red Army as a volunteer. These facts were sufficiently well known in the Main Cadres Directorate. Shchadenko[19] spoke about this. And Stalin did not trust Malinovskii.

Undoubtedly he was speaking about the 1954 denunciation, but given the passage of time Georgii Konstantinovich probably forgot that the main emphasis in the denunciation was not directed at Malinovskii's service in the Foreign Legion, but at his unacceptable social origins.

Khrushchev[20] did not let the denunciation proceed. Questions of Malinovskii's social origins did not bother him and Nikita Sergeevich did not doubt the marshal's loyalty. As the events of 1964 showed, he was deeply mistaken.

In his service biography, which was compiled on 28 December 1938, Brigade Commander Malinovskii described the early period of his life as follows.

I was born on 23 November 1898, new style, in the city of Odessa; I don't know who my father was and my birth certificate lists me as "illegitimate." I don't remember 1903, when my mother, Varvara Nikolaevna MALINOVSKAYA, lived with her married sister Yelena at Slobodka station on the Southwestern Railroad, where her husband, Mikhail Danilov, worked as a weight inspector in the freight office. Then, in 1904 my mother moved to the village of Sutiski, not far from Gnivan' station along the Southwestern Railroad, in what is now Vinnitsa Oblast', and there found work as a cook in the district hospital, bought a Singer sewing machine on credit and did some sewing. In 1908-09 the local landlady, Countess Geiden, who sometimes visited the hospital for charitable purposes, took her on and she worked as a housekeeper and often as a cook; because the cook was an inveterate drunk, and here she became acquainted with a young footman and was fired for this, after which she settled in the same village of Sutiski and took up sewing, which is how she earned her keep; it was in this village that I began to attend the village school (Sutiski was the hereditary estate of the Geidens and it is doubtful that the countess simply took on a housekeeper just like that, without a recommendation. One may assume that from the very start; that is, from 1904, Varvara Mikhailovna worked as a housekeeper on the Geidens' estate by someone's solid recommendation. And it's quite odd that they fired her for marrying a footman. The fact that a footman and a cook, or a footman and a housekeeper were husband and wife was a common occurrence for landed estates, B.S.). By the fall of 1910 she married this footman (why didn't

---

18 Editor's note. Aleksandr Vasil'evich Kolchak (1874-1920) joined the Russian navy in 1894 and took part in several expeditions to the Arctic and was appointed commander of the Black Sea Fleet during the First World War. During the civil war he joined the anti-Bolshevik forces in Siberia and became head of this movement following a military coup. He was later recognized as head of all anti-Bolshevik forces in Russia, but his armies were defeated during 1919. Kolchak was betrayed and turned over to pro-Bolshevik forces, who executed him in Irkutsk.

19 Editor's note. Yefim Afanas'evich Shchadenko (1885-1951) joined the Bolshevik faction of the social-democratic movement and later served in the First World War. During the civil war he served as a political officer with a number of formations and continued to rise in the armed forces' political apparatus between the wars. During World War II he served as a deputy defense commissar and member of the military council on several *fronts*. Shchadenko retired due to poor health in 1944.

20 Editor's note. Nikita Sergeevich Khrushchev (1894-1971) joined the Communist Party in 1918 and served as a political commissar during the civil war. He later gained Stalin's favor and rose rapidly through the party's ranks. During the Great Patriotic War he served as a political commissar with various *fronts*. Following the war, he was party boss in Ukraine in Moscow. After Stalin's death he gradually pushed aside his rivals and occupied the top posts in the party and government. Khrushchev was removed from his offices in 1964 and sent into retirement, where he wrote his clandestine memoirs.

she get married earlier and how did they live unmarried?, B.S.) and mama and I moved in with Sergei Zalesnyi in the village of Klishchev (seven kilometers from Sutiski) and mother took on the surname of Zalesnaya, while I remained Malinovskii; that is, I was not adopted. It was here in the spring of 1911 that I finished the parish church school in the village of Klishchev and it was this spring that this same Zalesnyi drove me out of the house, following lengthy arguments on this matter with mama. I left with some other boys from the village for landlord Yaroshinskii's Shenderov farm (three kilometers from the village of Klishchev) and began to work as a farm laborer at odd jobs, (I mostly worked as an animal driver and cleaned plows) plowing deeply to grow sugar beets, and in the winter I began to work in the bull shed and hauled manure to the fields) (the village of Shenderov in modern Tyvrovskii district, then Tyvrovskii county really exists. It is located between the villages of Fedorovka and Potush. There were 280 inhabitants in the beginning of the twenty first century, B.S.). So I worked until August 1913 and corresponded with my aunts and on the invitation of auntie Yelena, whose husband had been transferred from Slobodka station to the Odessa freight station and worked as a weight inspector, I arrived in Odessa in the fall of 1913 and, with the help of this uncle Danilov I began work in a fancy goods shop owned by the merchant M.P. Pripuskov, at 29 Torgovaya Street. This merchant often redeemed goods in the trade office and the weight inspectors knew him (it's of interest that in 1911 the merchant M.P. Pripuskov owned the village of Gulyaeva Gora (Il'yatino) in the Smolensk district of Vereya county. The village was located 26 kilometers from Dorokhovo station along the Belorussian Railroad. It's unknown whether this merchant was a relative of Malinovskii's employer, B.S.). I received five rubles per month, but in May 1914 I came down with scarlet fever and when I finally got out of the city hospital the merchant had hired another teenager in my place, and the merchant told me that I should take it easy for a month or two following my illness, and then we would see, and thus I became unemployed, and then the war began, and it just so happened that I had read a brochure about the war of 1812 and was full of desire to fight heroically at Borodino in 1812, although I was often without anything to do and would disappear at my uncle's work place in the goods wagons at the freight station, from where military freights were loaded. I secretly climbed onto one of the trains and left for the front with the soldiers.

Malinovskii's daughter recalled once how the habits acquired in Pripuskov's store came in handy.

I was leaving to see a pregnant friend and I clumsily wrapped up a box shaped like a basket, within which there were amazing candies, in strawberry-shaped wrappers with the scary name of "Radium." Papa looked for a long time over his glasses, then got up, took the box and then unbelievably skillfully and artistically, almost stylishly, wrapped up the box in a second and didn't even tie it up with a bow—but with a rose! Papa said that "you should do everything with flair!" and explained, "It's the Odessa way!"

This is what modern Ukrainian local historians write about Tyvrov:

The years passed and the village's owners came and went, the population put up with their oppressions and rose up when their patience came to an end. In June 1648 Maksim Krivonos's Cossack-peasant troops took Tyvrov by storm. Then the Poles and Turks came again, and then the Polish landlords. The estate was considered a rich one and grain was shipped to Danzig.
    In 1742 Tyvorv's owner, the Bratslav Second Lieutenant Mikhal Kalitinskii brought monks from the Dominican order here and built a new *klasztor* (a Catholic monastery, B.S.) for them on the site of the old one, which had been founded as early as 1569 and which had probably been destroyed by rebels. In 1744 Tyvrov was awarded the status of a small town. At that

time an event occurred, which was typical of the "enlightened" eighteenth century and not just for the Middle Ages. As early as 1590 Marianna Yaroshinskaya, having married Sevastian Kalitinskii, received Tyvrov as a dowry and the village thus passed to the house of Kalitinskii. When the line of direct descendants of this clan died out, the representatives of another branch of the Kalitinskiis and the Yaroshinskii clan began to make claims on the small town and the adjoining land. The "family conflict" was resolved in 1756 by force of arms. Upon launching a "raid"; that is, having attacked Tyvrov with a well-armed detachment, Zakharii Yaroshinskii won a bloody battle in which both sides even employed artillery.

His son established himself firmly: he built a large manor house opposite the monastery and built a large park and both architectural sites defined Tyvrov's silhouette and face for a long time…

And this is what is recounted about Tyvrov in a modern tourist site:

This is a regional center along the picturesque banks of the Southern Bug River, 30 kilometers from Vinnitsa. The town is first mentioned in 1505, when the Bratslav landowner F. Dashkevich was awarded the right to own Tyvrov. A Lithuanian and then a Polish fortress on the Tatar road. In 1648 M. Krivonos's Cossack detachments seized it and destroyed the old Catholic church, although the Poles soon returned to the town. In 1742 the Bratslav Second Lietenant M. Kalitinskii built a new church for the Dominicans' monastery (in Soviet times a factory for producing plastic articles was located in this building). In 1744 Tyvrov was awarded the status of a small town. In 1756 the Yaroshinskii clan won the right to own the town and they built a large manor house opposite the monastery and constructed a park. Later on the estate belonged to Count Geiden, who was engaged in beer brewing in the town. In 1898 the manor house suffered heavily in a fire, although the building still remains and is now a boarding school. The trade buildings from the XVIII century have also been preserved, as well as the water mill from the XIX-XX centuries. The wooded bank of the Southern Bug River, with it granite ledges here, are a popular rest area for people from Vinnitsa.

There was a theological academy in Tyvrov, the graduates of which had the right of preferential acceptance into theological seminaries. Its program was basically equal to four years of high school and thus its level was very different from the usual parish school. Only children of the clergy were accepted here on a tuition-free basis, while the rest had to pay.

In 1911 the estate no longer belonged to the Yaroshinskiis, but to that same Count Geiden and it was located in the district center of Tyvrov. It was locatred 16 kilometers from Gnivan' station.

According to the guidebook by Viktor Karlovich Gul'dman, *Estate Land Ownership in Podol'ya Province*, which was issued in 1898, Count Dmitrii Fedorovich Geiden, a nobleman from Saint Petersburg Province, owned the villages of Tarabanovka and Sutiski in the Vinnitsa district. There were no longer any landowners by the name of Yaroshinskii in the Vinnitsa district. There were only the heirs of Iosif Frantsevich Yaroshinskii, nobles from Podol'ya Province, who owned the villages of Klishchev, Komarov, Rovets, Biskupka, and Grizhintsy. It's not excluded that Count Geiden bought these villages from Yaroshinskii's heirs in 1900, when he established his Tyvrov brewing plant. No Shenderov farm is mentioned in the guidebook. It was probably one of the above-named estates, probably Klishchev (Klishchov), which is next to Shenderov, approximately eight kilometers to the southwest.

Thus Count Dmitrii Fedorovich Geiden (1862-1926), who supposedly at one time was Rodion Malinovskii's benefactor, was the owner of Sutiski. He completed Saint Petersburg University and joined the 12th Akhtyrka Hussar Regiment from civilian life and was later promoted an officer.

In 1891 he completed the Nikolai General Staff Academy and served as high as a colonel of the General Staff. He established a brewing plant in Tyvrov in 1900, in which 2,100,000 liters of beer were produced yearly. Geiden's beer enjoyed great popularity and was sold throughout the empire, even in the Grand Duchy of Finland.[21] Pilsener beer was primarily produced in the plant. The count retired following the Russo-Japanese War and he was elected a deputy to the State Duma.[22] With the beginning of the First World War in 1914 he returned to the army and was appointed acting duty general on the staff of General Brusilov's[23] 8th Army and remained at this post up to the end of 1917. The count joined the Volunteer Army[24] in 1918 and was appointed acting general for special assignments with the army's supply chief. During July-August 1919 General Wrangel[25] appointed him acting chief of the garrison of Tsaritsyn.[26] Geiden then came down with cholera and was evacuated. In 1920 was "at the disposal" of the supply chief of the Armed Forces of South Russia.[27] Following the evacuation from the Crimea,[28] he lived in Serbia and was a permanent faculty member at the Crimean Officer's School in the Kingdom of the Serbs, Croats and Slovenes.[29] After leaving the school, he moved to Zagreb, where he passed away on 23 May 1926. Dmitrii Fedorovich was decorated with a number of orders, was a Gentry Captain in the Vinnitsa district of Podol'ya Province, a representative of the Zhmerinka local board and, aside from Sutiski,

---

21 Editor's note. Before the revolution the Grand Duchy of Finland enjoyed a semi-autonomous status in the Russian Empire.

22 Editor's note. The State Duma (*Gosudarstvennaya Duma*), the first elected legislative body in Russian history, came about as a result of concessions made by Emperor Nicholas II during the revolution of 1905. There were four Dumas in all, lasting from 1906 to 1917, when the final Duma was abolished by the Provisional Government.

23 Editor's note. Aleksei Alekseevich Brusilov (1853-1926) joined the Russian army in 1872 and fought in the Russo-Turkish War of 1877-78. During the First World War he commanded an army and the Southwestern Front, whose summer offensive of 1916 came close to destroying the Austro-Hungarian army. He was appointed commander-in-chief of the Russian army in 1917, but was relieved shortly afterwards. Brusilov later joined the Red Army, but did not play an active role in the civil war.

24 Editor's note. The Volunteer Army (*Dobrovol'cheskaya Armiya*) was organized in south Russia at the end of 1917, in order to oppose the Bolsheviks, who had seized power in Russia in November. The army, which was based on a cadre of ex-officers and the Cossack population of the North Caucasus, spearheaded the drive on Moscow in 1919, where it was defeated by the Red Army. The Volunteer Army, severely reduced in numbers, was evacuated to the Crimea in 1920 and there merged with the remaining anti-Bolshevik forces.

25 Editor's note. Petr Nikolaevich Wrangel (1878-1928) joined the army in 1902 and fought in the Russo-Japanese War. During the First World War he rose to the command of a cavalry brigade. He joined the Volunteer Army in 1918 and commanded a division, corps and army, before resigning in a policy dispute. In 1920 he was appointed commander of all anti-Soviet forces in the Crimea and Northern Tavria. However, his forces were overwhelmed by the Red Army and he left for exile with the remnants of his force. Wrangel died in exile in Belgium.

26 Editor's note. The town of Tsaritsyn, on the lower course of the Volga River, was founded in 1589. During the civil war the city withstood several sieges by anti-Bolshevik forces, in which Joseph Stalin, the future Soviet dictator, played a notable part. The city was renamed Stalingrad in 1925 and during the Second World War was one of the turning points of the war. Stalingrad was renamed Volgograd in 1961, during the anti-Stalin campaign.

27 Editor's note. The Armed Forces of South Russia (*Vooruzhennye Sily Yuga Rossii*) were formed in early 1919, incorporating all anti-Bolshevik forces in Russia's south. This force was successively commanded by Anton I. Denikin and P.N. Wrangel, until its defeat and evacuation from the Crimea at the end of 1920.

28 Editor's note. This refers to the evacuation of the remnants of the anti-Soviet forces from the Crimean peninsula in November 1920, following their defeat by the Red Army.

29 Editor's note. The kingdom was established in December 1918, as the result of the defeat of Austria-Hungary in the First World War and included the kingdom of Serbia and the former Austro-Hungarian provinces of Croatia and Slovenia. In 1929 the country was renamed Yugoslavia.

he owned another 8,100 acres in Smolensk Province and another 1,080 in the Kuban'.[30] He was the first man in Podol'ya Province to establish telephone communications in a number of towns and small towns, and he built a number of factories, a distillery, a mill, and a school.

In a later service record, compiled by Marshal Malinovskii on 4 March 1948, the beginning of his life was laid out somewhat differently:

> I was born on 23 November 1898 in the city of Odessa. I don't know who my father was, because I was the illegitimate child of Varvara Nikolaevna MALINOVSKAYA, who lived with her sisters as a single mother, and who from 1903 lived in the village of Sutiski, Tyvrov district, Vinnitsa Oblast', and worked as a cook in a hospital and a housekeeper during 1908-09 at the estate of Count Geiden, also in Sutiski.
>
> In 1910 my mother married the peasant ZALESNYI and moved to the village of Klishchev and lived there until 1944 and was a member of a collective farm, and now lives in the city of Vinnitsa, with her daughter. I help my mother regularly and send her 400 rubles and often send packages and other things.
>
> In 1911 I finished the village school in Klishchev and my stepfather threw me out of the house, after which I began my independent working life, and from the spring of 1911 I worked as a farm laborer at the Shenderov farm (three kilometers from the village of Klishchev), which belonged to the landlord YAROSHINSKII, until the fall of 1913, and then left for the city of Odessa to my aunt, whose husband, DANILOV, worked as a weight inspector at the Odessa freight station, where they got me a job as a shop clerk in merchant PRIPUSKOV'S store at 29, Torgovaya Street.
>
> In the spring of 1914 I came down with scarlet fever and was without work upon being released from the hospital. I ran around the warehouse at my uncle's job at the freight station and, having gotten aboard a train full of soldiers, rode away with them to the front: this is how I ended up at the front and was enrolled in a machine gun crew of the 256th Yelizavetgrad[31] Infantry Regiment as a volunteer.

However, there exists quite a different version of Rodion Yakovlevich's early biography, which is supported by certain documents and seems to us to be closer to reality than that version which Malinovskii himself offered in his service reports.

On 15 October 1991 the agronomic scientist and specialist in potato diseases L.V. Rozhalin wrote in a letter to Natal'ya Rodionovna Malinovskaya about his meetings with Rodion Malinovskii in the village of Staryi Belous, Chernigov district, Chernigov Province:

> In January 1902 we had a lot of guests staying with us for the baptism of my sister Oksana. I well remember the burning candles at the font and the old priest with a long, grey beard. At this time it was evidently decided to build a new house for the Belous priest on the same site where the old house stood with the attached kitchen. It was necessary to tear this house down and we had to temporarily move to another place. In the spring my parents left to see the landlady Malinovskaya, in order to speak to her on this matter, and they took me with them. I remember well that this meeting took place in the courtyard near Malinovskaya's large house. During this meeting a large dog came up to me and sniffed me in a friendly way and licked

---

30 Editor's note. This refers to the territory in south Russia along the Kuban' River.
31 Editor's note. Yelizavetgrad was founded in 1752 in honor of the Empress Elizabeth. The Soviets changed its name to Zinov'evsk in 1924 and to Kirovograd in 1934. The current Ukrainian transcription is Kirovohrad.

my nose with its tongue. Perhaps I had a cold. At that moment a boy my height, in short pants and a white shirt, ran up to me and said: "Don't be afraid, she doesn't bite." This was Ron (Rodion), Malinovskaya's adopted son. We were the same age and both were already three.

There were three houses in Malinovskaya's spacious courtyard. The former owner's (Prince Kekuatov?) (the representatives of this princely clan of Tartar descent really did live in Chernigov province and their estate was in the village of Bigach, Borzenskii district, B.S.), in which Vera Nikolaevna Malinovskaya lived with her numerous friends. There was a two-room house near the gates to the farmstead; one room of which was filled with the pictures of Malinovskaya, who was an artist; the other room was used for sick people, as Malinovskaya was also a doctor. The third house remained unoccupied and was usually rented by boarders in the summer. Malinovskaya allowed our family to move into this house while they were working on our house. There was a large old carriage barn in the courtyard, with very high gates and which was completely empty. Almost every year Malinovskaya's acquaintances would arrive to spend the summer, because there was an empty house and a stream for bathing. A worker named Mikhailo lived on the farmstead and carried out various tasks: he guarded the farmstead in the winter and heated up the small greenhouse, where my father raised flowers and seedlings.

When our family became acquainted with Vera Nikolaevna Malinovskaya, she was probably more than 50 years old. She was already partially gray. Her friend, Rakhil' Modestovna Khir'yakova, with whom she lived, looked very much like an old lady.

Here it is necessary to make a small regression regarding the Khir'yakov family. I found the family tree of the Tove family on line, where there is listed a Yuliya Modestovna Khir'yakova, who was born in the middle of the 1840s and whose second marriage was to Lev (Leonel') L'vovich Tove, who was born in the second quarter of the XIX century. By the way, Leonel' Tove was an engineer at factories in the Urals and a British subject. Rakhil' Modestovna was Yuliya Modestovna's sister. If she, as a sister, was born in the 1840s, then she was probably no less than 60 years old in the first decade of the 1900s. One of Yuliya Modestovna's and Leonel' L'vovich's sons, Lev L'vovich Tove, later became a famous scientist and in 1912 served to the rank of state councilor. He was born in 1867 in the settlement of Lys'va in Perm' Province, but completed the famous Richelieu High School and then the Saint Petersburg Mining Institute. In 1902 Lev L'vovich Tove the younger became an adjunct professor in the Tomsk Technological Institute in the department of mining art. In 1902, as the leader of a mining party, he personally studied the gold mining enterprises of the Yenisei territory and visited many goldfields. The result of this work was his report on the gold industry in the territory. In 1894 Tove was engaged in searching for gold in the Amur and Maritime provinces. His researches also reached to Kamchatka. The result of this work was a large three-volume study on the Far East's gold industry. Lev Tove was a consultant for the Russian Society of Gold Manufacturers, a member of the board of the Tomsk Society for the Relief of Mining and Gold Extraction Laborers and Workers, and a member of the editorial board of the journal *Gold and Platinum*. He was a major specialist on gold in Russia and in 1904 began to teach a course on "gold mining" to students. At the same time, Lev L'vovich often visited the Lena goldfields and the gold mines of the Tomsk gold district. He committed suicide on 17 January 1917 as a state councilor and representative for fuel in Siberia and the Far East. At about 12 noon Lev Tove shot himself in the mouth with a revolver. This took place in the professor's lounge of the main building of the Tomsk Technological Institute. In a note he left behind, he said: "I must make way for the greater good and pass it on to firmer hands. I wish you success and that things move more quickly." In his obituary, a friend of the deceased, Aleksandr Vasil'evich Adrianov, a commentator and traveler, who was shot by the Bolsheviks in March 1920 for supporting Kolchak's government, wrote: "The huge amount of responsible work, which is connected with unimaginable difficulties, given our present confusion, and with the daily reproaches and demands of dissatisfied consumers, had so overstrained the nerves of the representative that he was deprived of rest and sleep. And when those near to him advised him to give up this work, L.L. found that he could not." The obituary states unclearly that L.L. Tove committed suicide "being unable to withstand such pressure and unable to find a way out of the developing situation," insofar as "the new responsibility in those conditions required the unimaginable straining of his physical and spiritual forces." Tove was a wealthy and good man, but he parted with money easily. As A.V. Adrianov remembered, the Tomsk bibliographer and publisher P.I. Makushin told him: "Lev L'vovich Tove used to come into my store all the time in order to send 25 or 50 rubles for someone in need that he had heard about, and each time, when sending the money, he asked me not to mention his name." He once contributed 500 rubles to the Society for Assisting the Establishment of Rational Recreation in the Villages of Tomsk Province, but only on the condition that his name would not be mentioned. It is not excluded that the suicide was linked to some sort of work abuses and a major embezzlement. According to Adrianov, "all they found on the deceased was 23 rubles and 50 kopecks, while he had debts of several hundred rubles in the relief office, while at the same time he earned a lot and lived very modestly." The post he occupied was open to a lot of corruption. According to Adrianov, Tove "had too soft of a nature and was unable to refuse anyone's request." A pension of 1,600 rubles per year was established for the family.

Lev L'vovich Tove had three children: Petr (born in 1901), Dmitrii (born in 1902) and a daughter Avgusta (born in 1906). This was his wife, Aleksandra Gavrilovna Myasnikova's second marriage and she had a daughter Nina (born in 1896) and a son Lev (born in 1898) by her first marriage.

In some documents the name "Khir'yakov" was written (or read) as Kir'yakov. For example, in the Ivanov family tree, whose forefather was Captain Agap Gavrilovich Ivanov (1763-1833), it is noted that Matvei Ivanovich Ivanov, a state councilor and mining engineer for the supervision of private factories, and his wife, *nee* Princess Sof'ya Nikolaevna Maksutova, had a son Dmitrii, born on 6 November 1869, who was baptized on 11 November in the Ascension Church in Kasimov. His godparents were the engineer and state councilor Modest Nikolaevich Kir'yakov and his daughter Rakhil' Modestovna Kir'yakova. This was undoubtedly Rakhil' Modestovna Khir'yakova. Since she kept her maiden name, it follows that she was not married. Her real surname really was Khir'yakov, insofar as there is an obituary devoted to her father, Modest Nikolaevich Khir'yakov, a mining engineer and state councilor, which was published in issue no. 6469 of the newspaper *Novoye Vremya* in 1894, which wrote:

On 27 February, at the age of 80, one of the oldest mining engineers and state councilor, Modest Nikolaevich Khir'yakov, passed away. The deceased, upon graduating from the course with a gold medal from the Officer Mining School, over the course of many years managed the Serebryansk, Kusa, Zlatoust, Kushva, and Nizhnyaya Tura factories, as well as Count Shuvalov's private factories. He introduced a number of improvements into factory affairs. Under his direction, the Zlatoust factory acquired a laboratory and they began to make iron according to the Contuas method. While a young mining engineer, the deceased was on assignment in Sweden, where he became closely acquainted with mining and factory affairs in a school in Falun . It was here that he learned Swedish, which later enabled him to translate several of Pushkin's works into Swedish. Young engineers, when departing on business to Swedish factories, always approached the deceased for advice and recommendations. As a man, M.N. had a pleasant character and loved to converse with young people. Despite the positions he occupied, he did not acquire a fortune and lately lived exclusively on his pension with his large family.

Thus Rakhil' Modestovna could not have an estate and the latter most likely belonged to Vera Nikolaevna's husband, who had died by this time. I should also note that M.N. Khir'yakov's son Aleksandr became a writer and at one time was close to Lev Tolstoi.

But let's return to Rozhalin's memoirs. He recalled:

Ron called Vera Nikolaevna "mama Vera" and Rakhil' Modestovna "mama Krona," because he could not yet correctly pronounce the word for godmother. This incorrect child's pronunciation remained in adulthood. Rakhil' Modestovna's brother, Aleksandr Modestovich Khir'yakov, and his sister, Natal'ya Modestovna also lived with Vera Nikolaevna. V.G. Chertkov,[32] together with Aleksandr Modestovich, distributed L.N. Tolstoi's philosophical sayings by publishing different photographs of L.N. Tolstoi with his philosophical sayings printed on them. Khir'yakov presented a set of such photographs to my father... Yefrosin'ya Dmitrievna (A.M. Khir'yakov's first wife was Ye.D. Kosmenko, 1858-1938, B.S.), Aleksandr Modestovich's wife, worked for a time for L.N. Tolstoi and accompanied our migrating Dukhobors[33] during their passage to Canada...

A major role in the "life" of V.N. Malinovskaya's family was played by a girl of about 20 years who worked for her, named Yelena Nikolaevna. Yelena Nikolaevna was born in Mariupol' and had a secondary education and a good character. She was a full-fledged member of Vera Nikolaevna's family over the course of many years. Her main responsibility was taking care of little Ron. When our family began to live in Malinovskaya's house while ours was being built, I automatically fell into Yelena Nikolaevna's orbit and got quite far away from observation by my nanny Kossovich. Almost every day Yelena Nikolaevna would lead Ron and me to the sandy bank of the Belous River, which was the eastern boundary of Malinovskaya's farmstead. There we would dig in the sand and dig little pools and catch minnows with a handkerchief and put them in our pools, where these small fish quickly died. Yelena Nikolaevna would shame us for tormenting the small fish. She would usually read a book or sing unfamiliar songs. The next year Yelena Nikolaevna, Ron and I began to cross the creek to a meadow on a bridge made of boards with handrails, and Yelena Nikolaevna would acquaint us with the names of various plants. I still recall from that long-ago time the medicinal plant "krovokhlebka," which I have never seen anywhere else. There was an old pine woods beyond the meadow. They bought Ron and me metal boxes and we made drawers with glazed lids for making collections of butterflies and beetles. Ron and I had a contest in making a collection and a fortunate incident helped me to win it.

We had an observation hive in a window in the living room of our new house, which housed bees. The hive consisted of one frame, which was glazed from two sides. Both of the frame's pieces of glass were closed by small doors. The bees would enter the hive through an opening cut in the window frame. Upon opening both small doors, you could see all the bees, without fearing that they would fly into the room. You could observe through the hive's glass how the bees fed and took care of the queen, how they cleaned the hive, how they kept thieves out of the hive, and how they fought against enemies, etc. Our guests would often sit

---

32   Editor's note. Vladimir Grigor'evich Chertkov (1854-1936) joined the Russian army in 1873, but left in 1880. He later met Tolstoi and became a devoted follower. Due to the czarist government's attitude to Tolstoi, Chertkov went into voluntary exile in 1897, but returned to Russia in 1908. Chertkov became the editor of Tolstoi's works following the latter's death in 1910.

33   Editor's note. The Dukhobors ("spiritual strugglers") were a splinter group of Russian Christians who arose sometime in the 18th century. Because of their pacifism and refusal to recognize the authority of the government and the official Orthodox Church, they were often persecuted. Large numbers of them immigrated to Canada at the end of the 19th century, aided by Tolstoi and other like-minded supporters.

near the hive's glasses. Once at night a large and rare night butterfly, by the name of "Death's Head," got into the hive, attracted by the smell of honey. My father heard a loud noise one night, which the bees had raised and upon opening the glass he saw the butterfly in the hive and pulled it out of the hive through a specially made opening. Thanks to this incident a very rare butterfly appeared in my collection. Ron clearly envied me.

In those years there were a lot of lizards in the Belous woods and Ron and I would compete in catching lizards. We would bring them home in boxes and release them in our gardens. We had unpleasant incidents with the lizards. While returning home after one such hunt along the village street, one of us dropped his box and it opened and the lizards scattered and started to hide under the barn wall, leading out into the street. The owner appeared while we were catching the lizards and began to shout that these reptiles would ruin her cow. Yelena Nikolaevna had to try and calm the woman down. I once caught it from my father in our house. It happened this way: upon coming back home from the hunt, I temporarily put the box with the lizards on the dining table and then let the lizards go in the garden. I didn't notice that when the box was lying on the table that one of the lizards had hidden under a napkin, which covered the bread that had been cut for lunch. My father came, took off the napkin and discovered the lizard! My father shouted at me loudly and I broke out in tears. Ron didn't know how to cry at all like other children do. If he was sternly punished, then he would begin to speak in a quivering and broken voice that he was innocent and that he was being punished "for nothing." There could be no question of Vera Nikolaevna employing physical or painful means of punishment. When punished, Ron would have to sit on a chair for a certain time in the middle of the room and the time he had to sit depended on the extent of the malfeasance. Vera Nikolaevna was a good woman, but it's possible that she was excessively stern and demanding of Ron. R.M. Khir'yakova ("mama Krona") was excessively condescending and forgave some of his misdeeds. R.M. Khir'yakova taught Ron French. At twelve years he would speak only French with her.

During the summer Vera Nikolaevna would study with us almost every day, trying to expand the knowledge we had received in school, and also taught us how to draw. Ron sometimes worked in the garden and cleaned up "mama Krona's" room, for which she paid him and the money was kept in an account in her room I found out about this following one unpleasant occurrence.

V.N. Malinovskaya's farmstead was large, with a probable area of about three hectares. There were no trees in the water meadow part of the farmstead and the land was rented for growing vegetables. There was a bathhouse on this part of the farmstead and a deep well had been dug near the bathhouse, from which they got water not only for the bathhouse, but for preparing food. Once, when we were near the well, Ron grabbed a large pumpkin which had grown next to the well, and threw it into the well. Because the well was shallow the spray from the pumpkin flew up higher than the well. He liked this. He grabbed another large pumpkin. I asked him not to throw it into the well, but he threw it in and said: "I'll pull them out with a pole." However, the pumpkins he speared with the pole would fall back into the well before he could grab them with his hands. All of our efforts ended with us splitting up the pumpkins. I went home, trying to avoid seeing the owners and didn't go to see the Malinovskiis for two days. Ron came to see me and said that Mikhailo had cleaned the well and they paid Mikhailo for this "with my own money, which were kept with mama Krona."

We suffered a terrible tragedy in the spring of 1905. My favorite brother, Tolya, drowned in the river in front of my own eyes. We took this tragedy very hard. When, following this accident, Yelena Nikolaevna took us for a swim, she brought along a rope, in order to keep hold of Ron on a leash while he swam. I didn't go swimming. Ron liked this kind of swimming. He got undressed, tied the knot on his own, fastening the rope to his waist. Then he gave the other end of the rope to Yelena Nikolaevna, boldly strode to the center of the river, went up to his chest in the water and shouted "I'm drowning, I'm drowning," dove under the water and hid there. Yelena Nikolaevna quickly began to work, pulling out the seven-year old boy from under the water. When I looked at her face I saw fear and tension, because it was not easy to pull. When she had dragged him closer to the bank, he got up; satisfied that he had pulled the joke off. Yelena Nikolaevna was upset. She untied the rope on Ron's stomach and ordered us to go to the garden. Following this incident, we didn't go swimming for a long time.

Mama Vera's and Mama Krona's efforts to keep Ron from smoking tobacco were without result. Relatives and acquaintances from Chernigov often rode or walked to see us. The Belous landlords, owners of farmsteads and small plots of land visited our family systematically. These were the Sikorskiis, Aleksei Osipovich, his wife Stefaniya Feofilovna and their children Lelya and Volodya. The children were already teenagers, but we organized a Christmas tree for them and I was there several times. The Grembitskiis, Fedor Fedorovich and his brother, Colonel Dmitrii Fedorovich. Fedor Fedorovich's wife, Agnessa Nikolaevna played the piano well, while another landowner, Pavel Grigor'evich Berezovskii, played the violin well. They would organize concerts for us together. Teachers also came to see us.

In 1901 the Holy Synod excommunicated L.N. Tolstoi from the church. One might have assumed that such active Tolstoyans such as V.N. Malinovskaya and her friends would treat my father, a priest and servant of the church, coldly. However, this did not happen and they not only visited us, but brought their friends and acquainted us with the family…

During the summer of 1912 professor Tove from Tomsk University, his wife and two children, lived with Vera Nikolaevna: Petya was my age and Nina was 15 or 16 years old (actually, according to the biographical guidebook *Professors of the Tomsk Technological University*, which was issued in 2000, Petr L'vovich Tove was born in 1901, while Nina was the daughter of Lev L'vovich Tove's wife, Aleksandra Gavrilovna Myasnikova, by her first marriage and was born in 1896, B.S.). During this time both the children and the grownups were crazy about croquet. Petya Tove had a bad character. When they would play croquet, Petya and Ron would sometimes have differences that threatened to turn into a fight and Nina, who never played croquet, would call Yelena Nikolaevna to put out the emerging fire. Ron really liked Nina and was already in love with her, tried to get on her good side, photographed her and gave her photo to me (I still have it), although he was unsuccessful. Nine behaved very haughtily in socializing with Ron and me. I didn't like her and treated her as I would an unpleasant grownup. The following incident in these relations upset me. We had guests and they were all sitting on the terrace, near which white lilies were blooming. We were in the garden near these lilies. My father's sisters, Manya, Sasha and Katya, and their friend, Manya Berezovskaya, were sitting with the guests and with them was Nina Tove. Without saying anything to me, Ron grabbed a single white lily from the bunch, went to the terrace, walked up to Nina and put the flower in the buttonhole of Nina's blouse. Nina kindly allowed him to do this. Then he backed off a little, rapturously looked at Nina and exclaimed "The Sistine Madonna." Everyone, particularly the girls, laughed out loud. I was very insulted by this humiliation of my friend, while he reacted quietly to it, like water off a duck.

In the summer of 1913 L.N. Tolstoi's favorite grandson, Il'yushok, (the son of Andrei L'vovich Tolstoi) (a future colonel in the American army, B.S.) and a tutor lived with V.N. Malinovskaya. We were warned of the day of their arrival. On this day we did not leave the farmstead and caught fish on the river bank, which was adjacent to the farmstead. When we were approached by a young man and a boy, we knew who had arrived. Il'yushok turned out to be younger than us (Il'ya Andreevich was born on 3 February 1903, B.S.). He was about 13 years old, while we were soon to turn 16.

We suggested going fishing with Il'yushka, but he refused and said that he didn't like to fish (which did not later interfere with his establishing the world's first dolphinarium, B.S.). We really enjoyed fishing and so his refusal surprised us. Ron and I had buzz cuts, so we never had a hair style, while Il'yushka had bangs on his forehead, which caused him to resemble a girl or a small boy, and so I asked him "Why did they cut your hair this way?" He replied: "There were a lot of people on the day of grandfather's funeral and we kids were playing in the stable and I fell down and hurt my forehead." He raised his bangs and I saw a small scar on his forehead. The tutor took no part in our conversation… Il'yushok was a very tender and happy boy… Sometimes his tenderness was too much. Once, when I was ordered to go to Chernigov on business, I put on my school uniform, with a service cap, decorated with the metal coat of arms of my school. Seeing me dressed in this fashion, Il'yushok gave me a big hug and said "My soldier boy." I felt uncomfortable among those present. Such "calf-like endearments" were not permitted in our boy's society. Il'yushok was physically much weaker than us and thus our relations with him were much more condescending than in relations between Ron and me. Some time following our first acquaintance, Ron began to call Il'yushka "Lyul'ka." Once in a secluded (place, B.S.), far away from grownups, Ron was demonstrating his superiority over Il'yushok to me, smoking cheap tobacco in a pipe, which was called a lyul'ka; I didn't like the tobacco smoke and Il'yushok said: "Don't call me your stinking 'Lyul'ka' anymore."

The tutor was never in our house during the entire time of his stay in Belous. Ron and Il'yushok often visited us. We had something of interest for them. We had a very high pole erected in the garden, on the top of which was attached an old wagon wheel, on which storks had built a nest. One baby stork fell out of the nest and it was very difficult to put him back in the nest, so we fed him. This is how we acquired a house stork. He lived in the garden and was not afraid of people in the least. In the same way, a very amusing domesticated magpie would fly into our house. We had an aquarium with small fish and in the living room there was a small observation hive, with bees, on the window. A "talking" parrot, Zhako, lived in our dining room. My mother would sometimes treat us to something tasty. The time came for Il'yushok and his tutor to go home. We set out for the last time with the tutor to our hiking woods, which was only about three kilometers from Chernigov. We were fortunate and found three large mushrooms in the woods. This was a great rarity for these woods. Ron photographed Il'yushok, the tutor and me with the mushrooms we had found. I still have this photograph. As we were coming home from our hiking woods, Il'yushok said to me: "Let's leave something in the woods for memory's sake." We found a small pine tree and stuck one of our mushrooms on one of its dry branches. I studied in Chernigov in the fall, but would often come home by foot, passing through our hiking woods. Once, during the winter, while passing through the woods on my way to Belous, I remembered Il'yushok's mushroom. I went through quite deep snow and found the mushroom. It had dried out but was sitting securely on the branch. It had been summer here just a few months before and my friends were here. I could never have imagined that this wonderful summer in Belous would be the last for me and that I would never meet either Ron or Il'yushok again.

In April 1914 our family moved to Lyubech, to where my father the priest had gone to work. In the spring of that year, when we were already living in Lyubech, we received a letter from M.N. Malinovskaya, in which she wrote that she had informed Ron about his mother and that the latter had allowed him to go see her, and he had left. "Let him help his mother in her work." Following this letter, our correspondence with V.N. Malinovskaya broke off completely. This greatly surprised us. When V.N. Malinovskaya lived in Mariupol' in the winter, my father would regularly correspond with her. Ron and I were forced to correspond with each other during the winter and we wrote letters to each other quite regularly. In

1915-16, while studying in Chernigov, I would go on foot to Belous, hoping to meet Ron or someone from the Malinovskaya "family," but their house was unoccupied and not even the guard Mikhaila was in the farmstead.

In 1917 I finished the high school in Chernigov and came home to Lyubech. Then suddenly, after an absence of almost three years, V.N. Malinovskaya arrived. She had to ride horses more than 50 kilometers in order to travel from Belous to see us in Lyubech. She told us how she had lived during the past war years as the chief of a front-line hospital, and other things. However, she didn't say anything about Ron, so I asked the question: "How's Ron getting along?" What she was able to tell me struck me so powerfully that I can now almost exactly reproduce it. This was her answer: "Ron didn't want to live with us. I sold Belous. He was with the army at the front. He's not in Russia right now. He's probably become a German prisoner. I'm going to leave here through Kiev to his mother. I plan to teach Rodion's sister the trade of a village schoolteacher. I hope that we'll be able to work together." To judge by the expression on her face and the tone in her voice when Vera Nikolaevna answered my question, I understood just what a deep moral blow Ron had inflicted on her and R.M. Khir'yakova, having failed to return home following his visit to see his mother and his departure for the army. These two very old women had given a lot of themselves in order to raise their adopted son. Of course, due to his youth, Ron didn't think about his old guardians. As a result of this, I didn't bring up Ron any more while Vera Nikolaevna was with us. While she was at our house, she devoted a lot of attention to me. I told her that I dreamed of studying in medical school. She told me how difficult it had been to work in a military hospital, where a lot of wounded did not die from their wounds, but from tetanus from an infected wound. Those infected with tetanus would undergo horrible seizures and pain before they died. She said that due to the features of my character, I should not become a doctor. After staying with us for two days, we escorted her to the steamship bound for Kiev. Upon parting, she promised to send her address following a meeting with Ron's mother. A few days later I received a letter from her from Kiev, in which the conditions for enrolling in the institute's agricultural department were described in detail, as well as the peculiarities of studying in that department. This was the last letter. We were unable to learn anything about her fate and the fate of her friends. Knowing her strong character and her devotion to carrying out her promises, I think that she died soon after leaving us, which is why she didn't send a return address.

In the years following the Great Patriotic War I read an article in one of our journals entitled "A Marshal's Baton out of a Soldier's Knapsack." The article described Marshal Malinovskii's "path" from solider to marshal. This article contained a photo of my childhood friend Ron, which had been taken in 1915. Ron should have been in the fifth class in school in this year, but in the picture he was in a soldier's uniform and a St. George's Cross stood out on his chest. I decided that this was not Ron, but some other kid who looked like him. After some time I remembered that Ron had a small outcropping of skin on his cheek next to his left nostril, probably the result of some childhood accident, which remained up to our final meeting in the fall of 1913. I inspected the published photos of Marshal Malinovskii with a magnifying glass and found this sign on several of them. I decided to meet up with him following his retirement, in order to show him the photographs made in 1912 and 1913, as well the pictures of people among whom we had lived in our childhood. However, Malinovskii passed away before he retired. Thus I had no opportunity to meet with him.

In the *Chernigov Yearbook for 1902*, which was issued in 1901, only one Malinovskii is mentioned, the district doctor Boleslav Stanislavovich. He practiced medicine in the Snovsk precinct and his office was located at Snovsk station (Korzhovka farm), Gorodnyansk district. This is now the town of Shchors, which is located 70 kilometers northeast of Chernigov; that is, sufficiently far from Staryi Belous. I should note that in the 1901 yearbook, which was published in 1900, there is no B.S. Malinovskii as yet and the district doctor in the Snovsk precinct is listed as Aleksandr Vasil'evich Kordobovskii. This may indicate that Malinovskii was appointed on in 1901, which might indirectly point to his youth. If this was his first appointment upon completing the university, then he could have been born in about 1875. One should not exclude the possibility that Boleslav Stanislavovich was in some way related to Vera Nikolaevna. His name and patronymic also indicates a Polish nationality. It's quite likely that Vera Nikolaevna, who was herself a doctor, could have recommended her relative to the provincial council as the district doctor for one of the districts.

And this is what the Kiev local historian Yelena Malyshko writes about her great grandmother's, Mariya Pavlovna Stefanova (*nee* Berezovskaya), search for information about the fate of her son, Oleg Aleksandrovich Stefanov, who perished in the Great Patriotic War:

In desperation and as a last possibility, my great grandmother decided to take advantage of her childhood friendship with Rodion Malinovskii, who in the 1950s was already a marshal of the Soviet Union and minister of defense. I well remember the conversations in our family about their worries during this period—great grandmother didn't want to let her dear acquaintance down, for obvious reasons, by setting before society a slightly different biography. The farmstead of Rodion Yakovlevich's aunt, Natal'ya Malinovskaya, a doctor and landowner, was next to the estate of Pavel Grigor'evich Berezovskii, which the old folks of Staryi Belous still recall.

When coming across a picture of her childhood friend in the postwar newspapers, great grandmother could only sigh mournfully. However, the desire to find out about her son's fate and find his final resting place overcame all doubts.

It's reliably known that there was no official reply from Moscow. However, later on geographical names appeared in our family conversations, which had not been indicated in the sparse lines of the burial notification: "Chernaya River" and the "Leningrad Front." Where did this data come from decades after the war? Perhaps Malinovskii nonetheless helped out, if only through intermediaries? Unfortunately, there's no way of finding this out now. Relatively recently, while preparing this material, I read a small notation in Wikipedia that the popular name for the Msta River, which flows through Borovichi—where the 281st Rifle Division was stationed—is translated as Chernaya from old Finnish.

We were unable to find out just what happened at the Borovichi training ground—was it a training accident, or was the division subjected to a bombing attack. The indifferent figures in the archival documents give a preliminary summary of the number of those "put out of action" of the number of officers in the veterinary service by the middle of 1942. It was only in 1944 that the leadership decided to finally inform the relatives.

In this case, what is particularly important is that Rodion Yakovlevich Malinovskii's connection to the village of Staryi Belous in the Chernigov region is indicated not only by L.V. Rozhalin's letter, but in the works of local historians, who have no connection with Rozhalin. To be sure, they mistakenly considered not Vera Nikolaevna, but Natal'ya Modestovna, Rakhil' Modestovna's sister, who was neither a doctor nor a Malinovskii, to be the owner of the farmstead.

Vera Nikolaevna Malinovskaya was a real person. In the *Yekaterinoslav Address Book for 1916* we read the following: "V.Ye. Ostoslavskaya's Mariupol' Girl's High School (Bol'nichnaya Street, Tregubov's building). Teachers: … Malinovskaya, Vera Nikolaevna. A teacher in the Mariupol' Girl's High School (she is the high school's doctor)." And in the address book *All of Mariupol' and its District*, which was issued by S.A. Kopkin in 1910, the home address of Vera Nikolaevna is listed: Malo-Sadovaya Street, the orphanage. It's quite possible that Vera Nikolaevna also worked in the orphanage as a doctor. And she could have easily hired Natal'ya Nikolaevna Malinovskaya as a nurse in the Kiev orphanage. Rodion Yakovlevich most likely studied in the Mariupol' Boy's Aleksandr High School. It was located on Georgii Street, in the building housing the city hall. The high school was founded on 15 September 1876 and consisted of one preparatory class, eight basic and seven parallel (first through seventh) classes. And he could have attended Giatsintov's high school, which was located on the corner of Torgovaya and Nikolaev streets, in Oksyuzov's building. The high school opened in 1906 and in June 1907 was changed to a private high school. There were five basic and two preparatory classes. It's not excluded that Rodion Malinovskii could have completed the Mariupol' Theological School, which was located on Metropolitan Street, before enrolling in the high school, or in one of the numerous city primary schools. He could have studied in the Gogol' Second City High School on Italian Street, which was located in the building of the Catholic community, or in the fourth class of the boy's high school on Fontannaya Street, opposite Goff's mill.

Mariupol' was the unofficial capital of the Greeks in Ukraine. However, in this major port city in the south of Russia there was not only no small number of Greeks, but Italians as well. The Italian consulate was located here. As we recall, Rodion's godmother was the Italian, Ludovica Bozelli.

In the denunciation cited above, the marshal's first wife, Larisa, maintained that Rodion Yakovlevich "never lost contact" with many of his relatives. And it is not excluded that by aunt Lidiya, who was supposedly a lady in waiting at court (this may only be a reflection of the fact, for example, that she finished the Smol'nyi Institute),[34] that Larisa Nikolaevna actually had in mind Vera Nikolaevna Malinovskaya. It is not excluded that Malinovskii maintained some kind of contact with her if, of course, she survived the civil war and did not emigrate, as did many other relatives on her side of the family. Thus he could have found out about the fate of Lev L'vovich Tove, while in his novel he linked some episodes in his biography with the biography of his uncle, Vasilii Antonovich. After all, in his service record Malinovskii wrote that uncle Vasilii was serving hard labor during the Russian-Japanese War, while in the novel *Soldiers of Russia*, the same uncle Vasilii was getting rich on military contracts. And Lev L'vovich Tove, with whom, as we have become convinced, Rodion also met at least once in his life; it seems he got rich thanks to gold mining but who, at the end, went bankrupt, which likely prompted his suicide. Nor is it excluded that his wife, for whom this was the second marriage, was earlier married to some high-ranking official, as was the wife of Vasilii Antonovich Grin'ko in *Soldiers of Russia*.

Most likely, the episode from this novel, where Vanya Grin'ko dreams about military school and they offer him a choice between either a military-medical school or an agricultural academy, reflects real-life conversations, only not with Count Geiden and the count's gardener, but with Vera Nikolaevna and Rakhil' Modestovna. Convinced Tolstoyans and enemies of violence, they, of course, could not approve Ron's idea of enrolling in the officer's school and becoming a professional officer. Thus they could have suggested to their adopted son either a medical or agricultural education. It's typical that Vera Nikolaevna suggested the same choice between medicine and agriculture to Rozhalin.

If the version with "mama Vera" and "mama Krona" corresponds to reality, then it becomes understandable why Rodion Yakovlevich carefully disguised his connection with these people all his life. A close connection with Tolstoyans was not a fact that would enable one to make a successful career in the Red Army. Also, many members of the Khir'yakov family ended up as

---

34   Editor's note. The Smol'nyi Institute was founded in the early 19th century by the Society for the Education of Noble Maidens and served as the first school for women in Russia. The Bolsheviks expropriated the building in 1917, where it served as their headquarters during the November coup, after it became the provincial party headquarters. The Smol'nyi Institute now houses the offices of the governor of St. Petersburg.

émigrés. For example, following the revolution the well-known writer, Aleksandr Mikhailovich Khir'yakov, a convinced Tolstoyan before the First World War, ended up in Poland. In 1906 he edited the SR[35] newspaper *The Voice*, and was sentenced to a year in a fortress for publishing anti-government materials. After the Bolsheviks came to power, A.M. Khir'yakov was arrested and escaped and, having traveled around the world, finally settled down in Poland. Aleksandr Modestovich took an active part in SR and Cadet[36] émigré periodicals and in the 1930s was the chairman of the *Union of Russian Writers and Journalists in Poland*. From the point of view of the NKVD,[37] he was considered a rabid anti-Soviet. A.M. Khir'yakov died in German-occupied Warsaw in the summer of 1940. It's understandable that with such a relative they certainly would not have let Malinovskii go to Spain and it's not likely that he would have been allowed to rise to the rank of general. Most likely, they would have cashiered him from the army, at the end of the 1920s, at the latest.

But who was Vera Nikolaevna and who was she to Rodion Yakovlevich? Let's examine all the possible variants of their kinship. Taking into account her patronymic, one may allow, purely theoretically, that she was the elder daughter of Nikolai Antonovich, while Rodion's mother, Varvara Nikolaevna, was his younger daughter. In this case, taking into account the approximately 30-year difference in age between Vera Nikolaevna and Varvara Nikolaevna, one must assume that Nikolai Antonovich had been married, at a minimum, twice. This version seems unlikely to me. Another version seems much more probable, according to which Vera Nikolaevna was either Nikolai Antonovich's wife and, therefore, Varvara Nikolaevna's mother and Rodion Yakovlevich's natural grandmother, or the wife of one of Nikolai Antonovich brothers and the natural aunt of Varvara Nikolaevna. In the latter case, Rodion would be Vera Nikolaevna's grandnephew.

One may also assume with a high degree of confidence that she came from the Khir'yakov family, otherwise the permanent residence of Rakhil' Modestovna in the farmstead in Staryi Belous and the frequent visits there of the other Khir'yakovs becomes inexplicable. Of course, Vera Nikolaevna could not have been Rakhil' Modestovna's natural sister, but could easily have been her cousin, if one allows that Modest Nikolaevich's natural brother was Nikolai Nikolaevich, whose daughter could have been Vera Nikolaevna.

If she really was the mother of Varvara Nikolaevna, then it seems perfectly explicable to us that she had adopted her grandson for more than ten years. Her wayward daughter had a child out of wedlock at 19, and moreover by a man more than forty years her senior and belonging to another class entirely. Such incidents are sufficiently common in life. A baby could have interfered with Varvara Nikolaevna's attempts to organize her personal life, particularly following the death of Yakim Ivanovich, when any kind of assistance on his part, if there was any, would have ended.

---

35   Editor's note. The Socialist Revolutionary (SR) Party was established in 1902 and its "combat organization" carried out several terrorist acts against czarist officials. The SRs joined the Provisional Government in 1917, although a left-wing faction allied itself with the Bolsheviks, who overthrew the government later that year. The SRs played only a small part in the anti-Bolshevik struggle during the civil war, before being suppressed altogether.

36   Editor's note. The Cadets was the informal name for the Constitutional-Democratic Party (*Konstitutsionno-Demokraticheskaya Partiya*), which appeared during the revolutionary events of 1905 as the result of the union of various liberal opposition groups. The Cadets formed the largest party in the First Duma, but their opposition to the government caused it to prorogue the parliament. Afterwards, the Cadets moderated their opposition and were active in the early days of the Provisional Government. The party was suppressed during the civil war and most of its leaders chose exile.

37   Editor's note. The NKVD (*Narodnyi Komissariat Vnutrennykh Del*), or People's Commissariat for Internal Affairs was created in 1934 on the basis of the OGPU. The NKVD was responsible for the secret police, foreign intelligence and the vast labor camp empire. The worst crimes of the Stalin era were carried out by the NKVD, which was renamed the MVD in 1946.

Thus it is quite natural that she tried to fob off her baby onto her mother or one of her relatives. In one of the following chapters, a reliable document will be cited to the effect that Varvara Nikolaevna did not raise her elder son Rodion, having turned him over to be raised by relatives not long after he was born. For this the son held a strong grudge against her for his entire life. It's quite possible that the statement in the novel about the death of Vanya Grin'ko's grandmother not long after the death of his grandfather is false. It could only be to mask Rodion's sufficiently close and prolonged tie to his grandfather's widow, who had powerfully influenced the formation of his personality.

There are very serious proofs that what was communicated in Rozhalin's letter is the truth. First of all, everybody that he mentions in the letter actually existed and the information that he relays about them is quite precise. Why would someone pass on such precise information for the sake of a single make-believe person? The main thing, as Natal'ya Rodionovna recalls, is the information about a small outgrowth of skin near Rodion Yakovlevich's left nostril as a result of a childhood accident, which is absolutely correct, and only someone who closely knew Rodion Yakovlevich could know about this defect. Aside from this, Natal'ya Rodionovna showed the photograph sent by Rozhalin, in which Ron Malinovskii is shown in Staryi Belous in 1913, to a criminal expert acquaintance who, upon comparing it with photographs of Marshal Malinovskii, came to the conclusion that Ron Malinovskii and Rodion Yakovlevich Malinovskii are one and the same person.

Malinovskii, as we see, had a very well-off childhood, with a governess, loving relatives, vacations in the countryside, and the full and free life of a landowner's son. However, this idyll did not last for too long. Some kind of conflict arose between Ron and Vera Nikolaevna even before the start of the First World War and it seems they parted forever. In all likelihood, the news that "mama Vera" was not his natural mother and that his real mother, Varvara Nikolaevna, had abandoned him in infancy, made a depressing impression on Malinovskii. It is impossible to pinpoint exactly when he left Vera Nikolaevna's hospitable home. To judge by Rozhalin's story, this would have happened no later than April 1914, although it is impossible to exclude that this happened as early as the end of the summer of 1913. Malinovskii had to drop his studies in the high school or school. There the academic year lasted from 17 August to 1 June. It is possible that Rodion did not even sit his exams to pass into the next class. Then the assertion in his service record of 1938 that he left for Odessa after August 1913 is true. Then he supposedly stopped working at the Shenderov farm. It's quite possible that he disguised Staryi Belous with this name, and Mariupol' with Gnivan'. It is most likely that following his vacation in Belous he headed for his mother's place in Klishchev, but couldn't get along with his stepfather there and left for his relatives in Odessa, where he began work as a salesman for the merchant Pripuskov. It's not excluded that he wanted to earn money in order to enter the officer's school. It's quite likely that Rodion didn't want to be a burden anymore to Vera Nikolaevna and decided to earn his own bread.

Malinovskii wrote in a form that from September 1913 through May 1914 he worked as a "gofer" in merchant Pripuskov's fancy goods store in Odessa. It's likely that Malinovskii related his true biography in forms from September 1913, although by all appearances Rodion worked as a full-fledged salesman. Malinovskii admits this in his novel.

Rodion Yakovlevich's daughter Natal'ya recalled:

> During his last trip to Odessa in the summer of 1966, papa, as if saying farewell, went around the places familiar to him from childhood. He showed mama the merchant Pripuskov's

house, the street and house where uncle Misha's family lived, business Odessa's back streets, Arkadievka and the harbor. We only avoided the square where, according to the rules regarding two-time heroes of the Soviet Union, a bust of papa by Vuchetich[38] stood.

"Shall we have a look?" mama suggested when all we had to do was to turn the corner.

"Go by yourself, if you like."

I don't think it was a matter of whether or not he liked what Vuchetich had done. One shouldn't stand in front of one's own bust.

On that day we dropped in on uncle Misha's son, papa's cousin Vadim Mikhailovich Danilov; we recalled the first meeting since childhood and the last with uncle Misha on the day of Odessa's liberation, 10 April 1944. An eyewitness, Anatolii Innokent'evich Fedenev, who at that time was a special duty officer with the *front* commander, told me.

Rodion Yakovlevich told the driver where to go and we immediately found the house on the outskirts of Odessa. We got out and people gathered round. I wanted to ask about Danilov, but Rodion Yakovlevich had already walked up to an old man standing at some distance. "Don't you recognize me, uncle Misha?" Although Mikhail Aleksandrovich knew about the amazing fate of his second cousin, he could still not believe that the fighting general standing in front of him was that same "poor relation," and gofher.

Insofar as people entered the first class of high school at the age of nine, in 1913 Malinovskii had most likely completed the fifth class. According to amendments made to the 1912 military conscription law, only people with a higher or secondary school education of no less than six classes of high school could join as officer candidates. Those who did not meet this requirement could take a special examination for six high school classes, with foreign languages excluded from the examination. Officer candidates were promoted to officer rank once they passed the special examination, which corresponded approximately to the course in a cadet school and included only specialized military disciplines. Insofar as Malinovskii entered the army not as an officer candidate, but only as a common volunteer (hunter), which was how he was entered on the lists of Russian servicemen sent to France as part of the Russian Expeditionary Corps in 1916, one may assume that he at some time wanted to take an external examination and enter a military (cadet) school. But then the war began. I think that Rodion entered the war from patriotic motives and a longstanding aptitude for military service, and not because he had no other way out, as he tried to present matters in his later service biographies and his novel. I think that no one fired Malinovskii from his job as a salesman and that he preferred to go to the front as a volunteer.

---

38   Editor's note. Yevgenii Viktorovich Vuchetich (1908-74) was a prominent Soviet sculptor who received many commissions during the postwar period. His works are unabashedly heroic and often quite large.

2

The First World War and the Civil War: Baptism of Fire

In his service biography, written on 28 December 1938, Malinovskii wrote how his military service began:

They introduced me to the commander even in the railroad car and I was officially enrolled as a volunteer in a machine gun crew of the 256th Yelizavetgrad Regiment; I was distinguished by my obstinate character and did not show much respect for the leadership, for which it did not care for me; I was in the line all the time, first as an ammunition carrier, then as a gunner, and then as machine gun commander; of course, I took part in all the fighting, but still didn't get any awards, although I did receive the Saint George's Cross, fourth class, although this was done by representation of another battalion commander, perhaps from the 290th Valuiki Regiment, for the support of which a battalion from our regiment was thrown in, as well as our machine gun platoon during the Germans' breakthrough in March 1915 near Kalwaria (north of Suwalki) (simultaneously, as was the case when one was awarded the Saint George's Cross, Malinovskii was promoted to corporal, B.S.). I was wounded in October 1915 near Smorgon' (here is at least indirect evidence that Rodion did not get along with his commanders, at least in Russia; the bearer of the first Saint George's Cross, 4th class, would receive the next one for being wounded; this is how, for example, Georgii Konstantinovich Zhukov received his second cross, 3rd class, but for this you needed to have good relations with your superiors; Malinovskii did not receive a cross for being wounded, B.S.) and was treated in Kazan' in the 66th city hospital, and upon completion of treatment I arrived at the 1st Reserve Machine Gun Regiment in Oranienbaum,[1] 6th Company, as a section commander, and at the end of December 1915 was assigned to a special machine gun team and I arrived in Samara with my team as part of the newly-formed 2nd Regiment, which in January 1916 was sent through Manchuria to be loaded onto a steamship in the port of Dairen, and from there through the Indian Ocean, the Suez Canal and to France through the port of Marseilles, where we arrived in April 1916; they equipped us in port and sent us to camp in Mailly, where all the kings and presidents carried out endless reviews and parades for an entire month, and in June the 1st Brigade (1st and 2nd regiments) was sent to the front near Mourmelon-le-Grand, not far from Reims and were then dispatched to Sillery, and then around Fort Brimont, where the

---

1   Editor's note. Oranienbaum was the site of an estate along the southern coast of the Gulf of Finland, which was granted by Peter the Great to one of his intimates in the early 18th century. The town of the same name was renamed Lomonosov in 1948.

February Revolution[2] caught us and at the front. Upon the appearance of Order No. 1,[3] I was elected chairman of the company committee and on 17 April 1917, following lengthy debates at meetings and delegate conferences, the brigade nevertheless adopted the decision to take part in the Allies' general April offensive[4] and we attacked Fort Brimont and on the attack's first day I was wounded in the left hand by an explosive bullet which smashed my hand, after which I underwent very lengthy treatment in hospitals in the towns of Bordeaux, St. Servan and St. Malo, where I was also elected to hospital committees. At the end of June 1917 the division of the brigades was carried out in the La Courtine camp on General Zankevich's[5] orders and I, not having properly finished my treatment, hurried back to my regiment and arrived in La Courtine, when the 1st Brigade was declared to be in mutiny, although there was actually no mutiny; rather the brigade simply refused to turn over its weapons and refused to leave for the front and demanded a return to Russia; upon arriving at my company I was once again elected to the company committee and a delegate from the detachment committee. At the end of August the detachment committee did not want to bring the matter to armed suppression and made the decision to turn over its weapons, which the soldiers at the meeting did not agree to and a new detachment committed was chosen right there at the meeting. At this time my wound opened up and with great difficulty (the camp had already been heavily isolated at the time and French units were arriving to surround the La Courtine camp) was sent back to the hospital at St. Servan, while around 15 September wounded soldiers arrived at the hospital and we found out that on 13 September the La Courtine camp had been fired on (that is; fire was opened on the camp and the camp surrendered). Upon discharge from the hospital, I was sent to the camp at Courneau (the other half of the Russian forces was there) and I was arrested and they even wanted to try me and all the other La Courtine committee members, but they only managed to interrogate me when the October Revolution took place, after which the French government issued an order to disarm all Russian troops, without distinction, and to put them to work, as if to say you can't eat for free during wartime and he who doesn't want to work will be sent to Africa for forced labor. I went to work in the Belfort area and, citing my wounded hand, neglected my work until I was arrested. The execution of two of our comrades—one was comrade Ushakov, while I don't remember the other one's name—showed our complete helplessness on the one hand, while I nevertheless felt a moral necessity to fight the Germans, who at this time were occupying Ukraine and mocking the

---

2   Editor's note. The February Revolution (23-27 February, Old Style, 8-12 March, New Style) was a spontaneous revolt against the czarist government's mismanagement of the war. The revolution, which was overall quite peaceful, led to the end of the Romanov dynasty and the establishment of the Provisional Government.

3   Editor's note. Order No. 1 was issued by the Petrograd (St. Petersburg) Soviet of Workers' and Soldiers' Deputies on 1 March 1917. The order instructed soldiers to obey their officers and the Provisional Government only if their orders did not contradict those of the soviet. This order did much to ruin discipline within the army, bringing about its virtual collapse within a few months.

4   Editor's note. The April offensive is known in the West as the Nivelle offensive, the brainchild of General Robert Georges Nivelle, who had been appointed commander-in-chief of the French army the previous December. Nivelle proposed breaking through the powerful German defenses along the Aisne River and ending the trench stalemate. The offensive began on 16 April 1917 and quickly bogged down, with the French suffering heavy casualties. The offensive ended in early May with minimal gains. Widespread mutinies in the French army broke out shortly afterward.

5   Editor's note.Mikhail Ippoliovich Zankevich (1872-1945) entered military service in 1891 and graduated from the General Staff Academy in 1899. During the First World War he served in staff and command positions and in 1917 was appointed the Provisional Government's representative in France. He returned to Russia in 1919 and fought on the White side in the civil war. Following the Whites' defeat, he returned to France and died there in exile.

people, and so I decided to go to the front and was sent to the Foreign Legion's 1st Moroccan Division, where I arrived in January 1918 (it follows from this that Malinovskii declared his readiness to join the Foreign Legion no later than January 1918, and possibly as early as December 1917. However, even in January 1918 the Germans in no way occupied Ukraine; quite the opposite, at this time Soviet troops were attacking in Ukraine and had occupied Kiev and pushed the troops of the Ukrainian Central Rada[6] back to the Austro-German lines. It follows that Malinovskii joined the Legion out of patriotic motivations of the most general kind and in no way because the Germans had seized his native Ukraine. However, to admit to the desire to voluntarily continue the "imperialist war" was not done in Soviet times. Therefore Rodion Yakovlevich made up the part about forced labor to which they had supposedly assigned him. In other words, it's better to fight than engage in pointless labor, B.S.) and in March 1918 the division was put in against the Germans' March breakthrough in Picardy,[7] and from this moment this division was mercilessly hammered in all of the heavy fighting of 1918; I was a machine gunner and then machine gun commander all the way up to the armistice. In January 1919 they removed all of us Russians from the Foreign Legion— except for those who had signed a contract to serve five or ten years, regardless of age, for which they received a one-time monetary bonus, and many fell for this bait—and gathered us in the village of Pleurs, not far from the town of Sezanne, where they first considered sending all of us to Denikin,[8] but encountered resistance because we signed up to fight the Germans, which was noted in our service books, although they nevertheless managed to dispatch a rifle company of 200 men to Novorossiisk, while the remainder, about 300 men, remained in the village until the signing of the Treaty of Versailles. In July they began to write down who wanted to return to where in Russia, by city, and 20 of us indicated Odessa, and in August 1919 they sent us to Marseilles and, having loaded us on the steamship *Paul Lec*, it turned out that they took us not to Odessa, but to Vladivostok, where we arrived on either 7 or 9 October 1919.

Here we should note that Malinovskii, as a hunter (volunteer) had the right to choose the arm he would serve in. This means that service in a machine gun company was evidently his own choice. Evidently Rodion was very strong back then. After all, he had to carry a heavy machine gun, which is far heavier than a 7.62mm rifle, on his back the entire war. And he fought well, both in Russia and in France, where they sent him also for his good knowledge of French. He served in the 4th machine gun command (later the 4th Machine Gun Company) of the 2nd Special Brigade's 2nd Special Regiment. Rodion was awarded a Saint George's Cross for bravery exhibited in the April 1917 offensive.

Rodion Yakovlevich's daughter testifies to the fact that

---

6   Editor's note. The Ukrainian Central Rada (Council) was established in March 1917 by a heterogeneous group of Ukrainian nationalists and other activists. Following the declaration of Ukrainian autonomy, the Rada quickly acquired the status of a national parliament. Pro-Bolshevik forces drove the Rada out of Kiev in November 1917.

7   Editor's note. This refers to the German army's large offensive (Operation Michael) against British forces in northern France, designed to take advantage of a temporary German numerical advantage on the Western Front before the arrival of sizable American forces. The offensive, which began on 21 March, at first achieved spectacular gains, but ultimately failed to split the Allied forces or reach the English Channel.

8   Editor's note. Anton Ivanovich Denikin (1872-1947) joined the army in 1890 and served in the Russo-Japanese War. During the First World War he commanded a brigade, division and a corps. Following the Bolshevik coup, Denikin and other high-ranking officers escaped to south Russia, where they founded the Volunteer Army. He later commanded the Volunteer Army and the Armed Forces of South Russia, before retiring in 1920. Denikin later lived in exile in Europe and the United States.

… He carried this document, a soldier's machine notebook as a machine gunner with the 256th Yelizavetgrad Regiment, through three wars—the civil war, the Spanish War, and the Second World War—as well as his ceremonial photograph with the Saint George's Cross and his pocket French country guide with the gold edging with printed, raspberry leather (on which he composed letters for his comrades in suffering—soldiers who were getting over their wounds—to French women with thanks for the Christmas presents they had sent.

Natal'ya Malinovskaya also recalled her mother's words:

As early as the First World War, in Poland, a fortune teller predicted a breathtaking career for papa, a marshal's baton and a high military position, but warned: "Don't start anything new or set out on a journey on Friday! This is a bad day for you." At first he didn't pay any attention to the warning and didn't take the prophecy seriously, but after his second wound (both on Friday, just like the third, thirty years later), he made it a rule to look at the calendar when setting the beginning of a new operation or planning trips. But you can't exclude Friday from the calendar and everything bad in the family inevitably occurred on a Friday. A Friday was the last day of papa's life—31 March 1967. Mama died thirty years later on a Friday.

One should mention that the 1st Reserve Machine Gun Regiment really was quartered in Oranienbaum. It was formed on 17 May 1915 from a reserve machine gun battalion and numbered 16 companies and 55 machine guns. Here Rodion Yakovlevich is absolutely correct.

In his 1948 service biography Marshal Malinovskii described the events of the First World War much more sparingly:

In October 1915 I was wounded in the fighting around Smorgon' and evacuated to the city of Kazan' for treatment, and upon recovering joined the 1st Reserve Machine Gun Regiment, from which in January 1916 I was assigned to the 2nd Special Infantry Regiment's 4th Machine Gun Team and sent to France, where the regiment arrived in April 1916 and soon left for the front.

With the beginning of the February Revolution, I was elected chairman of the company committee. On 17 April 1917 I was wounded and sent to the city of Bordeaux for treatment, and then to St. Servan and, upon being discharged from the hospital, due to the events in La Courtine among the Russian troops in France, I ended up on a work assignment.

Feeling a sense of deep insult for the Motherland—at this time the Germans had occupied almost all of Ukraine, I joined the Foreign Legion as a volunteer and the French army's 1st Moroccan Division and fought the Germans until the armistice of 1918.

In January 1919 they gathered us Russians from the Foreign Legion, who had signed a contract to fight the Germans to the end of the war, in the village of Pleurs, on the Marne, from where in August I left for Russia through Marseilles. They were preparing to send us through Odessa, but actually landed us in Vladivostok in October 1919.

It's amazing that twenty and thirty years later, Malinovskii repeated the fairy tale about the German occupation of Ukraine as the main reason for his joining the Legion. However, in 1948 he was already a marshal and it was uncomfortable for professional officers to correct Rodion Yakovlevich. However, at the end of 1938, when the campaign to unmask "enemies of the people" was just beginning to slacken, no one who read Malinovskii's service biography paid any attention to the obvious unreliability of the reason he gave for joining the Legion.

Natal'ya Rodionovna confirms:

He remembered the La Courtine camp and the hospital in St. Servan and knew from his own experience how difficult life is abroad. Its bread was bitter, even for those who remained in France by choice—in 1945 Timofei Vyatkin, who had long ago taken French citizenship and recognized from a newspaper photograph in the Russian marshal his old friend from the front, wrote: "Then I was sure that my decision was the most correct one, but with the passing of years I thought about those who, in spite of everything, returned… Who would have thought that I would be congratulating you—marshal and commander—upon receiving the Order of the Leion of Merit."

I want to put forward one artless story about the events in La Courtine. This is how the events in La Courtine were depicted in the "little diary" of an unknown Russian soldier, which was preserved in the Foreign Russian Archive in Prague. The soldier was probably from the 23rd Company, because the diary was written in this company's log. This company was part of the 2nd Special Regiment, in which Malinovskii served. This is its text:

On 24 September 1917. This is what I've gone through and seen in just a short period of our more than three-month stay in the La Courtine camp.

Everything is passing before my eyes. I was sent ahead to the camp before the arrival of my company and I immediately set about trying to arrange quarters for the soldiers, for the kitchen, for the company horses and, finally, a place for the company commander. Everything was ready and we only awaited the arrival of our regiment, and the 1st Regiment arrived first, and on the night of 12 June the 2nd Regiment's first echelon, the 1st Battalion arrived, and of course our company, and then the following echelons began to arrive, and finally the last one. The 1st and 2nd regiments had not even completely arrived when noisy meetings began and unrest was in the air. Everybody was awaiting the arrival of the 3rd Brigade, but they were delaying it for some reason. However, finally the 3rd Brigade arrived as well and crowds of our soldiers immediately went there and began to ask questions. They began talking about the current situation. Some said to go to the front, while others said it was necessary to go to Russia, although this was not limited to talking and two conflicting decisions began to emerge. One party demanded they be sent to Russia, while the other, headed by officers, passed a resolution to unconditionally subordinate themselves to the Provisional Government,[9] while at the same time demanding the payment of a wine allowance and the improvement of the condition of our wounded, as they had it very hard. And the party which demanded to be sent back to Russia took decisive action and set out for the 3rd Brigade, with music, to convince it to join the 1st Brigade, which is what we did several times. And finally, on 26 June, the 3rd Brigade left the La Courtine camp and 1,000 men remained in our brigade, and 600 left, having compiled beforehand last-minute appeals for everyone to join them the La Courtine camp, for which they printed many copies of the appeal in which they spoke about the 3rd Brigade being right and the 1st Brigade being wrong, although this had little effect and all the soldiers remained in La Courtine, except those who left. During all of these events preceding the explosion, orders were issued and the latest regimental and detachment meetings took place, in which the majority of members were for getting down to training. It was decided to defer the question to lower units for discussion. The majority of companies elected to train,

---

9   Editor's note. The Provisional Government was established by the Fourth Duma in March 1917, following the abdication of Nicholas II. The Provisional Government was at first dominated by the Cadet Party, but the locus of power later shifted to the socialists. Weakened by internal strife and attacks from left and right, the Provisional Government was easily overthrown in October (November) 1917.

but without backpacks, although the order came from the regimental commander to train in full military readiness. This order caused a great deal of commotion among the soldiers, as a result of which they did not go out to train, and then a schism arose. After the schism, they set about organizing company and regimental committees and a detachment committee and also set about insuring internal order, because all the officers abandoned their posts. Internal order was above reproach, because the soldiers themselves took care of it.

Following the schism, they immediaately tried to scare us with guns and machine guns, and also refused to pay our *per diem* and salary and called us not soldiers, but "traitors to the Motherland and the revolution," and they cancelled our brief two-day leave and we were thus cut off from the entire world. Rapp and a representative from General Zankevich came to see us from Paris and tried to convince us to join, but all of this accomplished nothing. Then delegates arrived, whose responsibilities were to go to a conference and there act according to their responsibility and authority, of which I will name the names of those I know, Smirnov and Gol'denberg, which is how they appeared on paper, as well as two others, although I don't remember their names, who also tried to convince us to unquestioningly submit to the Provisional Government, but the soldiers firmly refused, telling them that we submit to the Provisional Government, but not to its representatives, as they had fooled us more than once, which is why we can't trust them and will not go to the front here, because following the first offensive we saw how the French treated us, especially our wounded, and who can vouch that this won't happen the next time, and that we want to see our Motherland and show our mettle there. Thus the conference representatives weren't able to accomplish anything. Then comrades Rapp and Moroz and some others, whose names I can't remember, came. They also tried to convince us to submit, but again in vain, and they left us alone after these attempts and also didn't attempt to undertake anything. However, our people got the idea to compile a telegram to the Provisional Government and entrusted it to comrade Baltais, who left and then returned later to tell us that Zankevich refused to accept the telegram and began to ask us to submit to the Provisional Government, assuring us that things will get better, but if we don't submit, then they will get worse, and said that he had personally seen the machine guns and guns that had been prepared for us. But the soldiers once again refused to believe him and then he resigned his job and said: "Comrades! I beg you to listen to me, as you listened before and everything will be great." But the soldiers were very stirred up by this and did not want to obey him, and many were angry with Baltais and then went back; commissar Svatikov also came to see us. He sent us greetings from all of Russia and then began: "Comrades, let's unite," but they answered him sharply. Then Volkov went to Paris on business and upon returning from Paris renounced his post and tried to talk the soldiers into giving up on their plans and to submit to the Provisional Government. But the soldiers remained firm. Thus Baltais and Volkov had given up, and so the soldiers continued on their own and things went well. Fortunately, there was no violence or unruly conduct. However, on 19 June we received an order from the Provisional Government through Zankevich, in which it was ordered that undesirable elements should be removed from the 1st Brigade and that the remainder be made to submit, to introduce revolutionary courts and force the 1st Brigade to obey, with the 2nd Brigade, without interference from French troops. This order caused a big uproar. And they issued an ultimatum to the 1st Brigade: all of the La Courtine troops were to leave the camp for Clerneau station. They were to leave all of their weapons in La Courtine, both firearms and swords, and take their backpacks with them. 48 hours was given to carry the order out, with a deadline of 1000 on 21 June. A number of meetings were held on account of this and they decided on the following: let those who want to join the 3rd Brigade leave, and those who don't want to, let them stay, as a result of which about 500 men left, while the remainder stayed behind. Volkov, Baltais and Gusev left with the others. Those who stayed didn't leave because they had been ordered to leave without weapons and the soldiers decided under no circumstances to hand in their weapons, because you're not a soldier without a weapon and that this was inadmissible. The committees continued on how to act after 21 June. They decided thusly: to leave without their weapons and backpacks and to join the 3rd Brigade and then together with them go to the La Courtine camp, which they decided and did, telling General Zankevich about this beforehand. Thus on the morning of 21 June the 1st Brigade lined up with music and its officers and left for the 3rd Brigade.

Upon arriving at the appointed place, where the 3rd Brigade was supposed to be drawn up, we didn't find anyone, but then General Lokhvitskii[10] and some other officers arrived, as well as Colonel Gotua (Georgii Semyonovich Gotua was born on 1 January 1871 in Tiflis[11] and was a colonel in the 8th Turkestan Rifle Regiment before arriving in France, had been awarded a Saint George's weapon, and fought in Denikin's and Wrangel's armies during the civil war, was promoted to major general, and died in Belgrade on 13 January 1936. In *Soldiers of Russia* he is characterized as "a very demanding officer, both for himself and his subordinates," for which the soldiers did not like him and were afraid of him, B.S.), and then they brought those who had run away from La Courtine after the order had been issued, and G. Lokhvitskii told us: "Now we've met you; let's move on to where the 3rd Brigade is forming up." After some agitation, we passed one barrier, which was under guard, for what, was obvious, then a second and a third, which also stood under guard along the sides of the road, with machine guns in well-concealed places, and then they led us to the right of the road and here they wanted to split us away from the 1st Regiment, but the soldiers held tightly to each other. When they brought us to the place, a Colonel Kotovich appeared and ordered us to form up and then make ourselves comfortable, telling us that they would bring tents and kitchens and that they would deliver groceries to us along this road, but the soldiers shouted at him: "We didn't come here to live, but to join up with our comrades, and since you don't want us to, then we're leaving," and all of the soldiers turned decisively back. Then Kotovich shouted: "Form up, damn you, the general ordered it." But the soldiers cut him off immediately: "We ask that you not curse and say what you need to." Then he said: "General Zankevich is going to come now and will have a talk with you." The soldiers formed up and General Zankevich arrived to thank the 1st Brigade for coming and saving him from unpleasantness: "And now you'll go with your officers to the camp." We sat down and began to wait. After an hour had passed, the soldiers began to move out, but they asked them to wait a bit and within a few minutes three officers arrived from the 1st Regiment, but they began to demand that the soldiers turn over their delegates and submit unconditionally, but the soldiers didn't turn over anyone and moved to the camp. The officers, of course, moved out as well, but not a single officer from the 2nd Regiment. We found out the following upon arriving at the camp (it was about 7:00 in the evening). Soldiers from the 3rd Brigade had come and wanted to take the tents and kitchens for us, but the French commandant did not give them the tents and the soldiers who had remained in La Courtine refused to give them the kitchens and also did not give us any bread, because their bread had been sent on to us. Of course, the officers did not think we would return to La Courtine, so we had to dine on rusks. Going back a little, when General Zankevich issued the order for the officers to take up their posts, he added that you are going to La Courtine and tomorrow you will turn over

---

10   Editor's note. Nikolai Aleksandrovich Lokhvitskii (1867-1933) joined the army in 1887 and fought in the Russo-Japanese War. During the First World War he commanded a brigade and then a brigade and division with the Russian Expeditionary Corps. He later returned to Russia and joined the White movement and commanded a corps and armies, before emigrating in 1920. Lokhvitskii died in exile.

11   Editor's note. This is modern-day Tbilisi, the capital of Georgia.

your weapons. And on the second day following the events described here, the soldiers had prepared their weapons for turning in; that is, they had cleaned and oiled all of their weapons; some a machine gun, some a machine rifle and some a rifle and revolver, etc., etc., while the company committees had prepared lists for turning in their weapons. Everything seemed to be going smoothly, but then we received orders which mentioned turning in weapons, signed by commissar Rapp, after which everything fell apart. Why did Rapp issue the order and not Zankevich? We decided not to turn in our weapons until we receive a formal order from Zankevich. Then Rapp arrived and admonished us to turn over our weapons and demanded delegates from each company for this. But nothing helped. A division meeting took place in the evening, at which the question of handing in our weapons was discussed and during the discussion an officer from Rapp arrived and read a letter in which he once again admonished us to turn in our weapons and added a deadline of 6:00 in the evening of that very day. But nothing helped— neither the admonitions of the delegates, or Rapp's letter. We all decided not to turn in our weapons. Life went on after this. The soldiers did not pay any attention to threats or the French patrols. They didn't even pay attention when they reduced our food ration. After this, life went on and there was ideal order everywhere. At this time a delegation, consisting of three officers and seven soldiers, came to us from the 2nd Artillery Brigade, and this delegation promised to help us get out of the situation we were in and everyone explained to them how the schism had occurred, and after all the soldiers in the La Courtine camp had passed by in a ceremonial march and gone back to their barracks, the delegation went back Zankevich, and when the delegation arrived back from General Zankevich, they tried to convince us to turn in our weapons, explaining that this was the only way to do things, and a colonel climbed on to the rostrum and appealed to the soldiers this way: "Soldiers! Right now you are surrounded by French artillery, and if you don't believe me you can check by telephone, and they are going to start bombarding you soon." But the soldiers said: "Let them kill us, but we still won't turn over our weapons." Thus the first delegation from the 2nd Artillery Brigade was unable to convince the soldiers to turn over their weapons. After this, life went on without any particular adventures. Only that they passed a resolution in favor of Volkov and Baltais, as well as for all the delegates, hoping that they were being elected to fulfill the will of the soldiers and not as some kind of leaders. And then we requested General Zankevich that he improve the situation of those who had been arrested: he lowered our ration norms again and again, so that we received very little. This is what we got: 200 grams of meat, 600 grams of bread, 30 grams of sugar, 30 grams of fat, four grams of tea, etc., etc., while we didn't get any tobacco at all. So, it wasn't a very enviable life, but the soldiers would not leave to join the 3rd Brigade and stuck together even more. It was as if our deprivations made us stronger. But the 3rd Brigade wasn't sleeping either and tried a sly move in order to somewhat reduce the number of soldiers from La Courtine. It was only necessary to do a little, and this is what they did: no matter who got sick, even a little bit, he was either appointed to a commission or sent from La Courtine under some excuse, of which there were many (it's possible that Rodion Malinovskii was among them, B.S.). Of course, there were some who went, but the majority did not, even end up in the local police station. In this way, a lot of delegates left, who had been discharged while still in La Courtine, which they requested, although I don't know if they were actually discharged, or only the ones in La Courtine; I never saw a single one.

After everything described above it became quieter and a quiet life began for the soldiers from La Courtine, while the soldiers observed perfect order and training began, although this training did not last long, as they gave us very little food, so training ceased and life was peaceful. We sent a telegram to the French government, in which much was said and in which we requested the mediation of the French government between us; that is the La Courtine soldiers and representative General Zankevich and commissar Yevgenii Rapp. However, the

French authorities gave us this answer: "We don't interfere in your affairs." The soldiers said: "Well, if they're not interfering, then they shouldn't," and began to live peacefully again. Talented artists were found who put on a show and every evening the soldiers would go and watch and everybody was very satisfied, although I don't know what they were up to. Then a delegation from the 2nd Artillery Brigade again tried to convince us to turn over our weapons, otherwise things would get worse. They just told us that a lot of things were hanging over us and that we should turn over our weapons while there's still time, but the soldiers remained firm: "We'll die, but we won't turn over anything," and so for the second time the delegation was unable to convince the 1st Brigade to turn over its weapons. After this, a delegate, Vtorov, came from Russia, who had been sent in May by the 1st Regiment. He read a report with which he had traveled to Russia and which he had read to Kerenskii.[12] They began to ask him what he had heard. He told us in an hour that he hadn't heard anything but a single telegram, which related how a small part of the Russian troops in France had mutinied and that General Zankevich had temporarily stopped giving our *per diems* and pay and asked what we planned to do. That was it. And when we asked him about our present situation, Vtorov said the following: "Both sides have dug in their heels and it's impossible to understand who's right and who's wrong, but I advise you to turn over your weapons;" but they didn't listen to Vtorov. Once again things were supposedly quiet, but this was the calm before the approaching storm, which was not long in breaking out.

1 September 1917. In the final days of August there was a rumor that the 3rd Brigade had arrived from Courneau to Felletin, but no one knew yet why it had arrived, but on 1 September we saw live soldiers, from the 3rd Brigade, of course (we called them "the Felletin crowd"). They surrounded us and we could see how they were digging trenches and setting up machine guns where necessary (but thickly). However, this did not disturb the soldiers much. There had only been one meeting, during which we decided not to fire on our own (let them fire, but not us). Their delegation arrived on 1 September and tried to convince us to turn over our weapons, or it would get worse. After all, several French regiments, with artillery, had surrounded the 3rd Brigade. But once again the soldiers did not believe them and didn't turn over their weapons, didn't think about turning them in, while at the same time never thinking that they would open fire on the La Courtine soldiers. Then they received orders giving them an ultimatum until 10 o'clock in the morning on 3 September, that all the La Courtine soldiers abandon La Courtine and the paths they should take were pointed out, after which the distribution of food products for both people and horses would end, or as the old saying goes: "If a pitcher should fall on a rock, woe to the pitcher, and if a rock should fall on the pitcher, then woe to the pitcher again, so it's woe to the pitcher all around." But the soldiers decided to hold out to the last and not leave La Courtine, and there was a show on 2 September, with music, and on the morning of the 3rd and an hour before ten, music began to play and played for a long time. At ten o'clock the musicians moved back to their barracks and played a burial march, when suddenly an artillery salvo rang out. The salvo had been aimed at the 1st Regiment's last barracks and at the detachment council, where the musicians had arrived, and so the salvo hit the, taking two lives and wounding five others. They fire a few more rounds after the salvo, for an overall total of 17 shells on 3 September, but the soldiers didn't leave. Night came! It was nice during the day, but even worse at night.

12   Editor's note. Aleksandr Fedorovich Kerenskii (1881-1970) was a lawyer who became involved early on in revolutionary activity against the czarist government. He was elected to the Fourth Duma and following the February Revolution he served in various ministerial posts in the Provisional Government and later became prime minister and commander-in-chief of the armed forces. The Bolsheviks overthrew Kerenskii's government in November 1917 and he spent the rest of his life in exile in Europe and the United States.

Rifle fire didn't let up for a minute, while the machine guns rattled at night as if we were fighting off an attack. It was like this the entire night, and again at ten o'clock on 4 September they opened fire on us and fired off 66 rounds, after which the soldiers got all agitated and decided to surrender and hoisted a white flag. So everybody decided to form up in complete order and to leave along the 6th Regiment's path, without arms, of course; but we were not able to do this, because soldiers from the machine gun companies ran up and told us that the machine gunners had placed their machine guns opposite their regiments and would shoot everyone who came by (and the road along which the 1st Brigade wanted to go went by the machine gun companies), so we were unable to go properly. So everyone went the best way he could and our 1st Company reached La Courtine intact, where there remained only the company duty officer, an instructor, cooks, a tradesman, a supply clerk, and tailors. They all had remained with their things. We were met in La Courtine by our soldiers, who had left for the 3rd Brigade. They showed us where to go. When we began to approach the exit from La Courtine, we saw machine guns that had been set up and our brothers were beside them. At this point the French surrounded us and we moved on to the next village. Then they moved us to the field and ordered us to show our things and then simply began to frisk us and frisked us in the following manner: they put us in two files and put guards in front and behind and then began to frisk us, or simply steal from us. They took everything, binoculars, cameras and penknives. Of course, I can't speak for those who took revolvers, which they found on a few people. Why take personal items? After this, they led us to a French cemetery, where we settled in. We stood there until 5 o'clock in the afternoon and they gave us a piece of bread and a sardine for four people and at this time removed more than 30 men from the company. Those who had been selected beforehand spent the night of the 5th under the stars, but we didn't get much sleep because machine guns rattled and rifle fire all around La Courtine. It began in the morning. There was an endless cannonade. I began to count, but it was impossible. There was no way to keep up and I stopped counting after 100 rounds. The artillery fired all day, with the same thing at night, only worse, and then the machine guns chimed in; but none of this scared the dug-in machine gunners and they did not surrender.

They moved us further from La Courtine on the evening of 5 September and when we arrived at our destination they ordered us to make tents, and we were escorted by a French convoy with machine guns. Because our stopping place was a few kilometers from La Courtine, the sound of the machine guns and artillery reached us. They quartered us near a hillock and stationed guards all around, established watches in the corners, and a machine gun in the grove, so we were completely safe. We woke up on 6 September and the first question is what happened to the troops in La Courtine? However, no one could reply, but everyone understood that the soldiers in La Courtine had suffered a bitter fate, but nobody knew what kind. All of the soldiers were very weak, because they were still going hungry in La Courtine and when we left La Courtine we received only a cottage loaf for four. It was getting on toward lunchtime and we still hadn't gotten any bread. The soup had arrived, but there was no bread. But the soldiers were so weak that they couldn't wait until the food was handed out and everyone just lay down. They then decided to distribute the soup and eat it without bread, which is what they did, so the soldiers revived a little and started to make jokes. We're not submitting to Zankevich. Before long they brought bread and sugar and through them, the soldiers who brought the bread, we learned that it was all over with the soldiers from La Courtine, but they didn't know how. We stayed here until 9 September and they fed us once a day (as they say, "just enough to keep us alive", and on 9 Septmeber led us once again into La Courtine, where they formed us up and commissar Rapp and General Lokhvitskii and another general, Nikolaev, and other officers arrived. He read us a prayer, from which I gathered that we should try and make amends for what had happened and that we would be temporarily deprived of our committees and that power was to be transferred to the commanders of the battalions, companies, platoons, and sections. Then they took us to our barracks. It's impossible to describe what we saw here. It was a real Mamai battle,[13] where everything was tossed around and there, where the La Courtine soldiers had left their things, nothing remained, except boxes and other useless things, and I simply cannot describe everything I saw there, and it was impossible to think that they could so destroy the barracks, especially those that belonged to the 5th and 6th regiments. There were ten shell holes in one of the barracks. In a word, nothing was spared. Only I didn't see the people who had remained in La Courtine and haven't seen them since and don't know what fate befell them. Upon arriving in La Courtine, life went on as usual. Only the company officers wanted to reestablish discipline or something like that, but I didn't see anything special. There was 700 grams of bread a day per man. There were 250 grams of meat and 40 grams of sugar or fats. And life went on, only now we trained, went for wood in the forest and performed other work.

A trial began upon reaching La Courtine. A judge arrived from the camp at Courneau and they tried the NCOs and all the commanders and, of course, they demoted them after a trial. The NCOs began to quit their posts, but officers were found here and they ordered us to wear soldiers' stripes, saying that saying it wasn't a trial, and then issued a kind of an order, in which it was stated that it was impossible to travel to Russia before the spring and that the Provisional Government had authorized those who were willing to work for a salary of no less than three francs per day, with room and board. This upset a lot of soldiers, although there were those who agreed to go to work, including myself. The formation of the work groups began on the 27th. Colonel Kotovich (Mikhail Aleksandrovich Kotovich, born in 1880, was appointed commander of the 1st Special Infantry Regiment on 17 February 1917 and commanded the suppression of the uprising in the La Courtine camp and was commandant of the camp, B.S.) explained the following: "You'll go to work and they'll give you 700 grams of bread, 350 of beef, 60 grams of sugar, 70 grams of barley and rice and, besides this, will pay you three francs a day; so you'll go to work and earn the title of soldier and citizen, and then I'll see about getting you a salary, and then I'll form a unit and we'll go to the front and show what we're made of, and then I'll get you a *per diem* and I'll get you your company committees and company courts back, so Godspeed, boys," and he left. At 10:30 in the morning on 29 October we left La Courtine and at 1 p.m. we arrived in the town of Chartres, where they quartered us next to an enormous Catholic church, gave us cots and mattresses and delivered blankets, because there was no heating and it was cold. They fed us from the 102nd Regiment's stores. The food was good, but there wasn't much.

But it was already 4 November and there was no kind of entertainment, just walking every day to the 102nd Regiment to have lunch and dinner, at 10 and 5 o'clock, with the rest of the time just sitting in quarters, as we forbidden from going anywhere, except from 5 in the afternoon to 9 o'clock, when we went to have supper, which together took two hours, during which time it became completely dark.

6/19 November. They told us that 18 of us were going to work. We didn't have much time to get ready and as early as 6/19 November we left Chartres at 11:44 and arrived at our work site at 12:44. The owner to whom we had been assigned, met us and, having arrived before he did, they broke us up according to task, and I went with three others: there was myself,

---

13   Editor's note. A Mamai battle (*Mamaevo poboishche*) comes from Mamai, a Tatar khan from the Golden Horde, who launched a devastating raid in medieval Russia. He was defeated at Kulikovo Field by Muscovite forces under Grand Duke Dmitrii (Dmitrii Donskoi) in 1380, which marked the nascent Russian nation's first victory over the Tatars in nearly 150 years. The term, as used here, means an especially destructive battle or fight.

Bosik, Aleksandr Pomakhovich, and Vasilii Pomakhovich and we arrived at 3 o'clock on 6/19 November and we began to work. The work was simple and we were given peasant food. We had to thresh the wheat and the work wasn't hard and unfolded as follows. We got up at 5:30 in the morning, had breakfast at 6:00 and at 7:00 we began to work, finishing at 12:00, and from 12:00 to 1:00 lunch, and from 1:00 to 6:00 we worked again, every day, and on Sunday we rested. The food was good and they served it to us as follows: Meat, cheese, fish, apples and pears in the morning, which we washed down with cider. For lunch we had soup, cold and hot meat, baked potatoes, cheese, salad, and coffee. For supper we had soup, cold and hot meat, cheese, salad, potatoes, and baked apples. There was always enough bread. They served apple cider on Saturday for whoever wanted it. It was pretty good. We worked two weeks for French peasants and life was still pretty good. The only bad thing was carrying heavy 76-kilogram sacks of wheat high up. We slept in the stable with the horses or sheep and we were soaked through and it was very cold, but, as they say, you're not at home and there's no one to complain to. In general, however, it was a good life and the French treated us well, so I think that if you're good, then others will be good as well.

A list with a brief description of some personages listed is attached to this story: Individuals listed in this manuscript:

1) Baltais-Baltaitis—a delegate from military units which demanded to be returned to Russia (the 1st Special Brigade, located in the La Courtine camp).
2) Volkov—the same.
3) Rapp, Yevgenii Ivanovich, a lawyer with the Khar'kov District Judicial Chamber and an émigré since 1906, was appointed by Kerenskii's order a commissar of the Provisional Government with the Russian forces in France.
4) Zankevich, Mikhail Ippolitovich, general, representative of the Provisional Government to the Allied Forces High Command, a former General Staff quartermaster general.
5) Gotua, a colonel with the special detachment of Russian forces.
6) "Moroz," an émigré and anarchist.
7) Svatikov, Sergei Grigor'evich, a lawyer with the Saint Petersburg District Judicial Chamber, a commissar of the Provisional Government abroad, the former chief of the Main Directorate for Police Affairs.
8) Smirnov, a social-democrat, delegate from the Executive Committee of the Provisional Soviet of Workers' and Soldiers' Deputies.
9) Lokhvitskii, Nikolai Aleksandrovich, general, commander of the Special Detachment in France." (State Archives of the Russian Federation, fond 5881, opis' 1, delo 196, pp. 1-8)

One of the Russian Legion's officers, Staff Captain Vyacheslav Afanas'evich Vasil'ev, from the 2nd Special Regiment and who later became deacon of the Cathedral-Memorial at the Russian military cemetery in Mourmelon-le-Grand and who passed away on 14 December 1975 in Mourmelon-le-Grand (this graduate of the prestigious Pavlov Military School was born on 14 May 1898) left his memoirs about the mutiny in La Courtine. Aleksandr Solzhenitsyn recounts his meeting with him in France in the book *A Grain Fell Between Two Millstones*, although for some reason he demoted him to the rank of ensign. Vasil'ev recalled:

An unbridled and overly propagandized mob in soldiers' greatcoats, which had lost its human face, with angered and brutalized faces, is raging and getting drunk and behaving disgracefully in the La Courtine military camp.

The inhabitants of the neighboring villages lock their doors in the evening. The tragic situation of the Russian officers, who are being insulted by their own troops. No "threatening" orders from Petersburg are capable of pacifying this mob, which is being inflamed by sharp, non-Russian revolutionary-propagandists, who have crawled out of all the holes.

"Down with the war and home to Russia for the distribution of the land!" However, not all ranks of the 1st Special Infantry Brigade fell for this defeatist propaganda.

If the 1st Brigade (1st and 2nd regiments), which was assembled primarily from the factory element of the Moscow and Samara provinces, immediately began to put forward anti-militarist slogans and demand an immediate return to Russia, then the 3rd Brigade (5th and 6th special regiments), which had been assembled from the healthy peasant element of the Urals provinces, sought to resist the approaching anarchy.

A schism took place.

Early in the morning of 11 July 1917, at about 7:00 a.m., the loyal soldiers left the camp with all the officers and with gleaming bayonets loaded machine guns aimed at both sides of two walls of the infuriated mob, with their threatening fists and wild cries: "Sellouts!"

The rear is brought up by loyal Mishka—a bear, surrounded by a guard.

People throw rocks and sticks at him in helpless rage. To everyone's amazement, Mishka walked along with complete dignity, peacefully moving his paws and only growling a bit, as if wishing to say: "O the times, o the mores!" A detachment of loyal soldiers set up camp in tents near the town of Felletin, 23 kilometers from La Courtine.

On 10 August the detachment was transferred by rail to the summer camp of Courneau, near Arcachon.

In the beginning of September an order arrived from the Provisional Government to immediately and once and for all eliminate the La Courtine mutineers.

On the night of 15-16 September a composite regiment, which had been formed for this purpose, surrounded the mutinous camp.

Just in case, a French cavalry brigade was stationed behind as a second ring.

An ultimatum was issued to turn over weapons within three days.

Occasional shots by a Russian battery, which exploded in the air, gave them to understand that this is no time to kid around and that the unruly soldiers would have to choose: either surrender or accept battle. A large part of the La Courtine soldiers surrendered during the first two days. Only a few hundred leaders, who did not wish to submit, remained.

In order to avoid excessive losses in this first civil battle, it was decided to attack with the onset of darkness.

Spies reported that the holdouts had broken into the wine cellars and were "getting their courage up" by loading up on wine. Each company of "loyalists" received a precise assignment.

At midnight the composite regiment moved out.

By morning everything was over. The losses were minimal. Sorting out began.

The leaders and instigators were turned over to the French gendarmes and interned. The rest were broken up into "work companies" and scattered throughout France.

However, as Vasil'ev admits, revolutionary propaganda continued even after the suppression of the mutiny and even the "loyalist detachment" began to lose its military appearance under its influence.

The officers, who were unprepared for political upheavals, became confused, not knowing what to do.

Senior commanders did not receive any kind of instructions. Red Petrograd was silent.

Amidst this chaos, baseness and pusillanimity the bold voice of Colonel Gotua (the commander of the 2nd Special Regiment), who was born in Guria,[14] a knight without fear and reproach, rang out.

He called together the officers and soldiers to rise up and defend the trampled honor or Russia and the Russian uniform.

He called upon us to form a Russian Volunteer Detachment and to bring the struggle, together with the Allies, to a victorious conclusion, so that on the day of the armistice there would be at least one Russian unit with it national flag among the allied forces. Only a few answered this knightly summons.

Among these few was Rodion Malinovskii. One should keep in mind that his name was not on the lists of those who abandoned the La Courtine camp before the start of the assault, nor among those who were arrested following the seizure of the camp by units of the 3rd Brigade, which was faithful to the Provisional Government, or by individual servicemen from the 1st Brigade and the 2nd Artillery Brigade preparing to depart for the Salonika[15] front. This causes us to trust Rodion Yakovlevich's assertion that he had been sent from the camp among the wounded and sick before the start of the assault. Nor was he among those who took part in the assault on mutinous La Courtine, thus launching an internecine struggle. It seems quite likely that Malinovskii, as a well-educated corporal, became chairman of his machine gun company's committee after the revolution. However, the documents of the Expeditionary Corps' company committees have basically disappeared and for the time being we cannot confirm in documentary fashion Malinovskii's chairmanship of his company committee.

Rodion Yakovlevich undoubtedly took part in the mutiny at La Courtine, but he was not among those who were ready to offer armed opposition to other Russian soldiers who remained loyal to the Provisional Government. He supported the mutineers' demands about returning to Russia, but not the anti-war slogans, insofar as he wanted to continue fighting the Germans, but was only prepared to do this in his native land.

In his prewar forms and service biographies, Malinovskii pointed out that from November 1917 through January 1918 he was working in the Belfort area as a common laborer. However, the autobiographical hero of *Soldiers of Russia*, Ivan Grin'ko, did not serve in the work companies, but ended up in the Foreign Legion immediately after the hospital. Nor did Malinovskii mention being sent to work in several post-war service biographies, as, for example, the one which was written on 3 January 1946, in which he maintained that

> in April 1917, during the great French offensive (the Nivelle offensive), I was wounded and returned to my regiment in the La Courtine camp (France), where our regiment was located, from the hospital in the beginning of August 1917. We demanded to be sent back to Russia, but they didn't send us. In the end, our La Courtine mutiny was suppressed by force of arms and I was also subjected to repression as a committee member. The repressions grew following the October Revolution.

However, in the service biography of 4 March 1948 it is mentioned that "upon leaving the hospital and in connection with the La Courtine events among the Russian forces in France, I was

14 Editor's note. Guria is a region in southwestern Georgia. Its inhabitants speak a dialect of Georgian.
15 Editor's note. This refers to the large collection of Allied forces (British, French, Serbs, Russians, Italians, and Greeks) who manned the Greek-Serbian border following the Central Powers' defeat of Serbia in the fall of 1915. The Allied forces eventually defeated the Bulgarian troops along this front in September 1918.

sent to do labor." I am nevertheless inclined to believe that Rodion Yakovlevich did not do labor work in France, but just like his autobiographical hero Ivan Grin'ko, he immediately joined the Foreign Legion.

Following the assumption of power by the Bolsheviks in Russia the continuation of the war on the Western Front made no sense for the overwhelming majority of the Russian brigades' soldiers in France, although the committee of the detachment of Russian forces in France condemned the Bolshevik coup and supported the Provisional Government and the future Constituent Assembly.[16] But the Kerenskii government no longer existed and Lenin's government quickly came out in favor of the immediate conclusion of peace.

Thus on 16 November the then French minister of war, Georges Clemenceau,[17] issued an order, according to which servicemen in the special Russian brigades could choose between three possibilities: 1) service in the French army; 2) military-related work in the rear, or; 3) forced labor in French North Africa. Rear-area work was considered the most favorable. Particularly favorable was the variant with rear-area work, in which aside from retaining one's former salary (75 centimes per day; by comparison, a French soldier was paid a 25-centime *per diem*), one received another half-franc per day. 252 men signed up to serve in the French army (266, according to other data), and Rodion Malinovskii was among them.

Thus there was nothing in the way of self-serving interests in signing up to join the Legion, which Malinovskii tried to assure the postwar cadre officers (Malinovskii's early biography did not interest anyone after the war). We know how easy was the work to which they sent the Russian soldiers and which their French bosses stuffed with food. The majority of the Expeditionary Corps' servicemen preferred to wait out the end of the war in the rear. The mass enrollment into the Foreign Legion began in the last weeks of the war, particularly following the Armistice. Only a few, for whom the honor of Russian arms was dear, signed up in the Legion right away, and Rodion Malinovskii was among them. However, as fate would have it, the marshal had to hide his entire life the true motives for joining the Foreign Legion, which were actually quite honorable.

It should be noted that there were several Malinovskiis in the Expeditionary Corps. There was the adjutant of the Second Special Regiment's 2nd March Battalion, Ensign Konstantin Malinovskii, a sergeant major in the same battalion, Faddei Malinovskii, and a corporal and later a junior clerk with the staff of the 3rd Special Brigade's 6th Infantry Regiment, Ivan Malinovskii.

Rodion Yakovlevich Malinovskii always remembered his time spent with the Russian Expeditionary Corps with great feeling. As the British historian Jamie Cockfield writes,

> Malinovsky suggested that he and Khrushchev visit Champagne, where his old unit had been stationed. They went by car and Malinovsky easily found the old peasant's house where he had stayed at one point. The father had died but his wife and son, who now had children, still lived there and welcomed him graciously. A party spontaneously started, joined by the neighbors, and champagne flowed. Malinovsky asked about a bar he used to frequent, and

---

16   Editor's note. The All-Russian Constituent Assembly was elected through universal suffrage shortly after the Bolshevik coup, with the task of writing a constitution for the post-monarchical Russian state. The results of the election yielded a majority of Socialist Revolutionary delegates. The Assembly met in Petrograd on 18-19 January 1918, but was quickly dissolved by the Bolshevik authorities. Bits and pieces of the Constituent Assembly continued a twilight existence during the Russian Civil War, but the body never regained its previous importance.

17   Editor's note. Georges Benjamin Clemenceau (1841-1929) earned a medical degree but became involved in political journalism early on. He was later elected to parliament and served as prime minister during 1906-09. He became prime minister again in November 1917 and his uncompromising prosecution of the war was instrumental in keeping France in the conflict. Clemenceau demanded at harsh peace at the Versailles Conference but he lost the premiership in 1920.

the locals were amazed that he knew about it. He asked about a certain girl and learned that she had been dead for quite a while. Some of the denizens asked about their bear Mishka. Malinovsky reminisced and said that he was sorry that the Revolution had occurred when he was away from home.

According to Cockfield, "A story circulates today in the émigré community in Paris that Malinovsky was present for a memorial service for the Russian war dead in France held at the Russian cemetery at Mourmelon-le-Grand (one is still conducted each year to this day). These émigrés naturally flew the flag of old tsarist Russia. When the flag passed in review, Malinovsky, the defense minister of the Soviet Union, snapped to attention and saluted it!"

It's true that in 1960 Malinovskii, together with Khrushchev, visited the village where he was once quartered with the Russian Expeditionary Corps. Nikita Sergeevich recalled that Malinovskii precisely showed the road to this village, without asking anyone the way:

Malinovskii, who was already the USSR minister of defense, accompanied me on a trip to meet the heads of the great powers in Paris: the USA, Soviet Union, England, and France. The meeting broke down because immediately preceding it the Americans launched an intelligence aircraft over our territory.[18] This is a well-known fact in the story of our struggle against American imperialism, which had launched the "Cold War."

The conference opening was delayed and so when had a "window" of time. Malinovskii suggested: "Let's go to the village where our unit was located not far from Paris. I'll find the village and the peasant with whom we lived. Perhaps the peasant has already died, he was old, but his wife was young. She's probably still alive." That's what we did: we got in the car and set off along the French roads. The roads are pretty there. We found the village without any trouble.

Malinovskii remembered its layout. We found his landlady's house. The landlady really was alive. She had a son who was about 40 years old, a daughter-in-law and grandchildren. "My old man," she said, "died a long time ago." The son greeted us very kindly and they immediately began to organize a reception and wine appeared.

We had a drink and Malinovskii began to recall past days and began to put questions. "And here," he said, "was a tavern, where the peasants would gather." The French: "Do you remember?" "Yes, I remember it well."

"In that case, you probably recall what's her name," and they called some girl by her name. "Yes," Malinovskii said, "I remember." "Ha, ha, ha, he remembers. She was the local beauty. But she's been dead for a long time."

Other Frenchmen came up. They found out that the USSR defense minister was a soldier from that same Russian unit that was stationed in the village 50 years ago. "Of course, of course! We remember. You had a bear, too." "Yes," he replied, "we had a bear." Malinovskii told about how when they were traveling to France, someone got hold of a bear cub. The cub became attached to the soldiers and then was with them at the front. The peasants remembered this.

Malinovskii relayed some other events from his biography to me. "The fact hung over me very much," he said, "that I was part of the Expeditionary Corps." I can't recall exactly now what he told me, although I know from history that this corps returned to Russia with great difficulty. It seems that they sent it from someplace, so that its soldiers would land in territory

18   Editor's note. This is a reference to the downing of the U-2 reconnaissance aircraft by Soviet missiles in May 1960, on the eve of the Paris meeting.

controlled by the Whites. Malinovskii made a great trek before he ended up in the Red Army. This episode is important for understanding the spirit of Stalin's time.

The accusation that he was a member of the Expeditionary Corps in France and on territory occupied by the Whites, before he joined the Red Army, hung over Malinovskii like the sword of Damocles.

Nikita Sergeevich spoke about this somewhat differently another time.

We drove right up to the house where Malinovskii was quartered with a friend. No crowd had gathered, because we had arrived without warning. We got out of the car and the owner of the house, a man of about 45 years, came toward us. Malinovskii and I introduced ourselves and Rodion Yakovlevich asked whether his mother was alive and that she probably remembers that two Russian soldiers slept on the hay in her barn? The owner greeted us very warmly and invited us into the house, and his mother, the landlady in the old days, appeared. We greeted her and showed her all the courtesies. Malinovskii reminded her who he was, mentioned his friend's name and asked whether her husband was still alive. She answered that he had died. Malinovskii had earlier told me that the owner had been old and that the landlady was young and very pretty. Malinovskii's friend courted the landlady and she was in love with him. This was good for the soldiers, because the landlady fed them with milk, sour cream and tasty products of French cuisine. When he named his friend her glum face changed and came alive. She now looked like an old woman, although, according to her, she was younger than Rodion Yakovlevich.

At this point her son ran out and returned with bottles of wine, set the table and traditional French hors d'oeuvres appeared and the owners' soulful kindness and warmth was fully displayed. The son took care of us and treated us to wine. The old woman also had a drink. Malinovskii began to recall the past. The landlady evidently did not want to give way to recollections and kept very close control of herself with us. There was a certain indifference on her face, while her son displayed typical peasant conviviality, but without being obsequious.

Then everyone went out on the street. The inhabitants of the village had already gathered here. I remember many of them. These were middle-aged people. There were children, of course, as there are in all such cases in any village.

Malinovskii began to inquire about some of his acquaintances and addressed an old man in French: "Is your tavern still here? Do you still visit it?" The Frenchman smiled: "Yes, there's a tavern and we visit it the same way we used to, but the beautiful girl, whom you probably recall, has been dead for a long time." Malinovskii also began to smile and said: "I don't deny that I remember her." At this point everyone began to make a racket, recalling the girl from the tavern, a real beauty. It's obvious that the tavern owner kept her on to attract the young men, so that they would drink more of his wine. This was how he made his money. Malinovskii never mentioned any kind of familiarities with her or on her part. Evidently these were clean and good relations. He loved women, especially good-looking ones, about which he often told me openly, recalling his sojourn in Spain during the Republicans'[19] war against Franco.[20]

---

19   Editor's note. The Republicans were those forces loyal to the Spanish Republic during the Spanish Civil War (1936-39). Their opponents were commonly known as the Nationalists.

20   Editor's note. Generalissimo Francisco Franco (1892-1975) joined the Spanish army in 1907 and fought for several years against tribesmen in Spanish Morocco and thereafter quickly rose through the ranks. In 1936, as commander of the Army of Africa, he joined the Nationalist revolt against the Spanish Republic and gradually exerted his control over the state apparatus. Franco ruled Spain from as an absolute dictator

After Rodion Yakovlevich became minister of defense, veterans of the Russian Expeditionary Corps in France began to write him. For example, on 14 June 1960 Mikhail Andreevich Kostin wrote Malinovskii.

Dear Comrade Malinovskii!

I read with great emotion the meager lines in the newspaper communiqués about how, while you were in France you were able to, together with Nikita Sergeevich, to visit "beautiful Pleurs-sur-Marne."

I'm very, very glad for you and, to tell the truth, I envy you, as would any in my place.

You and I were together in Pleurs at one time, although we were not close; but that does not prevent me from giving way to reminiscences… Where could you have seen me in Pleurs?

Of course, you remember our "theater," which was located in a wooden barracks, the heart and organizer of which was "our" doctor—Dmitrii Alekseevich Vvedenskii, whose soldier's epaulets we changed for a colonel's during the farewell party organized by him. Our theater, which began with a display of acts with decorations, a picture of the Moscow Kremlin and a wanderer with a knapsack, who sang "Evening Bells" in a pleasant voice, backed up by a choir behind the curtain? That theater, where the operetta that caused a lot of controversy was performed, the prologue of which, "In Life's Stormy Days" Yermachenko soulfully sang? Our theater, on the boards of which performed short Karlusha, the "most terrible Bolshevik," with a flashlight, while making fun of the local priest, who was always unshaven and hated us Russians?

It was in the theater that I found my calling as a sort of "prima donna," performing in the chief women's roles (as Ol'-Ol'—Ol'ga Nikolaevna in L. Andreev's[21] play *Days of Our Life*, and a Vera Nikolaevna in Turgenev's[22] play *It Tears Where it's Fine*, and the widow in Chekhov's[23] play *The Bear*, and others.

Our "friend" Prachek liked the play *It Tears Where it's Fine* more than the others, as he said himself. Can one really forget him?

I don't know which café you visited. We actors gathered most often in the one, if memory serves me correctly, on that side of the street where the mayor's office (between the post office and the bakery, it seems) is. We also gathered lower down, where the owner's pretty daughter, Jeanne Monette, who was in love with Zamyslov, worked.

I was friends with the Boileau family. The landlord repaired bicycles, sewing machines and other things, while madame Boileau kept a kiosk and distributed papers daily to the subscribers. Our comrade, corpsman Ivan Pavlov, married one of the older daughters, Irene, and I was at his wedding celebration. I personally wooed Francine, whom I was crazy about and who was only 16 at the time. The youngest daughter, Carmen, was always at her knitting next to the gate and would quietly giggle when Prachek would walk by, loudly greeting her with 'Bon jour, Carmen,' with the stress on the letter o…

An entire life passed before Carmen could send me a New Year's card in 1960…

---

from 1939 to his death.

21   Editor's note. Leonid Nikolaevich Andreev (1871-1919) was a Russian playwright and short story writer, active in the so-called "Silver Age" of Russian literature. Andreev died an émigré in Finland.

22   Editor's note. Ivan Sergeevich Turgenev (1818-1883) was a Russian novelist, playwright and short story writer. He as the author of such novels as *Rudin* and *Fathers and Sons*. Turgenev died in France.

23   Editor's note. Anton Pavlovich Chekhov (1860-1904) was a Russian short story writer and foremost Russian playwright in history. He wrote such plays as *The Cherry Orchard* and *The Three Sisters*. Chekhov died of tuberculosis in Germany.

There's no one left in Pleurs out of the big Boileau family. The old folks have died and all the daughters got married and fanned out to all the corners of France. Pavlov's wife, Irene, wrote me two years ago that Jeanne perished in 1944 in the Resistance. She wrote me that they still remember the Russian Legion in Pleurs. Of course, she hasn't forgotten Francine… Last year I received a letter from the oldest sister, Henriette. She lived in Dr. Choquer's house, if you remember. She's now been living in Sezanne for many years. Lidi (Kostyrkin wooed her when we were there) sent me a postcard. All of them have long ago turned into grandmothers, as we have turned into grandfathers.

A few words about myself. I returned to Russia with the first group of Russian soldiers and since 1923 I have lived continuously in Central Asia. Of our old friends, I had the pleasure of meeting most often with Dmitrii Alekseevich Vvedenskii. He died four years ago as a venerable professor. Nikolai Borisovich Sergeev and Fedya Sorokin were in Tashkent and found me through the information bureau. But he is already a good 30 years of age.

I still do some work in the humble job of bookkeeper; although it's high time I retired. "I'm old and my mind's not what it used to be." My hearing is already bad. How an entire life has passed by unnoticed!

I have some consolation in my spiritual life. I read *L'Humanite*,[24] which I regularly receive through Moscow, and I sometimes manage to get hold of an issue of *Liberacion* and *L'Humanite Dimanche*, although very rarely, but even that's good. Making use of their material, I sometimes write on international affairs in the local press. I'm sending you a few articles (I have enough for a small book) as a keepsake. A small translation of mine was published last year in *The Star of the East*.[25] In a word, I'm still alive.

I guess that's all. Please excuse me for taking up so much of your time and talking so much. But what can you do! It's so pleasant to recall one's youth, and your trip to Pleurs awoke within me so many sleeping memories and reminded me of the irrevocable past. By the way, I'm sending you the song "Farewell Pleurs," which I rewrote from memory.

I wish you, dear comrade Malinovskii, as well as dear Nikita Sergeevich, that tireless warrior for the bright future of mankind, who with his visit has written, along with you, a brilliant page in the history of a small village, which has now become famous throughout the entire world, good health, long life and complete success in your difficult work toward the benefit of our beloved Fatherland and the cause of peace throughout the world.

Sincerely,

M. Kostin.

At that moment neither Malinovskii nor his regimental friend knew that within a little over four years one of them would be taking the most active part in the overthrow of "that tireless warrior for the bright future."

M.A. Kostin left his address: Islotan', Turkmen SSR, Zonal station.

Because he was so busy with state affairs, Rodion Yakovlevich managed to respond to his regimental friend only on 6 October. He wrote:

Hello, Mikhail Andreevich!

I received your letter, in which you were delighted with "beautiful Pleurs-sur-Marne."

---

24   Editor's note. *L'Humanite* was founded in 1904 as a socialist newspaper. It became the official organ of the French Communist Party following its split with the socialists in 1920.

25   Editor's note. *The Star of the East* (*Zvezda Vostoka*) was the official literary journal of the Uzbek SSR Writer's Union, published in Russian.

Just think, in 1960 I was in that very same Pleurs with N.S. Khrushchev and the entire village came out and accompanied us around the village to the church, and I stood with old man Piniar in the barn across from the church.

Of course, I remember everything well. And I remember you, the young soldier who was able to play Ol'-Ol in *Days of our Life*, but there's no longer a trace of the barracks where our theater was.

Just as from you, I received a letter from Konstantin Dmitrievich Lebedev, whom we then called "Marus'ka", and who played left center in soccer (he now lives in Kirov province, the town of Vyatskaya Polyana, 5a Azin St, apt. 5). For some reason he changed his name to Liberte (freedom).

I arrived in Russia at Vladivostok with Dmitrii Alekseevich Vvedenskii in 1919, but we parted there, and it's only now that I learn from you about him. Vasya Yermachenko and I served together in the 27th Division's 240th Tver' Regiment in the Red Army, but in January 1920 I came down with typhus and was in the hospital, where I survived by a miracle, while Vasya and the regiment left for the Polish front[26] and we lost track of each other.

We visited the café next to the mayor's office.

You see how many recollections I've stirred up within you. It turns out that you know French well, since you read and write French. I only read a little in *Le Nouvelles de Moscou* and some simple little books.

Thanks for your nice letter. Write me.

Sincerely,

R. Malinovskii.

In the novel *Soldiers of Russia*, Kostin is portrayed under his own name.

Rehearsals began. Vanyusha, as the "literate one," copied out all the roles and distributed them and got in his prompter's box. Ensign Shelkovyi had a lot of work to do. He had to teach Kostin to perform Clemente's sonata, while Kostin didn't play the piano very well. They didn't leave the instrument for days at a time. But perhaps this was useful to Vera Nikolaevna and Yevgeniya Andreevna, who wcre played by Kostin and ensign Shelkovyi and who got used to each other. Boris Sakharov, who was already well know for artistically designing sets, was in charge of the decorations.

It is also noted in the novel that Viktor Dmitrievskii, for whom Dmitrii Vvedenskii was the prototype as "the main leader and director of the circle literally did not leave the theater; that is, the old barracks on the outskirts of Pleurs."

Malinovskii maintained contact with the veterans of the Russian expeditionary forces in France, not only by exchanging letters. He had the pleasure of meeting several of them. Natal'ya Rodionovna recalled:

In about 1962 we had an amazing guest in our home—father's comrade from the expeditionary corps, an unusual man very unlike any I had ever seen, which is why I recall him. A long, lean and bald old man (he seemed much older than papa) in a black suit and a black bow tie of unbelievable dimensions—like a first-grade schoolgirl. He expressed himself in some kind of semi-understandable language, throwing in French words and ostentatiously rolling

---

26   Editor's note. Here Malinovskii is referring to the conflict between Soviet Russia and the reconstituted Polish state (April 1920-March 1921)

his rs in the French style. I don't know what he and papa talked about all Sunday, but judging by the heartfelt parting and excellent mood of both of them, the conversation was very interesting. It's a shame that I didn't ask papa then about this man, who either resembled a member of the State Duma (this is the notion I had of them at the time) or a provincial tragic actor. I don't know how his fate played out following his return from France and I don't even know his name. They recalled silly things, a bow and a vegetarian's homily over lunch.

One of the founders of the "Legion of Honor," Staff Captain V.A. Vasil'ev (then a lieutenant), recalled:

Only a few of them, volunteers to fight for the honor of Russia, got in the train cars. The first train carried seven officers, two doctors, an old priest, and 374 NCOs and soldiers. In order to make an example and to underscore the ideological content of this formation, Dr. Vedenskii from the 5th Special Infantry Regiment, joined as a private soldier.

Two officers were left behind at the Russian base to form march companies for reinforcements…

On 5 January the Russian Legion arrived in the combat zone and was commandeered to the famous Moroccan Shock Division, the best division in France.

This division, which consisted of a composite regiment from the Foreign Legion, the 8th Zouave, 7th Moroccan Rifle and 4th Moroccan Rifle regiments and the 12th Battalion of Malagasy riflemen, was placed in attacks exclusively to break through the enemy's fortified positions, or in counterattacks for closing up enemy breakthroughs.

This was the only division in France that didn't have a numerical designation. The division's combat glory stood so high that to serve in it was considered a great honor.

The division was resting. They met us like old friends.

The following day the Russian Legion was reviewed by the division commander, General DAUGAN.

The dashing mien of the Russian volunteers, among whom more than half were holders of all four St. George's medals, made an excellent impression.

The general, while reviewing the troops of the Russian Legion, would stop in front of the officers, shaking their hands, and having reached the left flank and looked in wonderment at the motionless Mishka and the two handlers at attention beside him.

Mishka, who was not used to the general's kepi, which was embroidered with gold, fixed his eyes on him; and the general on Mishka.

After a second's hesitation, the general smiled and raised his hand to his kepi. The staff officers around him repeated their chief's gesture. Mishka made a noise resembling approval, which he usually made when they gave him an orange or a small bottle of cognac, which he was a big fan of.

Mishka became a celebrity in the Moroccan Division.

He was assigned a soldier's ration by special order.

In the beginning of February 1918 the legion was transferred from the 4th Rifle Regiment to the 8th Zouave Regiment, where it became the 1st Battalion.

The Russian Legion had it first battle in April, repulsing the German offensive in northern France. V. Vasil'ev recounts:

The Moroccan Division was roused and loaded onto trucks. After a night's journey, it was unloaded in the area of the town of Beauvais. As always, it was held in the army reserve and was to be thrown into the fighting at the last minute.

The critical moment had arrived. The enemy had to be halted at any cost.

On the night of 25-26 April the division occupied its jumping-off position and counterattacked at dawn.

The Russian Legion, under the overall command of Colonel GOTUA; Captain LUPANOV, deputy legion commander and holder of four St. George's crosses. Captain MILEANT, Staff Captain IORDAN, and Staff Captain FRIDMAN, and lieutenants PRAVOSUDOVICH and MIRIMANOV were in the rifle company, and Captain RAZUMOV, Staff Captain PRACHEK, and doctors ZIL'BERSHTEIN and KLEIMAN in the machine gun company, and 359 officers and legionnaires were in the first echelon.

The Russian Legion's losses were large: among the wounded officers were Staff Captain MILEANT, Staff Captain FRIDMAN, Lieutenant PAVOSUDOVICH, with 34 NCOs and legionnaires killed, 76 wounded, and four missing.

Captain LUPANOV particularly distinguished himself and was awarded the cross of the Legion of Honor on the field (Mstislav Fedorovich Lupanov was born in May 1885 in St. Petersburg and passed away on 15 September 1976 in the small town of Mourmelon-le-Grand, near Paris, and since 1964 was the chairman of the Union of Officer Participants of the War on the French Front. He carved all of the metal fittings for the church in the Russian military cemetery in Mourmelon-le-Grand by himself, B.S.). The remaining officers received the Military Cross in varying degrees. Two legionnaires who distinguished themselves were awarded the Military Medal.

A large number of Military Crosses were distributed for their services to the NCOs and legionnaires. (The awarding of the Legion of Honor and the Military Medal for distinction in combat was accompanied at that time by the awarding of the Military Cross with a palm leaf. The Military Cross has four classes: with a palm for an army award, with a gold star for a corps award, with a silver star for a division award, and with a bronze star for a brigade award.)

The Moroccan Division remained in the line until 7 May, beating off the Germans' stubborn attacks. Having lost 74 officers and 4,000 soldiers, it was relieved by newly-arrived fresh units and pulled back for rest.

The road to Amiens had been closed to the enemy forever...

Some of the staff officers, following the example of Colonel GOTUA, began to form their own independent volunteer detachments.

These formations proved to be unlucky and only harmed the Russian name.

The Moroccan Division's 1st Russian Legion, which consisted of the best element and the morale of which was extremely high and which had already proven itself in battle, was in need of a rest in order to make good its losses. The newly-formed incomplete battalions, which siphoned off very needy reinforcements, were poorly organized and made up of an ill-assorted element and which had been undermined by extensive anti-militarist propaganda, gradually began to fall apart and, in the end, following a series of unpleasant incidents, were disbanded by the war ministry, without having contributed anything...

Colonel GOTUA'S role was that of an ideological leader. Of course, according to his rank, he could not command such a small unit, all the more so as the commander of the 8th Zouave Regiment, to which the Russian Legion had been attached as the 4th Battalion, he was a lieutenant colonel.

Colonel GOTUA was extremely energetic and threw his entire Caucasian nature into the cause of serving the Russian Legion.

He made the rounds of the "work companies" and explained the goal of creating the Russian Legion and chose volunteers and visited hospitals.

For drill purposes, the command of the Russian Legion fell to his deputy, Captain LUPANOV.

Besides, following the first battle, Colonel GOTUA, who had gone on leave for a couple of days, was not allowed to return to the Russian Legion…

The Legion next took part in the fighting in the Soissons area.
Vasil'ev recalls:

A march company of 108 NCOs and soldiers and three officers, which had been formed from newly enrolled volunteers, arrived from the Russian base. In the evenings we would sit around until midnight in a field meeting, having a pleasant conversation…

On 27 May the enemy put in his best forces and broke through the French army's front, and in a single leap passed through the Chemin des Dames, crossed the Aisne River and was approaching Chateau Thierry by forced march.

Soissons fell. The road to Paris was open.

The Moroccan Division was unloaded from trucks and occupied a position stretching ten kilometers along the Soissons—Paris road.

The enemy, drunk with success and supported by a colossal amount of artillery and buoyed by its numerical superiority, was easily developing his initial success.

The French units were retreating in disorder.

The Moroccan Division took upon itself the blow of the heavy German boot and, panting in desperation and with difficulty, held up the enemy stream with its last bit of energy. But all things come to an end! The Germans poured fresh forces into the fighting and pushed back the 8th Zouave Regiment.

At this critical moment, when it seemed that all was lost, the commander of the 8th Zouave Regiment threw his last reserve into the counterattack—the Russian Legion!

Under the overall command of Captain LUPANOV, with his adjutant, Guards Second Lieutenant RUDNIKOV, a rifle company under the command of Staff Captain IORDAN, and junior officers Lieutenant ORNATSKII, Lieutenant VASIL'EV, Lieutenant MIRIMANOV, and a machine gun company under the command of Captain RAZUMOV, Staff Captain PRACHEK, doctors ZIL'BERSHTEIN and KLEIMAN, the Russian Legion occupied its jumping-off position.

The rifle company, under the cover of the woods, moved forward. Soissons could be seen below. They didn't advance even a hundred paces, when the news made the rounds of the line: "Lieutenant ORNATSKII has been killed!" A stray bullet hit him in the head.

The lines emerged from the woods with the cry of "Hurrah" and vigorously threw themselves on the enemy…

However, having thrown itself so far ahead, the rifle company was, in turn, surrounded by a very powerful enemy.

One must speak of the outstanding feat by Junior Ensign D'YAKONOV, who heroically saved the remnants of the company.

Seriously wounded, he gathered around himself other wounded and, shouting to the officers: "Break out, I'll hold the Germans up," opened fire and thus focused all the enemy's attention on himself and enabled the remaining survivors to feel out a weak place in the enemy's ring and to break out of the encirclement and link up with their own forces.

D'YAKONOV probably perished. Glory to this hero!…

A difficult assignment fell to Captain RAZUMOV'S machine gunners.

Throwing them from one place to another into the thick of the fighting, they were attached to either the Zouaves or to the Moroccans; there where it was no longer possible to hold. Their appearance imparted new energy and raised the spirits of the exhausted and harassed soldiers.

"The Russians are with us" was passed down the line and their hopeful gazes were trained on these knights in defensive soldier's blouses, who picked up heavy Hotchkiss machine guns in a single bound, like a toy (these machine guns weighed 23.6 kilograms, B.S.).

It's not for nothing that they won all the first prizes in the division's sports competitions.

Their machine gun bursts literally mowed down the German lines, but in turn it brought about a murderous return fire by the enemy's artillery.

The machine gunners paid dearly for their shooting ability. Not many of them returned from the field…

One must also note the particularly high morale of the officers, who so as not to abandon their soldiers in this extremely difficult situation for them, remained among the French after being wounded and would remain in the line until the last opportunity; and only after the second or third wound were they removed unconscious from the battle field and evacuated. For example, Captain RAZUMOV, following a third wound in the head, Lieutenant GIRGENSON after a fourth wound in the stomach, and Lieutenant BATUEV, following a second wound in the hip.

Captain RAZUMOV and Staff Captain PRACHEK were awarded the Legion of Honor. All of the remaining officers received the Military Cross of various classes.

Three particularly distinguished legionnaires were awarded the Military Medal in the field. A large number of Military Crosses was distributed among the NCOs and legionnaires…

Corporal Rodion MALINOVSKII, a future marshal in the Red Army and minister of defense, served in the Legion…

Following the Soissons fighting, the Russian Legion received a banner as a token of the French government's gratitude. On the flagstaff was the white, blue and red Russian national flag…

All of June passes in extended defensive fighting, in order to block the enemy's entry into the VILLERS-COTTERETS woods.

At the end of June the exhausted division was pulled back to the Forest of Compiegne for a semi-rest.

In order to formulate the situation of the Russian volunteers, from the point of view of international law, the French government ordered all Russian volunteers to sign a second declaration, because there was no phrase in the first one about promising to fight "until the end of the war."

A wavering element, under the influence of propaganda, the long distance from home, exhaustion, the heavy fighting, and the heavy losses, took advantage of this detail and refused to sign a second declaration and was sent to the "work companies."

There were, of course, other very brave legionnaires, who believed that after the heroism they had displayed and the proof of the Russian Legion's selflessness, which had been recognized by the French command, the demand for a second declaration was an act of insulting lack of confidence in them and thus they refused to sign it out of principle and were forced to leave.

They dressed the Legion in the uniform of the colonial troops. Only on the left arm was there a band with the colors of the Russian national flag. And instead of the French coat of arms on their helmets, there were the letters L.R. (Legion Russe) in black. This was done so that the Russians, should they be captured by the Germans, would not face repressions as illegal combatants. After all, Russia had concluded the treaty of Brest-Litovsk[27] with Germany.

---

27   Editor's note. The Treaty of Brest-Litovsk peace treaty was signed on 3 March 1918 between the Soviet

This is what Vasil'ev recalled about the Russian Legion's concluding battles:

The command was transferred to Captain PRACHEK, and with him were two young officers—Lieutenant MIRIMANOV and Lieutenant VASIL'EV and about a hundred NCOs and legionnaires.

The Russian Legion entered the heavy July fighting in this reduced state.

Of course, one could not entrust an independent assignment to such a small detachment and it served as a "plug" and a mobile reserve. The Legion was thrown into those places where the enemy was applying heavy pressure, in order to support tired units…

On 15 July the enemy carried out a massed attack from Reims. However, the French army was itself getting ready to attack and had gathered in the Forest of VILLERS-COTTERETS.

The Germans' attack ran out of steam on the second day, having encountered a powerful rebuff.

At 4 o'clock in the morning of 18 July General MANGIN'S Tenth Army, which included the Moroccan Division, with the Russian Legion, emerged from the woods, pushed back the enemy and in ten days of fighting reached the important CHATEAU THIERRY road.

In this fighting the Moroccan Division was for the first time accompanied by tanks—little Renaults[28] and huge Schneiders.[29]

The RussianLegion, which had been reinforced by heavy machine guns, went in as a flank guard.

The Russian Legion lost the following officers wounded in the July fighting: Lieutenant MIRIMANOV, Lieutenant VASIL'EV, and a translator, the French officer Rouba. 17 NCOs and legionnaires were killed or wounded…

Major Tramuset, a combat staff officer in the Foreign Legion, was appointed to command the Russian Legion.

Guards Captain MARTYNOV was appointed deputy commander.

The battalion staff consisted of: a communications officer, the French Lieutenant Brenn, the officer translators lieutenants Rurco, Reerge and Rabote, doctors CHEREPOV and KLEIMAN, and the archpriest, Father BOGOSLOVSKII.

The 1st Rifle Company was commanded by Staff Captain SURIN (Boris). Lieutenants PRAVOSUDOVICH and PAVLOV, Second Lieutenant PRZHEVAL'SKII.

The 2nd Rifle Company was commanded by Staff Captain SURIN (Pavel). Second lieutenants SMIRNOV, KURILLO and TSVETAEV.

Lieutenant VASIL'EV was in temporary command of the machine gun company. Second Lieutenant URVACHEV…

The Moroccan Division was once again in General MANGIN'S Tenth Army, whose task was to break through the Germans' front between the Aisne River and the St. Gobain Heights in the direction of the town of LAON.

Russian government and the Central Powers (Germany, Austria-Hungary, Bulgaria, and the Ottoman Empire). The Soviets ceded the Baltic States to Germany and some territory in the Caucasus to the Turks and were forced to recognize the independence of Ukraine. The treaty was nullified by the Germans' defeat eight months later.

28 Editor's note. The Renault FT light tank, the first such vehicle to have a revolving turret, was produced during the First World War. One model weighed 6.5 tons and had a crew of two. It was armed with a 37mm gun or an 8mm machine gun.

29 Editor's note. The Schneider CA 1 was a French armored fighting vehicle used during the First World War. This model weighed 13.6 tons and carried a crew of six. The vehicle was armed with a 75mm gun and two 8mm machine guns.

The American 32nd Division ahead of them stumbled, halted and fell back and was relieved by the Moroccan Division.

At 5 a.m. on 2 September the rifle companies emerged from their trenches and threw themselves forward under a hurricane of artillery fire. The old priest and holder of four St. George's crosses, with a cross on a St. George's ribbon, archpriest BOGOSLOVSKII, disregarding all efforts to persuade him, emerged with the others from the trenches and walked under fire in the open.

Without a helmet, with his grey hair blowing in the wind, he raised his cross high in his right hand and blessed those going into the attack.

The Russian Legion's battalion had already jumped far ahead. The reserve units of Zouaves hurriedly crossed the place where the priest was standing.

The French Catholics, in running past the Orthodox priest, removed their helmets and crossed themselves, while the closest ones to him ran up and hurriedly kissed the cross. The first rays of the rising sun imparted an unforgettable impression to this picture.

At noon the sad news reached the first line. The priest has been killed!

He had been seriously wounded by a German shell that blew up next to him.

The medics, having bandaged him up, brought him back to the dressing station on a stretcher. Flocks of German airplanes, circling like kites and peppering the attacking troops with fire, finished off the priest, who was still on a stretcher, with a machine gun burst…

By order of the commander-in-chief, Father BOGOSLOVSKII was posthumously awarded the Legion of Honor and the Military Cross with a palm.

The 12th Battalion of Malagasy riflemen was given the assignment of taking the heavily fortified locale of Terny-Sorny. The Moroccan Division's flank support depended on the success of this operation.

Having begun their movement, they came under murderous fire from point 172, which pinned them to the ground.

Forced to detach part of their forces to parry the sudden danger from the flank, they were too weak to capture Terny-Sorny and hit the dirt, suffering enormous losses under the constantly increasing enemy fire.

The Russian Legion, following behind the Malagasy battalion and seeing their critical situation, threw themselves forward, maneuvering under the Germans' deadly barrage and, outflanking Terny-Sorny from the east, break into it and seize the enemy's fortified locale in a cruel hand-to-hand fight…

A salvo of heavy German artillery landed in the command post and killed the Legion's commander, Major Tramuset, the French communications officer, Lieutenant Brenn, Dr. KLEIMAN, and three Russian communications troops.

The command of the Russian Legion passed to Guards Captain MARTYNOV. The enemy attempts for three days to take back this very important strong point…

The entire fury of the German counterattacks, like the waves on the ocean, broke against the granite cliff of Russian bayonets.

The gallant Legion commander, Guards Captain MARTYNOV and the commander of the 2nd Company, SURIN (Pavel), were decorated on the battlefield by a telegram from the commander-in-chief of the Legion of Merit.

Four Military Medals were affixed to the chest of particularly distinguished Russian legionnaires on the battlefield.

The Russian Legion's losses are large. Killed were Major Tramuset, Lieutenant Brenn, Dr. KLEIMAN, archpriest BOGOSLOVSKII. Wounded were Lieutenant PAVLOV, Second Lieutenant TSVETAEV, Dr. CHEREPOV, and the French officer translators Rurco, Reerge and Rabote. 24 NCOs and legionnaires were killed and 78 wounded…

Our old acquaintance, the valiant commander of the 8th Zouave Regiment, Major DURAN, was appointed commander of the Russian Legion in place of the dead Major Tramuset.

On 13 September the exhausted Moroccan Division received orders to attack and break through the fortified Hindenburg Line,[30] the proud Teuton's last stronghold.

The Russian Legion moved in the first echelon, behind its artillery's rolling barrage.

At 5 a.m. on 14 September, having lunged forward, the 1st Rifle Company, supported by the 2nd Rifle Company following 150 meters behind, broke into the ROSSIGNOL key fortified trench in a lightning attack, peppered it with hand grenades and, without halting, took the Avance second fortified line in a bayonet attack.

Having cleared the seized lines of the enemy, the Russian Legion, having outstripped in its unlimited fervor its own artillery's barrage, pushed toward its last assigned target—the Chateau de la Motte third fortified line and broke into it with a bayonet attack.

A mighty Russian "Hurrah," which sprang from 400 Russian chests, so stunned the Germans that they had no time to put up resistance and surrendered in panic.

Red rocket flares soared up to warn our artillery and aviation that "We're already here, don't shoot, shift your fire further!"

The chief of the Moroccan Division stated in his report about this legendary fight:

> All of these actions were carried out so brilliantly and with such vigor that the Russian Legion's losses were relatively insignificant (nine killed and 25 wounded).

In recommending the Russian Legion for an award, he further wrote:

> A battalion of specially picked men, the uncompromising hatred for the enemy of which, combined with complete contempt for death, inspired all of their actions. The willingness to sacrifice, with which the Russian Legion carried out its maneuver, the boldness and courage with which it displayed under the hurricane fire of the enemy, and the amazing energy and hardiness displayed by them, requires the recommendation of the Russian Legion for the award they deserve.

All the ranks of the unit, which received a "fourragere," wear this award—a kind of aiguillette—on the left shoulder. Two palms gave one the right to a fourragere with the colors of the Military Cross, four palms, the colors of the Military Medal, six palms, the colors of the Legion of Honor, and eight palms, a double fourragere. By the end of the war all of the regiments in the Moroccan Division had been awarded with fourrageres with the colors of the Legion of Honor, except for the Foreign Legion's composite regiment which, together with the Alpine Rifle Regiment, had a double fourragere.

By the end of the war Doctor Vedenskii, as has been mentioned earlier, who joined the Russian Legion as a private soldier, had been awarded with the Legion of Honor and the Military Cross, with a palm, for distinction in combat.

Awarding a soldier the Legion of Honor is an extremely rare occurrence in the French army and there were only a few such cases during the entire war. Following the Armistice, Dr. Vedenskii was restored to his rank of military doctor. He left for Vladivostok to join Admiral KOLCHAK'S forces. His further fate is unknown.

---

30 Editor's note. The Hindenburg Line (*Siegfriedstellung*) was the popular name given to the defensive position to which the Germans withdrew in February-March 1917, in an attempt to conserve manpower. The Allies broke through the Hindenburg Line during September-October 1918.

Thus in ten months of combat service 24 officers, three doctors, a priest, seven French officers and translators, and 994 NCOs and legionnaires passed through the Russian Legion.

During this same period the Russian Legion lost in killed and wounded 16 officers, three doctors, one priest, six French officers and translators, and 523 NCOs and legionnaires.

Before the end of the war the Russian Legion, together with the Moroccan Division, was transferred to Lorraine, where the news of the armistice found it on 11 November. The Russian legionnaires then took part in the occupation of the Rhineland, occupying the town of Morsch, north of Friedrichshafen.

Vasil'ev notes ironically:

Following the conclusion of the armistice, the ranks of volunteers for the Russian Legion grew amazingly. Aside from soldiers who had transferred from the "work companies," and who now expressed a desire to serve in the ranks of the Russian Legion, legionnaires of Russian descent were transferred from the Foreign Legion, with the permission of the war minister, to the Russian Legion.

On 16 November 153 men arrived from the Foreign Legion, and another 42 on 3 December.

Unfortunately, as it proved later, this was mainly a heavily-propagandized element, for which the single goal, knowing that the Russian Legion would be sent back home before long, was just to reach Russia and go over to the Reds. He also notes that following the disbanding of the legion and before the departure for Russia to Denikin's, Kolchak's or Miller's[31] forces, the corpsmen and warrant officers were promoted to officer rank.

Rodion Malinovskii was just a corporal, although he occupied an officer's position—the commander of a machine gun company (as opposed to the commander of an infantry platoon, this was not an NCO position, but an officer's). I was unable to find traces of this last promotion to lieutenant, corpsman and warrant officer in the form of orders to the Russian forces in France. It's not excluded that there was no general order, but that an order was issued personally to each man together with an officer's service record. Practically no service records were preserved in the files of the Russian expeditionary forces. Evidently the officers took them with them when they were discharged.

In 1960, in a letter to the Parisian newspaper *Russkaya Mysl'*, one of Malinovskii's former commanders in the Russian Legion (most likely Captain Vasil'ev), maintained that Malinovskii "was a gloomy, disciplined veteran, who was always looking distrustfully around." In this context, the word "disciplined" renders his participation in the uprising in La Courtine unlikely, although the fact that Rodion Yakovlevich chose to write about precisely this event in his first literary work, speaks in favor of the notion that he really did take part in the La Courtine uprising.

To judge by one indirect bit of evidence, Corporal Rodion Malinovskii was nevertheless promoted to lieutenant. The fact is that as early as his service in the Red Army Rodion Yakovlevich wrote a play in seven scenes about the La Courtine uprising, *Feats of a Life*. Malinovskii dated the completion of his work on the play as 30 August 1920. The certificate that Malinovskii completed the junior commander's school, where he was sent in June 1920, is dated 21 August. One may assume that Rodion Yakovlevich wrote his play while attending school. To judge from everything, this was his first literary work. The author's dedication is on the first page: "I dedicate this to the detachment of

---

31   Editor's note. Yevgenii-Ludwig Karlovich Miller (1867-1939) joined the Russian army as a young man and commanded a military district and an army during the First World War. During the civil war he commanded White forces in northern Russia. He was active in émigré politics in France, but in 1937 he was kidnapped by Soviet agents and shipped to the Soviet Union. Miller was executed in Moscow.

Russian forces in France, who rose against the Kerenskii government in the La Courtine camp in June 1917." The main and obviously autobiographical hero of the play is Petr Stepin. In the author's remarks he is described in the following manner: "Petr Stepin is a young, persistent and smart soldier with a strong personality, who was born and grew up in a factory in one of the southern towns of Russia. He had a bold gaze and strength and confidence in his movements." As regards one of the southern towns, we should note that Mariupol' and Odessa fall equally under this category and Mariupol' perhaps, even more so. After all, Odessa is not just a town, but one of the largest and most unique cities of southern Russia. We should also note that in the play Malinovskii gave his hero a proletarian (factory) origin. The fourth scene concludes in France, following the suppression of the uprising. Before the fifth scene, the action of which takes place in Siberia, two years pass, which means that the events unfolding there occurred in the final months of 1919. Stepin and his comrade, the soldier Skvortsov, who is also pro-Bolshevik, arrive at Kolchak's army in worn-out uniforms characteristic of those who have been freed from German captivity. They present documents attesting that they are officers, although they present themselves under other people's names: "Scene 4. The same people, plus Lieutenant Ogloblin. Stepin: Pleased to meet you. I'm an agent with a special counterintelligence detachment, Lieutenant Ordyntsev, and this is my colleague (points to Skvortsov) from the same detachment, Cornet Bloufel (Stepin hands over two documents).

"Ogloblin (saluting): 'Forgive me, lieutenant!' Stepin and Skvortsov end up in a reserve battalion, where they convince the soldiers to go over to the red partisans, assuring them that "We're real Reds" and that their officer's documents are falsified. Stepin kills a Kolchak officer who attempts to interfere with them.

However, Malinovskii never once wrote either in official forms or in his service biography about any kind of connections with Siberian partisans or about such a favorable episode as the killing of a Kolchak officer. Thus one may assume, with a high degree of certainty, that all the episodes in the latter part of the play are a literary invention. However, it seems to me that the scene with the officers' documents have a certain basis in fact. Most likely, Malinovskii had a service record with him and other documents testifying to his officer's rank. And it's possible that the corresponding episode in the play was to convince those who knew anything about Malinovskii's officer's rank that the corresponding documents were forged and were only for the purpose of disguising himself. To all appearances, Malinovskii had the foresight to destroy them before going over to the Reds.

General Ye.Ye. Mal'tsev, then commissar of the 74th Rifle Division in the 48th Rifle Corps, which Malinovskii commanded in 1941, tells us, evidently in Rodion Yakovlevich's own words:

> Malinovskii, having passed through difficult front trials, a young, clever and intelligent soldier, could easily have become an officer when they proposed that he take an external examination in the reserve regiment to get into the military academy after he got well.
>
> "I won't go," he answered, already understanding what a great gulf existed between the mass of soldiers and the gentlemen officers, while remaining convinced that while remaining a Russian patriot, one doesn't have to become an officer…

As we can see, there is a hint of Malinovskii's possibly being an officer. And to propose that our hero simply enter a lieutenants' school, he would have to have sufficiently high educational credentials.

In the deep autumn of 1919, four combat friends—Malinovskii, Yermachenko, Tsyb, and Trofimov—having managed to get back to Russia, made their way from Vladivostok to Siberia to friendly forces; that is, to the Reds. His friends became soldiers in the Red Army. Rodion

Malinovskii accurately and bravely cut down the White guard lines with his "Maksim"[32] in the fighting for Achinsk, Chulymskaya and Taiga.

In all likelihood, the play was written for a divisional amateur theatrical, but it is unknown if it was ever performed. Rodion Yakovlevich sent it to Moscow for a competition. There the subject of the La Courtine uprising met with fervent approval, although the play itself was seen as weak. Somebody had the idea of turning it over to some literary type for a rewrite. On 12 August 1921 an unknown reviewer wrote the responsible party functionary Aleksei Ivanovich Angarov-Zykov, who later came to serve as the chief of the VKP(b)[33] Central Committee's section for cultural-enlightenment work and who was executed on 26 November 1937: "It's difficult to say who could rework this. Perhaps someone in the Pedagogical Academy could take this on?" However, in all likelihood, no literary rewriter could be found and the play was not performed.

However, let's return to France. Malinovskii faced a difficult journey home. On 31 July 1918 Clemenceau recommended to the minister of foreign affairs that Russian officers be used among the troops slated for intervention in Russia. He believed that one should propose such service, first of all, to the officers serving in the Russian expeditionary forces in France. The premier called upon these officers, as well as NCOs, to serve in Siberia. This, as the French command believed, would prevent the Central Powers from mobilizing the German and Austro-Hungarian prisoners who were still there. However, the project came to nothing due to the insufficient number of volunteers.

At the same time, the French government was paying those being repatriated to Kolchak an advance salary and half of a bonus if they would join the legion and go off to serve. According to Jamie Cockfield's evaluation, after the French quit paying a salary to officers in September 1919, by the end of November only 1,200 Russian officers from the expeditionary corps and former prisoners of war remained in France. However, in December about 25,000 Russians were still subordinate to the base command in Laval, including more than 20,000 in France and 4,000 in Algeria. Rodion Malinovskii was no longer among them.

His fellow soldier and friend, the military doctor D.A. Vvedenskii, helped him get to Russia.

Dmitrii Alekseevich Vvedenskii's (his name is written as Vedenskii in the Russian Legion's documents, while in the USSR he and his descendants wrote the name as Vvedenskii) daughter recalled her father:

He was very much a hale-fellow-well-met, loved to carouse and was handsome, while at the same time he was very interested in social questions and was an SR. He told us how students, including himself, traveled to L.N. Tolstoi's funeral and carried his coffin. He was proud that he showed up in the newsreel and went to watch it ten times (that was a rarity then!)…

I only remember one anecdote about the war. D.A. arrived in Moscow from the front (when, I don't know) and dropped into a tavern and naturally ordered some vodka. They can't give him any due to prohibition. "Well, then give me some cold tea, and no sugar." (He only drank that sort of tea all his life). They gave him a pair of cups—a big one with water, and a small one with brewing tea. He poured it and the big one contained vodka and the little one had cognac…

---

32   Editor's note. This was the Russian name for the machine gun invented by Hiram Maxim toward the end of the 19th century. The machine gun could fire up to 500 7.7mm rounds per minute. The Russian army purchased a large number of these machine guns and they were widely employed during the Russo-Japanese War, the Firsst World War, the Russian Civil War, and beyond.

33   Editor's note. This was the acronym for the All-Union Communist Party (Bolsheviks) (*Vsesoyuznaya Kommunisticheskaya Partiya, Bol'shevikov*). In 1952 the name was changed to the Communist Party of the Soviet Union (CPSU).

In 1916 Russian troops—the expeditionary corps—were sent to France (and to Macedonia).[34] Officers with a knowledge of French were offered the opportunity of joining this corps. D.A. joined up and was commandeered to the 5th Special Infantry Regiment and sent to France from Archangel to Brest. From July 1917 he was the regiment's senior doctor.

During his service in France (from 23 April 1916) he received four French military crosses—one with a bronze star, two with a golden star, and one with a palm leaf, and he also received a Saint George's Cross (in 1919), evidently while he was serving as a private soldier…

He was promoted to the rank of corporal for distinguished combat service at Villers Bretonneux.

D.A. served as a machine gunner. Judging from the number of attacks in which the Russian Legion took part, they put them into the hottest sectors. The following places are noted in his service record:

Villers Bretonneux (28 April 1918), Soissons (28 May 1918), Terny-Sorny (the Hindenburg Line, 2-14 September 1918), Chateau de la Motte (14-17 September), defending the Chalepenu sector (10-30 October 1918), moving from the village of Solsur to the village of Merville (November), and entered Germany on 19 November 1918. It was while serving in the Legion that D.A. received four French crosses. It was there he was decorated with the Order of the Legion of Honor. Such an award is very unusual for a soldier and there were probably few Russian officers with such an order…

He used to tell in a semi-sarcastic way that the commander recommended him for this high award, specially emphasizing in his order that soldier D.V. had set up his machine gun and beaten off an attack in his, the commander's, presence on the front line. And D.A. would note that he was in no way shooting where he should have been (however, this could relate to another episode, as he didn't make a hero out of himself)…

In February 1919 D.A. had the title of doctor and the rank of collegiate assessor restored to him and became the Legion's senior doctor. In August "he left for Marseilles in order to go to Russia," by ship, which was traveling to Vladivostok. He was eager to get to Russia and wanted to take part in building a new country (he was an SR…).

In a letter to his sister Aleksandra (in 1920-21, this letter is also in the Gor'kii[35] Museum), D.A. wrote that he didn't get along with the officers on the ship (they had very diverse political views) and that someone had written a denunciation of him. He told me (or in my presence) that he was friendly with the Czechs[36] in Vladivostok and that the Czechs "were always raising hell." A friend from the staff (papa was very sociable and had a lot of friends in his youth) said: "Mit'ka, get out of here." "And I," papa said, "had to carouse in a group together with Dumbadze, the chief of Kolchak's counterintelligence, and I heard his stories about how he used to shoot commissars, aiming at their anus" (this is probably Georgii Samsonovich Dumbadze, a captain in General Rozanov's staff and holder of the St. George's Cross, 4th

---

34   Editor's note. These were Russian troops sent to the Salonika front in Greece during the First World War.

35   Editor's note. This refers to Aleksei Maksimovich Gor'kii (Peshkov) (1868-1936), a Russian and Soviet writer who stressed social themes in his work. He was an early supporter of the Bolsheviks, but later broke with them, preferring to live abroad. Gor'kii returned to the USSR in 1932, but died four years later under mysterious circumstances.

36   Editor's note. This probably refers to the Czechoslovak Legion, which grew out of captured Austro-Hungarian troops of Czech and Slovak nationality who were captured on the Eastern Front. Following the Treaty of Brest-Litovsk, the Czechoslovak Legion sought to incline the Western Allies toward recognizing an independent Czechoslovak state by leaving Russia through Siberia and fighting on the Western Front. Evacuation arrangements with the Bolsheviks soon broke down and the Legion, numbering some 50,000 men, was inexorably drawn into the Russian Civil War on the White side. The final units of the Legion left Vladivostok only in 1920.

Class, who led operations against red partisans in Yenisei and Irkutsk provinces and who left his memoirs *That Which Facilitated Our Defeat in Siberia in the Civil War*. Insofar as G.S. Dumbadze took part in the Siberian Ice March,[37] there's no way he could have been in Vladivostok in October 1919. It's quite possible that D.A. Vvedenskii met with him later, when he was moving west. Nor is it excluded that in this case we are speaking of Georgii Samsonovich's uncle, Major General Iosif Antonovich Dumbadze, who was the commander of the 1st Vladivostok Fortress Artillery Brigade. G.S. Dumbadze died on 24 January 1989 in Los Angeles at the age of 92, B.S.). "How did you get away?" I asked. "I got on the train and left." He arrived in Tomsk, his home town, where his sister Vera lived and to where they sent some of the younger children. Since papa was an officer (or simply a doctor?), they sent him to the military hospital. In the previously mentioned letter it was mentioned that the hospital was infected (typhus was rampant) and D.A. expanded it to 900 cots, and that D.A. had trouble getting things arranged, as he did not understand how hospitals work. In December 1919 the Reds took Tomsk and the hospital (as I understood from his stories) became a Red Army hospital and papa a Red Army commander. D.A. wrote his sister that he did not agree either with the dictator Kolchak or the communist dictatorship, but that he supported the Soviet government and thus he should work, not get involved in social questions, ans stick to his medicine (there's a lot of civil enthusiasm in the letter). They sent a commissar, a sailor, to the hospital. A form was unearthed where D.A. had written that he was an SR. "You're a fool, Mit'ka." said the commissar, "You shouldn't have written that."

D.A. came down with typhus and severe complications and was sick for a long time, after which he was sent to another hospital, to the therapeutic section, which did not interest him professionally. He wanted to be involved in urology, prepare his dissertation and work in a university, and asked that they send him equipment from his father's office…

One should note that D.A. Vvedenskii was a member of the detachment committee in France and was in favor of continuing the war against the Germans. He had to hide this fact from the Kolchak people, who didn't take kindly to committee members, as well as the Reds.

Subsequently D.A. Vvedenskii, following his demobilization from the Red Army in March 1924 in Tashkent (he began serving on 24 December 1919), worked as a urologist, defended his doctoral dissertation, and in 1934-54 headed the Tashkent Medical Institute's urological clinic. From 9 January 1943 through 27 August 1945 he was again a volunteer in the Red Army as a military doctor-surgeon, became a lieutenant colonel and the chief of a medical reinforcement group on the First Ukrainian Front, and received the Order of the Red Banner. He died in Tashkent on 11 September 1956, at the age of 69. One should note that Dmitrii Alekseevich's sister, Nadezhda Alekseevna Peshkova (1901-71), whose nickname was "Timosha," was the wife of Maksim Gor'kii's son, Maksim Peshkov, and the mistress of the head of the NKVD, Genrikh Grigor'evich Yagoda.[38]

In his novel, Malinovskii portrayed Doctor Vvedenskii under the name of Vladimir Dmitrievskii. Ivan Grin'ko's own appearance in the Legion is described in the following manner:

The commander of the 1st Machine Gun Company, Captain Machek, a sunburnt blonde with a large mustache and kind and bright eyes (he was of Czech origin and served the Austrian emperor faithfully and now, having landed in the Moroccan Division, was serving France, but

---

37   Editor's note. This refers to the 2,000-kilometer retreat of Kolchak's army during the winter of 1919-20.
38   Editor's note. Genrikh Grigor'evich Yagoda (1891-1938) joined the Russian revolutionary movement as a young man and quickly rose through the ranks of the secret police following the Bolshevik coup. He was appointed chief of the NKVD in 1934, but was dismissed in 1936 and arrested the following year. Yagoda was convicted in the third of the great Moscow show trials and executed.

was utterly convinced that he was fighting for the liberation of his native Bohemia) amicably greeted the group of newly arrived volunteers and did not conceal his delight with the fact that they all turned out to be Russians. He loved Russians and considered them his brothers. Captain Machek spoke Russian passably and shook everyone's hand:

"'Greetings, friends!'"

This surprised the Russian volunteers no end.

Having examined the accompanying documents, the captain sent the entire group to the second platoon.

"There are already some Russians there," he informed us, "and the platoon is commanded by Senior Sergeant Timofei Vyatkin."

Capt. Machek twirled the document handed to him by Vanyusha for a particularly long time. He was considering something and finally said:

"And you, Private First Class Ivan Grin'ko, will have to take over the company's combat section. By the way, there's no permanent chief there. You'll have charge of 12 two-wheeled machine guns, 12 carriages for machine gun rounds, 27 horses and mules, and 14 soldiers—12 drivers, one horse attendant who's got his eye on my riding horse, and one driver for delivering forage…"

Training exercises went their usual way. The companies and teams went well out into the field and carried out firing. Exercises with live rounds took place. The 1st Machine Gun Company's scores were good and the regimental commander even thanked it. Captain Machek was very pleased with this and, while congratulating the machine gunners on their success, firmly shook the NCOs' hands. Vanyusha was also awarded this honor. He was not an NCO, and was only performing the duties of the machine gun company's chief of the combat park.

"Thank you, Corporal Grin'ko!"

These words meant that Vanyusha was no longer a private first class, but had been promoted to corporal Now he would have two red cloth stripes on his sleeve, instead of one.

Here Malinovskii awarded his autobiographical hero with a rank he didn't have himself. There is no document regarding the awarding of Rodion Malinovskii French crosses during the period of his service in the Legion where he is called corporal—only Private First Class.

Following the fighting at the end of April and beginning of May, Grin'ko received a promotion:

Captain Machek formed up the 1st Machine Gun Company and carried out an inspection. Following reinforcements, there were 12-14 men in each platoon. The captain halted in front of the second platoon and became thoughtful. The duties of the platoon commander were being temporarily performed by Sergeant Marlen, who was not distinguished by great bravery, and the captain did not want his subordinates conducting themselves in the fighting like their commander. Machek decided to strengthen the platoon with someone.

"Corporal Grin'ko," Machek called Vanyusha.

Vanyusha ran up from the company's left flank and stood at attention in front of the captain.

"You, friend Grin'ko, will have to join the line: I'm appointing you, Corporal Grin'ko, chief of the fourth machine gun, and I think we can transfer the command of the combat section to Kondratov. Do you think this is correct, friend Grin'ko?" Capt. Machek looked questioningly at Vanyusha.

"Correct, my captain," answered Vanyusha.

During the subsequent fighting, "Vanyusha dashingly observes through his binoculars the results of his machine gun's fire and sees how the mowed-down lines of Germans fall dead in the grain fields and rise no more. From time to time Vanyusha commands: 'A little bit lower!' or 'forward'."

It seems that Vanyusha Grin'ko remained only a machine gun commander until the end of the fighting, as Malinovskii wrote in all his forms, while at the same time he carried a revolver, which was likely authorized for platoon commanders. And while breaking through the Hindenburg Line, Vanyusha actually commanded all three machine guns in the second platoon, as was the case with Malinovskii, although nowhere is it mentioned that Grin'ko was appointed commander of a machine gun platoon. But even when Grin'ko is firing only from his own machine gun in April, May or June, the commander of his second platoon is nowhere mentioned.

And this is how Vladimir Dmitrievskii first appears on the novel's pages:

The machine gun barrel is already red and it's time to change it. While Vanyusha and Viktor Dmitrievskii, the machine gun's second crewman, were changing the barrel, the Germans approached. They are already clearly visible at 200 meters, no more… A long burst cuts down the enemy almost at point blank range…

Vanyusha began to rouse Viktor Dmitrievskii before dawn. There's no way the latter wanted to get up. When Viktor finally opened his eyes, Vanyusha commanded:

"Get up! Forward march."

"Where? What for," asked Dmitrievskii, not understanding.

"In order to shake the sleepy foolishness out of you."

He had to submit. When Vanyusha was convinced that Viktor had finally woken up, he turned over the guard of the machine gun to him and fell into a peaceful sleep, putting a box with shells under his head…

Unexpectedly the sunny blue sky is filled with the roar of motors. These are enemy planes. They hang over their heads and drop small bombs on the machine gunners and then rain lead on them from their machine guns. The machine gunners took cover in the wheat. But they can easily be made out from the planes and once again hand grenades rain down on them; now at strafing height. All kinds of planes were there! There were Turkish planes, with their half-moon insignias, Austrian, with their colorful squares and two-headed eagles, and German, with their sinister Maltese crosses. "The ravens have gathered from all over and there all coming at us," Vanyusha thought, quickly running toward the grove with the machine gun barrel. Viktor Dmitrievskii was running beside him and with the tripod over his soldier he looked like a stag beetle.

The machine gunners finally gathered in a copse. The sweat is rolling off everyone and all are exhausted. The battle rages around them: this means that the machine gun company and a handful of riflemen from the first battalion are surrounded. Everybody understands this. They also understand that they will not be able to break out of this ring. Captain Machek assigns firing sectors between the platoons, issuing short commands:

"First platoon to the east… second platoon to the north… third platoon to the west… fourth platoon to the south… Set up your machine guns and be ready to open fire!"

The sun turned crimson. Soon it will set beyond the horizon. "Maybe night will save us," Vanyusha thought and shares his thoughts with Viktor. His face is very pale and his black mustache and short beard stand out more clearly than usual.

"What? What's that?" he asks, not understanding. "Maybe I'm just as pale," Vanyusha thought. "If that's the case, then it's not from a surfeit of courage." And it was true; this time Grin'ko certainly did not feel the onset of moral strength. Then suddenly everybody heard Captain Machek's calm voice:

"Friends, who has a needle and thread?"

"What does he need a needle for? What's he planning to do, stick the Germans?"

"Here you go, *mon* captain," and one of the soldiers handed him a needle and thread.

And Captain Machek, without paying attention to the chatter of the rifles and machine guns around the small grove and at the whining and hissing of the bullets, having found the undone seam on the finger of his lacquered glove, began to slowly sew it up. Not a single muscle twitched on his dust-covered face, along which streams of sweat flowed. The captain's hands firmly held the needle and confidently pierced the leather of the glove. The captain's calm unintentionally spread to the machine gunners around him. Mighty "Zhizhka" wanted to offer his services, but the captain replied:

"Friend, you didn't even have a needle, so how are you going to sew a glove; I'll do it myself…"

The second machine gun platoon quickly moves behind the legionnaire infantry, but gets lost. Vanyusha takes turns carrying the barrel with another crewman and Viktor Dmitrievskii. The barrel, damn it, seems to weigh several tons and the rib-like upper part of the barrel cuts into his shoulder. The sweat runs down his face and gets into his eyes. But he can't slow down and as quickly as possible must get out of the flat area that is being enfiladed from the right flank by machine gun fire.

The story of Dmitrievskii (Vvedenskii) receiving the order of the Legion of Merit is described in the novel:

Before the division was pulled back into the rear, Captain Machek called together the first machine gun company in order to sum up the results of the recent fighting and to evaluate each platoon. The second platoon received the most praise and the captain emphasize that the main credit in this goes to Corporal Ivan Grin'ko. He managed to pull the platoon out from under artillery fire before the attack and then headed the platoon, replacing the wounded platoon NCO, Timofei Vyatkin. He coped with this task very well and showed bravery and valor, as one might expect from a holder of the Saint George's cross.

The captain was sparing in his praise and carefully chose his words that could express the essence of Vanyusha's courage, and then said slowly and authoritatively:

"Corporal Ivan Grin'ko showed heroism. Yes, real heroism."

Vanyusha didn't know where to hide his eyes from embarrassment. And the captain continued:

"Ivan Grin'ko s now a sergeant, so you can congratulate him."

Captain Machek went up to Vanyusha and firmly shook his hand:

"I sincerely congratulate you, friend!"

But that was not all. The captain informed us that the division command suggested that the company recommend one man for the order of the Legion of Merit, four for military medals, and to award an unlimited number of military crosses.

Captain Machek said "I propose to award a medal to each platoon and I leave the right to decide to nominate a soldier for the Legion of Merit; that is, the highest award, to the second platoon."

Everyone was very pleased with the fact that the second platoon had been singled out for its services. It gathered to decide the question of the candidate to receive the order of the Legion of Merit. Everyone immediately spoke out that the only candidate is Grin'ko.

"He's the most worthy!"

"He not only led us into the battle, but the Madagascans as well."

Vanyusha was the last to speak. He very much wanted to receive the order, but his innate humility didn't even allow him to think about this, so he said:

"Friends, you've really overrated me and I didn't do anything outstanding. I fought, just like all of you did. Our success belongs to the entire platoon. I request that you…" and Vanyusha became pensive, trying to restrain his great inner excitement. "There's a man among us who has struggled for the soldiers' interests and struggled in such a way that he brought upon himself the disapproval of the commanders and, as a result, was demoted to private and was deprived of his officer's rank. This is Viktor Dmitrievskii. For this he deserves, from us soldiers, this high decoration. Besides, in the recent fighting Viktor demonstrated great bravery and valor and behaved heroically during the breakthrough of the Hindenburg Line…"

Vanyusha, imitating Captain Machek, halted and looked attentively into Viktor's eyes. The latter grew embarrassed and objected:

"That's not true, I didn't display any heroism, and this is too much…"

"I repeat," Vanyusha said more firmly, "that Viktor Dmitrievskii unconditionally deserves to be awarded with the Order of the Legion of Merit. And I ask you, dear comrades, to take what I said into account. I haven't done half as much as Viktor has."

Vanyusha pronounced these final words with such obvious sincerity and conviction that the platoon's machine gunners believed them. Only Akhmed-Bela refused to agree for a long time, believing that it would be quite just to recommend Ivan Grin'ko for the Order of the Legion of Merit and Viktor Dmitrievskii for the Military Medal. The platoon never the less decided to recommend that Viktor Dmitrievskii be decorated with the Order of the Legion of Merit and Sergeant Ivan Grin'ko for the Military Medal; the rest, some for the second time and some for the first, would receive the Military Cross.

Captain Machek was amazed at this decision, because he had been sure that Vanyusha would surely receive the Order of the Legion of Merit. However, he knew how to respect the collective's opinion and filled out the recommendation the way the soldiers had decided…

The long-awaited order awarded Viktor Dmitrievskii the Order of the Legion of Merit and disrupted the Russian soldiers' boring existence in Pleurs. But they had expected this and were not surprised by the order. Something else was more interesting: Dmitrievskii was promoted to lieutenant colonel in the medical service. Now that was news!

The commanders got to work on time and prepared an officer's uniform for Dmitrievskii. He was to be appointed the battalion's senior doctor. The machine gun company's second platoon was ecstatic: now they would have their man in the battalion's medical unit.

About ten NCOs and soldiers, including Grin'ko, received military medals.

Of course, Vvedenskii was not an officer, but a military bureaucrat, and no one had demoted him, but rather he had joined the Legion as a volunteer, in order to fight at the front lines, and not to remain in the rear. And he had spoken in favor of continuing the war in the detachment committee, which is why he joined the Legion. And they did not restore him to the rank of lieutenant colonel in the medical service, for which there was no rank in the tsarist army, but in the rank of a collegiate assessor, which corresponded to the rank of army major, which had been abolished in 1884 and which since had been between the ranks of captain and lieutenant colonel.

The recommendation that Vvedenskii be awarded practically coincided with Malinovskii's.

Private First Class Dmitrii Vvedenskii of the Russian Legion, a soldier of extreme bravery and resilience in battle, combines within himself rare composure and very fortunate initiative. As a doctor in the Russian army, he was one of the first to sign up as a volunteer with the Russian Legion and took part in all its battles. On 14 September 1918 he was the first to go into the attack, showing contempt for danger and serving as an example to his comrades. He facilitated the successful repulse of the enemy's counterattack and, on his own initiative, set up his machine gun and, despite intensive enemy artillery fire, inflicted a complete defeat on the enemy with his flanking fire on the attacker. He received five decorations as a military doctor in the Russian army and was awarded the Military Cross with palms in the French army.

Actually, Malinovskii, to judge from the Legion's surviving documents, was never promoted to sergeant. However, in the recommendation for his second Saint George's Cross, he is not named as a soldier who had replaced the wounded platoon commander, but the full-fledged platoon commander.

In the novel Dmitrievskii at first works for Grin'ko, as machine gun commander, as a loader and, to judge from the award recommendations, in the September fighting Vvedenskii really was a machine gun commander and Malinovskii the commander of a machine gun platoon. At the same time, in the final battles Grin'ko is actually carrying out the duties of the commander of a machine gun platoon.

It is notable that the Captain Machek of the novel (actually Staff Captain Prachek) treats Grin'ko favorably and is always advancing his career. At the same time, in Vasil'ev's article, Staff Captain Prachek is mentioned as a Russian officer. It's highly unlikely that they would send a captured former officer in the Austrian army to France as a member of the Russian Expeditionary Corps. Staff Captain Prachek was without a doubt a Czech, but at the same time a Russian subject, born and raised in the Russian Empire.

In the "Memorial" data base there are five bearers of the last name "Prachek" among those who died and went missing in the Great Patriotic War, of which four were from the Novgorod-Severskii area of Chernigov Oblast', while the fifth was from the village of Novo-Pokrovka in the Ivanovskii area of Amur Oblast', where his family had probably arrived from Ukraine, as Novo-Pokrovka was founded by settlers from Poltava province. And thus Malinovskii and Prachek could have had common acquaintances in Chernigov province. So, perhaps Staff Captain Prachek favored Malinovskii as a compatriot?

Having made Prachek a former Austrian officer, it's possible that Malinovskii was hiding the Chernigov scent in his biography.

He also never mentioned being awarded a second Saint George's Cross in his service biography. It's not known whether he ever knew about this award. However, Vvedenskii, in speaking about his being awarded the Saint George's Cross for the same battle, allows himself to assume that Malinovskii managed to find out about his being awarded a second Saint George's Cross. On 4 September1919 Admiral Kolchak's representative in France, General D.G. Shcherbachev, issued an order awarding the soldiers of the Russian Legion. Among those awarded was Corporal Rodion Malinovskii. He was awarded the Saint George's Cross, Third Class, for "displaying personal bravery in the fighting on 14 September 1918, while breaking through the Hindenburg Line and, while commanding a machine gun platoon, inspired his men and broke through the space between the enemy's fortified machine gun nests and set up his machine gun there, which facilitated the decisive success in capturing the heavily fortified third trench line in the 'Hindenburg Line'." Malinovskii received yet another palm branch to his French Military Cross with swords. The fact that he's named as a corporal in the order does not in and of itself prove that he served at this rank in September 1919. As a rule, the award orders named the rank of the awardees which figured in the original recommendation. The recommendation was drawn up in the fall of 1918, when Malinovskii really was a corporal. If he had really been promoted to lieutenant, then this could have happened no earlier than the spring of 1919, after the Legion was disbanded.

By the way, promotion to an officer's rank enabled them to regulate the former legionnaires' material situation. The French government paid the officers being repatriated to Kolchak an advance on their pay and half of a bonus if they had served in the legion and were departing to serve in the army of the Omsk[39] or other anti-Bolshevik governments.

Malinovskii was awarded the Military Cross with a silver star for the breakthrough of the Hindenburg Line. In General Dogan's, the commander of the Moroccan Division, order of 15 September 1918, no. 181, which was reproduced in French and Russian at the Russian base in Laval, in order no. 163 of 12 October 1918, the following was said of Corporal Rodion Malinovskii, a machine gunner in the 2nd Regiment's 4th Machine Gun Company: "An excellent machine gunner. He particularly distinguished himself during the attack on 14 September, shooting down with his machine gun a group of enemy soldiers who were putting up stubborn resistance, while not paying any attention to the danger of the enemy's deadly artillery fire."

Earlier in 1917 Malinovskii had been awarded the Saint George's Cross. One should mention that according to the laws accepted in the French army, the soldiers and officers of the Russian Expeditionary Corps received award payments for Russian orders and medals, but only for those that had been bestowed upon them during their time in France. Rodion Malinovskii was also lucky enough to receive them although only for a short time, from the autumn of 1917, for the Saint George's Cross, 4th Class, which he had received during his time in the expeditionary corps.

In the novel it is related in detail how Dmitrievskii was presented the Order of the Legion of Merit:

> Lieutenant Colonel Dmitrievskii had settled into the battalion's medical unit and decided to celebrate, upon receiving his first officer's pay, his Order of the Legion of Merit, which already stood out on his chest on a red ribbon. And, of course, to "celebrate" his lieutenant colonel's epaulets in the proper fashion. The entire second platoon had been invited to this feast. A long table had been set in the garden, complete with wine and fried canned food, while a tasty salad had been prepared in large bowls. Everyone congratulated the battalion doctor and they drank a lot. The canned goods and salad were eaten in full. Tomatoes, radishes and cucumbers appeared immediately; the bowls were once again filled with salad, which had been well salted and peppered. The gourmets noted that only vinegar was missing.
>
> "Take a bottle of vinegar out of the nightstand and pour it on the salad," Dmitrievskii ordered the medic.
>
> The medic quickly poured out the contents of the bottle into the bowls with the salad and everyone threw themselves on the food, praising the spread. And this salad was eaten before long. Then they began to sing songs. The feast lasted until late in the evening.
>
> In the morning some of the participants of the feast appeared at the battalion medical unit in order to sober up.
>
> "Well, get a bottle of castor oil from the nightstand," ordered Lieutenant Colonel Dmitrievskii, addressing the medic.
>
> The medic fetched the bottle from the nightstand and gave it to Dmitrievskii. He looked at it, sniffed it and said:
>
> "Why did you give me vinegar; give me the other bottle."
>
> But there was no other bottle; it had gone into yesterday's salad instead of the vinegar.
>
> Viktor Dmitrievskii spat in anger and cursed:
>
> "Now, just you keep quiet!"

---

39   Editor's note. This refers to the All-Russian Provisional Government, based in the Siberian city of Omsk. Consisting of an unstable alliance of former SR and Cadet members of the disbanded Constituent Assembly, the government was overthrown in November 1918 and Admiral Kolchak proclaimed supreme ruler.

The medic grimaced; he had also eaten the salad yesterday. He grabbed his stomach and immediately threw up.

The departure for Russia with Dmitrievskii is described in the novel in the following way:

Once in the evening Vanyusha, Likanin and Viktor Dmitrievskii set out for a walk along a familiar path. They walked slowly. Viktor said:

"You know, I received assurances that I can organize a Red Cross detachment, and then the ARA (during 1919-23 the American Relief Administration distributed food and other relief to countries that suffered during the First World War, B.S.) will help us leave for Russia."

They argued for a long time and examined all the conditions in which they could get away to the Motherland.

"The ARA will send you where it wants, if we get mixed up with it, and they could send us to Denikin," said Vanyusha. "Then prove that you're not a camel."

Viktor insisted:

"I'm a doctor and a lieutenant colonel in the French army and have every right to head this detachment, and I guarantee that everything will turn out alright…"

Viktor Dmitrievskii went to Paris and got the French command's agreement and that of the ARA representatives to organize a medical detachment and send it to Russia. Vanyusha and Mikhail immediately signed up for this detachment. Aside from them, Stepan Kondratov, Petr Yermachenko, Protopopov, Semin, and Kruglov signed up.., in all, 22 people….

Viktor Dmitrievskii's efforts were crowned with success after only two weeks. Early in the morning in the middle of August, the medical detachment loaded onto the steamship.

The steamship *Loire* was a freight-passenger ship. The holds were filled with all kinds of freight… Viktor got permission from the ship's captain to quarter his medical detachment in the twin deck in the bow, with the right to walk on all the ship's decks. They settled them-selves more or less satisfactorily. The twin deck was closed with boards and covered with a tarpaulin, which protected it from the heat and rain.

In Shanghai the *Ryazan'*, a mail-passenger ship of the Russian volunteer merchant marine, hosted the Russians aboard. The ship had a small displacement—only about 5,000 tons. It was leaving Shanghai in the morning for Vladivostok.

The biggest surprise for Vanyusha was his meeting aboard ship with Serafim Aref'ev, a former weapons worker from the 256th Yelizavetgrad Regiment's machine gun team. They recognized each other at first sight and warmly embraced. Aref'ev was now a repairman on the *Ryazan'*. He spoke a lot about Russia, mainly about what was going on in Vladivostok. He then brought a flat can of alcohol, which had been soldered shut, and he and Vanyusha celebrated their meeting. They were joined by Misha Lilanin, Stepan Kondratov and Petr Yermachenko, who never turned down a chance to have a drink.

Malinovskii doesn't' mention anything in his novel about how that how they first planned, with the assistance of the ARA, to leave for Odessa and only found out on the steamship that they were being taken to Vladivostok, as he maintained in his service biography in 1938. Most likely, the Red Cross detachment was heading to Vladivostok and Kolchak from the very beginning and Malinovskii knew this. This meant that at the time he was still planning to serve in the Omsk government's forces. However, following his arrival in Vladivostok and particularly on the road to the front, Malinovskii probably became convinced that Kolchak's army was beaten and was falling apart. At this moment the intention of going over to the Reds had evidently matured in his mind. One may assume that Rodion Yakovlevich served as an officer with the Whites, just as the hero of the play *Feats of a Life*.

This is what Rodion Yakovlevich wrote in his service biography in 1938 regarding his participation in the civil war following his arrival in Vladivostok:

> They immediately wanted to put us in the White army and we began to approach everyone possible to let us go home, which we managed to do in the prisoners'a and refugees' committee, which the ARA had control over and, having received permission to leave for a furlough, we set out for Omsk, through Irkutsk: they started to delay us at the station and we took to our heels, each his own way—all of us were from the central provinces or Ukraine. We somehow made it to Omsk (the railroad workers in the railway guards teams on the freight trains were almost to a man against the Kolchak people and readily assisted us). It was hard to get beyond Omsk—only military trains were moving and they were breaking up the ice on the Irtysh River and, after a few days, when Petropavlovsk had already been take by the Red Army, I made my way across the Irtysh by way of an icebreaker's passage and went through the snow along the open fields, keeping the railroad's telegraph poles in sight, as one could not move along the roads because of the endless columns of Kolchak's retreating forces, passing by day and night, and by the evening of the next day I was completely worn out and reached the road, which was now empty of Kolchak's columns. Having gone a little ways, I ran into a reconnaissance team from the 27th Division's 240th Tver' Rifle Regiment, was stopped and searched and the scouts found in my pocket my French military cross (I had been awarded with the French Croix de Guerre three times during the 1918 fighting) with swords, which was the whole thing; the scouts decided that I wasn't a soldier, but an officer, because they never awarded soldiers crosses with swords, and decided to simply shoot me; after all, there were some bushes not far from the road, and I heard cries to take him into the bushes and finish him off. I got very offended and angry and I began to curse as I had never cursed before, and then one of the scouts chimed in that they should take me to headquarters, and they answered him that if you want to bother yourself with him, go ahead, and so the scout delivered me to a nearby village, where the battalion's headquarters was quartered for the night. The battalion commander heard me out and called the doctor so that the latter, being an educated man, could check my French documents; the doctor checked them and confirmed that they were indeed French—that is, my soldier's booklet and ration card, which had been issued in Marseilles while boarding the steamship, and I still have them. The following morning the headquarters of the 240th Rifle Regiment arrived at the village and in the headquarters I met another three comrades out of the group of 20 men with whom I had arrived with from France—these were comrades Vasilii Yermachenko, Sergei Trofimov and Ivan Tsyb. Someone from the deputy division commander of the 27th Division talked with us, clarifying the conditions of our stay in France and suggested that if we want to go home we can, but all four of us expressed a wish to serve in the ranks of the RKKA,[40] after which he sent us with a note to the commandant of the division staff, and the latter sent us with an accompanying document to serve in the 240th Tver' Rifle Regiment. This is how we joined the regimental machine gun crew and in the evening left for Omsk with the crew, which was 10 or 11 November 1919. By evening of the second day we entered Omsk following a brief exchange of fire and then continued the pursuit; there were small skirmishes near Kansk and Novo-Nikolaevsk and heavy fighting near Taiga station, against the Poles and troops from Votkinsk. Following the occupation of Mariinsk, our division rested and the 30th Division pursued Kolchak's forces further. Our machine gun crew was quartered in the village of Sobakino (it was also called

---

40   Editor's note. The RKKA (*Raboche-Krest'yanskaya Krasnaya Armiya*), or Worker's and Peasant's Red Army was the official name of the Soviet army from 1918 until after the Second World War.

Dmitrievskoe), not far, about 30 kilometers from Mariinsk, where we received reinforcements and began to train. I came down with a severe case of typhus in the beginning of February and they took me to the hospital in Mariinsk, where they were keeping all the typhus cases, including myself, who being sick with typhus for the second time, was extremely ill, and from Mariinsk they moved us to Tomsk to a better equipped hospital and where there were even sheets and blankets (in the square next to the Mariinsk clinic there stands an obelisk, where the victims of the civil war are buried, including the head doctor of the Mariinsk district, V.A. Paramonov, who became infected with typhus while treating the sick. Before this he had taken part in the 27th Division's combat activities. It is not excluded that he was the very doctor who saved Malinovskii's life, B.S.). I was discharged from the hospital in April, but was so weak that I could barely walk and went to the town commandant in order to be sent to my unit. The thaw had begun and streams of water flowed along the street, and I (as did everyone who had crowded into the commandant's office) had only felt boots and we all demanded at least down-at-the-heels shoes, but the commandant didn't have any, although he promised that boots would soon arrive, which is how we waited 20 days, until the commander declared that it was forbidden to sent typhus patients back to their units and in May they had already sent me to Kansk-Yeniseiskii to the 137the Independent Battalion for protecting the Siberian railroad. Upon arriving in Kansk-Yeniseiskii, I found out that the 27th Division had left for the Polish front[41] (for which it had departed during my illness) from the Minusinsk area. I was unable to catch up to my division, so I remained with the 137th Battalion and was dispatched to the young commander's training school with the 35th Independent Rifle Brigade for protecting the Siberian railroad, which I completed in August 1920 and was appointed machine gun chief in the second company of the 137th Battalion. On 3 December 1920 the 137th Independent Battalion was merged with another battalion to form the 246th Rifle Regiment and I was appointed commander of a machine gun platoon in the 2nd Company, and on 1 February 1921 the commander of a machine gun crew. On 28 February the regiment was renamed the 3rd Siberian Rifle Regiment and sent to the Trans-Baikal to guard the tunnels along the Trans-Baikal railroad and to guard the Mongolian border. In December 1921, after Ungern's[42] bands had been eliminated in Mongolia and after a battle in the Mysovaya station area, the 3rd Regiment was disbanded and I was appointed to the 35th Rifle Division's 309th Regiment, first as an assistant commander of a machine gun crew, and on 17 December 1921 commander of a machine gun crew.

Malinovskii was much more laconic in his 1948 service biography:

I managed to make it from Vladivostok as far as Omsk with difficulty and there, having crossed the front, I voluntarily joined the 240th Tver' Regiment of the Red Army's 27th Division on November 10 1919 and took part with the regiment in the capture of Omsk a few days later, and then as far as Mariinsk, where our division remained in reserve while the 30th Division moved on.

I came down with typhus and during this time the division left for the Polish front, and after recovering I joined the 35th Brigade's 137th Rifle Battalion and completed the brigade school for young commanders and in the fall of 1920 I was appointed a platoon commander

---

41   Editor's note. This is a reference to the Soviet-Polish War of 1920.
42   Editor's note. Baron Roman Nikolai Maximilian von Ungern-Sternberg (1885-1921) was born in Austria-Hungary, although his family later moved to Russia. He fought in the Russo-Japanese War and the First World War. He fought the Reds during the civil war, with the support of the Japanese. He raided Soviet territory from Mongolia, but was captured. Ungern-Sternberg was executed following a brief trial.

in the 137th Battalion's 2nd Company, and in January 1921 the commander of the 246th Regiment's (the 137th and 138th battalions were merged to form a regiment) and the regiment was renamed the 3rd Siberian Rifle Regiment.

In his 1938 service biography, Malinovskii declared: "I did not serve in the White army and I completed my service in the old army and French army as a corporal. I have not been tried or investigated. I have no relatives overseas. I know French and Spanish and can speak on my own, and write and read with the aid of a dictionary."

The question arises as to how Malinovskii made it from Vladivostok to Omsk through the rear of Kolchak's army, while being in a military uniform and obviously of draft age, but without a single document in Russian. The assumption is that he never the less had documents in Russian, only not those which one would want to show a mounted patrol of Reds, which was already prepared to send Rodion Yakovlevich to a better world without further ado.

From all appearances, Malinovskii was not quite precise as to the circumstances of his capture by the Reds. It was probably a mounted patrol and they were preparing not to shoot Rodion Yakovlevich, but to hack him to death (cartridges in Siberia at the time were worth their weight in gold).

And this is what, judging by everything, happened immediately before Malinovskii's encounter with the Red mounted patrol. The writer Vsevolod Vyacheslavovich Ivanov,[43] the author of the classic Soviet work on the civil war, the novella *Armored Train 14-69* (and the play by the same name), lived in 1918-19 in Omsk. In his autobiography, which was published in the journal *Literary Notes* on 1 August 1922, he recalled:

> I took part in the revolution from 1917. After the Czechs took Omsk (I was in the Red Guards[44] then) and when they shot and hung all my fellow classmates, I ran away to the Hungry Steppe[45] and, following the death of my father (the Cossacks thought that I had killed him because my father loved the czar and wanted to try me), I moved further beyond Semipalatinsk toward Mongolia.
>
> They caught me from time to time, because I took part in communist plots. So I wandered all over Kolchak's territory from the Urals to Chita, and when they mobilized me I was commandeered as a typesetter to the supreme commander's mobile printing press. I had a false passport under the name "Yevgenii Tarasov."
>
> Two incidents occurred later.
>
> When the partisans surrounded our train, the train commander, Lieutenant Malinovskii, told me:
>
> "Give me your greatcoat and take my beaver fur coat. I'm going to make a break for it; there's an open road over there."
>
> I gave him the greatcoat. The lieutenant didn't get away and they hacked him to death within half a kilometer. The partisans approached (they were in white overalls, so you couldn't see them in the snow), killed some old general by the rail cars and a midshipman with a frostbitten ear, and about 30 volunteers, who had been betrayed by the railroad workers.

---

43 Editor's note. Vsevolod Vyacheslavovich Ivanov (1895-1963) began to write at an early age and continued to do so while serving in the Russian Civil War with the Red Army. His works often have an eastern flavor.

44 Editor's note. The Red Guards were a volunteer group of urban workers, sailors and soldiers, who served as the Bolshevik Party's paramilitary force and helped it to seize power in 1917. Red Guard units later served as the basis for the formation of the Red Army.

45 Editor's note. The Hungry Steppe (*Golodnaya Step'*) is a broad plain along the left bank of the Syr Darya River, in what is now Uzbekistan.

It's of interest that Vsevolod Ivanov's comrade, Nikolai Ivanovich Anov, also a writer and also with the last name of Ivanov (Anov was a pseudonym), who met with him in Omsk, testifies in his memoirs that when he had to fight against the Czechs in 1918, Vsevolod served with the Reds as a machine gunner. And of all the types of weapons in the train, his chief attention is devoted to the machine guns. The train in which Vsevelod Ivanov served was most likely an armored train (it is not excluded that this was the armored train *Sibiryak*, which supposedly vanished somewhere in the area of Omsk), and Malinovskii could have been the chief of the machine gun crew. And the midshipman, who is mentioned among those shot, could have been the chief of the train's artillery and at the same time commander of the armored train (naval officers usually served as artillery men on the Whites' trains, as naval guns were often mounted on them). Ivanov did not kill the general by the train in his novella, but right in the town. If the hypothesis regarding the writer's service on the armored train is true, then Malinovskii could have served as the prototype of one of the story's and play's personages—Lieutenant Obaba. It's interesting that French sky blue leg wrappings are constantly associated with this personage, which could have remained with Malinovskii following his service in the legion. Of course, it's not known whether Malinovskii managed to fight against the Reds as a member of the armored train's crew. It's quite possible that in Ivanov's novella we're dealing with an uprising against the Whites in Vladivostok. But there was such an uprising in Omsk right before the Red Army's arrival.

As regards the lieutenant's beaver fur coat, Ivanov, most likely, gave rein to poetic license. It's well known that the British supplied Kolchak's forces with officer's greatcoats made out of kangaroo fur. It's most likely that Malinovskii had such a greatcoat. It's quite possible that Vsevolod Ivanov served on an armored train under his own name. He could actually have joined the Reds, as is known, precisely in the Omsk area, and not much further east, as he maintained in his autobiography. And it's not known whether the writer knew Malinovskii by name. And it was unlikely that he remembered the name of the soldier who saved his life by turning over his greatcoat. It is not excluded that the author of *Armored Train 14-69* did not find out that the lieutenant buried by him actually remained alive. There is no evidence that the author and marshal met at any time after 1919. However, one may allow that Vsevolod Ivanov recognized Malinovskii during the Great Patriotic War, when his pictures started appearing in the newspapers. And if they were never the less fated to meet, one can imagine the following conversation between them following the first bottle of cognac, which they both really loved:

"So, Rodion, why didn't the Reds hack you to death back then?
"Well, Seva, it was like this…"

3

Between Wars

Malinovskii did not take part in the civil war for long at all and did not manage to perform any kind of outstanding feats and did not receive any awards. In this regard, Rodion Yakovlevich stands out in striking fashion from the other "marshals of victory" of his generation. G.K. Zhukov managed to fight as a squadron commander against Wrangel and the Antonovites[1] in the Tambov area, for which he was awarded the Order of the Red Banner. And as early as May 1923 he was commanding a cavalry regiment. As early as January 1920 K.K. Rokossovskii[2] was commanding a cavalry regiment and in 1921 he was awarded the Order of the Red Banner for fighting against Baron Ungern's Asian Division.

L.A. Govorov,[3] although he fought for Kolchak as a second lieutenant and, having gone over to the Reds in Tomsk at the end of 1919, already commanded an artillery battalion in the battles against Wrangel in the autumn of 1920, for which he received the Order of the Red Banner. And as early as October 1923 Leonid Aleksandrovich became the artillery commander for a rifle division.

One does not even need to mention S.K. Timoshenko,[4] the glorious hero of the civil war and, just like Malinovskii, a machine gunner in the czarist army. As early as November 1919 he was commanding a cavalry division in the 1st Cavalry Army and during the civil war received three orders of the Red Banner and an honorary revolutionary weapon. It makes sense that he was promoted to marshal as early as 1940, the first of the generation of the "marshals of victory." A.M. Vasilevskii[5] managed to serve to the rank of staff captain in the czarist army and commanded

---

1   Editor's note. The Antonov Rebellion (*Antonovshchina*) was a large-scale peasant uprising during 1920-21 centered in the Tambov region. The rebellion was led by Aleksandr Stepanovich Antonov (1888-1922), a former SR who mobilized peasants dissatisfied with the Bolsheviks' grain requisition policies. The rebellion was suppressed by M.N. Tukhachevskii, who employed poison gas and a policy of shooting hostages.

2   Editor's note. Konstantin Konstantinovich Rokossovskii (1896-1968) joined the imperial army in 1914 and the Red Army in 1918. He was arrested in 1937 and freed only in 1940. During the Great Patriotic War he commanded a corps, army and several *fronts*. Following the war, he commanded Soviet occupation forces in Poland and during 1949-56 was the country's defense minister, due to his Polish ancestry. Following his return to the Soviet Union, Rokossovskii served as a deputy defense minister and commanded a military district.

3   Editor's note. Leonid Aleksandrovich Govorov (1897-1955) was drafted into the imperial army in 1916 and Kolchak's army in 1919, finally joining the Red Army in 1920. During the Great Patriotic War he commanded an army and later a front. Following the war, Govorov commanded a military district and was commander-in-chief of the National Air Defense Forces.

4   Editor's note. Semyon Konstantinovich Timoshenko (1895-1970) was drafted into the imperial army in 1914 and joined the Red Army in 1918 and commanded a cavalry division in the civil war. He later served as the commander of several military districts, commanded Soviet troops in the war with Finland, and served briefly as defense commissar. During the Great Patriotic War he commanded *fronts* and groups of *fronts*. Following the war, Timoshenko commanded several military districts and served in the central military apparatus.

5   Editor's note. Aleksandr Mikhailovich Vasilevskii (1895-1977) joined the imperial army in 1915 and the Red Army in 1918. During the Great Patriotic War he served as deputy chief and then chief of the General

an infantry battalion during the First World War. During the civil war Aleksandr Mikhailovich served as a regimental commander, although subsequently due to his unfavorable social origins (he was the son of a priest) and his officer's rank, he was demoted to the position of deputy commander of a rifle regiment at the end of 1919 and to the commander of an independent battalion in August 1920. He didn't receive any awards during the civil war and he became the commander of a rifle regiment only in 1922.

I.S. Konev,[6] just like Timoshenko, joined the Bolshevik Party as early as 1918 and was the commissar of an armored train, a rifle brigade, rifle division, and staff in the Far Eastern Republic's[7] National-Revolutionary Army, but was not decorated for his service in the civil war.

F.I. Tolbukhin[8] was a staff captain during the First World War and the commander of an infantry battalion, and during the civil war was the junior assistant of the chief of staff of a rifle division for operational work and chief of staff of provincial troops and the chief of the operational directorate of the staff for the Karelian region, and as early as March 1922 was chief of staff of a rifle division. Fedor Ivanovich was awarded an Order of the Red Banner for the civil war.

During the civil war K.A. Meretskov[9] was the assistant division chief of staff and during these years was the first of the future marshals to complete the General Staff Military Academy, and then commanded a training brigade in 1921 and was chief of staff of a cavalry division. Kirill Afanas'evich was the only "marshal of victory" who did not have service experience in the czarist army during the First World War. Meretskov was decorated with the Order of the Red Banner for the civil war, but only in 1928.

Thus following the civil war, Malinovskii occupied the lowest position in the Red Army, compared to the other "marshals of victory." He had not accomplished any outstanding feats during the civil war (I think that in his heart of hearts Rodion Yakovlevich was even happy that he had not taken to active a part in the internecine strife, for which reason his high-ranking fellow officers later teased him: "While we were slicing up the Whites, someone was taking it easy in France with the mademoiselles"), and upon the conclusion of the civil war in 1922 he had the shortest amount of service in the Red Army in comparison to the other future marshals. However, neither did he have any obvious minuses, such as service in the White armies as an officer (Govorov) or having served as an officer in the czarist army (Tolbukhin and Vasilevskii).

Staff during 1942-45. He also commanded a *front* and was commander-in-chief of Soviet forces during the war with Japan. Following the war, he again served as chief of staff and was later minister of the armed forces (1949-53). Vasilevskii was later relegated to secondary positions in the central military apparatus.

6   Editor's note. Ivan Stepanovich Konev (1897-1973) was drafted into the imperial army in 1916 and joined the Red Army in 1918. During the Great Patriotic War he commanded an army and several *fronts*. Following the war he commanded Soviet troops in Germany and Austria, and also commanded the ground forces and a military district. He later served as first deputy minister of defense and commander-in-chief of the Warsaw Pact forces. Konev briefly commanded Soviet forces in Germany in 1961-62.

7   Editor's note. The Far Eastern Republic (*Dal'nevostochnaya Respublika*) existed as a nominally independent state from 1920-22. It was actually subordinated to the central government in Moscow and was intended to serve as a buffer zone between Red forces in the Far East and Japanese-occupied Russian territory. With the collapse of the anti-Bolshevik position in the Far East at the end of 1922, the Republic was abolished.

8   Editor's note. Fedor Ivanovich Tolbukhin (1894-1949) joined the imperial army in 1914 and the Red Army in 1918. During the Great Patriotic War he served as a front chief of staff, and army commander and a *front* commander. Following the war, Tolbukhin served as commander-in-chief of the Southern Group of Forces and commanded a military district.

9   Editor's note. Kirill Afanas'evich Meretskov (1897-1968) joined the Red Army in 1920. He served as a military adviser during the Spanish Civil War and commanded Soviet troops against the Finns in 1939-40. He was arrested shortly after the start of the Great Patriotic War, but survived and returned to command an army and *fronts*. Following the war, Meretskov commanded military districts and was a deputy minister of defense.

If Malinovskii was even actually promoted an officer and served for a short period with Kolchak, without taking part in the fighting, he managed to hide these facts from the cadre organs and secret service. On the other hand, his mother's peasant origins spoke in his favor. Once again, nobody knew about his father, the chief of police.

Malinovskii was also aided by the fact that at the moment he joined the Red Army he had acquired quite a decent level of education. While he certainly was inferior in this regard to Tolbukhin, Vasilevskii, Govorov, and Meretskov, the latter of whom had already managed to complete the military academy as early as 1921, Malinovskii was on the same level as Rokossovskiii and was ahead of Timoshenko, Zhukov and Konev.

One of Malinovskii's few advantages was his relative youth. Tolbukhin and Rokossovskii were born in 1894 (Rokossovskii made himself younger by two years during his service in the Red Army and began to write in forms that he was born in 1896), Vasilevskii and Timoshenko in 1895, Zhukov in 1896, Govorov, Meretskov and Konev in 1897, and Malinovskii in 1898. Thus Rodion Yakovlevich proved to be not only the youngest of the "marshals of victory," but had the most headlong career. One should note that Rodion Yakovlevich became the youngest marshal during the Second World War of all the armies involved. Only L.P. Beria,[10] born in 1899 and awarded the rank of marshal of the Soviet Union on 9 July 1945, was younger. However, Lavrentii Pavlovich was only a political marshal and he received his rank not for his services as a commander, but simply by transforming his rank as general commissar of state security for that of a marshal. So Malinovskii was the youngest of any country's marshal-commanders.

Compared to the other future Soviet generals and marshals, Malinovskii had the completely unique experience of the First World War on the French front. Here he had to fight the Germans in conditions which differed significantly from the conditions on the Eastern Front. There was a much higher concentration of artillery and machine guns in the West, and thus the concentration of troops and the stability of the defense were significantly greater. Tanks (Malinovskii was able to observe the Allies' tank attacks during the war's final months) were employed by both sides and aviation was used more actively. Besides, the more combat-capable German divisions fought on the Western Front than on the Eastern, where there was a higher percentage of reserve, *Landwehr*[11] and *Landsturm*[12] divisions and brigades. The conditions in which Malinovskii had to fight reminded one more of the conditions of the Second World War than those in which the main body of czarist troops had to fight.

This is how Malinovskii described his service in the Red Army in his service biography from 1938:

> In August 1922 the 35th Division arrived in Irkutsk and was changed from a 9-regiment unit to a 3-regiment one, and I was appointed chief of the 309th Regiment's disbandment committee, and on 23 August I was appointed chief of the machine gun crew of the 35th Division's 104th Rifle Regiment. On 1 August 1923 I was appointed assistant to the

---

10   Editor's note. Lavrentii Pavlovich Beria (1899-1953) joined the Bolsheviks in 1917 and quickly rose through the ranks of the security organs. He was appointed chief of the Georgian party apparatus in 1931 and that of the entire Trans-Caucasus region the following year. He was appointed head of the NKVD in 1938. During the Great Patriotic War he presided over the deportation of several "suspect" national groups and was in charge of the Soviet atom bomb project. Beria was arrested shortly after Stalin's death and executed.

11   Editor's note. The *Landwehr* consisted of men regarded as too old for military service and who were relegated to guard or occupation duties.

12   Editor's note. The *Landsturm* consisted of those who were deemed unfit for military service, but served as a military reserve.

commander of this regiment's 1st Battalion, and at the end of October we were detached from the 35th Division as a second-line cadre and arrived in the town of Kaluga to form the 81st Rifle Division. On 18 November 1923 I was appointed commander of the 1st Battalion of the 243rd Rifle Division and served in this capacity until 1 October 1927. I later studied in the Frunze Military Academy[13] and completed it in the spring of 1930, and upon completion of the academy I was appointed chief of staff of the 67th Caucasian Cavalry Regiment (although I never had any affinity for the cavalry).

(Here one may put forward the testimony of Malinovskii's daughter, Natal'ya, to whom her father once confessed his dislike of the cavalry. She was surprised: "But papa, the cavalry has horses!' Here Rodion Yakovlevich noted: "Cavalry is not just horses. It's also swords!" Evidently the sight of a man being hacked up by a sword put Malinovskii off the cavalry for his whole life, B.S.) "On 25 January I was appointed assistant to the chief of the first section in the staff of the North Caucasus Military District, and on 15 February 1931 chief of the same section's second sector. On 10 January 1935 I was appointed chief of staff of the 3rd Cavalry Corps. On 19 June 1936 I was appointed assistant to the cavalry inspector for the operational section in the Belorussian Military District."

Malinovskii's first rating as a commander was compiled during the second half of 1922: "Disciplined, energetic and insistent. He enjoys the respect of his subordinates. He has a great deal of practical experience with the machine gun. Not being a party member, he is completely reliable and devoted to Soviet power. He fully corresponds to the position of the chief of the 104th Rifle Regiment's machine gun crew."

It's interesting that in the play, written a year earlier, Malinovskii noted insistence as one of the main qualities of his autobiographical hero, Petr Stepin.

The rating was just as favorable in 1924: "Disciplined and energetic. He is close to the masses, sometimes even to the detriment of his service position. He is well developed politically and is not weighed down by his service. He is worthy of being confirmed in the position of battalion commander."

In Malinovskii's 1925 rating, there was an indication as to his possible career growth: "He corresponds to his position as commander. For the purpose of his future promotion, it is necessary to commandeer him to 'Vystrel'"[14] (courses for improving the command element).

In 1926, as the commander of the 1st Battalion of the 243rd Rifle Regiment, Malinovskii once again received a high rating, with the prospects of further promotion:

> He possesses a firm and well expressed will and energy. He is disciplined and decisive in all of his actions. Firm and strict in his relations to his subordinates, he skillfully combines an element of comradely approach with reserve.
>
> He has no military education, being a natural talent in this case and, thanks to his persistence and insistence and independent study, he has acquired the necessary knowledge of military affairs by independent study. He is an active participant in the work of the OSO.[15]

---

13   Editor's note. The RKKA Military Academy (previously the RKKA General Staff Academy) was renamed the Frunze Military Academy in 1925, upon the death of the war commissar of the same name. As a rule, the most promsing offices studied here.

14   Editor's note. This is a reference to the higher officers' command school "Vystrel" ("shot"), which existed in the Red and Russian armies from 1918 to 2009.

15   Editor's note. The OSO (*osoboe soveshchanie*) was a non-judicial organ in early Soviet institutions with the power of reviewing criminal cases and handing out sentences.

He is irreproachable in his morals. He corresponds to the position of battalion commander. He deserves to be commandeered to the military academy.

Malinovskii's carrer was aided by the fact that he joined the party. In his 1938 service biography, he wrote that

I joined the party in 1923, while serving in the 243rd Rifle Regiment, and was made a full member in October 1926. I was accepted by the 81st Division's party commission in Kaluga. My party membership number is 1040844. I have no party reprimands and have not been subject to such. I worked for two years as a member of the assizes session of the 81st Division's military tribunal. I have not been a member of any other parties. I have not deviated from the general line of the party and during the Trotskyite opposition[16] of 1925-27 I looked into the entire counterrevolutionary essence of Trotskyism during the discussion in the Frunze Military Academy's discussion during the autumn of 1927, and in this struggle I firmly supported the line of our party's Central Committee.

Obviously, entry into the party was a mandatory condition for being commandeered to the military academy. As we recall, in the 1926 rating, Malinovskii was recognized as worthy of studying in the Frunze Military Academy. He only lacked full membership in the party. And following his transition from candidate to full member, the road to the academy was open.

Rodion Yakovlevich departed for the academy in October 1927. He was very nervous before taking his entrance examination. His daughter recalls how her father told her: "I decided right then and there: 'if I don't pass, I'll shoot myself. I must pass.'

"But why?" I asked in surprise. (The conversation took place on the eve of one of my own examinations, which was evidently the cause of it.)

"'Otherwise, I would cease to respect myself.'"

The completion of the academy, particularly in the first rank, opened up possibilities for his future career growth. This was all the more the case as the rating upon completing the academy was quite positive:

A student at the Frunze Military Academy. He mastered the general academic course. He was particularly active in his work while during his probationary service with a cavalry division. He is precise, conscientious and hard working. He is disciplined, modest and reserved.

He displays average activity in his social and political work. He has learned French well. He is qualified for both line and staff work. Conclusion—he may be appointed chief of the operational section of a rifle or cavalry division staff. He may be awarded the rank of chief of division commander as a political and military commander.

The only minus here is his average social-political activity. However, in the end, they forgave the natural talent's lack of desire to mouth nothings at party meetings. The recognition of the possibility of appointing Malinovskii a political and military commander, without a commissar, meant that he was fully trusted in the political sense.

---

16   Editor's note. The Trotskyite Opposition (or "Left Opposition") refers to a phase in the Communist Party's post-Lenin struggle for power. The opposition was headed by Lev Davidovich Trotskii (1879-1940), who was opposed by Joseph Stalin and Lev Borisovich Kamenev (1883-1936) and Grigorii Yevseevich Zinov'ev (1883-1936), Trotsky was defeated and removed from his post as war commissar in 1925, after which Kamenev and Zinov'ev had a falling out with Stalin. They then allied themselves with Trotskii, but were defeated and expelled from the party.

In his 1948 service biography, Rodion Yakovlevich stated:

> When the regiment (3rd Siberian Rifle, B.S.) was disbanded, I was transferred to the 35th Division's 309th Regiment, and in the reorganization of 1922 I was transferred to the 35th Division's 104th Rifle Regiment as chief of the machine gun crew, and then as assistant to the battalion commander.
>
> In October 1923 I was appointed commander of the 1st Battalion/243rd Rifle Regiment/81st Division in the town of Kaluga.
>
> In October 1927 I entered the Frunze Military Academy as a student and in May 1930 I completed it in the first rank and was appointed chief of staff of the 10th Cavalry Division's 67th Cavalry Regiment in the town of Kropotkin, where I temporarily commanded a regiment. In 1931 I was appointed assistant to the chief of the operational section of the staff of the North Caucasus Military District and worked for a long time on operational projects.
>
> In January 1935 I was appointed chief of staff of the 3rd Cavalry Corps and in June 1936 assistant to the army cavalry inspector in the Belorussian Military District.

In 1931, in connection with his appointment by order of the RVS[17] of 16 March to the staff of the Belorussian Military District, Malinovskii received the following rating:

> His military-theoretical training is good. He figures out the situation quickly and skillfully. He possesses the qualities for becoming a good staff commander at a high level. He has quite sufficient qualities of will for a commander and is more inclined to work in the role of a line commander.
>
> He's healthy, hardy and well trained in line work. He handles personal weapons excellently. He may be promoted to the position of the sector chief or commander of a rifle or cavalry regiment. He fully corresponds to the position of assistant to the chief of the third sector of the military district staff's first section.

In 1932 his rating was just as positive:

> He possesses a commander's qualities of will and makes an intelligent decision in exercises with the command element and firmly puts the decision into practice. He is well developed politically.
>
> He was worthy of an out-of-turn promotion to the position of chief of staff or commander of a rifle or cavalry regiment, as a political and military commander.
>
> He is worthy of promotion to sector chief of the military district staff's first section undere an army commander.

And finally, Malinovskii was appointed chief of the second sector of the Belorussian Military District staff's first section in an order of 14 March 1933. The ratings from 1933 and 1934 attest to his complete correspondence to his position and the possibility of appointing him political and military commander of a rifle regiment or chief of staff of a rifle division.

However, an unexpected promotion followed.

---

17   Editor's note. The RVS, or Revolutionary Military Council (*Revolyutsionnyi Voennyi Sovet*), was the Soviet Republic's highest military body during the civil war. It was created in September 1918 and was initially headed by L.D. Trotskii and also included a commander-in-chief of the armed forces. The RVS was abolished in 1934.

In an order of 10 January 1935, Malinovskii was appointed chief of staff of the 3rd Cavalry Corps, which was quartered in Minsk, to where Rodion Yakovlevich had to transfer from Smolensk. However, in June 1936 he was returned to the staff of the Belorussian Military District in Smolensk, having been appointed assistant to the army cavalry inspector's operational section.

Following the introduction of personal ranks in the Red Army on 22 September 1935, Malinovskii was awarded the rank of colonel.

What is remarkable is that Malinovskii, having risen to high staff positions, never commanded either a regiment or a division, although to judge from the results of his ratings he was often nominated for the post of regimental commander. Probably, despite the fact that Malinovskii always sought a line appointment, he was more regarded as a staff worker.

In principle, before being commandeered to Spain, Malinovskii's career was quite successful, although there was nothing particularly outstanding in it. There were hundreds of commanders in the Red Army with similar service records, who during the Great Patriotic War rose, at best, to the post of division or corps commander.

Malinovskii did not avoid denunciations during 1936-37. He later had the opportunity to read them, although he knew the informer even then. His daughter recalled:

I don't know where the frighteningly big folder (it's too bad I don't remember what it was called, although it was probably only by number) appeared from on papa's desk and which disappeared after a few days. I was curious, assuming that it was raw information, but the folder contained an unimaginable number of denunciations, filed in chronological order. (Now I can assume that at the end of the 1950s they acquainted some people with their personnel files. One can only guess why they did this and exactly whom they acquainted them with, but I believe that these folders were not returned, of course, to the archives.) Due to childlike simplicity and the large number of denunciations, I only read the first and last ones.

In the last one a personage familiar to me, with large stars on his epaulets, informed the proper people about the criminal fact, which he saw with his own eyes, of R.Ya. Malinovskii's conversation with some foreign diplomat in a foreign language at some kind of reception. The author of the paper could not say anything about the subject of the discussion, due to his lack of knowledge of languages, which he acknowledged. Thus the swear word "secret collaborator," which I had heard from my parents' conversations, for the first time acquired a real meaning. And, as luck would have it, the next day papa and I, while carrying a piece of Roquefort cheese from the "Cheese" store on Gor'kii Street, which was our traditional winter stroll, ran into the author of the denunciation! I wrinkled my nose. Papa greeted him, as if happy and, waiting a moment, said: "You should always greet your elders. Sort out things with people of your own age." Did this mean that children should not settle their parents' scores, or that scores should not be settled at all? Or are both answers right?

The story of the first denunciation is far longer. It stretches a half century in time and can no way be summed up in two paragraphs. Life arranged it oddly, neither a drama nor as a novel, mixing up the genres and changing the protagonists and tellers.

So, act one, just as in the document. In the paper (it's too bad that I didn't look where it was addressed and who wrote it), our neighbors in the communal apartment reported that Brigade Commander (or some such rank) Malinovskii, who lives next door, failed to take down the inscribed picture of the enemy of the people Uborevich[18] from the wall, although

---

18   Editor's note. Ieronim Petrovich Uborevich (1896-1937) joined the imperial army in 1915 and the Red Army in 1918. He commanded armies during the civil war. Following the war, he commanded military districts and was chief of the army's rearmament program. Uborevich was executed during the military purge.

the wives of the undersigned commanders "approached Malinovskii's wife with the corresponding reproof," and that on the following day she said that she had passed their words on to her husband and received the following reply: "I hung it up, and there it will stay…"

At least five years passed. The war was going on and it was the end of 1944 or the beginning of 1945. It's was almost night. The duty officer entered with a report:

"Comrade marshal! General so-and-so has arrived in connection with his appointment to some kind of post!" (The wording in my civilian account is naturally conventional.)

My father, in a calm and quiet voice:

"Tell that son of a bitch that he had better be gone within thirty seconds! If not, I'm going to personally smash his face."

This refers to the following incident. In 1937, or in the beginning of 1938, Malinovskii's neighbors in the communal apartment in Smolensk wrote a denunciation of him. The informants were Nikolai Dmitrievich Yakovlev, then the artillery chief for the Belorussian Military District and later an artillery marshal and chief of the Main Artillery Directorate, and Brigade Commander Ivan Andreevich Naidenov, who until February 1938 was the assistant to the cavalry inspector for the Belorussian Military District for communications and later a lieutenant general and chief of the RKKA Communications Directorate, although in 1940 he was demoted to deputy chief of the directorate. In the denunciation it was reported that a signed picture (something along the lines of "to my student") of the enemy of the people Uborevich was hanging in Rodion Yakovlevich's room. Insofar as Naidenov evidently moved to Moscow from Smolensk no later than the end of February 1938 and that there was nothing criminal in a picture of Uborevich before June 1937, then it's most likely that the denunciation was written between June 1937 through 1938, when Malinovskii was in Spain. It is not excluded that the insistent attempts to recall Rodion Yakovlevich from Spain were linked to this denunciation. It's most likely that Malinovskii was in no way punished for the picture of Uborevich, if only because he could not be blamed for links to Uborevich at the time of his departure for Spain and, in any event, he could not take down the ill-starred picture while he was in Spain.

In the beginning of the 1960s Natal'ya Rodionovna saw a pile of denunciations on Malinovskii's desk. The first was a denunciation of Uborevich and the second was from two weeks before. The second belonged to a marshal, their neighbor in the building on Granovskii Street, and was dedicated to the reception involving foreign guests. Afterwards, when they were going up in the elevator with this marshal, Malinovskii's daughter did not greet him. In this regard, Rodion Yakovlevich said: "Sort things out with people your own age, but show respect to your elders."

In all likelihood, the marshal who didn't rate a handshake was Filipp Ivanovich Golikov,[19] the chief of the GlavPU[20] until May 1962. In any event, the other neighbors who were marshals, Budennyi[21] and Meretskov, according to Natal'ya Rodionovna, were not at that reception.

---

19   Editor's note. Filipp Ivanovich Golikov (1900-80) served as a political commissar during the civil war. He later commanded an army and was head of military intelligence. During the Great Patriotic War he commanded fronts and was responsible for the repatriation of Soviet POWs. Following the war, Golikov served in the central military apparatus and was chief of the armed forces' political directorate.

20   Editor's note. The GlavPU, or Main Political Directorate (*Glavnoe Politicheskoe Upravlenie*) was created in 1919 as the All-Russian Bureau of Military Commissars and had several names during its existence. This body was responsible to the party Central Committee for political indoctrination in the armed forces.

21   Editor's note. Semyon Mikhailovich Budennyi (1883-1973) was drafted into the imperial army in 1903 and served in the Russo-Japanese and First World wars. During the civil war he raised cavalry detachments and commanded the 1st Cavalry Army. During the Great Patriotic War he was commander-in-chief of the Southwestern High Command and commanded *fronts*. Following the war, Budennyi was head of the army's cavalry branch.

Malinovskii rated Uborevich higher than all the others executed with Tukhachevskii,[22] including the marshal himself.

Without a doubt, Khrushchev spoke about Naidenov, who had written the denunciation of Malinovskii, in his memoirs:

> Once, while talking with him (Malinovskii, B.S.), I told him about how General Popov and I were wandering around Kalach, hanging around the corpses of the German soldiers and a grey horse. I also told him how we had met at night with a communications general, and I named him.
>
> He immediately reacted. I asked him: "Do you know him?" "Of course, I know him very well, we served together." He then related several details to me: "There was this incident. When I returned (after Spain, B.S.), I was supposed to report to the cadre section in the defense commissariat. The officer who met me in the cadre section, either through carelessness, or through lack of assiduousness, gave me my personnel file (or maybe that was necessary). I leafed through it and my hair stood on end: how is it that I'm still alive? So much false filth had been gathered against me.
>
> "One can only be amazed why I hadn't been arrested and shot, like many others. And among this filth lay that general's report.
>
> "He was evidently a secret agent. He had written such filthy things about me.
>
> "After this it was not only repulsive for me to offer my hand, but even repulsive to hear his name. He's a disgusting man. He dared dream up such slander against me that I don't know what kept Stalin from arresting and shooting me, just as he had a number of other honest people, but more prominent and worthy by the awards they had earned in the Red Army. It seems that I drew a lucky ticket in the lottery of life. That's the only way I can explain the fact that I remained alive."

Following his move to Moscow after the war, Malinovskii's neighbor (through the fence) at the dacha in Bakovka was Marshal of Artillery N.D. Yakovlev. In 1944 Yakovlev came to see Malinovskii on orders of the *Stavka*.[23] Malinovskii immediately told his adjutant: "Tell that swine that I give him three minutes to get the hell out of here. Then I'll come out myself and smash his face."

The loss of the Malinovskii family's favorite tomcat, Noire, is also linked to Marshal Yakovlev. N.D. Yakovlev's son, the well-known historian N.N. Yakovlev, shot the tomcat. His wife, Svetlana Dmitrievna Pozharskaya, a historian of Spain, told Natal'ya Rodionovna about this. The tomcat was in the habit of doing his business in the Yakovlevs' bedroom and the husband was forced to shoot him.

Natal'ya Rodionovna related in detail the story of the tragic death of the tomcat Noire in her memoirs. She doesn't' mention the marshal's last name. However, the story is undoubtedly about N.D. Yakovlev's dacha, insofar as it was the only one that had a common fence with Malinovskii's dacha.

---

22 Editor's note. Mikhail Nikolaevich Tukhachevskii (1893-1937) joined the imperial army in 1914 and was captured the following year. He escaped and returned to Russian in 1917 and joined the Red Army the following year. During the civil war he commanded armies and *fronts* and put down anti-Soviet uprisings. Following the civil war, he was chief of staff, commanded a military district, and was chief of the armed forces' rearmament program. Tukhachevskii was executed along with Uborevich and others.

23 Editor's note. The *Stavka* was the highest wartime military body in late-imperial Russia and the Soviet Union. During the Great Patriotic War the body's official name was the *Stavka* of the Supreme High Command.

As regards Naidenov, this lieutenant in the czarist army, who managed to join the RKP(b) as early as 1917, finished his career and then his life's journey without any kind of major shakeups. Following the war, Ivan Andreevich was the deputy chief of communications for the General Staff of the USSR Armed Forces, chief of communications for the General Staff of the USSR Armed Forces and, in 1950, a "well-known military communications expert," as they call him today in one of the articles dedicated to him, retired into the reserves. Naidenov died on 15 April 1975, at the age of 85.

Nikolai Dmitrievich Yakovlev didn't do as well and himself became the victim of a denunciation. In February 1952, as a marshal of artillery and chief of the Main Artillery Directorate and a deputy minister of the armed forces, he was arrested and accused of sabotage and deprived of his marshal's rank, although after Stalin's death he was released and restored to his marshal's rank. He was subsequently the deputy commander-in-chief and the commander-in-chief of the National Air Defense Forces and in 1960 was in the group of inspector generals. Yakovlev died on 9 May 1972 at the age of 73. It's revealing that Malinovskii, having become minister of defense, did not retire Yakovlev, but let him quietly serve until his pension.

Rodion Yakovlevich got married in 1925. This is what he reported about his wife and her relatives in his 1938 service biography:

> I got married in 1925, in Irkutsk, to where I had travelled specially from the town of Kaluga, to Larisa Nikolaevna Sharabarova, who was born in 1904 and with whom I became acquainted in 1923, when she worked as a typist in the headquarters of the 104th Rifle Regiment. She was raised by her grandfather and grandmother in the city of Irkutsk, 3 Stepan Razin Street. Her grandfather at first worked building and repairing chimneys, and then as a bricklayer, and then set up his own brick factory in the taiga, where he worked and hired laborers, after which he became a contractor and built homes. He died in 1920. He was an old man and did not serve in the White army. Her grandmother was a housewife. My wife's mother bore her out of wedlock, which is why she was raised by her grandfather and grandmother, and her mother began to cohabit with the postal worker Puchkov, who died in 1916 or 1917, while she herself worked at the post office as a telegraph operator and died in Irkutsk in 1919, following an operation, while her remaining children—Yevlogii and Andronik—also went to their grandmother to be raised, because my wife began to work at the age of 16, having given up her studies. My wife's younger brother Yevlogii, who was born approximately in 1909, began to sell small items at an auction as a young boy, and now works as a storehouse director at the Irkutsk Shoe Factory and did not serve in the Red Army (he got a medical deferment due to his pronounced crossed eyes). My wife's uncle, Fedor Mikhailovich Sharabarov (a son of the grandfather who raised my wife), who is now on pension, earlier worked as a builder and repairer of chimneys and as a bricklayer and then a conductor on mail trains, now lives in Irkutsk, 2 Stepan Razin Street. My wife's grandmother died in 1928.

According to the recollections of Malinovskii's friend, Major General Ivan Nikolaevich Burenin,[24] the marriage between Rodion Yakovlevich and Larisa Nikolaevna began to show signs of cracking even before his trip to Spain. Malinovskii did not hide the fact that he had affairs in Spain, which he honestly admitted to Khrushchev.

---

24   Editor's note. Ivan Nikolaevich Burenin (1896-1986) commanded a division during the Great Patriotic War and also served on an army and *front* staffs. Following the war, Burenin taught at the Frunze Military Academy and was a military adviser in China until his retirement in 1954.

4

In Spain

As Rodion Yakovlevich wrote in his 1938 service biography, "From January 1937 through May 1938 I was on a special state assignment in Spain."

There's no doubt that he was sent to Spain on the recommendation of the commander of the Belorussian Military District, I.P. Uborevich. On 2 June 1937, while speaking before an expanded session of the defense commissariat's Military Council, which was dedicated to unmasking "Tukhachevskii's military-fascist plot," Stalin announced: "Tukhachevskii and Uborevich requested us to send them to Spain. We say to this: 'We don't need big names. We'll send less well-known people to Spain.' Let's look and see what came of this. We told them that if we send you, then everyone will notice, so it's not worth it. So we sent unknown people, and they are working miracles there." Malinovskii was just such an unknown commander, whom no one in the country and the world knew, just like they didn't know Rodimtsev,[1] Batov,[2] Kuznetsov,[3] Pavlov,[4] and Kulik,[5] and tens of others heretofore unknown, or at least known only in a narrow circle of commanders, and whose pictures were not published in the newspapers. Of course, this was not the only reason Stalin didn't let Tukhachevskii and Uborevich go. He had already decided their fate for himself and had doomed these commanders to a shameful death. However, we shouldn't doubt that then, in the summer of 1936, he asked them to recommend bright "unknown" commanders to be sent to Spain, among whom Uborevich probably named Malinovskii. Neither Tukhachevskii nor Uborevich, nor the others who figured in the affair of the "military-fascist plot" knew that in sending unknown replacements instead of themselves to Spain that they were preparing replacements for themselves in the Soviet Union. And although some of the Soviet "Spaniards," particularly fliers, were shot after their return, the majority of them made a brilliant career, replacing

---

1   Editor's note. Aleksandr Il'ich Rodimtsev (1905-77) joined the Red Army in 1927 and was an adviser during the Spanish Civil War. During the Great Patriotic War he commanded divisions and a corps. Following the war, Rodimtsev served as a deputy military district commander.

2   Editor's note. Pavel Ivanovich Batov (1897-1985) joined the imperial army in 1916 and the Red Army in 1918, and later served as an adviser in Spain. During the Great Patriotic War he commanded a corps and armies. After the war, Batov commanded armies and a military district and was deputy chief of staff of the Warsaw Pact forces.

3   Editor's note. Nikolai Gerasimovich Kuznetsov (1904-74) joined the Red Navy in 1919 and fought in the civil war. During the interwar years he was Soviet naval attached in Spain and was appointed navy commissar in 1939, a post he held throughout the Great Patriotic War. Kuznetsov was demoted twice during the postwar period and was dismissed from his posts in 1956.

4   Editor's note. Dmitrii Grigor'evich Pavlov (1897-1941) served in the Firsst World War and joined the Red Army in 1919. He was an adviser in Spain and also served as head of the army's armored directorate. He commanded the Western Front at the beginning of the Great Patriotic War, but was shortly afterwards relieved. Pavlov was blamed for his front's poor performance and executed.

5   Editor's note. Grigorii Ivanovich Kulik (1890-1950) joined the imperial army in 1912 and the Red Army in 1918. He served as chief of the Main Artillery Directorate before the war. During the Great Patriotic War he commanded armies, but was so incompetent that he was demoted from marshal to major general and removed from command. Kulik was later accused of treason and executed.

those who were shot during the course of the bloody purge of 1937-38. Malinovskii was one of the "lucky ones."

One should note that from the very beginning of the war the Spanish Republicans were in a very unfavorable situation. 80 percent of the cadre army had risen up against them. Thus in the first months the Republican army was represented by a poorly trained militia. The majority of Spanish officers professed quite backward operational-tactical views. The Soviet advisers were faced with a very difficult task. They had no power of command and had to convince the Spanish commanders in the correctness of the advice they offered, displaying diplomatic skill.

In January 1937 Rodion Yakovlevich arrived at the Madrid defense zone. At first he served as adviser to the commander of the 3rd Corps, and then to the commander of the Maneuver Army along the Aragon (Eastern) front, and then adviser to the commander of the Aragon front. The Spanish communist and commander of the 11th Division, Enrique Lister,[6] recalled:

> Colonel Malino—Rodion Malinovskii, who later became a marshal of the Soviet Union and USSR defense minister, arrived at my division at the height of the fighting along the Jarama.[7] Shells fell like rain and bullets flew on my command post, which was located almost on the front line. When we had become acquainted I read in his half-surprised and half-mocking look a condemnation of the fact that I had located the command post in such a place.

Malinovskii recalled this meeting:

> Lister had arranged an original examination for me.
> Bullets whistle over our heads and over the stunted, leafless bushes. Lister and I pace from a small house to the courtyard fence, from the fence to the small house. The general looks like a man taking a stroll after lunch, so I also make it known that the bullets don't bother me any more than flies. We exchange brief, business-like phrases... It begins to grow dark. As if by accident, I examine the trace of a bullet on my torn sleeve.
> "Colonel Malino!" Lister exclaims with a smile. "We haven't yet celebrated our meeting."
> He summons his adjutant: "Bring a bottle of good wine!"

Lister warmly spoke of Rodion Yakovlevich, valuing him as a skillful and valiant commander:

> We were together until the end of the battle on the Jarama. From there he went to the 2nd Corps, and I to Guadalajara. We met again in March 1938 along the Aragon front, where he had arrived to visit us and once again saw me at the command post, being bombarded by the enemy's aimed fire. Not long before this, the enemy had broken through our line near La Condoneria and I had just thrown my last reserve—the special battalion, into the fighting. Thanks to the bravery of its soldiers, the newly-arrived reserves and nightfall, we managed to hold our positions. That was the last time I saw Colonel Malino in Spain. We became good friends during the time we fought together. He was distinguished not only by an unusual military toughness, but also the ability to rapidly, precisely and shrewdly resolve complex

---

6   Editor's note. Enrique Lister (1907-94) joined the Spanish Communist Party early on and participated in an uprising in Cuba in 1931. During the civil war he commanded a division and a corps. He took refuge in the USSR following the Republican defeat and served as a general in the Red Army during the Great Patriotic War. Lister returned to Spain in 1977, following Franco's death.

7   Editor's note. This refers to the Battle of the Jarama (6-27 February 1937), when the Nationalist forces sought to capture Madrid. They were held by fierce Republican resistance and halted. Both sides suffered very heavy casualties.

military problems at each stage of the fighting. Later these qualities manifested themselves more broadly and brilliantly. I most admired in him courage and firmness with which he defended his views, respect for the opinion of others, and forthrightness and honesty in his relations with people.

Malinovskii remembered the legendary general Lukacs, the noted Hungarian writer Mate Zalka[8] (Bela Frankl), who had lived in the USSR and who perished near Huesca in Spain in 1937…

The 5th Regiment, offspring of the party and the true forge of revolutionary combat cadres, became the soul of the defense of Madrid; the recently formed International Brigades[9]—the 11th, which was first commanded by Kleber[10] and then by the German Hans Kahle,[11] and the 12th, which was created and lead by the Hungarian (actually, a Hungarian Jew, B.S.) from the Soviet Union, Mate Zalka—played a decisive role in the battle against the insurgents. I had to search out General Cooper (Corps Commander Grigorii Ivanovich Kulik, the military adviser with the commander of the Madrid front, fought under this pseudonym in Spain, who was later awarded the rank of marshal, but who was demoted in 1942 and executed by Stalin in 1950, B.S.) and I left Madrid for the Galapagar area. Along the way I stopped in at the headquarters of the 12th International Brigade. The first person I met was the brigade's chief of staff, Colonel Belov—Karlo Lukanov,[12] a Bulgarian and later a noted political figure in the People's Republic of Bulgaria. General Lukacs (I didn't know at the time whose pseudonym this was) was not at the command post, but was along the front-line positions. I decided not to lose any time and asked Colonel Belov to acquaint me with the situation along the brigade's sector, which he did quite readily and soundly.

"And here's General Lukacs," said Colonel Belov, pointing toward two men who had gotten out of the car next to us.

"Who's the second one?"

"Colonel Fritz."

---

8   Editor's note. Mate Zalka (real name, Bela Frankl) (1896-1937) joined the Austro-Hungarian army in 1914 and was captured on the Eastern Front, where he converted to communism. He later fought on the Red side in the civil war and also against the Greeks in Turkey. He later joined the International Brigades in Spain. Zalka is mentioned in several of Hemingway's works.

9   Editor's note. The International Brigades were volunteer military units that served with the Spanish Republican forces during the civil war. The volunteers came from many countries and were usually communists or sympathizers. The brigades fought in Spain from the fall of 1936 to the fall of 1938, when they were disbanded and sent home.

10   Editor's note. Emilio Kleber (Manfred Stern) (1896-1954) was drafted into the Austro-Hungarian army during the First World War and captured by the Russians. He later became a Bolshevik and fought in the civil war. He later served as a spy in the US and a military adviser in China. He commanded a brigade and division during the Spanish Civil War. Following the war, he returned to the USSR, where he was arrested and sentenced to a labor camp, where he died.

11   Editor's note. Hans Kahle (1899-1947) fought in the First World War and was a prisoner of war in France. He later joined the German Communist Party. He commanded a battalion, brigade and division during the Spanish Civil War. Kahle returned to Germany after the Second World War and worked as a party functionary in the Soviet zone of occupation.

12   Editor's note. Karlo Todorov Lukanov (1897-1982) fought in the Bulgarian army during the First World War and later joined the country's communist party. He later moved to the USSR and fought in the Spanish Civil War with the international brigades. He returned to Moscow following the war and returned to Bulgaria in 1944, following the Soviet invasion of the country. Lukanov afterwards held a variety of party and governmental posts.

"Fritz! That means he's a German," I thought.

Mate Zalka's characteristic feature, of which I was convinced more than once, was his ability to win over those around him. We had not even managed to get acquainted and I was already in the power of his truly scintillating energy. He smiled broadly, displaying an even row of white teeth, was lively and was evidently aroused by what he had seen at the forward position.

"Let's put aside our pseudonyms for a minute!" exclaimed General Lukacs and turned to me: "Meet Colonel Batov."

"So that's Fritz!" I thought and shook Lukacs' companion's hand a second time. Pavel Ivanovich Batov was smart and well-proportioned and I could tell by his bearing that he was a born soldier. By the way, that's how he is today—twice Hero of the Soviet Union and a general of the army who earned glory during the Great Patriotic War.

"And I'm Mate Zalka. Have you heard of him?"

"Wait, wait, are you really the Hungarian writer Mate Zalka?"

I remembered the story "Khodya" and the story's Chinese hero who fought against the Whites during the civil war. I had read other works by Zalka, but for some reason I recalled "Khodya" very powerfully.

"One and the same. To be sure, I'm more of a writer than a commander, but what can you do; I had to trade in my pen for a bayonet," and a kind and childishly direct smile began to play on his lips. I did learn something in the civil war. Here, however, in Spain, we're going through a tough school. To be sure, we sometimes get a low grade. Isn't that right, dear Fritzi?"

"Well, the students aren't to blame. You could compare them to first-graders who have been dropped into the tenth grade."

Colonel Batov explained that the soldiers in the brigades are burning with internationalist enthusiasm, but that alone is not sufficient. The enemy is powerful and to fight him you need experience, while many people in the brigade are holding a rifle for the first time.

Pavel Ivanovich and I talked for a few minutes as professional military men.

"Yes, here we have to learn right on the battlefield. Now our Soviet T-26[13] tanks have appeared. Excellent vehicles! The Italian tanks, armed with machine guns, are no match for them! Ours have guns. This raises another problem: the infantry still doesn't know how to cooperate with the tanks. Given a skillful combination of forces, we can really beat them."

And Pavel Ivanovich told me about the fighting that had taken place on 1 January. This was along the Guadalajara sector, where the Republicans had decided to launch an attack against the enemy in the direction of Almadrones and Siguenza. The 12th International Brigade, with four batteries and a company of tanks, was to attack the insurgents in the flank, toward Mirabueno and Algora. They attacked the enemy positions unexpectedly toward evening and drove the fascists out of both inhabited locales. However, late at night a battalion of Internationalists, which had occupied Algora, was suddenly attacked by five companies of insurgents. A fierce bayonet fight broke out in the village. It was difficult to predict its outcome, but all of a sudden three of our tanks came up. They opened fire from their guns and machine guns along the streets. The fascists ran away, having lost more than 150 men in the village.

---

13   Editor's note. The T-26 was a light tank produced in large numbers in the Soviet Union during 1931-41. One model weighed 9.6 tons and carried a crew of three. This model had a 45mm gun and a 7.62mm machine gun.

In the meantime, General Lukacs paced back and forth beside us. It was obvious that he was intently mulling something over, and I thought to myself: "How quickly his mood changes!" Finally, he came up to us.

"Spain! The fascists are tearing its body apart and those who call themselves the friends of justice don't want to notice anything. Treason, that's what it is!"

General Lukacs knitted his dark brows and leaned against the table on which lay a military map.

"The class struggle is what it is! Just look who's fighting in our brigade. Fighters against fascism in Germany and Italy and volunteers from other countries. They made their way here, one by one; they avoided hundreds of obstacles created by that very same policy of non-interference and took up the cause of the Spanish people. And the bourgeois press calls them bandits. It's monstrous! Just who are these so-called bandits? There's Ludwig Renn,[14] whom Hitler put in prison on the Alexanderplatz for his anti-fascist books? Or Richard, the construction worker? Or you, dear Fritzi?"

General Lukacs, who was a great philanthropist, which is a quality everyone remembers about him now, told us with indignation about the fascist bombing of Madrid. I heard how German-made bombs exploded in the hospital of San Carlos and how the church of San Jeronimo and how people's blood flowed on the sidewalks of the Glorieta. For the first time my eyes were opened to the bared teeth of fascism. Within a few years I saw all of this in my own Soviet country…

They warmly saw me off—General Lukacs, Colonel Batov, Colonel Belov and another Bulgarian who had joined our group—Petrov, whose real name was Ferdinand Kozovskii—and advised me on how to find General Cooper…

The insurgents' third operation began to take Madrid—the Jarama operation.

The fascists had evidently decided to set up a real "Cannae" for the Republicans with a simultaneous attack from the northeast from Siguenza, and from the south, along the eastern bank of the Jarama River. To be sure, they were not able to launch a simultaneous attack. The first attack was made against the newly formed and untried Spanish brigades. The 12th International Brigade was moved up to defend the most dangerous axis, leading the enemy to the Madrid—Valencia highway.

My meeting with General Lukacs in the middle of February was not cheerful. He had just returned from the hospital where a lot of the brigade's wounded soldiers lay. His face was pale. The general was suffering and couldn't disguise the fact.

"Damned bridges! We should have blown them up and I don't understand why our command hasn't done that. I sent a company with four machine guns to the Pentoche bridge. Was that enough? Of course! Everything was quiet. Our boys had evidently let down their guard and during the night they were unexpectedly attacked by the Moroccans, without a single shot. Not one of the machine guns managed to open fire. Four men are left from the company. Do you understand, Colonel Malino?!"

The general didn't know what to do. He understood that the company commander had simply been careless.

"Again a lesson! But we're no longer first graders and we're not vigilant enough. The poor, poor soldiers…"

14 Ludwig Renn (1889-1979) was born into the Saxon nobility and fought in the First World War on the Western Front and later wrote a book about his service. He joined the German Communist Party in 1928 and fought in Spain during that country's civil war. Renn died in Berlin.

I tried to calm General Lukacs, but I understood immediately that words would not help his sorrow. He was the commander, and like every real commander he had fatherly feelings for his soldiers. He understood that you can't have war without blood, but the enemy must pay a high price for every drop.

As for the bridges, a big and irreparable mistake had indeed been made. After all, the Republicans had a very small bridgehead on the western bank of the Jarama, and they had not had time to consolidate it as needed. At the same time, the water in the river rose considerably in February and the Jarama represented a really serious obstacle for the insurgents. It was not difficult to guess that the insurgents would immediately begin an attack for the crossings. They were much more crucial to them than to the Republicans. Common sense suggested that we destroy the bridges. However, the Central Front command did not do this. It's difficult to discern the reasons. It was either a failure by the Spanish officers, many of whom were used to fighting according to the ossified canons of the royal army, to think things through, or the inertia of a previously conceived offensive plan. In any event, the bridges made it easier for the enemy to force the Jarama.

I nevertheless reminded General Lukacs that the events along the Jarama had begun to develop favorably for the Republican forces, and this was all the more pleasant because the Jarama operation was essentially the first operation on an army scale. This meant that their experience was growing. Now Soviet tanks completely dominated the battlefield. Soviet air power now represented a major force. It had appeared in the sky over Spain in November and the inhabitants of Madrid could see, with tears in their eyes, how the Soviet pilots scattered the fascist air pirates. During the Jarama operation the fascist were scared of our fighters like fire. They completely renounced their favorite move: "to pound" the same position of the Republicans for several hours. Now the bombers' raids were brief, and they often dropped their bombs on the first pass. But our fighters nevertheless were able to "grab" the insurgents over the battlefield, and then black plumes of smoke would rise to the sky…

By rights, Guadalajara became a symbol of the Republican Spain's valor and courage.

The enemy planned this operation in the form of a vigorous advance by the Italian Expeditionary Corps along the Zaragoza road. On 9 March the interventionists[15] planned to seize Torica, and then Madrid as early as 15 March. All of their calculations were based on the absence of any kind of serious Republican forces along the northwestern axis and on the possibility of an unbroken advance. However, these calculations proved to be short-sighted. Three divisions followed one behind the other (the fourth, the Littorio Division, was in reserve) along the narrow valley, bounded by the Samosierra mountain range and the bank of the Tagus River could be halted and defeated by much weaker forces.

This is exactly what happened. If on 8 March the interventionists moved 15 battalions, armed to the teeth, against three weakly equipped Republican battalions, then as early as the following day the Republican command threw the 11th International Brigade in here, with a company of tanks. By maneuvering and operating from ambushes, these tanks met the interventionists with heavy fire. Within another day Lister's 2nd Brigade and the 12th International Brigade entered the fighting. On 12 March the Republican forces already included three divisions and two battalions of T-26 tanks under the command of the Soviet volunteer, General Pavlov. Thanks to their stoutness, these forces, which were significantly inferior to the Italians, defeated the enemy. Bombing attacks and machine gun fire from our planes played a decisive role in their successful actions.

---

15   Editor's note. This refers to the Italian and German troops and fliers who supported the Nationalist forces during the civil war.

The Italian Expeditionary Corps was routed.

I personally did not take part in these battles: following the Jarama operation I was appointed adviser to the commander of the 2nd Madrid Corps. But I didn't lose contact with either Lister or Lukacs, and visited them near Guadalajara. And General Lukacs would come to Madrid; one minute he wouldn't be there due to the heat of battle, and then his happy face and energetic figure would show up, and then we would have time for a soulful conversation.

I remember how one of our meetings took place in the middle of March. As usual, Mate Zalka was aroused. We embraced each other and he began to tell me about the recent combat events. I had already heard about how his brigade had stubbornly defended and bravely attacked. And now Lukacs told me another bit of news: his brigade had taken the Palacio de Ibarra.

"It was quite an easy matter," Lukacs said, gesticulating. "Two of my battalions, including the Garibaldi Battalion, quietly approached the palace through the woods, with tanks. The tanks opened fire and the infantry began to surround the garrison. All they had to do was surrender, but they evidently feared payback for their atrocities. They resisted furiously. Then the tanks broke through the stone walls of the fence, followed by the infantry, and the Italians panicked. Those who were in one piece surrendered… Counterattacks then began, but we had already reached the edge of the woods; an open field lay before us, so it was hard to sneak up on them. To be sure, the Italians threw in yet another battalion against us, and then some kind of reserves and a tank company. This is where the falcons helped us out. Imagine: about 30 planes in the air!"

"And you call this a simple affair?"

General Lukacs was embarrassed: he didn't know how to brag, while at the same time he couldn't help but be glad for his troops.

"Of course, it wasn't simple." Mate Zalka's face grew dark. "We left eighty men in that damned palace. Eighty! On the other hand, the fascists had a bad time of it: two battalions ceased to exist, 150 prisoners, equipment, weapons and, to top it off, operational documents from the headquarters of the Italian 535th Battalion."

General Lukacs always took care of his people. However, he was not able to take care of himself. His death left a great void in our hearts. It was difficult and impossible to imagine that I would no longer see the impetuous and smiling Mate…

Colonel General Aleksandr Il'ich Rodimtsev, who was a major in Spain and who received the title of Hero of the Soviet Union, left a picture of Malinovskii in Spain in his memoirs:

In Madrid I was summoned to Colonel Malino.

The small room that I entered reminded me of a classroom: aside from a long table, covered by a large map, plus several chairs, there was nothing else. A broad shouldered and large man in a brown civilian suit was sitting at the table. Seeing me, he rapidly ran his hand through his bristly head of hair.

"How was your trip?"

"Alright."

He invited me to sit down. I followed the movements of his large and powerful hands, which were measuring something on the map with a compass. Beside him lay a thick notebook with a calico binding. Finally, the colonel turned to me and, having made a small triangle with a red pencil in the area of the small town of Villaverde and jammed it with his compass:

"You'll be here."

"The front line?" I asked.

"Almost. Lister's here right now."

Then, having thought a little, he added:

"Lister's going to receive orders soon to move with his brigade to the El Pardo area. That's northwest of Madrid, along the Mansanares River. It's very hard to find him. See that Franco doesn't catch you."

Malino bent over the map.

"When you get to the road junction, there'll be a destroyed two-story building. One road leads to the center of town, and the other to the right to the Lister's brigade's concentration area. You take this road."

I nodded. It seemed that Rodion Yakovlevich did not even notice this gesture. He continued to send me off in detail. He drew a thin and squiggly line on the map with his pencil. He noted our troops with a red pencil and the insurgents with a black one. He showed me what road to take to Lister's headquarters.

"Do you understand?" he asked, finished his instructions.

"Perfectly!" I answered.

"Well then, I wish you luck," and he firmly shook my hand…

Lister, having gotten a break, decided to devote it to training. Malino, who had been appointed adviser to the division, rendered him a great deal of aid and support.

Malino drew up a good schedule and carried out the exercises himself…

One time, having agreed with Lister and the division's chief of staff Iglesias, Malino was supposed to carry out exercises with the staff officers.

Everyone drove out to the field at the appointed time. An officer met us. He had a downcast look. We soon found out the reason. It transpired that only 20 officers had shown up out of 52, mainly commanders, sent by the 5th Communist Regiment.

"Should we cancel?" asked the officer.

"We'll carry out the exercise," Malino answered.

They had only begun to assign the task, when Lister and chief of staff Iglesias arrived. Seeing that only half of the commandeered officers were present, Lister said loudly, so that everyone could hear him:

"Begin the exercise, Malino. The chief of staff and I will learn as well."

And he began to dutifully carry out all the instructions. Finally, according to the conditions of the exercise, the officers had to force a rapid and deep river. Malino gave the order and everyone took to knocking together from whatever lay around rafts and little boats. Then barrels and boards from an old house were used. The officers crossed to the other bank and there they "stormed" the enemy positions. There was an unpleasant incident with one group: they threw together a flimsy and unprepossessing little raft, hoping that they wouldn't have to cross over the river on it. However, they had to sit in it and cross the river. At first, everything went alright, but in the middle of the river, where the current was particularly rapid and there were a lot of whirlpools, the raft began to break up under the unfortunate warriors. Within a few minutes the boards were rapidly moving along with the current, while the officers in the water began to shout: "Save us, help us!"

I was already getting ready to jump into the water, but Malino and Lister stopped me:

"Let them get themselves out of it. It'll be a lesson for their whole life."

It was only with difficulty that the soaked officers made it to the bank.

A new meeting between Rodimtsev and Malinovskii took place in June 1937. This is how Aleksandr Il'ich described it:

Malino summoned me at the end of June. When I arrived, he was sitting and drawing something on the operational map with a pencil, and from time to time making some kind of notes in a thick notebook. Taking a break from his work, he turned to me:

"How are things?"

"Good."

I felt that Malino had summoned me for a serious conversation.

"You're not tired, are you? Are you getting along with Lister?"

"It doesn't get any better."

"Then, here's the thing. You'll stay and work with Lister. There's a very serious operation coming up."

"What kind?" I asked, burning with impatience.

"Everything in its own time," said Malino, growing serious. "There's a lot of important and complex work ahead. We have to reform and train formations that have just been formed. And this will be difficult, due to the simple reason that the followers of the former prime minister and war minister, Largo Caballero,[16] who was recently removed from office, are carrying out an indecisive policy. They're not working very actively in the war ministry. Someone or other is putting the brakes on the formation and organization of a new army."

Malino grew quiet for a minute, drew his big palm over his bristly hair, and then suddenly smiled.

"No matter, we've already achieved something. The newly elected prime minister Negrin[17] has sped up the formation and restructuring of the Republican army. The commanders and commissars have begun to more boldly carry out their work to train and knock together the reserves. Of course, frictions in the government still make themselves felt. But things are moving forward somewhat."

I couldn't restrain myself and asked, "Are there any new units?"

"Yes," Malino answered. "The Republican army's 5th Corps has completed its formation, outfitting and training. It was created thanks to the insistent efforts of the Central Committee of the Spanish Communist Party and the Communist Party's Madrid committee, on the basis of the 5th Regiment and the International formations. The corps has three divisions: the 46th, 35th and 11th."

Malinovskii helped Lister and Rodimtsev during the subsequent fighting for Brunete. The latter testified:

"Let's meet in the division headquarters and contact Malino, and then make a decision," I suggested.

Lister agreed.

We quickly got in touch with Malino from the division headquarters. He related the situation on this sector of the front to us:

All of the strong holds—Llanos, Quijorna and Villenueva de la Canada—were in the insurgents' hands. As to Lister's question as to whether the brigade should continue attacking,

---

16   Editor's note. Franciso Largo Caballero (1869-1946) was a Spanish politician and trade union leader who served as prime minister of the second Spanish Republic during 1936-37. He fled to France in 1939 and was later imprisoned by the Germans. Caballero died in exile.

17   Editor's note. Juan Negrin u Lopez (1892-1956) was trained as a doctor and later joined the Spanish Socialist Worker's Party. He became prime minister of the Spanish Republic in 1937 and allied his government closely to the Soviet Union. An internal coup overthrew his government in 1939 and he fled to France. Negrin died in Paris.

Malino replied: "Decide according to the situation, but I wouldn't advise it." He recommended resuming the offensive when the tank company and artillery battalion arrived.

A few minutes after this conversation we were sitting together, going over our options. Having weighed everything, we decided to attempt to seize the crossings over the Guadarrama River. Of course, we had gotten deep into the enemy's rear. However, seizing the crossings would enable us to hold the captured positions.

Lister ordered the commanders of the 1st and 100th brigades to immediately commit their second echelons into the fighting and to storm the crossings. The offensive resumed. We eagerly awaited news from the brigades, but they were not soothing. All of our attempts to seize the crossings over the Guadarrama and heights 670, 640 and 620 were unsuccessful. The troops attacked several times, but were forced to fall back on their own trenches.

Lister was upset by the brigades' failure. At this moment the commander of the Madrid front called and chewed him out for standing in one place.

"This is what we've come to. They're accusing us of laziness and cowardice. But is it really possible to thrust forward, when we've already gotten 15 kilometers into the enemy's rear?"

Upset, he paced about the room, wanting to join in the attack himself. However, he soon thought better of it.

The entire following day the 1st and 100th brigades attacked the crossings and the adjacent heights. However, the results once again proved distressing. The enemy had strong fortified and our forces suffered heavy losses. If the division lost only four killed and five wounded in the storming of Brunete, then we lost 200 men in the attack on the crossings. 300 troops were wounded."

This time Malinovskii was right, and not Lister and Rodimtsev. They could not achieve success without artillery and tanks.

The former chief of staff of the Republican army's Northern front, Francisco Ciutat, emigrated to the Soviet Union after the Republic's defeat, and later worked as an adviser in Cuba for Fidel Castro's government. In a letter to the marshal's daughter, Natal'ya Rodionovna, not long after Rodion Yakovlevich's death, he recalled:

In all my life I have never met a man whom I respected more than your father and, without exaggeration; I can say that fate has put me together with various historic personalities.

I had the honor of being beside your father, whom we then modestly called *Coronel Malino*, in 1937-38. Colonel Malino always remained an unattainable example for me. I am obligated to him not only for acquiring professional skills, but also for the fact that even then I understood how necessary are a profound and thorough knowledge of the subject in military affairs is. But not only this! A commander needs no less an exacting mind and a good heart. Your father gave me not only a military lesson, but a lesson in valor, stalwartness and dignity. And, don't be surprised!—a lesson in delicacy. In carrying out the duties of an adviser, it's not easy to restrain oneself from the temptation of publicly instructing someone, and all of Colonel Malino's predecessors gave advice to Lister in the presence of his subordinates, or simply speaking, issued commands over his head, which not everyone could put up with. And even if the adviser is three times right, in hurting the commander's pride he undermines the soldiers' faith in him, and the overall cause suffers as a result. I know for certain that Colonel Malino would discuss the situation with Lister in a very small circle (I was present at these discussions several times). Colonel Malino would precisely describe the situation and lead one to a conclusion, but the final word remained for the commander, and often was not even present for promulgating the order. Your father stood shoulder to shoulder with us during the hour of our most difficult trials and later, already in Moscow, when we were separated from our homeland, how many of us did he help! We knew that we Spaniards had a deputy in the Soviet government—Colonel Malino.

This is how Malinovskii's daughter described Francisco Ciutat:

Don Francisco, eternal memory to him, fought in the Spanish Republican Army with Lister, when he was still quite young, lived nearly 30 years as an émigré in our country and another 20 in Cuba, where he became Castro's adviser on my father's recommendation, and returned to his homeland only at the end of his life. In telling me about his youth and friendship with my father, he noted: "It's very important, when you don't live in your native country that you have someone close in Russia." And then I recalled papa's words during a telephone conversation, which I accidentally overheard: "I very much request that you help the Spaniards. After all, you shouldn't forget that they don't live in their homeland. It's not easy to be an émigré."

Upon returning to the USSR, Malinovskii wrote "Operational-Tactical Conclusions from the Experience of the Spanish Civil War from the Start of the Uprising Through May 1938." The text for the report's final form is dated 23 August 1938. He noted that

The theater of military activities in Spain is primarily mountainous and extremely broken. This changes to very mountainous along many sectors of the front, which has an enormous influence on the development of military activities. Some combat arms sometimes simply cannot find employment in the fighting, but are forced to enter the fighting and operate in completely abnormal and unacceptable, for them, relief conditions (this is mainly in regard to tanks and field artillery, which are forced to operate not in the field, but in mountainous and extremely mountainous areas). It's clear that the experience of employing these combat arms in such specific conditions does not enable us to make any indisputable conclusions regarding these or other tactical tenets or methods for employing this equipment in a future war in our theaters of military operations.

Thus Rodion Yakovlevich well understood the uniqueness of the Spanish experience and its low applicability to a future major war in Europe. In this he differed from the main adviser for armored affairs, D.G. Pavlov, who, on the basis of the Spanish experience, came to the conclusion that it is expedient to employ tanks in the future on in small subunits and recommended renouncing the formation of large armored formations.

Malinovskii emphasized that in Spain the organization of anti-tank defense was made easier by the nature of the terrain:

The nature of the theater of military activities in the Spanish war greatly eases the organization of anti-tank defense. The theater represents an almost complete anti-tank area. It's very easy to put the majority of defensive lines into a tank-resistant condition: stone walls, fences, gullies, and terraces become ready-made anti-tank obstacles. In these conditions an anti-tank gun becomes almost an invulnerable and terrible weapon against a tank.

In other conditions, in the conditions of our theater of military activities, an anti-tank gun will be more vulnerable against a tank and its role in the overall system of anti-tank defense will decrease, but it is nevertheless necessary to recognize the fact that we underestimated its role in a future war, and in this sense the experience in Spain is particularly valuable for us. It showed just what a powerful enemy the anti-tank gun is for our tank and mechanized formations. The anti-tank gun is the main and chief element of the anti-tank defense.

Moreover, in employing a fragmentation grenade, it becomes an excellent means for accompanying the infantry attack. And in a war of maneuver, the anti-tank gun, as a highly-maneuverable weapon on the battlefield, which does not fall behind the infantry, will render great service, suppressing the enemy's remaining machine guns in the defense…

Passive anti-tank means, such as anti-tank ditches, escarpments, minefields, and stone walls are the second main element of anti-tank defense. They essentially comprise modern anti-tank defense. After all, the power of the anti-tank gun is great when it is located behind an anti-tank obstacle, artificial or natural, and the strength of an anti-tank obstacle is only great when it is protected by the fire of an anti-tank gun. These two main elements must always work together, which is where their strength lies.

One anti-tank gun near Villenueva de la Canada during the Brunete operation[18] repelled three attacks by Republican tanks and knocked out ten tanks thanks to the fact that it was located behind a ditch inaccessible for tanks.

The viability of an anti-tank gun depends on how carefully its firing position has been chosen, outfitted and camouflaged. The gun should not give away its position ahead of time. It's necessary to take into account the fact that it can open its most destructive fire against tanks at a range of 600 meters and closer. The gun must have several reserve firing positions and fire communications with neighboring anti-tank guns.

The anti-tank gun crew's resilience, calm and valor have great significance. In the fighting around La Codonera (the fighting in the Alcaniz area in March 1938) the Republican 33rd Brigade was powerfully attacked by the Italians and supported by numerous tankettes. A single 45mm anti-tank gun, which was serviced by International soldiers, was thrown in to support the 33rd Brigade. Upon arriving at the attack sector, the quickly removed the gun from the truck and, having rolled it directly out to the road, met the tankette attack with accurate fire in the open. The Italian attack was literally beaten back in the course of a few minutes: four tankettes remained on the battlefield and were seized by the Republicans. To be sure, almost the entire gun crew was lightly wounded, but refused to be evacuated and remained in the line.

Rodion Yakovlevich also described the effectiveness of other anti-tank weapons:

The Spanish war put forward a new and very powerful and simple means of combating the tank—a gasoline-filled bottle. The enemy infantry showers our tanks with these bottles at point-blank range and the tank's motor area gets heated up and catches fire, often causing the fuel tank to explode. However, some brave tank crewmen continued to pilot their burning tank, pulled it back 200-250 meters to a shelter and put out the fire with sand and clothing. The mixture of gasoline with a small percentage of sulphuric acid, in the bottle bursts into flames when the bottles breaks and its contents come into contact with the phosphorous powder glued to the paper in which the bottle is wrapped. Such a bottle, in breaking against a tank's smooth armored surface, burns with a high flame for eight minutes. If the burning liquid does not penetrate into the tank, then the fire will go out within eight minutes and the tank remains unharmed. It's another matter if the bottle breaks against the ribbed surface of the T-26 tank's motor area and the liquid gets on the heated motor. In this case, it is difficult to fight the fire on the tank when it is not caused by a special mixture, but by pure gasoline,

---

18   Editor's note. The Battle of Brunete (6-25 July 1937) was a Republican offensive west of Madrid designed to relieve Nationalist pressure on the capital. Although the initial attack was somewhat successful, Nationalist counterattacks drove the Republican's back and they suffered heavy casualties.

although there were incidents when the crews took the tanks out of line and extinguished the fire on the T-26, when the motor area was not engulfed in flame. The conclusion is simple— we must make a tank so that any burning liquid on it does not penetrate inside the tank and ignite if from within.

The hand grenade and a bundle of grenades proved to have little effect against the tank and were almost never employed. However, the armored-piercing bullet in the hands of stalwart infantry is a very effective method of fighting tanks, and was always readily employed by the Republican forces against the insurgents' tanks.

Tankettes were not employed much in the Great Patriotic War, and thus armor-piercing bullets had no role to play. Special anti-tank rifles appeared, although their effectiveness left much to be desired.

Malinovskii warned:

The traditional scheme of attack (the infantry gathers along the jumping-off line, the tanks bypass it, break into the forward edge, suppress the enemy's firing points, and the infantry moves behind the tanks, etc.) completely failed to justify itself in the conditions of the Spanish theater of military activities—and the Republicans were cruelly punished around Brunete, Zaragoza and Teruel, and other places.

In conditions of a mountainous theater of war, the combat power of the tank decreases. The fascists learned to fire on our tanks pretty well with their field artillery, furnishing each brigade with 2-4 anti-tank guns, and created an anti-tank artillery reserve, which they maneuvered pretty well. As a result (the terrain difficulties, plus accurate artillery fire), the fascists would stop the Republican tanks. The infantry would halt with the tanks and the attack break down.

Here's an example: in January 1938 Campesino's[19] 46th Infantry Division, which before this had been training for half a year near Madrid, arrived at the Teruel front. The division, reinforced with four companies of tanks, attacked the Alto de los Salados height along a narrow front, which was defended by one battalion with four anti-tank guns and three batteries of field artillery. All of the division's attacks were beaten off by the fascists and the division lost 14 tanks knocked out and partially left for the fascists. Following the first unsuccessful attack, Campesino declared: "The infanty will not move without tanks." From this one can see how and what the Republican army's units trained for. Everything was built around the successful tank attack. The infantry did not know how to employ its artillery and guns, of which Campesino had a lot, and the simplest fence proved impregnable for the infantry. The infantry is not trained to overcome barbed wire obstacles without tanks. The Republicans' artillery is very poorly trained, has traditionally been apart from the infantry, and in battle was subordinated only to the senior artillery commanders.

Aviation in Republican Spain is a completely separate combat arm and is not trained to cooperate with the infantry, artillery or tanks.

The Spanish fighters performed and are performing miracles in air battle. Their bombers fly extremely well and bomb well very important targets at the front and in the fascists' immediate rear. But crews are completely untrained to cooperate with the ground.

---

19 Editor's note. El Campesino ("The Peasant") was the *nom de guerre* of Valentin Gonzalez (1904-83), who joined the communist party early on. He commanded a brigade and division during the civil war, but was forced to flee to the Soviet Union following the Republican collapse. He later spent time in a Soviet labor camp, before escaping. Gonzalez returned to Spain following Franco's death.

In the final battles along the Teruel front and from May 1938 the Republicans managed to work out something approaching tactical cooperation between aviation and the infantry. The aviation began to sometimes bomb and strafe the enemy's attacking or gathering infantry, and his artillery and tanks. However, the Republican air crews continue to take off on their combat missions using road maps that don't show terrain features and with the Republicans' and fascists' positions very crudely noted. The air units' headquarters are not even linked with such ground force commanders as corps commanders, not to mention division commanders. To be sure, there are representatives from the higher air command in the corps headquarters of the Levante Army, but these are captains and lieutenants who don't understand a thing about their job.

The Spanish infantry is not trained for interacting with aviation. Even senior officers, not to mention the soldiers, still cannot distinguish their planes from fascist ones, although excellent guidebooks have been published showing the planes' silhouettes. The alarm is sounded amongst the troops at the front and in the rear at the appearance of any aircraft. Then everyone, from soldier to commander, hides in a shelter or disguises himself in the field. And since aviation often appears over the battlefield (3-4 fascist sorties, plus 3-4 Republican sorties), then the entire day is spent in alarms.

Even the anti-aircraft units' special observers often poorly understand these silhouettes, while there are no observers at all in the infantry, artillery and tank units.

The officers do not want to take on this matter at all. Attempts to introduce recognition markers in the infantry for communicating with the aviation were unsuccessful. The infantry would lay them out at the appearance of any aircraft, which attracted the fascist aviation.The Republican aviation, flying only at high altitudes, often did not see the markers.

Such a lack of troop training in the Republican army is sorely felt in combat actions. The Republican infantry does not attack without tanks. Moreover, it often does not attack even when the tanks, at the cost of heavy losses, reach the fascists' forward edge. The tanks cannot suppress all the machine guns located in special nests, while the infantry, upon encountering fire, lies down once again.

The infantry completely fails to maneuver in small subunits on the battlefield. There's no cooperation between fire and movement. The offensive tactics are very primitive. The infantry either rises up and moves forward in combat formations that remind one of a mob, or the entire combat formation hits the ground. Comparatively satisfactory cooperation within the infantry is sometimes achieved in training, but almost never in battle, which can be explained not only by the low level of the commanders' training, but also by very poor discipline. The heroism of individual soldiers can by no means always influence the course of the fighting.

Thus the Republicans, having overestimated the importance of tanks in conditions of a theater where they are not very useful, underestimated the importance of artillery and were unable to bring together the two combat arms closest to each other—the infantry and artillery.

Unfortunately, these same shortcomings, which were characteristic of the Spanish Republican army, manifested themselves to an even greater degree in the years of the Great Patriotic War. Soviet commanders were unable to intelligently organize the interaction of the infantry, artillery, tanks, and aviation, and the subunits, consisting overwhelmingly of untrained recruits, failed to learn how to maneuver on the battlefield and went into the attack in dense combat formations, which reminded one of a mob and which led to heavy losses.

Malinovskii gave credit to the enemy, against which the Spanish Republicans could oppose only a hastly formed militia:

The insurgent army, headed by cadre officers, 70-80 percent of which ended up on the insurgents' side, immediately began its triumphant progress through the country, while regular Moroccan units and the Foreign Legion from Spanish Morocco also appeared in the arena.

This organized and fearsome force got as far as Madrid itself, sowing fear and panic within the ranks of the hastily organized columns that the Republic managed to put forth for an open battle. The attempts by the Republican command to halt the insurgents' offensive with counterblows were unsuccessful. A stubborn struggle ensued along the immediate approaches to Madrid, which ended on 6 November with a powerful attack by the insurgents directly on Madrid. The fascists planned to capture the Spanish capital on the anniversary of the October Revolution. However, against all expectations, the Republican army held.

Malinovskii regarded the anarchists among the Republican commanders worst of all: "The most repulsive group of commanders is the anarchist group, which still maintains its weak authority among the anarchist units through outright demagoguery. This group is not large, but very poisonous."

He noted the low level of discipline in the Spanish Republican army:

Discipline has enormous significance for the army's combat effectiveness—not outwardly expressed, but profound internal discipline, which is based on the profound consciousness of one's duty and the struggle's clear goals, discipline that is supported by both measures of persuasion and education, as well as by measures of compulsion.

It is discipline that is the Republican army's Achilles heel. The command element does not feel responsibility and no one holds it to account; it is not judged by military tribunal, and if it is judged, then it is always excused. If an officer abandons his platoon, company or battalion in battalion and deserts it, he is not punished for his crime. Quite the opposite! There have been striking cases when an officer who has run away in battle has been promoted to a higher rank and appointed to a higher position. There are a lot of examples of this: the commander of the 17th Brigade, Madronero, who fled from the field, was almost immediately promoted from major to lieutenant colonel and appointed to command a division.

The lack of responsibility, which is encouraged by traitors of all stripes, who have wormed their way into the Republic's state and military apparatus, weakens the army's combat power. As a result of this, the commanders abandon their subunits and units to their fate at the first artillery bombardment or bombing raid by the enemy. The remaining commander-less soldiers, after having put up some resistance, abandon the field at the first treasonous shout of "We're being outflanked!" after their commanders. And these are basically good soldiers. However, having been deprived of their commander, they throw down their weapons and run, run, run in panic until they get tired, and then they come upon trucks and frighten the drivers into taking them to the rear. This is a typical picture of flight for the anarchists, confederalists and socialist or simply non-party units of the Republican army. Almost the entire Aragon front shamefully ran away during the latest operation, which concluded with such a major defeat for the Republican forces.

Quite the opposite, Rodion Yakovlevich emphasized, iron discipline reigns in Franco's army:

Franco maintains the cruelest discipline in his army by any means. The manifestation of cowardice, for either an officer or soldier, is punishable by death on the spot. No one has the right to abandon a defensive line without an order, and those who waver and fall back are shot on the spot. Such discipline is maintained with extreme violence, terrorizing any one who thinks differently, while a great deal of demagougic work is waged, including in the press.

It is worth noting that the officers of the Spanish Falange[20] live and eat together with their soldiers and receive almost the same salary as they do; they often serve their soldiers as an example of self sacrifice and courage. The entire officer corps feels this iron discipline on themselves and no one will ever be able to avoid responsibility and punishment for crimes in battle. The officer whose platoon or company runs from the field is the first to be shot. Thus while he is alive he will not permit anyone to leave the fight and will himself shoot the first man to waver. This is how corporals and sergeants behave who want to become officers guarantee themselves a prosperous life later on, after the war. This is what discipline in the insurgents' army rests upon.

The Republicans don't know of a single case when they easily captured any kind of position, hill or inhabited locale from the fascists. They took Kichorna and Belchite and many other villages from the fascists, but these places were defended by the fascists with great stubbornness. I never saw more stubbornness in defense, although I had occasion to take part in the World War of 1914-1918 and fight all this time against the Germans who, as is known, showed the greatest stubbornness in the defense.

The insurgents are much weaker in the offensive. Given the Republicans' stubborn defense (this also happened sometimes); the enemy quickly breaks himself against the defense more quickly than the Republicans in such a case.

In general and overall, one must admit that the insurgents have managed to retain a high degree of combat effectiveness in their army, which greatly exceeds the Republican army's combat capability...

One must suppose that the cruelty of the Franco regime shields, to a certain degree, his army against treason, espionage and demoralization, which are eating up the Republicans' armed forces...

One could say that the fascists have a good and modern air force and artillery, good anti-aircraft artillery, a large number of sapper units, a disciplined but poorly trained infantry, and unsatisfactory tanks.

To judge from combat activities, their troops' training is based on the complete cooperation between infantry, aviation and artillery, with the maximum employment of aviation and artillery.

In these conditions, it was not possible to realize the Republican forces' numerical superiority, even with the assistance of Soviet advisers and Soviet munitions and combat equipment, as well as the help of the International brigades.

Malinovskii maintained that:

The insurgents' armaments also greatly exceed those of the Republican army. For example, they have a lot of mortars—no less than four per battalion, plus the presence of special mortar subunits, which are attached to the divisions launching the main attack. For example, in January 1938, during the taking of the area of the extremely important heights of Alba de los Salados, El Muleton and Sierra Gorda), the fascists concentrated more than 100 mortars and inflicted through their fire heavy losses on the 39th, 35th and 68th infantry divisions.

However, not everything was so dark. Malinovskii cited examples of stalwart behavior and heroism by individual units of the Republican forces, commanded, as a rule, by communists:

---

20   Editor's note. The Falange was a semi-fascist organization founded in 1933 by Jose Antonio Primo de Rivera (1903-36). The movement was later coopted by Franco's more traditional forces.

After all, not everyone ran away! There were and are an entire series of great units, which fought and are fighting heroically—units lead by the heroic Spanish Communist Party, units led by Lister, Francisco Galan, Modesto, Duran, Campesino, Del Barrio, Tagueni, Toral, Cristobal, Vega, Santiago, and an entire series of other unknown and wonderful soldiers, commanders and commissar-communists. These units have waged a stubborn and unequal struggle, often against a numerically superior enemy. And only thanks to them does Republican Spain still continue to exist and struggle. Del Barrio's 27th Division, Toral's 70th Division fought just as stubbornly, as did Vega's 34th Division, which in the course of three days fought in almost complete encirclement in the area of Minas de Segura and La Os de la Fecha and which had been treasonously abandoned on both flanks by anarchist units on the Aragon front. Full of heroism are the battles of Tagueni's 3rd Division, Lister's 11th Division and the 45th International Division in the area of Alcaniz and Caspe.

But could they really have stopped the major fascist offensie on Catalonia? No, they could not. They suffered heavy losses and overexerted themselves in daily 15-20 hour stubborn battles against the enemy's great superiority in aviation and artillery. They did not reinforce them and relieve them with fresh units. They fell back and, driven to exhaustion, sometimes abandoned good positions, mountain passes, defiles, and previously prepared defensive lines without a fight. Can one really say that they have a low combat effectiveness? No! These are heroic and highly capable combat units, but there's a limit to everything. These fine units were pushed to the limit, which the spies and traitors that have wormed their way into the higher military staffs and headquarters had a hand in.

Rodion Yakovlevich pointed out the deleterious influence of the inter-party struggle within the Popular Front[21] on the course of combat operations:

The political struggle between the parties of the Popular Front was inevitably reflected and is reflected in the army's development. The anarchists and counterrevolutionary elements came out openly against the creation of a unified regular army and undermined its combat capability as best they could. Part of the anarchists began to instill discipline in the army and create regular units for the hidden goal of later employing them in a future struggle for state power. Another part of the anarchists continues to believe that the instillation of discipline in the army is outright treason to the principles of anarchism and continues to work to demoralize the army. An enormous band of spies, saboteurs, and open and hidden fascists, who are carrying out their foul work, have found a refuge among the anarchists and the "National Confederation of Labor," taking advantage of the weakness of the Republican state apparatus and its inability to carry out decisive actions. It is precisely in this that lies the reason for an entire series of failures on the front and and Republican army's latest major defeat on the Eastern front.

The striking lack of initiative among many of the Republican army's command elements, enables the enemy, given his shortage of human resources, to flexibly maneuver battalions, brigades and divisions, enabling them to rest and reorganize, and not even in the rear, but along passive sectors of the front.

The Republicans can't pull this off. Poor discipline and the historically evolved friendship of the battalion and brigade commanders with their senior commanders almost exclude

---

21   Editor's note. The Popular Front was a left-wing electoral coalition that won the parliamentary elections in Spain in 1936. The Front formed a government which waged the civil war until its defeat in 1939. The coalition was notorious for its infighting and occasional violence between members.

maneuver by battalions and brigades outside their divisions. For example, during the difficult April days in 1938 the Levante Army had prepared an offensive operation in the Terriente—Albarracin area. For this purpose, the 39th Infantry Division's (this communist division's best brigade, under the command of brigade commander Ivon, a communist) and the 68th Infantry Division's 218th Brigade were temporarily merged into Cartona's 64th Infantry Division. Both of these brigades, operating within a foreign division, basically foiled this operation, because they operated very sluggishly. The fascists, who disposed of six battalions against 16 and four batteries against 12 (plus 40 fascist planes), held their positions, giving up only one village—Masegoso and a height by the same name.

The training of the infantry, artillery and artillery of the Republicans and fascists is not very high and approximately equal. However, the insurgents' command element comes out ahead of the Republicans' in terms of initiative and discipline.

The belligerent sides' training of the combat arms to cooperate is completely dissimilar. Among the Republicans the troops' combat training was carried out independently, according to combat arms, but rarely in cooperation between the infantry and tanks. The officers of the Republican militia, who lack sufficient knowledge and experience, trained the infantry to exclusively cooperate with tanks, forgetting about cooperation with the other combat arms, while the the artillery's role was negated in the extreme. Aviation was not employed in exercises with the infantry and tanks.

Reserve units, where the training and instruction of mobilized contingents would be carried out, were not created in the Republican army. All of those mobilized are immediately dispatched to the armies, and from there to the corps and then to the divisions and brigades occupying positions. There are no reserve weapons in the brigades. There are not enough command personnel to go around for the established battalions. The recruits hang around for months in the brigades' rear, with no kind of training and gradually, one after the other, cover the active battalions' losses. During a withdrawal they turn into an unarmed panic-stricken mob, carrying along the armed units with them.

Even in a nightmare, Rodion Yakovlevich could not imagine that very soon, during the Great Patriotic War, the dreary experience of the Spanish Republicans would be several times worse in the Red Army: the training of recruits would practically cease and they would begin to conscript people from the liberated territories directly into the units and almost immediately throw them into the fighting unarmed and unclothed.

Rodion Yakovlevich noted in particular "the national character of the Spanish people—heroic and revolutionary. The people's combat qualities are striking: this is a people, hardy to an extreme degree, and modest in its demands, whose sincerity sometimes borders on naivete. This quality makes the work of spies easier."

Many officers among the Republican troops did not manifest the necessary concern for their troops. Malinovskii sadly noted:

The officers, particularly in the higher military staffs and headquarters, don't concern themselves much how the soldiers live, where they sleep and what they need.

The soldiers met the winter of 1938 not only in somewhat broken terrain, but in high mountain areas, not having warm clothing, blankets, gloves and the most elementary thing—shoes. The soldiers froze and walked through the snow and mud in canvas slippers, while at the same time the stores in all the towns were groaning under the weight of woolen and warm goods, cloth, jackets, blankets, and leather shoes—and all of this at cheap prices. Only the great patience, habitual need and uncomplaining nature of the Spanish people kept the soldiers from cleaning out the stores with shoes and warm jackets. All the army's lower levels and several front staffs insistently and ahead of time warned about this shortage, while the central supply apparatuses and the government kept on gathering and gathering its strength to disburse funds for meeting the army's urgent needs. The army is sitting without tobacco and the soldiers smoke wooden leaves and cabbage, and it's a holiday for the soldiers when they come across a few cigarettes. But after all, this weakens the army's combat capability.

He also noted:

… the absence of initiative among the command, the lack of flexibility at all levels, the lack of exactingness in carrying out combat orders. The absence of combat experience among the masses, which have not fought in a long time, especially among the command element, makes the situation worse.

And finally, the main thing is the absence of mutual assistance among the units: if a platoon or a company, a battalion or even a brigade is half surrounded, they will never rescue this unit from its misfortune; it will either surrender or perish, but they will not come to help it—there has never been one such incident. A striking example of this is the destruction of one of the 92nd Brigade's battalions in the La Rambla area, which had gotten into the enemy rear and there encircled during the operation near Segura de los Banos. Another example is the 43rd Division's isolated struggle near the French border.

Things are otherwise with the enemy: a half-encircled battalion of African riflemen near Costa de la Reina in September 1937 stubbornly fought for two days and was relieved by newly-arrived reserves. All of Franco's fierce counterattacks from Couda to Cocund during the encirclement of Teruel by the Republicans were dictated by the decisive wish to liberate the units besieged in Teruel, and it's not surprising that they fought so stubbornly in encirclement for almost an entire month. And the famous Alcazar de Toledo, which withstood the two-month encirclement of its units, while holding out to meet friendly forces! All of these examples are of another order and exert a colossal influence on the combat capability of the enemy's army.

Malinovskii highly rated the role of the International Brigades in the Spanish war:

The 11th International Brigade, whose core consisted of Germans, was the first one formed. It took part in the heaviest fighting around Madrid and performed miracles of bravery and heroism. The Thalmann[22] Brigade covered itself with eternal glory. One may forthrightly say that the brigade played a decisive role in the defense of Madrid. Its history is a chain of glorious feats of the greatest heroism, persistence and self-sacrifice.

After it, the 12th, 13th, 14th, and 15th international brigades and, recently, another one— the 129th International Brigade, were formed. All of these are wonderful combat units of the Republican army. The fascists have more than once experienced their strength and persistence. In essence, the fascists suffered a defeat on the Jarama only thanks to the international brigades. Franco smashed up his best units and the Foreign Legion against them. Also, along the Guadalajara Italian fascism smashed its teeth, having gotten into a fight with the Italian internationalists and Garabaldists and also suffered a defeat thanks to the heroism of the 11th

---

22 Editor's note. Ernst Thalmann (1886-1944) joined the German Social Democratic Party and later fought in the First World War. He was one of the founding members of the German Communist Party and later became its chairman. The Nazis arrested him in 1933 and he spent the rest of his life in a concentration camp. Thalmann was later executed.

and 12th international brigades. One can say outright: had international assistance for the workers had not arrived in time, fascism would have established its authority in Spain as early as the beginning of 1937. Both friends and enemies recognized this.

Malinovskii described in detail how the Frankists organize their attacks:

There tanks do not play a significant role in either the offensive or defensive. The fascists carried out an entire series of operations without tanks or with their minimal employment.
    The outline of their combat arms cooperation in the offensive is very simple and unvarying:

1. The detailed reconnaissance of the defensive zone from the air and ground,
2. The lengthy exhaustion of the defense's strength through aerial bombardment and artillery fire,

This exhaustion continues, depending on the steadfastness of individual Republican units—from one day (the operation near Alfambra) to up to five days (the operation to seize Teruel). Their aviation bombs strongholds in the Republican positions that stand out and operates uninterruptedly in small groups of 3-9 planes at altitudes of 800-1,200 meters throughout the daylight hours. The artillery indicates the targets with its fire and then the artillery layers its fire on the same targets, or shifts it to other targets.

Such a working over of the forward edge of the defense and the nearby depth continues 6-8 hours, usually from 0800 to 1400-1600, after which the fascist aviataion operating in this area (30 to 200 planes) once again appears over the field. Part of the bombers bomb the forward edge again, while the remainder bombed the areas of the Republicans' artillery positions and a small part penetrates into the immediate rear and bombs road junctions, stations and major inhabited locales, etc. Having bombed their targets, the bombers do not leave, but continue to circle over their targets, particularly over the areas of the Republicans' artillery positions, in order to keep the gun crews in their shelters. Assault aircraft (always just "Fiats"[23]) dive behind the bombers in groups of 3-9 planes. They form in a circle (carousel) at a distance of 100-200 meters from each other, and each such group begins to dive on its target in consecutive attempts. Depending on the number of targets, there may be 3-12 such diving groups along an attack front of 6-12 kilometers.

Such dive bombing produces an extreme morale effect on the Republican units and each soldier literally attempts to crawl into the earth. Psychologically, the soldiers do not suffer during the plane's descent and when he is shooting, but when he pulls out of the dive and the roar of the motors is at its loudest.

At the same time, other groups of assault aircraft are marauding in the immediate rear, shooting up the roads, troop concentrations and transport and not turning up their nose at hunting individual vehicles and motorcycles. At the same time, the fascists' artillery fires with full force on the targets not attacked by the aviation.

It is precisely at this moment that the infantry begins the attack at a distance of 800-1,200 meters. In nine months not once did the enemy infantry come out at night to occupy jumping-off positions for the attack, in order to attack during the day.

---

23   Editor's note. This may refer to the Fiat CR.32, an Italian fighter plane that saw service in the Spanish Civil War and World War II. This model had a crew of one and a top speed of 360 kilometers per hour. This model was armed with two 7.7mm or one 12.7mm machine guns and could carry up to 100 kilograms of bombs.

If the fascist infantry, having begun the offensive, encounters heavy fire from the Republicans' artillery and machine guns, the matter rarely gets as far as the attack. The attack is halted and from the morning of the following day the preparation for the attack begins from scratch.

The Republicans' most steadfast units have withstood 3-4 days of such a preparation. Unreliable units, with weak discipline (especially the Anarchists) have run away on the first day.

More often, the fascist infantry has occupied positions abandoned by the Republicans without a fight, and scouts with the fascist flag appeared there first, and then a half-organized mob of entire companies and battalions went in.

When the fascists took risks and attempted to crush the Republicans' defense through an infantry-tank attack, without the consecutive carrying out of the preparation described above, they suffered extremely heavy personnel losses and the attack was never successful. This was the case in December near Teruel, when four fascist divisions (81st, 82nd, 33rd, and 85th) smashed themselves against Lister's 11th Division and Cartona's 64th Division. And only in February did Franco, having gathered all his aviation and artillery near Teruel, achieve success, although the Republicans' best units fought against him.

In Malinovskii's opinion, "The insurgents would not have remained in power, if they had but once had inflicted upon them such a major defeat such as the Republicans suffered around Malaga, the north and in Catalonia. Franco's regime would have immediately been shaken to its foundations, but the tragedy is that the Republican army is not strong enough to launch such an attack on the enemy. Perhaps the future will yet show this." However, to judge by the overall tone of the report, which is critical of the Republican army, one feels that Rodion Yakovlevich did not believe in victory, particularly after Soviet military advisers and specialists and the soldiers of the international brigades were withdrawn from Spain.

Malinovskii maintained:

Stone is what has a great effect on the troops' activities. Almost the entire surface of Spain is covered by stone. They gather it in bunches while clearing fields and employ it to build stone walls along the fields. Rocks are used for building the peasants' homes and other structures, corrals for livestock and fences, etc. As a result of the fact that Spain's population of 21 million lives in villages, and there are almost 8,000 villages with a population of less than 3,000, and also that individual farmsteads are scattered throughout Spain, practically the entire territory of the country is covered with small inhabited locales and farmsteads made of stone.

These structures can well withstand fire from field artillery, small-caliber and tank artillery, and are completely invulnerable to incendiary bombs and shells. They represent real forts for defense, while the larger villages are small fortresses. The fascists take good advantage of them for stubborn defense, both against the Republicans' infantry and against their tanks.

Besides this, stones are used for building terraces along the slopes of the mountains. The peasants very stubbornly take back from the mountains and stones every bit of arable land (45 percent of Spain is unsuited for agriculture). Thus all the slopes of the mountains are covered with terraces that appear to be steps, with the steps one meter or higher, which are completely impassable for tanks. In those places where the soil isn't rocky and not too broken up, there is another obstacle: there are downpours in Spain and the rapid flows of water have cut it up with deep ravines with steep sides, which serve as an excellent shelter for the infantry against aviation and artillery fire and are at the same time insuperable obstacles for tanks.

As regards roads, one may consider Spain to be a rich country. There are almost no unpaved roads there and even the worst country roads are paved with stone and quite accessible for auto transportation. Thus auto transportation has completely squeezed the horse out of the army; the mule (chiefly) and the horse are employed almost exclusively as beasts of burden.

> Spanish roads are very good in quality; they are paved with bricks or asphalt or have a high-quality gravel cover with a wide thoroughfare."

It's not by accident that after Spain Malinovskii began to be considered a specialist in mountain warfare.

According to the experience of the Spanish war, Malinovskii reached the conclusion that

> The infantry's combat activities, which unfolded in Spain, showed that the infantry continues to remain the chief combat arm, which, supported by the other combat arms, decides the outcome of battles and, in the final analysis, the outcome of the war. It is the most stable and stalwart but, at the same time, fragile combat arm, although modern equipment will of course find employment in a future war on a large scale.

He stressed that:

> One can very easily and rapidly destroy infantry, which possesses all of the fine qualities—political-moral condition, modern weaponry and excellent fire and tactical training. Many of our people in Spain observed (and many participated themselves) in an infantry attack on the enemy defense, and then stated: "What awful infantry, even with Lister's and Campesino's troops! You can knock yourself out, but they won't attack! There's not way you can get them to attack! Our Soviet infantry would show then how to attack!"
>
> A profound and dangerous error. Our excellent infantry would have attacked an unsuppressed machine gun once, and then attacked a second time, but not a third. One should understand what a great crime it is to fling infantry against unsuppressed machine guns. This means to exterminate it at the beginning of the battle. A machine gun is a machine for exterminating living beings and it will exterminate and exterminate them, no matter how many people they put up against it. One should understand this once and for all. This is why the Republican infantry, even the best—Lister's and Campesino's—did not attack. One should never upbraid the infantry for not attacking. One should establish the reasons it does not attack and remove them, or, at least weaken the influence of these reasons as much as one can.
>
> The machine gun is a terrible weapon. It seems to me that many people have forgotten its role in the World War and Civil wars, and the Spanish war has reminded them. One must treat the light machine gun, and particularly the heavy machine gun, with the greatest respect. You cannot always suppress it with rifle and machine gun fire, as this can only be done by small-caliber artillery, if you fire accurately on the embrasure of the machine gun nest. You can suppress it with field artillery (you don't need a lot of artillery for this, just more skill), and with tanks and aerial bombardment. To be sure, this is difficult and takes effort, but it is necessary; otherwise the attacking infantry will suffer heavy losses, as there are generally a lot of machine guns in the defensive.
>
> One must once again imagine the prospect of a future war, when the breakthrough of the defense will become, just as it was for the attacker in the World War, an incredibly difficult problem, even given the attacker's tanks and aviation.
>
> One should renounce those flighty field exercises, where machine guns in the defensive were quickly suppressed in a blaze of rapidity and maneuverability, and where defensive zones were rapidly broken through. For two dozen machine guns emplaced behind a small but swampy and inaccessible creek may inflict a sobering and fatal blow to all of these planned successes. All of the infantry's planned hourly rates of advance will be overturned. It's necessary to teach our infantry the serious, complex and extremely stubborn offensive engagement

and the breakthrough of the enemy's defense in complex and skillfull interaction with the other combat arms.

Unfortunately, they paid no attention to his warnings. Too often during the Great Patriotic War Soviet infantry attacked the enemy's unsuppressed machine guns and artillery head on and suffered colossal losses.

Rodion Yakovlevich explained very sensibly in what direction infantry weaponry will evolve:

It wouldn't hurt us to consider that sooner or later the bayonet with the rifle will have to be removed, as it almost never comes to that in the modern engagement, while it interferes a lot: the chief of these is that the loss of the bayonet completely changes the rifle's engagement. We should teach the infantry to fire rapidly, but accurately. To not measure fire in seconds, but in fractions of seconds, is nothing but a useless expenditure of shells, as it's not easy to bring them up during the engagement. The modern engagement excludes haste in firing, but requires unhurried but accurate fire at short distances of 500 yards or closer. This is where accurate fire is needed, and at distances of 300 meters and closer. The fact that the rifling on the sight is for 2,000 yards cannot be justified. We should pave the way for the introduction of the short automatic rifle, first by about 20 percent, and then maybe the war will indicate 100 percent, but the production of this rifle should be organized and it employed now. We should have snipers in each section, always with the best weaponry and an optical sight, for firing at 1,000 meters or closer…

Our Maksim machine gun proved to be the best machine gun out of all the systems in the world and received general recognition. The German or any other Maksim is much inferior to ours. Its best distance for firing is no more than 1,200 yards and the most deadly and destructive strength of heavy machine gun fire begins at 1,000 and closer.

We should give our unconditional preference to firing over open sights and renounce firing from closed positions or against a closed target with machine gun batteries, which is the most wasteful means of expending ammunition and which yields a completely insignificant effect. In the same way, one should not resort, unless absolutely necessary, to firing from machine guns at distances over 1,500 meters and, all the more, more than 2,000 meters. The effectiveness of fire with an increase in distance declines so much that it's best to renounce it altogether and not expend so much ammunition and labor on training machine gunners in long-range fire.

It's extremely important to supply heavy machine guns with optical sights and to supply them with no less than 20 percent of tracer bullets, which greatly increase the effectiveness of their fire.

At the same time, he pointed out the good training of the enemy's anti-aircraft artillery: "The enemy's anti-aircraft units, predominantly German, are trained better than the Republican ones, have better equipment and very good high-explosive shells. The fascist artillery's accuracy is very high. From the second burst they shift to hitting the target and keep planes under accurate fire to the extent of their range. They wage defensive fire well in a particular zone."

Malinovskii was also concerned about reinforcement equipment for the infantry:

…it's extremely important to furnish the infantry with an 80-100mm mortar with a range of 2-3 kilometers, while keeping it light and maneuverable (like the 81mm "Stokes"[24] mortar). A rifle battalion should have no less than 3-4 of these mortars; that is, a mortar platoon.

---

24   Editor's note. Malinovskii is referring to the 81mm mortar designed by Wilfred Stokes (1860-1927) in 1915.

The battalion should also have a platoon of anti-tank artillery, 2-4 45mm guns; it will carry out tasks of accompanying the infantry in the attack, for which it must have 50 percent fragmentation shells. The infantry should have a heavy-caliber 12-20mm anti-aircraft machine gun with a tracer, armor-piercing bullet-shell; three such machine guns per battalion.

As regards the activities of the armored forces, Malinovskii highly rated the actions of Soviet crews and those of the Republican tank forces very low:

Our crews… manifested magnificent examples of combat work, while the Spanish crews, as a result of their low technical and tactical training, were afraid of getting involved in decisive fighting, which didn't save them from losses and yielded low combat results.

One may describe the actions of tanks with Spanish crews in the following manner. The attack is carried out at a very low speed, no more than 5-6 kilometers per hour, and often even slower. The attack against the enemy is carried out head-on. Upon discovering an anti-tank gun, the tanks halt and begin to fire; the field of view from the tank is poor and the fire of little effect. Meanwhile, the gun knocks them out in turn. The tanks suffer losses; the knocked-out tanks remain on the battlefield, while the surviving ones withdraw.

Repeat attacks are carried out differently. The tanks approach to a distance of 600-800 meters and halt in a shelter in such a manner that the enemy can only see the turret. The tank's gun, firing on the enemy's trenches, begins the so-called "fire attack": it rapidly exhausts its ammunition supply and the tanks withdraw from the battlefield and go to the rear for about 2-3 hours for refueling. Then they come on again, repeat the "fire attack," and once again leave to refuel, while the infantry continues lying down, waiting for the tanks to reach the enemy trenches and suppress the machine guns.

There were instances when 1-2 tanks with heroic crews reached as far as the enemy trenches and engaged them in single combat, while the infantry rose to the attack and success was achieved, although this happened extremely rarely. It ended otherwise in the majority of cases: they peppered the tanks with bottles of gas; the crews perished in the tank, or, were shot at point-blank range while leaping out of their tank. The remaining tanks and infantry observed this picture, without even thinking of supporting the attack by these brave men. Such was the usual picture of a tank attack with Spanish crews, without cooperation with the artillery and infantry, the result of which was heavy losses in tanks and the crews' hatred for their own infantry and artillery.

The pernicious methods of the tanks' "fire attack" penetrated into our tank subunits. There were incidents when our crews operated according to Spanish methods, although this was mostly an exception. There were cases when entire tank companies with our crews waited for the artillery to completely suppress the anti-tank guns without beginning their attack, and if the Republicans' artillery was unable to carry out this task, then the tanks would not emerge for the attack. We must understand that artillery alone (even in large numbers) is unable to destroy all the anti-tank guns in the enemy's defense, just as the tanks will not be able to suppress everything by themselves. Only the combination of the artillery's actions (even in small numbers) with those of the tanks will ensure the success of the tank attack. This is axiomatic.

In general, tanks with our crews operated well, with vigor and courage. They would close to a favorable distance, would halt and open a heavy fire against the enemy's defense for a short time. Under the cover of this fire, part of the tanks would move further and fire point blank on the embrasures of the anti-tank guns' nests, would suppress them, while the remaining tanks would hurl themselves into the attack against the trenches. And if the infantry followed behind the tanks into the attack, the attack was usually successful and it seized the enemy's trenches and broke through his defensive lines. Tanks with our crews also displayed magnificent examples of counterattacking the attacking enemy. After all, the single force holding off the insurgents' offensive around Madrid in the autumn of 1936 was our tank company.

Our crews mainly consist of excellent tank men who take their vehicles wherever they want. They have more than once literally saved the Republican army from a catastrophic defeat. The Spanish command knows this and often even abuses this, with our connivance. The sad story of the fighting around Fuentes de Ebro serves as a striking example of this, where almost 50 percent of our BT[25] tanks with our crews was knocked out and perished. This defeat of our tank crews was not justified by anything, and our wonderful tank drivers and turret and vehicle commanders were not guilty of anything, while those of our people were guilty who gave their consent to such an insane and poorly prepared tank attack.

There's nothing surprising here. After all, Soviet crews consisted entirely of professional tank men, as a rule, of officer rank, while the Spanish crews consisted of poorly trained recruits. Malinovskii did not know that in the Great Patriotic War, and in the Finnish War before that, Soviet tank crews, the majority of which had gotten into their tanks for the first time before the attack, reminded the Republicans' tank crews to a much greater degree. This is why Soviet tank losses were so great.

Rodion Yakovlevich warned: "One should not send a tank deep into the rear; that is, 15-20 kilometers, for they will be destroyed or will remain there without fuel and ammunition, and they will not always be able to get out and, upon encountering ten anti-tank guns and blown-up bridges, fore and aft, will be shot up."

Rodion Yakovlevich rated the Frankists' tanks very low:

The fascists' tank units chiefly consist of tankettes and are poorly trained. The best equipment in the enemy's tank units are tanks captured from the Republicans. On the battlefield the fascists' tankettes and tanks are very cautious, even cowardly and never push the attack to a conclusion given the presence of anti-tank artillery with the Republicans. Their tanks never break away from their infantry and always cooperate with their artillery. The enemy's tanks are brave to an impudent degree in pursuing the Republicans' retreating infantry and pull far away from their infantry, although always accompanied by low-caliber light artillery.

As regards the combat employment of aviation, Malinovskii noted:

The Republican aviation acquired enormous combat experience during the war and one may say that it unconditionally ruled the sky before the attack on Segovia in May 1937. Air superiority was chiefly maintained by the I-15[26] and I-16[27] fighters and the SB.[28] Beginning in

---

25 Editor's note. The BT (*bystrokhodnyi tank*) was the name of an entire series of light tanks produced in the Soviet Union during 1932-45. The popular BT-5 model weighed 11.5 tons and had a crew of three. It was armed with a 45mm gun and a 7.62mm machine gun.

26 Editor's note. The I-15 was a biplane fighter produced in the Soviet Union during 1934-37. One model had a maximum speed of 350 kilometers per hour. It had four 7.62mm and two 12.7mm machine guns and could carry up to 100 kilograms of bombs.

27 Editor's note. The I-16 was a monoplane fighter produced in the Soviet Union during 1934-42. It had a maximum speed of 525 kilometers per hour. It had two 7.62mm machine guns and two 20mm cannons and could carry up to 500 kilograms of bombs.

28 Editor's note. The Tupolev ANT-40 (*skorostnoi bombardirovshchik*) was a two-engine bomber produced in the Soviet Union during 1936-41. One model had a crew of three, a maximum speed of 450 kilometers per hour and a maximum range of 2,300 kilometers. It was armed with four 7.62mm machine guns and could

May 1937, the enemy achieved an almost two-to-one numerical superiority in the air: he received a large number of "Fiat" fighters, which withstand air battles well with our fighters, while we received a large number of RZ light bombers[29] ("erzety"), very slow planes which are extremely vulnerable to the enemy's fighters and requiring a large degree of fighter cover. As a result, the air superiority passed to the enemy.

Rodion Yakovlevich also pointed to the appearance of fast "Messerschmitts"[30] among the enemy:

Of the enemy's fighters, the best machine is the "Messerschmitt," which has a high-altitude motor, good armament and possesses great maneuverability at high altitudes (4,000 meters and higher). It is inferior in maneuverability to the Republican fighters at lesser altitudes. As a rule, the "Messerschmitts" fly at high altitudes, in small groups or singly. They rarely get into fights with large numbers of Republican fighters and love to suddenly throw themselves on single planes that have become separated. They really love to hunt for bombers, particularly if the latters' cover has been poorly organized.

For example, during the fascists' offensive in the Alfambra area in February 1938, a squadron of Republican bombers took off to bomb Perales del Alfambra from an airfield not far from Barcelona, while another squadron of Republican fighters was supposed to take off from the Barracas airfield to cover them. When ten Republican bombers had already appeared over Valbona, the Republican fighters were just taking off from the Barracas airfield, five minutes late. Eight "Messerschmitts" attacked the Republican bombers in a sharp dive from a great height and shot down four within less than a minute, putting the remainder into disorderly flight. Within a few minutes, eight Republican fighters attacked the "Messerschmitts" and shot down four vehicles, without losing a single plane. Had the Republican fighters not been late, the fascist planes would not have risked attacking the bombers.

Individual training among the fascists is more even than among the Republicans, among whom there are a lot of heroes and skilled pilots, but who have far more poorly trained pilots, with little flight time, particularly at high altitudes. A survey of captured German and Italian fliers reveals that each of them has no less than 40 hours of flying time (the Republican pilots have five hours). It's also known from prisoner testimony that combat training for German pilots is carried out in conditions close to combat: flights from unprepared field airfields, sorties and landings in groups, against the wind, with the wind, and at different angles to the wind. Bombers, in particular, fly in paired crews, exploiting their equipment to the fullest.

In his words, "The enemy's aviation has won air superiority and is over the target for the greater part of the day during major operations. The Republican aviation appeared in the air for a short time only to drop its bombs and leave." Malinovskii pointed out that "Our I-15 fights well and shoots down a lot of enemy planes, although it is slower than the enemy's 'Fiats' and 'Messerschmitts,' although it maneuvers better. The I-16 is faster than the 'Fiat' and is not inferior

---

carry up to 600 kilograms of bombs.

29   Editor's note. The RZ was a Soviet bomber biplane which first appeared in 1935. One model carried a crew of two men and was armed with three 7.62mm machine guns. This aircraft could also carry up to 400 kilograms of bombs.

30   Editor's note. This is probably a reference to the Messerschmitt Bf-109 single-seat fighter model, which was produced in Germany during 1936-45. One model had a maximum speed of 640 kilometers per hour. This model was armed with two 13mm machine guns, one 20-mm and one 30mm cannons. This model could also carry up to 250 kilograms of bombs.

in armament and maneuverability and possesses almost all of the qualities of the newest German fighter, the 'Messerschmitt,' and is even superior in maneuver.

However, he had a poor opinion of the SB bomber:

Our SB has a lot of shortcomings. It is very vulnerable to the enemy's fighters and his anti-aircraft artillery. Sufficient to say that a group of SBs (22 planes) was met by a group of German 'Messerschmitt' fighters while carrying out a combat mission on 7 February 1938, and met their attack. Our SBs quickly lost four planes, while the remained managed to escape. To be sure, this happened because a squadron of I-16s, under the command of Senior Lieutenant Kivotchenko, turned back in a cowardly manner, leaving our SBs with a weak fighter cover. We were never able to inflict such a defeat in a single attack by our planes against the German 'Heinkel-111'[31] bombers, although the fighting was very stubborn. The reason is that the enemy's planes are technically superior to ours, and are better outfitted with better armament and a greater bomb load.

Rodion Yakovlevich suggested the following:

Our SB should have:
a speed of 450 kilometers per hour and higher,
double guidance and autopilot,
good all-round machine gun defense against enemy fighters,
the fuel tanks should be well defended and it should be difficult to set them on fire (they should be wrapped with rubber or some other material),
they should consist of separate fuel tanks, and one tank—the back-up one—should be armored,
they should be outfitted for blind flying,
the pilot's cabin, or at least his seat, should be armored,
the construction of the equipment should enable the pilot to carry out bombing even if the remainder of the crew has perished,
the bomb load should be no less than two tons and allow for any combination, both as to the number and weight of bombs, and have a ceiling of no less than 6,000 meters with a full bomb load.
Our I-15 has proven to be an excellent fighter, but also has a number of shortcomings, which should be eliminated:
we should increase its speed, raising it to 420-450 kilometers (per hour),
remove the wheels,
increase its armament with a heavy-caliber machine gun,
protect the fuel tank,
as far as possible, make it difficult to ignite when hit by an incindiery bullet,
give the pilot an armored seat,
install an autopilot.

31   Editor's note. The Heinkel-111 was a cargo plane and bomber produced in Germany during 1935-44. One bomber version carried a crew five, had a maximum speed of 440 kilometers per hour and a maximum range of 2,300 kilometers. This model was armed with up to seven 7.92mm and one 13mm machine guns and one 20mm cannon. It could carry up to 2,000 kilograms in its bomb bay and more on its wings.

All of these qualities should be attached to the I-15, without sacrificing its most valuable quality—its maneuverability in the air battle. To be sure, it is difficult to combine high speed and maneuverability. For this, it is necessary to furnish it with a wide range of speeds, which will enable the I-15 to wage the air battle in approximately the same conditions in which it wages it right now.

We lack an assault plane and it is vitally necessary. The enemy's "Fiat" works successfully as an assault plane. Therefore, we could move along the lines of reinforcing the I-15's machine gun armament and give it an armored cabin for the pilot, hang several ten-kilogram bombs on it with powerful fragmentation effect and, having furnished it with a speed of around 400 kilometers and higher, get a good assault plane, capable of waging an air battle if necessary.

Our I-16 fighter has also proved to be a good modern fighter, but has the same defects as the I-15. It is very vulnerable and thus is in need of specific improvements:

it must be supplied with machine guns that can fire through the propeller; otherwise it is helpless with its widely separated 7.62mm machine guns;

armor the pilot's seat,

protect the fuel tank from catching fire,

give it a speed of 450 kilometers and higher, so that is not inferior to any high-speed fighter
     in the world,

improve its maneuverability in air combat,

put in an autopilot.

Malinovskii proposed seriously modernizing the airfield network:

The experience of war in Spain showed that it would be ideal to have an airfield network built according to another principle than the one we have now. We need an airfield-hotel. Aviation must enjoy complete freedom of maneuver, while the tail now attached to it, in the form of brigade air parks, terribly restricts our freedom of maneuver. Parks are needed as the main bases for air formations and necessary for field airfields, but we should have a main airfield network. For this, it is necessary to create a special airfield service, concerned with the exploitation of complete servicing of this network.

An air formation carries out its combat assignment and, upon returning, receives information by radio that its airfield has been destroyed and that this formation has been assigned another airfield for landing. This other airfield must take on the air formation and furnish it with everything necessary—refueling, fuel, a bomb load, the inspection and repair of aircraft, food, a shower, medical assistance, a hospital, an operating room, and complete rest for the tired crews, and even recreation—so that the air formation can fully put itself together within 6-8 hours and can take off to carry out its combat assignment. Such an airfield-hotel is what we need. In the opposite case, we will have what we have: a landing on a field where the crews inspect their planes themselves, they load their own bombs, bandage themselves up, dine on dry rations, and rest under a tree or on hay in a barn. These conditions quickly and inevitably make themselves felt in the condition of the flight crews. The more underground hangars on our airfields and in good shelters for the flight crews' rest, the better things will be.

Malinovskii called for great attention to be paid to the training of flight crews:

The problem of training and accumulating flight cadres is extremely important. Experience has shown that the Spanish fliers, who have been trained by us over the course of six months, both as bomber and (in particular) fighter pilots, in getting into battles with experienced (with 2-3 years of flying experience and more) German and Italians, quickly become their victims, and the lack of experience and skill in waging the air battle shows. It's also important that the Spanish fliers feel that the Germans and Italians are superior in fighting skill. Thus, as a rule, the Spanish crews give up and, of course, suffer losses.

Our pilots fight in a completely different manner. They would confidently enter the fighting with a numerically superior enemy and inflict a defeat on him. They displayed good training and skill in waging air combat. The enemy feared them and never got into a fight with them on equal terms or even a slight superiority. Only when he had 3-4 planes to our one would he fight and, following the first defeats (2-3 shot down planes), he would scatter and run away. Thus it is necessary to train flying cadres for fighter aviation carefully and in a sustained manner, and for a long time, for the outcome of air battles in a future war will depend on this.

However, once again the experience of Spain proved to be inapplicable to the Great Patriotic War. In Spain the Soviet pilots were represented by experienced pilots whose flight time was no less than that of their German and Italian enemies. During 1941-45 the majority of Soviet pilots completed flight schools, having barely mastered take off and landing, and became easy prey for the German aces.

Malinovskii noted the weakness of the Republicans' anti-aircraft artillery:

The training of the rank and file of the Republicans' anti-aircraft batteries is extremely poor. Inexperienced range finders prepare data and the anti-aircraft artillery fire is always behind the plane's flight path. A lot of shells are expended and explosions fill the entire sky, but the enemy's planes meanwhile maintain their course and carry out their missions…

The number of planes shot down by anti-aircraft artillery is not very great and requires the large expenditure of shells—up to 1,500 for one plane shot down. This is explained, besides the rank and file's poor training and by the worthlessness of our shrapnel shell.

Rodion Yakovlevich was concerned with civil defense, which was supposed to be able to withstand enemy air raids:

The experience of the war in Spain has shown that we have completely underestimated the role and importance of local anti-aircraft defense. If only we don't have to pay for this in heavy losses. It's necessary to put an end to this criminal negligence and very seriously take on the construction of strong shelters in our cities, particularly in the industrial areas; new buildings should be built with strong basements, capable of withstanding a 25-kilogram bomb (as is known, this bomb can penetrate all six floors and blows up in the basement, destroying the building). The conclusion: it is necessary to built strong reinforced concrete shelters and to bring public opinion and our urban organizations into this matter. In peacetime these basements may be used as warehouses and fruit basements, etc. We will have to build these in any event, and if we don't build them ahead of time, we'll have to do it during wartime, of course, already having suffered heavy losses.

All large and small depots of gasoline, kerosene and oils should be hidden under the ground; otherwise they will be destroyed at the very beginning of the war, regardless of any kind of ant-aircraft defense of these targets. This also applies to artillery depots. This is all terribly expensive, to be sure, but there is no other way out.

According to Malinovskii, cavalry did not play any kind of noticeable role in Spain:

Steadfast infantry almost always repelled cavalry attacks (the 27th Division near Singra, north of Teruel, and the 46th Infantry Division near Teruel). The less steady units, or those that had been worn out through extended fighting, ran away and more often than not became prey for the cavalry. For example, in the fighting for the Cedrillas—Valbona area in May 1938, there was a single cavalry regiment of eight squadrons operating on the fascists' side. It had badly torn up units of the Republicans' 39th Infantry Division, which had been worn out by three months of uninterrupted fighting. The inability of the Spanish infantry to stand up to the fascist cavalry is explained by the lack of knowledge about this combat arm and the memory of the beginning of the war, when the enemy's cavalry (mainly Moroccan) easily scattered and surrounded the poorly organized and completely unprepared Republican detachments.

The insurgents have only the single 58th Cavalry Division, under the command of General Monasterio, which has been employed by the enemy exclusively in the major offensive on Catalonia, with the single task of developing the success…

Only once during the Brunete operation in July 1937, near Kichorna, did we observe the successful and correct employment of cavalry—the Jesus Hernandez Cavalry Regiment—and then only because it was actually commanded by our Senior Lieutenant Fesenko…

Of course, this experience does not mean that cavalry did not find its place in the Spanish war. It would have found its very correct and useful employment, if it had existed, but neither side had a real and modern cavalry.

Malinovskii was not satisfied with the organization of the command and control of the Republican forces. He maintained:

On the whole, the staff organization of the Republican army is not different that in other modern armies, because the headquarters are cumbersome, with a lot of personal adjutants, clerks and service personnel. The command and control of troops is based only on written documents in the form of a general or individual combat order. Preliminary instructions are sometimes issued orally or by telephone, but they do not have the force of orders until they are confirmed by a signed and sealed written order. The commander does not sign orders—the chief of staff writes up the order in the commander's name and signs it himself. Following Prieto's[32] departure, an order may also be signed by the unit's or formation's commissar. As a rule, orders are very long and insufficiently specific; the imperative mood is almost never used. Either very polite forms ("I request," "as far as possible," "if the situation allows") are employed, or, most often, the order is written in the third person. The troops receive the order late, while a junior commander, even having received orally the most detailed instructions, does not set about carrying them out until he receives a written order. The single exception to this rule is a retreat. They retreat without orders, in opposition to the order, and, in the majority of cases, without being punished.

Rodion Yakovlevich was an enemy of staff bureaucracy. He believed that an order shout be short, precise, contain nothing extra, correspond to the situation, and be carried out unconditionally. Rodion Yakovlevich would grow indignant:

---

32   Editor's note. Indalecio Prieto (1883-1962) joined the Spanish Socialist Workers' Party as a young man and was active in the country's political life. He served as defense minister in the Republican government during the civil war. Following the Republic's defeat, Prieto chose exile in Mexico, where he died.

Upon issuing an order, all of the cadre officers, who for the most part occupied the positions of chiefs of staff, were more concerned that all the points recommended by the manual, were expressed in the order in the most detailed manner, independent of whether or not they were necessary there. It's not important to the professional officer that the order takes a long time to write (usually 2-3 hours, which is considered a hurried writing of an order). If the order is drawn up before the beginning of the operation, then they will write it up for entire days, and sometimes even longer.

The chief of staff is not concerned with the fact that the order will arrive late to the troops, but whether other cadre officers will criticize it, saying that he couldn't write an order, left out a point as directed by the manual! It's crazy, but it's true.

Thus it's hardly surprising that during the Brunete operation the commander of the 68th Brigade received an order from the division at 1045 on 11 July 1937, in which it was stated that at 0700 an artillery preparation against Villafranca del Castillo will begin and that the 68th Brigade will attack at 0745. What were the troops to do? The attack was carried out not in the morning, but in the evening.

Quite often an order will reach the division or corps 15-30 minutes before the start of operations indicated in the order. It has only been possible to alter this state of affairs to a slight degree. In the headquarters of such commanders as Modesto, Lister, Campesino, and Duran, the commanders themselves issue short written and oral orders from their observation and command posts, either personally or through adjutants, thus achieving flexible command and control. In other headquarters, where we don't have such great influence, everything is done according to the old Spanish custom: there's no command post, while the commander sits in his headquarters and sometimes doesn't even know what kind of orders and when his chief of staff is issuing, just as the chief of staff himself makes a decision (sometimes not even reporting the idea to his commander) and then issues and signs the order himself. (According to Spanish regulations, only the chief of staff signs an order and gives it legal authority by applying his seal.)

Experience has shown that the commander and his staff cannot manage the fighting without personally observing the course of the fighting and the troops' behavior in the battle. Thus there exists the mandatory condition—the command post of a brigade, division or corps commander and, preferably the army commander—is combined with the observation post, furnishing it with all kinds of communications equipment. Modern military equipment in the attack is so powerful that it can radically change the course of the fighting in a very short time. And if you are not able to grasp this moment through personal observation and instead wait for reports at your command post, which has no field of observation, time will be lost and modern attack means will be employed too late and it is unlikely that they will be able to equalize the situation or tear success from the enemy's hands.

In order to successfully manage the battle, one must see it.

Malinovskii noted that

In the Republican army the telephone plays too significant a role. The commander and chief of staff consider it their sacred duty to constantly be by the telephone during the fighting. Telephone conversations are often conducted, but they make little sense, for the orders issued orally or by telephone are not carried out (with the exception of some formations and units). The commander usually speaks for a very long time by telephone, without code and in a complete non-demanding way. The chief of staff sits next to him and takes notes, then formulates what has been said in the form of a written order and sends it to where it's supposed to go. Thus the telephone does nothing to speed up the command and control process, while at the same time tying the commanders to their headquarters, depriving them of the opportunity of seeing what is most important and personally influencing the course of the fighting, while at the same time the telephone keeps the numerous army of spies sitting in the headquarters and communications lines (all of the communications lines pass through civilian communications centers) abreast of things. Persistent attempts by a certain part of the officer corps to fix this useless system encountered stubborn resistance by the remainder.

The telegraph (the main apparatus is the key-stroke teletype and the auxiliary is the Morse system) has been instituted down to the corps staffs. Telegraphic orders have force, but then are almost always confirmed by written ones.

The radio is poorly developed among the Republicans and is almost never used for troop control. They have radios in the armies and in some corps. Reports are sometimes received by radio, but never orders. Code is not employed over the radio.

The delegate service is well developed, but one-sidedly, and in the final analysis not much good comes of it. Officers from the higher headquarters travel to the lower ones: from the army to the corps, from the corps to the division, etc. There they read reports in the operational sections and duplicate them word for word by telephone or telegraph, or personally. As a rule, it usually doesn't go so far as to see the situation or the fighting with one's own eyes. In the final analysis, the command does not know the situation.

The fate of reports and notifications and mutual information are organized poorly, although it may appear to be satisfactory: reports are often communicated by telephone, but they are not precise, for they are transmitted on the basis of subordinates' telephone reports. As a rule, the worst is dressed up and the best is inflated.

For example, during the Teruel operation on 15 December 1937, the commander of the 64th Infantry Division, Cartona, on the basis of a report by the commander of the 83rd Brigade, reported to the army commander through the corps that the 83rd Brigade had reached the San Blas area and established communications with Lister's division and thus completed the encirclement of Teruel, although this did not actually happen.

Here is yet another example proving the extreme harm of paper command and control. In the beginning of February the fascists began a major offensive operation in the Sierra Palomera area toward Alfambra, for the purpose of throwing the Republicans back from the main artery, the Teruel—Zaragoza road and capturing the Teruel—Alfambra—Alcaniz road and threatening Teruel from the north. The anarchist 42nd Infantry Division scattered completely on the first day of the attack, although the division staff reported through the corps to the army that the division was fighting. Actually, the 42nd Division no longer existed, while the 27th Infantry Division fell back in heavy fighting and with heavy losses from Lidon to Mesquita in the direction of Aliaga, and the front from Perales del Alfambra to the the Alto de los Salados height was not occupied by any Republican units.

Only the 39th Infantry Division, which had been relieved the previous evening along the Alto de los Salados sector and which had suffered extremely heavy losses there (the 22nd Brigade had 80 percent casualties, the 96th Brigade 50 percent, and the 64th 20 percent), was in Villaroya's army reserve.

It was at just this time that General Saravia received an order by telegraph from General Rojo "to hold the eastern bank of the Alfambra River at all costs." Saravia mechanically transmitted this order to the commander of the 39th Infantry Division, with the assignment to reach the Alfambra River by a night march and occupy the front from Canjada to Peralejos, which was more than 60 kilometers. He did not know the situation along the Alfambra River.

First of all, it was clear that the division could not cover the necessary 40 kilometers in the four remaining hours over no roads and, secondly, that this morally shaken and physically beaten division, upon getting involved in an unorganized meeting engagement along a broad front, would inevitably scatter and then the road through the El Pobo Range range from Alfambra to Alepus would be open to the fascists, which threat severe consequences.

In the morning the commander of the 39th Division reported the situation in detail to Saravia and his decision. Saravia approved it and immediately changed his previous order, issued a new one and sent a detailed report to Rojo, in which it was explained why he had made the decision to halt on the El Pobo, and not the Alfambra. During the day the fascists attempted to throw the 39th Infantry Division from the El Pobo, but were unsuccessful, and within six days, with the help of reserves, the Republicans reached and occupied the eastern bank of the Alfambra River.

At the same time Malinovskii rated the Frankists' command and control higher:

> To judge from the engagements and operations, troop control among the fascists is also poor, although better than among the Republicans.
>
> It also usually goes through a system of written orders. Written fascist combat documents, captured by the Republicans, are also wordy, although more categorical. Reports are long and highly colored.
>
> In the July fighting in the Onda—Artana area (southwest of Castellon), documents from the headquarters of the headquarters of the fascist 2nd Semi-Brigade/1st Brigade/84th Infantry Division were captured. Their close study confirmed that the fascists' written combat documents also suffer from overly flowery prose, lengthiness and a certain incomprehensibility.
>
> Their employment of field radio sets is organized better than among the Republicans and has been introduced down to the semi-brigade headquarters level. The Republicans sometimes intercepted their orders and reports over the radio; usually half coded (names and the most important words and phrases are coded, with the rest as is).
>
> The fascists employed optical communications equipment such as heliographs and lamps more broadly than did the Republicans.
>
> The fascists move their command posts up very close to the semi-brigades' combat formations (within several hundred meters during an attack), with the brigade command posts 1-1.5 kilometers, division command posts 2-3 kilometers, and corps command posts 6-8 kilometers. With the exception of individual commanders, the Republicans' command posts were somewhat further away.

Malinovskii noted that among the Republicans "all of their aviation is centralized and subordinated only to the war minister," and that "the aviation was not even subordinated to the commander of the army that was conducting the operation, and that he could only put in requests."

Malinovskii considered the radio the most important means of communications:

> Radio is the most wonderful means of technical communications in battle, given good training of the radio operaters and code clerks, of course. The employment of radio equipment at the front-army-corps level does not cause particular difficulties. Conversations by microphone at the battalion-regimetn level during the fighting itself may be coded in part, and often in the clear in a short fight. Higher-level conversations should be only coded and enciphered, mainly using a key.
>
> Radio sets were employed in the Republican army for duplicating communications with airfields, but due to the absence of experience and equipment were not broadly employed.
>
> The skillful employment of radio equipment may substantially ease the work of disinformation. For example, Franco would seriously confuse the Republican army command through his radio network. Having taken Teruel on 22 February 1938, the fascists began to shift all of

their forces to the east from 26.2 through 8.3 along the Teruel—Zaragoza road (which was reported everyday and in detail to Barcelona). Then the Republican intelligence uncovered a number of Spanish and Italian radio stations in the Guadalajara area, and the Republican command decided that the transfer of forces to Zaragoza was a maneuver and that the main attack would be launched against Guadalajara, and that this confidence held until the fascists captured Alcaniz.

The Spanish experience should have prompted some dark reflections on Malinovskii's part. For both German and Italy, as well as for the USSR, Spain became a sort of proving ground, upon which new weapons and combat equipment were tested. And, on the whole, the results of these tests were not in favor of the Soviet Union. The German-Italian aviation gained air superiority and the Frankist army, which had been trained by German instructors, showed itself to be significantly more combat-capable than the Republican army, which had been trained by Soviet advisers. Of course, the fact that four-fifths of the officers and soldiers of the regular Spanish army ended up with the Frankist, played a role as well. Also, an inter-party struggle was going on in the Republican army, while in the insurgent army everyone unconditionally subordinated themselves to Franco. However, as Malinovskii notes:

> The Moroccan units and the Foreign Legion were the most combat-capable and impressive force among the insurgents, which played a decisive role in the beginning of the civil war. The battle along the Jarama devastated the ranks of these troops and they lost their power. New, or young, or not too old reinforcements of Moroccans arrived; there were no reinforcements for the Foreign Legion, and it was reinforced with Spaniards. Thus these elite units were reduced to the general level of the insurgents' army. Now there most combat-capable units are the units from Navarre (the Falangists and the Rekete (the Rekete were members of the Carlists' militarized youth group—supporters of the pretender to the Spanish throne, Don Carlos the elder and his descendants, B.S.). The Italian Corps does not have a good combat reputation and its weakness was revealed in Guadalajara in March 1937. Following the shameful defeat at Guadalajara, the employment of the Italian Corps in the fighting was extremely cautious: the insurgents always placed it in the center of a shock group of forces, securely covering its flanks with Spanish corps.

Thus by the middle of the war the Frankist' most combat-capable regular units had been bled white and recruits took the place of veterans and professionals. And their high level of combat capability was to a great extent due to their German instructors. Typically, as Rodion Yakovlevich admitted, the Italian Corps was inferior to the Spanish units in combat capability. The Germans trained the Spanish Frankist forces better than the Soviet instructors did the Republican units. Malinovskii could not but understand that in its recruitment system the Red Army was closer to the Republicans than to the Francists and in a likely clash with the Wehrmacht it would find itself in a very difficult position. One senses that as early as August 1938 Rodion Yakovlevich understood that the Republicans, with whom, one could say, he had become close to during his stay in Spain, were going to lose the war, however sad. This lent a tragic tone to the entire report.

Having ended up an instructor in the Frunze Military Academy after Spain, Malinovskii transformed his report about the military experience of the Spanish war into a dissertation, which he was almost ready to defend. However, in March 1941 Rodion Yakovlevich was appointed commander of the 48th Rifle Corps along the Romanian border, and he had to forget about defending his dissertation for a long time. Later, after Malinovskii had become minister of defense, it was suggested that he defend his old dissertation and to immediately award him the academic degree of doctor of military sciences. One does not have to explain to the reader how difficult it would be for the minister of defense to defend his dissertation in a military academy subordinated to him. However, according to the marshal's daughter, when in 1960 "the academic council of the Frunze Academy informed my father of its intention to award him an academic degree for this dissertation (the defense did not take place back then, as the work was completed on the eve of the war), my father refused decisively: 'If I weren't a minister right now, they wouldn't even have remembered this work. So much for your body of work.'"

By the way, there's no doubt that they wouldn't even have required Rodion Yakovlevich to update the dissertation written before the war. If necessary, the academy instructors would probably have updated it. However, Malinovskii refused the offer to defend the dissertation. He was no longer interested in it, insofar as it didn't have any bearing on what he was doing then. And Rodion Yakovlevich never suffered from petty vanity and the marshal of the Soviet Union had no desire to show off his doctor's degree before others.

This is the way Malinovskii's daughter Natal'ya remembered her father's Spanish epic:

> Spain, which he fell in love with even before he set foot on its soil and which he left with the bitterness of unintentional guilt—"I wasn't able to help"… I remember the spinning, round labels with the dog next to the gramophone and the glossy white sleeve of the Spanish record: the crimson title and the swarthy female profile—the black lock of hair on her cheek, the rose behind her ear and the high comb in her curls. They put this record on often—"The Spanish record is playing."

Natal'ya Rodionovna told me that her father had a true love in Spain (by this time his relations with his first wife were completely ruined).

According to the translator Adelina Kondrat'eva (more about her below), another translator, Lidiya Kuper, was Rodion Yakovlevich's love. Following Malinovskii's departure from Spain, she married and immigrated to the USSR following the defeat of the Spanish republic and returned to Spain in 1957. In 2004 thr 89-year old Lidiya became the author of the first complete translation of Tolstoi's *War and Peace* into Spanish. She passed away in the beginning of 2013.

Spain always remained an important part of Malinovskii's life. Natal'ya Rodionovna recalls:

> I remember en route to Morocco (they took the family when it was necessary to impart a particularly friendly tone), at night papa called me to the porthole: "You see, shining like a star and the rays parting. Madrid" And I understood that papa didn't want to go to Morocco at all. This refrain continued throughout the entire trip: "See here, it's similar," and "the sunset is similar, as are the mountains against the horizon, and the name is Spanish—Casablanca, and the buildings are white, just like there, and oranges are blooming." In Morocco papa was introduced to a high-ranking military officer who had once fought on Franco's side. Then he and papa were enemies in the full sense of the word: they had fought along the same sectors of the front. And during the long automobile rides they spoke in Spanish about what their life was 20 years ago and how for others it was just a page of military history. I was struck then by, as it seemed to me, the interested and even friendly tone of their conversations. I don't know if this was the natural diplomatic norm or if time really had smoothed out their previous division and that although years had passed, it was possible that understanding had triumphed over confrontation.
>
> Three years later, when I enrolled in the language department's Spanish section, papa presented me with Aguilar's single volume of Lorca,[33] having guessed (or, maybe, predeter-

---

33 Editor's note. . Federico del Sagrado Corazon de Jesus Garcia Lorca (1898-1936) was a Spanish poet,

mined) my life's work, and a year later gave me an edition of *Blood Wedding*, brought by him from Spain.

A few years ago, while going through my archive, I found the draft of papa's undefended dissertation on the Spanish war—he was working on it on the eve of the Second World War and was unable to complete it. In one folder there were a lot of tiny photographs with the draft, papa's Spanish pictures. There were flowering almonds, a river, and a castle on a cliff, children by the roadside, a Madrid suburb, a mountain village, and the faces of friends. There are almost no signs of war in these photographs, but its bitterness is imprinted in them, an inerasable sign of the times, the orphanhood of that land and its light.

Among the things that were with Rodion Yakovlevich in the hospital was a pass enabling him to move freely around Madrid. Natal'ya Rodionovna describes it as follows:

Dark-pink cardboard, with the Madrid coat of arms in the left corner. In the middle "Free access everywhere" was written in large letters, and lower and in smaller letters, "with the right to bear arms," and even lower—"Malino is authorized." A seal. The date, 26 May 1937, and the signature of the military governor of Madrid. Papa carried this pass with him for nearly 30 years. Knowing the structure of his soul, I will say, without fear of being mistaken, that it was not only love, but a talisman, from 1937, which had migrated from an old notebook to a new one.

In Natal'ya Rodionovna's opinion, Spain saved her father from repressions:

He served three tours in Spain and returned only after the unambiguous instruction: "In case of delay, we will consider him a defector." I often think what it was like for him to come back after such a threat. And why did he nevertheless return, knowing what could be waiting for him. Papa's old friend, the military doctor N.M.Nevskii, who later became a major general in the medical service, told me that during their first meeting after Spain he and father talked for a long time about what was happening at home. In parting, papa said: "We may not see each other again, although there's no war on." But fate, which had saved him repeatedly earlier, protected him this time as well. ("First he sat tight in Spain, and then in the academy!"—was how one respected personage would joke, who also sat tight in a hot spot before the Second World War, but at the other end of the earth).

Malinovskii was decorated for the war in Spain with the Order of Lenin and the Order of the Red Banner. Natal'ya Rodionovna, as well as many fellow servicemen, believed that the mission to Spain saved Rodion Yakovlevich from the repressions. The marshal's daughter recalled her mother's words:

Of course, they repeatedly reminded your father about France, "where he took it easy while we were beating the Whites" (a traditional joke by one of the heroes of the civil war) and Spain, "where he slipped away in time" (we qualify this as a joke, repeated several times by another hero of a later war). I won't guess how father managed to survive—was it chance, fate?—but there can be no doubt that he was under constant suspicion. N.S. Khrushchev speaks in his memoirs about Stalin's lack of faith in my father and his order from on high "to not take your eyes off Malinovskii."

---

playwright and socialist activist. He was murdered by Nationalists at the start of the Spanish Civil War.

In Spain Malinovskii became acquainted with a 16-year old ninth-grader from Moscow, Adelina Venyaminovna Abramson (Serova from her first marriage and Kondrat'eva from her second), who came to Spain with her father, an SR bomb-maker, who immigrated to Argentina in 1910 and up to the beginning of the 1930s collected funds to help the USSR, together with his wife Rozaliya. Her older sister, Paulina-Marianna, was first a translator for the cameraman Roman Karmen,[34] and later a translator with Khadzhi Mamsurov,[35] whom she later married. Adelina worked as a translator in the headquarters of the Spanish Air Force. Both of them became acquainted in Madrid with Rodion Yakovlevich. Venyamin was a translator with the advisers on the Aragon front.

Later, in September 1942, Adelina was working in the intelligence section in the headquarters of the 66th Army, which Malinovskii commanded at the time. She was once captured, but managed to get away after a few days and, having crossed the front line, appeared before Malinovskii and honestly told him that she had been a prisoner. Rodion Yakovlevich looked into her eyes and said: "Adelina, remember, you weren't a prisoner."

After the war, in connection with the struggle against cosmopolitans,[36] they arrested Venyamin Abramson. Malinovskii was one of the few friends who called the Abramsons' apartment from Khabarovsk and asked: "Are you at home?" Abramson's wife wanted to tell him about her husband, but Malinovskii interrupted her: "I know, but I can't do anything. That's why I'm asking about you." Fortunately, they soon let Abramson go.

Paulina died in December 2000, and Adelina in December 2012, at the age of 92.

Malinovskii's service in Spain was rated sufficiently highly. In his 1938 service biography he noted that "On 11 July 1937 I was awarded the Order of Lenin by decree of the Presidium of the Central Executive Committee of the USSR and the Order of the Red Banner by decree of the Presidium of the Central Executive Committee of 22 October."

---

34   Editor's note. Roman Lazarevich Karmen (1906-78) was a Soviet camera man and film director. His documentary record of the Spanish Civil War and the Eastern Front during the Second World War were highly influential propaganda films.

35   Editor's note. Khadzhi Umar Mamsurov (1903-68), a native of Ossetia, joined the Red Army in 1918 and fought in the civil war. He was later involved in Soviet intelligence activities during the Spanish Civil War. Mamsurov later served as a division commander during the Great Patriotic War.

36   Editor's note. "Cosmopolitans," or "rootless cosmopolitans," were terms widely applied to those artists deemed insufficiently grounded in Russian-Soviet culture and too deferential to the West during the postwar ideological crackdown. Many of those accused were Jews. This campaign ended with Stalin's death in 1953.

5

Before Harsh Trials

Following his return from Spain, Malinovskii was appointed to his previous post as operational assistant to the cavalry inspector for the Belorussian Military District, which at the time was commanded by Army Commander Second Class M.P. Kovalev,[1] with whom Rodion Yakovlevich had not previously worked. Upon returning from Spain, Colonel Malinovskii was promoted to brigade commander on 15 July 1938.

On 10 February 1938 the following document appeared:

Party (political) description

For member of the VKP(b), Brigade Commander, comrade Malinovskii, Rodion Yakovlevich:

Comrade Malinovskii, Rodion Yakovlevich, was born in the city of Odessa in 1898. He is of peasant social origin. His social status is that of a white collar worker.

He has been a member of the VKP(b) since October 1926 and has party membership no. 1040844. He is a Ukrainian by nationality.

He has been in the RKKA since 1919. He was a participant in the civil war.

From 1916 through July 1918 he served as a corporal in the 2nd Infantry Regiment of Russian forces (Expeditionary Corps) in France and from July 1918 through August 1919 in the 1st Foreign Legion of the French Army as a private (actually, as we recall, Malinovskii joined the Foreign Legion's Russian Legion of Honor as early as January 1918, while at the time the 2nd Regiment no longer existed. In all likelihood, Malinovskii noted July 1918 here as the time when the Russian Legion fully lost its autonomy and French officers put in command and the soldiers and officers were dressed in French military uniforms. Strictly speaking, Malinovskii served in the French army not as a private, but as a soldier first class, which approximates the rank of "corporal" in the Russian and German armies. However, in the French army, where there is no rank of "corporal," he lacked some rights of a junior commander which a corporal had, B.S.).

For exemplary performance of his government assignment (in Spain, B.S.), he has been decorated with the orders of Lenin and the Red Banner.

He has been decorated with the medal "20 Years in the RKKA" on the twentieth anniversary of the RKKA.

He has no relatives on his or his wife's side abroad and none who have been repressed and deprived of their electoral rights.

---

1   Editor's note. Mikhail Prokop'evich Kovalev (1897-1967) joined the imperial army in 1915 and the Red Army in 1918. He commanded military districts and a front and army during the interwar period. During the Great Patriotic War he commanded a *front* in the Far East. Following the war, Kovalev commanded a military district.

He has served as operational assistant to the cavalry inspector for the Belorussian Military District since 1936 and since that time has been in the party organization of the Belorussian Military District headquarters.

During his stay in the party organization of the 1st, 9th and 10th sections of the Belorussian Military District headquarters and the cavalry inspectorate, comrade Malinovskii has made a positive impression. He is well developed politically. He is ideologically and morally steadfast. There have been no deviations from the general line of the party.

He often delivers reports and political information, the quality of which is good.

He takes an active part in party life. He carries out party assignments conscientiously and thoroughly.

He enjoys deserved authority. He has no party reprimands.

He is conscientious in his professional work. He is militarily well developed.

He is devoted to the party of Lenin and Stalin.

This party description was discussed and confirmed at a closed party meeting of the party organization of the 1st, 9th and 10th sections of the Belorussian Military District headquarters and the cavalry inspectorate on 10 February 1939, record no. 5.

Party organizer Tyukhov.

I confirm the signature of the party organizer of the 1st, 9th and 10th sections of the Belorussian Military District headquarters and the cavalry inspectorate, comrade A.A. Tyukhov.

Commissar of the Belorussian Military District headquarters, Regimental Commissar Berezkin.

As an instructor in the academy, Malinovskii was promoted to major general in June 1940. In the summer of 1940 Rodion Yakovlevich was awarded the title of "exemplary member of the academy." He was thinking about defending his dissertation, but fate decreed otherwise.

At the end of 1940 Malinovskii received the following recommendation: "He may be employed with the troops in the positions of division commander, corps chief of staff, or chief of the operational section of a group of armies."

This absolutey positive description, which failed to find any shortcomings in Malinovskii, opened good career prospects for him, all the more so because the repressions of 1937-1938 and the growth in the RKKA's size opened up a large number of vacancies for the command element. However, Stalin, defense commissar Voroshilov and chief of the General Staff Shaposhnikov[2] decided not to employ Rodion Yakovlevich on either staff or command positions, but sent him to teach in the academy. Evidently his work on the experience of the war in Spain, which the leadership of the defense commissariat liked, played a substantial role here. It was probably decided that with the start of the Second World War and the approach of the inevitable collision between the USSR and Germany, as many Red Army commanders as possible should be acquainted with the Spanish experience. One of the means of doing this was through teaching in the military academy. And thus by an order of 8 September 1939, Brigade Commander Malinovskii was appointed senior instructor in the headquarters service department of the Frunze Military Academy. The appointment was made at Stalin's order. In one of his notes in the autumn of 1939, he asked: "Has Malinovskii been recalled to Moscow"?

---

2   Editor's note. Boris Mikhailovich Shaposhnikov (1882-1945) joined the imperial army in 1901 and fought in the First World War. He joined the Red Army in 1918 and served in a variety of staff positions. He served as commander of military districts and was chief of the general staff three times. Shaposhnikov's last position was chief of the General Staff Academy.

It is not excluded that before his departure for Moscow, Malinovskii remained a few days in the headquarters of the Belorussian Military District, the forces of which were preparing for the invasion of eastern Poland, which took place on 17 September. As early as 3 September the Politburo of the VKP(b) Central Committee decided to extend by one month the RKKA service of privates and sergeants who had completed their service and who were to be demobilized (in all, 310,632 men). This announcement, as well as the increase of the mobilization strength of units in a number of military districts, as well as of auto transport, horses and tractors, and the readiness of National Air Defense emplacements in Leningrad, Velikie Luki, Minsk and Kiev was published on 5 September.On the night of 6-7 September a directive from the defense commissariat was received in seven military districts on conducting "major training exercises," which signified the Red Army's partial mobilization for seizing the eastern regions of Poland, which were to go to the Soviet Union, according to the secret protocol to the Molotov-Ribbentrop pact. The major training exercises began on the morning of 7 September and were conducted with a delay of 2-3 days. Auto transport, which was involved in bringing in the harvest, was not ready in time, while the railroads could not cope with shipments. They had to reduce the freight and passenger runs. On 11 September the Belorussian and Ukrainian special military districts received orders to deploy the districts' field headquarters into the Belorussian and Ukrainian fronts. On 14 September the military council of the Belorussian Special Military District (Army Commander Second Class M.P. Kovalev, Division Commissar P.Ye. Smokachev and chief of staff Corps Commander M.A. Purkaev)[3] received directive no. 16633 from the USSR people's commissar of defense Marshal of the Soviet Union K. Voroshilov and the chief of the RKKA General Staff, Army Commander First Class B. Shaposhnikov "On the Beginning of the Offensive Against Poland." It stated: "Secretly concentrate and be ready for a decisive offensive by the close of 16 September, for the purpose of launching a lightning attack and to defeat the enemy's opposing forces." Here specific tasks were assigned to various groups of forces. It also demanded that "a plan of action be presented by special courier by the morning of 17 September." On 15 September the chief of GlavPUR, L.Z. Mekhlis,[4] arrived at the headquarters of the Belorussian Special Military District and sent a telephonogram to the military districts' political directorate chiefs to immediately reprint in the district newspapers the lead editorial in *Pravda* "On the Internal Reasons for Poland's Military Defeat." Mass explanatory work among military personnel was to be undertaken on the basis of this article. According to L.Z. Mekhlis's instructions, subunits were created for carrying out propaganda directed against "gentry Poland."

It's possible that Malinovskii took part in planning the Polish campaign, but he was not fated to take a direct part in it.

One should also not exclude the idea that they may have suspected Polish origins in Rodion Yakovlevich's surname and recalled him from the war against the Poles, just in case. As we recall, Malinovskii did not take part in the Soviet-Polish War of 1920, because of typhus.

In the academy Malinovskii was awarded the academic title of assistant. What is even more important, in June 1940, in connection with the introduction of generals' ranks, Rodion Yakovlevich was awarded the rank of major general. By the way, in 1940 the overwhelming majority

---

3   Editor's note. Maksim Alekseevich Purkaev (1894-1953) was drafted into the imperial army in 1915 and joined the Red Army in 1918. During the Great Patriotic War he served as a *front* chief of staff and later commanded a *front*. Following the war, Purkaev commanded military districts.

4   Editor's note. Lev Zakharovich Mekhlis (1889-1953) joined the Russian army in 1911 and joined the Red Army in 1918. Following the civil war, he served as chief of the Armed Forces Political Administration and was instrumental in purging suspect officers. During the Great Patriotic War he served as political commissar on several *fronts*. Following the war, Mekhlis served as minister of state control until his retirement in 1950.

of brigade commanders were rated as colonels. The fact that Malinovskii became one of the few brigade commanders who were rated as major generals was probably the result of the fact that the new defense commissar, Semyon Konstantinovich Timoshenko, who knew Rodion Yakovlevich personally, insofar as from August 1933 through September 1935 he was deputy commander of the Belorussian Military District, valued him highly.

The description of Malinovskii during his attestation in the academy was just as glowing as the one from the party organization of the headquarters of the Belorussian Special Military District. It stated:

He is devoted to the party of Lenin and Stalin. He is politically and morally steadfast. He is closed linked to the masses and assigns them specific tasks for mastering knowledge supporting the preparation of a highly qualified commander. He systematically studies the experience of recent wars and is completing his dissertation and gaining the academic degree of candidate of military sciences.

Possessing a broad military world view and great experience in line and staff work, as well as combat experience in recent wars, comrade Malinovskii has achieved, while leading a study group of students with a great deal of combat experience, precise knowledge of theory and, on the whole, good results. While putting forward high requirements during studies and supporting good discipline in the study group, he carries out a great deal of educational work.

He has fully mastered the methodology of conducting lessons and turns in assignments for drawing up study materials on time. He draws up high quality assignments. He delivered lessons to a special group which were rich in content and on a high theoretical level (the academy's special group consisted of high-ranking commanders with great combat expeience, but who had not received a systematic military education, and the lectures were probably about Spain, B.S.).

He has been awarded the title of "exemplary member of the academy" for his work.

He is personally disciplined. He is suitable for field work.

He fully corresponds to his post. According to his work qualities, he may carry out important tasks in both the line and staffs.

With the troops he may be employed as a division commander, a corps chief of staff, or chief of the operational section in the headquarters of a group of armies.

Chief of the headquarters service deparment

Major General Tsvetkov.

As a result, Malinovskii was chosen neither as a division commander or a corps chief of staff, but immediately commander of the 48th Rifle Corps. This was due both to the deficit of senior commanders following the repressions of 1937-1938 and the accelerated deployment of new divisions, corps and armies due to the forthcoming war with Germany.

6

A Difficult Beginning

In his 1948 service biography, Malinovskii wrote:

In September 1939 I was appointed an instructor in the Frunze Military Academy, and in March 1941 commander of the 48th Rifle Corps in the Odessa Military District.

It was in this position that I began the war on 22 June 1941, along the Prut River; the corps fell back in heavy fighting from the Prut River toward Bel'tsy, Rybnitsa, Kotovsk, Kolosovka, Nikolaev, Kherson, and Kakhovka; the corps was encircled in Nikolaev, but broke through and got away.

I took over the command of the 6th Army at the end of August around Dnepropetrovsk and, in heavy fighting fell back safely with the army to the Donets River, toward Izyum, where the front securely stabilized from October 1941.

On 18 December 1941 I was appointed commander of the Southern Front and in this capacity successfully carried out the January operation toward Barvenkovo and Lozovaya with the forces of the 57th and 9th armies.

On orders from the *Stavka*, and due to the failures at Khar'kov and the withdrawal by the Southwestern Front's forces, the Southern Front began a systematic withdrawal and, during this withdrawal, being deeply turned in the flank and rear, was unable to hold Novocherkassk and Rostov and abandoned them without the *Stavka's* permission; the Southern Front was merged with the North Caucasus Front into a single North Caucasus Front. Marshal Budennyi was appointed commander and I, as his first deputy, headed the group of forces along the right flank, consisting of the 12th and 27th armies, and fell back on Kropotkin and Armavir, and from here the 12th Army fell back on Maikop and I was ordered to pull back units of the 37th Army, which was breaking out of encirclement, as well as some other units, to the Malka River toward Nal'chik—where I later turned these forces over to the Trans-Caucasus Front's Northern Group of Forces, and where I was ordered to place myself at the disposal of the chief of the General Staff in Moscow, where I arrived at the end of August 1942.

On 27 August 1942 I was appointed commander of the 66th Army, which I took over in the Kamyshin area and led to the Stalingrad area, and from their directly into an attack from the line of the Pichuga River along the right bank of the Volga River, although the offensive had very little success: an advance of 4-6 kilometers, and then heavy and extended fighting. In October I was appointed deputy commander of the Voronezh Front, and on 29 November 1942 commander of the 2nd Guards Army, with which I left the Tambov area to the Stalingrad area, and at the end of December the lead units of the 2nd Guards Army entered into heavy fighting with Manstein's[1] group, which was attempting to break

---

1   Editor's note. Erich von Manstein (1887-1973) joined the imperial army in 1906 and fought in the First World War on both fronts. During the Second World War he served as an army group chief of staff and corps commander in Poland and the West. During the Soviet campaign he commanded a tank corps, an army and an army group, before being relieved by Hitler in 1944. He was convicted of war crimes in 1949

through to Stalingrad, along the Myshkova River, to the south of Stalingrad, and on 26 December 1942, having gone over to a decisive offensive, routed Manstein's group, occupied Kotel'nikovo, Dubovskoe and Zimovniki, having defeated the flank of the enemy's Tormosin group of forces along the way.

In the middle of January 1943 the 2nd Guards Army reached Novocherkassk and Aksaiskaya. On 29 January 1943 I was once again appointed commander of the Southern Front (formerly the Stalingrad Front) and, continuing the offensive, the front's forces liberated Shakhty, Novocherkassk, and Rostov-on-Don and by the end of February reached the Mius River, but were unable to advance further.

On 22 March 1943 I was appointed commander of the Southwestern Front (later renamed the Third Ukrainian Front), which I commanded until 15 May 1944, having carried out a series of successful operations to liberate the Donbass, left- and right-bank Ukraine, including Dnepropetrovsk, Zaporozh'e, Krivoi Rog, Nikopol', Kherson, Nikolaev, Voznesensk, Tiraspol', and Odessa.

On 15 May 1944 I was appointed commander of the Second Ukrainian Front, whose forces, having begun the Iasi—Kishinev operation, routed a major enemy group of forces and liberated Romania, Hungary, part of Czechoslovakia, and Austria, and ended the war in the west in Prague and Vienna.

In July 1945 the *front* headquarters arrived in Chita and was put in charge of the Trans-Baikal Front, the forces of which launched a decisive attack on August 9 against the Japanese Kwantung Army[2] through Mongolia and occupied Changchun, Mukden and Port Arthur and concluded the war with Japan.

Thus on 14 March 1941 Malinovskii was appointed commander of the 48th Rifle Corps, which was based in Kirovograd. It is interesting that in the first draft of this order the former commander of the 15th Motorized Division, Major General Nikolai Nikanorovich Belov, who had commanded this division for only three days, was to have been appointed to this post. But Defense Commissar Timoshenko (or his messenger) changed this surname by hand to that of Malinovskii. And N.N. Belov perished along with his division in the Uman' pocket on 9 August 1941. He refused to be evacuated on the plane that had been sent for him.

According to testimony from Marshal Matvei Vasil'evich Zakharov,[3] who at this time was the chief of staff of the Odessa Military District, at first defense commissar Timoshenko had planned to appoint him, Zakharov, commander of the 48th Rifle Corps, as he had promised him, upon his appointment as chief of staff of the Odessa Military District, to give him a line command at the first opportunity. It was planned to appoint Malinovskii in Zakharov's place as chief of staff. However, the military district commander, Colonel General Ya.T. Cherevichenko,[4] requested that

---

and served four years in prison.

2   Editor's note. The Kwantung Army was formed in 1919 to guard Japanese holdings in southern Manchuria. Its command engineered the conquest of all of Manchuria in 1931-32 and took part in the opening phase of the war with China in 1937. As the war spread to the Pacific, the Kwantung Army lost much of its previous importance and it was easily routed by the Red Army in 1945.

3   Editor's note. Matvei Vasil'evich Zakharov (1898-1972) joined the Red Army in 1918 and fought in the civil war. During the Great Patriotic War he served as the chief of staff of a high command and of several *fronts*. Following the war he commanded Soviet forces in Germany and was twice chief of the General Staff Academy and chief of the General Staff.

4   Editor's note. Yakov Timofeevich Cherevichenko (1894-1976) was drafted into the imperial army in 1914 and joined the Red Army in 1918. During the Great Patriotic War he commanded armies and *fronts*, as well as a military district. Following the war, Cherevichenko commanded a rifle corps until his retirement in 1950.

Zakharov be retained as district chief of staff and, as a result, Malinovskii headed the 48th Corps. I should note that this appointment, in the conditions of the approaching war with Germany, would open the best prospects for career advancement. During the war, corps commanders (given successful command stints, of course) were promoted much more readily than army chiefs of staff (upon the beginning of the war, the Odessa Military District was transformed into the 9th Army).

Three days earlier, on 11 March, the plan for the Red Army's strategic deployment against Germany and its allies was drawn up. It was planned to launch the Soviet forces' main attack along the southwestern direction, where it was mistakenly believed that the German forces' main group of forces was concentrated. At the time, it was believed that "the deployment of the Red Army's main forces in the West, with the main forces against East Prussia and along the Warsaw axis, arouses serious fears that the struggle along this front may lead to extended fighting," due to the presence there of powerful German fortifications. In the section of the plan dedicated to the Red Army's activities along the southwestern direction, the deputy chief of the General Staff—the chief of the operational directorate—N.F. Vatutin[5] wrote in his own hand: "The offensive is to begin on 12.6."

Malinovskii's corps was supposed to move up to the Romanian frontier and begin combat operations in the case of an invasion of Soviet territory by German and Romanian forces, or once the Soviet forces had achieved success along the main, southwestern direction.

The Red Army leadership was not able to concentrate all of the necessary men and materiel and, as had been planned, in order to begin its offensive along the southwestern direction by 12 June. In the middle of May 1941, in the new deployment plan in the West, it was planned to launch the main attack, as before, in the southwest, in the direction of Krakow and Katowice, cutting Germany off from Romania and Hungary and placing the German group of forces in Poland under threat of an attack in the flank and rear. However, judging by the deadlines for concentrating forces, it was planned to begin the offensive no earlier than the middle of July. In the second half of May the 48th Corps began moving to the frontier along the Prut River and completed its movement in the middle of June.

In March 1941 Brigade Commander Aleksandr Grigor'evich Batyunya, a former ensign in the czarist army, was appointed chief of staff of the 48th Corps. He arrived at the corps not long after being freed from a camp. In 1958, when Malinovskii was defense minister, Aleksandr Grigor'evich was awarded the rank of colonel general, in which he finished his service in 1961. The corps, which consisted of the 30th Irkutsk Mountain-Rifle and 74th Rifle divisions defended along the Bel'tsy axis. They appointed as chief of the corps' political section Regimental Commissar Illarion Ivanovich Larin,[6] who managed to remain with Malinovskii almost all the time right up until his tragic death.

Malinovskii probably guessed that war with Germany would begin any day. For example, Military Doctor Kotlyarevskii, who was called up on 30 May 1941 to take part in the 45-day "training exercises" in the medical battalion of the 147th Rifle Division's, which was in Malinovskii's corps until June 1941 and where I.I. Larin was division commissar, testified as a prisoner that "On 7 June the medical personnel were informed in secret … that they would not be discharged upon the expiry of 45 days, because we would be fighting Germany within the near future."

---

5   Editor's note. Nikolai Fedorovich Vatutin (1901-44) was drafted into the Red Army in 1920 and completed the Frunze Military Academy and General Staff Academy. During the Great Patriotic War he served as deputy chief of the General Staff, front chief of staff and commander of several *fronts*. Vatutin was ambushed by anti-Soviet partisans and later died of his wounds.

6   Editor's note. Illarion Ivanovich Larin (1903-42) joined the Red Army in 1921 and served chiefly in political postings. During the Great Patriotic War he was a member of the military council of armies and a *front*. Larin committed suicide.

Yevdokim Yegorovich Mal'tsev, the commissar of the 74th Rifle Division and future general of the army, recalled how on the eve of the war Malinovskii had conducted an inspection as corps commander:

The short (Malinovskii was actually 175 centimeters tall and could in no way be considered short and, in any event, he was taller than Marshal Zhukov, B.S.), heavy-set corps commander got out of the car. The orders of Lenin and the Red Banner and the jubilee medal "20 Years in the RKKA" shone on his well sewn and ironed high-collared tunic. His had a stern, as if carved out of rock, and youngish and slightly full face, broad black eyebrows, large chin, and fixed eyes like poured lead…

Having heard the report by the division commander, the corps commander greeted everyone who met him and with an unhurried stride set out for the club, where the division's commanders and political workers had gathered for the critique. Everyone listened to Rodion Yakovlevich attentively. He was a man of few words. His speech was precise and intelligent and somewhat softened by a slight Ukrainian accent. The critique was brief but impressive. Everyone felt the corps commander's great life and military experience, his military and general erudition, his gift for profound theoretical thinking, and his lively speech.

"Early on, Peter the Great," Malinovskii said in a calm voice, "demanded that we teach how to behave in battle. A review, however, has shown that in the division conventionalities are allowed in the training of the troops and commanders, and this creates an incorrect idea as to the harsh reality of war. And we will pay with a lot of blood for this in battle…"

The hall grew quiet. It was stated too sharply. After all, we had only just received the draft of the new field manual, where it was stated that the Red Army's combat activities would be conducted to destroy, for the purpose of completely routing the enemy and achieving a decisive victory with light losses. Due to their insufficient theoretical and practical training, some commanders and political workers sometimes accepted the instructions in the draft field manual too literally and dogmatically. Rodion Yakovlevich, it seems, felt the auditorium's mood and continued:

"Yes, yes! It's easy to sing the song: 'We will rout the enemy with small losses and a mighty blow,' while in life we must do a very great deal in order that the blow against the enemy is mighty and the losses small."

And the corps commander began to unfold our existing shortcomings in the military training of units and subunits. He paid particular attention to the organization of cooperation between the combat arms on the battlefield. He mainly spoke of cooperation by the rifle subunits and units between themselves and the artillery. The infantry did not know how to keep to the rolling barrage and got separated from it, while the artillery had not learned to furnish fire support to the infantry in the depth of the enemy's defense.

"Lots of things happen in war. It may come to pass that the division will have to wage a defensive engagement," Rodion Yakovlevich said.

The auditorium grew quiet again. Many heard unfamiliar tenets from the lips of the corps commander. It was stated in the draft field manual: "We will wage an offensive war, shifting it to the enemy's territory."

"Let's remember," the corps commander continued, "how Vladimir Il'ich Lenin taught us. Here are his words: 'The conduct of that army that does not prepare to master all kinds of weapons, all means and forms of struggle that the enemy has or may have, is not smart and is even criminal… and without mastering all kinds of struggle we may suffer a huge, if not decisive, defeat… While mastering all the weapons of struggle, we will probably win.' Think about these words, comrade commanders and political workers of the 74th Division and

analyze whether the training of the units and subunits entrusted to you fulfill these requirements. It's unlikely, maybe, that the answer you give yourself will be positive…"

And the corps commander demanded that for the immediate future they teach the regiments and subunits to organize a defense and, most of all, its fundamental—anti-tank defense.
He spoke in detail about the role and place of the artillery, engineering subunits and assault
groups and recommended that the division command establish greater close cooperation with
the permanent firing points located in the fortified area where the division was stationed.

"The inspection has shown," said Rodion Yakovlevich, "that some commanders poorly
know the probable enemy. Other commanders display dangerous tendencies toward a belief
in easy victory. We have no basis at all for complacency. This is evidence of short-sightedness,
a lack of command culture and sometime simply a lack of responsibility and ignorance or
forgetfulness of military history."

I followed the hall closely. The collection of epithets addressed by the corps commander at
the belief in easy victory had its effect. Some lowered their heads even further.

"The most dangerous thing in war is to underestimate the enemy and to complacently
think that we are stronger. This is the most alarming thing that may bring about defeat in
war… This is what Lenin taught us," Rodion Yakovlevich stressed and began to speak in
detail about the combat training, weaponry and aggressive intentions of German fascism and
its accomplices. He stated directly that, judging from everything, that we would not be able
to avoid a war with Germany.

One could feel that Rodion Yakovlevich knew military history extremely well and he
employed his arsenal of knowledge for affirming each tenet he put forward.

"A commander in the Middle Ages was not a strategist, but simple the first knight of his
army," the corps commander began.

(I will note in passing that I first heard these words from Malinovskii and only many years
later, while studying A. Svechin's[7] fundamental work, *The Evolution of Military Art*, in the
General Staff Academy, I found out where Rodion Yakovlevich got them from.)

"…Almost until the end of the nineteenth century," the corps commander continued, "the
requirement of creativity remained the privilege of the supreme command. Even in Napoleon's
army the marshals and chief of staff Berthier[8] were, first of all, excellent executioners of the
emperor's will. But the Russo-Japanese War showed the great need for commanders of all
ranks to have a creative approach to command and for each soldier to show initiative. One
of the basic conclusions from that war is that it's impossible to have success in the modern
engagement without an enterprising and conscientious soldier or sailor. The maneuver nature
of the beginning of the First World War strengthened this tendency even further. Finally, the
nature of military operations in Spain and in fascist Germany's seizure of Poland shows that if
we have to wage a war, then the success of the engagement, operation and, on the whole, the
campaign will depend on the initiative and creativity of commanders and political workers
at all levels…"

---

7   Editor's note. Aleksandr Alekseevich Svechin (1878-1938) joined the imperial army in 1899 and fought in
     the Russo-Japanese War and First World War. He joined the Red Army in 1918 and served briefly as chief
     of the All-Russian General Staff, before moving on to academic work. During the interwar period he was
     the Red Army's leading theorist in the area of strategy. He was arrested in 1931 but released a year later.
     Svechin was arrested again in 1937 and shot the following year.

8   Editor's note. Louis-Alexandre Berthier (1753-1815) joined the army in 1770 and fought in the American
     Revolution. He stayed in the army to serve the First Republic and Napoleon. His excellent organizational
     skills made him Napoleon's *de facto* chief of staff during the latter's campaigns.

In this case, Malinovskii was speaking very much in the spirit of the Red Army's restructuring, which had been started by the new defense commissar following the unsuccessful Finnish war and which was directed at raising the level of combat training. According to Soviet plans, during the first days of war the divisions along the Romanian frontier really would have to wage defensive battles.

On 14 June the 48th Rifle Corps (30th Mountain-Rifle and 74th Rifle divisions) arrived by march to the Floresti—Rybnitsa area. the corps' third division, the 176th Rifle Division, had been transferred to the 35th Rifle Corps, and the fourth, the 147th Rifle Division, to the 7th Rifle Corps. The corps headquarters and the 74th Division were located in the reserve of the commander of the Odessa Military District, Colonel General Ya.T. Cherevichenko, who headed the 9th Army at the start of the war.

In 1961, following the war, the book by the famous publicist Lev Bezymenskii, *The German Generals with Hitler, and Without Him*, came out. On the margins of this book, across from the phrase "Now we know that the Soviet leadership committed a series of miscalculations in its evaluation of the military and political situation in the spring and summer of 1941," Rodion Yakovlevich left the following note: "These 'miscalculations' are nothing but a great crime against the Motherland by the people who made these 'miscalculations'." One feels that Rodion Yakovlevich did not care for Stalin, considering him, Molotov[9] and other political leaders the true criminals. From all appearances, he also held Timoshenko and Zhukov responsible for the unsuccessful start of the war, when the Red Army was preparing to attack, having missed the preparation for the German offensive.

In Field Marshal Erich von Manstein's memoirs, *Lost Victories*, Malinovskii particularly commented on that place where the field marshal described how following the victory over France: "On 19 June all of the army's higher leaders were summoned to Berlin to take part in a session of the Reichstag, where Hitler proclaimed the end of the western campaign. At this session he expressed the nation's gratitude by rendering honors to the higher military leadership. The scale of these honors spoke of the fact that Hitler considered the war already won." Malinovskii drew a parallel here between Hitler and Stalin: "And the victory parade and the reception in honor of the commanders in the Kremlin." Rodion Yakovlevich probably agreed with Manstein's following commentary on these celebrations: "Although the German people certainly considered the rendering of honors to deserving soldiers as a completely natural phenomenon, nevertheless, according to their forms and scope, these honors, at least as we soldiers of the army thought, went beyond the bounds of necessity."

Malinovskii also noted those places in Manstein's book, where the latter wrote about the concentration of Soviet forces on the borders and pointed out that these assertions did not correspond to reality. Manstein's assertion that "Hitler was always against the Soviet Union, although in 1939 he had concluded an agreement with Stalin," Malinovskii commented in the following manner: "Hitler's hat was on fire (p. 245), which is why he feared the USSR." Malinovskii evidently believed that once Hitler had decided to carry out aggression against the Soviet Union, then his hat, like a thief's, was burning; that is, his preparations for aggression could not remain unnoticed. This is

---

9   Editor's note. Vyacheslav Mikhailovich Molotov (Skryabin) (1890-1986) joined the Russian Social-Democratic Labor Party in 1906 and adhered to the Bolshevik faction under Lenin. Following the revolution, he became an ardent supporter of Stalin and was for many years the dictator's right-hand man. He served as chairman of the Council of People's Commissars during 1930-39 and was foreign affairs commissar/minister during 1939-49. During the Great Patriotic War he was a member of the State Defense Committee and the *Stavka*. He opposed Khrushchev's de-Stalinization campaign and was removed from his posts in 1957.

why he feared a Soviet retaliatory reaction. And when Manstein wrote about the threat that issued from the Soviet Union, Malinovskii noted that this was a threat to capitalism.

On the margins of *Lost Victories* Rodion Yakovlevich gave vent to his anti-German feelings, which had remained since the time of the First World War. By the way, in his comments he invariably spoke about the "Germans" and not about the "fascists." These were the same enemy for him, against which he had fought in the First World War. Of all the Soviet commanders of the Great Patriotic War, only Malinovskii had experience in the fighting on the Western Front in 1916-1918, and in an officer's position as commander of a machine gun platoon in the final months. There troop density and, what was more important, the density of artillery and machine guns, was several times higher than on the Russian Front. And the German divisions, which fought against the French and British, were more combat worthy than those on the Eastern Front. Then Malinovskii was able to observe a tank attack by the Allies and even help drag out a "Renault" tank that had become stuck in a ditch. He had his Spanish experience, when he became convinced what a serious opponent the *Luftwaffe* was. Rodion Yakovlevich knew that the Wehrmacht was a very powerful enemy and, in the depths of his soul he probably realized that the Red Army was weaker. Thus Malinovskii had no belief in an easy victory before the start of the war.

Manstein writes how in the famous Askaniya-Nova preserve, during a raid by Soviet aviation, the officers of the Eleventh Army's headquarters hurried to hide in the slit trench, but the chief of staff, Colonel Otto Wohler, the future commander of Army Group South and Malinovskii's enemy,

> suddenly stopped on the lower step like one struck dead. The voice of one of the officer's was heard from behind. "I beg to request you, Herr colonel, to move a little further. We're still standing outside." Wohler turned round in a fury and without having moved a single step, and shouted: "What do you mean further? I can't! There's a snake here!" And sure enough, everyone who came up saw a very unpleasant looking snake at the bottom of the slit trench. It had half drawn itself up and was fiercely shaking its head and giving off an evil hiss from time to time. The choice between the enemy planes and the snake was decided in favor of the planes. Malinovskii wrote opposite this place: "Even the snakes were against the Germans."

Mainstein, in describing the Eleventh Army's seizure of the Crimea in October-November 1941, mentioned that the XXX Army Corps' breakthrough "was concluded by the bold capture of the fort of Balaklava, which was carried out by the 105th Infantry Regiment under the commander of the bold Colonel Muller (later shot by the Greeks)." Malinovskii wrote opposite this: "Just what he deserved!" Colonel Friedrich Wilhelm Muller ended the war a general of infantry and holder of the Knight's Cross with Oak Leaves and Swords (this is approximately equivalent to the title of three times Hero of the Soviet Union) and commander of the Fourth Army in East Prussia. Following the general capitulation, he surrendered to Soviet forces and was handed over to Greece. He was shot in Athens on 20 May 1947 because, while the chief of the garrison of Crete, he carried out repressions against the civilian population. F.W. Muller even got the nickname of "the butcher of Crete." He was Malinovskii's enemy on the Southern Front in 1941 and later in Hungary, where he commanded the LXVIII Army Corps.

Rodion Yakovlevich also agreed with Manstein's assertion that:

> As a military leader, Hitler cannot simply be dismissed with the aid of that favorite expression, "a corporal from the First World War." He undoubtedly possessed a certain capability of analyzing operational possibilities, which manifested itself as early as that moment when he approved the plan for operations on the Western Front that was proposed by Army Group A: "this evaluation is evidently completely correct."

And the following passage about Hitler was worthy of a more expansive commentary. The field marshal wrote about Hitler that "He was lacking in strategic and operational competency." Rodion Yakovlevich noted on this score, hinting at Stalin: "He was not the only one who suffered from this shortcoming and there was something similar on the opposite side."

Manstein maintained: "When the first crisis around Moscow arrived, Hitler imitated Stalin's prescription for the stubborn holding of any position. This prescription brought the Soviet command to the edge of destruction in 1941, as a result of which it renounced this method during the German offensive in 1942." Here Malinovskii also agreed with the field marshal, although with a certain amazement: "It's strange, but there's a grain of truth here." In this case, Rodion Yakovlevich was probably struck by how, from the Soviet side this prescription led, as a rule, only to excessive losses, while on the German side it sometimes yielded an undoubted effect, as was the case around Moscow and in the Donbass in the winter of 1941.

Manstein wrote:

> Since time immemorial a strong feature of the German military command had been that it relied on the sense of responsibility, independence and initiative of commanders at all levels and it developed these qualities whenever possible. Thus "instructions" for the higher military levels and orders for the middle and lower levels mainly comprised the "assignment" for the subordinate formations, units and subunits.

Malinovskii objected to this: "This was not the case in practice. The Germans' operational art and strategy were very ponderous. The Germans were strong in tactics."

Actually, getting ahead of ourselves, one can say that at the tactical level the Germans practically always outplayed the Red Army, even in 1945. However, at the operational and, even more so the strategic level, beginning from the fall of 1942, they had no more successes either on the Eastern or the Western fronts.

The Red Army was very rarely superior to the Wehrmacht in the tactical sense. One can probably name only three or four battles in which this superiority really told. One was Stalingrad, where this superiority was to a great extent achieved at the expense of the Germans' allies, as well as in the Belorussian and Iasi—Kishinev operations, and also, perhaps, the siege and storming of Budapest. I should note that Malinovskii was directly connected to three of the four battles and played a decisive role in the latter two.

This is the way Malinovskii's elder son Robert recalled the first days of the war:

> I well remember the beginning of the war. It caught us in Kiev, where my father's aunt lived. We arrived there with my mother, Larisa Nikolaevna, and my younger brother, Eduard. We were getting ready to travel further to see my father, who at this time commanded a corps in the Moldavian town of Bel'tsy. However, we never made it there and we had to turn around to the east and be evacuated. It was difficult to leave from Kiev: the Germans were already bombing the railroads. I remember well how as young boys we observed these bombing raids. At first we would run into the shelters and then understood that they weren't bombing the city itself, but the stations. So we sailed along the Dnepr, reached the Poltava area, and then in Khar'kov we got on a train as far as Moscow. But they were bombing Moscow as well. It was scary, of course. And then our mama, a native of Siberia, took us there. I finished school still in Siberia.

On 22 June Malinovskii issued his first combat order to the corps:

On the morning of 22 June the enemy began combat operations against the USSR from Romanian territory. He was able to cross the Prut River along some sectors of the frontier in small units and occupy some villages along the bank. The enemy has been thrown back to the western bank at all points by a counterattack by our arriving forces, leaving behind dead on our bank. The enemy aviation bombed Bel'tsy and Kishinev several times…

However, as early as 30 June Malinovskii, together with chief of staff Batyunya, was forced to issue this following order to the corps:

1. The units' combat operations against the Romanian-German forces during 23-29 June showed that some subunits manifested weakness in the fighting, at a time when the majority of soldiers and the command element fought excellently and became convinced in action of the absolute combat worthlessness of the Romanian forces and the low combat capability of the German forces.

2. A whole series of commanders and soldiers showed in the fighting for our great socialist motherland, while defending the native soil of the mighty Soviet people, examples of extreme self-sacrifice, valor and bravery, and mutual support in the fighting. For example:
   1) A Red Army soldier from the 30th Rifle Division's cavalry squadron, comrade Al'dibergin, being seriously wounded in the fighting, continued to crawl forward with the cry: "Into the attack, comrades, only in to the attack!"
   2) The commander of a company in the 30th Rifle Division, comrade Koval'chuk, fearlessly led his company into the attack, inspiring the soldiers to fight through his personal example, and the enemy was put to flight. Despite his wound, comrade Koval'chuk continued to fight and only a second and serious wound put him out of action.
   3) A corporal from the 30th Rifle Division and section commander, comrade Amonov, with the cry of "Hurrah! For Stalin!," was the first to throw himself into the enemy's ranks and, having flung himself forward and surrounded by six Germans, whom he destroyed by fire and bayonet and, together with the arriving troops of a sapper company, continued to fight. Although he was wounded, he did not leave his position.
   4) Senior Lieutenant Lavrov, from the 256th Rifle Regiment, was wounded in the fighting, but he categorically refused to go to the hospital, declaring: "It's best that I command my subunit—that's my duty," and remained in the line.
   5) A private from the 74th Rifle Division's 142nd Independent Anti-Tank Battalion, comrade Mechleev, was wounded in the head but refused to give up his weapon and be evacuated to the hospital, declaring: "I won't give you my rifle and I'm going into battle. I still have the strength to do it."
   6) Private Maktsiryan, a private from the 109th Rifle Regiment, while wounded, continued to fight with his machine gun and did not leave the battlefield until he was carried off by the company commander's order.
   7) Junior Sergeant Masashvili, commander of a section in the 109th Rifle Regiment, was wounded in the fighting, and then two more times, but continued to direct his mortar until all the rounds had been expended.
   8) Comrade Bobin, a political leader from the 30th Rifle Division and assistant commander for political affairs of a cavalry squadron, took over command of a rifle subunit, which was without a commander, and led it into battle and was seriously wounded in the fighting.
   9) Comrade Lieutenant Vinogradov, a company commander in the 78th Rifle Regiment, killed several officers in a fight with the enemy and, having captured a German machine gun, opened fire with it on the Germans who were running away.

10) Comrade Shaliev, a private with the 176th Rifle Division, while on the eastern bank of the Prut River with a machine gun, prevented the enemy from constructing a crossing. He destroyed up to 60-80 enemy troops. The German barbarians, who boasted about their valor, opened fire with an entire battery against a single man. But comrade Shaliev fired until the end. It was only a serious wound that put him out of action.

11) Comrade Colonel Goncharov, the deputy commander of the 30th Rifle Division, personally led the troops into the attack on the village of Skulen', while inspiring them with the call: "For the Motherland, for Stalin, forward!" During the fighting he handled the cooperation between the rifle regiments and the artillery.

3. The list of the best sons of our mighty Soviet people, who serve as a model and example for all of us in the struggle with the bloodthirsty enemy who has impudently attacked our Soviet land, does not end with this. However, there are traitors and self seekers in our subunits, who have forgotten their duty to the motherland and the Soviet people and who have avoided the fighting and who thus, have betrayed their comrades in battle. These are:

1) Private Samokhin, of the 109th Rifle Regiment, shot himself in the hand in order to avoid the fighting and, having thrown down his rifle, left the battlefield. Samokhin has been condemned by a military tribunal to the highest form of punishment—to death by shooting.

   Death and shame to the traitor and coward. In the same way our revolutionary court has disposed of such scoundrels as Zvorich, from the 256th Rifle Regiment, and Istratiya and Zhigar'.

2) Lieutenant Petrenko from the 35th Rifle Regiment abandoned his company in battle and deserted to the rear. He has been caught and will suffer his deserved punishment.

3) Ten mid-level commanders, who lost their subunits and together with them the appearance of a commander and who had obviously avoided the fighting, were rounded up in the rear of the 591st Rifle Regiment. Here are their shameful names: Senior Lieutenant Venger, lieutenants Sharopan, Stepanenko, Kharitonov, Mas'kov, junior political leader Lidletskii, junior lieutenants Matveenko and Stepanov from the 591st Rifle Regiment, Lieutenant Taranenko from the 78th Rifle Regiment and Jr. Lt. Unev from the 404th Rifle Regiment.

The worst thing is when commanders, having reached the lowest level of cowardice, avoid the fighting and demoralize their subunits. This is the greatest crime which one can commit against the Soviet people. Shame to them.

Ten junior commanders were found: Kozlov, Maksimov and Marchenko from the 256th Rifle Regiment, and Romanov, Bandeladze, Izmalkov, Shchupikov, Tarasov, Pshenichnyi, and Bovmuto from the 591st Rifle Regiment. There is nothing more shameful than cowardice. This degrades a commander and the soldier to the lowest level. The entire country curses cowards and they are cursed by mothers, wives and sisters. Such commanders lose soldiers, their subunits are disrupted and they are transformed into a mob. This is why 97 soldiers were discovered with the commanders of these very subunits.

This shameful episode, which occurred in the 491st Rifle Regiment, forces me to address the entire command element of the corps' units, in order to tear out by the roots and burn out with a heated iron these shameful sores on our healthy body. The strength and fortitude of the units and subunits entrusted to them depends upon you, comrade commanders, on your strength of will, on your organizational abilities, on your scrupulous control over fulfillment of your combat assignment, and upon discipline, the creators of which are you.

The absolutely precise execution of an order received and its unshakeable nature is the foundation of success in battle. We are the people's emissaries for the defense of our great socialist motherland and will carry out our duty with great honor along the front line. With profound faith in ultimate victory over bloody fascism and with unshakeable faith in the triumph of the cause of Lenin and Stalin,

I order:

1) The mid-level and junior commanders named above as ones who have run away from the fighting, are to be immediately judged by our family of commanders and turned over to a comrades' court of honor to review their crimes. The division commanders are to report to me one the fulfillment of this order by 5 July of this year.
2) The corps prosecutor is to see to the fulfillment of this order and bring the guiltiest before the judgment of a military tribunal.
3) The order is to be read to the entire command element, down to section commander inclusively.

Nonetheless, the corps' units did sometimes not manifest the requisite steadfastness and the commanders often lost control of their troops. For example, on 3 July 1941 Malinovskii issued instructions to Major General Sergei Gavrilovich Galaktionov, the commander of the 30th Mountain-Rifle Division, who before long, on 8 August 1941, was executed for "sloppiness and inaction" and who was posthumously rehabilitated on 29 May 1961 (by the way, he is missing from the "Memorial" data base):

I categorically demand that you carry out my order and immediately furnish me with the exact location of the division in defense along the line Pynzaren' (this should be Pynzareni, B.S.)—Kalumar—Skumniya—Bashila, including the artillery's firing points.

2. Take your units firmly in hand, and if the enemy is in Bashila, throw him out of there and entrench solidly.
3. Direct heavy fire on the approaching enemy and destroy his individual breakthrough groups with brief counterattacks.

Mine and obstruct the approaches for tanks and for infantry movement in general. Send me prisoners for verifying information.

Operate bravely and decisively. Any withdrawal without my specific order is to be halted. It is necessary to immediately establish firm control in the division and representatives are to contact me every three hours.

On 8 July Malinovskii sent a report from Putinest to the commander of the 9th Army, General Ya.T.Cherevichenko:

1. The 176th Rifle Divisions (MARTSINKEVICH'S group) (Colonel Vladimir Nikolaevich Martsinkevich, the commander of the 176th Rifle Division, was mortally wounded on 30 July 1944, as commander of the 134th Rifle Division, with the rank of major general, and awarded the title of Hero of the Soviet Union, B.S.), consisting of 1st Bn/404th Rifle Regiment, 2nd Bn/389th Rifle Regiment, a composite battalion from the 591st Rifle Regiment, and the remnants of other battalions—or about 1,200 soldiers—is holding the line of the village of SOFIYA—PELENIYA—the height one kilometer to the southeast. They are faced by small groups of the enemy along the flank and 2-3 battalions from the German 198th Infantry Division.

At 1400 I personally spoke to MARTSINKEVICH and he reported to me that NOVOSEL'SKII had pulled back from behind MARTSINKEVICH'S right flank to the east.

I ordered MARTSINKEVICH to hold on while reconnoitering along his flanks. During the night of 9.7 I will send 300 soldiers in reinforcements to MARTSINKEVICH.

2. All night during 7.7-8.7 SHEVERDIN (F.Ye. Sheverdin, the commander of the 74th Rifle Division, B.S.) peppered me with panicky reports about the encirclement of the artillery's firing positions and the complete breakthrough of his front.

By morning it transpired that thanks to disorganization in the division some of the battalions had voluntarily left the front and begun to withdraw.

The corps chief of staff undertook measures and returned these units to the front, as well as the 360th Rifle Regiment, which supposedly had fallen back from PUTINESHT', supposedly on orders of the commander of the 74th Rifle Division, to its positions, and which upon returning to the front got into a fight with the enemy on the height southeast of GECHIU-VEK. I ordered him to throw the enemy out by turning his flank and to capture heights 243.4 and 268.2 southeast of GECHIU-NOU.

SHEVERDIN is holding the front of the railroad booth northeast of SYNGUREN'—height 184.1—height 111.1, east of BEL'TSY. He just reported at 1230 that his units are falling back and have abandoned both heights.

SHEVERDIN has more than 80 guns in his infantry regiments. I ordered him to immediately rake the enemy with fire and to restore the situation.

The 74th Rifle Division is facing in the BEL'TSY area up to one enemy infantry division (apparently the Romanian 22nd Infantry Division and units of the Romanian 8th Infantry Division).

I have no cable communications with the 30th Mountain-Rifle Division, while radio communications is spotty, and I send groups of messengers one after the other, and I haven't had precise data since 2400 on 7.7. I hear fighting in GONCHAROV'S direction (Major General Mikhail Dmitrievich Goncharov took up command of the 30th Mountain-Rifle Division following the removal and execution of S.G. Galaktionov. He was mortally wounded in Pomerania near Naugard and died on 6 March 1945, as deputy commander of the 2nd Guards Tank Army, B.S.).

GONCHAROV has the 256th Rifle Regiment, 35th Rifle Regiment and the 71st Rifle Regiment (I held up the latter regiment yesterday near PUTINESHT' and dispatched it to GONCHAROV), and the 369th Rifle Regiment, although I didn't know where GONCHAROV was yesterday evening. All of the 30th Mountain-Rifle Division's regiments are small, with 200-250 soldiers apiece, with the remaining Bessarabians not yet removed, although many of the Bessarabians are still fighting.

I'm waiting for reinforcements and have sent a commander to RYBNITSA to meet them. I'm going to give GONCHAROV 2,000 men (the remaining 2,000 will go to MARTSINKEVICH), when I pull the Bessarabians into the rear.

At the present, I assume that GONCHAROV is fighting along the heights 5-6 kilometers southwest of VRADOIYA. I'm waiting every minute for messengers from the 30th Mountain-Rifle Division. There are no less than two regiments of mixed Romanian-German infantry facing GONCHAROV, and although their number hasn't been established, prisoners report that these are units of the 210th Infantry Division.

4. The 321st Rifle Regiment is carrying out its assignment to support the 30th Mountain-Rifle Division's left flank in the SYNDZHEREI area and to conduct reconnaissance toward KISHKAREN' and BUSHILA.

5. I have organized blocking groups in the rear and have caught a lot of commanders and soldiers and am organizing their dispatch to the front. I'm going to compile a list and try them.

6   I still don't have a communications battalion, nor a medical battalion or information when they will be arriving here from KIROVOGRAD.

7. All of the Germans' strength is in their amazing cooperation between aviation and the ground forces (as quoted in the document, B.S.). I don't even have a single plane and we don't see our planes overhead, which greatly depresses the troops.

8. I decided to stubbornly hold the front. I'm preparing rear lines.

Due to the worsening of the situation, Malinovskii at 1540 on 9 July sent an urgent telegram to the 9th Army's headquarters.

The enemy has deeply outflanked the corps' left flank, entering the Tul' area, and is obviously attempting to cut the corps off from the crossings in the Rybnitsa area. I request orders to prepare crossings in the Malyi Rashkov area.

2) I request an attack by the 2nd Cavalry Corps, along with units of the 30th Mountain-Rifle Diivision, against the enemy rear in the Chutuleshty—Dragonesht'—Peaen' area, to destroy it in order to retain the opportunity for the troops' planned withdrawal to the Rybnitsa crossings.

On 18 July Malinovskii was forced to issue an order to retreat behind the Dnestr River. The withdrawal later continued. The 6th and 12th armies, which had withdrawn from the Romanian and Hungarian frontier, fell into the Uman' pocket.

Ye.Ye. Mal'tsev recalled:

On the evening of 10 August senior political leader Musti returned from behind the German lines. He informed us in alarm that the German 16th Panzer Division was moving from Krivoi Rog along the Ingulets River toward Nikolaev. It evidently had the task of closing the encirclement ring around the 9th Army in Nikolaev. This, at least, is what the commander of a German panzer corps told our political leader, with whom who had spoken. Before long the corps commander arrived at the division. Rodion Yakovlevich, with his blackened face and, emaciated and in a dust-covered uniform, immediately made the decision to remove A.V. Lapshov's 109th Regiment (how many times just this regiment!) from its positions and to dispatch it on captured vehicles to Nikolaev in the capacity of a covering group. Neither the corps commander nor the commander of the 9th Army could delegate large forces. General Malinovskii also issued orders for an organized but expedited withdrawal to the crossings in Nikolaev.

I was ordered to leave together with the 109th Rifle Regiment.

"All our hopes are on you," said the corps commander in parting. "Cover Nikolaev until our arrival. Subordinate all military units and subunits to yourself and get in touch with the city's party and Soviet organizations and put the people's militia into the line. The fate of the entire 9th Army depends on your actions."

"We'll do everything in our power, comrade general," I replied to the corps commander.

However, the enemy managed to preempt us. When we entered the city, which had been heavily destroyed by German aviation—there were craters on the streets, many buildings had been destroyed, and there were fires on the eastern outskirts—an anti-aircraft battalion was engaged in an unequal battle with German tanks. The anti-aircraft battalion's position was along a road leading to the east, to the Dnepr and Kherson. The Hitlerites, in attempting to cut this path of retreat, dispatched a group of tanks there. Having learned of their approach, the battalion commander, Major Shevelev, ordered his men to lower the barrels of their guns. The crews at first were amazed at such a command, because, after all, 'Junkers'[10] had appeared over the city. But the major had calculated correctly: the planes now represented the lesser danger. Having let the tanks approach to point-blank range, the artillery crews opened fire. Eight vehicles out of 12 ignited within the space of a few minutes.

The enemy's surprise attack had been repulsed. This enabled the 109th Regiment to occupy defensive positions in time…

The fighting lasted throughout 13 August. The soldiers of the 74th Rifle Division really pounded the fascists' 18th Panzer Division (the 18th Panzer Division was operating with Army Group Center and did not fight around Nikolaev. It's possible that this is a misprint and that what is meant is actually the 16th Panzer Division, B.S.) and carried out a mission of extreme importance for the entire 9th Army: it held the bridgehead on the left bank of the Ingulets. However, when our 9th Army's main forces fell back to Nikolaev, the German panzer division and the "Adolf Hitler" Motorized Division, while deciding to leave Lapshov's regiment in peace, closed the encirclement ring about 3-5 kilometers from the banks of the Ingulets, thus blocking the path of retreat to the Dnepr.

On 15 August the corps commander General Malinovskii summoned Colonel F.Ye. Sheverdin and me. R.Ya. Malinovskii began to discuss how to get out of the developing situation. The corps commander decided to organize his combat formations into three echelons: the 74th Rifle Division in the first echelon had already occupied its jumping-off position for the attack along the left bank of the Ingulets, while the other two divisions were to attempt to break through the encirclement front and broaden the flanks and give us the opportunity to evacuate the rear establishments and wounded.

During the conference, the corps chief of staff, General A.G. Batyunya, went into the next room and immediately returned. Usually calm and level-headed, he was upset this time.

"Comrade corps commander," said A.G. Batyunya to R.Ya. Malinovskii, "tanks have appeared on the bridge over the Sinyukha River!"

"How many?" Rodion Yakovlevich inquired. Within a minute the chief of staff reported: "Eight, comrade corps commander."

The tanks proved to be ours. The commander of the Southern Front, General of the Army I.V. Tyulenev,[11] was in one of them. He had just undertaken a risky flight over the front line and had come under heavy fire from German anti-aircraft guns. The pilot was able to land on the eastern outskirts of Nikolaev with difficulty.

Upon arriving at the headquarters of the 48th Corps, I.V. Tyulenev immediately summoned the commander of the 9th Army, General Ya.T. Cherevichenko and the commander of the 2nd Cavalry Corps, General P.A. Belov.[12]

---

10   Editor's note. This probably refers to one or more military aircraft models produced by the Junkers aircraft company for the German armed forces. This may included the Ju-86 bomber, the Ju-87 ("Stuka") dive bomber and the Ju-88 bomber.

11   Editor's note. Ivan Vladimirovich Tyulenev (1892-1978) was drafted into the imperial army in 1913 and he served in the First World War. He joined the Red Army in 1918. During the Great Patriotic War he commanded a military district and *fronts*. Following the war, Tyulenev commanded a military district and served in the central military apparatus.

12   Editor's note. Pavel Alekseevich Belov (1897-1962) was drafted into the imperial army in 1916 and joined the RKKA in 1918. During the Great Patriotic War he commanded a cavalry corps and an army. Following the war, Belov commanded military districts.

Insofar as the 48th Corps was on the eastern bank of the Ingulets, the front commander turned to R.Ya. Malinovskii:

"What do you intend to do to get out of the encirclement?"

Rodion Yakovlevich laid out his plan and declared that he would go in the corps' first echelon; that is, together with the 74th Division. The plan was approved.

The fight for the exit out of the encirclement began on the morning of 16 August. The 74th Taman' Rifle Division attacked units of the fascist 18th Panzer Division and the "Adolf Hitler" Motorized Division. The fighting lasted all day. We had almost no tanks. We suffered heavy losses. But the enemy bled as well and was running out of steam. The German tank troops could not hold out. The encirclement ring was broken and the flanks widened. The 9th Army's forces crossed over the Ingulets and received orders to fall back to the eastern bank of the Dnepr.

In Nikolaev the four divisions of Malinovskii's corps (the 30th Rifle Division, which had been unable to fall back on Odessa, joined up with him) were fighting the enemy's 16th Panzer Division. The Germans captured 103,000 prisoners and 317 tanks out of the 6th and 12th armies, including both commanders—Lieutenant General Ivan Nikolaevich Muzychenko[13] and Major General Pavel Grigor'evich Ponedelin.[14] Only about 11,000 men and 1,015 motor vehicles got out of the encirclement with their equipment. The majority of those who made it out belonged to the 48th Corps, which became the core of the reconstituted 6th Army.

On 14 August Stalin ordered S.M. Budennyi:

> Front commander Tyulenev proved to be incompetent. He doesn't know how to attack, nor does he even know how to withdraw troops. He lost two armies the way they don't even lose regiments. I suggest you go immediately to Tyulenev and personally investigate the situation and report immediately on a defense plan... It seems to me that Tyulenev is demoralized and is not capable of handling a front.

However, I.V. Tyulenev was seriously wounded on 29 August in the fighting around Dnepropetrovsk, which possible saved him from a military tribunal, insofar as his relief as *front* commander and his replacement by the commander of the 38th Army, Lieutenant General D.I. Ryabyshev,[15] had been made as early as 26 August.

On 15 August Malinovskii was appointed chief of staff of the Southern Front's reserve army. But as early as 25 August he was appointed commander of the reforming 6th Army, which had been created on the basis of the Southern Front's reserve army and the headquarters of the 48th Rifle Corps. I.I. Larin became a member of the 6th Army's military council, and A.G. Batyunya became the 6th Army's chief of staff. The 6th Army's forces unsuccessfully attempted to eliminate

---

13   Editor's note. Ivan Nikolaevich Muzychenko (1901-70) joined the imperial army in 1917 and the Red Army a year later. He commanded an army during the Great Patriotic War, but was captured early on and spent the rest of the war as a German prisoner. Muzychenko attended the General Staff Academy after the war, but retired in 1947 for health reasons.

14   Editor's note. Pavel Grigor'evich Ponedelin (1893-1950) joined the imperial army in 1914 and fought in the First World War. He joined the Red Army in 1918. During the Great Patriotic War he commanded an army, but was captured and spent almost the entire war in captivity. Ponedelin was arrested in 1945 and convicted of treason and shot.

15   Editor's note. Dmitrii Ivanovich Ryabyshev (1894-1985) joined the imperial army in 1915 and fought in the First World War. He joined the Red Army in 1918. During the Great Patriotic War he commanded a mechanized corps, an army and a *front*, but was later demoted to corps command. Following the war, Ryabyshev held a number of secondary positions and retired in 1950.

the enemy's bridgeheads on the left bank of the Dnepr in the Dnepropetrovsk area and some of the attacking units, particularly the Dnepropetrovsk Artillery School, lost up to half of their rank and file.

On 21 August a directive was issued by the commander of the Southern Front, I.V. Tyulenev, one of whose points read:

> The Zaporozh'e group consists of the 274th, 226th and 270th rifle divisions and an NKVD regiment. I'm entrusting the command of the group to the commander of the 48th Rifle Corps, Major General Malinovskii and his staff, who are to immediately travel to Zaporozh'e and take on the command of the group.
>
> The assignment: to capture the island of Khortitsa and, while securely defending along the eastern bank of the Dnepr River, maintain Zaporozh'e in our hands.
>
> Have no less than one regiment in reserve.
>
> The boundary on the left is Krivoi Rog—excluding Nikopol'—excluding Preobrazhenka—excluding Volnovakha.

Here are the dramatic conversations over the cable on 25 August, the day Dnepropetrovsk fell:

> Pokrovskii[16] speaking, the commander-in-chief's chief of staff.
>
> Hello Rodion Pavlovich (they still didn't know the name and patronymic of the newly appointed army commander in the headquarters of the Southwestern Direction,[17] B.S.). I request that you report on what is going on in the Dnepropetrovsk area. That's all.
>
> Malinovskii: I wish you good health, Aleksandr Petrovich. Today I arrived in this area at the very height of disorder, as a result of which the enemy managed to break onto the eastern bank over an unexploded crossing and at about 1400 he began firing on adjacent streets. We managed to gather stray detachments and throw them into the elimination of the enemy who had broken onto the bank. There's fighting going on now in the Lomovsk area. Approximately 2,000 soldiers have been dispatched there, as well as aviation and artillery fire. This effort is being lead by Major General Dratvin (the commander of the 275th Rifle Division, B.S.). Col. Kashkin (chief of staff of the reserve army, B.S.) has left for there, as well as Temnyi, who has been at the crossings all the time. I had still not made a decision, but also took part in organizing and dispatching these detachments, both from the Kamenka area and Podgorodnyaya. This is all that we were able to do to organize these groups of people. Chibisov[18] (the commander of the Odessa Military District and at the same time the commander of the reserve army, who was appointed deputy commander of the Bryansk Front at the end of August, B.S.) is there and is running things. A categorical order has been issued to eliminate this enemy group at all costs and to capture the bank. I'm now trying to establish

---

16 Editor's note. Aleksandr Petrovich Petrovskii (1898-1979) joined the imperial army in 1915 and fought in the First World War. He joined the Red Army in 1919. During the Great Patriotic War he served as the chief of staff of armies, *fronts* and the high command of the southwestern direction. Following the war, Pokrovskii served in the army's military-educational apparatus.

17 Editor's note. The high command of the southwestern direction was a strategic control organ that existed from July 1941 to June 1942. This body controlled at various times the Southwestern, Southern and Bryansk fronts.

18 Editor's note. Nikandr Yevlampievich Chibisov (1892-1959) joined the imperial army in 1913 and fought in the First World War. He joined the Red Army in 1918. During the Great Patriotic War he commanded a military district, armies and a *front*. Following the war, he headed the Frunze Military Academy and served in various military districts, before retiring in 1954.

contact with the units and am undertaking all the measures I can, so… I'll get in touch with the units along the threatened axis and take over command. That's the situation. That's all.

Pokrovskii: Do you have anything on hand? I ordered them to dispatch a composite regiment from the Poltava military school by vehicle from Kremenchug, but it may arrive only by morning. That's all.

Malinovskii: I have something on hand, but not yet in my hands, although I have nevertheless ordered 30 tanks to the Podgornoe area. If we can't manage to eliminate the bridgehead at night, then we'll try to do it tomorrow. Aside from this, I'm transferring units of one organization from far away to the Orekhovo area on vehicles and they will come under my control only during the day and evening tomorrow, so your regiment from Kremenchug will be just what we need. If we can get along without it, I will try to keep it for you. I request that you send that regiment and we will meet it in Spasskoe. That's all.

Pokrovskii: Please remember the route the regiment will take: Kremenchug, then directly to the east along the high road to Sokolki, Tsarichanka, Chaplinka, Spasskoe, Novomoskovsk. It would be nice if you dispatch a commander to intercept it on the road and, if necessary assign it a task on the spot. I may be able to send 10-12 heavy TB[19] aircraft to your area at night. That's all.

Malinovskii: I'll send a commander to meet the regiment along the indicated route. I request you dispatch the night bombers against the northern outskirts of Dnepropetrovsk so that they can drop their goodies on the enemy along the bank itself. We'll also send over our goodies there, but you can't ruin oatmeal with butter, because we really need to strike and strike the enemy very hard. That's all.

Pokrovskii: I have one request for you: maintain contact with us. If you should go off somewhere, leave a regimental commander behind. That's all.

Malinovskii: My chief of staff, Brigade Commander Batyunya, will always be at headquarters and will always report the situation to you. That's all. Goodbye.

Pokrovskii: Goodbye.

On 8 September 1941 Malinovskii was awarded his second Order of Lenin for halting the German offensive from the Dnepropetrovsk bridgehead.

This is how Colonel General Ya.T. Cherevichenko, who on 5 October became commander of the Southern Front and who during the first month of the war had commanded the 9th Army, which included the 48th Corps, rated Malinovskii:

A firm, decisive and strong-willed commander. From the first days of the war comrade Malinovskii had to take on divisions that were completely new to him. Despite this, in a short period he has learned the peculiarities of each division. He has skillfully led the troops in the difficult conditions of combat and along that sector where a difficult situation arose, he appeared there and through his personal example, fearlessness and confidence in victory he inspired the troops to defeat the enemy. In the course of a month of war, units of Malinovskii's corps have been continuously involved in stubborn fighting with the enemy's superior forces and have coped completely with the tasks assigned to them. Malinovskii himself has been recommended for an award.

---

19   Editor's note. This probably refers to the TB-3 heavy bomber, which first appeared in 1934. Although it was officially removed from service in 1939, it nevertheless saw action during the Great Patriotic War. One version carried a crew of four, had a maximum speed of 212 kilometers per hour and a maximum range of 2,000 kilometers. The TB-3 carried 5-8 7.62mm machine guns and could carry up to 2,000 kilograms of bombs.

This is what Konstantin Stepanovich Grushevoi, the former second secretary of the Dnepropetrovsk party provincial committee recalled about the fighting for Dnepropetrovsk:

Naidenov (the chairman of the Dnepropetrovsk City Executive Committee, B.S.) and I sought out General N.Ye. Chibisov in a schoolhouse. His office was in the former teacher's lounge, where bookcases with class journals, globes and stuffed birds still stood. L.I. Brezhnev[20] arrived to see General Chibisov.

Nikandr Yevlampievich, pale from exhaustion, unshaven and with inflamed eyelids, tried to speak calmly.

"We were unable to unable to hold the right bank," he said. "Right now the troops are occupying previously prepared positions along the left bank."

A very powerful explosion was heard during out conversation. The school building shook. Plaster flew off the ceiling and walls. We were literally covered with dust.

The door was flung open and a staff officer ran in.

"Comrade commander! I request permission to report! The two-tiered bridge has been blown up!"

"Direct the retreating forces, artillery and tanks to the second bridge… Are there communications with the troops?"

"We're in contact, comrade commander."

"Go!"

The commander's adjutant, who had been dispatched to the right flank, returned unexpectedly. Stopping at the door, he stood at attention to deliver his report. At that moment blood flowed along the adjutant's left temple and left cheek. He involuntarily raised his hand and wiped his cheek with a bloody handkerchief.

"Are you wounded!" Chibisov quickly asked. "Where? In the head?"

"I got nicked a bit."

"A bullet?"

"Yes. All the glass in the car was smashed."

"Where and how did this happen?"

"They were shooting from behind the wall of the Comintern Factory. The Germans are there."

"That can't be!" exclaimed Chibisov.

"It's the Germans, comrade General. That's for sure. They say that they infiltrated at night during all the confusion."

Chibisov began to categorically demand from someone that they immediately drive the enemy from the territory of the Comintern Factory. L.I. Brezhnev, P.A. Naidenov and I set out to search for the front commander.

It transpired that General Tyulenev had left for the bank of the Dnepr and we caught sight of him only during the second half of the day. The commander was seeing General R.Ya. Malinovskii and Brigade Commissar I.I. Larin, who had arrived in Dnepropetrovsk. It became known that the reserve army was being renamed the 6th Army and that R.Ya. Malinovskii had been appointed the 6th Army commander, and I.I. Larin the member of the military council.

---

20   Editor's note. Leonid Il'ich Brezhnev (1906-82) joined the communist party in 1931 and rose through its ranks in Ukraine. During the Great Patriotic War he served in political posts at the army and *front* level. Following the war he served as leader of provincial and republican party posts and was chief political officer of the navy. Brezhnev replaced Khrushchev in October 1964, upon the latter's ouster.

The fighting continued with unrelenting force. They reported that a battalion from an artillery school, under the command of Colonel Baklanov, was successfully attacking the Hitlerites on the territory of the Comintern Factory, but that the enemy was holding on to individual areas of the left bank.

I.V. Tyulenev turned to me with a request to help the 6th Army Command set up its headquarters in Novomoskovsk…

The 6th Army's headquarters set up in the building of the Novomoskovsk high school and neighboring buildings. We didn't take down the school sign and it continued to hang, as before, by the broad doors, which were guarded by a sentry.

We found the 6th Army commander, R.Ya. Malinovskii and member of the military council I.I. Larin in the former office of the school principal.

Rodion Yakovlevich Malinovskii looked decisive and upbeat, although he manifested a natural reserve in his evaluation of the situation. I recall that he said that the enemy's attempts to overcome the Dnepr from the march had suffered a complete defeat and that the Dnepr is a sufficiently powerful water line for organizing a stable defense, and then worriedly emphasized that the fascists had seized bridgeheads in the area of the Comintern Factory and the sawmill.

"The enemy will attempt to expand these bridgeheads. However, we are taking measures to eliminate them," Malinovskii concluded.

"Consider that the retreat has ended. We won't let the Hitlerites get any further," added Larin."

Malinovskii evidently met Brezhnev, who at the time was a brigade commissar and the first deputy chief of the Southern Front's political directorate, for the first time in Dnepropetrovsk. In Dnepropetrovsk he was commandeered with Grushevoi, as the former secretary of the Dnepropetrovsk provincial committee for the defense industry, in order to assist in evacuating equipment from the Dnepropetrovsk factories.

On 30 August the *Stavka* of the VGK received a report, signed by the chief of the General Staff, Marshal B.M. Shaposhnikov, about the fighting in the Dnepropetrovsk area:

> According to available information, the enemy managed to cross at Dnepropetrovsk thanks to the commanders' criminal carelessness and lack of responsibility. The bridges and retreat of the troops were not covered, which enabled the enemy to break onto the left bank of the river on the heels of the retreating troops. A number of serious errors were committed in eliminating the enemy: slowness of operations, poor discipline among the troops, the absence of coordination, and the loss of control by the commanders, etc., all of which led to excessive losses.
>
> Take the appropriate measures on the spot and punish the guilty. I request that you inform me of the measures taken.

On the evening of 31 August (the message was received at 2130) Malinovskii was reporting to the staff of the Southern Front:

> Please call Ryabyshev or Antonov.[21] Malinovskii's asking.

---

21   Editor's note. Aleksei Innokent'evich Antonov (1896-1962) was drafted into the imperial army in 1916 and wounded in the First World War. He joined the Red Army in 1919. During the Great Patriotic War he served as chief of staff of a military district and *fronts*. He was then called to Moscow and became deputy chief and later chief of the General Staff. Following the war, Antonov was again appointed deputy chief of staff and commanded a military district and was chief of staff of the Warsaw Pact forces.

Major General Antonov on the line.

Major General Malinovskii reporting: With the onset of darkness, the situation in the Lomovka—Manuilovka area is as follows: In reply to our night attack, the enemy launched a counteroffensive at dawn and, as a result, pressed our units back to the northeast and captured all of Manuilovka. The artillery and Poltava schools have held his offensive up with great difficulty. A regiment from the 226th Rifle Division, which was committed into the fighting, threw the enemy back somewhat in the direction of Lomovka and captured the northern outskirts of Lomovka. At 1700 the enemy, having gathered his forces, attacked for a second time and broke through to Nizhnedneprovsk station and the village of Klochko. The enemy along the southern outskirts of the village of Klochko was halted by forces moved by motor vehicle, and a group of tanks and the resistance of an artillery school and with the onset of darkness was thrown back to the railroad. Our units maintained their position along the western outskirts of Lomovka. As before, the enemy is near the Comintern Factory and Factory No. 165. Thus the enemy is holding all of Manuilovka and the eastern half of Lomovka and has no less than a motorized division on the left bank. I had no air power today. I strafed the enemy with the small group of planes left to me. My decision for tomorrow is to commit the entire 226th Rifle Division into the fighting in the direction of the main attack from Mogila Staraya toward the western outskirts of Klochko village and along the railroad. As before, a very weak group under the command of Major General Dratvin and consisting of units of the 276th Rifle Division, a regiment from the 8th Tank Division and a group from the 26th Cavalry Division, will attack the railroad bridge from the right. Today Dratvin's group suffered heavy losses and will number about 400 men. The group from the artillery school and the Poltava school, under the overall command of Brigade Commander Petrov, will attack from the left toward the east of the road. Its strength will also not exceed 400-500 men. All of the artillery operating along this axis is being brought in. A battalion from the 8th Tank Division and seven guns from the 275th Rifle Division will cooperate with Dratvin's group. I'm bringing in the 274th Rifle Regiment, numbering 30 guns, with the 274th Rifle Division, and the 671st Rifle Regiment, numbering 24 guns, with Brigade Commander Petrov's group, as a long-range group. I have set the artillery preparation for 0800, and it is to last two hours, after which the attack will be launched. I'm now supplying this operation with materiel. The forces that I have designated are insufficient, but I have nothing else. I'm making my last exertion. I can't say with confidence that success will be achieved, because the experience of fighting the enemy in the factories' reinforced concrete buildings and other structures shows that this is a task very difficult of resolution. That's all from me.

Antonov: First of all; has all of the 26th Division been brought in, and what is the 28th Division doing, and where are the divisions' motorized-tank regiments? Secondly; Have you organized artillery observation posts? How many tanks will take part? Has a plan of cooperation been drawn up for the aviation, artillery and infantry? Third; why are you so unsure of victory? Answer these questions. Will you be able to transfer up to one regiment from the 169th Division before the start of the operation? That's all. Answer.

Malinovskii: My reply: 1) The entire 26th Division has been brought in, but it is very small. 2) the 28th Division is in the Voroshilovka—Niklaevka (northern) area and I'm not committing it into the fighting, because it is supporting the parrying of the enemy's possible crossings along the 273rd Rifle Division's sector.

Antonov: There's no reason to make a report. Go on.

Malinovskii: I continue to reply: The motor-tank regiment has been completely brought in, but it numbers no more than a hundred. The tanks will operate with the 226th Division, but there are only ten of them. I have delivered communications equipment, so that the artillery observers can be with the infantry. I have no aviation, and that which is here will be covering the group. Maybe Pokrovskii will be able to help us with something. Now, as to lack of confidence: I did not come to this mood alone. I acquired it as the result of six days of fighting, which cost me dearly. But I am operating with the greatest decisiveness, in order to carry out the orders.

Antonov: Can't you take up to one regiment from the 169th Division and employ it as a reserve along your axis? Answer.

Malinovskii: Your captain told me that it is concentrating in my area. I can take one regiment for my reserve, but it is designated as your mobile reserve. Pokrovskii informed me through his operational commander that it will be subordinated to me, but I haven't received it yet. By the way, it is badly organized and short of weapons. That's all.

Comrades Ryabyshev and Borodin on the line. Cooperation should be organized in the attack, chiefly cooperation with the aviation, artillery and infantry. If the operation is not ready by the designated time, then it's better to extend the deadline for its beginning. Pay particular attention to moving up the artillery observation posts, which are located with the infantry and indicate targets and the enemy's firing points for the artillery. You should open our artillery crews' eyes. I'm afraid that they are firing to no purpose by area, without causing the enemy any harm. You have such powerful artillery, which is capable of destroying the enemy without the assistance of the infantry, only it is necessary to employ it correctly. Use your aviation intelligently. We can't give you any more aviation tomorrow. If you can, bring in a regiment from the 169th Division for your reserve along this axis. Take care of your cavalry and don't expend it for nothing. Take on the enemy who has consolidated in the buildings and set them on fire with all your weapons. That's all.

Inform us more often about the situation. Member of the military council, comrade Vlasov, is coming to see you. He will tell you my instructions. Tell me the name of your corps commissar. He is being appointed to you as a member of the military council. He may take up his duties. We will send additional orders. Send us your suggestion for your assistant for rear area affairs. That's all.

I understand. Malinovskii and Krainyukov[22] on the line. We will completely carry out your orders. The organization of the artillery support is our main concern. My commissar's surname is Larin. We don't have any candidate for the rear position. That's all.

On 1 September organizational conclusions regarding N.Ye. Chibisov and his command, who were not able to hold Dnepropetrovsk, followed in a *Stavka* directive signed by B.M. Shaposhnikov:

According to information possessed by the General Staff, there are serious shortcomings in the work of the headquarters of the Odessa Military District. For example, the order by the Southern Front command on the formation of a headquarters for the reserve army at the expense of the district headquarters went essentially unfulfilled. The district commander, Lieutenant General Chibisov, who was also entrusted with the command of the reserve army, while considering this measure a temporary one, did not set about forming an army headquarters and instead of a headquarters, ordered the formation of casual operational groups carrying out the functions of an operational section, intelligence section and rear section.

---

22 Editor's note. Konstantin Vasil'evich Krainyukov (1902-75) joined the Red Army in 1919 and rose through the army's political ranks. During the Great Patriotic War he served as a member of the military council of armies and a *front*. Following the war, Krainyukov served in political positions in the provinces and in the central military apparatus. He retired in 1969.

Major General Ivanov, who had arrived at the district, was appointed chief of the reserve army staff, and Colonel Zakharov chief of the operational section.

A few days later Colonel Korzhenevich, who had arrived from the Southern Front, was appointed to that same post of chief of the operational section, in connection with which Zakharov formally remained as chief of combat training, while actually working together with Korzhenevich.

Somewhat later the front headquarters appointed Major General Yegorov, who arrived at the headquarters of the Odessa Military District, to that same post and, without taking up his duties until 15 August of this year, got drunk in the command element's sanatorium. Yegorov has been arrested (On 7 September Major General Daniil Grigor'evich Yegorov, a former ensign in the czarist army, was turned over to a revolutionary tribunal "for drunkenness and failure to carry out a combat order." He was demoted to another post and on 26 October was appointed to command the 150th Rifle Division. He got into the Khar'kov encirclement with his division and perished on 25 May 1942, B.S.).

Major General Polikarpov works as the chief of the armored section with Major Vasil'chenko. Neither knows who is subordinated to whom and what their functions are. Colonel Kashkin, the district chief of staff, panics and openly declares among the commanders: "The German will defeat us, as we have nothing to fight with."

The majority of the section chiefs did not know the reserve army's tasks, nor do they know what troops are coming into the district from the front and which units need to be fitted out, and what to do with the rear organs of the 6th and 12th armies.

The formation deadline for new formations, as a rule, is not maintained. The organization and mobilization section is not interested in the quality of the forming formations' rank and file and doesn't know what kind of troops the formation is being filled out with.

I am communicating the above-listed facts and request that you take the corresponding measures. I request you inform me of the measures taken.

On 3 September, in a combat report sent at 2100, Malinovskii noted that "The 226th Rifle Division suffered heavy losses; the division is demoralized by the command's poor leadership, and has 1,500 soldiers. Colonel Chugunov, the division commander, has been removed and steps taken to turn him over to a court." The commander of the 6th Army also noted that "aside from the 60th Motorized Division, the enemy has committed units of an SS division, reinforced with artillery and a large amount of mortar and automatic weaponry."

As K.S. Grushevoi recalled, in the beginning of September he arrived at the army's command post in the village of Podgorodnee with very sad news:

The 6th Army command was quartered in a typical peasant hut.

Stooping over, I cross the threshold.

R.Ya. Malinovskii, the thickset and broad-shouldered army commander, measures the chamber with broad steps. He is saying something to the members of the military council, brigade commissars I.I. Larin and K.V. Krainyukov.

Larin is lying on a wooden bed, covered with a patchwork blanket. Krainyukov is sitting at a long table, which is dark from time and polished by the elbows of several generations of local owners. There's a plate with salt in front of Krainyukov. It shakes and slowly moves toward the edge of the table with each artillery burst. The burning lamp under the icons sways in time to the firing nearby.

My appearance interrupts their conversation. Malinovskii halts, answers my greeting and invites me to sit down.

"What's going on, comrade provincial party secretary?" he asks.

"A GKO[23] directive, signed by comrade Stalin, requires that in retreating we burn the unharvested wheat down to the roots," I tell him. "In connection with this, the Dnepropetrovsk provincial committee would like to know exactly the situation in the 6th Army's sector."

"Burn it to the roots?" Malinovskii asks again. "But that's impossible!" He looks back at the members of the military council. "If the soldiers see that everything is burning behind their backs, they won't be able to fight! We will demoralize the army! I won't do that!"

Krainyukov grabs the plate that was falling off the table; Larin rises from the bed and tightens his belt, sits on the bench and sullenly looks at his feet.

"The directive demands that in case of a withdrawal that the wheat be burned!" I repeated.

"Put yourself in the position of the soldier sitting in a trench!" Rodion Yakovlevich says passionately. "Try to understand what the soldier feels who has received an order to fight to the last drop of blood, but not to retreat, and seeing at the same time that they're burning everything behind his back! After all, if they're burning things down, it means that they don't believe that the enemy will be held!"

"There's truth in the army commander's words. I understand Malinovskii. But I also understand that it's impossible to leave the wheat to the enemy. So I remind him that the GKO directive has been signed by I.V. Stalin and it must be carried out at any cost."

"I understand" Malinovskii answers. He turns sharply and puts his hands behind his back and looks out the window…

Larin breaks the silence.

"We will carry out the demands of the directive," he confirms.

On 13 September Malinovskii was forced to issue an order for the 6th Army to go over to the defensive. He ordered:

> All the army's forces, occupying defensive positions near the Dnepr River, are to dig in deep, so that neither aviation, artillery, mortars nor an enemy attack will scare them.
>
> Erect wire obstacles, create minefields and supply the units with a sufficient amount of bottles with flammable liquid against tanks.
>
> Create an auto transport group within each division for maneuvering troops according to the situation, and particularly supply the 169th and 226th rifle divisions with auto transport.
>
> Severely economize shells, particularly large-caliber ones, by broadly employing fire from division and regimental artillery, mortars, machine guns, automatic rifles, rifles, and hand grenades, for repelling any attempts by the enemy to cross the Dnepr River or to develop his success along the Nizhnedneprovsk axis.
>
> Secure reliable communications with units, in order to quickly understand the situation and to render assistance and repel all of the enemy's attempts to penetrate onto the left bank of the Dnepr River, broadly employing maneuver by artillery fire.
>
> Carry out the most intensive reconnaissance along all sectors of the army's front, penetrating onto the right bank of the Dnepr River for this, for the purpose of extracting information on the location of the enemy's forces, trying at all times to capture prisoners for interrogation. Each night must be filled with our scouts' bold nighttime searches.

---

23   Editor's note. The GKO (*Gosudarstvennyi Komitet Oborony*), or State Defense Committee, was formed on 30 June 1941, in response to the German invasion of the Soviet Union. Chaired by Stalin, it was the highest wartime body in the Soviet Union, concentrating all political, economic and military power in its hands.

On 20 September a directive by the commander of the Southern Front ordered the 6th Army: "The 6th Army, in its previous strength, is to securely hold the line of the Orel' and Dnepr rivers in its hands. It is to prevent through active defense the enemy's spreading to the east from the Orel' River and the expansion of his Lomov bridgehead."

On 27 September the 6th Army, consisting of the 26th and 28th cavalry divisions and the 255th Rifle Division was transferred from the Southern Front to the Southwestern Front.

On 6 November 1941 Malinovskii was awarded his third Order of Lenin "for the exemplary completion of the command's combat assignments along the fighting front against the German aggressors and the valor and courage displayed therein," and on 9 November he was promoted to lieutenant general. The two orders of Lenin, which were received during less than five months of war, when awards weren't tossed around at all, and the promotion to the next rank, speak to the fact that Stalin liked Malinovskii's actions and he singled him out from among the other generals.

In the award citation, which is preserved in an electronic data base, there are no data regarding his date of birth, nationality, party status, and other biographical information, although there is the requirement on the citation itself: "All the columns should be filled out completely." The text of the citation was typed up. It's not excluded that this was a later copy. The declaration states:

> While commander of the 48th Rifle Corps, and then as commander of the 6th Army, Lieutenant Geneal MALINOVSKII displayed an example of bravery and Bolshevik steadfastness in a number of responsible operations.
>
> Dedicated to the party of LENIN-STALIN, Lieutenant General MALINOVSKII firmly controls his troops' combat activities, maintains their combat capability at the proper level and always energetically and in a considered way carries out the plans of the assigned operations.
>
> During the critical period of the fighting, Lieutenant General MALINOVSKII decisively put things in order through his personal participation on the front lines.

Here the text breaks off. In the 6 November order Malinovskii is still a major general, when he is already being called a lieutenant general in the declaration. This confirms us in the opinion that we are dealing with a later copy here, which we don't' know who signed, although logic dictates that this should have been done by the then-commander of the Southwestern Front, Marshal Timoshenko.

Malinovskii was undoubtedly decorated for the fact that he was able to halt the Germans in the Dnepropetrovsk area. Unfortunately, this had no strategic significance. The enemy, upon encountering resistance near Dnepropetrovsk, was able to launch an attack into the rear of the Southwestern Front's forces from another, the Kremenchug, bridgehead. The Southwestern Front's main forces were encircled and destroyed in the Kiev area.

As the Rostov historian, V.I. Afanasenko writes, "the Southern Front's overall losses from 29 September through 31 December 1941 amount to 291,135 soldiers, which exceed the official data published in *The Great Patriotic War Unclassified. The Book of Losses* by 118,361 men."

The German Seventeenth Army and the First Tank Group, which were fighting against the forces of the Southern Front, lost 30,171 killed, wounded and missing in action, including 6,989 permanently, from 1 October through 31 December 1941. Besides this, during this period the Italian Expeditionary Corps and a Slovak Motorized Division were fighting against the Southern Front. Overall, from 22 June 1941 through 31 October 1942, the Slovak forces on the Eastern Front lost 2,502 men, including 715 permanently. The losses of the 1st Motorized Division in October-December 1941 could hardly have exceeded 500 men. During 28-30 September 1941 the Italian Expeditionary Corps lost 87 killed, 190 wounded and 14 missing in action in fighting against the Southern Front. The Italians lost approximately another 1,500 before the end of the year, so that their overall losses may be considered to be 1,800 men. The Germans' and allied forces' overall losses in the fighting against the Southern Front during the period 29 September through 31 December

1941 may be listed as 33,000 men, which is 8.8 times less than the Southern Front's overall losses. The correlation of irretrievable losses was even less favorable for the Southern Front, because killed and captured predominated in their losses, while wounded predominated in the enemy's losses.

On 25 December Malinovskii was appointed commander of the Southern Front, relieving Ya.T. Cherevichenko. Lieutenant General A.I. Antonov, the future chief of the General Staff, remained chief of staff. I.I. Larin was appointed member of the military council, in place of A.I. Zaporozhets.[24]

By this time the Soviet forces had already driven the Germans back from Moscow and had recaptured Rostov-on-Don. Now the Southern Front was supposed to liberate the Donbass.

According to Khrushchev's memoirs, Malinovskii "was the most stable commander and remained for quite a long time in the post of commander of the Southern Front. As they say, there's good with the bad, because in 1942 he gave up Rostov to the enemy for the second time. His troops were defeated, as were the forces of the Southwestern Front. Malinovskii fell out of favor and was removed from command."

Khrushchev recalled one quite intelligent saying of Malinovskii about orders:

Comrade Khrushchev, we have a way of doing things. When we make a decision and issue an order to the front, you have to calculate the time beforehand. Such and such an amount of time is required to transmit these orders to the armies; a certain amount of time is needed in order that the orders received by the armies are transmitted to the corps; a certain amount of time is needed in order for the corps commanders to transmit these orders to the divisions, and so on. On the whole, this is quite a lot of time. If right now, we, having just issued an order, will begin to check on its being carried out, then instead of facilitating the most rapid transmittal of this order to the troops, we'll pull people away from their work and they, by reporting to us, will not tell us that the order is not being carried out, but will say something else. Thus we force people to make up things and paralyze their work. Thus if I've issued an order, I have to allow for a period of time for the order to reach the combat units. Then the officers will begin, each along his particular line, to check on the correct understanding of the order and observe the established order that every officer is taught.

Rodion Yakovlevich expressed these very same thoughts in his report on the Spanish war.

The *Stavka* of the Supreme High Command planned the encirclement and defeat of the enemy's Donbass—Taganrog group of forces. It was planned to break through the Germans' defense along the adjacent flanks of the Southwestern and Southern fronts between Balakleya and Artemovsk and reach the lower course of the Dnepr.

From 18 January through 2 February 1942 the forces of the Southwestern and Southern fronts carried out the Barvenkovo—Lozovaya offensive operation. As a result, they managed to push the Germans back 90-100 kilometers to the southwest and to occupy Barvenkovo, Lozovaya and Izyum, creating on the bank of the Severskii Donets a bridgehead for an offensive on Khar'kov. But all of this entailed heavy losses.

As the contemporary Khar'kov local historian, Vadim Dzhuvaga notes:

---

24   Editor's note. Aleksandr Ivanovich Zaporozhets (1899-1959) joined the Red Army in 1918 and rose through the army's political ranks. During the Great Patriotic War he served as a member of the military council in various *fronts*, armies and military districts. Following the war, Zaporozhets continued his political work in provincial and central postings.

for the first time in history, during the offensive on Khar'kov, there appeared the so-called "jacket people," or "people in civilian dress," as the common people called them. In the villages occupied by the RKKA, men ranging in age from 17 to 55 years of age, who had not been previously called up into the army, for various reasons, before the occupation, were hurriedly conscripted into the army. They didn't dress them in military uniform and quickly distributed them among the subunits and immediately threw them into the fighting without any kind of training, and often even without weapons. Thus the name of the "jacket people." This was widely practiced in 1943, during the battle for the Dnepr from the Chernigov area to Tavriya.

The fate of the "jacket people," including women, was tragic. A German captain, a battalion commander from the 294th Infantry Division, who was defending the strong point of Peschanoe, wrote in his diary on 16 April 1942: "I saw a battlefield here which one may encounter only in this campaign. Hundreds of killed Russians, with German soldiers among them. The majority of them are half dressed, without boots, and with terrible wounds and stiffened extremities. Among them were Russian civilians and women."

Actually, the first "jacket people" appeared as early as the Soviet counteroffensive around Moscow in December 1941. However, it is not excluded that direct induction into units was practiced even earlier, during the Soviet forces' retreat.

On 22 April 1942 Malinovskii wrote a report on the Barvenkovo operation. This is how he evaluated the outcome of the preceding battles:

A) The Rostov operation concluded with the defeat of Kleist's[25] group.
B) The fight against Group Schwedler along the 12th Army's front, concluded with the halting of Schwedler's offensive on Voroshilovgrad, and the launching by the 12th Army, together with the 6th Army, of a counteroffensive, concluded with the pushing back of Group Schwedler from the Lisichansk and Sintyanovka area and the significant improvement of the 12th Army's position.
C) The 18th Army's December operation in the area of Kulinatskii siding, along the Orlovo-Ivanovka—Serditaya axis, which did not yield success, nevertheless taught us good lessons.

Malinovskii believed: "The enemy disposed of the following against the entire Southern Front:

"19 divisions along the front;
"10-11 divisions and one cavalry brigade in reserve;
"About 300 tanks;
"About 879-900 guns;
"About 250-300 planes."

On 3 January 1942 the Southern Front was reinforced with the 57th Army. As Malinovskii noted, the forces of the Southern Front, the *Stavka* and high command of the southwestern direction were faced with quite decisive tasks:

---

25   Editor's note. Paul Ludwig Ewald von Kleist (1881-1954) joined the imperial army in 1900 and fought in the First World War. During the Second World War he commanded panzer corps and a panzer army, and then an army group. He was relieved by Hitler in 1944 and captured a year later. Kleist was convicted of war crimes in 1952 and died in Soviet captivity.

… to defeat the Germans' Seventeenth Army, Group Schwedler and the remnants of Kleist's tank army, followed by the arrival at the middle course of the Dnepr.

The front's decision came down to the following: to securely cover the Rostov and Kamenka axes with the forces of the 56th and 18th armies (11 rifle divisions, two rifle brigades and three anti-tank artillery regiments), launch the main attack with superior forces from the front Izyum—Novoe Verkovo in the general direction of Pavlograd, to win the flank and the deep rear of the enemy's Donbass group of forces and through a follow-up attack toward Zaporozh'e and Bol'shoi Tokmak—to press the enemy's main group of forces to the shores of the Sea of Azov, to cut off its path of retreat to the west and, in conjunction with the front's right-wing armies, encircle and destroy it.

Malinovskii divided the operation into three stages:

The first stage is preparatory, from 1-12.42, and involves the regrouping of forces to the axis of the main attack, their reinforcement, rearming, the organization of their materiel support, the organization of the operation, and the cooperation of the combat arms.

The second stage is the defeat of the Seventeenth Army and Group Schwedler and the arrival of the infantry units to the line Lozovaya—Sofievka—Artemovka—Aleksandrovka—Skotovataya—Kuteinikovo—Nosovo, and the mobile units (cavalry, reinforced with tanks) to the Pavlograd—Chaplino area.

The 57th and 37th armies (12 rifle divisions, seven cavalry divisions, seven tank brigades, and nine artillery regiments) launches the main attack from the front Izyum—Nyrkovo in the general direction of Slavyansk and Pavlograd (the attack front is 90 kilometers).

A supporting attack is to be launched with the forces of the 12th Army (five rifle divisions, two artillery regiments and one tank brigade) in the general direction of Luganskoe and Dzerzhinsk, in order to tie down the enemy's Donbass group of forces and to secure the left flank of the front's shock group of forces.

The success of the formations along the axis of the main attack is to be developed by the commitment of two cavalry corps, reinforced by two of the best tank brigades, along the boundary between the 57th and 37th armies in the general direction of Slavyansk and Troitskoe, with the task of reaching the Pavlograd—Chaplino area and, by operating against the enemy's rear, to facilitate the destruction of the units of the Seventeenth Army and Group Schwedler and to support the subsequent development of the offensive operation.

The length of this stage is 7-8 days (13.21.1). The depth of penetration is 85-90 kilometers.

The third stage is the encirclement and rout of the enemy's main group of forces, the seizure of crossings over the Dnepr River near Dnepropetrovsk and Zaporozh'e and arrival at the front Pervoe Maya—Sukhachevka—Pavlov—Bol'shoi Tokmak.

The fulfillment of this assignment is to be achieved by developing the 57th Army's offensive in the general direction of Pavlograd and Dnepropetrovsk and the commitment of the 9th Army along the boundary between the 57th and 37th armies in the general direction of Krasnoarmeiskoe and Bol'shoi Tokmak and an offensive by the 18th and 56th armies to the west.

This stage's duration is 15-16 days (21.1-5.2.42); its depth is 140-190 kilometers.

The duration of the entire operation is determined at 23-25 days. The depth of the operation's development is 250-300 kilometers.

This is how Malinovskii formulated his "Results of the Operation and Conclusions":

1. The idea and its realization. The gap between the idea and its realization. May one that the operation was unsuccessful and that we did not achieve our assigned objectives? No, one cannot, as the operation was successful and concluded with the complete breakthrough of the front along an 80-kilometer sector and its development to 100 kilometers in depth. The 57th Army's units had an open road to Dnepropetrovsk and the enemy along this axis was seized with panic and confusion, and if the 57th Army's divisions were halted, then it was only due to the higher command's considerations and decisions, so as to concentrate all of the troops' efforts along the southern axis and to shake the entire foundation of the enemy's combat formation in the Donbass. In this operation the Southern Front's forces, closely cooperating with the Southwestern Front's 6th Army, inflicted enormous losses in men and materiel on the enemy...

2. The operation forced the enemy to throw his deep reserves into the fighting along a broad front, foiled his plan to restore the defeated forces of Kleist's army. The population of the Donbass once again was convinced of the indestructible power of the Red Army, which routed no less than five German infantry divisions in the Donbass, as well as all kinds of Belgian, Croatian and Romanian units, which were hurriedly, as in a fire, thrown against the breakthrough front, and a large operational wedge was driven into the enemy's defense and hangs as a real threat over the middle Dnepr.

3. The operation showed the great military skill of the higher command in the sense of the irreproachable cooperation of the two fronts, which usually, in the history of preceding wars, was a problem and which was of particular concern for the high command. This operation was conducted along the boundary between two fronts and concluded in a major operational success, which secures us a jumping-off point for the subsequent development of our offensive operations.

   We cannot pass over in silence ... the fascist liars, who seek to justify their defeat that we were helped by the winter. On this score, one must emphasize in particular that the situation was just the opposite. The winter and the Russian frosts, in general, saved them from a complete and final rout, particularly along the southern front. The winter and frosts, which one should say, were particularly brutal during this operation, created special conditions, which were determined by extreme difficulty for our attacking forces.

   First of all, inhabited locales acquired particular significance in the defensive system: the defending enemy took up positions in them and we had to experience particular deprivations, while remaining in the open field for several days straight, and in heavy frosts, while attacking these inhabited locales and blockading them.

   Secondly, the blizzards and heavy snowfalls made extremely difficult the delivery of supplies and feeding of the attacking forces, which cut loose from their supply bases with the development of the operation into the depth. This certainly weakened the strength of our attack and lowered the pace of the operation's development, and sometimes simply halted it for several days. All of this eased the defense by the enemy, who was falling back on his own bases and supplies and probably made our offensive more difficult.

   Had it not been for the winter, with its frosts and blizzards, then the operational idea might have been completely carried out.

   In these extremely difficult conditions, our troops, commanders and political workers displayed undying firmness, bravery and enormous persistence in their invincible desire to defeat the enemy. Deeply infused with faith in their just cause, they overcame all difficulties of winter and displayed amazing examples of their combat work: the raid by detachments from the 130th Tank Brigade against Gavrilovka station and Yazykovo station; the vigorous offensive by the 341st, 351st and 255th rifle divisions; the remarkable attack by the 5th Cavalry Corps against Barvenkovo; the amazing combat work of the 121st Tank Brigade; the artillerists of the 229th and 4th Guards heavy artillery regiments; the outstanding air battles waged by our Stalinist falcons. And, finally, the all-conquering will to crush the enemy at whatever cost; the fighting for Cherkasskaya, Yelizavetovka and Yakovlevka and the fighting to eliminate the Kirovo—Zvonovka—Vyemka salient—all of this showed that the will of our soldiers is unshakeable and that it crushes the enemy's will. And this is the most amazing and most valuable thing that one can have in war and in battle. Our main task is to assist our soldier, so that he feels in himself this strength, which is hidden inside him; that he know what a skillful and powerful soldier he is and that the enemy gave in, and that when he grows even more he will fight even better and no kinds of fairy tales about a "spring" offensive, no kinds of tanks and SS types will make him fearful, and that he will emerge the victor from any fight, no matter how complex it may be.

What kind of operational-tactical conclusions can we draw from this operation?

Infantry. Our infantry has gotten used to tank attacks and has learned to fight them. It has mastered and is not afraid of automatic rifle (from which there's a lot of noise, but few losses) (and this is absolutely correct, insofar as the effective range of automatic rifle fire is significantly less than that of a carbine or rifle. However, Stalin, with maniacal insistence, demanded that the troops be saturated with automatic weaponry and that entire companies of automatic riflemen be created, which, as opposed to the widespread misunderstanding, the Germans did not have. There was a lot of noise, but little sense from Soviet automatic riflemen, B.S.), mortar and artillery fire. It was drawn into night-time regroupings and this enables it to launch unexpected attacks on the enemy at dawn. It has significantly increased its offensive skill, knows how to solidly hold the defense and has acquired the habits of cooperating with tanks and artillery.

What must we develop in our infantry?

1) It is necessary to train it to quickly entrench, to construct defensive structures and to mask them. To rapidly construct obstacles in front of it, by employing all manner of available means. To trick the enemy, building false structures and, while carefully hiding their real strong holds, from which they will fend off any enemy attack.

2) We must particularly train it in intelligence gathering, vigilance and being sharp-sighted in preserving secrets. People who like this should be chosen for intelligence gathering, and good scouts must be encouraged in every way.

3) The infantry must be taught the types of street fighting, to blockade and seize earth and wooden pillboxes and strong holds and to quickly configure them for our defense.

4) The infantry should be taught as broadly as possible to employ their weapons and to greatly increase the accuracy of fire. The infantry should not strive toward heavy, but toward accurate, fire, and for this purpose to let the enemy come closer and closer, and then to reliably and without missing "dispatch" him.

5) We very much need to train the infantry in the art of the offensive engagement. This is such a part of training that one can never say that we have already learned it. What does know how to attack mean?—it means to know how to combine one's movement with fire from all weapons—from mortars, artillery, tanks, and aviation; to never lie down under enemy fire and to always strive to get out from under fire by surging forward, quickly entrenching, to once again combine one's surge with fire, and forward again. To not get off course, to mark out one's route of leaps beforehand, not to bunch up, but to keep in sight one's section and platoon commander. These simple truths are old and always new.

Artillery—

1) To master the art of the artillery offensive means to attack with one's own fire;
2) To increase our maneuver using wheels and fire, to always support one's infantry in the attack in time, and in defense. As a rule, have one's eyes (infantry observation posts) right in the infantry during the attack and along the front line in the defense.
3) To rapidly and smartly repel the enemy's tanks, for which we must always have prepared positions for rolling out light systems. Firing positions should be skillfully echeloned in depth, achieving their fire coordination during the enemy's tank attack.
4) Anti-tank artillery and cannon artillery should never fall behind the infantry and must render constant support to it.
5) To train it to cooperate with tanks and aviation.
6) To instruct it in centralized control, massed fire and to carry out brief but powerful barrages against targets.

Tank units—

1) To work out problems of close cooperation with the infantry, sappers, artillery, and aviation.
2) To train in the massed employment of tanks together with motorized infantry and cavalry.
3) To learn to lure the enemy tanks and fire on them from the site and from ambush, and to finish off the disrupted combat formations of the enemy's tanks through a decisive leap into the attack.
4) The most important thing is to learn to conserve our tanks and to quickly restore them.
5) To forbid our crews from quickly and senselessly firing off their combat load, so as to quickly as possible leave in order to "refuel and reload," which basically means deserting the battlefield.
6) To train the tanks to quickly operate at night.

Army aviation—

1) To fully work out practical methods of organizing the coordination of aviation with the ground forces on the battlefield. Each sortie should be linked to the troops' activities on the ground.
2) To prevent the scattering our forces along the entire front and to strive to fully concentrate our efforts along the main axis.
3) While appearing over the battlefield, to operate against the enemy as much as possible, because only in this manner can we achieve the best support for the attacking or defending infantry.
4) To learn to suppress the enemy's firing points and his artillery.
5) To increase the effectiveness of one's combat effect on the enemy: fire and bomb accurately.
6) To learn to fly in any weather.
7) To infinitely raise the art of the air battle.

Engineer troops. The troops should be taught to quickly dig the simplest earth shelters, to build artificial obstacles, to lay mines and clear mines, to build tank traps and hidden firing points for anti-tank rifles and for concentrated machine gun fire. To sharply increase the masking of structures. To teach the infantry to build defensive centers and lines on reverse slopes.

Chemical training. To achieve chemical discipline: the preservation of gas masks and other types of chemical defense. To prepare the troops to defend against the massive employment of poisonous substances by the enemy.

Troop control.

1) Division commanders and their staffs must see the engagement along the decisive sector and quickly react to the developing situation.
2) To sharply raise the topographical training of the command element at all levels and thus eliminate unclear, and sometimes false, reports.
3) To increase accountability in all areas of the troops' operational and tactical activities: troops, weapons, captures, losses, ammunition expenditure, etc.
4) To prevent the troops' unprepared activities.
5) To allot the troops (battalion, artillery battalion, regiment, and tank brigade) the maximum time for training and organizing cooperation: to avoid "eating up" their time in division and army headquarters. To radically alter the situation in which the main executioners—the company or battalion commander—barely has time to shout "Forward, after me," instead of carefully working out the problems of the offensive engagement with his subordinate company and platoon commanders and the commanders of the artillery battalions, batteries and squadrons, where it is necessary to agree on the terrain, order and methods of the offensive and attack, on signals, and on shifting the fire of tanks and men.
6) It should be a rule that the commander of the platoon or section should explain the mission to the troops and the methods for carrying it out.

Cavalry.

1) Return the horse to life, to employ it not only as a means of movement, but also as a means of combat, which means to treat it and preserve it in working condition through any means.
2) To master maneuver on the battlefield and to completely eliminate frontal attacks, to only observe from the front and to always strike from the flank and rear.
3) Learn to cooperate with the tanks in broad maneuver, and also with aviation.
4) Learn to quickly construct an anti-tank defense and to shelter one's horse behind it. Lead the enemy's tanks into natural anti-tank obstacles. Always go over to active operations against enemy tanks at night, swooping in on their rear and fuel bases, destroying the tank crews and tanks.
5) Train the cavalry for nighttime actions and deep raids against communications, communications lines and supply bases.
6) Intelligence gathering in the cavalry should be better and deeper than in the other combat arms.

Not all the problems of the Barvenkovo operation have been covered by what has been elucidated here, although they do yield a certain amount of experience, which by generalizing and analyzing we can better prepare ourselves, or command organs and the combat arms, in order to operate better, more decisively and correctly in the forthcoming spring-summer operations, while leading the army entrusted to us to its decisive goal—the complete rout of the German occupiers and clearing them from our Soviet land.

According to Grushevoi, Malinovskii, while already commanding the Southern Front, was skeptical of the "mortar-shovel," which fired 37mm mortar rounds, pointing out the low effectiveness of small-caliber mortars. And the mortar-shovel had already shown its ineffectiveness as early as the Finnish War. However, they put it into production again, which led to a pointless expenditure of men and materiel.

Svetlana V'yunichenko, a journalist from Slavyansk, quotes the opinion of Aleksandr Bol'shego, a local researcher that:

> In February 1942 the first stage of the Izyum—Barvenkovo operation began, when our forces attempted to break through to the Dnepr. The operation failed due to the shortage of human resources and equipment, and the absence of communications. But it could have changed the course of the war. Fierce fighting raged in the Slavyansk area. Our forces held territory as far as Bylbasovka to the middle of the spring. According to archival information, a naval battalion once ended up and fought here.
>
> The sailors were holding Makatykha. The Germans could not occupy it until the sailors left.

S. V'yunichenko continues:

> The "Memorial" data base archives, which have opened access to combat reports after 70 years, report that the 11th Independent Rifle Brigade fought against the Germans on the approaches to Slavyansk at the end of the winter of 1942. It essentially consisted of cadets. Almost all the teenagers died in Semenovka, Seleznevka and Chervonyi Molochar. Old timers recall that there was even fighting at the end of Shevchenko Street. According to military archival reports, many soldiers died not from bullets and shells, but from the cold. There are reports that in the harsh winter of 1941-1942 the northern lights were observed over the Slavyansk area.
>
> The town's outskirts were very well fortified from Severnyi. The Germans had managed to build pillboxes here. These days search groups assume think that they reached as far as Novosadovskaya Square and the mechanical factory. They name as one of the reasons for the operation's failure Kleist's tank division, which was located in Adamovka. Soviet intelligence "overlooked" its existence and it proved to be a surprise for our forces.
>
> "In those years, aside from the heavy losses on our side, the mass seizure of prisoners was observed," says Aleksandr Bol'shego. "When we consult the information, we are mainly speaking about the winter and spring of 1942. A year later instances of being captured were quite few. Then both sides preferred to shoot prisoners on the spot."

On 22 March 1942 The *Stavka* of the VGK received a report from the high command of the Southwestern Direction No. 00137/op on the situation that had developed by the middle of March 1942 along the Southwestern Direction's *fronts* and its thoughts on the prospects of the direction's combat activities during the spring-summer period of 1942. There it was maintained that:

> If one allows that all the tank and motorized divisions, located at the present time against the southwestern direction, will be reinforced again to the level of the beginning of the war, then we will have against the forces of the Southwestern Direction… 7,400 tanks according to the first scenario, and 3,700 according to the second. However, taking into account the enemy's significant losses throughout the entire course of the war against us, it is more likely that he will be able to put against the Southwestern Direction a number of tanks according to the second scenario; that is, up to 3,700 vehicles.

The Germans did not have so many tanks and assault guns (3,700 vehicles) along the entire Eastern Front. By the first scenario, the high command of the Southwestern Direction meant a division at authorized strength, which in its opinion had 500 tanks for a panzer division and 250 tanks for a motorized division, while by the second, under strength scenario, meant correspondingly, 250 and 50 tanks. Actually, the authorized strength of a German panzer division, in which only one of three regiments had tanks, consisted of from 150 to 220 tanks (for the second- and third-battalion panzer regiments, accordingly).

Given an average strength of a full-strength panzer division as 170-180 tanks, the sinister role that this catastrophic overestimation of the enemy's forces in the Khar'kov operation becomes understandable.

As a result of the January-February and March-April operations, the Southwestern Direction's forces lost, according to the report, an average of 110-130,000 men per month and as early as the middle of March, when it was still a long time before the end of the fighting (the German 3rd Panzer Division, for example, had not yet launched its attack against Moskalenko's[26] forces), there was a personnel shortage of 370,888 men in the rifle formations alone.

In the Dobropol' are alone they had to bury the victims of the offensive operation as late as the spring.

K.S. Grushevoi recalled:

> I should say that we veterans of the Dnepropetrovsk fighting were always interested in the fate of our comrades and were glad of their successes. It was with great emotion that we learned in March that L.I. Brezhnev had been decorated with the Order of the Red Banner for the fighting near Barvenkovo.
>
> During a meeting with L.I. Brezhnev in one of the 9th Army's divisions, I warmly congratulated him and, of course, sought to learn the details of the fighting. However, Leonid Il'ich, having thanked me for the congratulations, did not divulge any details and only said that "it was hot"… I later learned from participants in the fighting near Barvenkovo that during the offensive by our forces L.I. Brezhnev had been in the combat formations of one of the rifle regiments.
>
> I should note that the halting of the offensive in the Lozovaya and Barvenkovo area was viewed by us at the time as only a temporary measure. In the TsK KP(b)U[27] confirmed that the formation of the Dnepropetrovsk province's party and Soviet organs remained the most important task of our group, which was located in Voroshilovgrad. We were busy with this formation work, all the more so as up to 100 party and Soviet workers from the Dnepropetrovsk area, who had arrived by our summons from the army and the country's rear, had already gathered in Voroshilovgrad.
>
> The first group of workers from the Yur'ev district, headed by the secretary of the district party committee, N.K. Kishenei, was dispatched to the 57th Army, which was literally defending several tens of kilometers from the borders of Dnepropetrovsk province. It was assumed that in the event of a new offensive by our forces, it was precisely the Yur'ev district of the Dnepropetrovsk province would be the first to be liberated from the enemy.

---

26   Editor's note. Kirill Semyonovich Moskalenko (1902-85) joined the Red Army in 1920. During the Great Patriotic War he commanded an anti-tank brigade, cavalry corps and several armies. Following the war, Moskalenko commanded a military district and was commander-in-chief of the Strategic Rocket Forces.

27   Editor's note. The Central Committee of the Communist Party (Bolsheviks) of Ukraine.

Without a doubt, Brezhnev was decorated with the Order of the Red Banner with Malinovskii's knowledge, and that this was suggested by Larin, to whom Leonid Il'ich was directly subordinated. One can assume that Rodion Yakovlevich remembered Leonid Il'ich as early as from the fighting near Dnepropetrovsk and that he decided to note this during the course of the offensive, which he and the *Stavka* at the time recognized as successful and was not stingy with the decorations. In the wording to the decoration, which, by all appearances, had been compiled by the front's military council, it was stated:

> Leonid Il'ich Brezhnev summoned from the first days of the Fatherland War from the position of secretary of the Dnepropetrovsk provincial committee of the VKP(b). Before September he worked in special designation group under the front military council on fulfilling tasks directly among the troops for supporting combat operations. The military council highly valued comrade Brezhnev's work.
>
> Since October he has worked as deputy chief of the front political directorate.
>
> He has skillfully organized work in this position, putting all of his energy into the task.
>
> Throughout the month he was with a group of workers from the political directorate in the 57th Army's units for supporting combat operations. Having skillfully distributed the forces of the group and workers of the army's political section, he was able to mobilize the formations' political organs for supporting the operation. He was directly with the units during the fighting, removing shortcomings in the party-political work and in the units' combat activities.
>
> In a difficult moment, when the roads were covered with snow and vehicles fell behind, he was able to organize the uninterrupted supply of the troops with all the necessities. Comrade Brezhnev received a high evaluation from the front's military council for this work.
>
> He is fully deserving of a government decoration.

And on 27 March 1942 Brezhnev was decorated with the Order of the Red Banner.

This citation is not for the totality of services, but for a specific reason—organizing supply to the troops of the 57th Army during the Barvenkovo operation. The fact that Brezhnev, as his first decoration, received the quite important Order of the Red Banner was probably to a great degree Malinovskii's doing. Brezhnev probably valued this. Their longtime acquaintance, which by all appearances, began as early as the war years, and their liking of each other, helped Leonid Il'ich and Rodion Yakovlevich find a common language when they were preparing to overthrow Khrushchev.

The Barvenkovo operation, although it was crowned with relative success, had placed the Southern Front's forces in a complex situation. The captured Barvenkovo bridgehead had a very small base, and thus there was always a risk that the Germans would cut it off by launching attacks along converging axes. This is what happened during the large-scale offensive by Soviet forces around Khar'kov in May 1942.

On 7 June 1942 the Southern Front's military council, consisting of Malinovskii, member of the military council Larin, and chief of staff Antonov, dispatched a "Report on the Breakthrough by the Enemy of the Defensive Zone of the Southern Front's 9th Army on 17-20.1942" to the chief of the Red Army General Staff, Colonel General Vasilevskii, and a copy to the commander-in-chief of the Southwestern Direction, Marshal Timoshenko. The report was stamped "Top Secret."

On 6 April Timoshenko ordered the Southern Front command to securely consolidate along the lines attained and support from the flank the offensive by the Southwestern Front on Khar'kov and to cover Voroshilovgrad and Rostov. As noted in the report:

By 17.4 the 216th Rifle Division had been pulled into the 9th Army reserve in the area to the east of Barvenkovo. By this time the 15th Guards Rifle Division, on orders from the *Stavka*, had been removed from the 18th Army and dispatched to the Moscow Military District for deployment into a corps.

As a result of this, there remained only three rifle divisions, and these were not up to authorized strength, along the 18th Army's 80-kilometer front.

The 255th Rifle Division, which had been pulled back to the Voroshilovgrad area, where it had not finished refitting and had 5,424 men in its ranks.

It was necessary to immediately reinforce the 18th Army, in order to securely cover the Voroshilovgrad axis. For this reason, the 9th Army's 216th Rifle Division was shifted to reinforce the 18th Army…

The 57th Army had five rifle divisions, one tank brigade and artillery reinforcements along a defensive front of 80 kilometers. The average strength of the divisions was 6-7,000 men. The 9th Army had seven rifle divisions, one rifle brigade, two tank brigades, and artillery reinforcements along a 90-kilometer front. The average strength of these divisions was 5-6,000 men. The front reserve contained the 5th Cavalry Corps and the 12th Tank Brigade in the Brazhovka—Kurul'ka—Golaya Dolina area, the 255th Rifle Division and the 2nd Tank Brigade in Voroshilovgrad, and the 347th Rifle Division and the 4th Guards Tank Brigade in Roven'ki. As was noted in the report:

Since 7.5.42 the 9th Army's military council, on its own initiative and with the permission of the Southern Front's military council, began a local operation for the purpose of capturing Mayaki. The following units were to be brought in to take part in this operation: (the 33rd Rifle Division's 1120th Rifle Regiment (filled in with pencil, B.S.), a rifle regiment from the 51st Rifle Division, the 78th Rifle Brigade, the 15th Tank Brigade, and a dismounted battalion from the 30th Cavalry Division. On 9.5, following the capture of height 165.5 and the western outskirts of Mayaki, in light of the 9th Army commander's reserves along this axis, he was authorized to employ the entire 30th Cavalry Division to develop the success.

Nevertheless, the 9th Army commander was unable to develop the success initially achieved before 10.5, and in order to carry out his assigned task and capture the Mayaki area and the adjacent heights, thus improving the 9th Army's position along the Slavyansk axis, the 9th Army commander was ordered to relieve the weak 15th Tank Brigade with the more powerful 121st Tank Brigade and bring in one of the 333rd Rifle Division's rifle regiments. The main attack was to be launched through the wooded area to outflank Mayaki from the south.

On 13.5 Lieutenant General Antonov, the *front* chief of staff, was commandeered to the headquarters of the 9th Army to observe the course of the operation on the spot.

Following a study of the situation on the spot, on the morning of 14.5 Lieutenant General Antonov reported his findings to the military council that the enemy had brought up 2-3 infantry regiments to the Mayaki area and that the forces that had been committed into the fighting to carry out the assigned task were insufficient. It was necessary to reinforce the 9th Army's shock group, which could only be done with the 333rd Rifle Division, and to support it with front aviation. Moreover, if positive results could not be achieved by 15.5, then the operation should be halted.

On the basis of this, the military council of the Southern Front issued instructions to transfer the 333rd Rifle Division to the Mayaki area, leaving one rifle regiment behind in Barvenkovo. In exchange for the 333rd Rifle Division, the 34th Cavalry Division would be moved to the Barvenkovo area and the 333rd Rifle Division's regiment there subordinated to it.

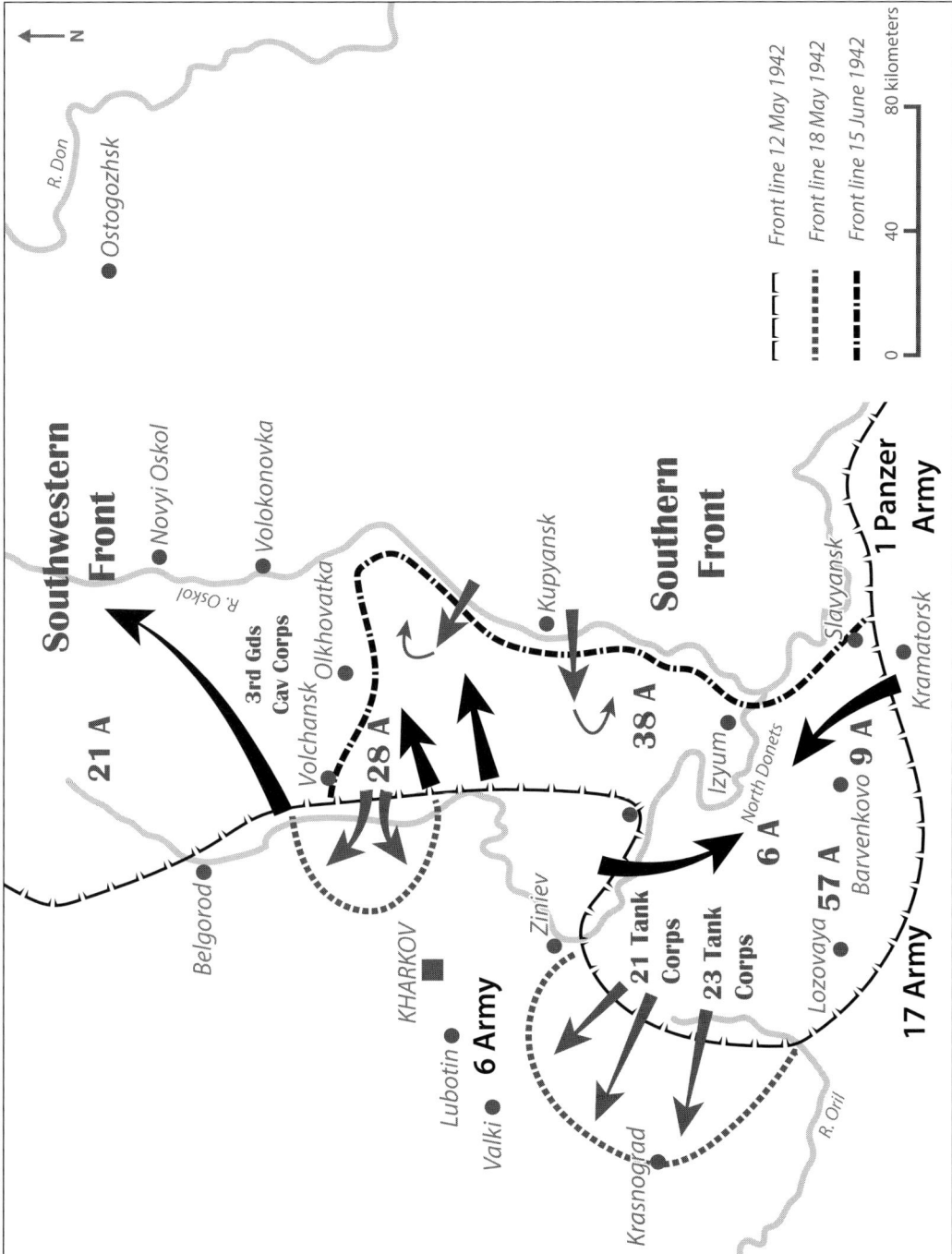

Map 1   Operations in the Khar'kov area, May–June 1942.

Legend:
- Front line 12 May 1942
- Front line 18 May 1942
- Front line 15 June 1942

Scale: 0 — 40 — 80 kilometers

Map labels:
- R. Don
- Ostogozhsk
- Southwestern Front
- Novyi Oskol
- Volokonovka
- R. Oskol
- 21 A
- 3rd Gds Cav Corps
- Volchansk
- Olkhovatka
- 28 A
- Kupyansk
- 38 A
- Belgorod
- KHARKOV
- Ziniev
- Izyum
- North Donets
- 6 A
- Slavyansk
- Kramatorsk
- 1 Panzer Army
- Southern Front
- 9 A
- Barvenkovo
- 57 A
- Lozovaya
- 21 Tank Corps
- 23 Tank Corps
- Lubotin
- Valki
- 6 Army
- Krasnograd
- R. Oril
- 17 Army

This regrouping was carried out, but the offensive on 15.5 did not yield substantial results and on the evening of 15.5 the commander of the 9th Army was ordered to halt the operation and go over to a firm defense.

Taking into account the prolonged location of the armies' headquarters in the same place, all of the armies' headquarters and that of the front changed their locations during 15-30 April.

On 14.5, on the basis of the *Stavka's* instructions, the headquarters were ordered to once again change their locations during the course of two days. In particular, the headquarters of the 9th Army was ordered to move from Dolgen'kaya to Kamenka.

On 16.5 the army's headquarters moved to Kamenka, but due to the incomplete readiness of communications at the new site, an auxiliary command post remained in Dolgen'kaya.

By 16.5 the situation of the 341st, 106th, 349th, and 335th rifle divisions' units was as before.

On 16.5 the 51st Rifle Division occupied the line excluding the fishing collective farm (west of Slavyansk)—Glubokaya—Nakatykha—excluding the woods. On the night of 16-17.5 the division, having received the 1120th Rifle Regiment and an assault battalion from the 333rd Rifle Division, was to relieve the 30th Cavalry Division's subunits and take over and organize the defense along the sector of the woods—western part of Mayaki—height 165.5.

333rd Rifle Division: the 1116th Rifle Regiment was concentrated in the woods in the area of height 222.1; the 1118th Rifle Regiment remained in the Barvenkovo area.

On the night of 16-17.5 the division headquarters and the 1116th Rifle Regiment were to carry out a march to the Barvenkovo area, with a stop on 17.5 in the area of Kurul'ka-2.

On 16.5 the 121st Tank Brigade remained in the woods (two kilometers northeast of Sharabany), with the task of moving to Barvenkovo on the night of 17-18.5, after relieving the units of the 30th Cavalry Division.

On 16.5 the 15th Tank Brigade was to remain in the woods in the area of height 178.1, with the task of moving to the Bogorodichnoe area during the night of 17-18.5.

The 78th Rifle Brigade occupied height 165.5 with part of its forces (up to a rifle battalion), with two companies in a gully (two kilometers southeast of Mayaki), which were to cross over to the left bank of the Severskii Donets on the night of 16-17.5 to take up defensive positions.

Thus, by the start of the enemy's offensive on 17.5, the 9th Army had still not completed its regrouping, due to the halting of the local operation against Mayaki.

On 16.5 the units of the 5th Cavalry Corps were located as follows:

On the night of 16-17.5 the 30th Cavalry Division was to turn its sector over to the 61st Rifle Division and concentrate in the woods (west of Mayaki), so as to move to the Golaya Dolina—Bogorodichnoe area on the night of 17-18.5.

The 34th Cavalry Division, along with the attached 1118th Rifle Regiment, was occupying defensive positions along the line Barvenkovo—Petrovka; the 50th Cavalry Division remained in the woods south of Dolgen'kaya; the 12th Tank Brigade was in Golaya Dolina.

The 9th Army, following the conclusion of the Slavyansk—Kramatorsk operation, and having taken up the defensive, set about strengthening its defensive zone from the beginning of April. As the result of a month and a half of work, fully outfitted trenches, with communications trenches, dugouts and light covers had basically been created in the divisions and work had begun on building wood and earthen pillboxes; there was a limited number of anti-personnel and anti-tank obstacles. Not much work on configuring inhabited locales for defense had been done. Matters were especially poor in regard to creating a deep defense in the divisional sectors.

This depended, on the one hand, on the shortage of strength in the units and on the shortage of explosives and anti-tank and anti-personnel mines and barbed wire, which began to arrive from the center to the front's engineer directorate only following the beginning of the enemy's offensive.

These shortcomings were noted in 9thArmy order No. 014 of 30.4.42, as well as by a group of commanders from the front headquarters, which was working in the army until the beginning of the enemy's offensive.

Given the limited number of active anti-tank weapons and the poorly developed anti-tank obstacles in the terrain, which was almost everywhere accessible for tanks, the army's defense was unable to withstand the massed attack by the enemy's tanks and was not elastic, because the divisions, due to their small size, were unable to organize their forces to a significant depth.

Units of the 1st Mountain Division, 100th Infantry Division, 14th Panzer Division, 60th Motorized Division, and the 68th Infantry Division were noted along the Barvenkovo axis along the sector Dobrinka—Sofievka—Andreevka—Golubovka—Indikovka.

Units of the 97th, 101st and 257th infantry divisions were operating along the Slavyansk—Izyum axis along the sector Indikovka—Bylbasovka—Mayaki—Raigorodok. The presence of Gablenz's units (384th Infantry Division) was noted in the Slavyansk area. The 16th Panzer Division was located in the Stalino area, to where it was assumed the 13th Panzer Division was concentrating.

The enemy was hurriedly reinforcing his units, which had been weakened in the winter fighting, both with men and materiel.

Thus 7-8 infantry divisions and 1-2 panzer divisions were opposite the 9th Army's front.

The enemy had 7-8 infantry and 1-2 panzer divisions (with an overall strength of 200-350 tanks) against our 6 ½ rifle divisions, three cavalry divisions and three tank brigades (with an overall strength of 23 heavy and medium tanks and 25 light tanks).

Taking into account the under strength condition of the 9th Army's units, the enemy had a superiority in infantry and an absolute superiority in tanks.

At about 0500 on 17.5 the enemy attacked, launching his attack along two axes:

A)   From the front Aleksandrovka—Golubovka in the general direction of Barvenkovo and Grushevakha, with the forces of the 1st Mountain Division, 100th Infantry Division, 14th Panzer Division, and the 60th Motorized Division;
B)   From the front Bylbasovka—Slavyansk in the general direction of Dolgen'kaya and Izyum, with the forces of the 97th, 101st, 257th, and the 384th infantry divisions, and the 16th Panzer Division.

The 68th Infantry Division operated between these shock groups.

The offensive was preceded by an extremely powerful aviation and mortar-artillery preparation, which began at 0400 and continued until 0500.

The enemy's aircraft, in groups of 20 and more planes, bombed the front line; the artillery's firing positions, headquarters, and communications lines. Simultaneously, the enemy's aviation subjected the crossings over the Severskii Donets River in the areas of Izyum and Bogorodichnoe to heavy bombing.

There followed from 0500 an attack by tanks and infantry on vehicles, accompanied by bombers. The tanks, with an overall strength of up to 150 vehicles along each axis, were organized into 2-3 echelons. Infantry on vehicles moved behind the tanks. Infantry, which was partially refinforced by small groups of tanks, attacked behind the mobile groups.

While bypassing the strong points and obstacles, the mobile groups broke through the defense en masse and reached the flanks and rear of the defense's combat formations.

By 1000, following a stubborn fight, the 9th Army's defensive front was broken along the axes of the enemy's main attack.

By 1400 the enemy had reached the Zaparo-Mar'evka—Nekremennoe—Kurul'ka—Ivanovskii—Khrestishche area and individual groups of tanks had broken through to the Barvenkovo area. Fierce fighting in the Barvenkovo—Novo-Pavlovka—Kurul'ka—Golaya Dolina area and the woods south of Bogorodichnoe continued to the end of the day on 17.5. Units of the 5th Cavalry Corps and the artillery units fought with particular stubbornness. On 17.5 units of the 5th Cavalry Corps destroyed up to 40 tanks and more than 50 motor vehicles with infantry. The 4th Guards Heavy Artillery Regiment along the main defensive line in the Nikol'skoe area held out until 1100 and up to 1800 in the Adamovka area. The 68th Guards Heavy Artillery Regiment was at its main firing points until 1300, after which, on orders from the 61st Rifle Division, it moved to the area north of Adamovka, where it remained until 1700.

Two batteries from the 186th Light Artillery Regiment from the High Command Reserve fought off three tank attacks over the course of 2.5 hours.

The infantry was also engaged in stubborn fighting, inflicting heavy losses on the enemy, particularly his motorized infantry, which was moving on vehicles.

Upon receiving a report from the headquarters of the 9th Army about the enemy's attack with major forces and his breakthrough along individual sectors of the frontline between 1100 and 1400, the front military council adopted the following measures:

1) The 5th Cavalry Corps in the front reserve was subordinated to the commander of the 9th Army;

2) The commander of the front's air force was ordered to direct its main efforts to supporting the 9th Army;

3) The commander of the 57th Army was ordered to adopted measures to securing the boundary with the 9th Army, for which the 14th Guards Rifle Division was to be regrouped to the left flank and render assistance to the 9th Army in holding the Barvenkovo area. The 2nd Cavalry Corps, which was to be subordinated to the commander of the 57th Army, was to be used for joined actions with the 14th Guards Rifle Division;

4) The commander of the 37th Army was to get ready to shift the 296th Rifle Division by auto transport and the 3rd Tank Brigade by rail;

5) At 1800 on 17.5 the member of the military council, Division Commissar comrade Larin, along with the deputy chief of the front staff's operational section and a group of commanders and political workers, left for the 9th and 57th armies. In the 9th Army's headquarters he adopted emergency measures to establish communications with the formations: through communications officers in cars and dispatched commanders and political workers from his group to the divisions, demanded that the army's military council firmly take control of the army in its hands, to stubbornly hold the attack by the enemy's tank groups and to support holding the crossings over the Severskii Donets River, particularly in the Izyum area. On 18.5 Larin demanded in the 57th Army's headquarters the adoption of all anti-tank defense measures, checking communications with formations and the precise fulfillment of the orders by the Southern Front's military council on moving up the 14th Guards Rifle Division and the 2nd Cavalry Corps.

6) At about 1400 on 17.5 a report was received from the headquarters of the 9th Army that enemy aviation had bombed Dolgen'kaya, where the headquarters' auxiliary command post was located. Major General Korzhenevich, the chief of staff, had been wounded. From this time on, cable and radio communications with the 9th Army's headquarters ceased. It later came to light that the 9th Army command, following the bombing of

Dolgen'kaya, moved to Kamenka at about 1300, and from there to the woods (west of Izyum), without informing the front headquarters. It was only at 0015 on 18.5 that a radiogram was received from the 9th Army commander, from which it transpired that the 9th Army's headquarters was in the woods west of Peski. The 9th Army's military council reported that it only had radio communications with its units, that communications had been lost with the 341st, 106th and 383rd rifle divisions and that the army's situation was grave.

Thus instead of organizing cooperation among the divisions for eliminating the breakthrough and to prevent the enemy's tanks from spreading to the crossings over the Severskii Donets River, the commander of the 9th Army, Major General Kharitonov,[28] left his troops to their fate and hurried to take refuge in the woods west of Izyum, along the left bank of the Severskii Donets River. As a result of this, from the second half of 17.5 command and control over the army was completely lost and the troops, no longer led by anyone, waged the fight on their own. At the same time, the commander of the 9th Army had complete freedom to make use of the headquarters and communications equipment of the 5th Cavalry Corps, which was located next to him in Brazhovka and which remained there until 1200 on 18.5, in order to control its forces.

In reply to this radiogram, the commander of the 9th Army was ordered at 0130 on 18.5 to leave for the 5th Cavalry Corps, to restore the lost command and control over his forces and to securely hold the occupied line. He was to employ the 343rd Rifle Division, which was to arrive at 1200 on 18.5 from the high command commander-in-chief's reserve for occupying Semyonovka, Malaya Kamyshevakha, Sukhaya Kamenka, and Senicheno.

The commanders of the 9th and 57th armies, and the commanders of the 2nd and 5th cavalry corps, upon the breakthrough of the enemy's tanks into the depth of the defense, were to restore the front, cutting off the enemy's infantry and destroying the tanks that have broken through.

This is what the overall conclusions came down to:

The chief reasons behind the enemy's breakthrough of the 9th Army's defensive zone and its withdrawal behind the Severskii Donets River and its heavy losses in men and materiel are as follows:

1. The absence of second echelons in all divisions, with the exception of the 51st Rifle Division, due to the small size of the units and the divisions' broad defensive front. Thus the tactical depth of the defense did not exceed the defensive depth of a regimental sector; that is, 3-4 kilometers.
2. The 333rd Rifle Division and the 121st Tank Brigade comprised the 9th Army's reserve and had not completed their regrouping by the start of the operation.
3. The massed attack by enemy aviation and tanks, which was deeply echeloned and which broke through along a narrow front.
4. We were not able to discover on 16.5 the movement of the enemy's 16th Panzer Division, which had been roused in Stalino and brought up to the breakthrough sector on the night of 16-17.5, which had evidently been prepared by the officers even before the movement, and which guaranteed the enemy's surprise attack.

---

28 Editor's note. Fedor Mikhailovich Kharitonov (1899-1943) joined the Red Army in 1919. During the Great Patriotic War he commanded and airborne corps and armies. Kharitonov later died of an illness.

5. The loss of control by the commander of the 9th Army, as a result of the movement of the army's headquarters to the woods (west of Peski).

The 9th Army's forces fought stubbornly and with persistence. Having begun the offensive at 0500, the enemy was able only by 0930-1000, and at the cost of heavy losses, to break through the 9th Army's tactical defense.

As the experience of the 9th Army's fighting shows, the enemy was able to increase the offensive pace only after overcoming the tactical depth of the defense… Before this the offensive pace was, even given the enemy's significant superiority in men and materiel, was no more than 1-1.5 kilometers per hour.

The enemy suffered heavy losses as a result of the fighting. During 17-19.5 he lost about 100 tanks knocked out and destroyed, 20 armored motor vehicles and more than 200 motor vehicles with infantry, while up to ten artillery and mortar batteries were suppressed and up to 10,000 enemy soldiers and officers killed (evidently the losses presented here are the ones inflicted on the enemy only by the ground troops. They are likely heavily inflated, as are the enemy's losses due to our air activity, B.S.). Besides this, during this period our aviation knocked out and destroyed 162 tanks, 980 motor vehicles and 19 guns.

While covering the left bank of the Severskii Donets River, the units of the 9th Army and 5th Cavalry Corps were able to return the materiel lost near the crossings and cross over to the left bank a significant amount of other weaponry and secure the removal of up to 15,000 men from the 57th and 6th armies.

Khrushchev recalled the unsuccessful operation to capture Mayaki:

I remember the operation that Malinovskii conducted to capture the village of Mayaki. The 9th Army was there, right on the boundary between the Southern and Southwestern fronts. Kharitonov commanded this army. They told me later that he died during the war. He was not a bad general and not a bad man. When they had prepared the offensive, I told Timoshenko that I was going to see Malinovskii in order to familiarize myself with the situation and that I would remain where the operation was to be conducted… I met with Malinovskii in the designated area and we left together, on sledges, to the village of Bogorodichnoe, where the headquarters of the Southern Front's 9th Army was located very near the front line… When we arrived at the army commander's, he reported that the offensive should begin within a couple of hours and said that he wasn't ready for the offensive, but that he had orders to attack. Then Malinovskii took up a pencil and compass, measured the distance needed to bring up ammunition (there was a shortage of shells), calculated that the shells would not arrive in time for the start of the offensive, and said that the offensive should be postponed. I agreed. The offensive was postponed until they could bring up ammunition.

The operation began on the following day. It was again unsuccessful. The enemy put up stubborn resistance and we lost people for nothing and halted the offensive along this sector, although I had been confident together with Timoshenko and Malinovskii that this operation would be successful.

Thus Nikita Sergeevich confirms that the ill-fated offensive against Mayaki was launched not only with the agreement of the Southwestern Direction's military council, but that he had personally observed the offensive in the 9th Army's headquarters. Thus they did not blame the rout at Khar'kov on Malinovskii.

General Nikolai Grigor'evich Lyashchenko, who served under Malinovskii on the Southern Front in 1941-42 as a regimental and division commander and who managed to get out of the

Khar'kov encirclement in one piece, later recalled: "Even in the most awful and almost hopeless situations of battle, Rodion Yakovlevich never lost his calm and self-possession and even a sort of deliberate politeness. There, where other commanders shouted hysterically, cursed and smashed faces, Malinovskii conducted himself exactly the same way as in a completely quiet situation."

7

From Rostov and Back. The Stalingrad Turning Point

Following the Red Army's Khar'kov defeat, the Germans began a general offensive along the southern wing of the Eastern Front at the end of June, preparing to seize the Caucasus and Stalingrad. The Soviet forces made a fighting withdrawal to the east.

The former chief of the General Staff's operational section, S.M. Shtemenko,[1] recalled:

> General R.Ya. Malinovskii, who commanded the Southern Front, at first decided to halt the German-Fascist forces along the line Millerovo—Petropavlovka—Cherkasskoe. However, he had to renounce this decision immediately, insofar as the enemy's more maneuverable units preempted us in reaching that line. The Southern Front had to bend its northern flank to the east, so as to prevent the enemy from turning this flank and breaking into the rear.
>
> The commander requested that the *Stavka* help with diversionary attacks by the Southwestern Front and to allot additional tanks and aviation, "in order to once and for all halt the enemy's attempt to move between the Don and Donets into my deep rear in the general direction of Stalingrad…"
>
> In the General Staff's opinion, it was expedient to gather all our forces, which were operating from Liski to the mouth of the Don, into a single front and subordinate it to R.Ya. Malinovskii. Of course, the front occupied an enormous area, but here you had an experienced and hard-working staff, led by General A.I. Antonov, and he, without a doubt, could have successfully controlled these forces.
>
> A.M. Vasilevskii reported the General Staff's thoughts to the Supreme Commander-in-Chief. It turned out that I.V. Stalin thought the same way. And when R.Ya. Malinovskii mentioned Stalingrad during conversations, the Supreme Commander-in-Chief dictated to him:
>
>> In the present situation, the Germans' main task is to reach Stalingrad, cut the sole remaining Stalingrad—Tikhoretskaya rail line, connecting the north with the south, and to thus cut the Soviet front in two and interrupt communications between the north and the three southern fronts, namely: the Southwestern, Southern and North Caucasus.
>>
>> This is now the greatest danger.
>>
>> The Southwestern Front is not in a condition to repel the enemy's advance, mainly because the front leadership has been deprived of communications with its units and is somewhat disorganized. It is not linked with the 9th Army and does not control it. The

---

1 Editor's note. Sergei Matveevich Shtemenko (1907-76) joined the Red Army in 1926 and later attended the General Staff Academy. During the Great Patriotic War he served as chief of the General Staff's operational section and deputy chief of staff. Following the war he served as chief of staff, before being demoted. Shtemenko's last position was as chief of staff of the Warsaw Pact forces.

21st Army has retired across the Don and is putting itself in order. Two armies are left in the front: the 28th and 38th, and Nikishev's group, with which the front does not have regular communications.

Things can't go on like this. We consider it timely to… unite the Southern Front's armies and the Southwestern Front's armies into the Southern Front, under your command, with the overall length of the front from Rostov to the Don in the area of Veshenskaya.

As regards the Southwestern Front; that is its headquarters and apparatus, we're thinking of transferring this entire apparatus to Stalingrad and to subordinate to it the 5th Reserve Army, the 7th Reserve Army—it's in Stalingrad—and the 1st Reserve Army, which will soon arrive in Stalingrad, so that all three armies, together with the 21st Army, comprise the Stalingrad Front, with the task of preventing the enemy from reaching the Don in the area of Stalingrad.

Following this, A.M. Vasilevskii sent to R.Ya. Malinovskii *Stavka* directive No. 170495, where the mission of the Stalingrad Front, which bordered on the Southern Front, was formulated as follows: "… to firmly occupy the Stalingrad line west of the Don River and under no conditions allow the enemy to break through east of this line toward Stalingrad." This directive was transmitted at 0245 on 12 July 1942.

On 14 July 1942 Malinovskii reported the following to the *Stavka*:

… According to the observations of our officers, Lopatin (the temporary commander of the 9th Army, B.S.) has preserved control over his forces. Units of the 28th, 57th and 38th armies are forcing their way through in groups between the attacking German tank columns in the general direction of Millerovo and Kamensk, and their commanders have fled beyond the Don River to Kazanskaya, Veshenskaya and Kletsko-Pochtovskii. Moskalenko (the commander of the 38th Army) reports that he is gathering his forces along the Don between Kalach and Veshenskaya. The remnants of these armies will be merged with existing formations. I have intelligence information that Verkhnyaya Tarasovka is burning and has been occupied by the fascists, and I am checking this data. The enemy's aviation has bombed communications centers in Kamensk, Roven'ki, Krasnodon, and Likhaya. My headquarters and I moved to the Krasnyi Sulin area this night.

Further on, Rodion Yakovlevich stated that insofar as the 28th, 57th and 38th armies no longer exist as combat units, then it is impossible to close with them the Southern Front's right flank along the Don in the Serafimovich or Veshenskaya area. He believed that "it is now necessary to adopt measures to halt the enemy north of the railroad from Surovikino to Tatsinskaya. If this is not done, then we will have to organize a defense along the Severskii Donets River and then to the east along the Don. In this case, the Konstantinovskaya—Voroshilovgrad—Taganrog wedge acquires extreme importance."

On 16 July A.M. Vasilevskii proposed, in the *Stavka*'s name, to Malinovskii that he not pull the 9th Army behind the Severskii Donets, but direct it to the east, in the direction of Morozovsk, while reinforcing it with one tank corps.

But Malinovskii objected:

To pull back Lopatin's army to the Morozovsk area is not possible in the present situation. Taking into account that the straight-line distance from Verkhnetarasovka to Morozovsk is almost 150 kilometers (that's 6-8 difficult and fighting marches for our infantry, both day and night, and a maximum of two marches for the German motorized infantry), it should be pulled back to the south in the general direction of Kamensk and the Severskii Donets, and the front's military council has already made the decision.

In the meantime, on 16 July a message was received that the Germans had encircled the 176th Rifle Division along the boundary between the 12th and 18th armies, and Malinovskii requested permission to pull back the 12th Army's left flank. Vasilevskii broke off the discussions for a few minutes, in order to speak to Stalin and, upon returning, stated: "the *Stavka* demands that you firmly and directly tell it: are you in a condition to hold the occupied salient with your available men and materiel and to detach, aside from Koroteev's[2] detachment (Major General K.A. Koroteev at this time was an assistant to the commander of the Southern Front, B.S.) some other kind of additional units for covering the sector between the Severskii Donets and Tsimla?"

Malinovskii replied honestly:

> No, I'm not in a condition, taking into account the situation of the 12th Army and the right flank of the 18th Army, and also the fact that Lopatin's group has still not fallen back on the Severskii Donets…
>
> The Southern Front's military council, having discussed the situation, proposes pulling the troops behind the Don, while at the same time holding the Rostov fortified area along its defensive line.

Within a few minutes permission for the withdrawal was given.

However, on the morning of 21 July German troops forced the Severskii Donets. The 18th, 12th and 56th armies fell back on the outer rim of the Rostov fortified area. Discussions took place on the following day between the Southern Front's military council and the *Stavka*:

> Top Secret
> Discussions over cable between comrade Stalin and comrades Malinovskii, Larin and Korniets (Southern Front).
> 22.VII.1942.

> Malinovskii, Larin and Korniets on the line.
>   Stalin on the line. Greetings. Can you not take upon yourself the defense of the southern bank of the Don from Bataisk to Tsimlyanskaya inclusively, so that the units of the North Caucasus Front located along this bank would be subordinated to you?
>   Malinovskii. We hope you are well. We report the following:
>   1. The situation has become more serious since this morning. Thus we will begin by reporting on the situation and our measures for receiving instructions from you.
>   I report: the communications officer dispatched by us from the headquarters of the 51st Army reported that according to information received in the army headquarters, by 0500 on 22.VII the enemy forced the Don near Tsimlyanskaya and had occupied the following in strength up to a division: Krasnoyarskaya, Popov and Boguchary. The enemy also crossed near Nikolaevskaya and occupied Morozov, Dubentsovskaya and Pirozhok. There's no information about the Konstantinovskaya sector in the 51st Army's headquarters. Our aviation, while carrying out reconnaissance along the Don and upon returning from its mission observed the

---

2   Editor's note. Konstantin Apollonovich Koroteev (1901-53) joined the imperial army in 1916 and the Red Army two years later. During the Great Patriotic War he commanded a number of corps and armies. Following the war, Koroteev commanded a military district.

following: at 1140 on 22.VII, 15 tanks and 60 other vehicles from the direction of Zapadno-Kagal'nitskii in the direction of Oblivnoi. At the same time, 25 tanks and 150 other vehicles were moving from Vislovskii in the direction of Bol'shaya Orlovka. 200 motor vehicles were moving from Zolotarevskaya in the direction of Nizhnii and Verkhnii Solenyi, while our reconnaissance aircraft were fired upon by anti-aircraft fire from the latter column and there were two Messerschmitts above this column. Ground reconnaissance has been dispatched; a repeat air reconnaissance and the headquarters commander have been dispatched to determine the identity of this column. I am hurriedly moving up to the crossing over the Manych Canal in the Veselyi area some units from the 9th Army, which have gathered in the Verkhnii Khomutets area with an overall strength of between 1,500 and 2,000 men, with the task of holding these crossings and to prevent the enemy from crossing the Manych Canal to the south. The headquarters commander left with this order an hour agao, followed by comrade Lopatin, in order to transfer these forces to the command of Parkhomenko, the commander of the 5th Cavalry Corps.

Lopatin is preparing to fly to see you tomorrow morning.

We are taking all possible measures to move the 68th Rifle Brigade from the Bataisk area to the Veselyi area to reinforce this group of Parkhomenko.

2. Along the 56th Army's sector the enemy attacked at 0900 today along the front Kamyshevka—Kamennyi Brod with tanks and motorized infantry, and along the sector Nesvetai—General'skoe, with up to 100 tanks, and broke through the line near General'skoe and attacked toward Sultan-Saly. They captured Sultan-Saly at 1600 and Krasnyi Krym at 1700.

A radio order has been transmitted to the commander of the 56th Army that he occupy defensive lines with units of the 216th Rifle Division in the Krasnyi Krym area. the area in the direction of Chaltyr' is to be occupied by units of the 16th Rifle Brigade, and the 31st Rifle Division the line from the Aksai River to Shchepkin. I have subordinated the 176th Rifle Division in the Rakovka—Bol'shoi Log area to the commander of the 56th Army. I have ordered the commander of the 18th Army to occupy the Rostov area with three divisions that have fallen back and to securely occupy the Rostov defensive line with three divisions and to continue crossing troops to the south bank of the Don, gathering the army in the Krasnoarmeisk—Stanitsa Zlodeiskaya—Stanitsa Kagal'nik area.

During the night the military council was working on the crossings. The 68th Brigade's artillery was crossing and the auto transport along the crossings over Zelenyi Island and along the railroad bridge.

The enemy is once again heavily bombing the Rostov crossings from 0600. Following our discussions with you, the members of the military council are once again heading out to the crossings in order to speed up the movement of troops to the southern bank of the Don.

3. We have reliable information, acquired from radio intercepts from the Romanians on 21 July, from which it is clear that: the enemy group of forces along the front Biryukovo—Matveev Kurgan is army group Ruoff, then the German Seventeenth Army along the front Kamensk—Biryukovo, the First Panzer Army along the from Kamensk—Belokalitvenskaya in the direction of Novocherkassk, the Fourth Panzer Army along the front Belokalitvenskaya—Tatsinskaya, also in the direction of Novocherkassk, and the Second Panzer Army along the front Tatsinskaya—Morozovskii toward the south, in the direction of Tsimlyanskaya and Nikolaevskaya.

In this message the Romanians are reporting to their general staff that the Germans' offensive on Voronezh and to the north is not successful and that the fighting for the Caucasus will begin in the near future by List's Army Group A, consisting of the above-named panzer armies, the Seventeenth Army and army group Ruoff, while Army Group B, with all the allied forces—the Italian, Romanian and Hungarian armies—will defend along the Don River and attack toward the Volga.

4. It is very necessary to quickly reinforce the 51st Army, chiefly with tank and motorized forces, at the expense of troops in the Caucasus, and to operate with a group for the 64th Army and tank brigades from the direction of Stalingrad in the general direction of Remontnaya and along the southern bank of the Don.

5. According to a report just received from our communications officer, the 37th Army crossed over units of the 295th Rifle Division to the Kostylevskii rea, the 230th Rifle Divisoin to the Yelkin area, and is crossing the 74th Rifle Division, gathering it toward Kalinin.

The enemy has occupied Melekhovskaya and is attempting to force the Don River, but his attacks have been beaten off; the 37th Army's headquarters is occupying Kalinin, under the cover of the 110th Cavalry Division, which is occupying defensive positions along the Don from Semikarakovskaya to Bogaevskaya. An order has been issued to the 37th Army to move to the area of Nizhnii and Verkhnii Solenyi and Bol'shaya Orlovka and, if I have time, I will seize a line along the Sal River and, if that works out, I will move the 37th Army to reinforce the 51st Army's units along the Nikolaevskaya—Konstantinovskaya sector. The 37th Army has also crossed over its artillery.

6. We are very much in need of aviation fuel, which we are trying to find along all the railroads, but we can't find the numbers of the transports indicated for us, or any kind of aviation fuel.

Due to the developing situation, it is necessary to subordinate the 51st Army to us, as well as all units located from Semikarakovskaya to Bataisk. They should immediately be issued orders commensurate with the developing situation. The lack of clarity in subordination is perniciously reflected in combat activities and command.

We believe that all our aviation, together with the aviation of the North Caucasus and Stalingrad fronts, should operate against the enemy from Tsimlyanskaya to Rostov. We need to radically reinforce our aviation against these panzer armies and make all efforts to deliver aviation fuel.

That's all for us.

Stalin. Your intelligence data is not very reliable. We have the intercept of Colonel Antonescu's message. We don't attach much significance to telegrams to Antonescu. Your aerial reconnaissance information is also not worth much. Our pilots don't know the ground forces' combat formations. Each vehicle seems like a tank to them, nor are they capable of determining just whose forces are moving in this or that direction. That's why we view with a critical eye reports from aerial reconnaissance, and with a large grain of salt. The only reliable intelligence is troop intelligence, but you precisely lack troop intelligence, or it's weak.

A critical examination of all the aerial reports leads us to the following conclusions:

1. The enemy has only insignificant groups along the Don from Konstantinovskaya to Tsimlyanskaya.

2. Our sham commanders are seized with fear of the Kraut and, as the saying goes, fear has big eyes, and thus it is understandable that each small German group is seen as an infantry or panzer division.

You must immediately occupy the southern bank of the Don as far as Konstantinovskaya inclusively and support the defense of the southern bank in this zone. The southern bank of the Don in this area is hilly and high, while the northern one is low. Thus, given good management, this zone can be secured. All units of the North Caucasus Front located in this zone are subordinated to you. The aviation of the Southern and North Caucasus fronts must be united in your hands. As regards the area from Konstantinovskaya to Verkhne-Kurmoyarskaya, the Stalingrad Front's aviation will secure it.

Stalin. What comments do you have?

Malinovskii. It's not clear to whom the units occupying the Don from Konstantinovskaya to the east will be subordinated. The rest is clear. On the basis of your instructions, I am subordinating to myself all of the units from Konstantinovskaya to the mouth of the Don and am uniting the aviation in my hands.

Stalin. The area from Konstantinovskaya to Verkhne-Kurmoyarskaya will remain under Budennyi for the time being, and then, depending on the situation, will be resubordinated to either you or Gordov,[3] who from today has been appointed commander of the Stalingrad Front in place of Timoshenko. That's all. Stalin.

Malinovskii: Everything is clear. We will act and await your order.

Stalin. The corresponding *Stavka* order will be transmitted to you, Budennyi and the Stalingrad Front, and you may immediately set about carrying out your assignment, in accordance with the order received. That's all.

Malinovskii: We will carry it out. That's all.[4]

The Germans occupied Rostov two days later. Malinovskii proved to be right and not Stalin, and the German plans were correctly reflected in the intercepted Romanian report.

Following the war, in 1946, in replying to a question from the journal *Ogonyok*, "What day of the war is most memorable for you?" the marshal replied:

My most bitter day of the war is the most memorable—when we had to abandon Rostov. It was a great sorrow to me that we were not able to delay the Hitlerite military machine. Since that time, no matter where I was fighting, the thought of Rostov never left me. I fought with this idea at Stalingrad, when the 2nd Guards Army barred the way to Manstein's panzer group.

And, finally, the long-awaited hour arrived: the storming of Rostov began on the night of 13-14 February 1943. At six o'clock in the morning the city was liberated. Within three hours N.S. Khrushchev and I were already on the streets of Rostov and saw tears of joy in the eyes of its residents. This was my first joyful day in the war.

We should note that Malinovskii, to judge from everything, abandoned Rostov at his own peril, without waiting for an order from above. He thus saved the Southern Front's remaining forces from the encirclement that threatened them following the forcing of the Severskii Donets by the Germans, but earned Stalin's enmity. On 28 July the leader, in connection with the fall of Rostov-on-Don issued his famous order no. 227 "Not a step back!" Following the war, while reading Manstein's book *Lost Victories*, Rodion Yakovlevich turned his attention to the following quotation of the field marshal regarding the battle of Stalingrad:

Paulus[5] should have told himself that following his speech at the Sportpalast,[6] Hitler would never agree to abandon the city. The name of the city was linked for the dictator to his mili-

---

3   Editor's note. Vasilii Nikolaevich Gordov (1896-1950) joined the Red Army in 1918. During the Great Patriotic War he commanded armies and a *front*. Gordov was arrested in 1947 and executed in 1950.

4   RGASPI, fond 558, opis' 11, delo 489, pp. 65-70.

5   Editor's note. Friedrich Wilhelm Ernst Paulus (1890-1957) joined the imperial army in 1910 and served in France and the Balkans during the First World War. During the Second World War he served as chief of staff of a corps and army and was later promoted to deputy chief of the General Staff. He commanded the German Sixth Army during the summer campaign of 1942 and was encircled and captured at Stalingrad. He later joined the anti-Hitler National Committee for a Free Germany. Paulus was later allowed to return to East Germany.

6   Editor's note. This refers to Hitler's 30 September speech that German troops would never leave the Volga around Stalingrad.

tary prestige. Thus the only thing possible would have been, upon leading his army from the Stalingrad area, to place Hitler before an accomplished fact, all the more so as the high command, as is accurately known, was mysteriously silent for 36 hours. To be sure, it is possible that such actions could have cost General Paulus his head.

Malinovskii continued the phrase about the accomplished fact: "And Paulus himself could have been shot." He commented on the words about the 36 hours thusly: "This reminds me of Rostov in 1942." One can understand this to mean that for an extended time the *Stavka* also failed to reply to Rodion Yakovlevich's request to abandon Rostov, in which case he could have been accused of failing to carry out the order to hold the city at all costs. This is all the more so, as Major General Platon Vasil'evich Chernyaev, the deputy commander of the Southern Front for the fortified areas of the Rostov defensive area was killed while crossing the Don as early as 23 July.

Rodion Yakovlevich very accurately discerned the enemy group of forces in the south and determined the axes of the main attacks. The Supreme Commander-in-Chief thought that the Germans were launching their main attack not only along the Stalingrad and Caucasian directions, but also near Voronezh, in order to outflank Moscow from the south, and that the Germans had neither tanks nor vans on the Don bridgeheads near Rostov. Thus he didn't allocate any reserves to Malinovskii, but expended them in fruitless counterattacks along the Voronezh axis, where the German forces had long since gone over to the defensive. And it was at just this moment, in order to shift the blame, order No. 227 appeared, in which it was asserted that "part of the Southern Front's forces, following panic mongers, abandoned Rostov and Novocherkassk without serious resistance and without orders from Moscow, covering their banners with shame." However, in his heart of hearts Stalin understood that Malinovskii had been right and, although he removed him from command of the Southern Front, he retained his faith in Rodion Yakovlevich. Before long Malinovskii was appointed to command the elite 2nd Guards Army, and later once again came to command a front.

Ye.Ye. Mal'tsev recalled:

> Taking into account the actually developing situation, the commander of the Southern Front, Lieutenant General R.Ya. Malinovskii, in order to improve his operational position, issued orders on the night of 27-28 July to pull back the front's left-wing forces to a line running along the southern bank of the Kagal'nik River and the Manych Canal. However, by this time the enemy had reinforced his forces with fresh reserves and launched new and powerful attacks on our units and formations. In these conditions, they could by no means fall back to the designated lines in an organized manner. The headquarters of the front and some armies often lost contact with their forces and did not always have precise information about the subordinate units' situation. In two days the enemy's tank forces advanced significantly along the Sal'sk axis.
>
> By the close of 28 July large gaps had appeared between the front's armies and the defense was disrupted. The troops, particularly the front's left wing, not being in a condition to hold off the pressure of the Hitlerites' significantly superior forces, continued to fall back to the southeast.
>
> During these days I had the opportunity to meet with Rodion Yakovlevich Malinovskii. He had lost weight and was stoop-shouldered, and with a gray face from constantly being tired, and in dusty clothes, the front commander nevertheless retained his inherent high spirits and liveliness. However, it was impossible not to guess what a heavy burden now lay on General Malinovskii's heart.
>
> There was nothing with which to hold the enemy's tank divisions. The commander of the Southern Front had little more than a hundred tanks to oppose a thousand and more fascist

tanks, and 130 planes against a thousand-plane armada. The front's forces received orders to cover an enormous territory and to defend the riches of the Caucasus. And now they were saying that Rodion Yakovlevich, who was already quiet enough without that, would not pronounce so much as a word for hours, being submerged in his heavy thoughts.

"Fall back" he would sometimes repeat in a crushed voice the same question. "But until when? After all, we will have sufficient forces to halt the enemy! Meanwhile, we're trying to hew wood with a whip… This is a pointless exercise. We need fresh forces… And we will find them…"

On 28 July the Southern and North Caucasus fronts were reorganized into a single North Caucasus Front. Marshal of the Soviet Union S.M. Budennyi was appointed commander of the North Caucasus Front and had the Black Sea Fleet and Azov Military Flotilla operationally subordinated to him. Lieutenant General R.Ya. Malinovskii and Colonel General Ya.T. Cherevichenko became deputy commanders and Lieutenant General A.I. Antonov the front chief of staff.

The Wehrmacht lacked sufficient forces to hold the constantly expanding offensive front. Even if the encirclement of Paulus's army had not occurred, the Germans would have been forced to hand over everything they had conquered in the summer campaign and undertake a new offensive with strategic aims in 1943 in Russia, without any chances of success. After they failed to destroy the Soviet forces in the areas of Voronezh, Voroshilovgrad, Millerovo, and Rostov, operation *Blau* had essentially failed. By the end of July the Bryansk, Southwestern and Southern fronts of Golikov, Timoshenko and Malinovskii, while suffering heavy losses, were able to fall back behind the Don, although they earned the unflattering order No. 227 for this. But this withdrawal had actually saved the Red Army. The Germans were able to capture all of 88,689 prisoners, 1,007 tanks and 1,688 guns west of the Don, which was significantly less than at Khar'kov and in the Crimea. Beyond Rostov the German front continued to increase and the Germans lacked the strength to hold it. Stalin had large reserves. On 1 May 1942 the *Stavka* reserve contained ten rifle and four cavalry divisions, 15 rifle and motorized rifle and three tank brigades. There were 74 rifle and mountain rifle and 19 cavalry divisions, 60 rifle, motorized rifle and airborne brigades and 23 anti-tank and 85 tank brigades in the internal military districts, not counting the 15 divisions and eight brigades of the NKVD's operational forces, which were also designated for combat activities. Aside from this, there were 40 divisions and 36 brigades in Iran and the Far East, a significant part of which were subsequently employed along the Soviet-German front. And new divisions and brigades were being formed all the time. The Germans had practically no reserves. From October 1942 through March 1943 they were able to transfer to the East only 13 infantry and four panzer divisions, which had been formed or reconstituted in the West, and 16 recently-formed *Luftwaffe* field divisions, which had a low combat value.

Lieutenant General Aleksei Ivanovich Nesterenko, who from May 1942 headed an operational group of guards mortar units on the Southern Front, recalled how on the morning of 7 August

I met R.Ya. Malinovskii in Belorechenskaya and reported to him on the condition of my units and on the combat orders we had issued. As always, Rodion Yakovlevich quietly and attentively heard us out and recommended we go to Maikop, in order to reinforce the defense of this very important axis with guards mortar battalions.

In our headquarters we quickly drew up an order, which was issued orally in Labinsk, and left for Maikop. A completely independent task was assigned in the order to the guards mortar units—to maintain their defensive positions, cover the withdrawal of our forces on Maikop, and to fight the enemy tanks…

On the night of 8-9 August the headquarters of the operational group was located in Khadyzhenskaya, along its northwestern outskirts. In the morning we were to present ourselves to Marshal of the Soviet Union S.M. Budennyi. The staff was preparing information for us on the condition of our units. And suddenly Moskvin appeared. He had a concerned look on his face.

"What's happened, Arsenii Petrovich," I asked.

"The enemy's tank have forced the Laba River south of Labinsk and they're outflanking us from the right and heading toward Maikop. All of the Hitlerites' attempts to force the Laba along the Kurgannaya—Labinsk sector have been repulsed by us. I request permission to immediately withdraw the battalions toward Maikop."

Moskvin was right: we ought to have immediately removed the battalions from the line of the Laba River and throw them into the defense of Maikop. However, for this we needed the authorization of Marshal S.M. Budennyi. Lomakovskii, Moskvin and I immediately left for his headquarters. We were traveling with an alarming report and an unpleasant request… However, there was no other way out of this. If our units did not fall back toward Maikop, then the fascist tanks and motorized infantry could break into it and close the exit into the mountains.

At about 0500 we drove up to the front's auxiliary command post. Our unexpected appearance and request upset Semyon Mikhailovich Budennyi. We had to listen to many bitter reproaches. However, the situation was such that it was impossible not to agree with our arguments. We had to pull back the "katyushas"[7] and prepare for decisive fighting in the mountains.

Upon receiving permission, we returned to our own headquarters. The chief of staff ordered the battalions to fall back on Maikop by radio.

By evening of 9 August the enemy's tank subunits and motorized infantry broke into Maikop. Our units managed to fall back behind the Belaya River: the 67th Guards Mortar Regiment with the 12th Army, and Moskvin's, Sidorov's and Kabul'nikov's battalions with the 18th Army. We managed to send a large number of M-13s and M-8s from the North Caucasus Front's operational group of guards mortar units from Stanitsa Saratovskaya beyond the Goitkhskii Pass. We later supplied our units with these shells.

Maikop was easily captured by the Germans to a great extent because of a reconnaissance-diversionary subunit the "Brandenburg-800" Regiment, headed by Lieutenant Adrian von Felkersam, who were dressed in NKVD military uniforms. They destroyed or captured communications centers and issued false radio messages and sowed panic. Those who dared to question instructions received from NKVD officials were immediately reminded of order No. 227. Felkersam's people also managed to capture part of the equipment for procuring oil, having prevented it from being destroyed. The Germans even manage to organize the symbolic extraction of Maikop oil, although this did not have any kind of practical significance. There were no oil-processing factories in Maikop and the Germans had not yet reached the nearest oil processing factories in Groznyi or Baku. To ship the Maikop oil to Germany for refining would mean additionally burdening the already overloaded railroad along which the Germans' Caucasian group of forces was supplied.

However, Malinovskii did not bear direct responsibility for the defense of Maikop and was not punished. I.V. Tyulenev recalled:

---

7   Editor's note. "Katyusha" was the nickname for several kinds (BM-13, BM-8 and BM-31) multiple rocket launchers employed by the Red Army during the Great Patriotic War. These weapons first saw action in July 1941. These weapons constituted the guards mortar units.

Following the fall of Krasnodar and Armavir, there remained only a small group of troops under Lieutenant General R.Ya. Malinovskii along the entire area from the Urukh and Terek rivers to the Kuban' River. The Germans had the opportunity to attack unhindered along the following axes: Cherkessk, Budennovsk—Mozdok, Budennovsk—Georgievsk—Prokhladnyi, Voroshilovsk—Mineral'nye Vody—Pyatigorsk—Nal'chik. A threat hung over the very rich areas of the Northern Caucasus... and mobile detachments were formed and departed toward Mineral'nye Vody to assist General Malinovskii's group...

General R.Ya. Malinovskii's units fought selflessly along the Ordzhonikidze—Groznyi axis. They repeatedly counterattacked the enemy in the Mineral'nye Vody area, inflicted heavy losses on him and, nevertheless in the second half of August, they were forced to fall back to the Pyatigorsk—Prokhladnyi—Nal'chik area. General R.Ya. Malinovskii's units successfully repulsed the Germans' repeated attempts to break through to these towns and themselves counterattacked the Hitlerites who were attempting to capture the defensive area along the Baksan River from the march. Many inhabited locales changed hands several times.

On 25 August Malinovskii was appointed commander of the 8th Reserve Army, which on 27 August was renamed the 66th Army and included in the Stalingrad Front. At the end of September the Stalingrad Front was renamed the Don Front, headed by K.K. Rokossovskii.

In September 1942 Malinovskii commanded the 66th Army, which as part of the Don Front attempted to break through to Stalingrad from the north and encircle the enemy group of forces. The commander of the Don Front, Konstantin Konstantinovich Rokossovskii, spoke of how difficult it had been to search out Malinovskii for the first time:

Upon arriving at the 66th Army's command post, I did not find the army commander. "He's left for the front," reported the army's chief of staff, General Korzhenevich, and would have summoned the army commander to the command post, but I said that I would find him myself. I spent time in division and regimental command posts. I made it to a battalion command post, where, having learned that the army commander was with one of the companies, decided to go there. I should mention that on this day there was quite a lively exchange of artillery and mortar fire and it looked like the enemy was preparing a sortie. Moving along the half-buried trenches and communications trench, sometimes standing up and sometimes hunched over, I made it to the front line. Here I saw a thickset general of medium height. Following the ceremony of officially introducing ourselves and a brief conversation, I hinted to the army commander this it hardly made any sense for him to be crawling around a company position. Rodion Yakovlevich heard out my observation attentively. His face lightened up:

"I understand," he smiled, "but the big brass is wearing me out, and so I get away from it as far as I can. And my people are calmer when I'm here."

We parted as friends, having achieved complete mutual understanding.

Soviet losses during the street fighting exceeded the Germans' by several times, insofar as the German troops were better trained for such fighting, had developed tactics for their storm groups and had organized cooperation between the infantry, artillery, tanks, and aviation. Thus after the war, Marshal Rodion Malinovskii, as minister of defense, maintained that for the Soviet troops the optimal form of operations during the summer and fall of 1942 would have been a planned withdrawal behind the Volga, with the preliminary evacuation of the population of Stalingrad and the equipment from the city's main factories. Then the Soviet infantry would not have suffered such heavy losses in the street fighting, while Soviet artillery from the left bank of the Volga could have uninterruptedly shelled the positions of the German forces in Stalingrad, which would have inflicted serious losses on them. With a powerful group of Soviet troops facing it, the German

Sixth Army would not have risked continuing the offensive toward Astrakhan'. Besides, powerful Soviet armies would have threatened Paulus's flanks. However, due to considerations of prestige, Stalin did not want to give up Stalingrad and demanded that Chuikov's[8] troops, which had been pinned to the Volga, hold the ruins in Stalingrad at all costs. Thus Malinovskii's proposal could not have been accepted, although it made sense and, in the event of its realization, the correlation of losses would have been more favorable for the Red Army.

On 22 October 1957 Khrushchev spoke at a party meeting of the central directorates of the defense ministry, the Moscow Military District and the Moscow Anti-Aircraft District. He touched upon the history of the battle of Stalingrad:

> You can get the documents in the General Staff and check that A.I. Yeremenko[9] and I wrote Stalin and laid out our point of view, and wrote that what if, and you could only write this way, it were possible and if there are reserves of munitions and we see that the enemy's flanks are empty and we carried out a reconnaissance—there was a division commander with a Ukrainian surname, ending in chenko—who faced the Romanians and said "Let me carry out a reconnaissance," and he did (in reality, this was Colonel Ye.F. Kakarchuk, the commander of the 302nd Rifle Division, which carried out a raid on the village of Sadovoe in the beginning of October 1942, B.S.).
>
> He came and killed so many people there that we cursed him out. He collected lots of prisoners. They later brought individual units of soldiers and waged propaganda against us (this refers to the killing of Romanian prisoners by the soldiers of the 302nd Rifle Division, B.S.). The same kinds of operations were carried out in other areas.
>
> The enemy had concentrated large forces against Stalingrad. Our 28th Army was in Astrakhan', where there was no front, but individual oases. I'm convinced that there are a sufficient number of commanders who know that time and these places. I don't mean to say that Yeremenko and I were the smartest ones and wrote about that. Comrade Rokossovskii also wrote about that, I'm convinced. The late Vatutin commanded the Voronezh Front and wrote the same thing. R.Ya. Malinovskii wrote that I also wrote about this to Stalin.
>
> This is natural, as these are military people, and not complete idiots.

Khrushchev's testimony is the single one today in which Malinovskii is mentioned as one of the co-authors of the plan for the Stalingrad counteroffensive.

The opinion was widespread among the German commanders that it wasn't worth storming Stalingrad, insofar as the city had no strategic significance and had been put out of commission by the *Luftwaffe* as an industrial and transportation center. They ascribe the desire to take Stalingrad to Hitler's political ambitions, not the least of all because of its name. However, Malinovskii more than once expressed the idea that Stalingrad should have been abandoned and the troops pulled behind the Volga. In 1965, during one of the meetings with the military intelligentsia, Rodion Yakovlevich said approximately this:

---

8   Editor's note. Vasilii Ivanovich Chuikov (1900-82) joined the Red Army in 1918 and commanded armies during the 1939 invasion of Poland and the 1939-40 war with Finland. During the Great Patriotic War he served as a military adviser in China before being appointed to command the 62nd Army's defense of Stalingrad. Following the war, Chuikov commanded a military district, the Group of Soviet Forces in Germany, the ground forces, and was also head of the country's civil defense program.

9   Editor's note. Andrei Ivanovich Yeremenko (1892-1970) was drafted into the imperial army in 1913 and served in the First World War. He joined the Red Army in 1918. During the Great Patriotic War he commanded and army and several *fronts*. Following the war, Yeremenko commanded several military districts.

I believe that Stalingrad should not have been defended. It would have been simpler to pull back our troops to the eastern bank of the Volga. The Volga is too serious a barrier for the Germans to quickly force it. Those troops which were ground up in the fighting for the city could have been better employed for counterblows against the enemy's flanks. Then our losses would have been much less than the Germans', as they were several times greater during the course of the defensive fighting.

One should note here that if the Soviet forces had left Stalingrad, then the Germans would not have had to keep as much men and materiel there, insofar as they would have been covered by such a mighty barrier as the Volga along its middle course. Then they would have had the opportunity to detach sufficient forces to defend the corridor between the Don and the Volga and the encirclement of the Sixth Army, in any case, would not have followed. Aside from this, they would have sent part of the divisions from the Stalingrad area to the Caucasus, although it's doubtful that this would have brought Army Group A decisive success there. To be sure, sooner or later the Germans would have been forced to leave Stalingrad, but, perhaps without such losses as were suffered by them as a result of the destruction of the Sixth Army. As regards the German generals' idea to not take Stalingrad, but to limit themselves to its destruction by air, the economy of force would nevertheless not have been that great. After all, the Germans would still have had to hold off the pressure from a group of Soviet forces in the Stalingrad area along the front of the Don River.

The Soviet forces suffered heavy losses, attempting to encircle Paulus's army by an attack from the north. According to the combat journal, on 18 September 1942 978 men were killed and 2,030 were wounded, with the number of missing in action not ascertained, in the 1st Guards Army's 258th Rifle Division (the future 96th Guards Rifle) alone, which was next to the 66th Army. It is necessary to stress that those irretrievable losses, which were fixed by name in the regiments' and divisions' combat journals, according to the experience of searchers, in all instances exceeded by several times the irretrievable losses mentioned in the combat report for the same day, while the difference could be as great as ten times. By comparison, the German Sixth Army during the ten-day period during September 11-20 lost only a few more irretrievably: 1,538 killed, 5,846 wounded and 223 missing in action. At the same time, all of the Sixth Army's divisions during this period were engaged in active combat operations: during the 11-12 and 18-20 September they were repelling an offensive by more than 20 Soviet divisions and were attacking in Stalingrad all ten days.

Let's compare the Sixth Army's losses over different months. In August, when there was not yet fighting in Stalingrad, they amounted to 6,177 killed, 19,582 wounded and 946 missing in action, or 26,706 casualties overall. In September, when the street fighting was already going on, Paulus lost 5,194 men killed, 19,615 wounded and 780 missing in action, for a total of 25,589; that is, 1,117 men less, particularly as the reduction came about completely due to irretrievable losses. To be sure, the Fourth Panzer Army's XLVIII Panzer Corps took part in the storming of the city, although it operated in the southern part of the city, where the fighting was much less fierce, than in the center and north in the factory area. Later the Fourth Panzer Army's divisions operating in the city were subordinated to the Sixth Army. The Fourth Panzer Army's losses in August amounted to 2,241 killed, 8,705 wounded and 240 missing in action, for a total of 11,186 men. In September the Fourth Panzer Army's losses fell to 1,619 killed, 5,982 wounded and 152 missing in action, for a total of 7,753 men. There is no information on wounded and missing in action for the last ten days of September, but insofar as the number of killed fell by nearly four times—549 to 142—compared to the preceding ten days, there couldn't have been a lot of wounded and missing in action. In October the Sixth Army lost 4,055 killed, 13,553 wounded and 736 missing in action, for a total of 18,344 men, which was 7,245 men, or 1.4 times, less than in September. In October the Fourth Panzer Army did not suffer any losses. Finally, during the first twenty days of November the Sixth Army lost 1,207 killed, 4,658 wounded and 199 missing in action, for a total of 6,064 men, which is 5,136 men, or 1.8 times, less than the losses for the first twenty days of October. In November the Fourth Panzer Army suffered losses only in the first quarter, and they were insignificant—1 killed and 11 wounded. Thus we are convinced that as opposed to widespread opinion, the German forces' losses since the beginning of the street fighting in Stalingrad did not increase, but decreased. And this is despite the fact that the strength of the Sixth Army was increased by the inclusion of the Fourth Panzer Army's formations. It's most likely that the correlation of losses was less favorable for the Soviet forces than during the fighting in the Don steppes, including the heavy losses incurred while sending reinforcements across the Volga. The Germans had experience in urban fighting and had been the first to create storm groups, and their coordination between the combat arms was much more precisely organized, and the level of training for the soldiers and commanders was significantly higher. On the other hand, in conditions of urban fighting it was much harder for them to employ their superiority in mobility. And the *Luftwaffe's* capabilities were more limited, as there was the great risk of hitting their own men. But it was far more important that the German soldiers and officers were better trained and showed more initiative and freedom in their actions and proved to be better acclimated to the conditions of urban fighting.

The chief thing was that the turning point in the correlation of losses between the Soviet and German forces took place as early as August; that is before the beginning of the fighting in Stalingrad. The German losses on the Eastern Front in January 1942 were 87,082 men, including 18,074 killed and 7,175 missing in action. The Red Army's irretrievable losses (killed and missing in action) in January 1942 amounted to 628,000 men, which yields a correlation of losses of 24.9:1. In February 1942 the German losses in the East amounted to 87,651 men, including 18,776 killed and 4,355 missing in action. The Soviet losses in February reached 523,000 men and were 22.6 times more than the Germans' irretrievable losses.

In March 1942 the German losses on the Eastern Front amounted to 102,194 men, including 12,808 killed and 5,217 missing in action. Soviet losses in March 1942 amounted to 625,000 killed and missing in action. This yields a "record" correlation of losses of 34.7:1. In April, when the Soviet offensive began to die out and the Soviet forces' losses in men captured were still quite few, the Germans' losses amounted to 60,005 men, including 12,690 killed and 2,573 missing in action. Soviet losses during this month amounted to 435,000 killed and missing in action. The correlation of losses is 28.5:1.

In May 1942 the Red Army suffered heavy losses in captured as the result of its unsuccessful offensive around Khar'kov and the successful German offensive on the Kerch' peninsula, while its irretrievable losses, according to the defense commissariat, were 433,000 men. This figure has been most likely significantly lowered. After all, the Germans took nearly 400,000 prisoners in May alone and, compared with April, when there were almost no prisoners; the losses even fell by 13,000 men, with a decline in the index of those wounded in battle by only three points. Thus it is impossible to establish the correlation of irretrievable losses in May 1942.

Soviet irretrievable losses for June amounted to 519,000 men. German losses for that month were 84,670 men, including 14,644 killed and 3,059 missing in action. The correlation of irretrievable losses was 29.3:1.

During July 1942 the German land army in the east lost 96,341 men, including 17,782 killed and 3,290 missing in action. Soviet losses in July 1942 were 330,000 men overall. The correlation of irretrievable losses is thus 15.7:1.

The true turning point in the correlation of irretrievable losses took place in August 1942, when the German forces were attacking toward Stalingrad and the Caucasus, and the Soviet forces in the Rzhev area. In August 1942 the German army in the East lost 160,294 men, including 31,713 killed and 7,443 missing in action. Soviet losses during this month were 385,000 killed and missing in action. The correlation of losses is thus 9.8:1; that is, the best for the Red Army in 1942. Hitler felt this turning point, realizing that there was no longer any chance of seizing the Caucasus. It is not by accident that it was precisely in August 1942 that the fuhrer, according to W. Schulenberg, admitted for the first time the possibility that Germany would lose the war, and there followed in September the noisy resignations of the chief of the General Staff of the OKH, F. Halder,[10] and Field Marshal W. List, the commander-in-chief of Army Group A, which was operating in the Caucasus.

In September the Germans' losses in the East were equal to 132,049 men, including 25,772 killed and 5,031 missing in action. Soviet irretrievable losses reached 473,000 men, which yield a correlation of irretrievable losses of 15.4:1.

In October Soviet irretrievable losses of 819,000 men were increased several times because the uncounted losses of the preceding months, particularly May, were taken into account. Thus it is impossible to accurately establish a correlation of losses for this month.

In November the German army lost 47,928 men in the East, including 9,968 killed and 1,993 missing in action. Soviet losses in killed and missing in action were 413,000 men. The correlation of losses rose to 34.5:1 as the result of heavy losses suffered in the course of the Soviet offensives around Stalingrad and in the Rzhev—Vyaz'ma bridgehead. In reality, however, if you take into account the large irretrievable losses suffered by Germany's allies, whose losses exceeded the German ones, then the real correlation of losses will probably be close to those in September and will remain at 15:1.

In December the German army in the East lost 84,675 men, including 18,233 killed and 4,837 missing in action. The Red Army's irretrievable losses reached 318,000 men, which yields a correlation of 13.8:1. However, by taking into account the heavy irretrievable losses suffered by the Romanians and the Germans' other allies, the real correlation of losses is probable close to that in August.

It is likely that if Hitler had renounced his campaign in the south in 1942 and, following the rout of the Soviet forces around Khar'kov and in the Crimea, had mounted a general offensive from the Rzhev—Vyaz'ma bridgehead, he would probably, taking into account the German forces' flanking position, have managed to encircle and destroy significant forces of the Western and Kalinin fronts. Then it is likely that the military career of Zhukov, Konev and possibly Vasilevskii would have been ended, although it is possible that Timoshenko and Malinovskii could have played a more significant role in the subsequent battles. And even if the Germans had not taken Moscow, they would have shortened their front line. They could have limited themselves in the south to taking Rostov and the Taman' peninsula. In this case the Wehrmacht would have avoided a catastrophe similar to the one at Stalingrad. And then the war would possibly have lasted a few months longer and would have ended with the American atomic bombing of Germany.

By the beginning of the Stalingrad counteroffensive the Red Army enjoyed a significant numerical superiority over the enemy. On 1 November 1942 the active army numbered 367 rifle and 24 cavalry divisions, 36 fortified areas, 164 rifle, motorized rifle, airborne and ski brigades, 15 anti-tank brigades, and 120 tank and mechanized brigades, for a total of 6,124,000 men, 77,180 guns and mortars 76mm and higher (not counting anti-aircraft guns), 1,724 rocket artillery launchers, 7,350 tanks, and 4,544 planes (only fighters, bombers and assault aircraft, and not counting anti-aircraft and naval aviation). In the beginning of November the *Stavka* had in reserve 27 rifle

---

10   Editor's note. Franz Halder (1884-1972) joined the imperial army in 1902 and served in the First World War. He was appointed army chief of staff in 1938 and was instrumental in planning its first campaigns during the Second World War. Hitler relieved Halder in 1942 and he took no further part in the war. Following the war, Halder served as an advisory historian for the US Army.

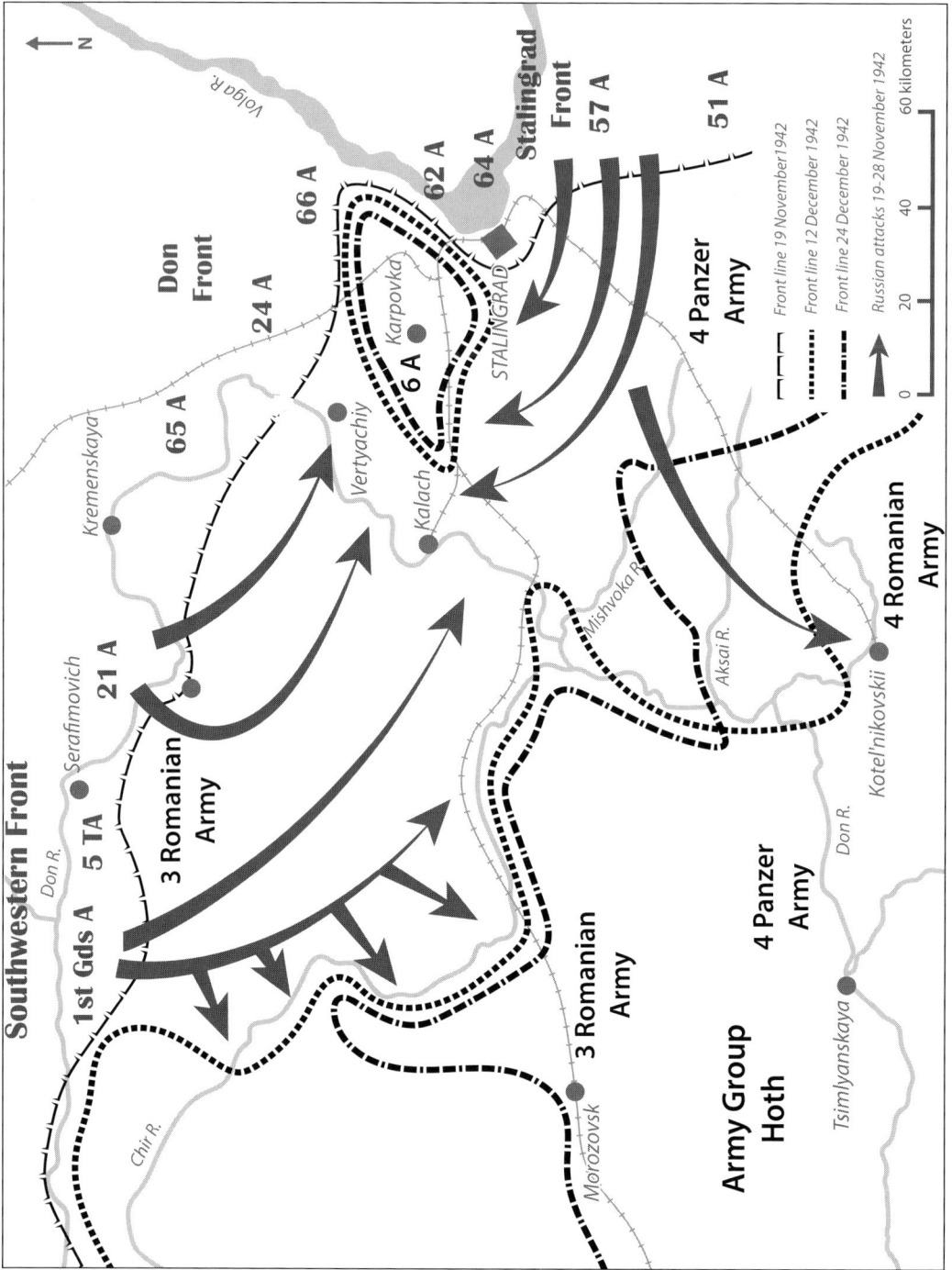

Map 2 Stalingrad, November-December 1942.

divisions, ten rifle and motorized rifle and 15 tank brigades, numbering more than 350,000 men, more than 1,000 tanks and 1,600 planes. There were another nine rifle and two cavalry divisions, 83 ski, motorized rifle, and airborne brigades, 32 tank and eight mechanized brigades in internal military districts. 29 divisions, 15 fortified areas and 51 brigades remained in Iran and the Far East. Aside from this the NKVD's operational forces numbered 18 divisions and 11 brigades, of which five divisions were in the Red Army.

By 1 November the German army on the Eastern Front had 172 divisions and three brigades, numbering about three million men, 1,288 tanks (not counting assault guns), 1,361 fighters, bombers and assault aircraft. Their allies' forces numbered 66 divisions and 13 brigades. According to the number of equivalent divisions on the front, the Red Army had a superiority of 2.1:1. The Soviet superiority of reserves in the rear was overwhelming. Up until March 1943 the Germans were only able to shift 27 divisions to the Eastern Front. The Red Army, not counting its forces in Iran and the Far East, had the equivalent of 131 divisions, including NKVD divisions, in reserve and in the internal military districts; that is, almost five times more. In the Stalingrad area the Red Army had 66 rifle and eight cavalry divisions, six fortified areas, seven tank and one mechanized corps, 18 rifle and motorized rifle brigades, one anti-tank brigade, 14 independent tank brigades, and four independent tank regiments. They were faced by 53 divisions and two security formations of low combat quality: 13 German, five Italian and 18 Romanian infantry divisions, three Italian Alpine divisions, four German and one Romanian panzer division, four Romanian cavalry divisions, and also one German and one Italian security divisions, which yield a Soviet superiority of 1.8:1. Taking into account that the 32 German-allied divisions were significantly inferior to the Germans in combat quality, this superiority was even more significant. The Germans had 313 combat aircraft in the Stalingrad area, including 175 combat-ready, while the Romanians had 130, the Italians 60 and the Hungarians 25. There were 1,916 planes on the Soviet side, including 1,414 combat ready. Moreover, 245 combat-ready aircraft from Long-Range Aviation were also employed. The Soviet numerical superiority in the air was 4.1:1. And the air force operating in the Stalingrad area received another 387 planes during the counteroffensive.

In October Malinovskii became the deputy commander of the Voronezh Front. There then followed the successful counteroffensive at Stalingrad and the encirclement of Paulus's army.

On 29 November a *Stavka* order appointed Malinovskii the commander of the 2nd Guards Army (the former 1st Reserve). He was relieved of the position of deputy commander of the Voronezh Front. I.I. Larin, who was appointed to major general following the abolition of the institution of military commissars in the Red Army on 9 October 1942, was appointed a member of the military council.

On 3 December the army began to move along two routes in 165 trains: from the areas of Tambov, Rada and Platonovka to Balashov, and from the areas of Morshansk, Michurinsk, Ranenburg, and Lev Tolstoi to Gryazi. On 10 December these troops began to detrain at the Ilovlya, Archeda, Kalinino, Lipki, and Nachalino stations and the Tishkin and 586th kilometer sidings.

At first, the 2nd Guards Army was supposed to take part in the elimination of Paulus's encircled group of forces in Stalingrad as part of the Don Front.

Marshal Aleksandr Mikhailovich Vasilevskii, then the chief of the General Staff, recalled:

> The plan called for the splitting up and elimination of the encircled group of forces consecutively and in three stages: in the first stage the forces of the Don Front were to destroy the four infantry divisions west of the Rossoshka River; in the second stage an attack by the Don Front, primarily by the 2nd Guards Army, to the southeast toward Voroponovo and a meeting attack by the Stalingrad Front's 64th Army through Peschanka and toward Voroponovo, was to isolate and then capture the enemy forces in the southern part of the encircled group

of forces; finally, the third stage called for an attack by all of the Don and Stalingrad fronts' armies operating along the internal front, in the general direction of Gumrak, in order to finally crush the resistance of the encircled enemy and finish him off.

Stalin confirmed this plan on 10 December, telegraphing Zhukov: "I think we can approve Vasilevskii's plan. The start of the 2nd Guards Army's commitment should be on the 18th. The entire operation to eliminate the encircled enemy should be completed by 25-26 December. I await your reply."

Zhukov did not object and on the 11th Vasilevskii's plan was confirmed.

However, on 12 December the offensive by Hoth's[11] Fourth Panzer Army to relieve the Sixth Army began. As early as evening on this same day Vasilevskii had begun to consider turning the 2nd Guards Army against Hoth. He recalled:

> … I set out for Zavarygin, in order, upon informing the *Stavka*, to take more decisive measures against the Hitlerites attacking from Kotel'nikovo. I was not able to immediately get in touch with the Supreme Commander-in-Chief. I then informed the commander of the Don Front, K.K. Rokossovskii, who happened at that time to be at the headquarters of the commander of the 2nd Guards Army, about the situation in the south and that I was determined to request the *Stavka* that we immediately dispatch the 2nd Guards Army's formations to the south of Stalingrad, as they arrived, toward Manstein's attacking forces. I proposed to Malinovskii that he immediately set about organizing the transfer of his army's ready units and formations by forced march to the Myshkova River, so as to preempt the enemy and launch a decisive repulse along the line of the Myshkova. I should note that by that time of the 165 trains involved in transporting the guards army, only 60 had arrived and unloaded in the area to the northwest of Stalingrad. The army headquarters and the 1st Rifle Corps had arrived with them.

On the night of 12-13 December a conversation between Vasilevskii and Stalin took place. At first the Supreme Commander-in-Chief did not agree with the chief of the General Staff and said that he would review the question of turning the 2nd Guards Army at a session of the GKO. It was only at 0500 that Stalin's sanction for the transfer of Malinovskii's army to the Stalingrad Front followed and its employment against the Kotel'nikovo group of forces was at last received.

Rokossovskii protested passionately against the 2nd Guards Army being taken away from him. According to Vasilevskii:

> The commander of the Don Front, my friend K.K. Rokossovskii, did not agree with the transfer of the 2nd Guards Army to the Stalingrad Front. Moreover, he insistently asked that I not do this and tried to win over I.V. Stalin to his side.
>
> He recalled this more than once after the war.
>
> "You were nonetheless wrong then," Konstantin Konstantinovich would say. "With the 2nd Guards Army, I would have defeated Paulus's starving and frozen divisions even before Manstein's arrival."

---

11   Editor's note. Hermann Hoth (1885-1971) joined the imperial army in 1903 and served in the First World War. During the Second World War he commanded a motorized corps in Poland and France. He commanded panzer and infantry armies on the Eastern Front, before being relieved in 1943. Following the war, Hoth was found guilty of war crimes, but was released in 1954.

It is likely that Rokossovskii's objections delayed somewhat the issuance of the corresponding directive, which was received by Vasilevskii only at 2230 on 14 December.

By this Stalin sanctioned the turn of the 2nd Guards Army against Hoth, which had actually been in progress since 13 December, on Vasilevskii's initiative, and which was based upon Stalin's oral agreement.

According to Aleksandr Mikhailovich:

> Yet another very important decision by the *Stavka* followed on the night of 13-14 December: to change the direction of the attack by the Southwestern and the left wing of the Voronezh fronts. If, according to the plan for operation "Saturn," it was planned to move due south, through Millerovo and on Rostov, then now it was decided that following the defeat of the Italian army along the middle course of the Don, to direct the attack to the southeast, toward Morozovsk and Tormosin; that is, in the rear of Manstein's relief group.

Insofar as the *Stavka's* decision is of particular interest and arouses doubts about its correctness among those writing about it, I will dwell on this matter in greater detail. First of all, what was the *Stavka* guided by in renouncing the conduct of such an important strategic decision, which was already prepared for exectuion? The answer to this question is contained in the Supreme Commander-in-Chief's directive of 13 December, which was addressed to Voronov,[12] Vatutin and Golikov. The directive noted that at the end of November, when operation "Saturn" was being worked out, the situation was favorable for it and the operation was well justified.

> Subsequently, however, the situation changed in a way unfavorable to us. Romanenko[13] and Lelyushenko[14] are defending and cannot advance, because during this time the enemy was able to bring up a number of infantry (called rifle in the document, B.S.) divisions and tank formations from the west, which are holding them back. Thus an attack from the north will not meet up with direct support from Romanenko from the east, because an offensive toward Kamensk and Rostov cannot be successful.

Further on the Supreme Commander-in-Chief noted that the 2nd Guards Army cannot be employed for operation "Saturn," because it is working on another front.

Now the 2nd Guards Army's mission was, in conjunction with the 51st Army, to defeat the enemy's Kotel'nikovo group of forces, occupy Kotel'nikovo and securely consolidate there.

It was during this dramatic period, probably on 15 December, that Malinovskii's conversation by cable took place:

> Where's Malinovskii?
> Malinovskii is out with the troops right now.

---

12 Editor's note. Nikolai Nikolaevich Voronov (1899-1968) joined the Red Army in 1918. During the Great Patriotic War he commanded National Air Defense Forces and was head of the army's artillery branch. He also served as a *Stavka* representative to several *fronts*. Following the war, Voronov was primarily engaged in academic work.
13 Editor's note. Prokofii Logvinovich Romanenko (1897-1949) joined the imperial army in 1914 and fought in the First World War. During the Great Patriotic War he commanded both field and tank armies. Following the war, Romanenko commanded a military district.
14 Editor's note. Dmitrii Danilovich Lelyushenko (1901-87) joined the Red Army in 1918. During the Great Patriotic War he commanded a mechanized and a rifle corps and a field army and a tank army. Following the war, Lelyushenko commanded military districts.

There's a permanent place there, from where we are speaking. This means he's with you. Exactly.

I'll determine this this minute.

The Big Boss is asking for him. I request that you determine exactly where Malinovskii is.

Regarding comrade Malinovskii. He's just returned and has himself reported to the Big Boss. They've asked him to wait for five minutes, as there will be instructions for him.

I don't understand the last two bits of data. I have information from Korovyakov as of 1800 on 14.12.42.

They just informed us that there will be no instructions for comrade Malinovskii, but they ordered him to report his location by 0900.

Malinovskii's auxiliary command post was located along the southern outskirts of the Verkhnee—Tsaritsynskii farm. At 0600 on 17 December a combat order for the 2nd Guards Army was issued. It stated:

1. The enemy is attempting to link up with his blockaded Stalingrad group of forces through an attack from the southwest to the north and northeast.
2. The army's forces, while securely holding its lines, are preparing counterblows for the purpose of eliminating the enemy's possible breakthrough.
3. The 1st Guards Rifle Corps is to prepare counterblows with the forces of the 98th Rifle Division
   1) from Fifth Tavriya on Nizhnii Kumskii
   2) from Fifth Tavriya on Gromoslavka
4. The 13th Guards Rifle Corps is to prepare counterblows with the forces of the 3rd Guards Rifle Division
   1) from the Krep' State Farm on Ivanovka
   2) from farm no. 1 on Vasil'evka
5. 2nd Guards Mechanized Corps
   1) from the Kosh area (six kilometers southwest of Zety) in the direction of height 164.0, Ivanovka and Gromoslavka
   2) the Yurkin State Farm (ten kilometers south of Zety) on Tevektenerovo and Kapkinka
   3) along the railroad toward Abganerovo station and Gniloaksaiskaya
   4) north in the direction of Nariman and Gavrilovka
      Note that there's a tank brigade in Gniloaksaiskaya and the 13th Tank Brigade in Aksai, which may take part in a joint counterattack.
6. Report the results of reconnaissance to the army headquarters by the close of 17.12.42.
   Commander of the 2nd Guards Army
   Lieutenanat General Malinovskii
   Member of the military council, Major General Larin.

At 1830 on 17 December 1942 Malinovskii issued combat order no. 3:

1. The enemy, in strength up to 60-100 tanks, has launched an offensive from the area of the Nezhinskaya ravine in the general direction of Gromoslavka, and by 1500 on 17.12.42 had thrown the 20th Anti-Tank Brigade from its position on height 140.9, while continuing to attack along the road to Gromoslavka. By this time the 20th Anti-Tank Brigade's retreating units were seen in the area of height 121.3. At 1500 on 17.12 up to a battalion of infantry and armored cars were noted in the Rassypnaya ravine.

2. Units of the 4th Mechanized Corps, while holding the line March 8 Collective Farm—height 147.0—Zagotskot, are attacking with a group of tanks the flank of the enemy attacking from the area of Zagotskot.

   Units of the 13th Tank Corps are holding the area immediately to the west of Kruglyakov.

3. The 1st Guards Rifle Corps, having subordinated the 87th Rifle Division (minus the 1382nd Rifle Regiment) to itself, is to occupy the prepared defensive line Nizhnii Kumskii—Ivanovka by 0500 on 18.12.42 and is by no means to allow the enemy to break through to the north. The headquarters of the 1st Guards Rifle Corps is in Yeriko-Krepinskii.

   Two regiments from the 300th Rifle Division are defending to the right along the line Kobylevskii—Nizhne-Kumskii.

   The remaining units of the corps that are arriving are to be concentrated in the Novo-Petrovskii—Fifth Tavriya—Yerik (Yeriko-Krepinskii) area.

   The boundary on the left is excluding Rubezhnyi—excluding the Krep' State Farm—Ivanovka—Shestakov.

4. The 18th Guards Rifle Corps, having subordinated to itself the 87th Rifle Division's 1382nd Rifle Regiment and the 3rd Guards Rifle Division, by 0500 on 18.12.42 is to occupy the prepared defense along the line excluding Ivanovka—Kapkinka (Kapkinskii), having occupied Birzovoi with a powerful forward detachment, and is to in no way allow the enemy to break through to the north.

   The headquarters of the 13th Guards Rifle Corps is in the Krep' State Farm.

   The corps' remaining units are to be concentrated in the area Buzinovka—Krep' State Farm—excluding Zety.

5. The 2nd Guards Mechanized Corps, while occupying the Zety—Yurkin State Farm (12 kilometers to the south)—the 74th kilometer rail siding area, is to occupy Tevektenerovo—Abganerovo station area, taking into account the fact that this line is occupied by units of the 38th Guards Rifle Division. The corps is to establish communications with the tank brigade at Gniloaksaiskaya station and with the tank brigade in Aksai, with the idea of launching a joint counterblow, upon receiving special orders, with them against the enemy operating in the height 149.6—Zagotskot—Shestakov area facing the 1st and 13th guards rifle corps.

6. My auxiliary command post is in Verkhnii Tsaritsynskii and the army headquarters is in Kolpachki.

   Reports are to be sent to me at the auxiliary command post by 2400 on 17.12.42 and then every three hours on the movement of the formations and their readiness for defense.

At 1600 on 18 December Malinovskii and Larin issued a new order:

1. The enemy, in force up to 100-150 tanks and motorized infantry, has been launching stubborn attacks throughout 16-18.12.42 for the purpose of breaking through to the north in the Verkhnii Kumskii area.

2. Our forces are successfully beating back and throwing back the enemy to the south with decisive obstinacy, having thrown him out of Verkhnii Kumskii.

3. In order to decisively destroy the enemy north of the Aksai River, units of the 4th Mechanized Corps and the reinforced 87th Rifle Division, are to counterattack on 19.12.42, destroy the enemy and reach the Aksai River.

I order the following:

4. The 4th Mechanized Corps, with all its reinforcements, while pinning down the enemy along the front height 143.7—height 147.0—height 146.9 is to launch a decisive counterattack along the sector height 130.7—height 143.7 in the general direction of Chikov, launching its attack against the rear and flank of the enemy operating in the direction of Verkhnii Kumskii. The corps is to destroy the enemy and reach the Aksai River along the Lesnoi Kurgan—Chikov sector.

5. The 87th Rifle Division (minus one regiment, which is operating as part of the 4th Mechanized Corps) and the 13th Tank Brigade are to decisively counterattack from the sector Luch (14 kilometers south of Ivanovka)—Kosh—the Shirokaya ravine in the general direction of Klykov, to destroy the enemy and reach the Aksai River along the line Klykov—Antonov.

6. The 4th Cavalry Corps is to support the 4th Mechanized Corps' attack and securely hold the line of the Aksai River along the sector Don River—Lesnoi Kurgan.

7. The start of the counterattack is 1300 on 19.12.42.

Report to me on decisions adopted and orders issued by 1000 on 19.12.42, and then every three hours.

On 23 December *Stavka* representative A.M. Vasilevskii and the commander of the Stalingrad Front, A.I. Yeremenko, held a meeting with the command of the armies and corps at the 57th Army's command post. The plan for defeating the enemy's Kotel'nikovo group of forces, which was approved by the *Stavka* on 19 December, was examined. During the first stage the forces of the 2nd Guards and 51st armies were supposed to encircle and destroy the enemy's shock group along the northern bank of the Aksai River, and during the second stage launch an attack against the Kotel'nikovo group of forces, outflanking it from the northwest and southwest. The 2nd Guards Army was to make the main attack and the 51st Army a supporting attack, along with the 13th Tank and 3rd Guards Mechanized corps.

As early as 22 December Malinovskii reported the plan for the operation to Yeremenko:

Top Secret.
Very Important.
To the commander of the Stalingrad Front.
22.12.42.
1:200,000 map.

I'm reporting the decision for the 2nd Guards Army's offensive operation for destroying the enemy's Aksai—Kotel'nikovo group.

1. The operation is to begin on the morning of 25 December, with the 2nd Guards Army in the following operational formation: the 1st Guards Rifle Corps, consisting of the 24th, 98th and 33rd rifle divisions, the 1095th Corps Artillery Regiment (12 152mm gun-howitzers), the 648th Artillery Regiment (18 152mm gun-howitzers) and the 48th Guards Mortar Regiment (17 M-13 launchers). The main attack is to be launched along the front Chernomorov—Gromoslavka and by the close of the first day the offensive is to capture the line Generalovskii—Vodnyanskii. By the close of the second day the offensive is to capture the line Nizhne-Yablochnyi—Sredne-Yablochnyi. The army is to subsequently attack toward the line Maiorskii—Kotel'nikovo.

The boundary line on the right is Budennyi—Chernomorov—Generalovskii. The boundary on the left is Rubezhnyi—Krep' State Farm—Ivanovka—Zalivskii—Verkhne-Yablochnyi.

The 13th Guards Rifle Corps, consisting of the 3rd, 49th and 387th rifle divisions, the 506th Corps Artillery Regiment (12 152mm gun-howitzers), the 1100th and 1101st artillery regiments (12 122mm guns each), the 1250th Anti-Tank Artillery Regiment (15 45mm guns), the 23rd Guards Mortar Regiment (20 M-13 launchers), and two corps tank regiments. The corps is to launch its main attack along the front Vasil'evka—Birzovoi and by the close of the first day of the offensive it is to capture the line of the Neklinskaya ravine—Zarya. By the close of the second day it is to occupy the line of the Bol'shaya Yablochnaya ravine—Chilyakovo. The corps will subsequently attack toward Kotel'nikovo and Pimen-Cherni.

The boundary on the left is Zety—Tebektenerovo—Kruglyakov—Chilyakovo.

The 2nd Guards Mechanized Corps and the 6th Mechanized Corps will comprise the shock group and are to reach the Aksai—Peregruznyi—Shelestov area by the close of 24.12, and from the morning of 25.12 are to attack as follows: the 2nd Guards Mechanized Corps in the direction of Samokhin and Chilyakovo, capturing the Chilyakovo area on the first day, from where on the offensive's second day it is to operate against the enemy's rear in order to destroy him in the Shestakov—Klykov area. It will subsequently be employed according to the situation.

The 6th Mechanized Corps is to attack on the morning of 25.12 from the Peregruznyi area in the direction of Zhutov-2 and Darganov and by the close of the first day of the offensive is to capture the Gremyachaya—Pimen-Cherni area. On the offensive's second day it is to capture Kotel'nikovo with its main forces and Dubovskoe with a forward detachment, while carrying out reconnaissance of Andreevskaya, Gur'ev and Shabalin.

It is necessary that the 51st Army's group, consisting of the 38th Guards Rifle Division and the 13th, 56th and 254th tank brigades, under the command of the commander and his staff, attack in the direction of Gniloaksaiskaya and Kruglyakov, and the 3rd Guards Mechanized Corps, with the task, in conjunction with the 13th Guards Rifle Corps, of destroying the enemy in the Kruglyakov—Vasil'evka—Zagotskot area, after which it will comprise your reserve.

The 300th Rifle Division must attack on the right, launching an attack along its left flank in the direction of Chausovskii, with the task of capturing the line Verkhnii Rubezhnyi—Potemkinskii and covering the right flank of the 2nd Guards Army along the Don River.

The 4th Cavalry Corps will enter the breach between the 300th Rifle Division and the 1st Guards Rifle Corps, with the task of capturing Verkhnyaya Kurmoyarskaya on the first day of the offensive and Nagaevskaya on the second day, and to cover the army's right flank.

The 7th Tank Corps is to be in the army's second echelon and will be employed as the situation dictates, with it quite likely that it will have to take part in the first day's fighting to destroy the enemy together with the 13th Guards Rifle Division and the 51st Army's group in the Vasil'evka—Shestakov—Zagotskot area, launching its attack behind the 1st Guards Rifle Corps in the direction of Nizhnii Kumskii, Zagotskot and Gniloaksaiskaya. After this, it is to be employed as the 2nd Guards Army's reserve, depending on the situation.

2. An evaluation of the enemy's strength: one may assume that the enemy's 23rd and 6th panzer divisions are now operating in the Kruglyakov—Gniloaksaiskaya—Vasil'evka—Ivanovka

area. The 17th Panzer Division is in the Gromoslavka—Nizhnii Kumskii—Zagotskot area. It is not excluded that the 11th Panzer Division is also operating in the Zagotskot—Verkhnii Kumskii area and it is possible that it has not yet gotten involved in the fighting and may end up along the Vasil'evka axis or along the rail line to Abganerovo. One should take into consideration the fact that the enemy has up to 400 tanks and 1-2 infantry divisions north of the Aksai River. Thus the fighting will be very stubborn.

3. The Stalingrad Front's aviation must be fully committed for assisting the offensive of the 1st and 13th guards rifle corps' offensive and for opposing the enemy's aviation.

4. An artillery preparation will not be conducted, and the attack is to begin simultaneously with a 15-minute fire onslaught from all guns, as well as infantry weapons, including heavy machine guns.

I am reporting the decision outlined here for your confirmation.
Supplement—a 1:200,000 map.
The commander of the 2nd Guards Army.
Lieutenant General Malinovskii
Member of the military council
Larin
Drawn up in two copies by Malinovskii.

The following appeared within the confines of this plan:

Combat Order no. 14, 25.12.42. Map 1:100,000.
To the commander of the 6th Mechanized Corps.

1. The enemy, while covering himself with rearguard units, is trying to consolidate along the southern bank of the Aksai River, in order to secure an orderly withdrawal to the southwest.
2. The 2nd Guards Army is continuing the offensive for the purpose of seizing the line of the Aksai River and further pursuing the enemy's retreating units.
3. At dawn on 26.12.42 the 6th Mechanized Corps is to launch a decisive attack in the direction of Zhutov-2, Pimen-Chernya and Gremyachaya to cut off the enemy's path of retreat from the Aksai River and to capture Pimen-Chernya and Gremyachaya.
4. The 7th Tank Corps is to attack Verkhne-Yablochnyi in the morning and capture Kotel'nikovo.
5. Communications are to be maintained by radio, according to the radio signals table, coordinates and cipher. Reports by radio are to be sent every three hours and every six hours through a communications officer.

This combat order was signed by Malinovskii, Larin and the chief of the army staff, S.S. Biryuzov.[15] It was received in the mechanized corps' headquarters at 1320.

---

15   Editor's note. Sergei Semyonovich Biryuzov (1904-64) joined the Red Army in 1922. During the Great Patriotic War he commanded a division and an army and was a front chief of staff. Following the war, he served in the Soviet occupation forces in Austria and Hungary and in the central military apparatus. Biryuzov was appointed chief of the General Staff in 1963 and died in an airplane crash the following year.

The 2nd Guards Army's chief of staff, Major General Sergei Semyonovich Biryuzov became one of Malinovskii's closest friends. In 1961, when Biryuzov's memoirs, *When the Guns Roared*, came out, on 29 April he wrote a gift inscription to Malinovskii: "Dear Rodion Yakovlevich!"

"As a sign of my deep respect for you and that education which I received under your leadership in the years of the Great Patriotic War, particularly in the 2nd Guards Army, as well as during the postwar period.

"With sincere respect,

"Marshal of the Soviet Union Biryuzov."

General Erhard Rauss, the former commander of the 6th Panzer Division, the main strike force of operation "Winter Storm" (*Wintergewitter*), which was called upon to relieve the German Sixth Army in Stalingrad, recalled the situation that had arisen on 20 December:

The Soviet command realized the degree of danger that the ring around Stalingrad might be broken from the south and was hurriedly bringing up to the battlefield all the units it could scrape up, in order to cut off the tip of the Fourth Panzer Army's wedge. The Russian tank corps no longer possessed the power necessary to carry out this mission, having suffered such heavy losses over the last week and thus ceasing to represent a serious threat. Thus the Russians returned to their time-tested practice of attempting to crush the bridgehead in the Bol'shaya Vasil'evka area with the aid of concentrated artillery and mortar fire, and then to "wash" it away with massed infantry attacks. The 2nd Guards Army, which was taken from the forces besieging Stalingrad, was reinforced with reserves from the eastern bank of the Volga and was now located on the hills to the north and in the valley to the south of Bol'shaya Vasil'evka for a decisive attack against the 6th Panzer Division's positions.

Thousands of Red Army soldiers filled the snow-covered fields, slopes and low-lying areas of the endless steppes. The German soldiers had never seen such massive attacks. The first rows were mowed down by a hail of high-explosive shells, but newer and newer waves followed behind them. All the attempts by the Russian masses to reach our positions were cut down by fire from machine guns, artillery and other heavy weapons. The frontal offensive was stopped in its tracks.

Several hours later the Russians poured into Bol'shaya Vasil'evka from the east, like a stream of lava, pushing back the flank of the 4th Panzer Grenadier Regiment 100 meters. Not long after this they wedged themselves into the gap between the 6th and 23rd panzer divisions and turned into the rear of our forces along the bridgehead. We lost the eastern half of the village and the area around the graveyard, but the 6th Panzer Division's main defensive positions on the bridgehead remained unshaken, like a cliff among the roaring waves. Just at that moment, when the encirclement was nearly complete, a sudden and concentrated fire from all of Colonel Grundherr's guns cut down the Russian infantry. Despite the shells exploding in the combat formations, the 150 tanks of the 11th Panzer Regiment moved out of the village, and at that same moment Major Koch's 42 StuG-III assault guns hit the Russians from the rear. Shaken, even the enemy's powerful nerves could not withstand this onslaught of steel and fire. The Russian soldiers threw down their weapons and, like madmen, sought to run away from the hellish crossfire and the fatal armored grip. And then something took place which rarely happened during the Second World War. A crowd of Red Army soldiers ran to the west, even under the fire of their own artillery and "katyushas," to the only open place in the area, where they surrendered to our covering forces.

The battle continued to rage, but its culmination point had already passed and the crisis was over. The threatening masses on our flanks and in our rear had either been destroyed or taken prisoner. Even the Soviet combat method of last resort, which had so often yielded good results, failed this time around. The 6th Panzer Division's defensive battle on the Myshkova River was crowned with an important victory.

On 23 December Colonel Unrein's 4th Panzer Grenadier Regiment once again, supported by artillery and tanks, launched a counterattack and once again seized the eastern part of Bol'shaya Vasil'evka and the cemetery to the south of the river, which had earlier been occupied by the Russians. This final operation completely restored the situation to what it had been on 20 December. However, what was even more important was the fact that now the Soviet tanks and infantry masses had been defeated so that there were no longer any insuperable obstacles between the liberators and Stalingrad. The initiative had now shifted to German hands and the troops expected the Sixth Army's long-awaited attack to break out of the ring. Such an attack could only have been eased by the defeat of significant forces from the surrounding group of forces along the Myshkova River. That the order to begin the breakout was not issued immediately after our victory near Bol'shaya Vasil'evka struck everyone as inexplicable.

It seemed as though the orders issued by General Hoth's headquarters on 23 December had finally erased all doubts. These orders called for an attack to a depth of 33 kilometers to be undertaken by the combined armored units of all three of the LVII Panzer Corps' divisions on Christmas eve day. This column was to approach the encircled city as closely as possible, in order to establish communications with the Sixth Army, which was evidently no longer in a condition to fight, in order to free up a route for itself. A panzer combat group was supposed to secure the escort for covering the withdrawal of the troops from Stalingrad to the Myshkova River, while the main forces of the 6th, 17th and 23rd panzer divisions were to cover their crossing of the river. This represented, at the very least, an unusual mission, but in the light of the Soviet defeat along the Myshkova, its success seemed possible, if not ensured. Insofar as the rail line no longer ran as far as the Aksai River and that later several thousand motor vehicles were placed at our disposal, the problem of supplying and evacuating these forces did not seem insuperable. We even assumed that the Sixth Army's soldiers which had been encircled for a month, would find the strength for a march to the Myshkova, if their lives and freedom were at stake.

All of the preparations for the final leap, which had been called upon to decide Stalingrad's fate, were quickly completed. The combat group, which consisted of 120 tanks, 40 StuG-III assault guns and 24 SdKfz 233 armored reconnaissance cars, a panzer grenadier battalion on armored transports, a motorcycle company, a sapper company, and a motorized artillery battalion, was ready for the final lunge on 23 December, when a counter order arrived, according to which the 6th Panzer Division was to be immediately withdrawn. We were supposed to cross the bridge over the Don near Potemkinskii during the night of 22-23 December and reach Morozovskaya by forced march.

It was clear to even the youngest soldier that this spelled defeat in Stalingrad. The LVII Panzer Corps' two remaining divisions, the 17th and 23rd, were insufficient to stand against the Russian forces on the Myshkova, much less thrown them back. Although no one knew the reason for which the order was given, the soldiers and officers guessed that something terrible must have happened.

By dawn on 24 December the 6th Panzer Division was in a march formation that stretched 130 kilometers, rolling toward an undefined future along the blood-covered steppes, where it had so successfully fought.

Raus was mistaken when he maintained that the 2nd Guards Army took part in the 20-23 December fighting against his division and that on 23 December, following the German victory at Bol'shaya Vasil'evka, almost no combat-capable Soviet forces remained between the Myshkova

River and Stalingrad. Actually, only two divisions from Malinovskii's army had been activated opposite Hoth's corps, and that its main forces were still blocking the LVII Corps' path to Stalingrad.

In "A Short Military-Historical Document on the 2nd Guards Army," it states:

> Manstein attacked with a force consisting of the 11th, 23rd, 17th, and 6th panzer divisions, the *Wiking* SS Division, and the 386th Infantry and 7th *Luftwaffe* Field divisions. The overall number of his tanks exceeded 500. This menacing armored force was met by our glorious units, which, on the instructions of Marshal of the Soviet Union, comrade A.M. Vasilevskii, had been united for fighting Manstein's group of forces under the leadership of the deputy commander of the Stalingrad Front, G.F. Zakharov.[16] His plan consisted of cutting off the "tail" of the armored ram in the most effective manner; that is, to separate the tanks moving ahead from the motorized infantry and rear organs and to defeat them in detail along the Aksai River in the area of Zhutovo station. For this purpose, General Zakharov decided to operate in the following manner:
>
> Units of the 51st Army's 302nd, 92nd and 126th rifle divisions were occupying defensive positions to the right (east) of the path of advance of Manstein's group. The 51st Army's headquarters was in Zhutovo-2 (the commander of the 51st Army was Major General Trufanov[17]).
>
> Major General Tanaschishin's 4th Mechanized Corps was ordered from the Aksai area and, moving to the west, attack the right flank of the attacking enemy in the area of Biryukovskaya station.
>
> The 35th Tank Brigade and a tank regiment, along with a mechanized brigade from Major General Vol'skii's 3rd Mechanized Corps, were to attack the enemy's left flank. Units of the Major General Shapkin's 4th Cavalry Corps had been concentrated somewhat to the south. Thus a corridor was formed, along which Manstein advanced, having our troops on both sides along his flanks and attempting to cut him into two parts by means of a simultaneous attack from the east and west.
>
> From the north, along the approaches to Verkhnii Kumskii, the way was blocked to the enemy by the 1378th Rifle Regiment of M.S. Diasamidze, later a Hero of the Soviet Union, 87th Rifle Division, Major General Vol'skii's tank regiment and the heroic 20th Anti-Tank Brigade, which was allotted by the commander of the 57th Army, Lieutenant General Tolbukhin (now a general of the army).
>
> Major General Vol'skii's 3rd (Guards, B.S.) Mechanized Corps was actively operating.
>
> The 4th Cavalry Corps had the task of covering the Aksai—Dorofeevskii area as far as the Don River.
>
> Events unfolded here in the following manner: General Tanaschishin's 4th Guards Mechanized Corps (the 13th Tank Corps up to 19 January 1943, B.S.) advanced right up to the enemy, drew off the 23rd Panzer Division onto itself and got into a fight with it, but did not launch an attack against the flank of the enemy's main group. However, having drawn off the enemy's panzer division on itself, it made the fighting against the remaining tanks easier.

---

16 Editor's note. Georgii Fedorovich Zakharov (1897-1957) joined the imperial army in 1915 and fought in the First World War. He joined the Red Army in 1918. During the Great Patriotic War he commanded armies and *fronts* and was the chief of staff for several *fronts*. Following the war, Zakharov commanded a military district and served in the central military apparatus.

17 Editor's note. Nikolai Ivanovich Trufanov (1900-82) joined the Red Army in 1919. During the Great Patriotic War he initially commanded armies, but was later demoted to corps command. Following the war he served with the Soviet occupation forces in Germany and in the Far East. Trufanov retired in 1960.

From the west, our 85th Tank Brigade, a tank regiment and a mechanized brigade from the 3rd (Guards, B.S.) Mechanized Corps drew the enemy's 17th Panzer Division upon itself and fought stubbornly, but suffered heavy losses.

Nonetheless Manstein continued moving along the corridor and crossed the Aksai River with his lead tanks and encountered here a fixed defense in the Verkhnii Kumskii area by the 87th Rifle Division's 1378th Rifle Regiment and the 20th Anti-Tank Brigade to the east along the line of heights 46 and 47 (a 1:200,000 map).

Fierce and bloody fighting unfolded. General Vol'skii's heroic 3rd (Guards,B.S.) Mechanized Corps suffered heavy losses, destroying a multitude of enemy tanks.

By 1500 on 17 December the enemy had almost destroyed the heroic 20th Anti-Tank Brigade and the 87th Rifle Division's 1378th Rifle Regiment, leaving tens of his damaged tanks on the battlefield. The 4th Cavalry Corps had been badly torn up, but honorably carried out its mission. Thus the enemy, having lost up to 400 tanks here, had been significantly roughed up, but continued to commit fresh forces into the fighting, ignoring his heavy losses.

Manstein's formations, which while very exhausted, nevertheless represented a very impressive force, encountered the 2nd Guards Army's forces along the line Nizhni Kumskii—Gromoslavka—Vasil'evka.

The march of the 2nd Guards Army to the battlefield is described in epic spirit:

The guards army carried out a march unparalleled in history. The troops covered 40-50 kilometers per day in conditions of a fierce winter, and the inhabited locales along its route of march were full of installations and hospitals, and keeping the army warm represented incredible difficulties, but the army moved on and the forward units of its 3rd and 49th guards rifle divisions, the 13th Guards Rifle Corps, 98th Rifle Division and the 70th Rifle Regiment/24th Guards Rifle Division/1st Guards Rifle Corps successfully arrived on time at the line Gromoslavka—Ivanovka—Kapkinka, preempting the enemy's actions. Despite the fact that the guards army's forward units entered the fighting while the anti-tank weapons were still on the march and there was a shortage of ammunition, the enemy did not advance further. The 2nd Guards Army stood like a steel wall across the enemy's path, defeated the remaining units of Manstein's group and began its offensive to the southwest, west and northwest.

By this time the 7th Tank, later the 3rd (Guards, B.S.) Corps and the 6th Mechanized Corps (later the 5th Guards Mechanized Corps) and several divisions, including the 300th Rifle Division (now the 87th Guards Rifle Division) had been included in the army...

Events unfolded in the following manner:

The army's forces entered the fighting by echelon.

At first the divisions of the 13th Guards Rifle Corps (8th and 49th) and the 1st Guards Rifle Corps' 98th Rifle Division were committed into the action, following a 180-kilometer march in harsh winter conditions, which deployed and entered the fighting along the line of the outer edge of the Stalingrad fortified area. On 20 December both rifle corps (1st and 13th guards rifle) reached the line of the Myshkova River, with the task of preventing the enemy from breaking through to save his Stalingrad group of forces.

The 98th Rifle and the 3rd and 49th guards rifle divisions had the task of holding German field marshal Manstein's fierce attacks along the line Gromoslavka—Ivanovka—Vasil'evka.

Here our infantry displayed miracles of mass heroism, covering their banners with unfading glory.

During this period the 2nd and 5th Guards mechanized corps did not take part in the fighting, but were carrying out countermaneuvers in the defensive depth in difficult and roadless condtions.

Major General Vol'skii's 3rd (Guards, B.S.) Mechanized Corps, which was assigned to the army, was pulled into the reserve following the heavy fighting near Verkhnii Kumskii, in light of its heavy losses and took no further part in the army's operations.

During 22-25 December the army's forces took up the pursuit of the defeated enemy. The army made a fighting advance of 60 kilometers in only two days.

The Germans threw in the Romanian 2nd and 18th divisions along the line of the Aksai River, while attempting to hold our forces, but the smooth and coordinated attacks by the infantry and tank formations spoiled the enemy's calculations here as well.

In order to assist the advance of the Shock Army, which had by this time fallen significantly behind, the 1st Guards Rifle Corps and the 2nd Guards Mechanized Corps, which had crossed the Don River in the Velikaya Kurmoyarskaya area, with an attack toward Tormosin (to the northwest) threw back the enemy, which had been facing the 5th Shock Army and occupied Tormosin (2nd Guards Mechanized Corps)…

At this time the 300th Rifle Division (now the 87th Guards Rifle Division) was carrying out its mission of covering the army's right flank by defending along the Don River.

Tormosin was a big food and ammunition base, which supported the enemy's Nizhnee-Chirskaya and Tormosin groups of forces…

The army's front, which at the beginning of its deployment stretched 40 kilometers, had reached 120 kilometers by 26 December. From the moment of the guards army's entry into the fighting it was already experiencing a serious shortage of fuel, while its supply lines stretched back 200 kilometers by the start of the heavy fighting. The repair and reconstitution units, rear organs, depots, and hospitals lagged behind, and there was a shortage of spare parts. By the start of the fighting the tank park contained 30-40 percent of vehicles that had fallen behind. Subsequently, while continuing the offensive, by the morning of 29 December the army's left group (7th Tank Corps, 24th Guards Rifle Division and the 98th Rifle Division) had completely cleared the town of Kotel'nikovo of the enemy.

Following the defeat of the enemy's Tormosin and Kotel'nikovo groups of forces, the situation of the army's forces required the following: first of all, the concentration of the army's scattered forces, in particular the concentration of the 1st Guards Rifle Corps, closer to the army's right flank in the Tsymlyanskaya area and the 2nd Guards Mechanized Corps in the Novo-Tsimlyanskaya area, and; secondly, the development of the success of the pursuit in the direction of Rostov and Novocherkassk.

Upon occupying Kotel'nikovo, the 3rd Guards Tank Corps (the former 7th Tank Corps) had completed a 130-kilometer raid to the Konstantinovskaya—Semikarakorskaya area.

During the 3-6.1.43 period the enemy, having discovered the movement of the 3rd Guards Tank Corps to the Semikarakorskaya area, concentrated a massive strike by his aviation against this corps' units and against the 300th and 98th (now the 86th Guards Rifle Division) rifle divisions moving up to reinforce it; 250-300 enemy sorties were carried out each day during this period.

On 7 January 1943 frequent enemy counterattacks began along the army's right flank in the Yermilov—Kondakov area, and in the center in the Razdorskaya area, and along the left flank.

The 33rd Guards Rifle Division suffered the fate of having to withstand more than ten counterattacks by enemy detachments, launched with a strength of 20-30 tanks and 1-2 battalions of infantry in the Yermilov—Belyanskii—Verbovskii area.

The division repelled all of the enemy's counterattacks and firmly supported the cover of the army's right flank. The 98th Rifle Division, the units of which had moved up from Martynovka, south of the Sal River, to the line Ryaska—Denisovskii, ended up in a more difficult situation, and in this area were subjected to a powerful attack by enemy tanks, which suffered heavy losses and were scattered.

During 8-11.1.43 the 3rd Guards Tank Corps was nevertheless unable to advance to the Bagaevskaya area for the purpose of securely holding the bridgehead along the Don River along the front Razdorskaya—Manychskaya; and then by the close of 11.1.43 the 2nd Guards Mechanized Corps was moving line Bol'shaya Orlovka—Tapilin—Oblivnoi with the task of parrying the attack by the enemy's group of forces from Batlaevskaya and to develop the success of the 3rd Guards Tank Corps.

During 8-11.1.43 units of the 3rd Guards Tank and 2nd Guards Mechanized corps pursued the retreating enemy along the northern bank of the Manych River. The pursuit was unsuccessful. The enemy slipped out from under the attack, pushed aside the screen and fell back through Veselyi.

On 15 January, in accordance with the Southern Front's order no 006/op of 14.1.43, the army's forces were assigned the following task: "The 2nd Guards Army is to launch an attack with its mechanized group (the so-called 'Don mechanized group'), consisting of the 3rd Guards Tank and 2nd and 5th guards mechanized corps and the 98th Rifle Division, under the command of the commander of the 3rd Guards Tank Corps, Lieutenant General Rotmistrov,[18] on the morning of 17.1.43 from the front Bagaevskaya—Veselyi toward Bataisk, with the task of seizing Bataisk by the morning of 18.1.43, while one mechanized corps is to capture Rostov."

By this time the army had the following tanks: eight KVs,[19] 48 T-34s[20] and 84 T-70s;[21] we were able to seize with these forces a bridgehead along the Manych River along the front Arpachin—Pustoshkin—Krasnyi—Veselyi and move toward the Bataisk area. However, on 20 January the enemy threw in 150 tanks and began launching frequent counterattacks with powerful aviation support.

Heavy fighting broke out here, during the course of which our glorious heroes—soldiers and officers—covered themselves with undying glory.

During 22-26.1.43 the enemy finally pushed back units of the 3rd Guards Tank and the 5th Guards Mechanized corps to the northern bank of the Manych River; during this period units of the 2nd Guards Mechanized Corps displayed examples of tenacity in the defense along the front Alitub—Arpachin—Manychskaya, literally fighting in semi-ecirclement.

---

18   Editor's note. Pavel Alekseevich Rotmistrov (1901-82) joined the Red Army in 1918. During the Great Patriotic War he served as chief of staff of a mechanized corps and later commanded a tank brigade, tank corps and a tank army. He was relieved of his army command in 1944 and appointed deputy chief of the army's armored forces. Following the war, Rotmistrov served in Germany and the Far East and in the central military academic apparatus.

19   Editor's note. The KV tanks were a series of heavy armored vehicles named in honor of Soviet defense commissar Kliment Voroshilov. The most common models were the KV-1 (45 tons, a crew of five, a 76.2mm gun, and four 7.62mm machine guns) and the KV-2 (53.1 tons, a crew of six, a 152mm gun, and two 7.62mm machine guns). Other models were produced as well, although in small amounts.

20   Editor's note. The T-34 was the Red Army's standard medium tank during the Great Patriotic War and afterwards. The 1941 model weighed 26.5 tons, carried a crew of our, was armed with a 76mm gun and two 7.62mm machine guns. A later model was fitted with an 85mm gun.

21   Editor's note. The T-70 was the Red Army's most common light tank, beginning in 1942. It weighed 9.2 tons, carried a crew of two, and was armed with a 45mm gun and a 7.62mm machine gun.

The enemy, with the forces of the newly-arrived 11th Panzer Division, numbering up to 100 tanks, and the forces of the 111th Infantry Division, as well as other units, and supported by 100 planes, was particularly active along the front Manychskaya—Usman'—Samodurovka—Krasnyi.

During the day he managed to seize Malaya Zapadenka, inflcting heavy losses here on the 3rd Guards Rifle and 98th (now the 86th Guards Rifle Division) rifle divisions, which had already been weakened. The 13th Guards Rifle Corps was unable to come to the assistance of our units operating in the Manychskaya—Konygin area, because it was tied down in fighting with the enemy's superior forces along the front Veselyi—Pozdneev—Krasnoe Znamya.

The recent ten days of fighting from 20 January were so exhausting for the army's units and formations, particularly for the tank and mechanized forces, that one did not consider counting these formations in calculating our forces. Suffice it to say that by 20 January 1943; that is, a month since the start of the fighting; the army had lost half of its manpower...

At the end of the first ten days in February, the army began stubborn fighting for Novocherkassk. Here the enemy's Rostov group of forces was ground up and on 13 February the army's forces (the 13th Guards Rifle Corps, with the active assistance of the 387th and 33rd Guards rifle divisions) captured Novocherkassk... The army continued to pursue the enemy and on 16 February reached the enemy's heavily fortified Mius defense line. Our artillery played an outstanding role in continuing the entire operation... By 18 February, at the time of the fighting along the Mius, the army did not represent a force capable of attacking further. The army had lost its shock and fire power.

The time had arrived for reconstituting the army.

During the course of its offensive as far as the Mius River, the infantry had made a fighting advance of 600 kilometers, captured 1,300 prisoners, 14 tanks, 589 motor vehicles, 20 armored cars, eight tows, 32 motorcycles, 57 bicycles, 148 guns, 47 mortars, 105 heavy and 441 light machine guns, 68 rail cars, six radio sets on motor vehicles, 12 depots with ammunition, six clothing depots, eight food depots, 11 depots with arms, 2,027 rifles, 1,077 horses, 1,725 wagons, and 4,000 head of livestock.

During this time the enemy lost 32,500 soldiers and officers killed, 27 planes were shot down, 352 tanks destroyed, as well as 290 motor vehicles, 50 armored cars, 148 guns, 636 wagons, 77 mortars, and 150 heavy machine guns.

The following conclusion was drawn about the December 1942-February 1943 fighting:

The 2nd Guards Army carried out its historic role, defeated the remnants of the Manstein group's still large and serious forces, crushed them and went over to the offensive.

The army's first offensive cost the blood of many Soviet people. During the offensive, the infantry—the guards army's main force, demonstrated a lot of shortcomings, to pass over which would insult the glorious memory of the knight-heroes who died for the victory of our beloved Motherland. But the army carried out its decisive assignment.

The main mass of infantry was able to operate according to the methods of group tactics. The new combat formations had not yet been mastered and, as a result, during the preparation the combat formations were dense along the front and in depth, and as they approached the target of their attack they became extremely dense, covering gaps and depriving us of the opportunity to fire from the depth. Subsequent combat experience showed just how pernicious the echeloned organization of the infantry's combat formations was. There, where the infantry attacked in linear combat formations, there were fewer losses and the greatest success was achieved. The command element of small subunits had not yet been sufficiently trained in managing their subunits. The entire system of command consisted of commanding "forward," without combining fire and maneuver. The love for maneuvering weapons and personnel on the battlefield had not been inculcated. The commanders did not know how to search out weak places in the enemy's combat formations and did not search for ways to outflank and envelop him and did not seek out opportunities for infiltrating amidst the enemy's combat formations.

The enemy was thrown into the fighting, counting on its shock strength and hand-to-hand combat.

We did not concern ourselves much with the firefight and employing our weapons with maximum intensity.

The weak and dispersed fire preparation and support for the attack and the frontal attack by the mass of infantry were the basic combat method in the small subunits.

The composition of the 2nd Guards Army, which had been formed in Tambov on the basis of the 1st Reserve Army, was as follows by 2 November: 1st Guards Rifle, 13th Guards Rifle and the 2nd Guards Mechanized corps.

By 1 December the 17th Guards Corps Artillery Regiment, the 54th Guards Independent Anti-Tank Artillery Battalion, the 408th Independent Guards Mortar Battalion, and the 355th Independent Engineer Battalion had been added.

By 1 January 1943 the 4th Cavalry Corps, 300th Rifle Division, 648th Army Artillery Regiment, 506th Artillery Regiment, 1095th Artillery Regiment, 1100th Artillery Regiment, 1101st Artillery Regiment, 535th Anti-Tank Artillery Regiment, 1250th Anti-Tank Artillery Regiment, 23rd Guards Mortar Regiment, 88th Guards Mortar Regiment, 90th Guards Mortar Regiment (minus the 373rd Battalion), 15th Anti-Aircraft Artillery Division, 3rd Guards Tank Corps, 6th Mechanized Corps, (became the 5th Guards Mechanized Corps on 1 February), 52nd Independent Tank Regiment, 128th Independent Tank Regiment, 223rd Independent Tank Regiment, and the 742nd Independent Mine-Sapper Battalion had been added to the army.

By 1 February 1943 the 4th Cavalry Corps and the 90th Guards Mortar Regiment had been removed from the army. In place of them, the 488th Mortar Regiment and the 4th Guards Mortar Regiment were added, as well as the 136th Independent Tank Regiment and the 1st Pontoon-Bridge Brigade.

As of 20 December 1942 the 2nd Guards Army numbered 80,779 men, and only 39,110 on 20 January 1943. Thus not even counting possible reinforcements, the army's losses were no less than 41,669 men. However, the 2nd Guards Army's actual losses were significantly greater.

"A Short Military-Historical Document on the 2nd Guards Army as of 20 December 1942" maintains that by 25 November the six rifle divisions of the 1st and 13th guards rifle corps numbered 21,077 combat troops. By 3 December, when orders were received to embark the army, "the combat strength reached 80,779 men." However, it is impossible to understand how during a week the 2nd Guards Army's combat strength increased by nearly four times. After all, during this time the army's strength was increased by the inclusion of the 2nd Mechanized Corps, which had an authorized strength of 13,559 men, as well as the 17th Guards Corps Artillery Regiment, 54th Guards Independent Anti-Tank Artillery Battalion, the 408th Independent Guards Mortar Battalion, and the 355th Independent Engineer Battalion, which altogether did not number more than 3,000 men. It is most likely that in this case the figure of 80,779 men represents the army's numerical, and not combat, strength.

After 20 December the army was reinforced by an infantry division, a cavalry corps, 13 artillery and mortar regiments, one anti-aircraft division, one mechanized corps, one tank corps, four independent tank regiments, one mine-sapper battalion, and one pontoon-bridge brigade. And this does not include reinforcements marching in. Thus by 20 December 1942 the 2nd Guards Army had two rifle and one mechanized corps, one artillery regiment, one artillery and one mortar battalion, and one engineer battalion. According to A.I. Yeremenko, during 20-29 December just two of the 51st Army's mechanized corps received 3,000 reinforcements from the rear military districts. It's hard to believe that the 2nd Guards Army's two mechanized corps received less than 3,000 men in reinforcements during the month following 20 December. The proviso that "during the vigorous offensive a certain number of enlisted men fell behind their units and attached themselves to formations that were not a part of the army," does not change matters. Besides this, a pontoon-bridge brigade had an authorized strength of 1,813 men and a mine-sapper battalion about 400 men. The mechanized, tank and cavalry corps, as well as a rifle division, even if their strength was less than authorized when they became part of the 2nd Guards Army, taken together probably represented a reinforcement of no less than 30,000 men. On 20 November the 4th Cavalry Corps numbered 10,284 men, 9,284 horses, 7,354 rifles and carbines, 566 PPSh[22] automatic rifles, 264 light machine guns, 140 anti-tank rifles, 70 76mm, 24 45mm and eight 37mm guns, 16 107mm and 120mm mortars, 46 82mm and 116 50mm mortars. However, at the moment it was transferred to Malinovskii's army it had already suffered heavy losses. Its 81st Cavalry Division lost 1,897 men killed, wounded and missing in the 4 December fighting alone, plus 1,860 horses. Thus the 4th Cavalry Corps arrived at Malinovskii's army probably not having more than a third of its initial personnel strength. The authorized strength of a tank regiment was 339 men, so that four regiments could increase the army's strength by 1,356 men. Artillery and mortar regiments at the end of 1942 and the beginning of 1943 numbered 758-1,120 men and an anti-aircraft division 1,345 men. The strength of Malinovskii's army could have increased by approximately 13,500 men by the inclusion of the additional artillery units. Aside from this, there were reinforcements. Even if one assumes that the other combat units were reinforced at the same level as the two mechanized corps, then they would have received by 20 January no less than 10,000 reinforcements. However, it's entirely possible that the mechanized corps and the other formations received more reinforcements. One should not doubt that during the 20 December 1942-20 January 1943 period the number of people who passed through the 2nd Guards Army was not 80,779 men, but a minimum of 140,900 men. Taking this into account, the army's losses did not number 41,669 men, but a minimum of 101,800 men.

The German Fourth Panzer Army faced the 2nd Guards Army. The panzer army lost 404 men killed, 1,216 wounded and 53 missing in action during the last ten days of December 1942. During the first ten days of January 1943 the Fourth Panzer Army lost 135 killed, 425 wounded and 103 missing in action, and during the second ten days 394 killed, 1,117 wounded and 50 missing in action. Even if you compare these losses with those of the 2nd Guards Army alone, then the correlation is 26.1:1 in favor of the Germans. However, at this time the Germans' Fourth Panzer Army was faced by, besides the 2nd Guards Army, the 51st and 5th Shock armies, the total losses of which were unlikely to have been less than those of the 2nd Guards Army. Besides this, the remnants of the Romanian 2nd and 18th divisions, as well as the 15th Air Field Division, were fighting against the 2nd Guards Army, although their total losses, in any event, were less than those of the Soviet 51st Army. And taking into account the fact that among the Soviet losses the proportion of irretrievable losses was higher than those of the Wehrmacht, then the real correlation of irretrievable losses for the German Fourth Panzer Army and the opposing group of Soviet forces may be on the order of 35-40:1. The more favorable correlation of losses for the Soviets in 1943 is only due to the enormous irretrievable losses in the Stalingrad area, which amount to 30.3 percent of all the Germans' irretrievable losses in 1943.

---

22   Editor's note. The PPSh (*pistolet-pulemet Shpagina*) was a popular light machine gun model in the Red Army during the Great Patriotic War. It was designed by Georgii Shpagin (1897-1952) and weighed 3.63 kilograms unloaded and could fire 900-1,000 7.62mm rounds per minute.

We should note that the losses of the *Luftwaffe's* air field divisions before their transfer to the ground army on 1 November 1943 can be determined only approximately. In all, from October 1942 to 1 November 1943 about 250,000 men served in the *Luftwaffe* field divisions, and at the time they were transferred to the ground army these divisions numbered about 160,000 men. Thus their total losses in killed, wounded, missing in action and sick men evacuated to the rear may be estimated at 90,000 men. Taking into account the relatively low combat capability of the air field divisions, as well as the fact that at the end of 1942 and in 1943 the Red Army predominantly attacked, one may then assume that no less than a third of the losses of the *Luftwaffe* field divisions are irretrievable losses. This means 30,000 killed and missing in action and 60,000 wounded and evacuated sick. Taking into account the fact that of the 21 *Luftwaffe* field divisions formed, one division (14th) took no part in the fighting right up until the end of the war, remaining in Norway, and that in 1943 another six divisions were in the West, the Southeast and in Denmark and took no part in the fighting, then the 1942-43 losses are actually being proportioned among 14 divisions, which yields average losses of 6,400 men per division. Insofar as the 15th *Luftwaffe* Field Division was employed more actively at the end of 1942 and in 1943 than the majority of the other air field divisions, then one may assume that this division's losses were no less than 10,000 men. The 15th *Luftwaffe* Field Division was engaged in active combat operations from the end of December 1942 to the middle of February 1943. It was then involved in fighting from the middle of July through September 1943 and suffered particularly heavy losses during the retreat to the Dnepr in August-September. Taking into account the fact that during the period 20 December 1942-20 January 1943 its losses were not likely more than one-fifth of the total; that is, about 2,000 killed, wounded and missing in action, then these can hardly influence in a significant way the correlation of losses between the 2nd Guards Army and the enemy forces opposing it.

During these days when the 2nd Guards Army was successfully attacking, a tragedy occurred that personally touched Rodion Yakovlevich. His friend and comrade-in-arms, member of the army's military council Major General Illarion Ivanovich Larin, perished. This is what the documents say about this incident:

To the GKO, comrade Stalin and comrade Molotov.
27 December 1942.

According to a report by the Special Section of the Stalingrad Front NKVD, during the night of 26-27 December of this year, Major General Larin, member of the 2nd Guards Army's military council, shot himself in his apartment.

Larin left a note containing the following: "I have nothing to do with it. I ask that you not touch my family. Rodion is a smart man. Long live Lenin."

Rodion is the commander of the 2nd Guard Army, comrade Malinovskii.

On 19 December, while traveling to the front line, Larin acted nervously, walked around at full height and was slightly wounded in the leg, creating the impression that he was looking to die.

Comrade Selivanovskii, the chief of the NKVD's Special Section for the front is conducting an investigation.

People's Commissar of Internal Affairs of the USSR, L. Beria.[23]

---

23   RGASPI, fond 83, opis' 1, delo 19, p. 8.

Malinovskii's mother,
Varvara Nikolaevna
Malinovskaya, 1898.

Odessa police
chief Yakov
Ivanovich
Bunin (in the
center, upper
row), presumed
father of R.Ya.
Malinovskii.

R.Ya. Malinovskii in France, May 1916.

R.Ya. Malinovskii (wearing helmet) in France, 1916.

R.Ya. Malinovskii (in the center) with the 137th Independent Rifle Battalion. Kansk-Yeniseiskii, 1922.

Colonel R.Ya. Malinovskii with his mother, 1930s.

R.Ya. Malinovskii.
Madrid, 1937.

R.Ya. Malinovskii, Spain, 1937.

Brigade Commander R.Ya. Malinovskii, 1938.

Major General R.Ya. Malinovskii, winter 1941-42.

Lieutenant General R.Ya. Malinovskii with regimental commissar I.M. Larin, December 1941.

Lieutenant General
R.Ya. Malinovskii,
winter 1941-42.

Lieutenant General
R.Ya. Malinovskii with
I.M. Larin, member of
the Southern Front's
military council, 1942.

R.Ya. Malinovskii with N.S. Khrushchev and P.A. Rotmistrov, 19 January 1943.

R.Ya. Malinovskii with member of the Southern Front military council Major General A.I. Kirichenko, N.S. Khrushchev and secretary of the Rostov provincial party committee B.A. Dvinskii, Rostov, 18 February 1943.

Transfer of command of the Second Ukrainian Front. Sitting (left to right), General R.Ya. Malinovskii and Marshal I.S. Konev. Standing (left to right), Major General M.M. Stakhurskii and Lieutenant General of Tank Troops I.Z. Susaikov, members of the Second Ukrainian Front military council. Miranden, Romania, May 1944.

Marshal R.Ya. Malinovskii and M.V. Zakharov studying a map, Second Ukrainian Front.

Marshal R.Ya. Malinovskii
in Hungary, end of 1944.

Marshal R.Ya. Malinovskii in Krepice, Czechoslovakia (near Brno), April 1945.

Marshal R.Ya. Malinovskii
with his second wife, Raisa
Yakovlevna Kucherenko,
9 May 1945.

Marshals A.M. Vasilevskii, R.Ya. Malinovskii and K.A. Meretskov. Port Arthur,
September 1945.

Commanders and members of the Trans-Baikal Front's military council at General Yamada's palace. Marshal R.Ya. Malinovskii in the center. Second from left is Lieutenant General K.A. Zykov, chief of the Trans-Baikal Front's political administration. Changchun, China, September 1945.

Marshal R.Ya. Malinovskii with Mongolian Marshal Kh. Choibalsan, Ulan Bator, Mongolia, May 1946.

Marshal R.Ya. Malinovskii in Khabarovsk, 7 November 1946.

Marshal R.Ya. Malinovskii with wife Raisa and daughter Natal'ya, 1950s.

Yu.A. Gagarin, marshals R.Ya. Malinovskii and A.A. Grechko, N.S. Khrushchev, and marshals M.V. Zakharov and K.S. Moskalenko, 1960s.

Marshal R.Ya. Malinovskii with N.S. Khrushchev on the Lenin Mausoleum. Moscow, 7 November 1962.

Marshal R.Ya. Malinovskii fishing in the Adriatic Sea, June 1964.

Marshal R.Ya. Malinovskii with Marshal S.S. Biryuzov aboard an airplane, 1960s.

Left to right: Marshal R.Ya.
Malinovskii, unknown, A.A.
Gromyko, and L.I. Brezhnev in
the Belovezhskaya Woods, 1965.

Marshal R.Ya. Malinovskii with
his wife Raisa and daughter
Natal'ya, 9 May 1965.

Marshal R.Ya. Malinovskii and French president Charles De Gaulle with the Taman' Division, June 1966.

Marshal R.Ya. Malinovskii, 1966.

The Chekists[24] suspected that one of the reasons for the suicide was an incident that took place four months earlier. The former secretary of the Southern Front military council, Senior Battalion Commissar A. Fedenev, wrote about the flight in August 1942 of Captain Sirenko, the adjutant of the former commander of the Southern Front, in a letter to Malenkov[25] on 29 December 1942:

To the secretary of the TsK VKP(b), comrade Malenkov.
From Battalion Commissar A. Fedenev.
29.XII.42.

I, being the secretary of the Southern Front military council, following its disbanding, was part of the Don operational group under the command of Lieutenant General Malinovskii and throughout the entire period of its existence was together with comrade Malinovskii.

During this group's existence, in approximately the middle of August 1942, when the group's headquarters was located in Nal'chik, the following incident occurred.

A Captain Sirenko served under the front commander Lieutenant General Malinovskii as a permanent staff member for special assignments. Sirenko arrived at the Southern Front military council together with comrade Malinovskii from the army where he served him as an adjutant and was with him throughout the entire period of Malinovskii's sojourn at the Southern Front. He was also together with Malinovskii in the operational group until the time of its arrival in Nal'chik.

In Nal'chik we received instructions from the *Stavka* of the High Command to merge Malinovskii's group with the Trans-Caucasus Front's northern group of forces and that Lieutenant General Malinovskii was to leave and be at the disposal of the commander of the Trans-Caucasus Front.

Upon receiving this order, comrade Malinovskii ordered the group staff to travel to the town of Ordzhonikidze, where he was himself to travel in order to meet the commander of the northern group, Lieutenant General Maslennikov.[26]

I don't remember the date, but in the morning, when all the vehicles of the group's staff and security were ready to leave for the town of Ordzhonikidze, the absence of Captain Sirenko and comrade Malinovskii's driver, Technical Lieutenant Letinskii, was noted. The departure was scheduled for 0700, but they were still not there at 0800. Several people were dispatched to find them, because they assumed that Sirenko, together with Letinskii and the former driver of Division Commissar comrade Larin, had gone to the latter's apartment, because he was a local and his parents were in Nal'chik.

---

24   Editor's note. The name "Chekist" is derived from the word "Cheka," itself a shortened form of the Russian name for the "Extraordinary Commission" (*Chrezvychainaya Kommissiya*), the first secret police organization established by the Bolsheviks at the end of 1917. Since then the term "chekist" was applied to all secret police operatives, no matter what the name of the organization.

25   Editor's note. Georgii Maksimilianovich Malenkov (1902-88) joined the Red Army in 1918. Thereafter he quickly rose through the party ranks and became a protégé of Stalin. He played an active role in the party purge of the late 1930s and was head of the party's cadre directorate and a secretary of the Central Committee. During the Great Patriotic War he was a member of the GKO in charge of aircraft production. Following Stalin's death, he briefly held the top government and party posts, but was later eclipsed by Khrushchev. Following an attempt to overthrow his rival, Malenkov and several others were stripped of their posts.

26   Editor's note. Ivan Ivanovich Maslennikov (1900-54) joined the Red Army in 1918 and later advanced in the NKVD apparatus. During the Great Patriotic War he commanded armies and fronts. Following the war he commanded military districts and later returned to secret police work.

While the search was going on, Malinovskii summoned me and gave me a letter to read, which he found in his briefcase and which was addressed to me. The letter proved to be from Captain Sirenko. Addressing me, he wrote that the situation at the front had become very difficult and that supposedly our generals had shown themselves incapable of commanding, had become demoralized, were drinking and engaged in debauchery, such as that old roué General Zhuk (Major General Zhuk was the Southern Front deputy commander for artillery and had arrived at the front headquarters together with Malinovskii from the 6th Army). He said that the generals travel with various "wives" and "daughters," or simply prostitutes. Having witnessed all of this, he, Sirenko, decided that he must actively fight the Germans in his homeland and had decided to join the partisans. He said that there was already a small detachment of three men, but that it would grow and they would still hear from him, Sirenko. He signed the letter already as the commander of a partisan detachment.

After this it became clear that Sirenko had run away and had taken Malinovskii's driver in the car, so we left for Ordzhonikidze.

Malinovskii left for Ordzhonikidze alone, while we were directed along the road to Groznyi. On the way to Groznyi Malinovskii caught up to us and I was with him together in the northern group's military council. In the city of Groznyi Malinovskii told me that he had reported the disappearance of Sirenko to the Special Section and that instructions had been issued for his search and detainment. I then spoke to the operational representative, whose name I don't know, as I saw him for the first time. While located with the North Caucasus Front in September, Senior Major for State Security, comrade Zilenin, the chief of the front's Special Section, spoke with me, from which I concluded that this fact was known to the special organs.

29.XII.42. Senior Battalion Commissar A. Fedenev.[27]

The incident with the flight of Malinovskii's adjutant and driver and Larin's driver probably provoked fears in Larin that the special section operatives would cook up a political case against him and Malinovskii in connection with Sirenko's flight. During the days of the victory at Stalingrad Soviet generals sometimes feared the special section operatives more than they did the Germans.

In "Memorial's" data base on deaths in the Great Patriotic War, there is an order by the People's Commissariat for Defense's Main Administration for Cadres of 12 May 1945 to exclude from its list "Captain Aleksandr Ivanovich Sirenko, who was at the disposal of the military council of the Southern Front. He was missing in action in August 1942. His wife, Aleksandra Konstantinovna Sirenko, resides in the city of Kremenchug, 31 Shevchenko Street"

This excerpt from a postwar order by the Defense Commissariat's Main Administration for Cadres about exclusion from the lists on 12 May 1945, was evidently based on the wife's declaration, which was delivered to the Poltava provincial military commissariat. We should note that at this time by no means all Soviet prisoners of war had been repatriated from the western zones of occupation, so one may assume the most varied versions of Aleksandr Sirenko's fate. He could have perished in fighting the Germans. He could have been captured by them and repatriated to the motherland after the war, where he was threatened with a trial or execution for desertion, or the GULag.[28] If he was lucky, Sirenko could have remained in the West by passing himself off as

27   RGASPI, fond 83, opis' 1, delo 19, pp. 11-12.
28   Editor's note. GULag was the acronym of the Main Camp Administration (*Glavnoe Upravlenie Lagerei*), which was in charge of the extensive system of forced-labor camps in the USSR. The GULag was created in 1930 and was a part of the OGPU, NKVD and MVD apparatus until its disbandment in 1960.

a Ukrainian from former Polish territory and become an émigré, but it seems he did not write his memoirs.

I was able to find more detailed information on A.I. Sirenko in the electronic data base "The People's Feat in the Great Patriotic War of 1941-1945." This indicates his year of birth—1911; nationality—Ukrainian; party allegiance—Komsomol[29] member; beginning of his service in the Red Army—1933; place of conscription—the Kremenchug District Military Commissariat, Ukrainian SSR, Poltava Province, Kremenchug District, and; his position—adjutant to the commander of the Southern Front. Captain Sirenko had not been wounded and had no awards and had fought in the war since 22 June 1941 (his date of service is mistakenly given as 22 June 1942 on his award certificate). In the declaration for his being awarded the Order of the Red Star, it states that

> Captain Sirenko has fought from the first day of the Great Patriotic War against the German occupiers in the position of adjutant of the commander of the 48th Rifle Corps, then commander of the 6th Army and the commander of the Southern Front. Over the course of the entire struggle against the German occupiers, he has shown himself a loyal son of our socialist Motherland, has displayed bravery and fearlessness in battle, while carrying out responsible combat tasks such as the transmission of combat orders under direct fire. He manifested himself particularly in the fighting around Slobodka station and the town of Kotovskii in July 1941, and during an attack by tanks and motorized infantry on the head-quarters of the 48th Rifle Corps in August 1941, near Krinichki (in the Nikolaev area), as well as during the crossing of the corps' units over the Bug River under fire, and during the corps' escape from encirclement in the area of the city of Nikolaev.
>
> On 26 August 1941, during the fighting around Dnepropetrovsk, he personally carried out a reconnaissance of the islands in the area of the double railroad bridge over the Dnepr River and also decisively assisted in putting shaky troops in order during 15 days of stub-born fighting around Nizhnedneprovsk, turned them around into the battle, while subject-ing himself to the enemy's artillery and mortar fire. He often appeared together with me in the most dangerous places during the 6th Army's heavy fighting during the retreat from the Krasnograd—Pereshchepino area behind the Severskii Donets in October 1941 and he always showed himself a brave and selfless soldier-commander.
>
> He is worthy of being decorated with the Order of the Red Star.
>
> Commander of the Southern Front.
>
> Lieutenant General Malinovskii.
>
> 26 March 1942.

In the military council's conclusion, which was signed by Brigade Commissar Larin, it states: "As the military commissar for the 48th Rifle Corps and then a member of the military council of the 6th Army, I often observed comrade Sirenko's combat work. Comrade Sirenko is a fear-less combat commander. He copes honorably with combat assignments. He fully deserves being awarded the Order of the Red Star."

And on 18 April 1942 Sirenko received the order.

It's possible that we'll never know the further fate of Captain Sirenko.

---

29 Editor's note. The Komsomol (full name, *Vsesoyuznyi Leninskii Kommunisticheskii Soyuz Molodezhi*), or All-Union Leninist Communist Union of Youth, was founded in 1918 as the Communist Party's youth branch. It was disbanded in 1991.

There exists a legend that Larin supposedly shot himself as early as August in a room in the Hotel Moscow, awaiting an audience with Stalin and fearing that following the publication of order No. 227, he and Malinovskii could be turned over to a military tribunal for trial. According to the visitor's register in Stalin's Kremlin office, Larin and Malinovskii were there on 24 August 1942. Insofar as immediately after that, on 25 August, they were appointed to command the 8th Reserve Army (the future 66th Army), one can assume that Stalin summoned them precisely in connection with this appointment, in order to show that despite the formal demotion in position, his faith in Malinovskii and Larin had not changed. In principle, one cannot exclude that the matter of Sirenko's flight was discussed. However, the latter seems unlikely. First of all, we don't exactly precisely when the adjutant ran away. It's not excluded that this was after 24 August. Secondly, there is no information that news of this incident was immediately reported to Stalin. After all, Beria, when he had to report to Stalin on Larin's suicide at the end of December, sent him only Fedenev's testimony on the Sirenko affair, which was contained in a report to Malenkov at the end of December. Beria did not send Stalin any August documents concerning Sirenko's flight. It seems unlikely that Beria's subordinate, V.S. Abakumov,[30] the chief of the Directorate of Special Sections, sent Stalin a report on the Sirenko incident without having informed his immediate superior. It's most likely that the Sirenko affair did not go any further than the North Caucasus Front's Special Section in August. Evidence of this is the letter, cited below, from Stalin to Khrushchev, from which it follows that Stalin became aware of Sirenko's flight no earlier than the end of December.

We should also note that Malinovskii had an audience with Stalin in the latter's Kremlin office on 5 and 7 May 1942, 1-2 August 1944, and 19 June 1945. He probably met Stalin later as well, only these meeting did not take place in Stalin's Kremlin office, where Stalin rarely appeared after the war, usually when he met members of foreign delegations, and at one of his dachas, where no record of visitors was kept.

In connection with Larin's suicide, at the beginning of January 1943 Stalin sent the following coded message to Khrushchev:

> I received your coded message regarding your trip to the 2nd Guards Army for work there. I think that you should stay there for the next two months in the 2nd Guards Army's military council and seriously observe Malinovskii's work. It's not by accident that during the Southern Front's retreat Malinovskii's personal adjutant abandoned our front and supposedly joined the partisans, when he actually went over to the Germans. It's also not by accident that Larin, a member of the 2nd Guards Army's military council and Malinovskii's personal friend, committed suicide, leaving a note of incomprehensible and strange content. What does Larin's phrase that "I have nothing to do with it" in his note? What's he justifying himself for here? Nor is it comprehensible why did Larin think that we would touch his family. Why does Larin's note speak of Rodion as a smart man? And Malinovskii is silent, as if this does not concern him. Ask Malinovskii all about this, as well as about his personal adjutant, and let's see what he says. Take some men, experienced special operatives, with you and organize the strictest observation of Malinovskii with their assistance. If some kind of falsehood is revealed in Malinovskii's behavior, signal me immediately, in order to immediately relieve him for this or that plausible reason and replace him with someone else. Collect information on Kreizer,[31]

30   Editor's note. Viktor Semyonovich Abakumov (1908-54) joined the Red Army in 1922 and the OGPU in 1932. During the Great Patriotic War he headed the army's counterintelligence service (SMERSH). He was appointed head of the Ministry of State Security in 1946 and carried out purges of party and military officials under Stalin's orders. He was arrested in 1951 and later executed.
31   Editor's note. Yakov Grigor'evich Kreizer (1905-69) joined the Red Army in 1921. During the Second

as it's possible that he will fully qualify to replace Malinovskii, if his replacement should prove to be necessary. Inform me regularly about the results of your observations.

Khrushchev, who on that day stopped in the Verkhne-Tsaritsynskii farm, recalled Larin's suicide:

Suddenly Malinovskii storms in, still in his long coat, without having undressed, and very upset. I look at him and tears are flowing like a river. "What's going on? What's happened, Rodion Yakovlevich?" "A tragedy has occurred. Larin has committed suicide."

Larin was a member of the 2nd Guards Army's military council and a fighting man. He was great friends with Malinovskii and they served together before the war. When Malinovskii commanded a corps, Larin was his commissar. Malinovskii always requested that Larin remain with him, either as chief of the political section, or as commissar. He deserved respect as a political worker. He was wounded before all of this happened. I dropped in on him in his apartment. He could not walk, but the wound wasn't serious, in the fleshy part of the leg, with the bone undamaged and the bullet only grazing the shin. Larin was coherent when he spoke. A woman, an army doctor, took care of him. They later told me that before he shot himself he was talking quite gaily with her. Malinovskii was extremely upset by this event and bemoaned his death. I didn't know how to calm him. What had caused such an action? Why did Larin shoot himself? His adjutant later informed me under what circumstances this had occurred.

The circumstances were very unclear. Larin left for the front line and was observing the fighting under the cover of a haystack. He was walking around, as if looming in front of the enemy and obviously looking to die. There was no reason to behave that way. He was simply drawing fire on himself. Of course, he was soon wounded. Although the wound was not serious, he suddenly shot himself. What for? It happened that people shot themselves at the beginning of the war, when we were retreating. All of a sudden, we're attacking we've surrounded Paulus's forces and are fighting Manstein, one might say, at the turning point. We've long since stopped running away and a new stage in military operations against the enemy has begun. The 2nd Guards Army, a strong and powerful army, is successfully repelling Manstein's attack. And suddenly he shoots himself? Larin left a note, which was also very strange. I can't precisely reproduce its contents right now, but the sense of it was that he is committing suicide, followed by the words: "Long live Lenin." Then his signature. We immediately dispatched this note to Moscow…

I was immediately summoned to Moscow. The latest multi-hour dinner was taking place at Stalin's, with all the "supplements" and drinks, as well as a review of the events that had taken place during the past day.

Stalin asks me: "Just who is Malinovskii?" I reply: "I've reported to you about Malinovskii before. He's a famous general, who commanded a corps in the beginning of the war, then an army, and then the Southern Front. He had some failures there. You know that." Of course Stalin knew that this was the *front* that was outflanked by the enemy and fell apart. The enemy took Rostov with ease, for which Malinovskii was relieved of his post and sent to the rear…

Shcherbakov[32] understood that the anger against Malinovskii would be directed directly or obliquely against me. "All of this," Shcherbakov said, "is not accidental. Why didn't he write

---

World War he commanded a division and several armies. Following the war, Kreizer commanded several military districts.

32   Editor's note. Aleksandr Sergeevich Shcherbakov (1901-45) joined the Red Guards in 1917 and the

'Long live Stalin' and instead wrote 'Long live Lenin!'?" I answered: "I can't say. He evidently shot himself under the influence of some sort of psychologically abnormal condition. If he had been in a normal condition, then he wouldn't have shot himself. He had no reason to shoot himself." But no, Shcherbakov kept on rubbing salt in the wound. I had to put up with a lot of unpleasantness.

Of course, the best thing for me would have been to simply say that Larin was some kind of so-and-so and Malinovskii's the same. But I didn't agree with that and could not say that to Stalin. So, Stalin once again: "Just who is Malinovskii?" I replied: "I know Malinovskii. I know him only from the positive side. I can't say that I've known him for many years, but I've known him since the start of the war. He behaved himself well and firmly this whole time, both as a man and a general." A threat was evidently hanging over Malinovskii. Everything had come together here—the fall of Rostov and Larins's suicide—all of it tied up in a single knot. Stalin: "When you return to the front, you should keep an eye on Malinovskii. You should always be at the headquarters of the 2nd Guards Army. Keep an eye on all his actions and orders." In a word, I'm responsible for Malinovskii and his army and have to be the eye from the party and the *Stavka* observing Malinovskii. I said: "Alright comrade Stalin, as soon as I arrive I'll be inseparable from Malinovskii."

I took off for Verkhne-Tsaryntsinskii. And then I sort of forgot the road to the front headquarters, which was moving together with the 2nd Guards Army and always located next to Malinovskii. Malinovskii is a smart man. He understood that this was the result of Stalin's lack of faith in him. In my person he saw a controller over his activities. While we were shifting the headquarters, I had an apartment next to Malinovskii. It turned out that I was more a member of the 2nd Guards Army's military council than that of the entire *front*. Actually, the army was our main force along the front axis, so no real contradictions arose. And Malinovskii always coordinated with me all instructions and orders which he prepared, before he signed them. I didn't sign them because this was not my responsibility, but I knew all the orders and instructions, because Malinovskii reported everything to me.

Things were moving along well. I was satisfied with the situation at the front and with Malinovskii—his capabilities, his executive ability and his tact. In a word, who stood out in my eyes against the background of the other commanders and I treated him with respect. It was good to work with him.

At 2000 on 29 December Malinovskii issued an order to the deputy army commander, Major General Ya.G. Kreizer, to the commander of the 2nd Guards Mechanized Corps, Major General Sviridov, and to the commander of the 33rd Guards Rifle Division, Major General Utvenko:

1. The enemy, having been beaten in the Kotel'nikovo area, has abandoned Kotel'nikovo and is falling back to the southwest. He is simultaneously holding the Tormosin area.
2. At 2400 on 29.12 the 2nd Mechanized Corps is to cross over the Don River in the Verkhne-Kurmoyarskaya—Potemkinskii area and decisively attack in the direction of Balabanovskii and Tormosin and by the close of 30.12 capture the Aleshkinskii—Tormosin area, operating toward the left wing of the Southwestern Front, which is attacking from the Chernyshkovskii—Oblivskaya area. Upon capturing the Tormosin area, the corps is to push forward detachments toward Verkne-Aksenovskii, Tarasinskii and the west.

Communist Party a year later, quickly rising through the party's central and provincial apparatus. During the Great Patriotic War he was a secretary of the Central Committee, the head of the Moscow city party organization and chief of the armed forces Main Political Administration. He died of a heart attack.

Upon completing the mission, the corps headquarters is to be in Tormosin.

3. The 33rd Guards Rifle Division is to continue attacking at 0300 on 30.12 and by the end of the day is to capture the area Semyonov—Budarin—Yepifanov and support the 2nd Mechanized Corps' activities from the southwest and to push forward detachments to seize Belozerskii and Kupaly.

Upon completing the assignment, the division headquarters is to be located in Komarov.

4. The actions of the 2nd Guards Mechanized Corps and the 33rd Guards Rifle Division are to be united under the command of Major General Kreizer, with his auxiliary command post in Verkhne- Kurmoyarskaya.

5. The command post of the 2nd Guards Army's headquarters is in Gromoslavka.

Reports are to be made by radio every three hours, with the first report by 0300 on 30.12.

This order was signed for the first time by the new member of the army's military council— Guards Regimental Commissar Aleksandrov, and by Guards Colonel Gretsov for the chief of staff.

On 1 January 1943, when the failure of Manstein's plan to liberate the encircled group of forces became obvious, the Stalingrad Front was renamed the Southern Front and directed toward Rostov. A.I. Yeremenko considered such a decision to be incorrect and reported this to the Supreme Commander-in-Chief. But as Andrei Ivanovich noted in his diary, Stalin said: "Don't be upset, you played the main role in the Stalingrad battle… We are entrusting you with a more important task: to cut off the enemy's Caucasus group of forces by an attack on Rostov."

This idea was also discussed on 5 August 1943 during Stalin's meeting with Yeremenko in the village of Khoroshovo. Here are some short fragments from diary notes of this meeting.

… Comrade Stalin, who had been walking around the room until then, stopped in the middle and listened to my report. "Hello, comrade Yeremenko," he said, pronouncing my name with the accent on the third syllable, and extending his hand to me. "Your health, comrade Stalin!" I replied.

He smiled simply and warmly and politely shook my hand and, gazing fixedly at me, said: "It seems that you're still sore at me because I turned down your proposal during the final stage of the Stalingrad battle to finish off Paulus. You shouldn't be sore. We know and all our people know that you commanded two *fronts* during the battle of Stalingrad and played the chief role in the defeat of the fascist group of forces around Stalingrad and, as to who finished off the bound rabbit, does not play a special role."

I replied to what were essentially words of thanks: "Stalingrad is now history and its author is our people, party and you, personally, comrade Stalin."

At this point Stalin inserted: "Everyone lays everything on Stalin, 'Stalin this, Stalin that.' Of course, I issued directives, but you were in direct command there and ran this battle. Of course, the Soviet people, led by the great Russian people, won, but it had to be led."

Probably if Yeremenko had managed to rapidly capture Rostov and thus cut off the escape route of the Germans' Caucasian group of forces, his marshal's epaulets would have been guaranteed. However, Andrei Ivanovich did not command the Southern Front for long and was unsuccessful.

The 2nd Guards Army suffered the above-listed loss of 101,800 men not only in the fighting for the Kotel'nikovo bridgehead with Hoth's relief group of forces, but also during the unsuccessful offensive on Rostov and Bataisk, which was christened operation "Don." During this operation the 2nd Guards Army was supported by the 3rd Kotel'nikovo Tank, 2nd, 3rd Stalingrad, 4th Stalingrad, and 5th Zimovniki mechanized corps. In all, 11 rifle divisions, 13 mechanized and three tank brigades, nine tank regiments, 18 artillery and mortar regiments, and six independent artillery and mortar battalions attacked. However, the distance of the group of forces from the front supply bases by hundreds of kilometers created great problems for the timely receipt of fuel, food and ammunition. This also increased the irretrievable losses in tanks and motor vehicles, insofar as there was no place to repair damaged equipment.

The German 16th Motorized and 17th Panzer divisions, which disposed of 60-70 tanks and assault guns, were defending Rostov and Bataisk.

On 14 January 1943 Yeremenko, the commander of the Southern Front, the member of the front's military council, N.S. Khrushchev, and the front chief of staff, Major General Varennikov, signed operational directive no. 006 at 1600. The preamble stated:

> In carrying out the instructions of the *Stavka* of the VGK, the chief task of the Southern Front's forces is arriving at the line Shakhty—Novocherkassk—Rostov—Bataisk, in order cut off the path of retreat of the enemy's forces from the Northern Caucasus; in conjunction with the forces of the Trans-Caucasus Front, the Southern Front is to destroy the enemy's Caucasus group of forces and prevent its arrival at the Don River.

The "Don" mechanized group, consisting of the 3rd Tank and the 2nd and 5th guards mechanized corps, under the command of Lieutenant General of Tank Troops Pavel Alekseevich Rotmistrov, was ordered to attack on the morning of 17 January along the front Bagaevskaya—Veselyi toward Bataisk and by the morning of 18 January capture it, while another mechanized corps was to occupy Rostov. The 300th Rifle Division, attacking from Razdorskaya toward Novocherkassk, was to support Rotmistrov's group from the north. The 1st Guards Rifle Corps was to force the Severskii Donets on 18 January and move on Novocherkassk. The 13th Guards Rifle Corps, with its three divisions attacking behind Rotmistrov's group, was to reach the Bataisk—Ol'ginskaya area by 21 January. The 8th Air Army was to carry out an airborne landing in Bataisk with 306 parachutists, whose task consisted of seizing the bridges over the Don. If they could not hold the bridges, they were to blow them and the rail lines up.

However, due to a shortage of fuel and the units scattered positions, the start of the offensive had to be moved back a day. However, on 19 January only the 19th Guards Tank Brigade was ready to attack, and even it was not fully equipped.

On Rotmistrov's initiative, a detachment of 12 tanks, nine armored transports and five armored cars, and two companies of automatic riflemen from the 2nd Guards Motorized Rifle Brigade, under the command of the commander of the 19th Brigade, Guards Colonel A.V. Yegorov, left for Bataisk on the morning of 20 January. Five T-34 tanks, with a group of automatic riflemen, attacked an airfield 1.5 kilometers from Bataisk, while the main forces attacked the town. The group attacking the airfield damaged the landing strip and several depots, but was completely destroyed by retaliatory fire from 88mm anti-aircraft guns. The Germans lost one gun. The detachment's main forces, which were shelling the railroad station, lost three tanks, three armored cars and more than 50 men killed and wounded as a result of retaliatory fire. The remnants of the detachment took up defensive positions near the Lenin and OGPU state farms, awaiting Rotmistrov's and Malinovskii's main forces.

However, by this time Manstein had moved the 11th Panzer Division to Bataisk. On 19 January he attacked from Ol'ginskaya toward Manychskaya, crushing the 98th Rifle Division, whose remnants fell back to Manychskaya. On 21 January the 11th Panzer Division's units attacked Colonel Yegorov's detachment and forced it to fall back to the right bank of the Manych. Seven armored vehicles and 50 infantrymen survived.

On 22 January the 2nd and 5th Guards mechanized corps' brigades were finally ready for the attack and occupied Samodurovka farm, Cheryumkin, Krasnyi, Usman', and Nizhne-Podpol'nyi. To repel the offensive, the German 17th Panzer and 16th Motorized divisions were thrown in, and as early as 23 January threw the Soviet forces out of all the above-named locales. But by evening the 2nd Mechanized Corps' brigades were able to occupy Cheryumkin, Nizhne-Podpol'nyi and Krasnyi Lovets. Units of the 3rd Guards Tank Corps threw the enemy out of Pustoshkina. However, only 11 combat-ready tanks remained in the corps. By the morning of 25 January there were no more than 50 combat-ready tanks in the 2nd and 5th Guards mechanized corps.

The 13th Guards Rifle Corps was holding the line Pozdneevka—Krasnyi Kut—Veselyi with the forces of the 49th Guards Rifle Division. Two of the 3rd Guards Rifle Division's regiments were fighting along the line 500 meters north of Krasnoe Znamya farm.

On 23 January the commander of the 2nd Guards Army received the following instructions from Stalin:

> 23.1.43. Transmitted at 0853 and Malinovskii received it at 1230.
>
> By cable to comrade Yeremenko and Khrushchev, with a copy for comrade Malinovskii.
>
> The seizure of Bataisk by our forces has great historic significance. With the capture of Bataisk, we will bottle up the enemy's army in the Northern Caucasus and prevent 24 German and Romanian divisions from exiting to the Rostov—Taganrog—Donbass area. The enemy in the Northern Caucasus must be encircled and destroyed, just as he was encircled and is being destroyed around Stalingrad. It is necessary for the forces of the Southern Front to cut off the 24 enemy divisions in the Northern Caucasus from Rostov, and the forces of the Trans-Caucasus Front's Black Sea Group will close these divisions' escape route to the Taman' peninsula. The chief role in this matter belongs to the Southern Front, which must, together with the Trans-Caucasus Front's northern group, encircle and capture or destroy the enemy's forces in the Northern Caucasus. It is necessary to move the Southern Front's main forces, which are located in the Manych area and south of the Don, toward Bataisk, in order to take Bataisk and Azov and to cut the enemy's main routes of retreat and to encircle his retreating units, in order that all of his equipment remain. I request that you take these instructions as guidance and report on their fulfillment. I. Stalin.
>
> 23.1.42. 0630. Transmitted by Major General Shevchekno.

However, in practice, Malinovskii's army and the tank and mechanized corps attached to it had to defend, and not attack. On 24-25 January there was fighting in Manychskaya, which the Germans took at the close of the 25th. The remnants of the 2nd Guards Mechanized Corps fell back to the east, but during the day of 26 January the corps, together with the 2nd and 5th guards mechanized corps, once again attempted to force the Manych in the Manychskaya area, although they were repulsed with heavy losses. By the start of the attack the corps contained only 21 combat-ready tanks, including four KVs, seven T-34s and ten T-70s. Rotmistrov reported to Malinovskii on the evening of 26 January: "Units of the mechanized group, as a result of the developing situation and heavy losses are no longer capable of conducting independent combat operations."

The *Stavka* of the Supreme High Command, in its operational directive No. 30031, which was dispatched on 26 January at 2340 to the commander of the Southern Front, Colonel General Yeremenko, demanded:

1. Decisively improve the control of the front's troops.
2. Speed up the pace of the 51st and 28th armies' offensive and on 28.01.43 reach the line Ol'ginskaya—Bataisk.
3. The 2nd Guards Army's auxiliary command post should be immediately moved closer to the troops.
4. Control of the 2nd and 5th guards mechanized corps and the 3rd Guards Tank Corps should be subordinated directly to comrade Malinovskii.

5.   Confirm reception and report on fulfillment.
     I. Stalin.
     G. Zhukov.

It seems that Stalin was disappointed by how Rotmistrov, who had not been able to concentrate sufficient forces for an offensive on time and who was throwing units into the battle piecemeal, was managing the operations of the mobile group. Now Iosif Vissarionovich had transferred control of the tank and mechanized corps directly to Malinovskii, hoping that he could achieve something. After all, the prize for taking Bataisk and Rostov was enormous: all of German Army Group A, which was stuck in the North Caucasus. However, by this time the only thing left of the Soviet mobile corps was their names, and it was difficult for Rodion Yakovlevich to achieve rapid success.

Yeremenko immediately issued orders to the commanders of the 2nd Guards and 51st and 28th armies:

> The *Stavka* of the VGK has assigned the Southern Front the categorical task of reaching the Bataisk—Koisug area by the close of 28 January and cutting the Caucasus group's path of retreat. On 28 January the opposing enemy is to be defeated by decisive actions and the line Ol'ginskaya—Bataisk—Koisug reached. In order to carry out this task, the entire rank and file is to be mobilized. Dispatch responsible commanders to the units to help in organizing and carrying out a decisive offensive and to defeat the enemy.
>   Yeremenko. Khrushchev. Varennikov.

The hurriedly organized offensive ended without results. On 27 January the 24th Guards Rifle Division's regiments, together with the remnants of the 5th Guards Mechanized Corps, once again attempted to force the Manych and encountered powerful artillery fire and bombing and strafing attacks from the air. Nor did the 3rd and 49th guards rifle divisions, reinforced by the 128th, 136th, 158th, and 223rd independent tank battalions achieve anything. 20 tanks fell through the ice and as many were knocked out by enemy artillery. Old timers from the Tuzlukov farm recalled that "many soldiers killed remained in the reeds of the Manych. In the spring, when the river awoke, the current carried away the bodies of those killed. Where? No one knows. How many? No one counted…"

On 29-30 January Malinovskii's army just as unsuccessfully sought to force the Manych. On 30 January the *Luftwaffe* bombed the headquarters of the 2nd Guards Army in Nizhne-Solyonyi farm. Several officers were killed and a number of operational and registration documents burned. Thus the summary number of losses for the rank and file for 20-30 January 1943—17,802 men— who are shown in the report by the army staff, are by no means complete. By January 30 all of the tank and mechanized formations were essentially incapable of fighting:

The 3rd Guards Tank Corps had nine tanks and 350 motorized riflemen;

The 2nd Guards Mechanized Corps had eight tanks and about 1,000 motorized riflemen;

The 5th Guards Mechanized Corps had eight tanks and up to 2,000 motorized riflemen;

The 128th, 136th, 158th, and 223rd tank regiments disposed of 24 tanks, leaving a total of 49 tanks combat ready in the 2nd Guards Army.

The 4th and 3rd Guards mechanized corps, which were attached to the neighboring armies, had a corresponding two and four tanks apiece and occupied the Pavlov, Zolotaryov and Novo-Kalinovskii farms and the Rakovo-Tavricheskii and Radukhina Balka farms.

And only three weeks earlier there were 526 combat-ready tanks in the five corps and four tank regiments.

They hurriedly filled out a request in the Southern Front's headquarters for reinforcements, where it was noted that "the front needs reinforcements of 100,000 men, of which 50,000 are from guards units, and 500 tanks." This indicates that the main part of the tanks had been irretrievably lost.

Finally, on 31 January the guards troops of the 33rd, 24th and 49th divisions, supported by the surviving tanks, forced the Manych and began fighting along the left bank. However, on 1 February the attempts to take Samodurovka, Manychskaya and Krasnyi utterly failed. These inhabited areas were occupied only by the close of the following day. By 6 February units of the 2nd Guards Army reached the Usman'—Reznikov—Verkne-Podpol'nyi—Nizhne-Podpol'nyi area and halted on this line.

However, it was still impossible to take Bataisk, and even more so Rostov. The time had already passed and the First Panzer Army's main formations from the North Caucasus had managed to pass through Rostov.

Stalin blamed Yeremenko for the failure and for not being able to force the commanders of the 28th and 51st armies, generals V.F. Gerasimenko[33] and N.I. Trufanov, who were unable to take advantage of the fact that Malinovskii's army had diverted upon itself the most combat-capable formations of Army Group Don.

At 1400 on 2 February 1943 Yeremenko issued his final order to the Southern Front:

1. In its order no. 46017 of 29 January, the *Stavka* of the Supreme High Command has satisfied my request that in view of my illness (opened wounds) it has relieved me from command of the forces of the Southern Front.
2. At 2400 on 2 February I turned over command of the Southern Front's forces to Lieutenant General R.Ya. Malinovskii.

Simultaneously, Malinovskii confirmed with his order that he had entered upon the command of the front. In the beginning of February Nikolai Ivanovich Trufanov was removed from his post and until the end of the war was no longer appointed to command an army. On 11 February Lieutenant General G.F. Zakharov replaced him as commander of the 51st Army.

On 3 February Khrushchev send a coded telegram to Moscow, where it was noted, in particular, that:

The enemy facing the front of our troops' offensive continues to stubbornly resist and coun-terattack with infantry in his previous group of forces. The enemy was not engaged in active operations along the line Severskii Donets River—Kochetovskaya—Melekhovskaya. The enemy air force bombed the combat formations of the 2nd Guards and 51st armies in groups of 6-8 planes. The colonel general turned over the command of the front to Malinovskii.

Stalin probably feared that Yeremenko would prove stubborn and refuse to turn over command, appealing directly to the Supreme Commander-in-Chief, as had already been the case with his appointment as commander of the Southern Front. But this time everything turned out alright.

Khrushchev recalled that Stalin asked him who should be appointed to command the Southern Front in Yeremenko's place and Nikita Sergeevich recommended Malinovskii:

Of all the army commanders on our front, Malinovskii was the one who was the most prepared and who could cope with the task. But I resolved not to name him. Malinovskii was being blamed for everything then: Malinovskii surrendered Rostov, Malinovskii's member of

---

33   Editor's note. Vasilii Filippovich Gerasimenko (1900-61) joined the Red Army in 1918. During the Great Patriotic War he commanded armies and military districts. Following the war, Gerasimenko was deputy commander of a military district.

the military council, his friend and pal Larin, wrote a note of doubtful political content and concluded it with the words: "Long live Lenin!" and shot himself…

Stalin finally forced me to name a candidate for commander from among the Southern Front's leaders. Then I said: "Of course, Malinovskii. You know him and I know him." "Malinovskii? You name Malinovskii?" "Yes, I name Malinovskii." "Alright, I confirm Malinovskii!" And he turned to Molotov: "Write it down!" Molotov immediately grabbed a notebook and pencil and Stalin dictated the order to appoint Malinovskii commander of the Southern Front's forces.

It's indicative that Khrushchev admits that Stalin "forced" him to name Malinovskii's candidacy, but it was necessary for him that the proposal emanate from Khrushchev. In closing, Stalin said: "Now that we've relieved Yeremenko from his post and appointed Malinovskii, according to your suggestion, you will have to return to Malinovskii. There you must not move an inch from him, keep an eye on him and check on his actions."

Malinovskii, as front commander, ordered a general offensive to begin on 5 February.

The 51st Army was to operate in the areas of Ol'ginskaya and Bataisk, and then force the Don and Aksai rivers, occupy Aksaiskaya (Aksai), capture the rail and surface roads connecting Rostov with Novocherkassk, in order to cut the Hitlerites' path of retreat to the north, and to attack toward Rostov by turning its right flank to the west.

The 51st Army's offensive was planned for 7 February. Two days remained for preparations.

On 6 February the forces of the 28th Army, with the active support of the 51st Army's forces, occupied Bataisk. On 7 February the 44th Army and N.Ya. Kirichenko's cavalry-mechanized group, having taken the town and railway station of Azov, eliminated the enemy's bridgehead on the left bank of the Don.

The Germans were stubbornly defending along the right, hilly bank of the Don. General N.I. Trufanov ordered the 87th Rifle Division, together with units of the 3rd Guards Mechanized Corps, to attack toward Ol'ginskaya and to then force the Don and the Aksai, to capture Aksaiskaya station, and to attack toward Rostov.

At 2240 on 14 February Malinovskii, Khrushchev and the front chief of staff Varennikov, sent Stalin (with a copy to Zhukov) the long-awaited combat report No. 0047/op on the capture of Rostov:

1. Following prolonged and stubborn fighting, the front's forces captured on 14 February Rostov-on-Don and more than 20 other inhabited locales, including Alekseevka, Kuteinikovo, Budennyi, Kamennyi Brod, Grushevskaya, and Aksaiskaya.

2. The enemy continues to fall back to the west, holding the line Kalinin—Sinyavka—Morskoi Chulek. His air force has been operating in single planes.

3. At 1600 the 5th Shock Army, while overcoming the resistance of the enemy's rearguard units, reached the following line: the 3rd Guards Cavalry Corps, four kilometers west of Sokolovo-Kundryuchenskoe—Sambek—excluding Boldyrevka;
   The 4th Guards Mechanized Corps is fighting to capture Boldyrevka;
   The 315th Rifle Division is in the Krasnoznamenskii area;
   The 40th Guards Rifle Division is Popovo-Nesvetaiskii and Pavlenkov;
   The 4th Guards Rifle Division is four kilometers east of Rodionovo-Nesvetaiskoe.

4. While pursuing the enemy, the 2nd Guards Army reached the following line at 1600: the 2nd Guards Mechanized Corps if fighting for Novyi Sambek and Shchedrovskii;

The 13th Guards Rifle Corps captured Kuteinikovo, Kirbitovo and Budennyi, with the 300th Rifle Division along the eastern outskirts of Rodionovo—Nesvetaiskoe;

The 1st Guards Rifle Corps, while overcoming the enemy's resistance, was fighting four kilometers south of Budennyi and seeking to capture Shchepkin;

The 24th Rifle Division, the army reserve, is in Novocherkassk;

The 3rd Mechanized Corps has concentrated in the Kamyshevskaya—Grushevskaya area, with a tank regiment in Krivyanskaya.

The 51st Army captured Aksaiskaya in a night attack and is overcoming obstacles and mined areas and was fighting to capture Bol'shie Saly.

The 28th Army broke into Rostov at night and, while overcoming obstacles and mined sectors and the resistance of enemy covering detachments, captured it.

The 248th Rifle Division, under the command of Lieutenant Colonel Sivankov, the 34th Guards Rifle Division under the command of Colonel Dryakhlov, and the 159th Rifle Brigade, under the command of Major Dubrovin, distinguished themselves in the fighting for Rostov.

By 1200 the army was fighting to capture Myasnikovan and Leninovan.

The 44th Army was engaged in offensive fighting along the line Kalinin—Morskoi Chulek, but upon encountering the enemy's stubborn resistance, was unsuccessful.

Kirichenko's cavalry-mechanized group's main forces have concentrated in Kumzhenskii, Dugin and Obukhovka, with a forward detachment along the Khopryi—Martynovka rail siding—Nedvigovka sector.

4.   Throughout 15.2 the troops are continuing to develop the offensive to the west.

One could say that Malinovskii was promoted to colonel general two days before the liberation of Rostov, as an advance. Evidently Stalin did not doubt that he would take Rostov in the next few days. It's also most likely that Malinovskii's major role in the Stalingrad battle was noted by this rank. However, he had already received on 28 January 1943 the Order of Suvorov First Class directly for the defeat inflicted by the 2nd Guards Army on the Kotel'nikovo group of forces. One should note that Malinovskii also received the medals "For the Defense of Stalingrad" and "For the Defense of the Caucasus."

Khrushchev recalled that Malinovskii

really worked a lot. This was a very hard-working man, with a good head. I liked his judgments on military problems, and not only military ones. But he also rested. He always rested at a definite time in the day if, of course, the situation allowed…

Malinovskii told me a lot about his life. He did not know his father. It seems that his mother was not married and she did not bring up her son. He was raised by his aunt and spent his childhood in Odessa. He spoke of his mother in a very unrestrained, even insulting, way. He not only did not love her, but he retained a sort of injured feeling from his childhood years. He spoke of his aunt with tenderness, but spoke in anger about his mother. He also told me that he had worked as a salesman in Odessa as a boy. Then the First World War began. Having run away, he wormed his way into some sort of military train that was heading for the front. The soldiers took him with them. This is how he got into the army. He then ended up among the Russian troops who were sent to France and fought their as a machine gunner. This is where the revolution caught him (It's typical that Malinovskii told Khrushchev about how he had worked as a salesman in Odessa, which was undoubtedly the truth, although he did not say a word about any kind of agricultural work, where he worked as a seasonal laborer. Evidently he did not want to let his imagination get away with him in a heart-to-heart conversation with a member of the Politburo during this harsh wartime, all the more so as Nikita Sergeevich could have detected a falsehood. And since Rodion Yakovlevich honestly confessed that he had not lived with his mother before the First World War, then the version that he had worked for a landowner proved to be without merit. It was difficult to find such landowners In Mariupol' or Staryi Belous. And nowhere does he directly say that the aunt who raised him lived in Odessa. He probably meant his Mariupol' aunt, Vera Nikolaevna Malinovskaya. He did not get along with his mother, for the sake of whom he renounced his full and carefree life, and Malinovskii held a grudge against her his whole life, B.S.)…

Following Stalin's death Malinovskii and I met while hunting and I told him in a relaxed atmosphere how Stalin had reacted to Larin's suicide and how I had been entrusted with sticking close to Malinovskii and keeping an eye on him, when he went to bed, whether he closed his eyes, whether he's sleeping or pretending. In a word, to persistently keep an eye on him. This spying was unpleasant to me, because I knew that he felt all of this and understood why a member of the military council, a member of the Politburo of the party's Central Committee is following him around everywhere and is always beside him in any movement. And if I didn't demand that all of his instructions and orders should be reported to me, it was only because he himself observed a definite tact and informed me himself. He did not force me to demand this of him and in this way put himself in a more favorable position.

Malinovskii replied: "I saw that and can sincerely say that I was very satisfied that you were beside me the whole time. After all, I'm an honest man and did everything that, from my point of view, it was necessary to do. Thus I was satisfied that you would see everything and understand correctly." And I agreed with him, for this meant that the corresponding report would be made to Stalin. And this is what I reported to Stalin. Evidently life itself forced Stalin during the war to restrain his anger, which was directed at arresting and destroying people.

However, shortly after the capture of Rostov the offensive by the Southern Front's forces came to a standstill. Evidence of this is the report by the front's military council, which was dispatched at 2400 on 24 February:

1. Throughout 24.2.43 the front's forces continued to wage stubborn offensive battles along the right flank and in the center.

In overcoming the enemy's powerful fire resistance and engineering obstacles and repelling numerous enemy infantry and tank counterattacks, our units advanced 200-400 meters. One line of trenches along the flank, SKELYANSKII and height 114.9 were captured in the day's fighting.

Throughout the day, the enemy attacked the combat formations of units of the 5th Shock and 2nd Guards armies with groups of aircraft, and up to 20 planes simultaneously bombed the 51st Army's attacking forces. The infantry shot down three Ju-88s.

On the left flank the front's forces continued to actively defend their positions and relieved units.

The 5th Shock Army, while overcoming the enemy's powerful fire resistance along the entire front and infantry counterattacks along the right flank and in the center, occupied one line of enemy trenches by units of the 3rd Guards Cavalry Corps, while the 258th Rifle Division occupied the inhabited locale of SKELYANSKII. The army was unsuccessful along the rest of the front, repelling the enemy's attempts to return their lost positions.

The 2nd Guards Army, while developing the offensive in the direction of ZAKADYCHNOE station, repelled up to three enemy infantry and tank attacks during the day against the right flank and center, supported by aviation in groups up to 28 planes.

The 98th Rifle Division captured height 114.9. The army had no success along the remaining sectors.

Throughout the entire day the 51st Army repelled numerous attacks by the enemy's infantry and tanks, supported by aviation and, upon encountering powerful fire resistance, did not enjoy success. Height 101.0 was lost as the result of an enemy counterattack.

The 28th Army turned over its defensive sector to the 44th Army and has concentrated in the NOVAYA BESSERGENEVKA—BLAGODAT'—KALMYKOV area and has set about reinforcing its units.

The 44th Army went over to an active defense of the line: excluding RYASNYI—SADOVSKII—KOPANI and to the south along the eastern bank of the Sambek River.

The following enemy forces were destroyed during the day:

Up to two battalions of infantry;
20 machine guns;
6 guns;
8 earth and wooden pillboxes;
6 mortars;
12 tanks.

I HAVE DECIDED:

To bring up the artillery and mortar units during 25-26.2, to replenish their munitions and to organize a decisive attack on the morning of the twenty-seventh. The 5th Shock Army will attack along the sector Skelyanskii—Perepol'e, the 2nd Guards Army along the sector Aleksandrovka—Dorogany, and the 51st Army along the sector Stepanovskii—Ryazhenaya.

At this time the Germans had already begun their counteroffensive around Khar'kov and occupied Pavlograd on 22 February and Lozovaya on 25 February. In these conditions, Malinovskii could not count on any kind of reserves, and without them he could not continue his offensive to the lower reaches of the Dnepr, during the course of which he would have to overcome the Germans' powerful position along the Mius River.

In the meantime, the Germans occupied Khar'kov, and on 18 March Belgorod. The commander of the Voronezh Front, General F.I. Golikov, was relieved and the former commander of the Southwestern Front, N.F. Vatutin, was appointed in his place. Malinovskii became the commander of the Southwestern Front in place of Vatutin. F.I. Tolbukhin replaced him on the Southern Front. I should note that during the German counteroffensive, of the Southern Front's forces the 4th Guards Mechanized Corps, which was forcing the Mius in the area of Mamaev Kurgan and which on 18 February captured a bridgehead near Anastasievka, suffered the most. The corps then got into encirclement and had been almost completely destroyed by the close of 22 February. On 28 February the Southern Front's forces gave up their attempts to force the Mius and went over to the defensive.

8

From the Donbass to Odessa

On 22 March, during a quiet period, Malinovskii was appointed commander of the Southwestern Front, while Fedor Ivanovich Tolbukhin received the Southern Front from him. A representative British military delegation arrived at the Southwestern Front shortly afterward.

On 27 March 1943 Churchill wrote Stalin:

> I have appointed Lieutenant General Giffard Le Quesne Martel,[1] Knight Commander of the Order of the Bath 3rd Class, and holder of the Distinguished Service Order and Military Cross as head of the British military mission in the Soviet Union.
>
> General Martel is a high-ranking general, who has occupied high positions in the British army and commanded a division in France before Dunkirk and was recently the commander of the Royal Armored Corps. I specially selected him for this post, insofar as I believe that he possesses both military and personal qualities that you and the Soviet military authorities will like and which will guarantee the mission's success. In sending to the Soviet Union an outstanding officer, with a remarkable service record, I am emphasizing the great importance that I attach to the close cooperation between our countries and am placing at your disposal one of my best officers, whom I ask you to trust implicitly. He already had the opportunity in 1936 to see the Red Army during maneuvers and hopes to renew his acquaintance with it in the stern trials of war. I hope that you will issue the necessary instructions that he be given the opportunity to enjoy all the necessary conditions to achieve this goal.

It was precisely General Martel who was shortly to meet with Malinovskii and his subordinates.

General Sir Giffard Le Quesne (Q) Martel) was a well-known figure in the British army. In 1912 he was the boxing champion of the British armed forces. During the First World War Martel served in the engineer troops in France. In the summer of 1916 he was recalled to England. He was assigned to construct an obstacle zone, which was a copy of a sector of the front, for training the crews of the tanks undergoing development. In October 1916, not long after the first employment of tanks during the Battle of the Somme, Martel was appointed to the staff of the tank troops, where he worked under John Fuller.[2] He was promoted to major in 1917. As early as 1925 Martel built at his own expense the world's first super light tank, this was later known as the tankette. In 1936 he was promoted to colonel and sent to work in the war ministry as a junior director of

---

1   Editor's note. Sir Giffard Le Quesne Martel (1889-1958) joined the army in 1908 and served in the First World War. He was an early exponent of armored warfare and was an observer at the Red Army's 1936 maneuvers in Belorussia. He commanded a division in France in 1940 and was later appointed chief of the Royal Armored Corps. During 1943-44 he headed the British military mission to the Soviet Union. Martel retired in 1945.

2   Editor's note. John Frederick Charles Fuller (1878-1966) became chief of staff of the British tank forces during the First World War. Following the war, he wrote extensively on the subject of a future war, stressing the importance of armor and calling for the creation of small professional armies.

mechanization. In 1936 Martel was present at the exercises in the Belorussian Military District and there most likely met with Malinovskii. He was promoted to major general in February 1939.

Martel commanded the 50th Motorized Division in France from January 1940. In May 1940 he led the English counterattack near Arras, which forced the German tank columns to halt, which aided the success of the Dunkirk evacuation. In December 1940 Martel was appointed commander of the Royal Armored Corps. He was promoted to lieutenant general in 1942 and took part in planning military operations against Rommel[3] in North Africa and first suggested weakening his tank units in defensive fighting and then launching a counteroffensive. At the end of 1942 Martel was sent to serve in India and Burma.

From the end of March 1943 to February 1944 Lieutenant General Martel was chief of the British military mission in Moscow. He replaced Admiral Geoffrey Miles[4] at this post. He was received by Stalin on 12 April 1943. According to Martel's memoirs, during this meeting he acquainted the Soviet leader with his experience of fighting Rommel and the effectiveness of a well-prepared defense against German tank formations, which should be weakened as much as possible before one goes over to an offensive. The British general was convinced that it was precisely thanks to his advice that the Red Army adopted the tactic of pre-planned defense during the battle of Kursk. It's possible that Stalin took Martel's opinion into account, although the opinion of his own marshals and generals probably meant more to him. Not long after his return to England in March 1944, Martel was seriously wounded during an air raid and lost his right eye. The general retired in 1945 and began to write his memoirs and works on military matters. Lieutenant General Martel died in 1958 at the age of 68.

Shortly after Martel's arrival in the USSR, the English military mission visited the front. During this trip it visited the Southwestern Front. It's not excluded that Martel recalled Malinovskii from the 1936 maneuvers and therefore expressed a desire to visit the front he commanded.

By this time Malinovskii had already been promoted to general of the army on 28 April (Tolbukhin was promoted to colonel general on the same day). Once again, this was an advance for future victories. However, it's possible that Stalin took into account the fact that in February and March Malinovskii, as opposed to the commanders of neighboring fronts, did not suffer any particularly significant defeats and continued, although slowly, to advance. Malinovskii was now equal in rank with Rokossovskii and Vatutin, having bypassed Yeremenko and Govorov, and was ahead of Tolbukhin. This proves that Stalin looked upon him favorably.

The Supreme Commander-in-Chief tried somewhat to put in order the correlation of positions and ranks at the higher command level, so that by the eve of the summer campaign of 1943 the fronts were commanded by no less than colonel generals. And insofar as it was necessary to promote Tolbukhin, who commanded the Southern Front, to colonel general in this matter, in order to show that his neighbor occupied a more important place in the military hierarchy, Stalin considered it necessary to make Malinovskii a general of the army.

How the trip by the British delegation to the Southwestern Front was organized is of no little interest.

---

3   Editor's note. Erwin Johannes Eugen Rommel (1891-1944) joined the army in 1910 and took part in the First World War in France, Romania and Italy. During the Second World War he commanded a panzer division in France, the Afrika Corps during 1941-43, and German forces in Italy and France in 1943-44. Rommel was implicated in the plot to assassinate Hitler and forced to commit suicide.

4   Editor's note. Geoffrey John Audley Miles (1890-1986) joined the navy in 1905 and fought in the First World War. During World War II he commanded a warship and was chief of the British military mission in the Soviet Union during 1941-43. Following the war, Miles occupied a number of administrative posts and retired in 1948.

Here is the program for the trip by General Martel and his entourage:

Secret
Copy no. 2
I confirm
Chief of the Red Army General Staff
Marshal of the Soviet Union
(Vasilevskii)
Malinovskii's resolution:

To organize the reception of the mission and its accompaniment along the front in accordance with my personal instructions. My deputy, comrade Kotlyar (later a colonel general and Hero of the Soviet Union, L.Z. Kotlyar was the chief of engineer troops for the Southwestern Front, B.S.) and Colonel Rogov (the chief of the Southwestern Front's intelligence section, B.S.).
    Malinovskii

11.5.43.
The plan for the military mission of Great Britain to the front
The mission's members:
Lieutenant General Martel, chief of mission
Colonel Exham, deputy chief of mission
Colonel Hugo, a tank officer
Captain Theakstone, a translator
Major Turner, a General Staff officer
Purpose of the trip

1.   To become acquainted with the situation along the Southwestern Front along the Chuguev—Balakleya—Izyum sector.
2.   To discuss problems of the combat employment of the combat arms with the front, army, corps, and division commanders.

The route and sites to be acquainted with.
Moscow, Voronezh, Ostrogozhsk, Roven'ki, Svatovo, Izyum, Balakleya, Novaya Gnilitsa, Shevchenkovo, Kupyansk, Valuiki, Staryi Oskol, Voronezh, Moscow.
The length of the route is 2,000 kilometers, of which 1,000 is by air.
During the trip the mission is to become acquainted with:

A)   the battlefields in the areas of Voronezh, Korotoyak, Ostrogozhsk, and Staryi Oskol.
B)   with the operational situation and combat formations of our forces along the Severskii Donets River in the areas of Chuguev, Balakleya and Izyum.
C)   the organization and condition of a tank corps armed with Soviet tanks.

The mission is to visit:
The headquarters of the Southwestern Front, the headquarters of the 1st Guards and 6th armies, and the headquarters of the 6th and 30th rifle corps and the 23rd Tank Corps, where they are to be received by the commanders.

The calendar for the trip.
11 May (changed from 10 May, B.S.)

1000—departure from Moscow on a Douglas[5] aircraft.
1200-1400—arrival in Voronezh. Breakfast.
1400-2000—an automobile inspection of the battlefields in the Voronezh area. Sleeping accommodations and food at a site prepared by the headquarters of the Steppe Front.

12 May (changed from 11 May, B.S.)—trip to the headquarters of the Southwestern Front along the route Voronezh—Roven'ki and an inspection of the battlefields in the Korotoyak—Ostrogozhsk area. Breakfast en route.
    Arrival at the headquarters of the Southwestern Front. Received by General Malinovskii. Sleeping accommodations at a site prepared by the headquarters of the Southwestern Front. Eat.

13 May (changed from 12 May, B.S.)—trip to Nizhnee Solyonoe.
Arrival at the headquarters of the 1st Guards Army. Received by Lieutenant General Kuznetsov.[6] Sleeping accommodations at a site prepared by the headquarters of the Southwestern Front or the 1st Guards Army.

14 May (changed from 13 May, B.S.)—arrival in the Izyum area and acquaintance with the situation there. Meeting with the commander of the 6th Corps, Major General Alferov. Sleeping accommodations prepared by the 1st Guards Army staff.

15 May (changed from 14 May, B.S.)—arrival in the Savintsy—Balakleya area to become acquainted with the situation. Meeting with Lieutenant General Kharitonov (the commander of the 6th Army. On 28 May, shortly after meeting with the English, Lieutenant General Fedor Mikhailovich Kharitonov passed away at the age of 44 from a heart ailment, B.S.). Sleeping accommodations at a site prepared by the headquarters of the Southwestern Front and the 6th Army.

16 May (changed from 15 May), B.S.)—arrival in the Chuguev area (possible meeting with the commander of the 30th Corps, Major General Firsov). Trip to the Kupyansk area, where they will spend the night at a site prepared by the commander of the 23rd Tank Corps. Received by Lieutenant General Pushkin.

17 May (changed from 16 May, B.S.)—travel to Voronezh, with an en-route visit to the Staryi Oskol area. Rest and sleeping accommodations at a site depending on the time and speed of the trip.
Arrival in Voronezh, rest.

19 May (changed from 18 May, B.S.)—return to Moscow by Douglas aircraft.

---

5   Editor's note. This is probably a reference to the Douglas C-47 transport aircraft, which the Soviets received in large amounts through Lend-Lease during the war.
6   Editor's note. Vasilii Ivanovich Kuznetsov (1894-1964) joined the imperial army in 1915 and the Red Army in 1918. During the Great Patriotic War he commanded several armies. Following the war, Kuznetsov commanded an army and military district and also worked in the central military apparatus.

Items for familiarization:

1. It is authorized to acquaint the mission in all headquarters with available information about the enemy. Conversations with captured enemy soldiers and officers are authorized. The inspection of all captured equipment is authorized.

2. It is authorized to pass on information about our forces within the bounds of necessity, in order to explain the operational situation in general terms. It is forbidden to discuss the prospect of possible or planned operations.

   You may show the front line on a map. It is forbidden to show the location of reserves.

   In the headquarters of those divisions to be visited by the mission, it is authorized to show the divisions' combat formations on a map and at the site, but without indicating their strength and combat composition.

3. As for questions of waging combat operations and tactics, it is authorized to discuss these within the confines of the tenets of the infantry combat manuals, parts I and II, the draft of the new field manual, and answers, which will be given by us to the Imperial General Staff's questionnaire.

4. It is authorized to acquaint them, in general terms, with the operations conducted during the winter offensive and in detail with the fighting in the areas of Voronezh, Korotoyak, Ostrogozhsk, and Staryi Oskol.

5. One may show armaments, with the exception of self-propelled artillery. One may communicate accurate tactical-technical details, except for the RS.[7]

Organizational questions:

A) Means of travel—a Douglas aircraft, by order to the Air Force chief of staff. Five Willys[8] (as in the document, B.S.) motor vehicles, by order of the chief of the Main Automobile Administration, are to be sent to Voronezh by the close of 5.5, with a communications officer from the foreign relations section, Captain Kozlovskii.

   Quartering and food:
   Quarters are being prepared in the Voronezh area for housing the members of the British military mission and for six of our people, Colonel Muromtsev and six senior officers, as well as for six motor vehicles. Bear in mind that on the day of their landing, the mission is to be served lunch and dinner, and a hot breakfast on the following day. The headquarters of the Steppe Front is preparing this. This is to be ready by 7 May. Bear in mind rest and food on the return trip to Moscow. Captain Kozlovskii, the communications officers from the foreign relations section, will check this.

   In the area of the Southwestern Front's headquarters (within a radius of 10-15 kilometers) a site is being prepared to house the mission and its accompanying officers, as well as food (lunch, dinner and breakfast). Slit trenches should be provided.

   Sleeping and eating quarters are to be determined by the commander of the Southwestern Front for the trips to the Izyum, Balakleya, Chuguev, and Kupyansk areas.

---

7   Editor's note. RS (*reaktivnyi snaryad*) refers to the rocket-propelled shells employed on Soviet BM-8 and BM-13 platforms, popularly known as "katyusha."
8   Editor's note. This is a reference to the Willys MB jeep, which the Soviets received in large amounts through Lend-Lease.

There may be one rear-area site from which they will travel to see the troops and to which they will return to spend the night.

Field snacks may be arranged at the armies', corps' and divisions' command posts, with hot food mandatory by evening.

For feeding and rest en route, as well as for spending the night outside of the planned sites, the foreign affairs section is to have a sufficient amount of food products, field cots and linen in a special truck (to be allotted by the Main Automobile Administration).

B)   Security:

The mission is to be covered by fighters during the Moscow—Voronezh leg of the trip, by order of the Air Force chief of staff. At stops and places for spending the night, as well as en route, ground and air support, in accordance with the situation, is to be organized by order of the commanders of the Steppe and Southwestern fronts. Guards from junior lieutenant courses are to be detailed for security.

The following are to accompany the mission:
Colonel Muromtsev.
Colonel Kostin—the senior General Staff officer with the headquarters of the Voronezh Front, who will explain the situation while visiting the battlefields.
Lieutenant Colonel Motinov and Captain Kozlovskii from the foreign relations section.
For accompanying the mission within the confines of the Southwestern Front.
The deputy front commander or the deputy front chief of staff for the auxiliary command post are appointed to escort the mission within the confines of the Southwestern Front.
The deputy army commanders and the formation commanders are to accompany them in the armies, corps and divisions.
Major General (Dubinin) (Nikolai Ivanovich Dubinin was the chief of the special group of General Staff officers for communications with the troops, B.S.)
7 May1943.

Resolution: To maintain one's dignity, to ask few questions and to be modest and exact with one's answers. Lieutenant General Kotlyar and Colonel Rogov are to accompany the mission with the Southwestern Front.

The following are forbidden:

1.   To speak about the second front.[9]
2.   To speak about the quality of Allied arms delivered to us.
3.   To make toasts to the close alliance of the Soviet Union and England.

Lieutenant General S.P. Ivanov. (Semyon Pavlovich Ivanov—chief of staff of the Southwestern Front from the end of May through November 1943, chief of staff of the Voronezh Front and then of the First Ukrainian Front, who was then removed from his post for making false reports on the situation in the Kiev area and appointed chief of staff of the Caucasus Front, and from 29 October 1944 through June 1945 chief of staff of the Third Ukrainian Front; from June 1945 through March 1946 he was chief of staff of the High Command of Soviet Forces in the Far East; Colonel General S.P. Ivanov was awarded the title of Hero of the Soviet Union for the Soviet-Japanese war, B.S.)

---

9   Editor's note. This is a reference to what the Soviets viewed as the Western Allies' delay in opening a new front in Europe against Germany.

The chief of the Southwestern and Third Ukrainian fronts' intelligence section, Major General Aleksandr Semyonovich Rogov, recalled Malinovskii:

> Our commander was a demanding but just man. He was very charming in simple human interaction. Many recall his smile. It did not appear often and was never hackneyed and greatly changed his face—something childlike, boyish and open would appear. Rodion Yakovlevich possessed a remarkable sense of humor and one could sense a real resident of Odessa in him. He well understood that in a difficult situation it was necessary to relax and knew how to relieve the pressure with a joke, while at the same time not insulting anyone's vanity.

Rogov was later unlucky. On 9 March 1963 the deputy chief of the General Staff's Main Intelligence Directorate, Colonel General A.S. Rogov, was reduced in rank to a major general and retired in connection with the uncovering of GRU Colonel O.V. Pen'kovskii[10] as an agent of American and British intelligence. This time Malinovskii was unable to defend his former subordinate against Khrushchev's anger. Rogov outlived him by many years and passed away in 1992 at the age of 91.

Judging by the reception plan for the delegation, they were to treat the members of the delegation less like allies than as potential spies, and it was authorized to inform them about the course of the fighting in only the most general terms. The taboo on making toasts in favor of a close alliance between the USSR and England is indicative. This aroused the amazement of the English, who themselves sought to share to a maximum degree their combat experience. The lack of desire to initiate the allies into plans for future operations may be explained by the desire to preserve military secrets. After all, a leak could later come from British sources. However, it is logically very difficult to explain certain limitations on what one could and what one could not communicate to the British guests. For example, why was it forbidden to communicate data about our reserves and to show their location on a map? Why did the combat and numerical strength of the Soviet divisions have to remain a secret for the allies? It's completely mysterious as to why it was forbidden to communicate tactical-technical data about Soviet self-propelled guns and "Katyushas." The SU-76,[11] which had only just been mastered by Soviet industry, was by no means the most successful vehicle of this type and the somewhat more successful SU-76M began serial production only from the end of May and these vehicles were not yet with the troops. As regards the "Katyushas," after two years of their being employed at the front, the Germans already had captured platforms and were fully aware of their combat qualities.

It's interesting that the taboo on speaking about the second front and the quality of the weaponry being delivered through Lend-Lease[12] was laid down in order not to upset the members of the British mission. Soviet generals and officers were perfectly capable, particularly after a hefty dose of spirituous liquors of being quite impartial in their comments about the delay in opening the second front, and they often expressed a low opinion about the quality of Allied military equipment. American and British planes and tanks were not so bad, despite what postwar Soviet

---

10   Editor's note. Oleg Vladimirovich Pen'kovskii (1919-63 joined the Red Army in 1939 and fought in Finland and in the Great Patriotic War. Following the war he became an intelligence officer, but passed secrets to the US and Great Britain in the early 1960s. He was arrested in the fall of 1962 and executed the following year.

11   Editor's note. The SU-76 was a self-propelled gun produced in the Soviet Union during 1942-45. Mounted on a T-70 tank chassis, it had a crew of four and was armed with a 76mm gun.

12   Editor's note. Lend-Lease was the US program to arm, feed and fuel allied countries during the Second World War1. Initially intended for the United Kingdom and China, the program was later expanded to include the Soviet Union and other countries.

propaganda maintained. However, they were significantly more complex to control and sensitive to observing all the technical norms. And the level of the Soviet pilots' and tank troops' training was, on the average, significantly lower than their British and American colleagues and they had difficulty in mastering foreign equipment. Aces had no problem with it, however. It's sufficient to recall that three times Hero of the Soviet Union Aleksandr Ivanovich Pokryshkin[13] scored the majority of his victories in an American "Airacobra."[14]

This is how General Martel himself recalled this trip. In his memoirs, *The Russian Outlook*, which appeared in 1947, he wrote:

> Russia has always been ruled by cold-hearted people, although the Russian people are wonderful and kind. To a certain degree, a cruel and authoritarian rule is probably inevitable, given their Asiatic origins. A numerically small, but consisting of picked members, communist aristocracy must maintain a high level of prestige and fully employ a secret police in order to maintain control over the state. Life and human suffering are often not taken into account, which explains the authorities' obvious lack of attention to these matters…
>
> I had a long conversation with Marshal Stalin (this meeting took place on 12 April 1943, not long after Martel's arrival in the USSR, B.S.). We discussed many military matters in detail. This was a pleasant and interesting conversation.

There is a widespread opinion in English historiography, based upon Martel's later memoirs, *An Outspoken Soldier: His Views and Memoirs*, which appeared in 1949, that it was precisely during this conversation that Martel proposed to the Soviet leader that he halt the expected offensive by major German armored forces through a stubborn defense, in order to knock out the enemy's tanks and then, in turn, go over to the offensive with one's own tank formations. The general, as commander-in-chief of the Royal Armored Corps, had proposed employing such a tactic against Rommel at El Alamein and this had been successful. Here one must once again make the proviso that Stalin and his generals could have arrived at this tactic without the advice of the British general. However, the recommendation by a recognized authority in the area of tank warfare could have reinforced the Supreme Commander-in-Chief in his intention to meet the expected German attack in the area of Kursk with a previously-prepared defense.

The Southwestern Front was chosen for the trip by Martel and Colonel Exham, Lieutenant Colonel Hugo and the interpreter Captain Theakstone, who accompanied him, insofar as the roads were supposed to be dry there earlier than along the Western Front, which was closest to Moscow. Martel recalled:

> We flew and motored southwards from Moscow, visiting places of interest on the way, and arrived on the second night at the headquarters of the southern group of armies and met General Malinovsky the next day. We then went on to the headquarters of the Army Commander on the Upper Donetz front (F.M. Kharitonov's 6th Army was defending here,

---

13   Editor's note. Aleksandr Ivanovich Pokryshkin (1913-85) worked for several years as an aircraft mechanic before finishing flight school in 1939. He is credited with shooting down 65 enemy aircraft during the Great Patriotic War and was awarded the Hero of the Soviet Union three times. Following the war, Pokryshkin held a number of command and administrative posts.

14   Editor's note. The Bell P-39 Airacobra was a single-engine fighter aircraft produced in the United States during 1940-44 and also exported to the Soviet Union and other allied countries. The standard model had a crew of one and a maximum speed of 605 kilometers per hour and a range of 840 kilometers. The aircraft was armed with one 37mm cannon and four 12.7mm machine guns and could carry up to 230 kilograms of bombs.

B.S.). We sat round a table with the Army Commander and a map was spread out in front of us. Half the map was covered with a sheet of paper, which probably concealed the Russian dispositions. The other half showed us all the German dispositions. The Army Commander explained all the German defense system very clearly. He was a fine soldier and described the situation very well. When he had finished I thanked him and said: "Now I want you to tell me all the Russian dispositions and strength because, quite clearly, I cannot appreciate the situation unless I know both sides." He looked at me for a few moments and then replied: "We never tell anyone anything about Russian dispositions or strength." This, of course, was the moment for the tough stuff! Trying to look very angry I spoke out strongly and said: "Do you imagine that I have come all the way out from England to put up with tomfoolery of that sort. I have never been so insulted before in my life. I certainly do not propose to put up with that kind of treatment for a moment." The Army Commander was taken aback. He had not expected such plain speaking and became very red in the face and looked at me for perhaps half a minute. He was not sure of himself. Suddenly he put his hand on the sheet of paper that covered half the map and tore it off with a flourish and a gesture. "There you are," he said, "there are all the Russian dispositions and strengths." They had all been concealed under the sheet of paper. I was determined to cash in on this success and replied: "When I visit your corps and divisions at the front is this same tomfoolery going to happen or are they going to treat me properly?" He had not yet invited me to visit his divisions at this front, but this seemed a sound line to pursue. This time he answered almost at once: "I am going to tell them to tell you everything." I was, of course, immensely relieved at the result of the interview.

During the trips to the front, as well as to the headquarters, Martel and his associates were treated to bounteous breakfasts, lunches and dinners and, as the general admits, they began to drink vodka and other spirituous liquors at 0800. The general recalled:

On the first day after our arrival at the headquarters of the Southwestern Front, it was suggested that we take a hot bath in a place located about a kilometer from the headquarters. As it was already quite late and one had to walk more than a mile both ways, we replied that we really didn't need a bath. This, of course, was a mistake, as shower cabins had been specially prepared for us. We went there the following morning and saw a tent with a large number of shower heads, which were located quite high over the ground. We had a wonderful shower. It was later explained that the commander of the Southern Front's engineer troops had never seen British officers before, but he had been told that they really love to take baths and that they are all very tall. When we arrived we chose to forego a bath and proved to be quite short. This was not a very good beginning. He chose the tallest among the Russians that he could find and adjusted the shower heads to their size. Not a single one of us could reach the shower head, but we enjoyed it.

After this we all felt good when we arrived the following day at army headquarters. Here they showed us several prisoners, the majority of whom were barefoot. The Russians told us that, of course, their boys had taken the prisoners' boots, if they liked them. Despite this, all of the prisoners stated that they were being treated well. They had all expected that they would be shot or something even worse…

The Army Commander asked me if we would like to have a concert party the next day. As we had already had one each day and spent several hours over each meal, I asked him if he would excuse us if we did not have a concert party next day, as we had a long programme. We discussed the programme, and it was arranged that we should get back at 6 p.m. so as to leave time for a discussion with himself and his Chief of Staff. I was most insistent on this, and was assured that this would be all right. As it happened, we had to spend hours over meals the next day, and in spite of every effort on our part, we did not get back till 8 p.m. On arrival, I met the Army Commander, who said that the concert party was all ready! I made a mild protest, but this went so badly that I had quickly to pretend that the concert was the one thing we wanted to have! We had to curtail our discussion and then have the concert party out of doors in the dark, and then dined about midnight.

We had a long programme the next day, and asked if we might have breakfast at 8 a.m. without fail. We all arrived at the hut at 8 a.m. They said that as it was dark last night, we could not have seen much, so we were to have it all again. I replied that we had heard frightfully well in the dark, so we managed to cut out the singing, and only had the dancing again. This enabled us to have breakfast about 8:30 a.m. and then get away.

They treated us with the utmost hospitality throughout our tour, and were so out to do everything possible for us, that it seems perhaps unfair to criticise even in jest. The time we spent in this way, however, was out of all proportion. We could have done ever so much more if it had not been for this hospitality, but this position had evidently to be accepted with good will. This form of celebrating did not seem to have been affected in the smallest degree by the war. Most of us failed, at one time or another, in the drinking bouts. On the third day, I could not do any 'bottoms up,' but recovered later. On the whole, we held our own fairly well, but the older Russian officers left us standing.

In reality, the bounteous Russian hospitality had a clearly defined purpose—to reduce to a minimum the socializing by the members of the British mission with the Soviet officers and generals, lest the English, God forbid, should learn something that was forbidden. On the Southwestern and other fronts where Malinovskii commanded, there was a special general, whose job it was to outdrink foreigners visiting the front. This was Lieutenant General of communications troops Aleksei Ivanovich Leonov, the chief of the communications directorate for the Southwestern Front and later the Third and Second Ukrainian and Trans-Baikal fronts. He was famous, in particular, for the fact that in Romania in 1944 he got the French ambassador Pierre Cota, who was representing "Free France," drunk. There's no doubt that he had to compete in a drinking bout with Martel. Leonov, who was trained and had been born in 1902, was almost 13 years younger than Martel, which was no small advantage (while Aleksei Ivanovich was only seven years younger than Pierre Cota). However, Leonov and the other Russian generals outdrank the younger members of the British delegation. They got foreigners drunk in order to learn some kind of information from them and, chiefly, in order to reduce to a minimum their free interaction with Soviet officers and generals.

As regards Leonov, aside from the fact that he was the life of the party and an excellent master of ceremonies, he was also a pretty good communications officer, which is why Malinovskii always took him with him from front to front; well understanding that success in battle depends to an enormous degree on well established communications.

Aleksei Ivanovich's career continued successfully after the war. He served together with Malinovskii in the Far East, and in 1951 was appointed chief of communications for the Air Force. In 1953 Aleksei Ivanovich headed the central courses for improving the communication troops' officer corps, which was a bit of a demotion, but with Malinovskii's appointment as head of the Ministry of Defense, Leonov's career took off again. In 1957 he was the first deputy chief of the Ministry of Defense's communications troops and, in 1958 chief of the Ground Forces' communications troops and, in the same year, chief of the Ministry of Defense's communications troops. In May 1961 Aleksei Ivanovich was promoted to the rank of Marshal of Communications Troops—the highest rank for a communications officer. Leonov outlived Malinovskii by more than five years and died in November 1972.

On 27 May 1943 Malinovskii received a thank-you letter from Martel, which had been passed through the General Staff, which was dated 20 May:

> Dear General Malinowski:
> I am thanking you in this letter for your hospitality during out stay at your headquarters and for the very interesting conversations with you and your chief of staff. All of your commanders, with whom we met during our trip to your area of the front, did everything possible to help us become acquainted with the military methods employed by the Germans at various times, as well as with those methods, which were worked out by you, which enabled you to defeat them.
>
> Your commanders also showed us your front's forward defensive lines and bridgeheads. As a result of many interesting conversations we acquired a great deal of information of interest to us.
>
> We were accorded the greatest hospitality everywhere and feel that the trip was a successful one for us.
>
> I discussed military operations in North Africa with many of your officers and they asked me for further information on certain questions. I will study these questions and send my replies to the chief of the Red Army General Staff in Moscow for employment as he sees fit.
> Yours sincerely,
> Quc. Martel
> (Lieutenant General Martel)
> To the commander of the Southwestern Front, General of the Army R.Ya. Malinovskii.

Another letter from Martel to Malinovskii was signed "Kupyansk, 17 May 1943," and was also forwarded to Rodion Yakovlevich:

> Dear General Malinowski:
> During my stay at your headquarters I did not understand that I would not have the opportunity to say goodbye to you before your departure.
>
> I am taking the opportunity to write you and sincerely thank you for your hospitality and for the excellent preparations which you carried out for our trip around your front.
>
> All of your commanders did everything they could to insure that we would be able to observe everything we wanted and to receive all the information we required.
>
> I cannot express in words my thanks to you for the assistance you rendered us.
>
> Lieutenant General Kotlyar took care of all the preparations for our reception. He helped us in every way and I had a number of pleasant conversations with him.
> Yours sincerely,
> Que. Martel
> (Lieutenant General Martel)
> To the commander of the Southwestern Front, General of the Army Malinovskii.

It's possible that General Martel never found out that General Kharitonov died less than two weeks after meeting with him. It's quite likely that the conversation with the British general provoked a fatal exacerbation of the Soviet general's heart disease. Kharitonov probably suffered over the fact that Martel provoked him to violate his instructions, forcing him to show the Soviet reserves, and thought all the time about whether he would be punished or not. It seems that Martel never quite understood what country he had landed in and could not even imagine that his desire to learn more about the Red Army, which was motivated by his sincere desire to help an ally in the struggle with the Germans, could cost his interlocutor his life.

At the concluding stage of the Battle of Kursk, the Southwestern Front's forces launched an offensive against the Donbass, taking advantage of the fact that the main German forces had been pulled into the fighting in the area of the Kursk salient.

Rodion Yakovlevich recalled:

On 17 July 1943 the forces of the Southwestern Front launched an offensive with the forcing of the Severskii Donets, where a powerfully fortified defensive line had been prepared by the enemy. The fighting was bitter and stubborn. At the same time the troops of the Southern Front launched an offensive for the purpose breaking through the defense along the Mius. Despite the fact that the formations enjoyed insignificant success, they tied down major enemy forces and deprived him of the opportunity of transferring his formations to the Kursk direction, which made it easier for our forces to carry out their tasks in the Battle of Kursk.

In August, alongside the offensive on Khar'kov, the Soviet forces began a new offensive in the Donbass. Malinovskii recalled:

On 13 August combat operations by the Southwestern Front's right-wing forces began and, on 16 August, those of the shock group, which had been created in the center of the front. On 18 August the Southern Front's forces went over to the offensive.

The Southwestern Front's 3rd Guards Army, under the command of Lieutenant General D.D. Lelyushenko (the Southwestern Front's 57th Army was attacking on Khar'kov, B.S.) was fighting directly for the Donbass. It forced the Severskii Donets River and on the night of 1-2 September captured Lisichansk with the forces of the 32nd Rifle Corps, and then, having bypassed many of the enemy's strong points, occupied Artemovsk on 5 September and Kramatorsk and Konstantinovka a day later.

At this time the Southern Front's forces were developing the offensive in the direction of Stalino. The enemy was half encircled. The German-Fascist forces threw away their weapons and equipment in panic and hurriedly began to fall back to the west. The Southwestern Front's forces, while crushing the resistance of the enemy's rearguards, rapidly advanced toward Krasnoarmeisk with mobile formations. This made it easier for the Southern Front's forces to carry out their assignment to liberate Stalino.

Under the threat of encirclement, the German-Fascist command sought to more rapidly pull its forces back to the west and southwest. The commander of Army Group South, Manstein, issued an order in which he demanded that the troops conduct a mobile defense and increase their formations' steadfastness in order to fall back on the Dnepr in an organized fashion. Simultaneously, the Army Group South command issued a top secret directive "On the Evacuation, Destruction and Removal of Property," in which it assigned its troops the task of completely destroying the areas being abandoned.

I, as a witness and participant in these events, saw this terrible picture of Hitler's evil deeds. We then paid attention to the fact that the enemy was falling back along country back roads and not along paved roads or improved country roads. The Hitlerites had mined the paved roads, blown up bridges, inhabited locales, industrial centers, factories, plants, and equipment, burned and destroyed wheat and agricultural equipment, and flooded the mines. The enemy was carrying out "scorched earth tactics."

Losses were heavy. For example, according to an entry in the 230th Rifle Division's combat journal, during 15-24 July 1943 the division lost 628 killed and 2,943 wounded. Insofar as there were 4.7 wounded for each man killed, one may assume that the number of killed has been lowered at the expense of those missing in action, data on which are not presented in the combat journal.

This is how the journalist Svetlana V'yunichenko describes the liberation of Slavyansk:

The operation that finally led to the complete liberation of the town began on 17 July 1943. It entered the annals of history under the name of the Izyum—Barvenkovskaya cauldron. The goal remained as before—to encircle the Germans' Donets group of forces and break through to the Dnepr. The grand design was to draw off German panzer divisions from the Kursk bulge. The command essentially gathered all its forces in order to stand to the death. And they stood. The forcing of the Severskii Donets took place in Svyatogorsk, Prishib and Sidorovo. On the operation's first day some units of the 244th Rifle Division were able to reach as far as Khrestishch. There they remained. Our intelligence did not report that a German panzer regiment was based in the village…

The Soviet side's losses were colossal. Batyuk's 79th Division lost 2,000 soldiers and officers in one day of fighting around Prishib. Many of them lay down in the Donets earth. They remained forever on the battlefield in common graves.

Aleksandr Bol'shii relates that "The field military commissariats called up many young men from the liberated villages. They didn't even have time to issue them soldier's identity books. And if they had time to issue them, they didn't have time to gather them from the dead in this fiery cauldron. Therefore, having perished in the fighting, literally within a kilometer of their homes, they are still listed as missing in action. Now the identities of 17-18 year old boys are being established using copies of their Komsomol membership cards published in the "Memorial" data base, bonds and school certificates…"

According to archival data, two armies went missing here. According to various calculations—from 350,000 to 600,000 men.

The 79th Rifle Division was almost completely destroyed around Golaya Dolina. They did not make it as far as Slavyansk.

The 61st Guards and 297th rifle divisions liberated the town. They were then awarded the title of Slavyansk. A major offensive began here only after Soviet forces had won a victory along the Kursk bulge.

When the Soviet army entered the town on 6 September the population understood that this was for good.

According to the recollections of eyewitnesses, these were well-trained and experienced soldiers. There was a lot of equipment, including tanks. They only stayed in Slavyansk for two days and then moved on, toward the Dnepr. However, it was clear that the enemy would not enter the town again.

In September 1943 about 10,000 citizens remained out of a population of nearly 80,000. No one has yet counted the losses of the Soviet divisions that took the city.

On 17 September 1943 Malinovskii was awarded the Order of Kutuzov First Class for the liberation of the Donbass. The fact that this was not the Order of Suvorov, but one lower in status, speaks to the fact that Stalin was not quite satisfied with the Southwestern Front's operations, as was the case with the Southern Front, both of which had been unable to rout the enemy in the Donbass and only to push the Germans out of the territory of the coal-producing basin.

Here I want to cite letters by the member of the military council of the Southern Front, Ye.A. Shchadenko, to G.M. Malenkov and A.S. Shcherbakov, which date to the beginning of October 1943. It paints a picture of the reinforcement situation in the front next to Malinovskii's. However, the situation there does not differ in principle from that which existed at the same time on the Southwestern Front.

Shchadenko wrote:

Top Secret.
To the secretary of the TsK VKP(b), Malenkov G.M.
From Ye. Shchadenko
6 October 1943

Deeply respected Georgii Maksimilianovich.
I'm sending you a copy of my report to comrade Shcherbakov on the measures toward strengthening the combat capability of the Southern Front's armies, in connection with the significant reinforcement of the front's forces from the mobilized population of territory liberated from the enemy.

I request that you familiarize yourself with and, if you find it possible, to report to comrade Stalin. This question is very topical, not only for the Southern, but also for the Southwestern, Voronezh, Steppe, Central, and other fronts, where the mobilized population is being fed into our units without the necessary checkin and training.

I believe that this question of great political importance cannot be resolved without the intervention of the State Defense Committee. The existing practice of calling up the draft-age population in areas liberated from German occupation, which is being carried out in an atmosphere of extreme haste, will inevitably lead to and has led to the dilution of our troops, chiefly the infantry, and to the sharp decline in their combat capability.

The local contingent, having its own huts and families in the immediate rear, looks back and becomes an unreliable element in our army. Thus it would be well to remove this contingent to a better prepared and reliable internal district. At the same time, it is absolutely necessary that those called up on one front, following a corresponding checking and training in the internal military districts, be dispatched to reinforce the troops along other fronts.

Such a measure will sharply reduce the rate of desertion and enable us to more successfully fight enemy intelligence, and will yield us a better trained and prepared reinforcement.

As regards the Southern Front (particularly the Odessa axis), one of its features is that the majority of the population here is well-off and there are a lot of German colonies (which means that the troops have to be reinforced with potentially unreliable Germans, B.S.).

The German colonists, who are falling back to a man with the German army, are carrying all of their livestock with them, as well as their property and equipment, and they are destroying and burning everything (structures, stacks of hay and straw) everything they can't take with them.

Naturally, the German colonists, having been called upon by Hitler and following suitable processing in the Hitlerite army, become the most inveterate and rabid enemies of Soviet power.

These circumstances require that particular attention be paid to the Southern Front.

There are 3-4 times as many troops on the Southern Front as the enemy has (an amazing admission, refuting the widespread opinion that even after Stalingrad the Red Army did not enjoy a great numerical superiority over the Wehrmacht, B.S.). There is also powerful equipment in the reliable hands of skilled and devoted people. But if we continue to adhere to the fallacious practice of filling out units from local resources, without their suitable verification and training outside the fronts, then we'll get what we already had on the Southwestern and Southern fronts in 1942: as our armies advanced they took in a lot of unreliable and untrained men and, when the situation became more difficult and when we withdrew these people ran away to their villages, throwing away their equipment and taking their weapons with them.

I consider it to be very necessary to immediately turn over to the Southern front 30,000-35,000 well-trained replacements from the internal military districts and, in exchange, removing the same number of draftees and those liable for service, who are in desperate need of extensive military training and political education.

This would significantly strengthen our units' combat capability and enable us to successfully resolve the tasks facing the front.

6 October 1943
Top Secret
To the chief of the Red Army's Main Political Administration, Colonel General comrade A.S. Shcherbakov

Having familiarized myself close-up with the situation in the 28th, 51st, 44th, 5th Shock, and 2nd Guards armies,

I can report:
The latest reinforcements were added to the divisions during the second half of September from the mobilized population of Zaporozh'e Oblast', which was recently liberated from the enemy. The overall strength of those mobilized is 115,000 men for September alone, of which 2,000-4,000 men joined each division.

The smallest number entered the 5th Shock Army's divisions, the numerical strength of which at present does not exceed 4,500-5,000 men.

16 percent (18,675) of the reinforcements consists of draftees born in 1922-25; that is, of people who are completely untrained; all the others are former servicemen and those liable for service in the Red Army, who for this or that reason remained in territory occupied by the enemy.

A significant part of the latter represents an element which is not completely reliable, either in the combat or the political sense of the word. Aside from a large percentage of deserters, among them there were incidents (2nd Guards and 44th armies), when any kind of difficulties or serious obstacles arose, particularly regarding enemy tanks or aircraft, when these elements obey their commanders poorly. There have been incidents of withdrawing without the commander's orders, as well as provocative shouts on the part of panicked and unreliable elements: "We're being surrounded," "We've been outflanked," and "It's every man for himself," etc.

Right now I'm investigating undoubtedly reliable reports of these elements partially going over to the enemy. There have been incidents of open and hostile agitation against being drafted into the Red Army and contrasting and praising the order of things in the Hitlerite army.

Having consulted with comrade Vasilevskii, the chief of the political directorate and other of the front's responsible workers and having familiarized myself with propaganda and "SMERSH"[15] materials, I have raised the question before the front's military council of scrupulously checking and removing from the divisions people not fully reliable as well as completely untrained in the military sense.

---

15   Editor's note. SMERSH (*Smert' Shpionam*, or "Death to Spies") was the acronym for Red Army counterintelligence. The organization was formally established in 1943, although it may have existed prior to that date. The organization was headed throughout by Victor Sergeevich Abakumov and was officially disbanded in 1946 and its duties transferred to other organizations.

As a result, on 4 October the *front's* military council issued orders to the front's troops for the immediately checking and removal of unreliable people, for which special commissions have been established consisting of workers from the front, armies and divisions. The commissions have been ordered to carry out this checking within a three-day period, to transfer those removed from the divisions to separate battalions in the divisions' rear and then carry out a more careful checking, study, education, and combat training of those people remaining in the divisions.

It has been ordered to concentrate all of the called-up youth who have not undergone military service in reserve army and front regiments for training according to a month-long combat program, along with the corresponding education.

The *front's* military council is convinced that these measures will undoubtedly make healthier our combat organisms, mainly the infantry. There will be fewer people in the divisions, but on the other hand, they will be more capable of resolving their combat tasks.

In connection to the armies' preparation for the planned serious operation to defeat the enemy who has fortified himself along the line Zaporozh'e—Melitopol'—Molochnaya River, on 4 October the front's military council made the decision to immediately organize through the front's armies' and corps' political apparatus a mass checking, political training and bringing up all levels of the *front* organism to the level of the task facing the armies, for the purpose of specifically assisting the command to successfully carry out this operation.

The plan for this work, which has been worked out together with the Political Administration and approved by the *front's* military council, will be conducted not only during the preparatory period, but almost during the operation's decisive phase. All of the party and non-party activists, exemplary soldiers, both veterans and new arrivals, who must visibly demonstrate their ability to resolve any tasks set by the command, are aimed at this.

This measure must mobilize everyone to eliminate the placid and irresponsible attitude toward their obligations, both on the part of the armies' command-political and officers and rank and file, to inculcate order and military instruction in the divisions' and armies' immediate rear.

All of our preparatory work for the forthcoming operation is being carried out according to the following slogans:

"Everyone to defeat the enemy along the line Zaporozh'e—Melitopol'—Molochnaya River,"

"Prevent the enemy's remaining divisions and rear services from leaving the Crimea."

Member of the Southern Front military council

Colonel General Ye. Shchadenko

5 October 1943.[16]

In the majority of cases, they resolved the problem of unreliable and untrained conscripts from the occupied territories in a more radical manner than that suggested by the former chief of the Main Administration for the Formation and Maintenance of Troops and the deputy defense commissar, Yefim Afanas'evich Shchadenko. They simply threw them into frontal and unprepared attacks against German positions.

For the sake of comparison, here is a description of an attack by a punishment battalion, written by the commander of the signals company, Lieutenant Valentin Dyatlov:

---

16   RGASPI, fond 83, opis' 1, delo 29, pp. 75-77.

Two of our regiment's battalions took part in the ten-minute fire onslaught—that was all. Following the onslaught, there were a few seconds of silence. Then the battalion commander jumped up on the parapet: "Guuuuuys! For the Motherland! For Stalin! Follow me! Hurraah!" The punishment soldiers slowly crawled out of the trench and then, as if waiting for the last ones, they raised their rifles across their chests and ran forward. A groan or a cry, with a prolonged "Aaaaah," rolled from left to right and left again, first lessening and then increasing. We also jumped out of the trench and ran forward. The Germans set off a series of red rockets toward the attackers and immediately opened a powerful mortar-artillery fire. The lines hit the dirt, as did we a little ways behind in a longitudinal furrow. It was impossible to raise one's head. Who could make out the enemy targets in this hell? His artillery fired from hidden positions and far away from the flanks. Heavy guns also fired. Several tanks fired over open sights and their iron shells flew over our heads with a wail…

The punishment troops were lying in front of the German trench in an open field with small bushes, while the German "threshed" this field, plowing up again the earth, bushes and bodies of men… Seven men fell back together with the punishment battalion, whereas together they had numbered 306 (there was nevertheless no attack along this sector).

One may put forward the testimony from a letter home by a German soldier in the summer of 1943:

The Red Army called up the entire population, men and women, from the newly-occupied territory. The labor battalions formed from these people are used for increasing the mass of the attackers. It made no difference that these recruits were untrained, the majority of them without weapons, and many without boots. The prisoners taken by us stated that it was calculated that the unarmed would take the weapons of the fallen. These unarmed people, who were forced to attack, were suspected of collaborating with us and literally paid with their lives for this suspicion.

The attacks that were undertaken by units, made up of "occupied people," in no way differed from attacks by punishment companies and battalions. The same Dyatlov describes a battle in Belorussia in December 1943.

A line of people in civilian dress, with enormous sacks on their backs, went by me along the communications trench. "Guys, who are you and where are you from?" I asked. "We're from the Orel area, as reinforcements." "What kind of reinforcement is that, when you're in civilian clothes and don't have rifles?" "They said we'd get them in the fighting…"

The artillery fire against the enemy lasted about five minutes. 36 guns from our artillery regiments "smashed" the Germans' front line. Visibility became worse from the shell explosions…

And now the attack. A line rose up, twisting like a crooked black snake, and a second one behind it. And these black twisting and moving snakes were so ridiculous and so unnatural on the gray-white earth! The color black against the snow is an excellent target. And the Germans "watered" these lines with thick lead. Many firing points awoke. Heavy-caliber machine guns were firing from the second line of trenches. The lines hit the dirt. The battalion commander howled: "Forward, you mother fuckers! Forward! Into the battle! Forward, or I'll shoot you!" But it was impossible to raise oneself. Just try and get off the ground under artillery, machine gun and automatic rifle fire…

The commanders nevertheless managed to raise up the "black" village infantry several times. The enemy fire was so dense that having run a few steps, people would fall as if they had been scythed. We artillerists were also unable to help, as there was no visibility and the Germans' firing positions had been well camouflaged, and, what is most likely, the bulk of fire was coming from pillboxes, and thus the fire from our guns did not yield the necessary results.

The situation of the "occupied ones"; that is, those who had been called up from among those who had been under enemy occupation, in no way differed from that of those in punishment battalions. The latter were given worn out uniforms with holes in them, often taken off corpses and they were not due decorations or stars on their forage caps. The former were not even in uniform and often not even armed. The "bast shoe" infantry went into battle in coats and jackets, realizing in practice the slogan familiar since the First World War: "You'll get your weapon in battle!" The chance of someone in the punishment battalions dying was even less than among the recruits from the occupied territories. The punishment troops were at least somewhat able to fight. The "occupied ones," the majority of whom lacked any kind of combat training, and sometimes even weapons, became only good targets for the German guns, mortars and machine guns in their attacks on an unsuppressed defensive system.

Here was not only the Soviet command's general negligence from top to bottom, but also a definite political calculation. The inhabitants of the occupied territories were all suspected of collaborating with the Germans. It did not bother Stalin, Beria, Abakumov and the lower ranks of the NKVD and SMERSH that the main body of collaborators, especially those who had stained themselves by taking part in shootings of Jews, Gypsies and hostages and in operations against the partisans and who had served in the Wehrmacht and SS, retreated together with the Germans. Those remaining had been subjected to Nazi propaganda, served in the occupation establishments and worked in schools and hospitals, with the permission of the occupiers. Although in this they were also guilty before Soviet power and now had to expiate their guilt with blood. This way the NKVD would have less work to do after the war. In any event, there was no opportunity to clothe and arm those called up directly into the units. After all, there was practically no additional clothing in the units and there was only a small supply of rifle weaponry, which had been gathered from the battlefield or taken from the wounded before they were sent to the hospital. This is how it came about that the "people in jackets" had, at best, one rifle per three men, and sometimes for ten. Their main task was to blow up minefields with their bodies, force the Germans to expend their supply of ammunition firing on the attackers, and to exhaust the enemy, so that later more combat-capable cadre units (where the reinforcements mainly came from hospitals and areas in the deep rear and who had undergone some kind of training), could throw the weakened enemy from his occupied positions. Those "occupied people" who had the good fortune to survive in the first attacks, subsequently and gradually received weapons and a uniform and were no longer distinguished from ordinary soldiers, just like the punishment troops who had expiated their guilt.

This is what former prisoners of war I.A. Dugas and F.Ya. Cheron write:

> As a rule, having liberated a particular territory from the Germans, the Soviet command would gather all of the draft-eligible population and would drive it into battle, often without weapons and uniforms. This was the case, for example, in the Khar'kov offensive in May 1942. The soldiers called the hastily mobilized men "crows" (because of their dark civilian clothes). In the attack a "crow" could be armed with a shovel or a bayonet, and in rare instances with a rifle, which he did not know how to fire. Question: What should these "crows" that were captured be considered—soldiers, civilians or partisans? The Germans acted in the following manner: if the "crow" had a buzz cut or had a rifle, the "crow" was considered a prisoner of war. Sometimes the Germans simply drove the "crows" off, without even examining their haircuts. It was a crime on the part of the Soviet command to send these people into battle.

One should not doubt that the unfortunate "crows" should nevertheless be considered Red Army soldiers. After all, the Germans also expended ammunition in repelling their insane attacks, just the same as when Red Army soldiers in uniform attacked. With the passage of time, the surviving "crows" received rifles and uniforms, but they had little chance of surviving to the end of the war.

When the Soviet soldiers shifted combat operations to Germany and its allied and occupied countries the reserve for drafts directly into the units became those prisoners of war and "Ostarbeiters" liberated from the camps. For example, on 7 April 1945 the chief of the First Ukrainian Front's political administration, Major General Yashechkin, reported to Shcherbakov, the chief of the Red Army's Main Political Administration:

> During the fighting on German territory, the front's formations and units somewhat made up their combat losses in personnel at the expense of Soviet citizens of draft age who had been liberated from German imprisonment. More than 40,000 men have been dispatched to units as of 20 March.
>
> The overwhelming majority of these reinforcements consist of Ukrainians and Russians up to 35 years in age. Among the reinforcements are military personnel who had been in German captivity, including officers with the rank of junior lieutenant, lieutenant, senior lieutenant, and captain. Some soldiers and officers, who had been liberated from German captivity, had wounds and government decorations received in battle against the German aggressors up to the time of their capture by the Germans.
>
> Almost all of the young soldiers have an incomplete or complete average education, with only an insignificant part of them with higher and elementary education. There are only a handful of illiterate or semi-literate.
>
> Of the 3,870 people who entered units and formations in the 13th Army in February, where Major General Voronov is the chief of the political section, 873 were former soldiers and 2,997 newly called into the army, including 784 women. By age, there were 1,922 younger than 25, 780 between 25 and 30, 523 between 30 and 35, 422 between 35 and 40, and 223 older than 40. By nationality, there were 2,014 Ukrainians, 1,173 Russians, 221 Azerbaidzhanis, 125 Belorussians, ten Armenians, 50 Uzbeks, and 125 of other nationalities. Of these reinforcements, 70 percent had worked in German industry, 15-20 percent in agriculture, and up to 10 percent were prisoners in German prisons and concentration camps.

If we assume that the proportions between the various categories of those called up directly into the 13th Army's units were approximately the same throughout the entire First Ukrainian Front, then one can say that among the draftees about 9,000 had been prisoners of war and more than 31,000 were "Ostarbeiters," while there were no less than 8,000 women among the latter. Besides this, recalling the experience of employing "jacket" reinforcements, there is every reason to suspect that they could have employed women not only in bathhouse and laundry battalions and medical battalions, but directly in attacks against enemy positions.

The troops that Malinovskii commanded had to fight in Romania, Hungary, Yugoslavia, Austria, and Czechoslovakia. Of these countries, there were no Soviet prisoners or "Ostarbeiters" in Hungary and Yugoslavia and in Romania only prisoners liberated following their joining the anti-Hitler coalition, who reinforced Tolbukhin's and Malinovskii's armies. There were prisoners and eastern workers in Austria and Czechoslovakia, which were called up directly into the units of the Second Ukrainian Front.

However, it was still a long way to the capitals of Europe. Meanwhile, the Southwestern Front, in conjunction with the Southern Front, was wresting southern Ukraine from the Germans and Romanians. On 14 October Malinovskii's forces liberated Zaporozh'e and saved the Dnepr Dam from complete destruction. Erich von Manstein, the commander of Army Group South, wrote about this in his memoirs:

> … following an artillery preparation, the intensity of which we had yet seen no equal on his part (artillery divisions operated here for the first time), the enemy managed to penetrate into our bridgehead with up to ten divisions, supported by a large number of tanks. We had to abandon it following heavy fighting. Although we managed to withdraw across the Dnepr the forces that had been defending the bridgehead, as well as to blow up the railroad bridge that had been restored just a few months before, and to cross over the dam, the divisions that had been defending on the bridgehead were very worn out.

On 20 October 1943 the Southwestern Front was renamed the Third Ukrainian Front. On 25 October its forces liberated Dnepropetrovsk and Dneprodzerzhinsk and seized a broad bridgehead on the right bank of the Dnepr.

In the fighting for the Dnepr Malinovskii's forces had to cooperate closely with the Fourth Ukrainian (formerly Southern) Front, commanded by F.I. Tolbukhin. One must say that Malinovskii treated with sufficient skepticism Tolbukhin's qualities as a military commander. On the borders of S.S. Biryuzov's book, *When the Guns Roared*, in those places where Biryuzov's service is detailed as chief of staff of the Southern Front, while Tolbukhin commanded the front, Rodion Yakovlevich left a pair of caustic comments aimed at Fedor Ivanovich. There, where Biryuzov, while describing the fighting on the approaches to the Crimea in the beginning of November 1943, wrote that "it began when the commander of the 4th Kuban' Cavalry Corps, General N.Ya. Kirichenko, demonstrated a slowness that was unusual for him, and at first threw far fewer forces against Perekop than he could and should have" (this prevented us from seizing Perekop from the march and breaking into the Crimea), Rodion Yakovlevich noted: "In 1941 Kirichenko behaved repulsively" (at the end of 1941 Nikolai Yakovlevich Kirichenko commanded the 38th Cavalry Division, which was part of the 18th Army of the Southern Front, which was commanded by Malinovskii, B.S.). I don't know if Malinovskii read the denunciation to the TsK VKP(b) by the deputy commander of the 4th Guards Kuban' Cavalry Corps, Vasilii Vladimirovich Bardadin against the corps commander Nikolai Yakovlevich Kirichenko on 28 October 1942, from which followed that Kirichenko was one of the most outstanding commanders in the Red Army for his skill in transforming (but only on paper) defeats into victories. Bardadin related how the unsuccessful attack by the corps' divisions against stanitsa[17] Kushchevka (Kushchevskaya) along the Kuban' had been transformed into a major victory in the headquarters' report:

> The attack at 0800 on 29 July did not take place, because two regiments of the 13th Cavalry Division were late, and upon their arrival at the jumping-off position the attack began at 1130. The enemy poured artillery, mortar and machine gun fire on the attacking groups of cavalry at the start of the attack, as a result of which the regiments suffered heavy losses in men and horses, the attack died out and the cavalry turned back. The 15th Cavalry Division's dismounted units reached the southern outskirts of Kushchevka and could advance no further. The 24th Regiment did not take part in the slaughter and turned back, having suffered heavy losses from enemy fire. The 13th Cavalry Division's 33rd Regiment took part in this slaughter, suffering greater losses than the 24th Regiment. The regiment operating along the supporting axis did not take part in the attack, as there were no communications with it, and it was only at 1500 that the regimental commander decided, on his personal initiative, to carry out his

---

17   Editor's note. A *stanitsa* is the name of a Cossack village in southern Russia.

assigned task, ran up against the enemy's organized fire, suffered losses and fell back to his jumping-off position.

As a result of the attack, our units failed to capture stanitsa Kushchevka and the enemy remained in his positions. Our losses were 400 men killed and wounded and about 200 horses. The enemy suffered a maximum of 100-150 chopped up and crippled and three captured. We captured six mules, five automatic rifles… In all, along the entire front Kushchevka—Shkurinskaya—Kanelovskaya, no more than 500-600 Germans were killed and 13 captured. In the report written in the front headquarters, it was pointed out that the Cossacks had chopped up 5,000 men and captured 300, which in no way corresponds to reality.

In Bardadin's opinion, "the operation was poorly organized and thought out and the cavalry attack was directed against a water line, which had been occupied by a well-organized system of enemy fire."

Bardadin also related how during the withdrawal behind the Kuban' River in August 1942 Colonel Millerov's 13th Cavalry Division ran away in panic from four German tanks and two planes, and ran away so fast that they were only able to gather them up and put them back into relative order after two days. As a result of the disorderly retreat by Millerov's cavalry troops, the neighboring 13th Cavalry Division came under enemy attack and suffered heavy losses—up to 40 percent of the soldiers and commanders.

The corps commander and commissar, despite Bardadin's proposal that the division commanders be tried "for cowardice and panic mongering," recommended them for decorations and new ranks. And although the entire contribution of the newly-minted generals Millerov and Tutarinov consisted of the fact that they, due to their own stupidity, unnecessarily threw in a mass of equipment and wore out men and horses to the point of exhaustion, while they were retreating over mountainous paths from an enemy who had no thought of pursuing them.

On the other hand, General Kirichenko enjoyed outstanding victories on the front of love. He awarded his mistress, a medical orderly from the 200th Mobile Field Hospital, O.S. Brazhnik, the Order of Lenin, because she had supposedly removed 131 wounded from the battlefield in 1941-42, although she never left the corps headquarters, or earlier in 1941 the headquarters of the 38th Cavalry Division, which Kirichenko then commanded, while she had already been awarded the Order of the Red Star in 1941.

And when Biryuzov wrote in his book that on 3 November 1943 that "The *Stavka* ordered that General Kirichenko, the commander of the 4th Cavalry Corps, be removed," Malinovskii noted on the margins: "This was absolutely correct!"

This is what Sergei Semyonovich wrote about Tolbukhin in the same memoirs: "F.I. Tolbukhin simultaneously entrusted me with the task of personally traveling to Perekop, to look deeply into the matter and the situation that had arisen there and adopt all necessary measures on the spot to increase the force of our attack." Rodion Yakovlevich commented quite sarcastically on this part: "Czar Fedor Ivanovich was always entrusting things, while sitting tight at the command post." And when Biryuzov stated that following snowfalls that paralyzed combat operations in Northern Tavriya, "even Fedor Ivanovich, who usually did not like being pulled away from his main command post, now often visited the armies' and corps' command posts and would speak at length with the generals, clarifying all the details of the forthcoming offensive on the spot," Malinovskii noted ironically: "It was evidently not dangerous at all to travel."

Here Biryuzov admitted: "I had to travel more often." On this note, Rodion Yakovlevich noted on the margins, but this time without irony: "That's another matter and the author is a brave and military man."

Marshal Vasilevskii, who was coordinating the activities of the Third and Fourth Ukrainian fronts, as a *Stavka* representative, recalled:

On 29 December, having discussed the problem with the commanders of these fronts, we came to the conclusion that in the conditions of the situation, as it had developed, it was not likely that the enemy would continue to seriously resist in the Dnepr bend and along the Nikopol' bridgehead. We believed that the enemy, having abandoned the territory between Nikopol' and Krivoi Rog and having pulled back his forces behind the Ingulets River, and then behind the Southern Bug and having sharply shortened his defensive front, would try and free up a part of his forces, mainly panzer divisions, in order to immediately shift them to those axes most dangerous for him—to Zhmerinka, Gaisin and Pervomaisk, for operations against Vatutin's and Konev's forces.

In order to prevent the fascist forces' planned withdrawal, Malinovskii, Tolbukhin and I decided, despite the lousy weather, to immediately begin active operations by the Third Ukrainian Front's forces along the Sholokhovo—Apostolovo axis and with the Fourth Ukrainian Front's 3rd Guards, 5th Guards and 28th armies (the command of which had been taken over by Lieutenant General A.A. Grechkin[18]) along the Bol'shaya Lepetikha axis and then also toward Apostolovo, with the immediate task of defeating the enemy's Nikopol' group of forces through the common efforts of the two fronts. It was planned that following the capture of Nikopol' and Krivoi Rog we would develop the offensive in the direction of Pervomaisk and Voznesensk with the forces of the Third Ukrainian Front and launch an attack with the forces of the Fourth Ukrainian Front from the Kakhovka—Tsyurupinsk area toward Nikolaev and upwards along the western bank of the Southern Bug toward Voznesensk, toward the forces of the Third Ukrainian Front.

This plan was corrected in the *Stavka*, which decided to renounce an immediate attack on Nikolaev, in order to concentrate on the elimination of the Krivoi Rog group of forces. As Vasilevskii admitted (in January 1944, B.S.):

The Third and Fourth Ukrainian fronts made repeated attempts to defeat the enemy's Nikopol'—Krivoi Rog group of forces, but were unsuccessful: there was a shortage of men and materiel and a serious shortage of ammunition. The Hitlerites, contrary to our expectations, not only did not want to abandon this area, but were doing everything in order to transform it into a continuous and well-prepared strong points, skillfully linked with each other by fire. In the middle of January, with the permission of the *Stavka*, we halted the attacks.

In connection with this failure, that same January his "sworn friend" Zhukov wrote a denunciation of Malinovskii to Stalin: "To comrade Ivanov.[19] Despite all of his fine qualities, Malinovskii does not like to actively fight. In order to move the Third Ukrainian Front forward, it is necessary to replace the commander. I advise you to put Yeremenko in Malinovskii's place. I assure you that this will be better. 17.1.1944. Yur'ev."[20]

Evidently, for Zhukov to "actively fight" meant to lay down one's soldiers without number. However, Vasilevskii was supervising the southern fronts at this moment, and not Zhukov. He evidently stood up for Malinovskii. And it suited Stalin when his commanders could not stand one another: just in case, it would be easier to find a counterweight to Zhukov.

---

18 Editor's note. Aleksei Aleksandrovich Grechkin (1893-1964) joined the imperial army in 1914 and fought in the First World War. He joined the Red Army in 1918 and fought in the civil war. During the Great Patriotic War he commanded a division, corps and armies and was also deputy commander of a *front*. Following the war, Grechkin worked in the army's educational apparatus before retiring in 1954.

19 Editor's note. This was one of Stalin's code names used in correspondence with his commanders.

20 Editor's note. This was one of Zhukov's code names used in correspondence.

In order to continue the operation, Vasilevskii proposed to Stalin that they turn part of the forces of Konev's Second Ukrainian Front against the Nikopol'—Krivoi Rog group of forces and reinforce Tolbukhin's front with reserves. However, Stalin ordered them to get by with the Third and Fourth Ukrainian fronts' available forces. However, the Supreme Commander-in-Chief nevertheless subsequently sanctioned their regrouping. The Second Ukrainian Front's 37th Army was transferred to the Third Ukrainian Front, which was to launch the main attack from the area northeast of Krivoi Rog toward Apostolovo. Malinovskii got the 31st Guards Rifle Corps from the *Stavka* reserve and the 4th Guards Mechanized Corps from the Fourth Ukrainian Front.

The offensive was resumed at the end of January. Apostolovo was liberated on 5 February. Tolbukhin's forces reached the Dnepr south of Nikopol'. The Germans abandoned the Nikopol' bridgehead and abandoned their heavy weapons and equipment, which they were unable to evacuate due to the washed-out roads. After this, part of Tolbukhin's forces was transferred to Malinovskii, who was concentrated on defeating the Krivoi Rog group of forces. They had to use Po-2[21] aircraft and tractors to supply the troops with ammunition, because of the washed-out roads. On 22 February Krivoi Rog was liberated.

Manstein recalled:

> On 31 January the enemy's new and powerful attacks began along the northern sector of the Sixth Army east of Krivoi Rog, as well as from the south against the Nikopol' bridgehead. They led to an enemy penetration along the latter bridgehead. Following three days of fighting, the enemy managed to accomplish a breakthrough with major forces along the Sixth Army's northern sector. Here the XXX Army Corps, against which 12 rifle divisions and two tank corps were operating, suffered heavy losses, although the correlation of forces, according to the number of divisions, was only two to one in favor of the enemy. Six divisions occupied the corps' first position and two panzer divisions the second position. However, these divisions, in light of their insufficient reinforcement with men and materiel, represented only combat groups. By this time there were only five battle-worthy tanks in both divisions!...
>
> With the enemy's breakthrough along the Sixth Army's northern flank, both corps, which were located along this flank, as well as both corps operating along the Nikopol' bridgehead, were almost encircled. The army group command had long predicted this result. Now, Hitler at last saw that it was necessary to agree to give up the eastern part of the Dnepr bend and the Nikopol' bridgehead. The Sixth Amy was actually able to get its corps out of the noose in heavy fighting, although it suffered heavy losses in equipment. The timely renunciation of this bastion, which we would not have been able to hold in any event, not only would have enabled us to pull back in good order all of our units located there, but also to free up divisions for the much more important northern flank of the army group.

On 19 March 1944 Malinovskii was awarded the Order of Suvorov First Class. This is how the successes connected to the liberation of Krivoi Rog and Nikopol', as well as other services in the battle for the Dnepr, were noted. Officially, he was decorated "for the successful forcing of the Dnepr River, the capture of the cities of Dnepropetrovsk and Dneprodzerzhinsk, the conduct of the Nikopol' and Krivoi Rog operations, and the breakthrough of the Germans' defense along the Ingulets River."

---

21   Editor's note. The Po-2 (also known as the U-2) was a general purpose Soviet biplane that first appeard in 1929. One model had a crew of one and a maximum speed of 152 kilometers per hour. It was armed with one 7.62mm machine gun and could carry six 50-kilogram bombs.

Now the path of the Third Ukrainian Front, whose left flank rested on the Black Sea, lay toward Odessa and the Romanian border, as the Fourth Ukrainian Front was to capture the Crimea. On 6 March Malinovskii's armies began an offensive toward Nikolaev. The 8th Guards and 46th armies were to launch the main attack toward the town of Novyi Bug. I.A. Pliev's[22] cavalry-mechanized group supported their operations. Novyi Bug was liberated on 8 March and on 12 March units of the KMG[23] reached Snigirevka, cutting off the path of retreat of 13 divisions of Colonel General Karl-Adolf Hollidt's[24] Sixth Army. On 18 March units of the 28th Army occupied Kherson. However, the encircled German divisions managed to break through beyond the Ingul and Southern Bug rivers, abandoning their supply trains and combat equipment. By 18 March the forces of the Third Ukrainian Front had reached the line of the Southern Bug and had set about forcing it. On 28 March Nikopol' was taken. Rodion Yakovlevich managed to liberate those cities that he had abandoned in 1941. Ochakov was occupied in the beginning of April.

At 0030 on 11 April Malinovskii reported to Stalin and Vasilevskii on the liberation of his home town of Odessa:

> On the front's left flank, the forces of the 8th Guards, 6th and 5th Shock armies and Pliev's group, having crushed the enemy's resistance, at 1000 on 10.4 captured by storm the Germans' powerful defensive strong point along the shore of the Black Sea, a major industrial center, railroad junction, important port on the Black Sea, and administrative center of Ukraine— the city of Odessa.

And he recounted all of the property captured thanks to the victory over the enemy:

> According to preliminary data, in the fighting for the city of Odessa the front's forces captured the following equipment: 207 locomotives, 3,957 train cars with various freight and factory equipment, 8,080 motor vehicles (the majority of which are not in working order), 169 tanks, ten armored transports, 273 guns of various caliber, 250 machine guns, 150 motorcycles (the majority of which are not in working order), 171 tractors and tows, 300 automobile tows, 1,400 carts, 31 depots with munitions, 21 depots with food stores, 233 mortars, more than 5,300 rifles, seven aircraft, 150 head of large livestock, and 1,500 head of small livestock. The counting of prizes is continuing…
> During this time 5,000 soldiers and officers were killed and 1,100 men taken prisoner.

In March 1944 the German Sixth Army, which was facing the Third Ukrainian Front, lost 2,549 men killed, 7,348 wounded and 3,827 missing in action. Its losses for the first ten days of April amounted to 522 killed, 1,792 wounded and 1,218 missing in action. During the second ten days of April the Sixth Army lost 1,594 killed, 6,097 wounded and 2,114 missing in action.

---

22 Editor's note. Issa Aleksandrovich Pliev (1903-79) joined the Red Army in 1922. During the Great Patriotic War he commanded a cavalry division and corps and later a cavalry-mechanized group in Europe and the Far East. Following the Great Patriotic War he commanded armies and a military district and was the commander of Soviet forces in Cuba during the Missile Crisis.

23 Editor's note. The KMG (*konno-mekhanizirovannaya gruppa*), or cavalry-mechanized group was a Soviet formation standing somewhere between a corps and an army. The KMGs generally included a cavalry and a tank corps, plus other smaller units and were employed for exploiting breakthroughs in the enemy's defense.

24 Editor's note. Karl-Adolf Hollidt (1891-1985) joined the army in 1910 and fought in the First World War. During the Second World War he commanded a division, a corps and an army. He was relieved from command of the Sixth Army in 1944. Following the war, Hollidt was convicted of war crimes, but served a little more than a year in prison.

During the third ten days of April the army lost 1,539 killed, 5,967 wounded and 776 missing in action.

The Third Ukrainian Front's losses in March and April are unknown.

Rodion Yakovlevich met his true love during the war. This is what his daughter Natal'ya recalled:

> The war found mama in Leningrad, where following graduation from the Library Institute she worked in the Mechanical Institute's library. Following her evacuation from blockaded Leningrad along the "Road of Life"[25] to Groznyi in April 1942, she went into the army and began her army life in a bathhouse-laundry plant and got out of encirclement twice. The second time was fateful—she met papa. In the summer of 1942, when they were getting out of encirclement, she and two other soldiers broke out through a corn field and counted German tanks. This information evidently proved to be important because mama was recommended for the Order of the Red Star, which my father awarded her. They told him that there were two soldiers and with them a girl with a blue kerchief… She probably made some kind of impression on papa even then, although it was only a year later that he had her transferred to his front headquarters. In 1944 mama was appointed chief of the military council's mess. When the commanders were on the front line—in dugouts or trenches—it was necessary to deliver all the dishes and food. Mama had young girls under her—after all, it was dangerous on the front line—but she went by herself. And Aleksandr Mikhailovich Vasilevskii always took a touching interest: "Well, how did it go, Raisa Yakovlevna, is everything in order?" Papa never asked her about that. Once mama decided to find out whether he was worried about her. Papa said: "I wasn't worried. I knew precisely that nothing would happen to you."

Natal'ya Rodionovna also explained why her father's co-workers called her mother countess and that her mother recounted the history of this nickname:

> When they took Budapest, they decorated all the girls who worked in the military council's mess: we held foreign currency in our hands for the first time. We went and bought ourselves beautiful dresses and suede leather high-heeled shoes with small buttons! And the dress was gray, almost blue, with folds and frills. I put on this dress the first time, when we were supposed to go to Budapest to the theater—to the opera theater! I'm coming out of the mess and a co-worker, Grisha Romanchikov, says: "Countess!" That's how it got started. Actually, mama was born in Ukraine, in the village of Bogorodichnoe, in a poor family with lots of children.
>
> There's a continuation to the story about the countess. Mama had a brother, Aleksei. He lived in Slavyansk at the start of the war and left for the front. By 1945, not having any news of his sister, he no longer hoped to see her alive. And then he, who had fought for two whole years in a neighboring army, turned up in Budapest also in the opera theater. Papa is sitting next to mama in the central box among the generals, while the soldiers and officers are in the stalls—in a word, the entire *front*. Naturally, they're observing not only the actors, but those sitting in the box. And here uncle Lonya sees a girl in the box with braids like a crown and cannot believe his eyes: "Raya? Or is it someone who looks like her? It can't be!" He goes to the box and there are soldiers standing guard. While he was explaining to them that he would like to call the girl, an adjutant, Anatolii Innokent'evich Fedenev, came out. He asked what the matter was. "That girl there looks like my sister…" "What's her name?" "Raya." "Raisa

Yakovlevna?" "Yakovlevna." Within a minute my mother appeared at the door. A meeting just like in the movies!

This is the way Natal'ya Rodionovna laid out her mother's biography:

My mama very much wanted to study and stayed with her sister in Leningrad and first enrolled in library courses and then in the Library Institute. By this time they were transferring her sister's family somewhere and mama stayed alone, a 15-year old girl, in Leningrad. It was nothing and she survived. She studied and completed her library courses and the Library Institute and began to work, first as a library inspector for the north, and traveled as a library inspector to Monchegorsk and around the villages. She said that no matter how difficult it was in Ukraine, and she had been there when the Ukrainian famine[26] hit…, where she had her first bout with dystrophy. Nevertheless, it seemed to her that it was harder for people in the north. This sensation was not motivated by anything. Maybe it was simply because Ukraine was home to her and the south, while it was uncomfortable and cold in the north. In the 1930s she traveled on a horse with another library inspector to deliver lectures and traveled God knows how among backwoods villages. Then she settled, as she told me, in a wonderful place with a beautiful name—Lodeinoe Pole, where she was already the head of the library. She loved her work fanatically, loved books and loved not only to hand out books, but she also organized readers' conferences. She was very proud of the fact that writers from Leningrad traveled to her conference. The height of her rapture was the arrival of Yurii German.[27] She managed to talk him into it and managed to arrange a meeting. And she later married and left with her husband for Leningrad. And here she wound up in a very intellectual family, where they somewhat dismissively called her "our Komsomol, Raya." They were all very well educated people—architects and translators with a university education going back many generations and she just didn't fit in with them. She had a son, whom she named German, in honor of her favorite opera, *The Queen of Spades*. This caused my brother no end of unpleasantness in his life. Imagine a boy born in 1936 and his name is German. Just like Goring.[28] He so wanted to change his name to Aleksandr. Half of his life he wanted to change his name to Aleksandr. Mama worked in the library of the Mechanical Technical College. Naturally, her husband left for the front immediately and not long afterwards she received notice of his death. The blockade[29] began and all of his large family, in which everyone was older than her, died in her arms. She was the healthiest and youngest. They took her son and evacuated him together with the kindergartens, like the majority of Leningrad's children, and they didn't

---

26   Editor's note. The Ukrainian famine, or "Holodomor," cost millions of people their lives during 1932-33. This was part of a larger famine that swept the Soviet Union during this time as a result of the state's collectivization policies.

27   Editor's note. Yurii Pavlovich German (1910-67) was a Soviet author and screenplay writer and served as a correspondent at the front during the Great Patriotic War.

28   Editor's note. Hermann Wilhelm Goring (1893-1946) was a decorated fighter pilot during the First World War. He later joined the Nazi party and became one of Hitler's closest associates. He was later appointed Hitler's deputy, chief of the air force and head of the country's economic program. He gradually lost influence during the Second World War, when his vaunted *Luftwaffe* failed to live up to expectations and was later stripped of all his titles. Goring was arrested and tried for war crimes, but committed suicide before his execution.

29   Editor's note. This refers to the blockade of Leningrad by German and Finnish forces during the Second World War, during which hundreds of thousands of residents starved or died from other causes. The blockade lasted from September 1941 to January 1943, when the Soviets opened a narrow land corridor to the city. German forces were not completely driven from the area until January 1944.

allow her to leave with him. However, at that time no one understood what was going on. It seemed that the children would spend two months somewhere while it was dangerous there, and then they would return. They could not imagine that they were saying goodbye to their children—some forever, and some for a long 4-5 years, and maybe more. After all, they later had to find each other. She would recall this scene later in her old age and how horrible it was. They were so small, such children and they are taking them away and don't allow her to leave, and then tell her: "And who will defend Leningrad?" "My God, how will I defend Leningrad? I'm a librarian. What can I do?" However, before long it became clear what had to be done—dig trenches, stand guard and then grab bombs and shove them into the sand…

She didn't recall the blockade often. I remember when Granin's[30] *The Blockade Book* came out and, upon reading the book, thought a long time whether to give it to mama, thinking it might be too depressing for her. I finally brought her *The Blockade Book* and then I came by and asked: "Well, how did you like it?" She replied: "It's all the truth, but such a small part of the truth." She didn't say anything more about *The Blockade Book*. Later some kind of completely improbable details would come through. Just the way the front-line soldiers didn't say anything, she didn't say anything about the blockade, or almost nothing, although one time someone asked her in my presence, she was on the front line, after all: "Raisa Yakovlevna, were you scared at the front?" She was quiet for a moment and then said: "After the blockade, not very much." There was nothing more horrible than the blockade. She knew for sure that to lie down was sure death. She told me about one terrible moment during the blockade. She came home and there were no longer any close relatives of her husband, although cousins or second cousins lived together with her in the apartment. Once when she came home she found that there were no relatives or even a stove. They had left for somewhere, with their ration cards and the stove. And then she sat down, and it was cold and she was hungry, and she set for several hours and then said to herself: "Alright you bastards, I'm going to survive just to spite you!" and began to think what she could sell in order to warm herself and buy something. And then, as she said, fate intervened. She found behind a sideboard, which had been chopped up for firewood, a lot of boxes with her mother-in-law's homeopathic medicines. The latter had treated herself homeopathically. For a long time she was sure that these homeopathic medicines, which she ate, saved her.

In another interview, Natal'ya Rodionovna recalled the following about her mother:

On 4 April 1942, the last day that cars ran on Lake Ladoga, mama, who was suffering from dystrophy, was evacuated and they moved them a month and a half to Groznyi. As before, they were hungry en route, which amazed me. Until summer she lived in a suburb of Groznyi, and when she learned that the area was going to be occupied she grabbed her small bundle and left, in the strict meaning of the word, "wherever her eyes took her." She knew for sure that she had not survived the blockade in order to end up under occupation. In her small bundle she had a piece of bread, a piece of soap and shoes for her son, which she had bought in Leningrad and carried throughout the war in her knapsack. She had no place to go. She walked and thought how she had never known such loneliness in her life and felt sorry for herself. In Leningrad her husband and all his relatives had perished and she did not know where her son was. Her parents and brother were living in occupied territory in Ukraine. So,

---

30   Editor's note. Daniil Aleksandrovich Granin (1919-) began writing in the 1930s while an engineering student. He continued his literary efforts after the war, of which *The Blockade Book* is probably the most well known.

crying, she reached a fork of three roads. She spent a long time making up her mind which one to take, and finally chose the one that finally led her to the front, where she became acquainted with my father…

When mama spoke about their meeting she didn't use words like "love at first sight." My parents were very restrained people and there were no stories about how talked and what words they spoke. I only know that before getting married, a man of my father's rank had to get an unofficial blessing from the Supreme Commander-in-Chief. Thus following the victory parade[31] papa and mama were present at a reception in the Kremlin, where she was presented to Stalin. Evidently the Supreme Commander-in-Chief found her worthy and following the reception the imperial imprimatur was received. My parents then married.

---

31   Editor's note. The victory parade referred to here took place on 24 June 1945 and featured representatives from all the *fronts* and armed services. The parade was followed that evening by a reception in the Kremlin.

9

From Bucharest to Prague

On 14 April 1944 the forces of Lieutenant General M.N. Sharokhin's[1] 37th Army forced the Dnestr River and seized the Kitskany bridgehead, which was up to 18 kilometers wide and 6-10 kilometers deep, with an overall territory of about 150 square kilometers. However, they were unable to immediately develop the offensive on Kishinev from this and other bridgeheads. Holding the bridgehead cost the army more than 3,200 killed.

In the second half of April the *Stavka* ordered Malinovskii's Third Ukrainian Front to prepare a new offensive on Kishinev from the bridgeheads along the Dnestr. In the first half of May Konev's Second Ukrainian Front was to attack toward Iasi, while Malinovskii's front was to join it in the second half of May. Rodion Yakovlevich requested the *Stavka* to turn over the Second Ukrainian Front's positions along the eastern bank of the Dnestr, opposite Tashlyk, to the Third Ukrainian Front. Chuikov's fresh 8th Guards Army and Tsvetaev's[2] 5th Shock Army were to relieve Zhadov's[3] 5th Guards Army, which was occupying positions opposite Tashlyk. The *Stavka* agreed with Malinovskii's proposal. By the middle of May Zhadov's army had been shifted to the front reserve in the Botosani area. Managarov's[4] 53rd Army from the Second Ukrainian Front was to support the offensive on Kishinev. However, on 6 May Malinovskii communicated the *Stavka's* new decision to front headquarters: halt all active operations along the Dnestr until August. The front's forces were ordered to organize a defense, although local offensive operations along individual sectors were authorized.

In order to eliminate the Soviet bridgehead, a group was formed from Maximilian de Angelis's[5] German Sixth Army under General Knobelsdorff, the commander of the XL Panzer Corps, which was occupying defensive positions along a 70-kilometer front along the Reut and Dnestr rivers

---

1 Editor's note. Mikhail Nikolaevich Sharokhin (1898-1974) joined the Red Guard in 1917 and the Red Army the following year. During the Great Patriotic War he served as deputy chief of the General Staff, an army chief of staff, and commanded an army. Following the war, Sharokhin served in the military-educational apparatus. He retired in 1960.

2 Editor's note. Vyacheslav Dmitrievich Tsvetaev (1893-1950) joined the imperial army in 1914 and fought in the First World War. He joined the Red Army in 1918 and fought in the civil war. He commanded armies during the Great Patriotic War. Following the war, Tsvetaev was head of the Frunze Military Academy.

3 Editor's note. Aleksei Semyonovich Zhadov (Zhidov) (1901-77) joined the Red Army in 1919 and fought in the civil war. During the Great Patriotic War he commanded an airborne and a cavalry corps, and then an army. Following the war, Zhadov served in the military-educational apparatus and commanded the central group of forces. Stalin ordered Zhidov to change his name to Zhadov during the war.

4 Editor's note. Ivan Mefod'evich Managarov (1898-1981) joined the imperial army in 1914 and fought in the First World War. He joined the Red Guard in 1917 and the Red Army a year later. During the Great Patriotic War he commanded a rifle and a cavalry corps and later armies in Europe and the Far East. Following the war, Managarov commanded an army before retiring.

5 Editor's note. Maximilian de Angelis (1889-1974) joined the Austro-Hungarian army and served in the First World War. He then served in the postwar Austiran army until its absorption by the German army in 1938. During the Second World War he commanded a division, corps and an army group. Following the war, de Angelis was imprisoned for war crimes, but was released in 1955.

from Orgeev to Speia, under a single command. The group included the XLIV Army Corps, which was defending the bank of the Dnestr north of Dubossary, and the XL Panzer Corps, which was defending the Orgeev sector, and the LII Army Corps, which was defending the sector from Dubossary as far as Grigoriopol'. As a result of the German forces' activities, the area of the bridgehead was seriously reduced up to a narrow strip along the western bank of the Dnestr, while Soviet troops suffered heavy losses.

In order to distract the German forces from the bridgehead in the Tashlyk area, the Soviet command undertook an offensive along the sector of the front from Grigoriopol' to Dubossary with the forces of Tsvetaev's 5th Shock Army of the Third Ukrainian Front. Three of the 34th Guards Rifle Corps' divisions were supposed to attack and destroy the German forces located in the "bottle" of Pogrebya—Dorotskoe—Vadul lui Voda. The German artillery's flanking fire from the "bottle" against the Tashlyk bridgehead inflicted heavy losses on Chuikov's 8th Guards Army.

The offensive against the German 17th Infantry Division began on 14 May. The 243rd and 203rd rifle divisions, with the support from the left of the 248th Rifle Division, attacked the German divisions and by the close of the day eliminated the bridgehead "bottle." The 17th Infantry Division pulled back to the western bank of the Dnestr.

Insofar as the western bank of the Dnestr is significantly higher than the eastern bank, the Soviet group of forces on the new bridgehead was under fire from three sides. During the second half of 14 May Eichstadt's 294th Infantry Division forced the Dnestr near Starye Dubossary (six kilometers south of Dorotskoe), while units of combat group F did the same near Koshnitsy. The counterattack was supported by a combat group from Unrein's 14th Panzer Division. During the night of 14-15 May the German forces completed their concentration and in the morning, following a powerful fire onslaught, began their attack simultaneously along four axes. Height 15.1 was stormed by two battalions with tanks from the peninsula north of Korzhevo and Pereryta by up to a battalion of infantry, Vadul lui Voda and the woods near Lake Dogma by up to two companies, while up to two companies attacked Koshnitsy from the orchards two kilometers west of the town. Heavy fighting went on all day. At night on 15-16 May the German forces attacked the northern outskirts of Koshnitsy with two battalions and cut the road to Dorotskoe, near the exit from the bend. The delivery of munitions to the encircled Soviet units and the evacuation of the wounded became practically impossible. The 49th Guards and 295th rifle divisions were thrown in to help them. However, on the night of 16-17 May the Germans laid down a bridge near the northern outskirts of Koshnitsy and, having crossed armored transports and assault guns over, with the support of 16 gun and seven mortar batteries and two batteries of six-barreled mortars and aviation, attacked in the morning and by midday had occupied the old defensive line, cutting off the neck of the bend (the "bottle"). The Soviet 243rd and 203rd rifle divisions were encircled.

All attempts to deliver munitions and food on armored transports and tanks to the encircled forces were unsuccessful. On 19 May the German forces took Koshnitsa. The bombardment of the Soviet forces did not stop. Losses increased with each day. On the night of 19-20 May the encircled forces sought to break out. On 18-19 May our artillery launched an attack on the German positions east of Koshnitsa and in the woods west of Dubossary. At night the remnants of the 203rd and 243rd divisions came out of the encirclement.

The 8th Guards, 5th Shock and 5th Guards armies suffered heavy losses. More than two thirds of the Tashlyk bridgehead had been recaptured by the Germans and the plans for an offensive on Kishinev had been foiled. The German 14th Panzer Division alone took 3,050 soldiers and officers prisoner, seized seven tanks and self-propelled guns, 447 guns, 193 mortars, 380 machine guns, 106 flamethrowers, and 102 anti-tank rifles. Losses for the 8th Guards Army alone were more than 30,000 killed, missing in action and captured. The 5th Shock Army lost more than 20,000 killed, missing and captured. The German Sixth Army's losses for the first ten days of May were 940 killed, 371 missing in action and 3,377 wounded, and in the second ten-day period 1,405 killed,

4,389 missing in action and 5,817 wounded. This totaled 16,299 men, including 2,345 killed and 4,760 missing in action. The correlation of irretrievable losses was 7:1 in favor of the Germans, and by taking into account the 5th Guards Army's losses and those of the Third Ukrainian Front's other armies, it probably approached 10:1.

On 15 May 1944 the decision was made to appoint Malinovskii to command the Second Ukrainian Front, which was considered stronger than the Third Ukrainian and was supposed to play the decisive role in the offensive in Romania. He left the headquarters of the Third Ukrainian Front on 20 May and took up his new position on 22 May, when his predecessor, Konev, was appointed to command the First Ukrainian Front. Fedor Ivanovich Tolbukhin took over the Third Ukrainian Front. His and Malinovskii's fronts had to fight in close cooperation to the end of the war.

The Romanian (Moldavian) population of Bessarabia greeted the Soviet troops warily, but did not put up any resistance and did not hurry to reinforce the Romanian troops as volunteers, already sensing that the USSR would win. However, liberation by the Red Army did not engender any particular joy. Naturally, the Moldavian peasantry carried the weight of the war on its soldiers, but nevertheless the brief return of the Romanians was a breathing spell between Soviet requisitions. In three years of Romanian rule in Bessarabia 417,000 tons of wheat was collected in the form of taxes and requisitions, and from June 1940 through June 1941, the first year of Soviet rule, the state took 356,000 tons for itself. Beginning with the spring of 1944, the newly-returned Soviet authorities extorted 480,000 tons from war-torn eastern Moldavia alone, even before the Iasi—Kishinev operation and the liberation of all of Bessarabia.

The commander of the 53rd Army, General Ivan Mefod'evich Managarov describes his first meeting with Malinovskii as follows:

> On 12 June Rodion Yakovlevich arrived at army headquarters with a member of the front's military council, I.Z. Susaikov[6]…
>
> By this time more than 20,000 men had accumulated in the 230th Reserve Regiment, which was station in the area of the town of Kotovsk. Half of them had been mobilized in the army's zone during the offensive, while the remainder had arrived following treatment in the hospitals. None of them had any weapons. I asked the *front* commander to give me the necessary weapons and uniforms for the mobilized men. R.Ya. Malinovskii intently heard out my request and promised to render assistance. We drew up a request for the lacking weapons and uniforms and sent it to the front headquarters. The front's other armies probably prepared analogous requests.
>
> I soon had this conversation with the front commander over the high-frequency radio.
>
> "Comrade Managarov! Did your army attack or retreat in the Uman'—Botosani operation?"
>
> "It attacked," I replied.
>
> "You submitted a request for such an enormous amount of various weapons, as if you're reforming an entire rifle corps. I ask you, what did you do with the weapons? Your troops were fully armed before the offensive. These are my orders: create the necessary number of groups, furnish them with transportation, and throughout the army's entire sector as far back as Zvenigorodka ransack all the groves, bushes and hollows and gather up all the weapons thrown down by the wounded. I believe that those who are lightly wounded should arrive at

---

6   Editor's note. Ivan Zakharovich Susaikov (1903-62) joined the Red Army in 1924 and became a political commissar. During the Great Patriotic War he served as a member of the military council on various *fronts*. Following the war, Susaikov continued to serve in the political apparatus until his retirement in 1962.

the hospitals with their weapons. Check all the hospitals. It's necessary to bring in the civilian population to gather up weapons. Put the gathered weapons in order. You won't get a single automatic rifle or machine gun."

I was not insulted by this reprimand. In carrying out the *front* commander's order, we gathered up such an amount of weapons that we were able to equip with them the soldiers in the 230th Reserve Regiment.

Here we see the character of Malinovskii's desire to arm the soldiers called up directly into the units, which should have somewhat increased their chances of survival in battle. By the way, to judge from everything, he nevertheless gave Managarov some amount of weapons. After all, he only promised not to give the newly mobilized men automatic rifles and machine guns.

Malinovskii's family came to see him before the Iasi—Kishinev operation. His son, Robert, recalled:

Father left for the front in 1941 and it was only in 1944, when victory was approaching, that he invited us to see him at the front. Their headquarters was in Moldavia at the time, in the village of Balan. We arrived from evacuation, first by train to Moscow, and then we traveled for several days by car: we traveled in a ZIS-101, accompanied by an officer, to Moldavia, passing through ruined cities and villages. I well remember, for example, destroyed Dnepropetrovsk, the streets under piles of bricks, among which a passage had been cleared.

The headquarters itself was in a village hut; there were no inhabitants, because everyone was quartered in huts. Father met us when we drove up. Of course, there were hugs, as we had not seen each other in more than three years. And then we lived with him for a month. He was constantly visiting the troops in a captured Opel Admiral. This car could go up to 150 kilometers per hour without its folding top, and father's bodyguard, which moved around on American jeeps, complained that it couldn't keep up with him. There were a lot of captured cars and Allied ones, chiefly American-made, particularly trucks. I even learned how to drive one of them, an old Mercedes.

I remember how Stalin called father several times late in the evening. He spoke with him only in military fashion, without any personal notes and did not engage in sentimentalities. They sent us back two weeks before the Iasi—Kishinev offensive operation.

On 9 September 1944 Malinovskii wrote his son Robert:

Dear Robusik! So, how was your trip? You probably got very tired on the road and now you should rest well and then get back to your studies. How's mama and her health? How is Edyunya? He's already gone to school and probably now plays the accordion less. Now we've advanced very far and have beaten the Romanians, so that they no longer threaten our motherland. Robusik, the Germans shot me up a bit, but not much; the bullet grazed my side but did not go through and the wound is already healing and soon will be completely healed. And I am only proud of this, for to spill one's blood for our Soviet motherland is the greatest honor for a military man. I kiss you very strongly, so kiss mama and Edik for me.

Your papa.

It's typical that the letter is addressed to the son and not the mother. It appears that the estrangement between Larisa Nikolaevna and Malinovskii was already growing. And the accordion on which Eduard played was a captured Romanian one, legally acquired by Rodion Yakovlevich through the prize commission.

On 20 August 1944 the Iasi—Kishinev operation began. When they reported to Malinovskii that the 27th Army had broken through the enemy's defense northwest of Iasi and forced the Balui River, he got into immediate touch with the divisions, checked out the information, and then decided to commit Kravchenko's[7] 6th Tank Army into the breach, although it was planned to do this only on the operation's second day. Rodion Yakovlevich decided not to give the German-Romanian forces time to occupy defensive positions along the Seret River, covering the narrow defile of the "Focsani Gates." *Stavka* representative Timoshenko approved Malinovskii's decision.

On the margins of the book *The Iasi—Kishinev Cannae*, which was issued by the "Nauka" publishing house in 1964 and edited by him, Malinovskii made the following curious notes (these are highlighted in italics, B.S.). Following the phrase

> There was a tense silence in the forward observation post, which was located on height 195.0. Here were *Stavka representative Marshal of the Soviet Union Timoshenko, Marshal of Aviation Khudyakov*, the front commander General Malinovskii, and generals and officers from their [corrected from: his] operational groups.

Rodion Yakovlevich added:

> *They arrived here on the evening of 19 August. The enemy, foreseeing something bad, his aviation methodically bombed the area of height 195.0 all evening and the beginning of night, but he was unable to change anything and awaited events like a criminal condemned to death. He still had a ray of hope, that perhaps mother will come out with a white shawl, which was a sign that the king had spared him and that there would be no execution. But in the morning his mother came out in a black shawl and the execution took place (Moritz Hartmann's "The White Shawl").*[8]

In the book's text this passage reads as follows:

> There was a tense silence in the Second Ukrainian Front's forward observation post, which was located on height 195.0. Here were *Stavka* representative Marshal of the Soviet Union Timoshenko, Marshal of Aviation Khudyakov, the *front* commander General Malinovskii, and generals and officers of the operational groups. They arrived here on the evening of 19 August. On this evening and in the first hours of night on the 20th, the enemy's aviation methodically bombed the area of height 195.0. The enemy evidently sensed something, but he was unable to change anything and awaited events like a criminal condemned to death. He still had a ray of hope, just like the hero of Moritz Hartmanns's famous poem, that he would catch sight of a white shawl. However, the fascist criminal, who had dyed his hands crimson with the blood of millions of innocent victims, could not count on mercy. And the "mother" in the form of just vengeance, emerged in a black shawl and the execution took place.

Of course, Rodion Yakovlevich does not bear responsibility for the editorial inserts and ideological stock phrases.

---

7   Editor's note. Andrei Grigor'evich Kravchenko (1899-1963) joined the Red Army in 1918 and fought in the civil war and the Soviet-Finnish War. During the Great Patriotic War he commanded a tank brigade and a tank corps, and then a tank army in Europe and the Far East. Following the war, Kravchenko commanded an army and retired in 1955.

8   Editor's note. Mortiz Hartmann (1821-72) was a German-Jewish poet and author, who also took part in the 1848 Revolution in Germany and the Austrian Empire.

I should note that in the Austrian poet Hartmann's poem the mother, in order to reinforce the courage of her son, a Hungarian count, comes out in a white shawl to convince him that the king had pardoned him, when the execution actually took place.

Actually, although the commander of Army Group South Ukraine, Colonel General Johannes Friessner,[9] had learned earlier of the Soviet offensive, He lacked powerful reserves and did not receive permission to pull back his forces to a shorter defensive position, although this does not mean that a withdrawal would have helped matters, all the more so as the Romanian troops would completely lose their combat capability during a retreat.

According to I.M. Managarov's reminiscences, on 4 September Malinovskii arrived at the 53rd Army's headquarters:

> The representative of the *Stavka* of the Supreme High Command, Marshal S.K. Timoshenko, who was then with us, awarded R.Ya. Malinovskii his marshal's epaulets and congratulated him with being awarded the rank of marshal of the Soviet Union.
>
> The *front* commander gave me an order regarding the army's further operations, after which I escorted Rodion Yakovlevich to the airfield and he flew off to his headquarters. Upon returning, I reported on this to Marshal S.K. Timoshenko.
>
> At approximately 1500-1600 they called me from the airfield and informed me to go there immediately. I arrive to see R.Ya. Malinovskii sitting on a lounger chair with a canvas back. He was very pale. The lounge chair's back was covered with blood. At headquarters, to where we brought the front commander, the army's chief surgeon, A.S. Rovnov, gave him first aid. Fortunately, the wound did not prove dangerous.

It's interesting to note, if one believes Managarov, that Stalin made the decision to award the rank of marshal to Malinovskii as early as 4 September (without Stalin's sanction, Timoshenko would not have risked awarding Malinovskii his marshal's epaulets), although the order to promote him to the rank of Marshal of the Soviet Union appeared only on 10 September 1944. In nominating him for this rank, S.K. Timoshenko wrote Stalin:

> Today is the day of the rout of the German-Romanian troops in Bessarabia (where Semyon Konstantinovich was from himself, B.S.) and on the territory of Romania, west of the Prut River… The enemy's main Kishinev group of forces has been encircled and is being destroyed. In observing the skillful leadership of the troops…, I consider it my duty to request you to petition the Presidium of the USSR Supreme Soviet to award the military rank of "Marshal of the Soviet Union" to General of the Army Malinovskii…

There is also the testimony of the marshal's adjutant, Anatolii Innoket'evich Fedenev on Malinovskii's wounding in Romania:

> On 28 August, while determining where it was more effective to commit the 4th Guards Army into the offensive, R.Ya. Malinovskii, together with the deputy chief of the General Staff, Lieutenant General V.D. Ivanov,[10] were examining the terrain in the Husi area aboard

---

9   Editor's note. Johannes Friessner (1892-1971) joined the army in 1911 and served in the First World War. During the Second World War he commanded a division and a corps, and later on commanded army groups before being relieved in late 1944.

10 Editor's note. Vladimir Dmitrievich Ivanov (1900-68) joined the Red Army in 1918 and fought in the civil war. During the Great Patriotic War he served as an army chief of staff and as deputy chief of the General Staff was often dispatched to the various *fronts* to help with the planning and conduct of military

two Po-2 aircraft. There was a fierce battle raging under the low-flying planes. The aircraft was shot at and the pilot increased the altitude. Upon returning to the airfield, V.D. Ivanov told Rodion Yakovlevich: "There are 12 holes in my plane!"

"I don't know how many holes are in the plane," replied Rodion Yakovlevich, "but I have one in my back."

The pilot first learned of Malinovskii's wounding on the ground and was amazed by the fact that Rodion Yakovlevich didn't say a single word to him, so as not to distract him from his duties and upset him.

As we can see, Fedenev dates Malinovskii's wounding significantly earlier than Managarov—28 August. Malinovskii himself confirms this in his service biography from 1946. "I was slightly wounded by a bullet on 28 August 1944." If this date is correct, then Rodion Yakovlevich's flight was not linked to the commitment of the 4th Guards Army into the fighting, insofar as by 28 August the front was already finishing off the encircled enemy group of forces.

On 22 August the Second Ukrainian Front's 4th Guards Army, while attacking along the left bank of the Prut, captured two crossings and advanced 25 kilometers in the direction of Husi, in order to link up with the Third Ukrainian Front's forces. However, Tolbukhin sent a protest to the *Stavka*, declaring that the 4th Guards Army's offensive was supposedly hindering the offensive by the forces of the Third Ukrainian Front.

The wound proved to be a shallow one, insofar as the bullet that hit Rodion Yakovlevich was fired from the ground and already spent. Following treatment of his wound, he returned to duty, refusing to go to the hospital.

On 24 August the encirclement ring closed. The forces of the Second Ukrainian Front's 4th Guards and 53rd armies and the 18th Tank Corps reached the Prut River along the line west of Husi and Kotumori and linked up with the Third Ukrainian Front's forward units. The problem of the 4th Guards Army lost its immediacy, although Malinovskii had been forced to turn over the area occupied by the 4th Guards Army to the Third Ukrainian Front's forces.

During the Iasi—Kishinev operation the forces of the Second and Third Ukrainian fronts were opposed by Army Group South Ukraine. By the start of the Soviet offensive it included the following German divisions: 3rd and 4th mountain infantry, 8th and 97th light infantry, 10th motorized, 13th Panzer, and the 9th, 15th, 46th, 76th, 79th, 106th, 257th, 258th, 282nd, 294th, 302nd, 306th, 320th, 335th, 370th, 376th, and 384th infantry divisions, the 153rd Field Training Division, as well as corps groups A (161st Infantry Division) and F (62nd Infantry Division). Of all of these divisions, only the 3rd and 4th mountain infantry, 8th and 97th light infantry and the 153rd Field Training divisions were able to avoid encirclement and more or less safely fall back into Hungary.

On 1 March 1945 the headquarters of the no-longer-active Army Group South Ukraine toted up the depressing results, which are presented in the following table.

The average strength of the divisions destroyed in Romania was 11,668 men. If we assume that five of the German divisions that more or less safely retreated from Romania numbered approximately the same number of soldiers and officers before the start of the Iasi—Kishinev operation, then one may place their total strength at 58,340 men and the strength of all the German troops in Army Group South Ukraine at 337,000 men. Approximately another 40,000 men could have been from the military personnel and civilian personnel from the *Luftwaffe* and Navy in Constanta, Bucharest, Ploesti and several other rear areas (including 25,000 in the Ploesti area and about

operations. He was a deputy *front* commander during the war with Japan. Following the war, Ivanov served in the central military apparatus and was the chief of the General Staff Academy.

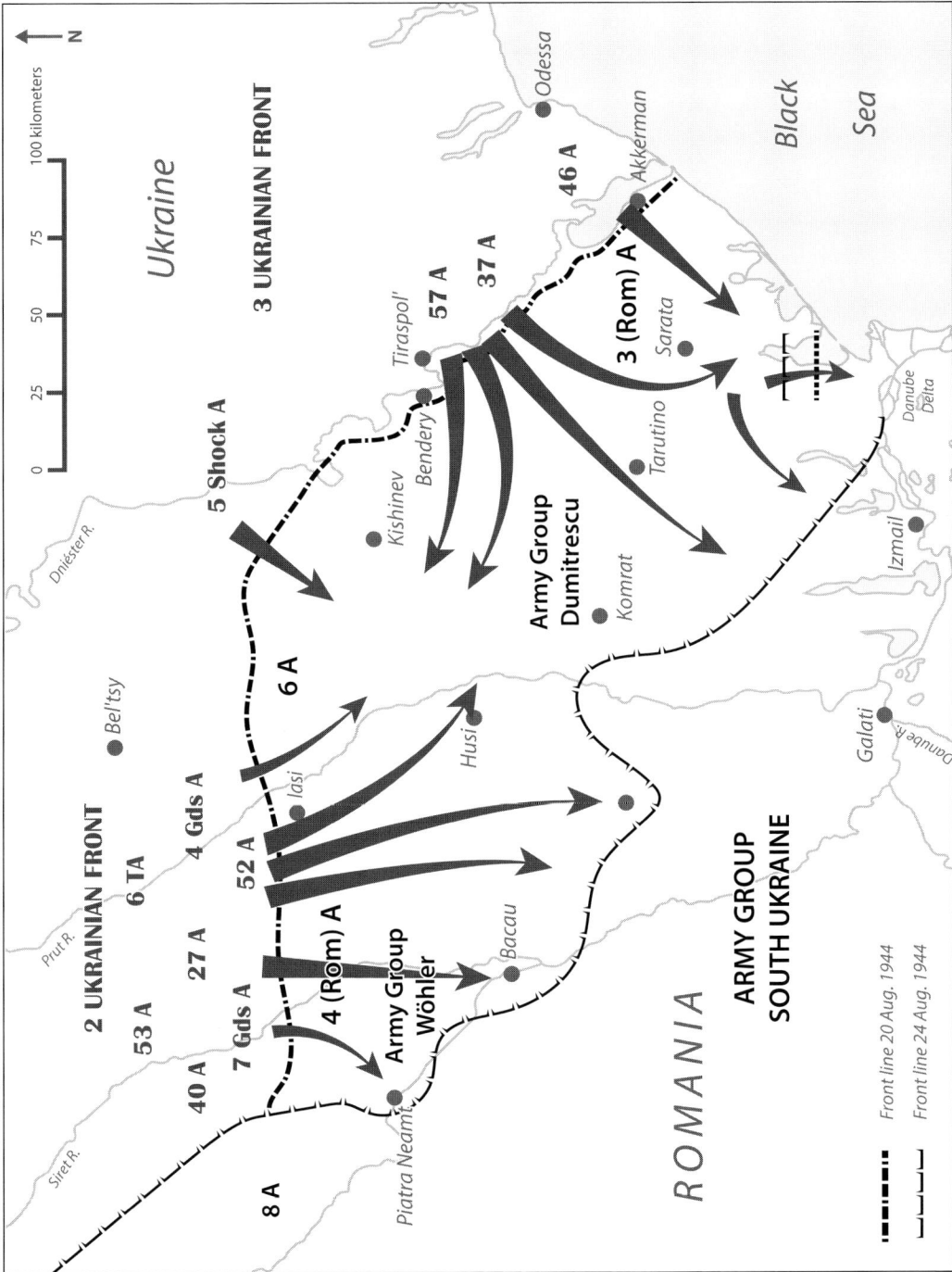

Map 3 The Iasi-Kishinev Operation, August 1944.

11,000 in the Bucharest area). At the start of the battle they were subordinated to the Army Group South Ukraine command but, in all likelihood, were not counted by the defunct headquarters. According to German data, the *Luftwaffe's* overall losses in Romania in August and the beginning of September were 16,134 men, mainly as prisoners. This figure includes 125 flight crews, 4,500 airfield personnel, 8,565 from air defense, and 2,944 from signals units.

There are no exact figures for the Romanian forces' strength. The following Romanian formations were part of Army Group South Ukraine by the start of the battle: 1st Guards Division; "Greater Romania" Motorized Division; 1st and 5th cavalry divisions 1st, 2nd, 3rd, 4th, 5th, 6th, 7th, 8th, 9th, 11th, 13th, 14th, 16th, 20th, and 21st infantry divisions; 18th Mountain Infantry Division' 110th Infantry Brigade, and; 4th, 101st, 102nd, 103rd, and 104th mountain infantry divisions. Besides this, the army group included Romanian border units and the commandant's office for the mouth of the Danube, as well as the headquarters of the Third and Fourth armies and seven army corps (I through VII). This yields total of 20 divisions and five brigades. It is known that the Romanian Fourth Army, which had just arrived in the Stalingrad area in the beginning of October 1942, numbered by the start of the Soviet counteroffensive 75,580 men in the VI and VII army corps, which included the 1st, 2nd, 4th, 18th, and 20th infantry divisions, as well as the 5th and 8th cavalry divisions. In all, there were five infantry and two cavalry divisions. This army was practically newly formed in Romania and by the start of the Stalingrad counteroffensive had suffered heavy losses. The Romanian Third Army then numbered 152,492 Romanian and 11,211 German military personnel. It included the I, II, IV, and V Romanian army corps and the German XLVIII Panzer Corps, which included the German 22nd Panzer and the Romanian 5th, 6th, 7th, 9th, 11th, 14th, and 15th infantry, and 7th Cavalry and 1st Panzer divisions. In all, there were seven Romanian infantry, one cavalry and one panzer divisions. Thus a single division in the Romanian Fourth Army had an average strength of 10,797 men and 16,944 in the Third Army. The difference is due to a significant degree to the presence in the Third Army of a number of motorized artillery units (2nd, 4th, 5th, and 8th motorized heavy artillery regiments and the 41st Independent Motorized Heavy Artillery Battalion), which were not in the Fourth Army. The average strength of a Romanian division in the two armies is equal to 14,254 men. We will employ this figure for calculating the strength of the Romanian forces in Army Group South Ukraine. At the same time, we calculate that two brigades are equal to one division. Then the strength of the Romanian forces with Army Group South Ukraine by the start of the Soviet offensive may be placed at 321,000 men.

Thus the overall strength of the German-Romanian forces opposing the Second and Third Ukrainian fronts amounted to about 658,000 men. The two Soviet *fronts* facing them numbered 1,314,200 men (including 771,200 men in Malinovskii's front); that is, they enjoyed a two-to-one numerical superiority. They disposed of 16,000 guns and mortars, 1,870 tanks and self-propelled guns, 2,200 planes as part of the 5th and 17th air armies and the Black Sea Fleet's aviation. According to Soviet estimates, the enemy had 900,000 men, 7,600 guns and mortars, 400 tanks and assault guns, and 800 combat aircraft. As regards the German-Romanian forces, this data is considerably exaggerated. Soviet historians have relied on the statement by Friessner, the commander of Army Group South Ukraine, to the effect that: "At the time I took command of the German-Romanian forces I disposed of two German and two Romanian armies, consisting of 44 divisions with an overall strength of about 900,000 men, including personnel from the rear units." However, he took over command of the army group on 25 July 1944. From that time and right up to the start of the Soviet offensive on 20 August, 12 German divisions were transferred to other fronts, chiefly to Poland, including six panzer and one motorized divisions. All of these were from the 44 German and Romanian divisions present on 25 July 1944. Due to this fact, the strength of the army group could have fallen by 245,500 men, which approximately coincides with our previous calculations.

Losses by the Destroyed German Forces of Army Group South Ukraine, August-September 1944

Army	Division	Strength as of 19.8.1944	Remaining Alive	Killed and Died	Missing in Action	Fate Unknown
Eighth	79th	10,500	2,855	63	4,838	2,744
Eighth	258th	11,750	2,142	70	3,828	5,710
Eighth	376th	13,500	2,990	27	3,195	7,288
Sixth	106th	12,420	850	6	1,985	9,579
Sixth	370th	13,500	1,113	20	2,977	9,390
Sixth	282nd	11,700	700	2	3,497	7,501
Sixth	9th	11,600	2,262	46	2,152	7,140
Sixth	62nd	11,000	439	8	4,025	6,528
Sixth	13th	13,905	500	8	620	12,777
Sixth	335th	10,453	318	12	3,520	6,603
Sixth	161st	12,561	476	3	4,717	7,365
Sixth	294th	11,332	473	10	6,485	4,364
Sixth	320th	10,885	324	27	4,468	6,066
Sixth	384th	9,855	112	2	4,023	5,718
Sixth	15th	11,611	1,576	42	4,978	5,015
Sixth	257th	9,491	558	15	5,773	3,145
Sixth	302nd	12,962	900	20	4,950	7,092
Sixth	306th	11,000	3,059	257	1,675	6,009
	Security Units and *Landsturm* Battalions	17,500	230	0	3,650	13,620
	Units subordinated to the Army High Command	22,000	2,853	76	3,838	15,233
	Corps troops	17,000	1,491	0	2,016	13,493
	Rhodes garrison	12,000	521	42	408	11,029
	Total	278,525	26,742	756	77,618	173,409

As we are convinced, Soviet data the strength of these forces has been exaggerated 1.4 times. The figure of 400 tanks and assault guns also appears to be an exaggeration. The German 13th Panzer Division had only 40 tanks and almost all of them were lost during the breakout from the encirclement. Its individual subunits managed to make it to the German positions in Transylvania. Other remnants of the division (including the part commanded by General Troger) fell back into Bulgaria, where they were interned and turned over to Soviet forces. The Romanian "Mikhai the Great" 1st Panzer Division numbered 48 German Pz-IVH tanks and 12 German StuG-IIIs. The German 286th Assault Gun Brigade numbered 25 guns. There were 43 assault guns in the 10th Motorized Division's 7th Panzer Battalion, which was armed with assault guns. From all appearances, the overall number of tanks and assault guns in Army Group South Ukraine did not exceed 300, if one assumes that 25 guns apiece could be in the 236th, 243rd, 911th, and 325th assault gun brigades, which were also operating in Romania. The 278th Brigade there disposed of 21 assault guns, while by the start of the Iasi—Kishinev operation the 239th Brigade was very short of equipment and it was unlikely that it had more than ten guns. Almost all of the enemy's armored equipment was destroyed or captured by Soviet forces. Only the 286th Brigade retained a large part of its vehicles.

The main mass of German and Romanian aviation was defending Bucharest and Ploesti against powerful strikes by Anglo-American strategic bombers. The Western Allies began their air offensive against Romania on 4 April 1944, in order to create the impression among the Germans that they were preparing to land in the Balkans (Hungary and Bulgaria also suffered) and to distract attention from the real landing area in France. The offensive continued all the way up to 19 August; that is right up to the beginning of the Soviet offensive. The Americans' losses in Romania were 223 bombers and 36 fighters, while the British, who carried out night raids, lost 48 bombers. The *Luftwaffe* lost 145 fighters and the Romanian Air Force 80. 121 German and Romanian pilots died. Losses on the ground amounted to 7,444 killed (6,979 civilians and 455 military) and 7,696 wounded (6,968 civilians and 728 military). The Allies had irretrievable losses of about 2,200 men, of which 1,095 were Americans and 52 British, while those who had been captured were repatriated in September 1944. The German Fourth Air Fleet, which was covering Romania and the Balkans, numbered only 200 planes by the beginning of August, including 30 long-range and 35 night bombers, 30 single-engine and 40 two-engine fighters, and 25 long-range and 40 tactical reconnaissance aircraft, while it was also obliged to assist Army Group North Ukraine. By the start of the Soviet offensive, this figure had declined even further due to losses. There were about 60 German fighters operating against the Allied air force. There were no more than 140 German planes facing the 17th and 5th air armies and the Black Sea Fleet's aviation. With the start of the offensive, 40 Ju-87s from Estonia and 30 Fw-190 fighters from Army Group North Ukraine were transferred to the Silistea airfield, but it was already too late. The Romanian air force employed 305 planes in combat operations. Thus German and Romania could oppose only about 445 planes to 2,200 Soviet ones, which gave the Soviets a five-fold superiority. The royal Romanian air forces lost 25 planes in the fighting against our air armies. According to official figures, Soviet aviation suffered irretrievable losses of 111 combat aircraft in the Iasi—Kishinev operation. By all appearances, this data is somewhat understated. It's more than likely that no less than half of these losses were inflicted not by the Romanian Royal Air force, but by the *Luftwaffe*. Also, according to official data, the two fronts suffered irretrievable losses of 75 tanks and self-propelled guns and 108 guns and mortars.

Friessner maintained: "In order to stay atop the situation, it was necessary to resolve the following two tasks:

1)   to pull back the army group's front back behind the Prut in time, possibly to the previously-prepared defensive line Galati—Focsani—eastern spurs of the Carpathians;
2)   to concentrate all the German forces in the rear area under my command.

Friessner put forth these proposals before the OKH[11] and Hitler, and he was supported by the Romanian dictator Ion Antonescu.[12] However, they were not accepted right up to the start of the Soviet offensive.

---

11   Editor's note. The OKH (*Oberkommando des Heeres*) was established in 1935 as the supreme high command of the German army. Together with the air force and navy, the OKH was subordinated to the OKW (*Oberkommando der Wehrmacht*). Hitler took over the OKH in 1941, after which its influence *vis a vis* the OKW steadily declined.

12   Editor's note. Ion Victor Antonescu (1882-1946) joined the Romanian army in 1904 and served in the Second Balkan War and the First World War. During the interwar period he rose rapidly through the

According to Friessner,

> As early as my first trips to the front…, we were hearing rumors about the doubtful reliability of the Romanian officers. Although at first there was no concrete proof, everything pointed to the fact that things were far from in order here. For example, the replacement of the higher Romanian officers was ordered by the Romanian minister of war, and the German commander was not informed of this. All of this took place on the eve of the Russian offensive!...
>
> The regular conferences between political figures and generals, which were taking place in the town of Alba Iulia… seemed very suspicious. We suspected that these people were conducting negotiations with enemy powers and were preparing to overthrow Antonescu's government. It was clear that a new government, formed by these politicians, would occupy a hostile position in relation to Germany…
>
> The crossing of military personnel of the front line to the enemy became a daily occurrence.

On 3 August Friessner wrote Hitler: "If symptoms of ferment appear once again among the Romanian units at the front, it will be necessary to issue an order to pull back the army group behind the Prut and farther to the line Galati—Focsani—the spurs of the Eastern Carpathians." Friessner recalled:

> The enemy managed to break through the Romanian 4th Mountain Infantry Division's front and advance several kilometers. The division was completely routed. As a result, the neighboring Romanian 21st Infantry Division was shaken and ran away following the capture of Rasceti by the Russians. A significant part of the rank and file of both divisions abandoned their positions as early as the artillery preparation. For this reason, the entire burden of the defense lay almost exclusively on the German divisions…
>
> The enemy was able to unexpectedly rapidly deeply penetrate into the positions of the Romanian 7th and 5th infantry divisions, which abandoned their positions without a fight, at the same time that the German formations, particularly the 76th and 79th infantry divisions, which had gotten into an extremely difficult situation, having been abandoned on the right and left by their Romanian neighbors, fought heroically and held their positions.

In the opinion of the then-chief of the General Staff of the ground forces, Heinz Guderian,[13] a timely withdrawal to the line Galati—Focsani—the crest of the Carpathians, would have disrupted the Russians' plans and "contracted the length of the front in such a way as to enable us to hold the front without help from Romania."

However, withdrawing the German forces to the indicated line before the start of the Soviet offensive and pulling back the unreliable Romanian forces would still have failed to avert the catastrophe. The Soviet superiority was too great. If the Romanian forces' front had been pulled back, the Soviet superiority would have become four to one according to overall troop strength and even more so in combat units. The Second and Third Ukrainian fronts' forces could easily create a 7-8:1

---

ranks and became defense minister. He early on associated himself with the Iron Guard and came to power in a 1940 coup. He aligned Romania with Nazi Germany and took his country into war against the Soviet Union. Antonescu was deposed in August 1944 and arrested. He was later tried and executed.

13   Editor's note. Heinz Guderian (1888-1953). Guderian joined the imperial German army in 1908 and served on the Western Front during World War I. He was Germany's leading exponent of armored warfare during the interwar period and later commanded panzer corps in Poland and the West. He was relieved of command in December 1941, although he was later appointed inspector general of panzer troops. He was promoted chief of the general staff in 1944, but was relieved by Hitler the following year.

numerical superiority along the axis of the main attacks, which guaranteed the rapid breakthrough of the defense. A withdrawal would have demoralized the Romanian forces even further and their withdrawal from the front would only have made the overthrow of Antonescu, the preparation for which had been underway since the end of July, easier. The German forces would have had to abandon Bucharest and Ploesti under pressure from Soviet forces and fall back into Hungarian Transylvania, and this would have guaranteed that the Romanians, who had no desire to fight side by side with the Hungarians, and who dreamed of returning Transylvania, would simply have surrendered to Soviet forces.

On 21 August Friessner met with Antonescu. The German general recalled:

> In reply to my remark on the suspicious behavior of the Romanian forces on the eve of and during the first day of the battle, Antonescu said that the Romanian troops' lack of desire to fight was completely unexpected for him. During his trips to the front he had gotten the impression that the units that had given up their positions had no reasons to fall back. He completely agreed that the Romanians had fought badly.
>
> However, the marshal was not inclined to agree that the real reason for the Romanian forces' insufficient firmness was the political intrigues. He said that, of course, there was no comparing the Romanian soldiers with the German ones, and that this concerned the officer corps most of all. According to him, he had ordered that the harshest measures be applied to deserters and cowards and he had evidently kept his word. He had visited the troops himself and had personally restored order where it was needed. I was aware, for example, that he had organized officer blocking groups to combat desertion, which were accorded great powers.

The following correlation of forces was created on the Kitsany bridgehead and north of Iasi: 6:1 in men, 5.5:1 in field guns of various calibers, 5.4:1 in tanks and self-propelled guns, 4.3:1 in machine guns, 6.7:1 in mortars, and 3:1 in aircraft in favor of the Soviet forces. The factor that up to 80 percent of the enlisted men in the rifle units consisted of reinforcements from those conscripted in the Ukrainian provinces liberated in the spring of 1944 is worthy of mention; also, more than 20,000 conscripts from Moldavia joined the troops.

According to official data in the collection *The Stamp of Secrecy Removed*, the Soviet forces' losses during the Iasi—Kishinev operation amounted to 13,197 killed and missing in action (1 percent of the overall strength of the two fronts' forces) and 53,933 wounded. These have most likely been reduced, particularly as concerns irretrievable losses. Insofar as the overall Soviet losses in killed and missing in action in the collection, *The Stamp of Secrecy Removed*, have been reduced by approximately a factor of three for the entire war, then one may assume that the Soviet forces' losses in the Iasi—Kishinev operation in filled and missing in action were about 40,000 men, while overall losses were about 134,000 men. However, even when taking this into account, they were several times less than those of the Germans. After all, the irretrievable losses of the divisions and units that fell into the Iasi—Kishinev cauldron amounted to about 252,000 men. The overall German losses, including also the wounded whom they managed to evacuate before they were encircled, and the losses of the divisions that did not fall into the cauldron, probably exceeded 270,000 men, which was more than twice that of the overall Soviet losses, even putting aside the Romanian losses (the Romanians lost up to 130,000 men in prisoners alone during the Iasi—Kishinev operation). If we include the Romanian losses, which also include several tens of thousands of killed and wounded, the overall Soviet losses are 3.5 times less than the German-Romanian ones, and more than ten times in irretrievable losses. This is the Red Army's best correlation of losses for the entire war, and it was achieved during an operation that was led by Malinovskii and Tolbukhin.

One cannot say that the coup of 23 August, which put an end to the adventurist dictatorship of Ion Antonescu and which put Romania into the ranks of the anti-Hitler coalition, did not have decisive significance for the Iasi—Kishinev operation's success. If this had not happened, then it's possible that the German forces which got into the encirclement would have managed to break out. But they were in the cauldron before the coup. And the Romanian forces would nevertheless have fought significantly worse than the Germans, even if they had not overthrown Antonescu.

In principle, among Germany's allies the Romanians had one of the most combat-capable armies and were inferior only to the Finnish army. The Romanian soldiers and officers could fight the Red Army as equals, but only in conditions of an approximate equality of men and materiel. Given a significant Soviet superiority, the Romanians' successful defense depended completely upon the abilities of the German forces to render them sufficient support. However, by August 1944 both the German group of forces in Romania and the ability of the Romanian forces to fight had been seriously weakened. Following the heavy losses suffered by the Romanians in the Stalingrad area and in south Russia in 1942-43 and during the fighting in the Crimea and the evacuation of the peninsula in the spring of 1944, the main part of the Romanian cadre army had been put out of action. In August 1944 Tolbukhin's and Malinovskii's forces were, for the most part, opposed by recently drafted conscripts. However, what is more important is that following the Allied landings in Normandy in June 1944 practically no one in Romania, including the soldiers and officers, doubted that Germany had lost the war and Romania should get out of it as soon as possible. So, even without the coup, the Romanian forces would not likely have put up fierce resistance to the attacking Red Army. The majority of them would either have surrendered, or retreated into the rear. And with the loss of Romanian territory, which was inevitable within the next few weeks, the Romanian army would have ceased to exist.

Thus even without the coup of 23 August, the results of the Iasi—Kishinev operation would have been catastrophic for Germany. She would have been completely deprived of Romania and its oil fields and refining industry. To be sure, the German army's irretrievable losses in Romania, in this case, would have been less, but this would have been of little comfort.

The single substantial win for the Soviet side from the coup of 23 August is that it received at its disposal the Romanian army, which conducted combat operations in Hungary and Czechoslovakia, drawing on its self part of the German and Hungarian forces.

One may say that a factor in favor of Romania was the fact that Hitler trusted Antonescu more than the Hungarian regent, Miklos Horthy,[14] whom he, and not without reason, suspected of intending to reach a separate peace. Thus as early as March 1944, with the approach of the front to the borders of Hungary, German forces occupied the country.

The Hungarian army was much weaker than the Romanian. The reason for this was that, as opposed to Romania, according to the conditions of the Peace Treaty of Trianon[15] of 1920, which concluded the First World War, Hungary did not have the right to have a mass army and have a peacetime military draft. Only in 1941 did it renounce the limitations of the Trianon treaty and begin to develop its army. Thus the Hungarians had practically no reservists with experience of military service. In the beginning of 1943 the greater part of the Hungarian Second Army, which

---

14   Editor's note. Admiral Miklos Horthy (1868-1957) joined the Austro-Hungarian navy in 1896 and fought in the First World War. He was appointed commander-in-chief of the navy in 1918 and in 1919 he was named regent of Hungary, following the collapse of the Austro-Hungarian Empire. During the 1930s he allied Hungary with Germany and participated in the invasion of the Soviet Union. He concluded an armistice with the Soviets in October 1944, but his government was deposed and replaced by an overtly pro-German government under Ferenc Szalasi. Horthy was taken to Germany and arrested by US forces in 1945. Horthy later lived in exile in Germany and Portugal.

15   Editor's note. The Treaty of Trianon (1920) formally ended hostilities between the Kingdom of Hungary and the main Allied powers from the First World War. According to the treaty, Hungary lost most of its prewar territory and an outlet to the sea, while large numbers of Hungarian-speaking populations were left in other countries.

included the most combat-capable formations, perished in the Don steppes. Two Hungarian armies, which were sent to the front in April 1944, chiefly consisted of poorly trained conscripts and were distinguished by their low combat quality and lack of desire to fight. However, these forces were of no use in liberating Budapest from German units, of which there were as many as Hungarian units. Thus Horthy's attempt to leave the war in the middle of October, which we will discuss below, failed.

In Romania Hitler trusted Antonescu to the end and did not believe that he could be over-thrown. Thus Romania was not occupied and there were few German troops in Bucharest and other rear-area cities, and they were considerably inferior in strength to the Romanian garrisons. Also, there were mostly *Luftwaffe* units in the Romanian rear areas, which were supporting anti-aircraft defense and which were of little combat value.

The main thing is that the main mass of German forces in Romania was encircled and was unable to break out toward Bucharest, which the Second Ukrainian Front's forces entered by 31 August. On 10 September 1944 Malinovskii was awarded the rank of Marshal of the Soviet Union for the Iasi—Kishinev Cannae. Tolbukhin was honored with the same rank, although this happened on 12 September, two days later. In this way Stalin underscored Malinovskii's seniority over Tolbukhin in his marshal's rank.

On 3 October Malinovskii's front completed the Bucharest—Arad operation, which it had begun on 30 August, along with the Romanian forces. During the operation all of Romanian territory and part of Transylvania was cleared of German-Hungarian forces. By the start of the operation the Second Ukrainian Front numbered 681,556 men and, if one believes the official statistics, it had lost 55,286 men, 8,447 irretrievably.

On 13 September Army Group South Ukraine, which faced the Second Ukrainian Front, consisted of the following German divisions, among which the following were on the march: 46th and 76th infantry, 3rd and 4th mountain infantry, the "Hoffbach" divisional group, the "Kessel" covering detachment, 4th SS Police Motorized Division, 8th Light Infantry Division, 8th and 22nd SS cavalry divisions, 23rd Panzer Division, and the 110th Panzer Brigade, for a total of nine divisions, one brigade and two divisional groups, each of which were the equivalent of a brigade, including: five infantry, two motorized, two cavalry, and 1 ½ panzer divisions, which is equivalent to 10 ½ divisions. Aside from this, the following Hungarian formations were part of the army group: 20th and 25th infantry divisions, 1st and 2nd reserve mountain infantry brigades; the 27th Light Infantry Division and the 9th Light Infantry Border Security Brigade; the Szekely Border Detachment; 2nd, 4th, 6th, 7th, 8th, 9th, and 12th reserve divisions; 1st and 2nd panzer divisions. Altogether—12 divisions, three brigades and one detachment, which was equivalent to a brigade, including ten infantry and mountain infantry, two motorized and two panzer divisions, which was equivalent to 14 divisions. In all, the army group included 24 ½ divisions, of which only 10 ½ were German. Given the same strength that existed before the start of the Iasi—Kishinev operation and the presence of approximately the same strength of *Luftwaffe* and navy units, then Friessner's forces should have numbered about 500,000 men. Taking into account the fact that half of the German divisions suffered losses in Romania and also that few *Luftwaffe* units remained, and also that there were no naval units at all, then the strength of the army group in the beginning of October probably did not exceed 450,000 men.

Ahead was Hungary. Upon entering this country, Rodion Yakovlevich probably recalled Spain and his friendship with the Hungarian writer and soldier Mate Zalka. On 6 October 1944 the forces of the Second Ukrainian Front began the Debrecen operation, in order to reach the Tisza River along the Chop—Szeged sector and assist the Fourth Ukrainian Front in crossing the Carpathians and capturing the trans-Carpathian area. Malinovskii had 59 divisions and 698,200 men and 825 tanks. Before the start of the operation, the Second Ukrainian Front had been reinforced with the 46th Army, 7th Guards Mechanized Corps, and the 7th Breakthrough Artillery Division, as well as with 75,000 reinforcements. This proves that the data on the losses in the Bucharest—Arad operation had been significantly lowered. If they had been correct, then the Second Ukrainian Front should have numbered, with reinforcements alone, 701,270 men, and by taking into account the addition of units and formations, no less than 800,000 men, insofar as the 46th Army had nine rifle divisions—of which eight were guards units—and three guards rifle corps. Given the army's authorized strength, together with the 7th Artillery Breakthrough Division's authorized strength of 10,707 men, this would yield more than 140,000 men and, even given the units' being understrength, this would not likely be less than 100,000 men. The mechanized corps contained about 16,000 men. Accordingly, the losses in the Bucharest—Arad operation should have been no less than 167,000 men, of which up to half could have been irretrievable. Army Group South, which was opposing the Second Ukrainian Front, had 26 ½ divisions and 293 tanks and assault guns, for a total of about 450,000 German and Hungarian troops. On 13 October Army Group South included the following German divisions: 15th, 46th and 76th infantry, 3rd and 4th mountain infantry, 8th Light Infantry, and 4th Motorized SS Police divisions, a combat group from the *Feldherrenhalle* Motorized Division, the 8th SS Cavalry Division, and a combat group from the 22nd SS Cavalry Division, and the 1st, 13th, 23rd, and 24th panzer divisions. This came to 12 German divisions and two combat groups, each of which was equivalent to a brigade, including five infantry and mountain infantry, 2 ½ motorized, 1 ½ cavalry, and four panzer divisions, which was equivalent to 13 divisions. Aside from this, the following Hungarian divisions were subordinated to Friessner: 20th and 23rd infantry; the remnants of the 25th Infantry Division; 27th Light Infantry Division; 9th Light Infantry Border Security Brigade; 1st Cavalry Division; 1st and 2nd panzer divisions; 2nd, 4th, 7th, 8th, 9th, and 12th reserve divisions and; the 2nd Reserve Mountain Infantry Brigade. In all, 12 divisions, two brigades and the remnants of one division, which was equivalent to a brigade, or nine infantry divisions, 1 ½ motorized, one cavalry and two panzer divisions, which was equivalent to 13 ½ divisions. Thus there were more Hungarian troops in Army Group South than German. If the strength of the German and Hungarian divisions was the same as the German and Romanian divisions on the eve of the Iasi—Kishinev operation, then there should have been about 540,000 men in Army Group South. However, considering the losses suffered in the Iasi—Kishinev operation and in the fighting in Transylvania, as well as the high rate of desertion among the Hungarians (according to Friessner's memoirs, 700 Hungarian soldiers deserted from the Szekely salient alone in September), the real strength of the divisions was considerably lower, then Army Group South probably did not number more than 450,000 men (on the condition that the new divisions and reinforcements were approximately equal to the losses suffered in the 13 September-13 October time period.

The Romanian 1st and 4th armies, which numbered 22 divisions, were operationally subordinated to Malinovskii. They probably did not have in their ranks more than 150,000 men. Thus the Second Ukrainian Front enjoyed a two-fold superiority over the enemy. On 12 October the Germans planned operation "Gypsy Baron," in the course of which they attempted to encircle part of the Second Ukrainian Front's forces. As a result of the Soviet offensive, they began their operation earlier, as early as 10 October, and cut off the 6th Tank Army. An armored meeting battle unfolded in the Debrecen area between this army and two German panzer divisions. It continued until 14 October, when the Soviet tank troops managed to break through the encirclement ring. On 20 October the 6th Guards Tank Army and the 33rd Rifle Corps captured Debrecen. On 22 October General Pliev's cavalry-mechanized group, which included both of General Gorshkov's corps, captured Nyiregyhaza and reached the Tisza River. However, as a result of the new German counterblow, it was cut off and was forced to abandon Nyiregyhaza, which it recaptured, with the assistance of the 27th Army, only on 29 October. By that time the Second Ukrainian Front's forces had reached the Tisza along the entire length of the front and the 46th Army had seized a large bridgehead in the area between the Tisza and the Danube.

In September 1944 the losses of Army Group South's German troops were 2,194 killed, 7,591 wounded and no less than 1,298 missing in action. In the last ten days of September 157,706 missing in action were included in the Sixth Army's losses, although this mainly concerned those who had died or been taken prisoner in August, during the Iasi—Kishinev operation. If we assume that the Sixth Army's losses in missing in action during the last ten days of September were a little more than the corresponding losses of the Eighth Army, which lost only a little less than the Sixth Army in killed and wounded, then the overall losses among those missing in action from Army Group South in September should be increased by 940 men—to 2,238, while the overall losses should be increased to 12,023, including 4,432 irretrievably.

According to German data, in September 1944 the Hungarian losses were 292 killed, 2,015 wounded and 66 missing in action, for a total of 2,373 men, and in October they were 270 killed, 2,519 wounded and 102 missing in action, or 2,891 men. These data undoubtedly deal only with those German troops who were fighting directly as part of their armies and do not include losses in the Hungarian Second and Third armies, which suffered particularly heavy losses in captured and deserters. Suffice it to say that as a result of the losses suffered during September-November, the Hungarian Second Army was disbanded as early as 1 December. Its losses in September, according to Hungarian data, were about 2,500 killed and about 7,500 missing in action. The Hungarian Third Army's losses were probably no less, at a minimum. The Hungarian troops' real losses in September, including captured and desertions could have amounted up to 5,000 wounded and up to 15,000 killed and captured.

In October 1944 Army Group South's losses were 1,655 killed, 7,234 wounded and 2,264 missing in action, for a total of 11,243 men. According to the evaluation by the author of the German official history, *The German Reich and the Second World War*, the Hungarian losses in the Debrecen battle were 20,000 men, while the German-Hungarian forces in this battle lost a total of 18,000 captured. Insofar as the Hungarian losses in killed and wounded in October were 2,789 men and 102 missing in action, who can probably be included among the killed, then the Hungarian losses in captured men may be put at 17,000 men and the Germans at 1,000. The Hungarian historian Ungvary puts the Romanians' losses in the Debrecen battle at 33,500 and Soviet losses at 84,000.

In September 1944 Army Group South Ukraine captured 2,101 men, chiefly Romanians, and in October, having been renamed Army Group South, 11,796 men.

This is the way S.M. Shtemenko, the chief of the General Staff's operational directorate, recalled Hungary's attempts to leave the war:

> The Soviet side, in accordance with the agreement with the Hungarians, dispatched the commander of the Second Ukrainian Front, R.Ya. Malinovskii, to Szeged for negotiations about the Hungarian government's fulfillment of the preliminary conditions of the armistice. Great was Malinovskii's surprise when a Hungarian colonel and senior lieutenant arrived in Szeged, completely unprepared to conduct negotiations on important matters. The colonel was a section chief in the Hungarian general staff, responsible for questions of internment and prisoners of war, and was unable to conduct negotiations. He did not offer any kind of data on the location of Hungarian and German forces, but reported that the Hungarian First Army had received orders to pull out of the Debrecen area to the Miskolc area.
>
> R.Ya. Malinovskii attempted to ascertain why Hungarian troops had not been pulled back from the line of the Tisza River, but did not receive a coherent answer. The commander got the impression that "the Hungarians want to win time in order to pull their forces out of the pocket into which they had gotten in Transylvania." He dictated the following demands to the representatives of the Hungarian government:

1) Immediately set about withdrawing Hungarian forces from the Tisza River toward Budapest, and launch an attack with part of these forces against the German troops facing the front in the Szolnok area;

2) Immediately issue an order to the Hungarian forces to undertake military operations against the German troops, upon having established contact with the Red Army;

3) Deliver to Szeged by 0800 on 16.10.44 complete data on the situation of the Hungarian and German forces and in the future furnish information about combat operations and their location.

I.V. Stalin, having received Malinovskii's report, ordered A.I. Antonov to make a representation to the chief of the Hungarian mission on this matter and dictated the text. On the evening of 14 October it was presented to Gabor Farago. It was stated in the representation:

The Hungarian representative, Colonel Utasi Lourend, is completely uninformed and, as a result, cannot conduct negotiations with representatives of the Soviet command concerning questions of the Hungarian government's fulfilling the preliminary conditions of the armistice.

The Hungarian government requested the Soviet government to halt its offensive in the direction of Budapest, so that it could remove its forces from this axis and direct them to Budapest.

The Soviet government carried out this request by the Hungarian government. However, the latter has not only did not remove its forces from the Tisza River for dispatch to Budapest, but has activated the combat operations of its forces, particularly in the Szolnok area.

The circumstances related above testify to the fact that the Hungarian government has evidently embarked on the path of not carrying out the preliminary conditions for an armistice that it took upon itself.

Because of this, the High Command of Soviet forces demands of the Hungarian government that within 48 hours of receiving this representation that it carry out the obligations which it has taken upon itself according to the preliminary conditions for an armistice, particularly:

1. To break off any kind of relations with the Germans and to begin active military operations against their forces.

2. To set about pulling back Hungarian forces from the territory of Romania, Yugoslavia and Czechoslovakia.

3. To deliver by 0800 on 16 October through Szeged to the representatives of the Soviet command complete information on the location of German and Hungarian forces and at the same time report to the above-indicated Soviet representatives the progress of carrying out the preliminary conditions for an armistice.

As authorized by the High Command of Soviet forces—deputy chief of the Red Army General Staff, General of the Army Antonov. 14 October 1944, 1925 hrs.

As early as 10 October the Hungarian command had transferred to Budapest the VI Army Corps and the 10th Infantry Division, which had been removed from the Carpathian front, which aroused the indignation of the Germans. This movement was probably carried out within the confines of Horthy's plan to take Hungary out of the war. These divisions later came in handy for the defense of Budapest.

On 15 October Miklos Horthy addressed the Hungarian people and announced the break with Germany and the signing of an armistice agreement. However, pro-German units, with the support of German troops, removed Horthy from power. The admiral surrendered after Otto Skorzeny's[16] people and special SS troops kidnapped his son, and he was interned on German territory. The new regent, Ferenc Szalasi,[17] the leader of the pro-fascist Arrow Cross Party, ordered the Hungarian army to continue the struggle on the side of Germany.

Skorzeny himself, who had led the seizure of the regent's palace on Castle Hill in Budapest, wrote in his memoirs, which were issued not long before his death:

> In 1954 A. Gatkevich, a retired Hungarian colonel, wrote me a letter, dated 15 January. In it the author stated that on 12 October he had accompanied his immediate superior, Colonel Roland von Utasi (this is without a doubt that same man who is referred to as Louren Utasi in Soviet sources, and Gatkevich was that second Hungarian officer who took part in the negotiations, and the oberleutnant about whom Shtemenko writes as accompanying the colonel. Evidently someone, either Skorzeny or Shtemenko, confused the rank of this second officer. The fact is that in German these ranks sound very similar—Oberleutnant (senior lieutenant) and Oberstleutnant (lieutenant colonel)—while establishing communications with the Soviet Supreme Command on orders from the regent, B.S.). On the morning of 13 October, following a ceasefire agreed to by both sides, two men left their positions in the area of the town of Szeged and departed for the Russians, on the other bank of the Tisza. I will quote Gatkevich's letter:
> "… at approximately 2200 we were informed that Marshal Rodion Malinovskii had arrived. Before long he entered the room, where we were expected him, accompanied by a small suite. This was a handsome fifty-year old man, with light-colored hair and the figure of a Hercules and his palms the size of a tennis racket. Intelligent and sly blue eyes stood out on his simple face with straight features. He more closely resembled a successful butcher than a high-ranking officer. He came up to us with outstretched hands and greeted us warmly."

Through an interpreter Malinovskii asked the parliamentarians about the situation on the German-Hungarian front. When Colonel von Utasi reported incorrect information, the marshal was surprised. He laid out before the amazed colonel a detailed and exact description of the operational situation.

> … The marshal presented us with the following conditions for a possible separate peace: the withdrawal of our forces from the Debrecen area, the cessation of combat operations along the entire front, an attack on the German forces from the rear in agreement with the approaching Soviet units, in order to force the Germans to capitulate. Unfortunately, I've already forgotten many details. When I asked him about Hungary's fate, he made a contemptuous gesture:

---

16   Editor's note. Otto Skorzeny (1908-75) was an Austrian who joined the SS in 1939. He fought in the West, Yugoslavia and the Soviet Union. His most famous exploit was freeing the deposed Italian dictator Benito Mussolini from captivity and bringing him to Germany. He was imprisoned after the war, but escaped and later served as an adviser to the Egyptian army. Skorzeny died in Spain.

17   Editor's note. Ferenc Szalasi (1897-1946) joined the Austro-Hungarian army and fought in the First World War. He left the Hungarian army in 1935 and became involved in politics and later helped found the fascist Arrow Cross Party. Following Horthy's removal in October 1944, the Germans installed Szalasi as head of the government. During his brief tenure in power, he increased the persecution of Hungary's Jewish population and helped the German effort under Adolf Eichmann. Szalasi was captured by US forces in 1945 and was returned to Hungary, where he was tried and executed in 1946.

"We don't need anything from the Hungarians, but the Germans…," and a grimace of hatred distorted his face, "… the Germans we will destroy," he said.

The parliamentarians were given 48 hours to accept the conditions presented by Malinovskii. In parting, he declared to both officers that "he hoped for a quick meeting with us as friends and comrades in arms." Gatkevich added that General Miklos organized the meeting…

When Gatkevich and his chief returned to the Hungarian positions, the latter had already been evacuated. In order to reach the battalion from which they had departed to meet the Russians, they had to go through ten kilometers of mud. Upon returning to Budapest on the morning of 14 October, they left for Castle Hill. Two days later at dawn I captured Colonel von Utasi; he was in uniform, but was wearing slippers, as his feet had swollen from the difficult march and could not fit in his officer's boots. Gatkevich had run away through the gardens before we arrived. In a letter sent to me, he added that he had presented an account of his mission to the Hungarian staff and then to an SD[18] functionary who interrogated him.

I should note that Malinovskii had chestnut-colored hair, but by 1944 it was already heavily streaked with grey, which is why the memoirist said he had light-colored hair. Gatkevich also emphasized Malinovskii's sincere hatred for the Germans, which had formed as early as the First World War.

S.M. Shtemenko recalled:

On 20 October 1944 R.Ya. Malinovskii sent an impassioned request, to be delivered personally to the Supreme Commander-in-Chief, to reinforce his *front* with tanks. "The enemy has evidently correctly determined that the Second Ukrainian Front's forces are moving along a very important operational-strategic direction and have thrown eight panzer divisions into the fighting against the *front*… The *front* will have to wage stubborn fighting. The enemy is not going to give up Hungary easily, because this is his most vulnerable area, while the Hungarians continue to stubbornly fight under Szalasi's leadership," the commander wrote.

He added that the enemy had lost up to 400 tanks in the latest fighting, but that we had lost 300 tanks.

In reality, by this time the Germans and Hungarians had lost only 133 tanks and assault guns destroyed and damaged, while the Second Ukrainian Front had lost about 500 tanks and self-propelled guns.

According to Shtemenko, Stalin, believing the optimistic reports by L.Z. Mekhlis, the member of the Fourth Ukrainian Front's military council, on the rapid dissolution of the Hungarian forces, "inquired of the General Staff how best to attack Budapest in order to capture it more quickly." Shtemenko continued:

Not suspecting anything, we replied that it would be best to take advantage of the broad bridgehead, which had been seized along the Second Ukrainian Front's left flank in the area between the Tisza and Danube. Here it was not necessary to force a river and the enemy disposed of a smaller number of troops than along other axes. Aside from this, the relatively fresh 46th Army had been moved up here. Following a breakthrough, it could be turned to the

---

18   Editor's note. The SD (*Sichendeitsdienst*) security service, established in 1931, was the intelligence branch of the SS. It was involved in numerous atrocities during the war.

north of the enemy's defense behind the Tisza and thus assist a direct attack by Shumilov's[19] 7th Guards Army and the Romanian 1st Army against Budapest from the east.

I.V. Stalin, having mulled over the General Staff's ideas, phoned R.Ya. Malinovskii and demanded that the Second Ukrainian Front immediately capture Budapest. Even A.I. Antonov, who reported the situation without embellishments, was unable to prove to the Supreme Commander-in-Chief that L.Z. Mekhlis' reports did not correspond to reality, particularly in the Budapest area.

A dramatic conversation occurred between Stalin and Malinovskii at 2200 on 28 October.

Stalin: We must capture Budapest, the capital of Hungary, as quickly as possible within the next few days. We must do this. Are you in a condition to carry out the operation?

Malinovskii: This assignment could be carried out in five days, but only on the condition that the 46th Army's 4th Guards Mechanized Corps be brought up…

Stalin: The *Stavka* can't give these five days. Try to understand, finally, that we must seize Budapest as soon as possible, for political reasons.

Malinovskii: I understand completely that the quickest possible capture of Budapest cannot be put off for political reasons. However, we can count on success only if the forces of the 4th Guards Corps take part in the operation.

Stalin: We cannot agree for any reason to postpone the offensive… The offensive on Budapest should be begun immediately.

Malinovskii: If you give me five days, then I'll capture Budapest during the following five days. If we undertake the storming without delay, then the end result will be that the 46th Army will get bogged down in extended fighting on the approaches to the Hungarian capital. In other words, it will not be in a condition to take Budapest.

Stalin: Why are you so stubbornly defending your position? You obviously don't completely understand the political significance of an immediate military offensive on Budapest.

Malinovskii: I understand just what great significance the capture of Budapest has. It is precisely for this reason that I'm asking for five days.

Stalin: I'm ordering you to begin the offensive on Budapest.

He had to carry out the order, although Malinovskii was certain that Stalin was mistaken and that his order would lead to extended fighting for Budapest. This is exactly what happened.

The Germans were able to concentrate the 13th, 23rd and 24th panzer divisions and the *Feldherrnhalle* Motorized Division for repelling the offensive on Budapest, while Malinovskii, following the battle for Debrecen and Nyiregyhaza, was catastrophically short of armored equipment, which he had been unable to replenish.

According to the Hungarian historian, Krisztian Ungvary, the Hungarian 10th Infantry, 5th, 8th and 23rd reserve, 1st Hussar, and 1st Panzer divisions and the German 20th Infantry and 23rd and 24th panzer divisions, which had been concentrated between the Danube and Tisza by 31 October, consisted of only 17,400 combat troops and disposed of 97 armored vehicles and 188 field guns.

---

19   Editor's note. Mikhail Stepanovich Shumilov (1895-1975) joined the army in 1916 and fought in the First World War. He joined the Red Army in 1918 and fought in the civil war and later in Spain and Finland. During the Great Patriotic War he commanded a corps and an army. Following the war, Shumilov commanded military districts until his retirement in 1956.

The forces of the Second Ukrainian Front, which were facing them, consisted of the following: 2nd Guards Mechanized Corps, which included 12,000 combat troops, 248 tanks and self-propelled guns; the 4th Guards Mechanized Corps, which numbered 6,000 combat troops, 73 tanks and self-propelled guns; the 23rd Rifle Corps, which numbered 10,000 combat troops; the 31st Guards Rifle Corps, which numbered 8,000 combat troops, and; the 37th Rifle Corps, which numbered 8,000 combat troops. In all, the Soviet group of forces numbered 52,000 combat troops and disposed of 321 armored vehicles and 4,470 field guns. It strikes us that the combat strength has been significantly undercounted—on both sides. If the figure of 12,000 combat troops in the 2nd Guards Mechanized Corps, which had an authorized strength of 16,442 men, strikes us as plausible, then a combat strength of 10,000 men for the three-division 23rd Rifle Corps, replenished to its authorized strength, seems far from reality. One of the divisions, the 68th Guards Rifle, should have had an authorized strength of about 12,600 men. The other two, the 99th and 316th would have had an authorized strength of 9,380 men apiece according to the table of 1943, while their authorized strength grew to 11,706 men by December 1944. However, even if they had been brought up to full 1943 strength, then calculating the combat element as 60 percent of the overall strength, there should have been about 19,000 combat troops in the 23rd Corps. The combat strength of the German-Hungarian forces was probably reduced by the same proportion. However, without a doubt the Soviet numerical superiority was no less than threefold.

The 23rd Rifle Corps' chief of staff, Sergei Aleksandrovich Andryushchenko, recalled his meeting with Rodion Yakovlevich on the eve of the offensive on Budapest:

> Malinovskii got up noisily to greet us, shaking our hands. He was tall and broad-shouldered. The marshal's eyes looked intently and with a great deal of good will. Sitting down beside us, Rodion Yakovlevich asked how the trip had been. A warm smile would play around his round face from time to time…
>
> At the end of the discussion, R.Ya. Malinovskii said:
> "Tomorrow, or the day after tomorrow, at the latest, you will receive orders to subordinate the corps to the 46th Army. The army commander, General Shlyomin,[20] will issue you the combat assignment to attack. You can expect difficult fighting, so don't count on an easy victory. The fascists will fight with the stubbornness of the condemned."

Malinovskii had requested five days for preparations, but Stalin demanded that the attack begin the next day, 29 October. The corresponding directive was issued on the evening of 28 October. At first only the 46th Army, along with the 2nd Guards Mechanized Corps, attacked, but they advanced slowly and with losses. Then the 7th Guards and Romanian 1st Army came to assist them.

As is known, the fighting for Budapest stretched out until the middle of February 1945, but Stalin, perhaps understanding with the benefit of hindsight that he had been hasty in attacking the Hungarian capital, later never blamed Malinovskii for the fact that the siege of Budapest extended for three and one-half months.

The Hungarian defensive front was pierced on the first day of the offensive and Soviet forces advanced 25 kilometers. On the morning of 30 October units of the 46th Army repelled a

---

20   Editor's note. Ivan Timofeevich Shlyomin (1898-1969) joined the army in 1917 and fought in the First World War. He joined the Red Army the following year and fought in the civil war. During the Great Patriotic War he served as an army and *front* chief of staff and later commanded several armies. Following the war, Shlyomin served in higher troops staffs and taught at the General Staff Academy until his retirement in 1962.

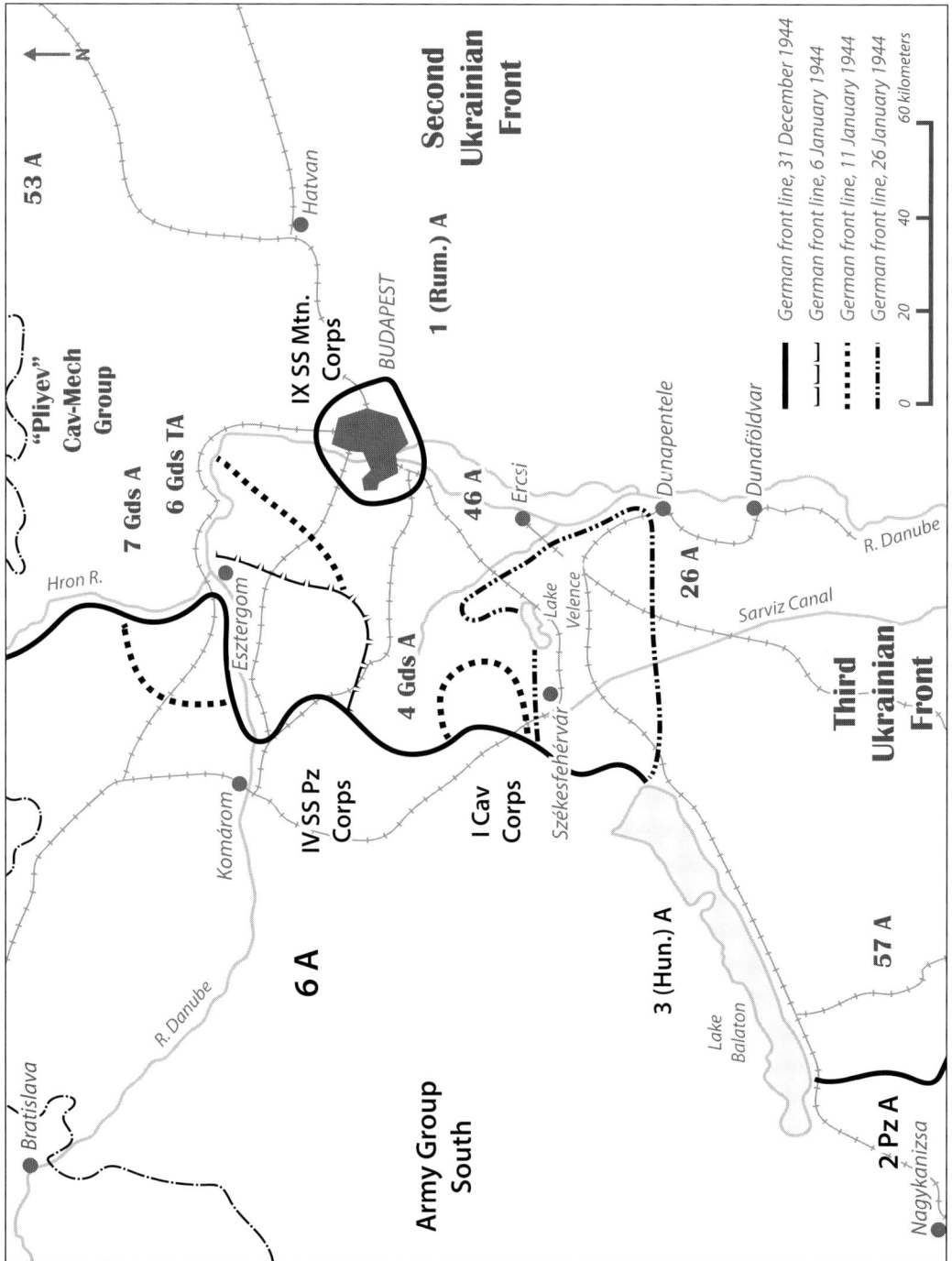

Map 4 The capture of Budapest, December 1944–January 1945.

Second Ukrainian Front

53 A

Hatvan

1 (Rum.) A

BUDAPEST

IX SS Mtn. Corps

"Pliyev" Cav-Mech Group

7 Gds A

6 Gds TA

Hron R.

Esztergom

46 A

Ercsi

Dunapentele

Dunaföldvár

R. Danube

26 A

Lake Velence

Sarviz Canal

4 Gds A

Komárom

IV SS Pz Corps

I Cav Corps

Székesfehérvár

6 A

R. Danube

Third Ukrainian Front

3 (Hun.) A

Lake Balaton

57 A

Army Group South

Bratislava

2 Pz A

Nagykanizsa

German front line, 31 December 1944
German front line, 6 January 1944
German front line, 11 January 1944
German front line, 26 January 1944

0   20   40   60 kilometers

counterattack by the 23rd Panzer Division and began fighting on the outskirts of Kecskemet. However, the Soviet offensive was halted here.

The 7th Guards Army's divisions forced the Tisza but were unable to widen the bridgehead. On 31 October the second echelon's formations—the 23rd Rifle and 4th Guards Mechanized corps—which had been committed into the fighting, began storming Kecskemet. Upon capturing Kecskemet, they were supposed to force the Danube and outflank Budapest from the east, while the 2nd Guards Mechanized Corps was to attack Budapest from the south.

On 2 November Soviet mechanized forces reached the line Alsonemedi—Ocsa—Gomba, 15 kilometers from Budapest. However, they were unable to advance further, due to German and Hungarian counterattacks.

By the close of 3 November the advance by the Soviet forces had been halted 10-15 kilometers to the south and southeast of Budapest. On 10 November the 7th Guards, 53rd, 27th, and 40th armies began to outflank Budapest from the north and northeast, while Pliev's cavalry-mechanized group attacked to the north in the Szolnok area, in order to roll up the enemy's defense along the Tisza River.

According to Friessner, in November

> Even in the Hungarian 10th and 12th divisions, which had heretofore been considered reliable and which were operating east of Budapest, there appeared signs of dissolution. The Hungarian soldiers, singly or in large groups up to 100 men, went over to the enemy with white flags. In all, over 2-3 days five officers and 1,200 soldiers went over to the Russians. Faith in the Hungarian army had been completely lost and it could no longer be relied on.

Placing no hope in the Hungarians, the German command transferred the III, IV and LVII panzer corps. Stubborn fighting broke out. On 14 November the Second Ukrainian Front received 200 tanks and 40,000 reinforcements. However, the attempts by the 6th Guards Tank and 7th Guards armies to penetrate into the Hungarian capital from the north were unsuccessful. On the other hand, by 21 November the 46th Army had seized a significant part of Czepeli Island.

A Hungarian reserve Hussar, Lieutenant Aurel Salamon, recalled the fighting in Budapest around 20 November, when the Soviet forces attempt to throw the enemy off Czepeli Island:

> By evening our positions were being attacked by the so-called Russian punishment battalions, which consisted of political prisoners. They were greeted by hurricane salvos from machine guns and mortars and tanks, buried in the earth up to their turrets, and even from fast-moving cutters on the Danube, which poured forth a hail of fire on the attackers. The attack soon died out and the Russians suffered enormous losses. Hundreds of dying and wounded remained lying in front of our positions. We most often heard cries of "My God!" alongside loud but weakening calls for help. Our corpsmen tried to drag them out, but each times they fell back, met by machine gun fire. These people were simply supposed to die. We were unable to help them and on the following day they grew silent.

During the fighting for Budapest Army Group South captured the following number of prisoners: 2,495 in November 1944, 3,943 in December 1944, 5,517 in January 1945, and 2,240 in February.

S.A. Andryushchenko recalled:

> Thus the 46th Army, as well as other field forces, was not able to capture the city from the march, as called for by the operational plan. Naturally, there were reasons for this, which were objectively stated in the report by the *Stavka* representative, Marshal of the Soviet Union S.K.

Timoshenko, on 26 November 1944. First of all, the front's forces had operated in a dispersed manner, along three axes—Miskolc, Eger and Hatvan, which prevented us from created a significant superiority of forces over the enemy along any one of them. The Hitlerites' opportunities and capabilities for rapid maneuver had been underestimated.

Here one should recall that Malinovskii did not have time to regroup his troops and concentrate his forces along a single axis, insofar as Stalin had ordered him to attack immediately.

In Timoshenko's report, which was dated 24 November, it states:

The Second Ukrainian Front is one of the most powerful *fronts*. It disposes of enormous potential, allowing it to defeat the defending enemy. However, despite this, it has been unable to mark up significant successes to its credit. In my opinion, the chief reasons for the operations' lack of success lie in the following:

1. The command, presupposing a quite relative superiority for attaining success, is attempting to simultaneously defeat the enemy groups of forces along several axes (Miskolc, Eger and Hatvan).

2. These efforts… lead to a dispersal of combat power, as a result of which our units are not able to face the enemy with a real superiority of combat force. As a result, for example, the front's main group of forces (27th, 53rd and 7th Guards armies), which number 24 rifle divisions, three mechanized and one tank corps, as well as the 2nd Cavalry Corps, ended up being concentrated along several axes:
    a) the 27th Army, consisting of eight rifle divisions, is fighting along a 50-kilometer front along the Miskolc axis;
    b) the 53rd Army, consisting of seven rifle divisions, is fighting along a 45-kilometer front along the Eger axis;
    c) the 7th Guards Army, consisting of nine rifle divisions, in operating near Hatvan. There are three mechanized, two cavalry and one tank corps along this same sector.

The infantry units are equally distributed along these axes among the corresponding armies. Only the 7th Guards Army, to which units of Pliev's group and the 2nd and 4th mechanized corps have been attached, has a definite superiority. However, as a result of the prolonged fighting against superior enemy forces, both Pliev's group and the mechanized corps are in a weakened state…

3. The command of the units, as well as their headquarters, have been spoiled to a certain extent by the events in Romania and Transylvania, as a result of which cooperation between the different combat arms is not being organized with the necessary thoroughness.
    On the basis of what has been elucidated above, I consider it expedient to demand the following from the commander of the Second Ukrainian Front:
    1. He must review all of his preceding decisions and form combat groups of forces which would, while disposing of an absolute superiority, launch an attack against the enemy in two places:
        a. Hatvan and Balassagyarmat, as the main axis.
        b. Miskolc, as the secondary axis.

Despite the fact that he was not able to take Budapest, on 3 November 1944 Malinovskii received his second Order of the Red Banner, which they now began awarding for time in service.

Rodion Yakovlevich was honored with it for 25 years of irreproachable service in the RKKA. The same decree awarded the Order of the Red Banner to Marshal Voroshilov for time in service, and who thus became the first five-time recipient of the first Soviet medal.

The Third Ukrainian Front's divisions were moved up to assist the Second Ukrainian Front. On 3 November Tolbukhin's forces, which had been reinforced with the fresh 4th Guards Army, began an offensive on Budapest from the Kiskeszeg area. Malinovskii transferred the 31st Guards Rifle and 5th Cavalry corps to Tolbukhin. As a result, the Third Ukrainian Front outflanked Budapest from the southwest. On 1 December Tolbukhin's forces took Szekszard and Paks, and on 2 December they forced the Danube along a broad front south of Dunafelvara.

On 5 December the 46th Army forced the Danube with heavy losses and seized a bridgehead on the right bank near Erd Ofalu. Another seven small bridgeheads were seized the following day in the Ercsi area. The losses were extremely heavy. Emil Tomka, a Hungarian colonel, wrote in his diary:

> Our artillery uninterruptedly shot up the Russians attempting to cross the river. German bombers also pinned them down. Three mortars fired on them from nearby positions. However, despite this the Russians continued to force the river. Groups of Soviet soldiers were ferried over on boats and ferries. I saw how a German bomb fell on a small barge, which was filled to the brim with people and went straight to the bottom. The most horrible things took place along that part of the bank where the Germans were. They fired on the landing troops from machine guns. There was very little chance of surviving. He who had not been cut down by a bullet was forced to fire back, standing up to his chest in the freezing water and mud. Having gotten his fill of all this, one hussar turned to me and said: "Colonel, what do the Russians do to their enemies if they treat their own soldiers so cruelly"

115 men were awarded the title of Hero of the Soviet Union—many posthumously—for forcing the Danube. On 8 December the forces of the 46th Army linked up with Tolbukhin's forces. Their joint efforts pushed the Hungarian 1st Hussar and German 271st *Volksgrenadier*[21] divisions, after which the 46th Army was transferred to the Third Ukrainian Front.

On 5 December Malinovskii's forces broke through the front northeast of Budapest. The 7th Guards and the 6th Guards Tank armies streamed toward Vacs. By this time all the German reserves had been pinned down to the south of Budapest. Army Group South had no forces to defend the space between Vacs and Budapest. On 9 December the tank forces of Kravchenko's 6th Guards Tank Army seized Balassagyarmat and reached the Danube in the vicinity of Vacs. A combat group from the *Feldherrnhalle* Division and Hungarian parachute, police and sapper battalions were thrown in against them.

According to K. Ungvari's evaluation, by this time the Second Ukrainian Front, not counting the Romanian armies, numbered 528,000 combat troops, 10,867 guns, 3,974 mortars, and 565 tanks and self-propelled guns, while the opposing German and Hungarian formations from Army Group South had 127,000 combat troops, 2,800 guns, 800 mortars, and 140 tanks and assault guns.

---

21   Editor's note. The *volksgrenadier* divisions were emergency units formed to meet the manpower crisis in the German army from the autumn of 1944. These divisions generally consisted of six battalions, instead of the standard nine. They also lacked much of the regular divisions' heavy equipment and were generally more configured for defensive fighting than attacking.

But let's return to Budapest. At 2100 on 21 December Malinovskii sent a coded message to Stalin for approval of "a plan for the Second Ukrainian Front's further operation." The operation's goal was "to capture the city of Budapest and by 25-28.12.44 reach the front Gella—Krivany—Bany—Stiavnica—Vrable—Surany—Nove Zamky—Komarno."

The front's right wing, consisting of the 40th and 27th armies (13 rifle divisions, two fortified areas, on three-brigade artillery division, and ten Romanian divisions) was to reach the front Smolnik—Ochtina—Rybnik—Odzany—Filiakovo—Lasuite—Svaty Benedik by 20 December. The front's left wing, consisting of the 53rd, 7th Guards and 6th Guards Tank armies, and Pliev's cavalry-mechanized group (22 rifle divisions, six cavalry divisions, two artillery breakthrough divisions, two mechanized corps, one tank corps, and three Romanian divisions) was to seize Budapest and by 25-28 December reach the line Vrable—Surany—Nove Zamky—Komarno.

On 21 December the 6th Guards Tank Army forced the Hron River. The Third Ukrainian Front's forces had broken through the defense along the Hungarian forces' sector between Lake Velence and Baracska. The Hungarians simply scattered. The Germans held firm and even launched counterattacks, but were forced to fall back under the pressure of an enemy that was 4-5 times superior to him in men and materiel.

The losses were significant. The Romanian 7th Army Corps, which at first numbered 36,348 men, had by the middle of January 1945, during the course of the fighting for Budapest, lost more than half its soldiers (about 20,000).

On the morning of 23 December units of the Third Ukrainian Front's 4th Guards Army captured Szekesfehervar and reached the line Bicske—Herceghalom—Bia. In this way the Vienna—Budapest railroad was cut. Only the narrow-gauge Esztergom—Budapest railroad, along which only a limited amount of food and munitions could be delivered, remained in German and Hungarian hands. On this day units of the 2nd Mechanized Corps reached Herceghalom.

On 24 December Soviet tanks reached the "Sepilon" trolley car park, five kilometers from Buda castle.

The 8th SS Cavalry Division was pulled back to Budapest and the IV SS Panzer Corps began to move from the Warsaw area to western Hungary. In this manner the Second and Third Ukrainian fronts' forces substantially aided the forthcoming offensive along the Vistula by the forces of the First Ukrainian and First Belorussian fronts in the area between the Vistula and the Oder rivers, which began in the middle of January 1945.

On 23 December Hitler replaced Friessner from his post as commander of Army Group South with the former commander of the Eighth Army, Otto Wohler[22] (General Hans Kreysing[23] replaced him). Hermann Balck,[24] the former commander of Army Group G in the West, replaced Fretter-Pico[25] as commander of the Sixth Army.

On the night of 22-23 December Soviet forces forced the Danube in the Nagyteteny area. However, a panzer group, consisting of the *Feldherrnhalle* Motorized Division and part of the 13th

---

22   Editor's note. Otto Wohler (1895-1987) fought in the German army in the First World War. During the Second World War he was chief of staff of an army and army group and later commanded same. Wohler was later convicted of war crimes, but was released in 1950.

23   Editor's note. Hans Kreysing (1890-1969) joined the German army in 1909 and fought in the First World War. During the Second World War he commanded a regiment, division, corps, and an army.

24   Editor's note. Hermann Balck (1897-1982) joined the army in 1913 and fought in the First World War in France, Russia, Italy, and the Balkans. During World War II he commanded a tank regiment, division, corps, and army in the East and later commanded an army group in the West. He was convicted of war crimes, but released in 1950.

25   Editor's note. Maximilian Ludwig Julius Franz Fretter-Pico (1892-1984) joined the army in 1910 and fought in the First World War. During the Second World War he commanded a division, corps and an army.

Panzer Division, were able to was able to recapture Torokbalint and break out of the encirclement at the last moment.

On 24 December 20 Soviet tanks, with small detachments of infantry, broke into the outskirts of Buda. Several tanks were knocked out and the Soviet tanks halted due to a lack of infantry. At around midday on 25 December several Soviet soldiers raised the red banner on Janos hill.

On 26 December units of the 7th Guards Army occupied Esztergom and a bridgehead was seized across the Hron, from which it was not far to Vienna.

On 28 December, with the seizure of Visegrad by Soviet forces, the encirclement ring was closed around Budapest. But they were unable to occupy the city at this time, as had been planned. During the fighting for Budapest Soviet losses in tanks and self-propelled guns during 20-31 December alone amounted to 169 vehicles.

How many men were defending Budapest? Among the Hungarian units and formations in the encirclement were: the 10th Infantry Division (7,500 men, but only 1,000 combat troops), the 1st Panzer Division (5,000 men, but 500 combat troops), the 1st and 2nd university assault battalions (1,000 men, 1,000 combat troops), the "Vannay" Battalion (1,000 men, 800 combat troops), units of the 1st Hussar Division (1,000 men, 200 combat troops), the 6th Assault Gun Battalion (2,000 men, 1,000 combat troops), six battalions of anti-aircraft artillery (2,000 men, 800 combat troops), five battalions of gendarmes (1,500 men, 1,000 combat troops), technical and sapper detachments (7,000 men, 2,000 combat troops), the Budapest Security Battalion (800 men, of which all were combat troops), the 1st and 2nd Budapest assault companies (800 men, of which all were combat troops), combat groups formed from volunteers in Budapest (2,000 men, of which 1,600 were combat troops), the Budapest Security Battalion (300 men, of which all were combat troops), militarized detachments of the Budapest police (7,000 men, of which 2,000 were combat troops), and combat groups from the Arrow Cross Party[26] (1,500 men, of which 500 were combat troops). Besides this, some army rear services and personnel from a military institute remained in Budapest, as well as militia battalions from the security forces, which did not take any part in the city's defense. Also, a significant part of the enumerated unit's muster rolls did not actually participate in the defense and many of them deserted. Thus at the end of December 1944 a battalion from the 12th Reserve Division consisted of 30-40 men, while the remainder had deserted, although nobody searched for them. In the same manner, part of the police battalions received rations, but nevertheless took no part in the fighting and, at best, only maintained order in the rear areas. And those Hungarians who were listed as combat troops, preferred to avoid combat operations, rightly believing that the war was already lost. The soldier and officers of the 1st Panzer Division, in particular, took no part in the fighting. The combat value of the Hungarian garrison in Budapest was extremely small, and those who really wanted to fight— Szalasi supporters, students from the university battalions and other Budapest volunteers had not, as a rule, been trained for combat. The overall strength of those Hungarians who could more or less be classified as servicemen according to their status and functions, in Ungvary's opinion, did not exceed 38,100, of which only 13,050 were combat troops. Of this number, half of the soldiers did not even have basic military training, while one out of six fought in units that had been formed during the siege. They disposed of 37-39 tanks and assault guns, 250-260 field and 55 anti-tank guns. However, for example, after 30 December the 2nd Regiment's 4th Artillery Battery did not fire a single shell, although shells were available. In Ungvary's expression, "a large part of the

---

26   Editor's note. The Arrow Cross Party was a political party of the national socialist type which arose in Hungary during the 1930s with a mixed message of anti-capitalism, anti-communism and anti-Semitism. Following Horthy's overthrow by the Germans, the Arrow Cross Party ruled Hungary from October 1944 to March 1945. Several of its leaders were convicted of war crimes after the war.

Hungarian military command during the siege only created the impression of carrying out its service obligations. In carrying out its duties, it sought to minimize losses among the Hungarians."

Well, here the Hungarian historian is correct. In wars large nations seek to win, or, at a minimum, not to lose, while small ones seek to survive.

The German units, which were defending Budapest, were also not distinguished by a high level of combat capability, while in conditions of the siege the overall numbers of forces and their combat strength were almost identical. The following German formations and units ended up in Budapest: the 8th SS Cavalry Division "Florian Geyer" (about 8,000 men), the "Maria Theresa" 22nd SS Cavalry Division (11,345 men), units of the *Feldherrnhalle* Motorized Division (7,255 men), the 13th Panzer Division (4,983 men), units of the 271st *Volksgrenadier* Division (about 1,000 men), the 1st SS Police Regiment (about 700 men), a battalion of heavy anti-aircraft artillery (about 100 men), other combat groups (about 1,500 men), the 12th Assault Anti-Aircraft Artillery Regiment (about 1,000 men), the 573rd Anti-Aircraft Artillery Battalion (about 200 men), the "Europa" Battalion (about 300 men), training battalions (about 200 men), other non-combat groups (about 2,500 men), and units of the IX SS Mountain Infantry Corps (about 1,500 men) and the sick and wounded who remained in Budapest (1,500 men). In all, there were approximately 42,600 Germans in Budapest, or 41,100 when not counting the sick and wounded. They disposed of 87 tanks and assault guns and 234 field and 62 anti-tank guns. In all, taking into account the Hungarian garrison, there were 79,000 defenders in Budapest, with 125 tanks and assault guns, 489 field and anti-aircraft guns, and 117 anti-tank guns.

Half of the German garrison in Budapest was not distinguished by any particular combat capability. The 8th and 22nd SS cavalry divisions consisted primarily of Hungarian Germans with only a smattering of military training (there were also no small number of Romanian *Volksdeutsche*[27] in the 8th Division). Before October 1944 only the 8th SS Cavalry Division, which had gotten into an encirclement and which far from being at full strength, had any combat experience, but it had earlier been mainly used for anti-partisan operations.

Two other divisions—*Feldherrnhalle* and the 13th Panzer—were far more capable, but they, just like the "Florian Geyer" Division, were not in Budapest in full strength (the *Feldherrnhalle* panzer battalion had avoided encirclement).

The German command refused to declare Budapest an open city and there was no place to evacuate the million-strong population of the Hungarian capital.

At the time of the encirclement there were 450 tons of munitions, 120 tons of fuel and a five-day supply of food for the more than 800,000 residents who remained in the city. To be sure, the inhabitants had some supplies of their own. The garrison required 80 tons of food per day, of which only 47 tons were delivered by air, which accounted for a little more than 500 grams of food for each serviceman (and this was in conditions that the 800,000-strong civilian population fed exclusively on the Holy Ghost. Moreover, the besieged ate 25,000 horses that remained without forage. From all appearances, the official data on food supplies were underestimated and some kinds of unaccounted-for supplies remained in the city. Otherwise, it is incomprehensible how the population of Budapest did not die from hunger in almost two months of blockade. The airfields capable of handling Ju-52[28] transport aircraft had been seized by Soviet troops as early as the end of December. Transport aircraft could also land on the race course that remained in German hands until 9 January, when Romanian forces captured it. From this day there was no more evacuation

---

27   Editor's note. This term refers to those ethnic Germans living outside the boundaries of the German state.
28   Editor's note. The Ju-52 was a German-tri-motor transport plane which first appeared in 1931. During the Second World War the plane was used to transport freight and paratroopers and was also employed as a medium bomber.

of wounded from Budapest (3,800 wounded had already accumulated by this time) and supplies were primarily dropped from the air. Food was delivered by 73 DFS-200 type gliders, of which 32 were shot down, as well as by small "Fiesler Storch"[29] communications aircraft. On the best days 93 were unloaded, which enabled them to carry 86 percent of all necessary freight. In all, 1,975 tons of supplies were delivered or dropped during the siege.

According to K. Ungvary's estimate, the Second Ukrainian Front's forces lost about 80,000 men during 1-25 November. This estimate is based on data that during this period the average combat strength of the *front's* divisions fell, on the average, from 5,500 to 4,500 men, while 40,000 reinforcements were received. We should note that the real losses could be even greater, insofar as in practice the decline of strength in the combat subunits was partially compensated by reducing the strength of the rear organs. On 1 November the Second Ukrainian Front had 44 rifle divisions, including one Romanian—the "Tudor Vladimescu"—as well as two fortified areas, three cavalry, three tank, and four mechanized corps. Excluding the Romanian division and assuming that two fortified areas are approximately equal to a rifle division, that the strength of a cavalry corps is approximately equal to the strength of a rifle division, that the strength of a tank corps is approximately equal to 1.2 rifle divisions, and that the strength of a mechanized corps is 1.6 times greater than the strength of a rifle division, the overall reduction of combat strength in these formations, not counting artillery, engineer and independent tank and mechanized units and formations, may be about 58,000 men. Taking into account reinforcements, the front's overall losses during 1-25 November 1944 may be calculated at approximately 98,000 men, and by taking into account losses from other units—no less than 100,000 men.

Again, according to K. Ungvary's calculations, the overall number of troops from the Second Ukrainian Front which took a direct part in the storming of Budapest was 177,000 men, not counting reinforcements and the Romanian 7th Army Corps, which numbered 36,000 men.

The strength of the Budapest garrison, according to ration strength, fell from 79,000 on 24 December 1944 to 70,000 on 3 January 1945, to 45,000 by 20 January 1945, and to 32,000 by 11 February, at the time of the breakthrough. On these dates the combat units numbered, correspondingly, 35,000, 30,000, 16,000, and 11,000 men.

On 24 December the opposing Soviet and Romanian forces numbered 156,000 men, including 85,000 combat troops. On 3 January their strength had fallen to 145,000 men (80,000 combat troops), to 80,000 (40,000) on 20 January, and 75,000 (36,000) on 11 February. It seems to us that Ungvary is lowering the Soviet forces' combat strength, which when taking into account reinforcements, which were dispatched only to the combat units, reached no less than 60 percent of overall strength. When taking this into account, the Soviets actually enjoyed a numerical superiority of 3-4:1 in combat units. Actually, it was even greater, when taking into account the serious shortage of munitions among the besieged, their absence of support from the air, the low combat capability of the Hungarian forces, which accounted for a third of their combat strength, and the low combat capability of half of the German forces. In Budapest the Hungarians were significantly inferior in combat capability to the Soviet forces, as well as the Romanian ones, while the soldiers of the two SS cavalry divisions were approximately equal, according to their combat capability, to the Soviet troops, while only the soldiers of the other SS units, as well as the panzer and motorized divisions, were superior in combat capability to the opposing Soviet and Romanian troops.

There were incidents of theft in Budapest among the German troops, but they were sufficiently harshly suppressed by the command and concerned only foodstuffs. One German soldier was

---

29   Editors note. The Fieseler F-156 Storch was a single-engine passenger aircraft which first appeared in 1936. During the Second World War it was used as a light passenger and reconnaissance plane.

sentenced to death for stealing a half kilo of coffee, but Pfeffer-Wildenbruch[30] changed death by firing squad to ten days in the guardhouse, taking into account the insignificance of the theft. Food was requisitioned in those quarters occupied by Soviet forces. Either nothing was paid for this, or vouchers were handed out, with which it was very difficult to purchase anything with later.

Malinovskii did not hurry to take Budapest, so as to avoid increasing Soviet losses for no good reason. On 1 January 1945 the 30th Rifle and 18th Guards Rifle corps took part in storming the city, as did the Romanian 7th Army Corps, for a total of seven rifle divisions, two Romanian infantry divisions, and one Romanian cavalry divisions, supported by several tens of tanks, self-propelled guns and 1,037 guns, which yielded a more than threefold superiority in artillery over the German-Hungarian garrison. Actually, their superiority was even greater, because the defenders had few munitions, particularly in heavy-caliber artillery. On 11 January the troops operating in the city were unified into Group Budapest, headed by the commander of the 18th Independent Rifle Corps, Lieutenant General Ivan Mikhailovich Afonin. On 24 January he was severely wounded and replaced by Lieutenant General Ivan Mefod'evich Managarov.

The Romanian 7th Corps was pulled out of Budapest on 15 January. It had lost 2,548 killed and wounded in the immediate fighting in the city. According to Soviet data, which is possibly understated, during 1-10 January 1945 the 18th Guards Rifle Corps lost 791 killed, 50 missing in action, one died for non-combat reasons, 2,567 wounded, and 72 sick soldiers evacuated. The tank units attached to it lost 20 tanks irreparably. From 18 January, following the occupation of Pest by Soviet forces, the storming of Buda began. It was conducted by the 18th, 37th and 75th guards rifle corps, which numbered 11 rifle divisions and one brigade of naval infantry. By 1 February they were being supported by 650 field and 134 anti-tank guns, 589 mortars, and 24 rocket-powered shell platforms ("Katyusha"). During February 1-10 the Budapest group of Soviet forces, according to possibly underreported data, lost 1,044 men, killed, 52 missing in action, four died of non-combat-related causes, 3,407 wounded, and 276 sick. Nine tanks were lost irretrievably and three damaged.

On 27 January Hitler authorized the Budapest group to break out of the encirclement, if necessary. On 9 February the fuhrer issued his final authorization for the breakout.

Taking into account the fact that the Soviet forces operating in Budapest were not inferior to the enemy in combat capability, and were even superior to the Hungarians, the situation with regard to street fighting was completely different than in Stalingrad. Also, the Soviets were superior in artillery, aviation, tanks, and ammunition supply. Thus is was more advantageous for Malinovskii's forces to be involved in street fighting than to fight in the field, and their losses in Budapest probably did not exceed those of the enemy.

Lieutenant General Aleksandr Ivanovich Mal'chevskii, who commanded the 110th Guards Rifle Division during 1944-45, testified about this period in the fighting to liberate Czechoslovakia:

> The commander of the Second Ukrainian Front, Marshal Rodion Malinovskii, in bidding me farewell, emphasized in particular, "Your job is to carry out my assignment and to spare people. I demand that you spare the soldiers and to always cover them with fire. I'm going to severely demand an accounting for losses. If you can get by with just fire, don't send people there." To tell the truth, in three years of war I heard this demand for the first time. That's the way I remember this commander—equable, calm and not one to raise his voice to his

---

30   Editor's note. Karl Pfeffer-Wildenbruch (1888-1971) joined the army in 1907 and served in the First World War in Mesopotamia and France. During the Second World War he commanded an SS police division and SS corps. He commanded the Axis garrison in Budapest until his capture. The Soviets released Pfeffer-Wildenbruch in 1955.

subordinates. It was striking how sparingly, respectfully, tactfully, and, in the fullest sense of the word, humanely he treated people. He never lost his presence of mind and did not lose his self control.

In January the Germans, with the aid of the IV SS Panzer Corps, undertook an attempt to relieve Budapest. The flat area in the Szekesfehervar area, to the southwest of the Hungarian capital, was more suitable for tank operations. However, the transfer of two panzer divisions there would have required five extra days and a significant expenditure of deficit fuel compared to the offensive variant from positions northwest of Budapest, where, however, the tanks would have to attempt to overcome mountainous terrain. Taking into account the time factor, the German command chose the northwestern variant. The operation to relieve Budapest was given the code name "Conrad."

It began on the evening of 1 January 1945. The IV SS Panzer Corps (the 3rd SS Panzer Division *Totenkopf*), 5th SS Panzer Division *Wiking*, and the 96th Infantry Division attacked from the Tata area (east of Komarno) in the direction of Budapest. Two thirds of *Totenkopf's* subunits took part in the offensive and only a third of *Wiking's* subunits. At the time the 96th Infantry Division had only a little more than 40 percent of its forces. The missing units arrived only on 6 January.

The Hungarian command's proposal to employ the Hungarian 1st Hussar, 2nd Panzer and 23rd Reserve divisions in the offensive was rejected due to their complete lack of combat worth. Their participation in "Conrad" was limited to two Hungarian battalions from combat group "Ney."

On 6 January the Third Ukrainian Front committed its reserves into the fighting. On 7 January the 5th SS Panzer Division *Wiking* took Czabdi, but was halted by the 18th Tank Corps near Bicske, 28 kilometers from Budapest. The attempt to encircle ten Soviet divisions was not successful.

None the less, Tolbukhin saw the situation as critical. He did not exclude the breakthrough of the encirclement ring and the withdrawal by Soviet troops from Budapest. The marshal ordered the creation of defensive lines with anti-tank guns.

By the start of the offensive the 3rd SS Panzer Division *Totenkopf* had 16 Panzer IVs,[31] 29 "Panthers,"[32] 11 "Tigers,"[33] and about 20 "Jagdpanzer-IVs,"[34] and four assault guns. Combat group Pape had 59 "Panthers," 20 "Jagdpanzer-IVs" and five "Jagdpanzer-38s."[35] The opposing Soviet 18th Tank Corps had (120 T-34s, 19 IS-2s[36] and 11 SU-85s[37]), 1st Guards Mechanized Corps (62 SU-100s and 184 "Shermans"[38]) and 2nd Guards Mechanized Corps (35 T-34s, eight IS-2s and

---

31   Editor's note. The Panzer IV was a German medium tank that first appeared in 1939. One model weighed 25 tons and had a crew of five. It was armed with a 75mm gun and two 7.92 machine guns.

32   Editor's note. The Panzer V ("Panther") was a German medium tank which first appeared in 1943. One model weighed 44.8 tons and carried a crew of five. It was armed with a 75mm gun and two 7.92mm machine guns.

33   Editor's note. The Panzer VI ("Tiger") was a German heavy tank which first appeared in 1943. One model weighed 54 tons and carried a crew of five. It was armed with an 88mm gun and two 7.92 machine guns.

34   Editor's note. The Jagdpanzer IV was a German tank destroyer vehicle mounted on a Panzer IV chassis and which first appeared in 1943. One model weighed 25.8 tons and carried a crew of four. It was armed with a 75mm gun and a 7.92mm machine gun.

35   Editor's note. The Jagdpanzer 38 was a German light tank destroyer mounted on a prewar Czech tank chassis. It first appeared in 1944 and weighed 15.75 tons, while carrying a crew of four. It was armed with a 75mm gun and a 7.92mm machine gun.

36   Editor's note. The IS-2 (Iosif Stalin) was a Soviet heavy tank which first appeared in 1944. One model weighed 46 tons and carried a crew of four. It was armed with a 122mm gun and three 7.62mm machine guns.

37   Editor's note. The SU-85 was a Soviet self-propelled gun which first appeared in 1943. One model weighed 29.6 tons and carried a crew of four. It was armed with an 85mm gun.

38   Editor's note. The M-4 "Sherman" was a US-made medium tank which first appeared in 1942. One model

11 SU-85s). During 1-7 January the IV SS Panzer Corps lost 529 killed, 2,652 wounded and 358 missing in action, and 39 destroyed and damaged tanks and assault guns.

On 8 January the second attempt to relieve the forces encircled in Budapest began, and within three days a thaw began and the roads became almost impassable. A panzer group from the 1st Panzer Division, the 23rd Panzer Division, 4th Cavalry Brigade, Weimann's panzer group, the *Feldherrnhalle* Division's panzer battalion, and the 3rd Panzer Division took part in the new offensive as well. They disposed of three Panzer-IIs,[39] 30 Panzer-IVs, 48 "Panthers," six "King Tigers,"[40] 24 assault guns, and five "Jagdpanzer-IVs."

On 6 January Malinovskii's forces counterattacked toward Komarom (Komarno) and on 8 January were at the city's walls. At this time Soviet tanks were already near Kisafelda, from where the road to Bratislava and Vienna opened.

On 9 January General Breith's German III Panzer Corps, consisting of the 1st, 3rd and 23rd panzer divisions and the 503rd Heavy Panzer Battalion, attacked. However, it was halted near Zamoy on 12 January.

On 9 January a new offensive on Esztergom began by General Gelle's corps. The newly-arrived 711th Infantry Division managed to take Dobogoko. The 3rd and 5th SS panzer divisions' combat groups crossed the crest of the Pilis Mountains, where they were halted. On 11 January the *Wiking* Division took Pilisszentkereszt, and on 12 January reached Csobanka, 17 kilometers from Budapest, but received orders to fall back, because the Army Group South command feared that Gille's corps would end up in the Pilis sack in the event of a Soviet offensive.

On the night of 12-13 January units of the IV SS Panzer Corps abandoned their positions and began to move under their own power 100 kilometers to the south, to the area east of Veszprem. On 15 January there was a frost and the roads became iced over, which was somewhat easier for armored equipment than the mud of the thaw.

Four panzer divisions (3rd SS Panzer Division *Totenkopf*, 5th SS Panzer Division *Wiking*, and the 1st and 3rd panzer divisions) were united in the IV SS Panzer Corps to take part in the final attempt to relieve Budapest. The offensive began on 18 January along the front between Sarkeresztur and Lake Balaton. On 19 January German tanks reached the Danube in the Dunapentele area. The Soviet 133rd Rifle and 18th Tank corps were encircled, but Gille had no infantry to creat a solid encirclement ring and the Soviet forces easily got out of the non-existent ring.

On 20 January *Totenkopf's* panzer subunits advanced to the northeast along the southern shore of Lake Velence through Gardony and by evening had reached the outskirts of Kis Velence. At the same time a detachment from *Wiking* reached the village and railroad junction of Szabolcs.

On 23 January the 1st Panzer Division and the "Ney" Hungarian combat group occupied Szekesfehervar. Soviet forces counterattacked the forward detachments of the 3rd and 5th SS panzer divisions. The 3rd SS Panzer Division *Totenkopf* halted near the village of Baracska, seizing its southern part on 24 January. Units of the 5th SS Panzer Division *Wiking* seized Ivancsa and reached the Vali River, where they were halted by Soviet artillery.

The 509th Heavy Panzer Battalion, which was armed with "King Tigers," attempted to force the Vali. It was unable to seize the northeastern part of Baracska, having encountered powerful

---

weighed 30.3 tons and carried a crew of five. It was armed with a 75mm gun, a 50 caliber machine gun and two 30.06 machine guns. The tanks referred to here were probably obtained by the Red Army through Lend-Lease.

39 Editor's note. The Panzer II was a light German tank which first appeared in 1936. One model weighed 8.9 tons and carried a crew of three. It was armed with a 20mm gun and a 7.92mm machine gun.

40 Editor's note. The Tiger II ("King Tiger") was a heavy German tank which first appeared in 1944. One model weighed 68.5 tonsand carried a crew of five. It was armed with an 88mm gun and two 7.92mm machine guns.

fire from Soviet anti-tank guns. However, the 3rd Panzer Division took the town of Dunapentele on 25 January.

As early as 21 January Soviet sappers had destroyed the crossings in the Dunapentele and Dunafoldvar areas, in order to keep the Germans from reaching the eastern bank.

On 27 January the Soviet counteroffensive along the southern sector of the front between the Sarviz and the Danube began, while in the north Soviet forces forced the Vali River and committed the 23rd Tank Corps, which had lost more than 122 tanks, into the fighting.

During the night of 27-28 January orders were received to call of operation "Conrad." Units of the IV SS Panzer Corps fell back to the Bakony Forest to the north of Lake Balaton.

According to official and obviously understated data, the 4th Guards Army, which repelled the attempts to relieve Budapest, lost in January 1945 3,588 killed, 4,543 missing in action, 132 dead from non-combat related reasons, 11,552 wounded, and 1,682 evacuated sick. During this same time the 5th Guards Cavalry Corps lost 2,165 men, the 18th Tank Corps lost 1,740 men, and the 23rd Tank Corps 313 killed and 659 wounded.

During the repulse of the three German offensives within the confines of operation "Conrad," the Third Ukrainian Front's losses were about 60,000 wounded, about 15,000 killed and 5,100 taken prisoner, while the German-Hungarian forces lost during the course of the operation about 26,000 wounded, about 8,000 killed and about 1,000 taken prisoner.

On 23 January 1945 Army Group South's armored group was distributed in the following manner:

> 23rd Panzer Division—2 Panzer-IVs, six "Panthers," three assault guns, and eight "Jagdpanzer-IVs".
> 4th Cavalry Brigade—one Panzer-IV and nine "Jagdpanzer-IVs."
> Hungarian 2nd Armored Division—26 Panzer-IVs, three "Jagdpanzer-IVs and four assault guns.
> 6th Panzer Division—12 Panzer-IVs, four "Panthers" and four "Jagdpanzer-IVs".
> 96th Infantry Division—three assault guns.
> 711th Infantry Division—seven "Jagdpanzer-IVs".
> 3rd Cavalry Division—eight "Jagdpanzer-IVs."
> The Stauwasser Regimental Group—one assault gun and one "Jagdpanzer-IV."
> The 211th *Volksgrenadier* Division—11 "Jagdpanzer-IVs."
> 8th Panzer Division—three Panzer-IVs, one "Panther" and two "Jagdpanzer-IVs."
> 3rd Panzer Division—nine Panzer-IVs, 12 "Panthers," eight "Jagdpanzer-IVs," and four assault guns.
> 5th SS Panzer Division—three Panzer-IVs, five "Panthers" and four "Jagdpanzer-IVs."
> 3rd SS Panzer Division—three Panzer-IVs, five "Panthers" and four "Jagdpanzer-IVs."
> 1st Panzer Division—25 "Panthers" and seven "Jagdpanzer-IVs."

There is no data regarding the armored equipment of the IX SS Mountain Corps, the *Feldherrnhalle* Panzer Division, 13th Panzer Division, 8th SS "Florian Geyer" Cavalry Division, and the 22nd SS "Maria Theresa" Cavalry Division, which were encircled in Budapest.

In all, this amounted to 274 tanks and assault guns.

On the evening of 11 February Pfeffer-Wildenbruch, the commandant of Budapest, sent out his final report:

> All food supplies have been expended and our ammunition will soon be exhausted. There remains a choice between capitulation and ending the battle for Budapest. For this reason, I'm undertaking an offensive operation with the last combat-capable units of the German

army, the Honved[41] and the Arrow Cross Party units. I will begin the breakout on February, with the onset of darkness. I plan to exit the encirclement between Szomor and Mariahalom. If this is not successful, then the attack will be launched along the Pilis Mountains. I request you prepare to meet us northwest of Piliszentlelek. The recognition signals are two green rockets to designate friendly troops. The forces at hand are 23,900 Germans, of which 9,600 are wounded, and 20,000 Hungarians, of which 2,000 are wounded.

After this, the German radio stations were destroyed.
Here is the historic report on the capture of Budapest, written by Malinovskii in his own hand:

In code over Baudot communications system
Moscow
To Comrade Semyonov
The Second Ukrainian Front's Extraordinary Combat Report
13 February 1945
1200 hrs
200,000:1 map

I report that the front's left-wing forces, having broken through a series of heavily fortified defensive lines, both on the approaches and within the city of Budapest, as a result of many days of bitter street fighting, took every building and block by storm, and by 1000 on 13 February of this year routed the encircled enemy group of forces, consisting of the IX SS Army Corps—the German 13th Panzer Division, the *Feldherrnhalle* Motorized Division, the 8th and 22nd SS cavalry divisions, and the 271st Infantry Division (minus the 979th Infantry Regiment), the 239th Assault Gun Brigade, the 1st Police Regiment, and 127th Motorized Sapper Brigade, the Hungarian I Army Corps, the 10th and 12th infantry divisions, the "Saint Laszlo" Infantry Division, independent subunits of the 9th, 19th and 20th infantry divisions, the 1st Panzer Division, the University Battalion, four gendarme battalions, a battalion from the "Louis" Military Academy, the "Vona" combat group, the "Vigaros" combat group, the "Volod" Battalion, the 201st, 202nd, 203rd, and 204th anti-aircraft battalions, independent detachments of Szalasite Hungarians, and German and Hungarian army and corps subunits, and completely captured the capital of Hungary—the city of Budapest—an extremely important rail and road junction in Europe, a major port along the Danube, and the chief center for all of Hungarian industry.

During the fighting to capture the city of Budapest the front's forces killed and destroyed the following from the encircled enemy group of forces: 49,982 soldiers and officers, 203 tanks and self-propelled guns, 367 guns of various caliber, 253 armored cars and armored transports, 490 mortars, 1,591 machine guns, and 189 aircraft.

According to incomplete data, we captured the following: 127,202 soldiers and officers, including the commander of the Budapest group of forces, SS Colonel General Pfeffer-Wildenbruch and his chief of staff, Colonel Lindenau, the commander of the 10th Infantry Division, Colonel Legotsky Laios, the quartermaster of the Hungarian Air Force, Major General Csanjasi Imre, 15 colonels, 19 lieutenant colonels and 12 majors who occupied various positions, three colonel generals, three lieutenant generals, and seven retired major generals; 269 tanks and self-propelled guns, 1,257 guns of various calibers, 83 armored cars and armored transports, 476 mortars, 1,434 machine guns, 41,000 rifles and automatic rifles,

---

41   Editor's note. This refers to the Hungarian Army.

15 aircraft, 194 locomotives, 9,475 train cars, 30 fuel tanks, 195 grenade launchers, 1,326 motorcycles, 32 gliders, 5,153 motor vechicles, 7,585 horses, 3,925 carts with various military equipment, and 46 depots with various military equipment.

This was followed by a list of names of unit and formation commanders who had distinguished themselves in the fighting for Budapest.

In combat reports nos. 0047 and 0048, which were sent at 2325 on 13 February and 2315 on 14 February, the same destroyed units and subunits from the German and Hungarian armies were listed, although at the same time a number of corrections were made. For example, in the first of these it was reported that "individual small enemy groups are being successfully destroyed in the woods northwest of the city of Budapest," and that

during 13.2.45 up to 17,000 prisoners, belonging to the German 8th and 22nd SS cavalry divisions, the 13th Panzer Division, the *Feldherrnhalle* Mechanized Division, and 271st Infantry Division, and the Hungarian 10th, 12th and 24th infantry divisions, were captured in Buda and northwest of Buda. Among the prisoners was the commander of the Hungarian I Army Corps, Colonel General Hindy (commander of the Hungarian garrison in Budapest), the commander of the Hungarian 12th Infantry Division, Major General Bauman, the commandant of the city of Budapest, Major General Csinkes Erno, and the commander of the IX SS Army Corps' artillery, Colonel Ernst Leding.

In report No. 0048 it was noted that "our forces were fighting along the left flank with an enemy group that had broken through, in the woods northwest of Budapest, and by the close of the day had basically completed its destruction," and that

during 14.2.45 256 prisoners belonging to the German 13th Panzer Division, the *Feldherrnhalle* Motorized Division, the 15th, 76th, 211th, and 271st infantry divisions, the 101st Mountain Infantry Division, and the 8th and 22nd SS cavalry divisions, and the Hungarian 5th, 10th, 12th, and 24th infantry divisions. Among those captured were the chief of staff of the Hungarian I Army Corps, Colonel Horvath, the commander of the 8th Cavalry Division's 16th Cavalry Regiment, Major Hoening Gall. Corpses were found on the battlefield that were identified by the prisoners and captured documents as the commander of the 22nd SS Cavalry Division, Major General Seichender, and the commander of the 8th SS Cavalry Division, Major General Joachim Rumohr.

Malinovskii's adjutant, A.I. Fedenev, recalled:

Budapest cost our Second Ukrainian Front dearly... And when they sing the song to Isakovskii's[42] poem, "The Enemies Have Burned my Native Hut," tears come to your eyes when you hear these lines:
"I spent four years coming to you,
"I subdued three powers..."
And all of us comrades-in-arms recall that this poem is about a soldier from our front:
"'And on his chest there glistened
"The medal for the city of Budapest."

42 Editor's note. Mikhail Vasil'evich Isakovskii (1900-73) was a Soviet-era poet, many of whose works were later set to music.

Rodion Yakovlevich said that this was the best of the war songs—the saddest and most truthful.

On a page in *The Iasi—Kishinev Cannae*, next to the phrase "We believe that Friessner worries not so much about Fretter-Pico's honor as about his own," Malinovskii underlined Fretter-Pico's name and made the following entry: "By the way, let it be known that this unlucky SS general was captured near Budapest in extremely confusing conditions. He was pulled by our soldiers out of a sewage pipe, in which he wanted to get away from encircled Budapest, in a soldier's body warmer, with all the accompanying smells, and before we could interrogate him, we had to sanitize him. This alone is enough to characterize Friessner's fascist general."

However, in this case, Rodion Yakovlevich was mistaken. Neither the commander of the Sixth Army, General Maximilian Fretter-Pico, nor the commander of Army Group South, Colonel General Johannes Friessner, served in the SS and were not captured by the Soviets. They were removed from their posts in December 1944, long before the fall of Budapest, and were captured by the Americans. Another general entirely was captured in Budapest in circumstances described by Malinovskii—the commander of the Budapest garrison, Karl von Pfeffer-Wildenbruch, whose surname was written next to Malinovskii's note by an unknown editor. He was an SS obergruppenfuehrer and SS and police general and remained in Soviet captivity until 1955. The episode about his capture was moved to the section about the liberation of Hungary from another book, *Budapest—Vienna—Prague*, which also appeared under Malinovskii's editorship in 1965. Here it sounds as follows:

> The commander of the encircled group of forces, General Pfeffer-Wildenbruch, and his staff, attempted to escape from the encirclement. No, his path lay not along the surface of the earth, because shells from Soviet artillery were still ringing, while the motors of Soviet assault aircraft still howled in the air, while Soviet infantrymen were still combing the hilly terrain of Buda. The general chose another path—a large sewage pipe. He managed to get to the surface through it and he considered himself safe. But Soviet soldiers appeared and the commander of the encircled group of forces, which had ceased to exist, raised his hands. I should note that the journey through the sewage pipe had left on him such traces that before talking with him we had to prepare a bath for him, in the literal sense of that word.

I should note that Skorzeny, describing in his memoirs how Horthy found refuge in the headquarters of Karl von Pfeffer-Wildenbruch on the morning of 16 December, reports that Pfeffer-Wildenbruch was on friendly terms with the last German Kaiser, Wilhelm II and resembled him to an amazing degree, directly hinting that this SS general could have been Wilhelm II's out-of-wedlock son. In principle, one cannot exclude this, as Pfeffer-Wildenbruch was born in 1888 in the Berlin suburb of Kalkberge.

Of the 28,000 Germans and Hungarians who attempted to break out of Budapest, approximately 800 soldiers and officers were able to do so, including approximately 700 Germans and 80 Hungarians, of which 44 were civilians. According to K. Ungvary's calculations, about 19,250 German and Hungarian servicemen died in trying to break out, while approximately 22,350 were captured. About 40,000 civilians became victims of the fighting and hunger in Budapest. Besides this, between 15 October 1944 and 13 February 1945 the number of Jews in Budapest fell by 105,500 people. The majorty of them were deported to Germany by the German security organs, with the assistance of the government and the Arrow Cross Party, and many became victims of the Szalasists' terror. Approximately 6,000 Jews died from hunger during the siege and 7,000 ended up in Soviet captivity.

The Swedish diplomat Rauol Wallenberg[43] saved approximately 20,000 Jews from Budapest from death and deportation, supplying them with temporary Swedish passports. On 17 January 1945 the deputy people's defense commissar, N.A. Bulganin, ordered Malinovskii to arrest Wallenberg, who had established contact with Soviet forces on 13 January, and to deliver him to Moscow. It's possible that Stalin suspected that Wallenberg was involved in separate contacts between Germany and the Western Allies, and when that assumption was not confirmed, he preferred to get rid of him as an unwanted witness. Wallenberg was arrested on 19 January and sent to Moscow on 25 January 1945. In all probability, he was killed (probably poisoned) in the Lubyanka prison between 23 July and 15 October 1947. Of course, in arresting and sending the Swedish diplomat to Moscow, Rodion Yakovlevich could not know what kind of tragic fate awaited Wallenberg. Nor could Malinovskii not carry out an order by the deputy defense commissar, behind which Stalin himself probably stood.

I should note that soldiers from Tolbukhin's Third Ukrainian Front carried out one of the most notorious of the Red Army's crimes in Hungary—the shooting of 32 Hungarians and *Volksdeutsche*, aged 16 to 50, in the village of Olasfalu on 22 March 1945. However, in this particular case this is not significant, because many armies passed from the Second Ukrainian Front to the Third Ukrainian Front and back. The soldiers in both *fronts*, just like in the remaining Soviet *fronts*, were essentially the same.

According to Ungvary's calculations, between 3 November 1944 and 11 February 1945 the Second and Third Ukrainian fronts lost about 130,000 wounded, about 44,000 killed and about 2,000 captured during the fighting for Budapest, while the Romanians lost about 12,000 wounded, about 11,000 killed, and about 1,000 captured. The German-Hungarian garrison's losses amounted to about 40,000 killed and 62,000 captured.

On 21 February 1945 Malinovskii, together with a large group of marshals and generals, was awarded for long service (more than 25 years of irreproachable service) a second time, and this time with the Order of Lenin. And only two weeks later serious trouble fell on his head.

On 6 March 1945, on the day of the beginning of a major German attack in the Lake Balaton area, a menacing directive was issued by the *Stavka*, which concerned Malinovskii's and Tolbukhin's *fronts*.

STAVKA OF THE VGK DIRECTIVE NO. 11036 TO THE *FRONT* COMMANDERS ON IMPROVING THE ORGANIZATION OF COMBAT OPERATIONS.
Copy: To the *Stavka* representative
6 March 1945, 0130 hrs

Lately on some *fronts* there have been incidents of carelessness and idleness, which the enemy has managed to take advantage of to launch perceptible surprise attacks against us. As a result of these attacks, our troops have been forced to retreat. The retreat in these cases was carried out in an unorganized manner, the troops suffered heavy losses in personnel and, in particular, equipment. For example:

1. The Second Ukrainian Front's 7th Guards Army, which was defending east of Komarno, upon being attacked by the enemy, was unable to repulse his offensive, despite the fact that it disposed of a sufficient number of men and materiel, abandoned its operationally important

---

43   Editor's note. Rauol Gustav Wallenberg (1912-47?) was a Swedish businessman and diplomat who saved thousands of Hungarian Jews from the Nazis and Szalasists, by providing them with false passports. He was arrested by Soviet authorities and transported to the Soviet Union, where he later died.

bridgehead (along the western bank of the Hron River) and lost 8,194 rank and file, 459 guns of various calibers (of these, 374 were 76mm or more) and 54 tanks and self-propelled guns.

Units of the Third Ukrainian Front's 26th Army, while attacking along the Sarviz Canal, penetrated 3-5 kilometers into the enemy's defense. The enemy, having launched a counterattack, broke through our attacking forces' combat formations, which lacked artillery support, without difficulty, because all of their artillery had been simultaneously removed from their positions and was moving forward. As a result of two days of fighting, units of the 26th Army's 133rd and 135th rifle corps lost 42 mortars and 90 guns of various calibers and were thrown back to their jumping-off positions.

The *Stavka* of the Supreme High Command considers that the incidents related here could have taken place only as a result of criminal carelessness, the poor organization of defense and the absence of reconnaissance and control on the part of the higher commanders and their staffs of the troops' situation and actions.

The commanders of the Second and Third Ukrainian fronts did not consider it necessary to report these shameful facts to the *Stavka*, evidently wishing to disguise them, and the General Staff had to gather this information from the *front* headquarters over the heads of the front commanders.

The *Stavka* points out to the commnader of the Second Ukrainian Front, Marshal of the Soviet Union Malinovskii, and the commander of the Third Ukrainian Front, Marshal of the Soviet Union Tolbukhin the poor control of the soldiers' actions, the unsatisfactory organization of intelligence and the inadmissibility of the report presented to the *Stavka* regarding the losses indicated above.

The Stavka orders:

    a)   the commander of the 7th Guards Army, Colonel General Shumilov, is to be reprimanded for carelessness and the poor organization of the defense;

    b)   the commanders of the Second and Third Ukrainian fronts are to conduct a thorough investigation of these incidents and hold the guilty parties responsible.

Report on the results of the investigation and the measures adopted.
Stavka of the Supreme High Command
I. STALIN, A. ANTONOV

What had brought on the Supreme Commander-in-Chief's anger? On 17 February the bridgehead aimed at Vienna, which was occupied by the 7th Guards Army, was attacked by the Sixth SS Panzer Army's I SS Panzer Corps, under the command of Obergruppenfuehrer Hermann Priss. Soviet, British and American intelligence had failed to spot the transfer of this army from the Western Front to Hungary. The I Corps consisted of the 1st SS Panzer Division *Leibstandarte Adolph Hitler* and the 12th SS *Hitlerjugend* Division. By the start of the offensive, the *Leibstandarte*, according to the British military historian, Major General Michael Reynolds, numbered 19,000 men, 37 Panzer-IVs, 41 Panzer-V "Panthers," 21 tank destroyer "Jagdpanzer-IVs," three assault guns, 175 armored transports, and also 36 "King Tigers" from the 501st SS Heavy Panzer Battalion, which had been attached to the division. The *Hitlerjugend* division numbered 17,000 men, 38 Panzer-IVs, 44 "Panthers," 21 "Jagdpanzer-IVs," and 165 armored transports, as well as 21 "Jagdpanzer-IVs" and 16 "Panthers" in the 560 SS Heavy Tank Destroyer Battalion, which had been attached to the division. In all, this amounted to 278 tanks and assault guns, which were four armored vehicles more than the 274 tanks and assault guns in Army Group South on 23 January 1945.

However, this data appears exaggerated regarding the personnel strength of the German divisions. According to the final report on the *Hitlerjugend* division, during the fighting on the Eastern

Front from 10 February through 8 May 1945, it lost 96 officers (53 killed and missing in action), 380 NCOs (125 killed) and 3,900 soldiers (1,320 killed and missing in action), for a total of 4,376 men (1,498 killed and missing in action). At the same time, within the confines of the overall capitulation near the town of Enns, southeast of Linz (Austria), 328 officers, 1,698 NCOs and 7,844 soldiers surrendered to the American 65th Infantry Division, for a total of 9,870 soldiers from the 12th *Hitlerjugend* Division. Taking into account the losses on 10 February 1945, there should have been approximately 14,246 men in the division, but by no means 17,000. It's likely that the strength of the *Leibstandarte* Division, which could have had 16-16,500 men by 10 February, was increased by Reynolds to the same degree.

The fact of the matter is that the German divisions' paper strength also included wounded, sick and missing in action for the last four weeks. And the Sixth SS Panzer Army's divisions arrived on the Eastern Front following the Ardennes offensive, in which they suffered significant losses, including wounded and missing in action. By taking into account these losses, the *Leibstandarte's* paper strength exceeded its authorized strength by 1,000 men.

This figure probably does not include "Hiwis"—"volunteer helpers," of former Soviet citizens, who carried out rear-area functions that did not involve carrying arms. On 20 September 1944, before the Ardennes offensive, there were 1,029 "Hiwis" in the *Leibstandarte*. There were evidently no "Hiwis" in the *Hitlerjugend* division, which had not fought on the Eastern Front, before February 1945.

About 10,000 soldiers and officers (not counting "Hiwis") from *Leibstandarte* were captured by the Americans in the Steyr area.

And there was also somewhat less combat-ready armored equipment in the I SS Panzer Corps. The 560th SS Heavy Tank Destroyer Battalion did not take part in Operation "Südwind" ("South Wind") (the attack against the bridgehead near Hron) and without it there were 160 tanks and assault guns in the two SS divisions, of which only 102 were ready for combat by the start of the attack.

This is what Michael Reynolds writes about the Operation "Südwind": "On 13 February the headquarters of Army Group South issued an order to the commander of the German Eighth Army:

> Upon concentrating all available infantry and tanks strength, attack, even at the expense of weakening the remaining sectors of the front, along with the recently-arrived I Panzer Corps. Following a short artillery preparation, launch an attack from the north, in order to destroy the enemy forces on the bridgehead near the Hron River.
>
> Although the bridgehead had existed an entire month, the Germans did not have detailed information about Soviet forces and their location. The only thing they were able to establish, through the aid of aerial reconnaissance, was that the Russians were prepared for defense and that a mechanized corps was occupying the center of the bridgehead, while a guards mechanized corps and tank corps, which had been attached to the 6th Guards Tank Army, were probably stationed in the rear east of Hron. The Germans understood that in the event of necessity, these formations could rapidly appear on the bridgehead. The Germans also knew that the Russians had created a powerful anti-tank defensive zone to the west of Bruta and also that the Parisz Canal would enable them to flood the area. Although the roads had already begun to thaw out, they had not yet become soft. Two bridges over the Hron remained—near Bina and Kamenin.
>
> The Russians had actually concentrated far more troops than the Germans suspected. The 4th Guards Mechanized Corps was in reserve, while the 24th and 25th guards rifle corps, which totaled seven rifle divisions, occupied the bridgehead. Five of these divisions were located along the defensive perimeter, while two were in reserve positions. Although these

divisions were under strength, they nevertheless numbered about 60,000 men, 100-230 tanks and self-propelled guns, more than 100 anti-tank guns, about 200 heavy mortars, and 200 guns and howitzers.

Three German and one Hungarian division blocked the bridgehead, suppored by elements of the 13th Panzer Division.

The Germans decided correctly that the Soviet forces had gone over to the defensive. Although preparations for a new offensive had already begun, it was not supposed to start before the middle of March. The troops on the bridgehead were in constant danger, because this was a tiny bit of land, 20 by 20 kilometers, and behind them was a river up to 40 meters wide.

However, the Germans had enough problems of their own. It was simply impossible to launch an attack from the south over the Danube, while to the west the terrain was very difficult, and thus the Germans decided to launch an attack from the north, although here they were to come up against some difficulties as well. The Parisz Canal was the main obstacle, which was full of snow melt. At the end of the operation, the attacking troops would be drawn into a narrow corridor between the ridge south of Luba and the Danube.

It was planned to carry out Operation "South Wind" with the forces of the *Feldherrnhalle* Panzer Corps. This corps consisted of three divisions and a whole 25 tanks (although, these were "King Tiger" tanks from the corps' heavy tank battalion). Its first task was to seize the commanding heights, particularly height 190 south of Svodin. However, the villages of Svodin and Bruta had to be taken through an attack from the rear, and it was strictly forbidden to get involved in fighting there, in order not to slow down the offensive to the south. The I SS Panzer Corps was supposed to follow behind *Feldherrnhalle*. Following the forcing of the Parisz Canal, it had been ordered to seize the ridge running to the east from Gbelce, and then turn toward the Danube and Sturovo. The "Hupe" reinforced combat group was to cross over the Danube from the south and create a small bridgehead near Obida.

As a result of Operation "Südwind," which lasted from 17-24 February 1945, the Soviet bridgehead beyoond the Hron River was eliminated and the forces of Lieutenant General Mikhail Stepanovich Shumilov's 7th Guards Army, which were defending it, suffered heavy losses.

Two panzer corps—the I SS and *Feldherrnhalle* (the latter was commanded by General Ulrich Kleeman)—which had been subordinated to General Hans Kreysing's Eighth Army—took part in the operation. The corps consisted of six divisions: 1st and 2nd SS panzer, 44th *Reichsgrenadier Hoch und Deutschmeister*, 46th and 711th infantry, and the 211th *Volksgrenadier* divisions, as well as the "Hupe" (this included about 20 assault guns) and "Staubwasser" combat groups. They disposed of 286 tanks and assault guns. They were opposed by the 24th and 25th rifle and 4th Guards Mechanized corps. These included seven divisions and six brigades: 72nd, 81st and 93rd guards rifle, 6th Guards Airborne, the 53rd, and the 375th and 401st rifle divisions, as well as the 27th Independent Tank, 36th Tank, 13th, 14th and 15th guards mechanized brigades, and the 38th Guards Tank, 292nd Independent Guards Medium Self-Propelled Artillery and 352nd Independent Guards Heavy Self-Propelled Artillery regiments. There is no exact data on the number of tanks and self-propelled guns. If one takes Reynolds's upper figure of 230 tanks and self-propelled guns, then the strengths were almost equal. If one supposes that the lower figure of 230 armored vehicles is correct, then the Germans had a superiority of 2.9 to one. If the two SS divisions had just been replenished, although they had not been brought up to authorized strength, then there had been no reinforcements in *Feldherrnhalle* Corps' units for a long time and they were significantly under strength, just as the 7th Guards Army's units. One may assume that the strength of the German and Soviet rank and file was approximately equal—about 80,000 men on both sides. There were six divisions and one brigade on the German side, which are equal to two regimental combat groups. At the same time, we can equate the strength of the *Feldherrnhalle's* Corps' four divisions and a brigade to the strength of the I SS Corps. We can equate the six Soviet brigades and three regiments to 3.5 divisions, and believe that the 10.5 Soviet divisions are approximately equal in strength to six German divisions and one brigade.

The former chief of the 13th Guards Mechanized Brigade, Gennadii Ivanovich Obaturov, recalled:

> On the evening of 22 February the brigade celebrated the 27th anniversary of the Red Army, and Colonel Tolubko called me during the night and said:
>
> "I'm relaying the corps commander's orders: gather up what you can and place it in defense along the eastern bank of the Hron River, along the sector opposite the village of Kamenin, with the task of rendering assistance to our retreating troops crossing the river and to prevent the Hitlerites from breaking through to the eastern bank of the Hron River. Subunits of the 15th Mechanized Brigade will be on the right near Bina."
>
> "So, Volodya, is it bad?"
>
> "Yes, it's bad."
>
> "I understand. I'll carry out your orders."
>
> Having informed Colonel Goryachev, I put the automatic rifle and anti-tank rifle companies and the anti-aircraft machine gun and engineer-mining companies on alert and by 0800 on 23 February had placed them in defensive positions along the indicated sector and ordered them to dig in immediately. I placed my observation post on a height in a grove opposite the bridge in Kamenin. Senior signals officers, captians Babenko and Zhukhovitskii, led by I.P. Yartsev, who had already become a major, were with me. Radio communications were working well.
>
> By this time the corps had broken out of the encirclement and had fallen back on Kamenin and occupied defensive positions ahead of the bridge.
>
> We had taken up defensive positions at the right time. We could see that tens of tanks and lines of Hitlerite infantry were approaching the river along the entire visible area from Bina and south of Kamenin.
>
> Fire from "Erlikon"[44] guns and DShK[45] anti-aircraft machine guns, and thcn from heavy machine guns, delayed the fascists at a range of 1,200-1,000 meters and aided the withdrawal of our subunits to the bridges. We had to observe with concern how our tanks were heroically fighting to the last shell, falling back to the bridge in Kamenin, and burned.
>
> Our composite team was engaged in defensive fighting until the close of 24 February. Units of the 7th Guards Army relieved it on the night of 24-25 February.

The losses for the German Eighth Army, which included the I SS Panzer Corps, during 11-28 February; that is, when Operation "Südwind" was being conducted, amounted to 1,425 killed, 6,839 wounded and 1,064 missing in action, for a total of 9,328, including 2,489 irretrievalbe. According to some estimates, approximately 6,000 of this number were due to Operation "Südwind," including about 1,000 killed. During 11-20 February Army Group South captured 1,061 prisoners, 622 prisoners during 1-10 February, and 2,240 for all of February. Of these, about 1,800 men may be ascribed to the operation against the Hron bridgehead.

---

44   Editor's note. The Erlikon was a 20mm anti-aircraft machine gun.
45   Editor's note. The DShK was a 12.7mm machine gun capable of firing up to 600 rounds per minute.

The I SS Panzer Corps announced the capture of 537 prisoners and the destruction or capture of 71 tanks, 45 field guns and howitzers and 75 anti-tank guns, as well as three aircraft by 22 February. 2,069 corpses of Red Army soldiers were found on the battlefield. According to an estimate by the I SS Panzer Corps command, about another 850 Soviet soldiers were also killed. If one assumes that these figures are close to reality and that the *Feldherrnhalle* Corps inflicted similar losses on the Soviet forces, then the 7th Guards Army's overall losses in killed may be estimated at approximately 6,000 men. One may also assume that about 1,250 Soviet prisoners were taken by the *Feldherrnhalle* Corps for the entire operation, which may include prisoners taken by the SS on 23-24 February. The I SS Corps' losses were 2,989 men, including 413 killed. The *Feldherrnhalle's* were probably not more than the SS losses. In this case, the German forces' overall losses in Operation "Südwind" may be estimated at 6,000 men, including about 1,000 killed. The SS panzer corps' armored irretrievable losses were three Panzer IVs, six "Panthers" and two "King Tigers." The *Feldherrnhalle* Corps's irretrievable losses in armor, of which it had five times less than the SS troops, could not have been significant and likely did not exceed three tanks and assault guns. When we take into account the fact that the *Feldherrnhalle* Corps destroyed and captured 59 guns and anti-tank guns, it also destroyed several tens of tanks and self-propelled guns. The 7th Guards Army's aggregate losses in armored equipment could have reached 100 vehicles.

We estimate Soviet losses in the 17-24 February 1945 fighting for the Hron bridgehead at 6,000 killed and 1,800 captured. This is close to the losses presented in the *Stavka* directive—8,194 men, but it's not clear whether the latter is speaking of all losses or just irretrievable ones. To all appearances, the number of wounded Red Army men was, at a minimum, not less than the number killed. In that case, the 7th Guards Army's overall losses could have reached about 14,000 men.

On 6 March the German operation "Spring Awakening" (Frühlingserwachen), which was to inflict a defeat on the Third Ukrainian Front and restore the German defense along the Danube, began in the area of Lake Balaton. This was one of the measures for realizing the "Alpine Fortress" plan, according to which the remnants of the German armies, as well as the government, were to sit it out in the Austrian and Bavarian Alps until the USSR and the Western Allies quarreled with each other. However, there was no military industry in the Alps, or sources of fuel. In order to render the "Alpine Fortress" in any way viable, it was necessary to hold the Czech lands and Bavaria, with their military industry, as well as Austria and western Hungary, with their oil deposits and oil-refining factories. Thus Hitler wanted to restore the defense along the Danube, in order to cover the oil deposits and oil-refining factories in Austria and Hungary.

Soviet, and afterwards Russian, historiography tradionally considers the battle near Lake Balaton in March 1945 as an outstanding victory by the Red Army, which bled the elite Sixth SS Panzer Army and the Wehrmacht's other shock divisions white in stubborn fighting. However, given the approximately equal strengths of the sides, the Germans supposedly enjoyed a significant superiority in the number of tanks and assault guns committed into the fighting. At first they maintained that the Third Ukrainian Front's forces that fought around Lake Balaton numbered 400,000 men and 877 tanks and self-propeleld guns. The initial figure for German Hungarian losses, according to the former chief of staff of the Third Ukrainian Front, S.P. Ivanov, in a collection of articles dedicated to the 25th anniversary of victory, was up to 45,000 killed, wounded and captured and 500 destroyed tanks and assault guns during 6-15 March. In 1979, in the 12-volume *History of the Second World War*, the number for the Wehrmacht's personnel losses near Lake Balaton was put at more than 40,000 men, while the armor losses, as before were put at 500 tanks and assault guns. In 2001, in the book *Russia and the USSR in the Wars of the XX Century*, another figure for the Third Ukrainian Front's strength at the beginning of the Balaton defensive operation was given—465,000 men. Here the Soviet losses around Lake Balaton were presented for the first time—32,899 men, including 8,492 irretrievable. Aside from all of the armies in Tolbukhin's front, there were operating against the Germans' Army Group South and the XCI Corps from

Army Group F, which was later subordinated to Army Group E, the 5th Air Army and two brigades of self-propelled artillery from the Second Ukrainian Front and also the Bulgarian 1st Army and two divisions from the People's Liberation Army of Yugoslavia's 12th Corps. There were 100,000 men in the Bulgarian 1st Army and not likely more than 30,000 men in the two Yugoslav divisions. The Third Ukrainian Front numbered 465,000 men. It's easy to show that the official figures on Soviet losses in the Balaton operation have been undercounted by approximately a factor of three. The fact is that by the start of the Vienna offensive operation on 16 March, the strength of the Third Ukrainian Front's forces had increased to 536,700 men by the inclusion of the 6th Guards Tank and 9th Guards armies. The 9th Guards Army consisted of three guards corps and nine guards rifle divisions. These formations were entering the fighting for the first time since the beginning of the war. They were fully up to authorized strength. Each division numbered 12,600 men. Besides this, the army included three mortar regiments, three independent anti-aircraft battalions, a signals regiment, an engineer brigade, and an independent flamethrower battalion. Together with corps and army units, the 9th Guards Army had no less than 135,000 men. The 6th Guards Tank Army had been in reserve since the beginning of February and had been brought up to authorized strength. It consisted of the 9th Guards Mechanized Corps—16,318 men, 183 tanks and 63 self-propelled guns, and the 5th Guards Tank Corps—12,010 men, 207 tanks and 63 self-propelled guns. Aside from this,the army included the three-regiment 202nd Light Artillery Brigade, the 51st Guards and 207th self-propelled artillery brigades, the 49th Guards Heavy Tank Regiment, the 364th Guards Heavy Self-Propelled Artillery Regiment, the 4th Guards Motorcycle Regiment, the 207th Guards Army Signals Regiment, and the 22nd Motorized Engineer Brigade. According to a strength table for 1945, a light artillery brigade would number about 3,000 men, the 207th Self-Propelled Artillery Brigade, which also took part in the Balaton operation—1,492 men, and the 51st Guards Self-Propelled Artillery Brigade—1,804 men. A motorcycle regiment had an authorized strength of 1,118 men, a heavy self-propelled artillery regiment—420 men, a heavy tank regiment—374 men, a motorized engineer brigade—1,180 men, and an army signals regiment—525 men. In all, the 6th Guards Tank Army, counting rear subunits, numbered about 40,000 men and 406 tanks and self-propelled guns. Moreover, the 209th Self-Propelled Artillery Brigade was attached to the Third Ukrainian Front during the Balaton fighting.

Therefore, by taking into account the addition of new armies and not even counting reinforcements, the troop strength of the Third Ukrainian Front by the start of the Vienna operation grew by 175,000 men. Had it not been for losses during the second Balaton operation, the front's troop strength should have been about 640,000 men, while only 536,700 remained. This means that its losses during 6-15 March were no less than 103,300 men. However, on 10 March the Third Ukrainian Front received quite an extensive reinforcement in armored equipment and one should not doubt that then the front received reinforcements, the size of which could in no way be less than 10,000 men (they simply did not dispatch fewer to the front). By taking this into account, the Third Ukrainian Front's losses in the Balaton operation could have numbered about 113,000 killed, wounded and captured. In March 1945 Army Group South's forces took 2,980 prisoners. Probably nearly all of these came from the Balaton operation. In that case, the overall number of killed and wounded may be placed at 113,000 men. Insofar as the undercounting of losses in the Red Army chiefly took place at the expense of killed and missing in action, one may assume that in the Balaton operation the number of killed was approximately equal to the number of wounded. Then the Third Ukrainian Front's losses in killed may be placed at 55,000 men, and all irretrievable losses at 58,000 men.

According to a report by the Third Ukrainian Front command, during 6-15 March the enemy lost about 28,065 (according to a later count, 28,175) soldiers and officers killed and captured. 128 guns, 88 mortars, 441 machine guns, and 88 automobiles were destroyed. 19 German planes were shot down by land-based anti-aircraft weapons and 77 by the 17th Air Army's fighters. The front's forces destroyed 391 tanks and 104 armored transports and knocked out 334 tanks and armored transports. Under the pen of Soviet historians, these figures were subsequently and magically transformed into 45,000 killed and captured enemy soldiers and officers, and more than 300 guns and mortars, about 500 tanks and assault guns, about 500 armored transports, more than 1,300 motor vehicles,and more than 200 planes. Here the actual German figures have been raised several times.

The following units took part in Operation "Spring Awakening" on the German side. The Sixth Army (army group Balck) consisted of the III Panzer Corps (1st and 3rd and, from 12 March, 6th panzer divisions, and the 356th Infantry Division). The Sixth SS Panzer Army consisted of the I SS Panzer Corps (1st and 2nd SS panzer divisions and, from 10 March, the 23rd Panzer Division), the II SS Panzer Corps (9th and 12th SS panzer divisions and the 44th *Reichsgrenadier* Division), and the I Cavalry Corps (3rd and 4th cavalry divisions and, from 10 March, the Hungarian 25th Infantry Division. The Second Panzer Army from Army Group South was to carry out a supporting operation—Icebreaker (Eisbrecher). It included the LXVIII Army Corps (16th SS Motorized Division and 71st Infantry Division) and the XXII Mountain Infantry Corps (118th Jaeger and 1st *Volksgrenadier* divisions). The XCI Army Corps (104th Jaeger, 297th Infantry, 11th *Luftwaffe* Field, and 1st Cossack Cavalry divisions), which was subordinated to Army Group Southeast (Army Group E) was to conduct yet another operation—"Wood Goblin" (Waldteuffel).

The numerical strength of the attacking German forces, according to German data, was as follows: Sixth Army—three divisions, 45,000 men and 77 tanks and assault guns; Sixth SS Panzer Army—eight divisions, (not counting a Hungarian division), 125,000 men and 320 tanks and assault guns; Second Panzer Army—four divisions, 50,000 men and 70 tanks and assault guns. In all, this amounted to 220,000 men and 467 tanks and assault guns (only combat-ready).

The German divisions' strength was as follows:

> Sixth SS Panzer Army command, together with army units—1,416;
> I Corps command, together with corps units—3,883;
> 1st Panzer Division *Leibstandarte*—18,671;
> 12th Panzer Division *Hitlerjugend*—17,423;
> II Corps command, together with corps units—3,036;
> 2nd SS Panzer Division *Reich*—19,542;
> 9th SS Panzer Division *Hohenstaufen*—17,229;
> Total—81,400.
> I Cavalry Corps command, together with corps units—2,600;
> 3rd Cavlary Division—7,000;
> 4th Cavalry Division—8,000;
> 44th Imperial Grenadier Division (Royal Kaiser and Master of the Teutonic Order)—14,000;
> 23rd Panzer Division (the army group reserve)—12,000;
> Sixth Army (army group Balck):
> Command of the III Panzer Corps, together with corps units—3,000;
> 1st Panzer Division—16,000;
> 3rd Panzer Division—15,000;
> 356th Infantry Division—11,000.
> Total for the northern attack group—170,000.
> Second Panzer Army's attack group—50,000.
> Thus the German group of forces attacking around Lake Balaton numbered 220,000 men.

In this case, we are speaking of forces at hand, which also includes wounded, sick and missing in action for the past four weeks. For example, on 12 February 1945 the 1st SS Panzer Division had an authorized strength of 615 officers, 4,037 NCOs and 13,723 enlisted men, for a total of 18,375, while the division actually had 513 officers, 3,105 NCOs and 15,377, for a total of 19,055 men. This strength actually included 28 wounded and sick officers, 179 NCOs and 1,037 enlisted men, for a total of 1,244 wounded and sick for the last month. Besides this, this figure included 300 missing in action for this period, which yields an overall 1,544 missing in action, wounded and sick. Thus with the exception of those missing in action, wounded and sick, by the start of Operation "Südwind" there were actually 17,511 men fit for service in *Leibstandarte*. The number of missing in action, wounded and sick accounted for 8.1 percent of strength at hand. By the start of Operation "Frühlingserwachen" the actual strength of the 1st SS Panzer Division had been reduced by 384 men, which probably approximately corresponds to the size of the the number of killed during Operation "Südwind." If one assumes that in the on-hand strength of all German forces that took part in Operation "Spring Awakening" about 8 percent consisted of those missing in action, wounded and sick, then there were actually 202,400 troops on hand.

The strength of the Hungarian 25th Division may be put at 10,000 men and that of the XCI Army Corps at 40,000. These divisions had no tanks. The XCI Corps mainly fought against the Bulgarian 1st Army and two Yugoslav divisions. Two Soviet rifle divisions operated against it for only a brief period of time, so we can remove it from our calculations, along with the Bulgarian 1st Army and the two Yugoslav divisions.

During 6-13 March the 1st SS Panzer Division lost 211 men killed, 1,059 wounded and 149 missing in action. By 16 March its losses had increased by another 16 wounded, as the division no longer had any irretrievable losses. The 12th SS Panzer Division lost during 6-13 March 148 killed, 656 wounded and 153 missing in action. In all, during this period the I SS Corps lost 2,392 men, including 359 killed and 302 missin in action.

The 2nd SS Panzer Division *Reich* lost 132 killed, 679 wounded and 194 missing in action during 6-13 March. The 9th SS *Hohenstaufen* Division lost during the same period 153 killed, 536 wounded and 105 missing in action. The II SS Panzer Corps lost 1,799 men, including 285 killed and 299 missing in action.

During 6-13 March the 3rd Cavalry Divisoin lost 87 killed, 433 wounded and 13 missing in action, while the 4th Cavalry Division lost 70 killed, 300 wounded and eight missing in action. In all, the I Cavalry Corps lost 911 men, including 157 killed and 21 missing in action.

During 6-13 March the Sixth SS Panzer Army's overall losses amounted to 5,919 men, including 963 killed, 4,328 wounded and 658 missing in action.

The 2nd Panzer Division lost 3,562 men, including 508 killed, 2,798 wounded and 157 missing in action.

Army group Balck lost 2,877 men, including 474 killed, 2,093 wounded and 310 missing in action.

In all, Army Group South lost 12,358 men, including 1,945 killed, 9,318 wounded and 1,095 missing in action.

During this period Army Group Southeast (E) lost 2,460 men, including 506 killed, 1,798 wounded and 156 missing in action.

In all, during 6-13 March ther German forces taking part in operation "Spring Awakening" lost 14,818 men, including 2,451 killed, 11,116 wounded and 1,251 missing in action. When including losses for the 14-15 March fighting, their overall losses could exceed 16,000 men, taking into account the much reduced intensity of the fighting during the last two days of the operation. Of these losses, about 13,500, including 4,000 irretrievable—were from Army Group South.

The Germans' irretrievable losses in armored equipment for the Sixth SS Panzer Army were 31 tanks, 11 assault guns and one armored transport, including from the 1st SS Panzer Division—12 tanks and one assault gun; 12th SS Panzer Division—five tanks and two assault guns, four tanks and five assault guns in the 2nd SS Panzer Division, four tanks in the 9th SS Division, and six tanks, three assault guns and one armored transport in the 23rd Panzer Division.

The Hungarian Second Army, which consisted of three weak infantry divisions and most likely did not exceed 50,000 men, also took part on the German side. It suffered practically no losses, insofar as it was located along passive sectors of the offensive front.

The correlation of overall losses in the Third Ukrainian Front's Balaton operation (not counting Bulgarian and Yugoslav forces) and Army Group South was 8.4:1 in favor of the Germans. For irretrievable losses, the correlation may reach as high as 14.5:1 in favor of the Germans, which proves to be compatible with the correlation of losses in men during Operation Citadel near Kursk in July 1943.

Usually in Soviet reports about personnel losses, the overall losses are reduced by a factor of two, and irretrievable losses by a factor of three. In his report on losses during the Balaton operation, Tolbukhin, to all appearances, went even further, lowering overall losses by 3.5 times and irretrievable ones by seven times.

Things were no better in the Third Ukrainian Front with the correlation of armored equipment losses. By the close of 5 March 1945 the Third Ukrainian Front numbered 157 T-34-85 tanks (another four vehicles were undergoing repairs), 13 IS tanks,[46] 95 SU-76s,[47] 12 SU-85s, and 80 SU-100s[48] (with two vehicles undergoing repairs), 23 ISU-122s,[49] (one vehicle was undergoing repairs), 10 ISU-152s[50] (with one vehicle undergoing repairs), 47 M4A2 "Shermans" (one vehicle undergoing repairs), three MZA1 "Stuart, " as well as seven T-70s,[51] one captured tank and three captured self-propelled guns, for a total of 479 battle-ready tanks and self-propelled guns and ten undergoing repairs.

By the evening of 16 March the Third Ukrainian Front (minus the 6th Guards Tank Army, but counting the 9th Guards Army's armored equipment) numbered 99 T-34s (with another 11 undergoing repairs), four ISs, 227 SU-76s (with one undergoing repairs), two SU-85s, 142 SU-100s (with another nine undergoing repairs), 18 ISU-122s, ten ISU-152, 60 "Shermans," (with one undergoing repairs), one "Stuart," as well as five SU-57s,[52] nine captured tanks, and 12 captured self-propelled guns, for a total of 589 combat-ready tanks and self-propelled guns. Another 22 vehicles were undergoing repairs.

During the Balaton fighting the 22nd Tank Regiment, 207th and 209th self-propelled artillery brigades, the 1094th and 1922nd self-propelled artillery regiments, and an indepdent self-propelled artillery division from the 27th Army were added to the Soviet forces. At the same time, the armored equipment of the 854th, 1891st and 1201st self-propelled artillery regiments, the 3rd

---

46   Editor's note. This refers to a series of heavy tanks produced for the Soviet army during the Second World War and afterwards. These included the IS-1, IS-2, IS-3, IS-4, IS-6, IS-7, and IS-10.

47   Editor's note. The SU-76 was a self-propelled gun that first appeared in 1942. It contained a crew of four and had a maximum weight of slightly over 11 tons. It was armed with a 76mm gun.

48   Editor's note. The SU-100 was a self-propelled gun that first appeared in 1944. It contained a crew of four and had a maximu weight of 31.6 tons. It was armed with a 100mm gun.

49   Editor's note. The ISU-122 was a self-propelled gun that first appeared in 1943. Depending on the model, it carried a crew of four or five men and had a maximum weight of 45.5 tons. It was armed with a 122mm gun and a 12.7mm machine gun.

50   Editor's note. The ISU-152 was a self-propelled gun that first appeared in 1943. Depending on the model, it carried a crew of four or five men and had a maximum weight of 45.5 tons. It was armed with a 122mm gun and a 12.7mm machine gun.

51   Editor's note. The T-70 was a light Soviet tank which first appeared in 1942. One model weighed 9.2 tons and carried a crew of two. It was armed with a 45mm gun and a 7.62mm machine gun.

52   Editor's note. The SU-57 was the Soviet designation for the US-built T48 gun motor carriage, which the Red Army received through Lend-Lease during the latter half of the war. The SU-57 carried a crew of five and was armede with a 57mm gun.

Guards, 58th, 72nd, and 432nd independent self-propelled artillery battalions, the 32nd Guards Motorized Rifle Brigade, and the 249th Tank Regiment were completely put out of action. Just by taking these units' losses into account, the front's armored equipment losses should have amounted to 43 T-34s, ten IS tanks, 30 SU-76s, 12 SU-85s, three captured self-propelled guns, and six T-70s. Moreover, taking into account the reduction in the overall strength of tanks and self-propelled guns, the 18th Tank Corps' irretrievable losses amounted to nine T-34s, four ISU-122s and one ISU-152. The losses for the 208th Self-Propelled Artillery Brigade, by taking into account the reduction in the overall number of tanks and self-propelled guns, amounted to 34 SU-100s, and the 23rd Tank Corps' losses amounted to two ISU-122s. For the same reason, the losses of the 366th Guards Self-Propelled Artillery Regiment amounted to two IS tanks and four ISU-152s, with the 1st Guards Mechanized Corps losing three SU-100s, the 5th Guards Cavalry Corps five T-34s and one "Stuart," the 4th Guards Army's independent self-propelled artillery battalion one T-70, and the 1202nd Self-Propelled Artillery Regiment three captured self-propelled guns. By taking into account these two factors alone, the Third Ukrainian Front's armored equipment losses can be calculated at 173 tanks and self-propeleld guns, which is already larger than the official figures of irretrievable losses from the report by the front command, which is cited by A.V. Isaev and M.V. Kolomiets—165 tanks and self-propelled guns, including 84 T-34s and 48 SU-100s. However, other units and formations, as well as the listed units and formations, for other types of armored equipment, the number of which on 16 March exceeded the number on 5 March, due to reinforcements. We should also take into account that the armored equipment of two unnumbered Soviet self-propelled gun battalions and one unnumbered tank battalion was completely destroyed or captured by the enemy, to the tune of 16 self-propelled guns and 11 tanks. It is known that the 207th Self-Propelled Artillery Brigade numbered 63 SU-100s upon being committed into the fighting, of which 20 remained on 20 March. It follows that its irretrievable losses were 43 SU-100s. The 209th Self-Propelled Artillery Brigade, from all appearances, also numbered 63 SU-100s, of which 46 were combat-ready on 16 March, with another two undergoing repairs. One may assume that the 209th Brigade lost 15 SU-100s irretrievably.

It is also known that during the Balation fighting the 363rd Guards Self-Propelled Artillery Regiment, consisting of 11 ISU-122s and six ISU-152s, was committed into the fighting along the 27th Army's sector. However, on 16 March there are no vehicles from this regiments listed among the Third Ukrainian Front's armored equipment, which makes one suspect that by that time they had all been irretrievably lost. The 22nd Tank Regiment, which had 11 T-34s, three SU-76s, one SU-85, and one KV-1, was put into the fighting along the 26th Army's sector. On 16 March it had six T-34s ready for combat and another six undergoing repairs, as well as two SU-85s, which proves that the regiment received reinforcements. It irretrievably lost, at a minimum, three SU-76s and one KV-1.

According to A.V. Isaev and M.V. Kolomiets, during 6-16 March the Third Ukrainian Front only once, on 10 March, received armored reinforcements: 75 SU-76s, 20 "Shermans" and 20 T-34s. At the same time, supposedly only the 23rd Tank Corps received T-34s, while the 1896th, 1891st and 1202nd regiments, the 18th Tank Corps and units of the 4th Guards Army received self-propelled guns. If these figures are correct, then one may approximately define the irretrievable losses in armored equipment by types as follows: 82 T-34s, 75 SU-76s and seven "Shermans." Besides this, one may also assume that a minimum of one SU-57 in the 209th Brigade, two "Stuarts," ten SU-85s, 164 SU-100s, one KV-1, six T-70s, nine IS tanks, 17 ISU-122s, seven ISU-152s, 11 captured tanks, and 19 captured self-propelled guns were destroyed. In all, the Third Ukrainian Front lost irretrievably no less than 411 tanks and self-propelled guns. Insofar as the front command reported losing irretrievably 84 T-34s, one may assume that two of the T-34s are losses from the 22nd Tank Regiment, compensated by the delivery of no less than three new vehicles. When taking this into account, as well as no less than one SU-85, which the 22nd Regiment received as reinforcements, the overall amount of irretrievably lost armored equipment increases to 414 tanks and self-propelled guns. Besides this, the 1094th and 1922nd self-propelled artillery regiments, which were committed during the battle, on 16 March numbered correspondingly 20 SU-100s (with one vehicle undergoing repairs) and 16 SU-100s (with one vehicle undergoing repairs). A regiment had an authorized strength of 21 SU-100s, so one may assume that the 1922nd Regiment lost irretrievably four self-propelled guns, which increases the overall irretrievable losses to 418 tanks and self-propelled guns.

The Sixth SS Panzer Army's irretrievable losses were 33 tanks (31 tanks, according to other data, although this may include a shorter time period), 11 assault guns and one armored transport. Taking into account the fact that Soviet captured equipment teams discovered about 279 damaged and abandoned tanks and assault guns in western Hungary at the end of March and beginning of April, Isaev and Kolomiets calculate the overall irretrievable armored losses of the Sixth SS Panzer Army, army group Balck and the Second Panzer Army during the Balaton fighting and for the beginning period of the Vienna operation at 250 tanks and assault guns. It's likely that this calculation is close to reality, taking into account the fact that some part of the equipment may have remained from the January fighting. However, one should keep in mind that a large part of this equipment had been knocked out or abandoned because of a lack of fuel as early as the Vienna operation. Also in this number are tanks damaged during "Spring Awakening," which proved impossible to evacuate during the retreat. Thus the Germans' overall irretrievable losses during the Balaton battle probably did not exceed 70 tanks and assault guns, which was approximately six times less than the Soviet irretrievable losses. This correlation was somewhat more favorable for the Red Army than during Operation Citadel, but it does impress for the final weeks of the war. It's not by accident that the in its report to the *Stavka* that the Third Ukrainian Front command preferred to lessen its armored losses by 2.5. It's possible that the *Stavka's* 6 March directive, which so frightened Tolbukhin before the start of "Spring Awakening," played a role in a similar undercounting.

It's interesting to compare the Sixth SS Panzer Army's personnel losses suffered in the West and the East. On the Western Front, during 11-31 January 1945 Sepp Dietrich's army lost 2,081 killed, 6,895 wounded and 5,891 missing in action, for a total of 14,867 men. On the Eastern Front, during 11-31 March 1945, the Sixth SS Panzer Army lost 1,313 killed, 6,529 wounded and 779 missing in action, for a total of 8,621 men. The army's overall losses on the Western Front were 1.7 times more and 3.8 times more for irretrievable losses. At the same time, one should take into account the fact that the report on the Sixth SS Panzer Army's losses for 11-20 March more than likely includes the losses for 6-10 March, from the beginning of the Balaton offensive. Moreover, four additional divisions joined the Sixth SS Panzer Army on the Eastern Front, thanks to which its strength rose from 81,400 to 122,400 men. Thus when calculating only the "old" divisions which had fought on the Western Front, the losses for Dietrich's army in Hungary were even less. Without a doubt, the size of the Germans' losses during the last year of the war was relatively higher than in the East.

To all appearances, Stalin found out about the Third Ukrainian Front's true losses during the Balaton operation. General Staff representatives assigned to the front and army headquarters, could have reported this to the *Stavka*, as well as the organs of SMERSH, among whose responsibilities were also to truthfully reflect the course of combat operations. Stalin did not bother to issue a new threatening directive, insofar as he had come to understand long ago that to struggle against the generals' and marshals' dishonest reports was the same as tilting at windmills. If he were to relieve people for false reports, within 2-3 months there would be no generals left at the front. It appears that Stalin also had strong doubts about Tolbukhin's command capabilities. Although the Balaton battle formally concluded in a victory for the Third Ukrainian Front, tactically speaking, it had been completely lost by Soviet forces, which outnumbered the enemy by more than two to one in personnel. Also, Stalin, in all probability, could not forgive Tolbukhin the fact that in spite of the large numbers of men and materiel allotted to him, the marshal was nevertheless unable to destroy the Sixth SS Panzer Army, which eventually surrendered to the Americans. Stalin nevertheless awarded Tolbukhin the "consolation prize" of an Order of Victory, but left him without the gold star of a Hero of the Soviet Union and did not send him to fight against Japan, where it was comparatively easy to earn such a star. On the other hand, Malinovskii departed for that war.

The idea for "Spring Awakening" somewhat reminds that for "Citadel." It was planned to encircle and pin to the Danube and destroy part of the Third Ukrainian Front. Only this time the attacks would be launched not along concentric but eccentric axes. However, if the Sixth SS Panzer Army, many of whose soldiers and officers had taken part in the Battle of Kursk, managed to advance quite far, the Sixth Field Army's group of forces was halted quite quickly. The correlation of forces was just as unfavorable for the Germans as during Operation "Citadel," which also predetermined the failure of "Spring Awakening."

As is well known, Operation "Citadel" was called off after the forces of the Western and Bryansk fronts began an offensive against the Germans' Orel salient. Evidently following the Battle of Kursk, Stalin decided to operate according to the same template in repelling major German offensives: first exhaust the attackers and then launch a counterblow. The same principle was adopted in the Balaton battle: we first exhaust the enemy, and then begin a general offensive on Vienna. At the same time, it was not taken into account that the situation in Central Europe in March 1945 was completely different than in the Kursk salient in July 1943. Let's begin with the fact that not one but many roads led to Vienna, the main strategic point and very important railroad junction in the south of the Soviet-German front, and that the Germans simply lacked the forces to cover even the majority of them. By no means did all the roads go through western Hungary, while an offensive in the Lake Balaton area could force the Soviet command to renounce a movement on Vienna only along this route. And following the beginning of "Spring Awakening" the most powerful reply from the Soviet side would be to begin an offensive on Vienna through Slovakia not immediately after the conclusion of the German offensive on Balaton, but within 4-5 days—say 9 or 10 March. If Malinovskii's Second Ukrainian Front had begun the Vienna offensive operation during these days through Esztergom and (or) the Bratislav—Brno operation, but aimed primarily not at Brno, but also at Vienna, particularly with the employment of two armies in reserve—the 9th Guards and 6th Guards Tank armies—the German defense would simply have collapsed. In these conditions, Operation "Spring Awakening" would have lost all meaning. Most likely, Hitler would then have ordered the operation in Hungary to be broken off and either all of the Sixth SS Panzer Army immediately shifted to defend Vienna, or at least one of its corps of three panzer divisions. As we recall, it took nine days to transfer the I SS Panzer Corps from the Esztergom area to the offensive area near Lake Balaton. Now, in order to carry out a reverse movement toward Esztergom, or more exactly toward Vienna, insofar as it would have been impossible to hold Esztergom would have required no less than 12 days, because the corps still had to be pulled out of battle. One must take into account that at this time Anglo-American aviation completely dominated all of the Germans' Eastern Front rear communications and that the Germans could carry out such a transfer only at night. At Kursk in July 1943 the German command was able to rapidly transfer troops from its shock group of forces to the Orel salient. However, in March 1945 such a rapid transfer was, in principle, impossible, and it is likely that the matter would have come down to a large part of three German panzer divisions traveling in train cars and deprived of the possibility of getting into the fighting. From all appearances, in this case the Red Army could have occupied all of Austria by itself. After all, in the middle of March the Anglo-American forces had not yet broken through the German front in northern Italy, and in the West the Allies had only just seized the Remagen bridgehead over the Rhine and had still not begun the offensive for the purpose of encircling the Ruhr group of forces. In any case, given such a development of events, the losses of the Third Ukrainian Front, which it incurred while repelling the German offensive, would have been significantly decreased. It's possible that the war could have been ended two to three weeks earlier and thus the lives of hundreds of thousands of Soviet soldiers could have been spared. However, Stalin preferred to operate according to his template.

It's not excluded that in this case the absence of *Stavka* representatives, which were eliminated as an institute at the end of 1944, at the front played a negative role. If, as before, the operations of Malinovskii's and Tolbukhin's fronts had been coordinated by Vasilevskii or Timoshenko, then each of them, on the spot, could have convinced Stalin of the utility of an immediate offensive on Vienna. Malinovskii considered Timoshenko an ideal *Stavka* representative, who would not interfere in the front commander's decisions without necessity and, if necessary, would defend the best operational variation to the Supreme Commander-in-Chief.

I should note that in the middle of March 1945 Anglo-American aviation launched a series of air strikes against strategic objectives in southern Austria, western Hungary and southern Slovakia. Airfields, railroad junctions, bridges and industrial targets were subjected to bombing. The main goal was the oil-refining plants, which according to the admission of the German command, led to a sharp decline in the production of fuel. On 15 March the OKW diary noted the following after an Allied raid of 14 March: "As a result of air raids on oil-refining plants in Komarno, the production of oil here has fallen by 70 percent... Due to the fact that army groups South and Center have previously been supplied with oil from Komarno, the consequences of these air raids will have an influence on operational decisions." One of the reasons for halting Operation "Spring Awakening" was exactly the shortage of fuel as a result of the damage which the bombings had done to the Komarno oil-refining plants.

The *Stavka* directive dealing with the failure in the fight for the Hron bridgehead aroused Malinovskii to speak quite sharply before the *front's* party activists on 11 March 1945, on the very eve of a new offensive:

> Comrades, as you recall, the last time I spoke so sharply before the party activists was about the fact that we not lose sight of our main task, and it is, as you are aware, directed at defeating the enemy. I don't argue, of course, that it is necessary to know philosophy, but we shouldn't forget our immediate tasks of defeating the enemy. Right now philosophy does not have decisive importance (laughter in the hall). If our artillery has been poorly trained for a breakthrough and if we poorly train and lead tanks and then they fall off a bridge into the Danube, as was the case not long ago, then no kind of philosophy and no kind of "grain" will help. Thus we must always remember that all of our work is combat work, and thus a good commander must be a good communist. Comrade Frunze wrote: "One may be a good communist and good Marxist and at the same time be a lousy commander." Why are communist knowledge and even a good knowledge of Marxist theory insufficient to be informed about all military questions? For we know that Marxist theory requires the attentive study of military affairs, by the commander first of all. Thus while examining the all-round and full-blooded work of each commander, each directorate and section, we come across such consoling thoughts. Everything's fine, the chiefs treated us well, our comrades came to this meeting with great enthusiasm, and people are studying, they help us out in the political section, and are studying some chapter in the history of the VKP(b),[53] and then move on to philosophy and philosophical problems, and all of this praise for oneself and other people

---

53   Editor's note. The VKP(b) (All Union Communist Party (Bolsheviks)) was the ruling political party in the Soviet Union during these years. Its name was changed to the Communist Party of the Soviet Union (CPSU) in 1952.

rings throughout each address by the comrades here. In my opinion, only comrade Alekseev put forward the question correctly, while everyone else said that everything is fine and dandy, but even if we carried out, for the most part, the mission assigned to us, if we have coped with our tasks and they aren't beating up on us, we don't have the right to say that everything is alright and forget that we still have a great deal of fighting ahead of us. This is why we must work several times better than we have before. There are a number of reasons for this. First of all, we are a long way from our native land and, naturally, we are surrounded by enemies and thus the troops must be very politically vigilant and tough in order to assure success. We just heard about incidents of people even going to church and getting married to Hungarian and Romanian women in order to demonstrate their feelings for them. We have an entire series of incidents of venereal diseases. All of this speaks to the fact that we are poor officers and if we were good officers and communists, then we wouldn't have such incidents, not to mention that such cases should not have a place in the *front's* field directorate, and yet we have heard that this is indeed the case with the *front's* field directorate, and this is an important report, a shameful report.

Further, I hear such conversations "I went to the front on detached service." We've gotten used to thinking that we're going to the front on detached service; meaning to sit here is our chief task. I said then and I'm saying it again that our main work is with the troops and that we must get rid of the words "I was on detached duty, but my staff work is the main thing" and to forget about detached duty. We should not phrase the question thusly, and it's very bad if we sit here and very good if a few workers remain here to carry out those orders which those comrades among the troops issue them, while we continue to view the matter that in going to the front we are on detached duty. I once again ask that you remember the the main work of officers and generals is work among the troops. I require this of my closest assistants. Do you often see comrade Fomin in the artillery headquarters? Do you often see comrade Kurkin at his headquarters? Do you often see comrade Tsirlin here in his headquarters, etc.? They spend almost all of their time among the troops. There's where their main work is, and it is only there that we should examine and make judgments about that knowledge that we still lack and how to add and increase our knowledge. We must not so modestly say that "We should study our manuals." We officers and generals of the front field directorate, which is the leading link, must not sit on these manuals and we should not only know them by heart, but we must also grow, if you like, and write these manuals ourselves, and I'm sure that the time will come when we must evaluate all of these manuals that have been written, while we are still shouting that we must know these manuals. We are very weak in this area, particularly in the operational directorate, which is the little brain of the front's field directorate. Comrade Markov spoke here and advocates (it's possible that there's a mistake in the stenographic record and the word reports should be used, B.S.) that we are studying the manual. I can say moreover that we must deeply pore over a journal like *Military Thought*.[54] Comrade Stalin issued a special order for this journal and removed the journal's editor, who couldn't handle this work. The journal was assigned new tasks and we must not only read it, but we must submit articles to this journal, and I am sure that our officer-communists have not submitted a single article to this journal. This would help from the point of view of multiplying our military habits, particularly as it relates to such workers who, as is their servicer responsibility, should be highly-qualified workers—the operational directorate, intelligence section and various combat arms. And it turns out here that all of these workers are only preparing to

---

54   Editor's note. *Military Thought* (*Voennaya Mysl'*) was the leading military journal in the Soviet Union and continues to perform the same function for the contemporary Russian armed forces.

study manuals. After all, the manuals only teach how to lead a battalion, regiment and division into battle, and how should one lead a corps or an army into battle, or artillery? This is not written up in our manuals. Do you really think I'm the only one who's going to do this, while the rest of you look on? Everyone must work on this matter.

The fact was put forward here that the representatives of the intelligence section and the commander of an intelligence company did not know anything about what the enemy intended, that they were not informed and missed what the enemy was planning and were sent running away without their pants. Where is your main work? This is where you should be looking! The fact that you missed what the enemy was planning and didn't inform me that the enemy was preparing to cross opposite the 7th Army's bridgehead, and the attack on the bridgehead came as a complete surprise. Shouldn't we consider this a crime? It follows that we should think not only about how great things are, but just the opposite, to multiply our efforts in order to actually achieve those tasks which comrade Stalin has assigned us. All the more so, as right now we have the opportunity, because we are faced with very intensive work in carrying out that order that comrade Stalin has assigned our *front*. For this work, we must all get out among the troops and, with our Bolshevik passion, direct all of our energy toward carrying out our leader's order (Applause).

Malinovskii's wonderful words about how "Right now philosophy does not have decisive importance" (he was speaking here about Marxist philosophy, of course, insofar as no other kind was recognized in the USSR), and that the main thing was to learn how to defeat the enemy. Such an opinion could get you a strict sanction, if not something worse, in peacetime. But these and even worse passages went by during the harsh war years.

In his quite emotional speech, Rodion Yakovlevich touched only briefly on the fact that the front's soldiers were not conducting themselves properly with the female population of Romania and Hungary. As a matter of fact, behind these words are tragic events characteristic of all Soviet *fronts* that had entered the territory of European countries (and then the countries of eastern Asia). I recall very well how one veteran, who had helped liberate Romania in 1944, told how he and some other comrades had raped the daughters of the local Orthodox priest—girls 16-18 years old—while one proved to be a virgin and the other not. I don't know which *front*, the Second or Third Ukrainian, this man fought on, although this does not really matter. Such things happened, to one degree or another, on all the *fronts* and little depended on the *front* commanders in this regard. However, the greater part of Romanian territory did not become a battlefield, while the Romanian forces were transformed into Soviet allies in the blink of an eye and the Romanian administration remained in place. Thus in Romania such excesses were nevertheless not widespread, and if Russian soldiers from time to time got together with Romanian girls this most often occurred out of love and mutual consent, although getting married in church aroused the dissatisfaction of Malinovskii and the political workers, who saw in this the undermining not only of ideological pillars, but of combat spirit as well.

Hungary remained a battlefield until the end of the war, the the Hungarian forces continued to fight on the German side. And it was here that excesses on the part of the Red Army took on a massive character.

I've had occasion to visit Hungary several times, particularly when contemporaries of the Second World War were still alive. And the Hungarians held it much more against Soviet forces not for suppressing the Hungarian revolution in November 1956, but for the massive rapes and depradations in 1944-45. To be sure, the Hungarian population was nevertheless fortunate in some respects. Red Army soldiers killed peaceful civilians in Hungary quite rarely and the destruction and torching of homes was a rarity. In this sense, it was much worse for the population of eastern Germany (including West and East Prussia, Silesia, and eastern Pomerania) As Aleksandr

Solzhenitsyn[55] wrote in *The Gulag Archipelago*: "Yes, the war was now in Germany… and each of us knew exactly that we could rape and shoot. This was almost the purpose of the battle." Here mass rapes were accompanied by mass murders and mass robberies—arson and the senseless destruction of property.

The Red Army soldiers were no doubt moved by a feeling of revenge. But not only this. If the rapes and murders in Romania, Germany and Hungary can be explained, to a certain extent, by this feeling, then how should one view similar excesses in Serbia? After all, the Serbs did not fight against the Soviet Union.

Soviet troops only spent a month in Serbia, during the Belgrade operation, which lasted until the end of September through the end of October 1944, and which was conducted in cooperation with the People's Liberation Army of Yugoslavia. On the Soviet side, the Third Ukrainian Front's 57th Army and the 10th Guards Rifle Corps from the Second Ukrainian Front's 46th Army took part. And the Red Army soldiers went all out during that month, raping a minimum of 121 women and killing 111 of them. The number of rapes was probably significantly higher, but many preferred not to talk about it. When the Yugoslav communists sent a delegation to Moscow, which included the future dissident Milovan Djilas,[56] and lodged a protest against the Red Army's conduct, according to Djilas, they failed to meet with Stalin's understanding and he refused to investigate the crimes and search for and punish the guilty parties, while at the same time accusing Djilas and his comrades of insulting the Red Army. One should not doubt that the soldiers of both the Second and Third Ukrainian fronts were guilty of rapes in Serbia and other countries. While killing and raping in Serbia, the Red Army soldiers vented their anger against the well-fed, by Soviet standards, European way of life. After all, the residents of Serbia and Voevodina, which were by no means the richest in Europe, lived much better than the Soviet kolkhoz workers.

Krisztian Ungvary quotes an account by the Swiss embassy in Budapest, where it was stated:

> The Hungarian population is suffering the most from the rapes of women. The rapes touch upon all age groups from ten to 70 years of age. The rapes are such a commonplace affair that there is hardly a woman in Hungary who has avoided them. They are sometimes accompanied by unbelievable cruelties. Many women prefer suicide to these horrors… The sufferings are magnified by the fact that many Russian soldiers suffer from venereal diseases and there are no medicines in Hungary.

In February 1945 the communists of the village of Kobanya, which is now in the tenth district of Budapest, made an appeal to the Soviet command:

> Over the course of decades the toilers of the entire world have looked upon Moscow just as the illiterate toilers looked upon Christ. It was precisely from there that they expected liberation from fascist barbarism. After long and torturous sufferings, the glorious and long-awaited Red Army arrived, but what did it prove to be!

---

55   Editor's note. Aleksandr Isaevich Solzhenitsyn (1918-2008) was a Russian-Soviet novelist and political dissident. He fought in the Great Patriotic War until his arrest in 1945, after which he spent eight years in labor camps. He first achieved literary notoriety in the 1960s, although he was no longer published after 1963. He was arrested and exiled in 1974 and eventually settled in the United States. Solzhenitsyn returned to Russia in 1994.

56   Editor's note. Milovan Djilas (1911-95) joined the Yugoslav Communist Party in 1932 and took part in the anti-German partisan struggle during the Second World War under Iosip Broz (Tito). Following the communist victory he was briefly president of Yugoslavia, but was dismissed from all his posts in 1954 for his criticism of Tito and the communist "new class." Djilas later spent several years in prison for his views.

The Red Army liberated Kobanya on 2 January, followed a stubborn fight for each house, and left behind destruction and desolation. And this is not because among the ruins of furniture in people's homes, whose residents were slaves for decades, one could find fascists. Among the toilers in Kobanya there are very few who sympathized with the Germans, while the majority hated the Nazis. But suddenly there was an explosion of insane and frenzied hatred. Drunken soldiers raped mothers before their children and husbands. Groups of 10-15 soldiers, among whom there were many who were sick with venereal diseases, took girls of 12 years from their fathers and mothers and raped them. After the first group there would come others, which followed the example of their predecessors. Several of our comrades were killed when they attempted to defend their wives and daughters…

The situation in the factories is terrible. The Russian officers have created unbearable conditions for work, ignoring the worker's committees in which there are a lot of communists. The workers toil for three pengoes an hour on an empty stomach, having the opportunity to eat peas or beans for lunch (in accordance with the 20 January 1945 agreement between the USSR and the new Hungarian government, the Soviet side received the right to print pengoes and carry out their emission to the end of 1945. "Red Army Command" was stamped on these "military pengoes." On 31 August 1945 1,320 pengoes were equal to one dollar and by 31 October their value had fallen to 8,200 penoes to the dollar. Thus even given a 1-hour working day a working man could earn per day, even according to the comparatively high August rate, no more than 2.5 American cents, which obviously could not support minimal needs, B.S.)… They treat the former fascist directors with much greater respect than they do the workers' committees, insofar as the directors supply the Russian officers with women… Marauding by the Russian soldiers continues to this day… We know that the most sensible representatives of the army are communists, but when we turn to them for help they become enraged and threaten to shoot us, declaring: "And what did you do in the Soviet Union? Did you really not rape our wives in front of our eyes, and then you killed them together with their children, burned our villages and reduced our cities to rubble." We know that Hungarian capitalism has committed its own sadistic cruelties… However, we don't understand why a soldier from Siberia says this sort of thing…, while the fascist attacks never even reached the Urals, the dream of the German fascists, much less Siberia.

It's no good to praise the Red Army on posters, in the party and factories, and elsewhere, at the same time that people who have lived through the Szalasi tyranny are now being driven along the roads like livestock by Russian soldiers, leaving behind them dead bodies (tens of thousands of Hungarians were deported to the USSR, B.S.)…

The comrades who have been sent to the countryside to carry out the redistribution of land, were peppered by questions: what's the use of this land if there's nothing to plow it with. The Russians took our horses. They can't plow with their noses. If such things are halted, that will neutralize all of the enemy propaganda and the Hungarian workers will treat the Russian soldiers like gods.

Similar appeals were sent by other organizations of Hungarian communists. Statistics about the number of raped women remain for only a few towns, which the German-Hungarian forces were able to recapture for a time. In Lajoskomarom 140 women out of approximately 1,000 were subjected to rape. In Szekesfehervar 5,000 to 7,000 women were raped in the 30 days Soviet soldiers were there, which amounted to 10-15 percent of all women. In K. Ungvary's opinion, up to 10 percent of the women in Budapest were raped.

Of course, the scope of violence against the civilian population in Hungary, Serbia, Czechoslovakia and even Austria was less than in Germany. Here a significant role was played by the fact that Ilya Ehrenburg's call to "Kill the German!" which was ceaselessly circulated by propaganda, affected the Red Army soldiers, although no one called upon them to "Kill the Hungarian!" or even more so "Kill the Serb!" or "Kill the Czech!" But in any case, this was mostly an elemental process, which not even a *front* commander could cope, even with the best will in the world.

The same thing occurred in other armies during the Second World War. This is not to speak of the German or Japanese armies, whose numerous crimes on occupied territory are well known and, as opposed to the Soviet ones, were for the most part organized. There were incidents of rapes, plundering and murders of innocent civilians among the Western armies in Germany as well. The French colonial regiments particularly "distinguished themselves" in this matter.

As regards the conduct of German forces in occupied Soviet territory, I will cite only two examples. While pulling back from the village of Myasoedovo, Belgorod district, the Germans burned the village and drove off the residents with them. In a report to the 21st Army's political section, it was stated:

> On 24 January six women from this village—60-year old A. Rusanova, 17-year old Ye. Kondrat'eva, 18-year old Z. Lupandina, M. Spesivtseva, the mother of three children, M. Murzaev, the mother of two children, A. Kondrat'eva, and a 15-year old boy N. Lupandin, decided to return to their native village. Along the road the women encountered a German intelligence patrol numbering 20 men. The fascist swine seized the defenseless women, took off their felt boots and boots, took them to the other end of the village toward the cellar, forced them all to their knees and shot them in order.

In June of the same year, during an attack by German units, the population of Bol'shaya Berezka, Bryansk Oblast', hid in the woods. They were ordered to return to the village and then, according to the report by the Bryansk Front's political administration, the following took place: "150 old men, women and children returned home. After this they were driven into the collective farm granaries, where they were stabbed with bayonets and clubbed with rifle butts. 11 children between 12-13 years were buried alive."

Let's return to the battles of the Second World War. The authors of the book *Budapest—Vienna—Prague* maintain that before the start of the Vienna operation

> the overall superiority of the front's (Third Ukrainian, B.S.) over the enemy along the shock group's 31-kilometer offensive sector from Gant to Lake Velence was quite significant. A high density of men and materiel was achieved here. For example, the 9th Guards Army had 180 guns and mortars per kilometer of front and about nine self-propelled guns, while the 4th Guards Army had 170 guns and mortars and more than 20 tanks and self-propelled guns per kilometer of front.
>
> The enemy in this sector was defending with the forces of the IV SS Panzer Corps, consisting of the 3rd Panzer Division *Totenkopf*, the Hungarian 2nd Panzer Division, the 5th Panzer Division *Wiking*, and several independent infantry battalions and subunits of special combat arms, which were being employed as infantry. On 16 March the corps had 35 motorized and infantry battalions, numbering more than 430 guns and mortars of all calibers and 185 tanks and assault guns. Thus the 4th and 9th guards armies, while enjoying only an equal correlation of tanks and self-propelled artillery with the enemy, outnumbered him as follows: 4:1 in personnel and 9:1 in guns and mortars of all calibers. One could really attack with such forces! Unfortunately, the shock group's low saturation with tanks and self-propelled guns for direct infantry support, as events showed, negatively told on the pace of the troops' advance.

The authors of this text obviously have problems with arithmetic. It works out that along the 4th and 9th guards armies' 31-kilometer sector there was an average of about 15 tanks and self-propelled guns per kilometer. This means that in all they disposed of approximately 465 armored vehicles, which was 2.5 times more, according to Soviet figures, than in the IV SS Corps.

Further on in the book *Budapest—Vienna—Prague* it states:

> By the close of the operation's first day the forces of the Third Ukrainian Front's right wing advanced only 3-7 kilometers and had only arrived at the northeastern outskirts of Szkesfehervar with part of their forces, having failed to carry out their assigned task.
>
> The *Stavka* of the Supreme High Command, while intensely following the course of the operation, decided to reinforce the Third Ukrainian Front by transferring to it the Second Ukrainian Front's mobile forces. This is how it was. In connection with the planned Vienna operation, the commander of the Second Ukrainian Front, R.Ya. Malinovskii, left for the Bia area with an operational group, where he organized his forward command post. The reasons for this were that Gen. Petrushevskii,[57] who commanded the 46th Army, was taking part in an army operation for the first time, and thus he wanted to be closer to him. On the other hand, it was necessary for the marshal to determine the time for committing the 6th Guards Tank Army into the battle, which was the prerogative of the front commander.
>
> And then completely unexpectedly a telephone conversation took place on the evening of 16 March between the commander of the Second Ukrainian Front and the Supreme Commander-in-Chief I.V. Stalin, during which instructions were issued to transfer the 6th Guards Tank Army to the Third Ukrainian Front. The 9th Guards Army had gotten bogged down and it was necessary, so to speak, to push it forward. Here the Supreme Commander-in-Chief state that since the Third Ukrainian Front's command post was far away and could not rapidly get in touch with the 6th Guards Tank Army, he requested that the commander of the Second Ukrainian Front personally issue orders to the tank crews and to commit the army into the fighting along the Balinka—Varpalota—Veszprem axis and subordinate it to the neighboring front from the march.

On 16 March 1945 the 6th Guards Tank Army numbered 426 battle-ready tanks and self-propelled guns (not counting the 207th Self-Propelled Artillery Brigade, which was transferred to it later).

Its commitment as part of the Second Ukrainian Front would have enabled us to launch an attack with the greatest number of forces against the weakest part of the German-Hungarian defense and to rapidly develop the offensive on Vienna. Stalin, however, decided to defeat the Sixth SS Panzer Army with the help of Kravchenko's tank troops, but this plan failed.

G.T. Zavizon and P.A. Kornyushin, the authors of a historical sketch of the 6th Guards Tank Army, note that before the Vienna offensive operation this army

> at first… remained with the Second Ukrainian Front and was designated for developing the success in the 46th Army's attack zone along the Second Ukrainian Front's left wing. However, its place in the operation changed sharply right before the start of the offensive. The 4th and 9th guards armies, which had been moved up to the Third Ukrainian Front's main axis, had only about 200 tanks and self-propelled guns. This was clearly insufficient for developing an offensive against the enemy's major armored group of forces, consisting of the

---

57   Editor's note. Aleksandr Vasil'evich Petrushevskii (1898-1976) joined the imperial army in 1915 and the Red Army in 1918. During the Great Patriotic War he served as an army chief of staff and commanded a rifle corps, before being promoted to command the 46th Army in March 1945. Following the war, Petrushevskii was a military advisor abroad and the chief of the Military Academy of the Soviet Army.

German IV SS Panzer Corps and the Hungarian VIII Army Corps, which had 270 tanks and assault guns. Thus on 16 March Stalin decided to transfer the 6th Guards Tank Army to the Third Ukrainian Front.

M. Reynolds writes:

When the Russians began their counteroffensive on 16 March, the Germans had no more than 400 combat-ready tanks. If one examines the reports, then it transpires that *Leibstandarte* had 37 tanks, four assault guns and nine "King Tigers' during this time. A number of "King Tigers" were blown up by their crews south of Szekesfehervar, because they were unable to evacuate them. *Hitlerjugend* had 18 tanks and 23 "Jagdpanzers." The 23rd Panzer Division had 28 combat-ready tanks and self-propelled guns. The II and IV SS panzer corps... and Balck's Sixth Army together had about 250 tanks.

At the same time, even without the 6th Guards Tank Army, by the evening of 16 March the Third Ukrainian Front disposed of 589 combat-ready tanks and self-propelled guns; that is, it had superiority of one and a half in the number of armored vehicles.

On 6 March 1945, according to German data, Army Group South's tanks were distributed as follows.

71st Infantry Division—seven "Jagdpanzer-IVs" and 20 assault guns.

1st *Volksgrenadier* Division—12 assault guns.

16th SS Motorized Division—24 assault guns.

7th *Jaeger* Division   seven assault guns.

3rd Cavalry Division—seven "Jagdpanzer IVs" and 11 assault guns (13 assault guns undergoing repairs).

4th Cavalry Division—four Pz-IVs, two "Jagdpanzer-IVsw (two Pz-IVs and 15 assault guns undergoing repairs).

1st SS Panzer Division—14 Pz-IVs, 26 "Panthers," 14 assault guns, as well as six "Flakpanzer-IV" anti-aircraft self-propelled guns, which were armed with a 37mm anti-aircraft gun and which was practically not employed in fighting against ground troops.

12th SS Panzer Division—12 Pz-IVs, nine "Panthers," 14 "Jagdpanzer-IVs," 13 assault guns, and two "Flakpanzer-IV" anti-aircraft self-propelled guns.

2nd SS Panzer Division—24 Pz-IVs, six "Panthers," nine "Jagdpanzer-IVs," 23 assault guns, and eight "Flakpanzer-IV" anti-aircraft self-propelled guns.

9th SS Panzer Division—19 Pz-IVs, 24 "Panthers," ten "Jagdpanzer-IVs," 16 assault guns, and five "Flakpanzer-IV" anti-aircraft self-propelled guns.

23rd Panzer Division—15 Pz-IVs, 14 "Panthers," 11 "Jagdpanzer-IVs," and 11 assault guns (41 tanks and 22 assault guns undergoing repairs).

44th *Reichsgrenadier* Division—three "Jagdpanzer-IVs" (five assault guns undergoing repairs).

1st Panzer Division—five Pz-IVs and 23 "Panthers."

3rd Panzer Division—12 Pz-IVs, 22 "Panthers," 13 "Jagdpanzer-IVs," and 26 assault guns.

5th SS Panzer Division—three Pz-IVs, nine "Panthers" and six "Jagdpanzer-IVs" (39 tanks and 49 assault guns undergoing repairs).

3rd SS Panzer Division—five Pz-IVs, 16 "Panthers," six "Tigers," and 12 assault guns (58 tanks and ten assault guns undergoing repairs).

509th Panzer Battalion—35 "King Tigers" and eight "Flakpanzer-IV" anti-aircraft self-propelled guns.

501st Panzer Battalion—31 "King Tigers" (23 "King Tigers" under going repairs).
560th Panzer Battalion—six "Tigers" and six "Jagdpanzer-IVs" (10 "Tigers" undergoing repairs).
1st Battalion of the 32nd Panzer Regiment—32 "Panthers."
The *Feldherrnhalle* Panzer Battalion—26 "Tigers" and seven "Flakpanzer-IV" ant-aircraft self-propelled guns.
Hungarian 2nd Armored Division—12 "Turan"[58] tanks and ten assault guns.
6th Panzer Division—22 Pz-IVs, 68 "Panthers" and 12 "Jagdpanzer-IVs."
Total—494 tanks, 276 assault guns and 41 anti-aircraft self-propelled guns.

The Soviet forces attacked on March 16, beginning the Vienna offensive operation. In the Third Ukrainian Front's sector the main attack was made by formations of the 9th Guards and 6th Guards Tank armies against positions held by the 3rd Panzer Division *Totenkopf* and against its boundary with the Hungarian 2nd Panzer Division. The German defense was pierced and contact between these two divisions was lost. Soviet forward detachments got into the rear of the 3rd SS Panzer Division *Totenkopf* and the 5th SS Panzer Division *Wiking*, which was located to the southeast, hanging over the entire German Sixth SS Panzer Army.

The 46th Army's forward detachments got into a fight on the evening of 16 March; that is, simultaneously with the offensive by the Third Ukrainian Front's forces. On the morning of 17 March the main defensive zone was broken through. The greatest success was achieved in the sector of Lieutenant General N.N. Shkodunovich's 68th Rifle Corps. On the morning of 19 March the 2nd Guards Mechanized Corps was committed into the breach along this sector.

On 18 March the 46th Army's forces forced the Altal River and by the close of 19 March had broken through two layers of the enemy's defense along 16-kilometer front to a depth of 30 kilometers. Before long the breakthrough had been expanded to 40 kilometers. The main forces of the Hungarian 1st Cavalry Division and part of the 96th Infantry Division were routed.

It was obvious that it would have been expedient to commit the 6th Guards Tank Army along the 46th Army's (Second Ukrainian Front) attack sector. There a significant part of the defenders consisted of ineffective Hungarian divisions and there were almost no German tank formations.

In the attack zone of the 9th Guards Army, which had been transferrecd to the Third Ukrainian Front, where on 19 March the 6th Guards Tank Army had been committed into the fighting, the German defense had not yet been pierced and the tank troops suffered heavy losses and were not able to develop a high offensive pace. The 9th Guards Army's slow advance could be explained by the fact that all of its divisions were fighting for the first time. Of course, there were a certain percentage of troops and commander with combat experience, but the commanders had never before commanded their units and subunits in battle, which told negatively on their cooperation and on their cohesiveness.The 3rd and 5th SS panzer divisions were in danger of being encircled. The I SS Panzer Corps was dispatched to eliminate the Soviet breakthrough and to prevent the encirclement of the formations of the IV SS Panzer Corps and the entire Balaton group of forces of Army Group South.

On 21 March, following fierce fighting, units of the 5th SS Panzer Division *Wiking* abandoned Szekesfehervar.

On 22 March the Third Ukrainian Front's forces had nearly completed the encirclement of the IV SS Panzer Corps' units (3rd SS Panzer Division *Totenkopf* and the 5th SS Panzer Division

---

58   Editor's note. This was a Hungarian medium tank which saw service during the Second World War. One model weighed 18.2 tons and carried a crew of five. It was armed with a 40mm gun and two 8mm machine guns, although a later model carried a 75mm gun.

Wiking) and the Sixth SS Panzer Army.There were only three kilometers left between the Soviet 6th Guards Tank Army's forward detachments and Lake Balaton, where there remained a withdrawal route for the German forces. In order to keep open a small corridor open near Berhid, north of Lake Balaton, for the withdrawal of the encircled divisions, the 9th SS Panzer Division *Hohenstaufen* was dispatched there. Having suffered heavy losses, it held out until 23 March, which enabled the main forces of the Sixth SS Panzer Army and the IV SS Panzer Corps to escape from the encirclement.

The *Stavka's* plan consisted of encircling the Sixth SS Panzer Army with the aid of Kravchenko's tank troops. However, this could not be done and Dietrich's army fell back to the west, through a narrow 2.5-3 kilometer corridor in the Fuzfo area, and the Soviet forces suffered heavy losses and as early as 2 April it was necessary to pull the 6th Guards Tank Army out of the fighting for refitting. On 20 March alone the I SS Panzer Corps reported destroying 66 Soviet tanks and self-propelled guns. Overall Soviet irretrievable armored losses in the Vienna operation, according to official data, consisted of 603 tanks and self-propelled guns. At the same time, if the 6th Guards Tank Army had been committed into the fighting in the 46th Army's offensive sector, as had originally been planned, then the Soviet forces along this axis, enjoying a two-fold superiority in tanks and self-propelled guns, would have advanced even more rapidly and achieved even greater successes, while attacking directly on Vienna. This is all the more so as the tank army was committed into the battle only after the the breakthrough of the enemy defense. In this case, the Sixth SS Panzer Army would have had to hurriedly retreat, abandoning a large part of its armored equipment due to a lack of fuel. It is likely then that the 6th Guards Tank Army's losses and those of the Third Ukrainian Front's other armies, would have been smaller and Vienna could have been taken a few days earlier.

Units of the Sixth SS Panzer Army fell back in the direction of northern Bergenland and then Vienna, pursued by three guards armies (6th Guards Tank and the 4th and 9th guards armies), at the same time the Sixth Army was falling back in the direction of southern Bergenland and Styria, pursued by the 26th and 27th armies.

Meanwhile, the 46th Army, along with the 2nd Guards Mechanized and 23rd Tank corps, while rapidly advancing along the southern shore of the Danube, captured Hungarian Komarom on 28 March, while Slovak Komarno along the opposite bank of the Danube remained in German hands. Malinovskii ordered the commander of the 46th Army, Lieutenant General A.V. Petrushevskii, to turn the 23rd Rifle Corps to the north and to force the Danube west of Komarno, where a landing was also to be made from the boats of the Danube Flotilla. They were, in conjunction with the 7th Guards Army's 25th Rifle Corps, to attack toward Bratislava, which they liberated on 4 April.

At 1230 on 1 April 1945 Malinovskii sent Stalin an extraordinary report:

> I can report that the *front's* forces, while developing the offensive along the Vienna direction south of the Danube River, today, 2 April 1945, stormed and captured the enemy's major road junction and powerful strong point and important center for the air and tank industries, the town of Magyarovar, and have entered Austrian territory.
> 130 tanks and more than 4,000 prisoners were seized in the fighting.

On 13 April the same sort of report was sent upon the occasion of the fall of the town of Hodonin, one of the district centers of Moravia, on the approaches to Brno. Vienna, in the storming of which by the forces of the Third Ukrainian Front, the Second Ukrainian Front's 46th Army also took part, was liberated. And at 1740 on 26 April Malinovskii reported the taking of Brno, "the center of a major military-industrial area," "a powerful defensive center" and "a major communications junction."

On this day Malinovskii, along with Tolbukhin, was awarded the highest commander's medal—the Order of Victory. They were awarded this medal for liberating the territory of Hungary and Austria, while Rodion Yakovlevich received order no. 8 and Fedor Ivanovich no. 9. Here Stalin sought to underscore Malinovskii's seniority.

This was followed by the Prague campaign, in the liberation of which Malinovskii's forces, together with the forces of the First and Fourth Ukrainian fronts, took part. The operation's chief goal was to prevent Army Group South's escape to the Americans. This task was basically accomplished.

At 2315 on 11 May the Second Ukrainian Front's final combat report was issued. There it was stated that

> On 11.5.1945 the front's forces continued to pursue the enemy and by the close of the day had advanced up to 50 kilometers and occupied the towns of Ledec, Netvorice, Neveklov, Bystrice, Sedlcany, Votice, Jankov, Sedlice, Vysibilunec, Petrovice, Borotin, Ledenice, Nem, and Benesov, and units of the 9th Guards and 46th armies met up with our American allies along the front Pisek—Ceske Budejovice—Perg.
>
> According to preliminary data, during 9-11 May 135,000 prisoners wre taken, belonging to the 13th, 6th, 15th, 16th, and 19th panzer divisions, the *Grossdeutschland* Panzer Division, the 46th, 48th, 75th, 78th, 96th, 211th, 320th, 253rd, 154th, 371st, 70th, 76th, 357th, and 711th infantry divisions, the 97th and 8th light infantry divisions, the 3rd and 101st mountain infantry divisions, and various independent battalions and artillery battalions. Among those captured were six generals—the commander of the LXXII Army Corps, Lieutenant General Werner Schmidt, the commander of the 6th Panzer Division, Major General Waldenfels, the commander of the 76th Infantry Division, Major General Berner, the commander of the 320th Infantry Division, Major General Gilian, the commander of the airfield area, Major General Nichus, the chief of staff of the 440th Construction Sector, Major General Gottschilk.
>
> According to incomplete data, during 9-11 May the following were captured: 291 tanks and self-propelled gun, 668 guns of various calibers, 269 armored transports, 9,000 motor vehicles, ten aircraft, 2,000 horses, and 12 radio sets. The counting of captured equipment is continuing.

Malinovskii's daughter, Natal'ya, recalled:

> On the fifth anniversary of our victory I asked mama: "What was in like on 9 May in '45?" And she replied: "It was a celebration. Your papa and I traveled from Modra to Vienna. We were in the Vienna Woods, in the zoo. They preserved all the animals there!" That's how I found out that my favorite photograph, the one where it seems that they were deliriously happy, was made in the Vienna zoo. So much has passed! Mama had the blockade winter of 1941, the evacuation to Groznyi, the front, encirclement… and meeting papa, and in 1943 he awarded her with the Order of the Red Star. In this picture she still doesn't know that for them the war isn't over and that the road to a peaceful life lies through the Khingan Mountains.

And in her more detailed memoirs, *Memory-Snow*, Natal'ya Rodionovna added:

> … and last year, while going through the family archive, I found a page from a notebook with papa's article for the *front* newspaper. He wrote about how torturous it was to retreat, how shameful it was, when falling back, to look into the eyes of people who remained—and not

only people: "It was particularly painful to abandon Aksaniya Nova, a wonderful southern natural park. It was unbearably bitter because the war had gotten this far. The animals looked at us with the same reproachfulness as did people. You wanted to lower your eyes…"

I well recall mama's story about the Victory Parade in '45. The trains were unloaded and the *front's* military council and the secretariat staff were put up in the Moscow Hotel. Preparations for the parade were well underway, but one could feel in everything that there was something else. Papa was too preoccupied and came home too late, and not from rehearsals for the parade, but from the General Staff, and he was took quiet and absorbed in something of his own. But the parade passed and everybody was soaked to the skin by the torrential rain, which nevertheless did not dampen the celebration, although there was sorrow for everyone who had been killed, tormented or missing in action…

Following the parade there was a reception in the Kremlin and a fireworks display in the evening, and later in the hotel room a photograph was taken that's hanging on my wall alongside the one made on 9 May '45 in Vienna. When Weil had packed up his equipment and left, everyone continued sitting together for a long time—papa, his officers for special assignments, and mama—and they reminisced and told jokes, and were quiet. Then mama suddenly heard Tevchenkov[59] purring to himself:

"Curl, curl, you curly forelock!
"Curl, you forelock, in the wind!
And, noticing that she was listening, he winked and began to sing louder:
"Mama, I'm not afraid of Siberia,
"After all, Siberia is also Russian land!
It was then that mama understood that the war was not over for them, and that they had to leave once again for the front, which acquired a new name—Trans-Baikal.

It's interesting to follow how they honored the marshals at the reception in the Kremlin on 24 May 1945, which was dedicated to the *front* commanders. Molotov made the toasts. They drank for marshal after marshal in this order: Zhukov, Konev, Rokossovskii, Govorov, Malinovskii, Tolbukhin, and Vasilevskii (the latter together with General Bagramyan,[60] in so much as their forces had fought in East Prussia). There then followed toasts for Meretskov (he was not at the reception, because he was already in the Far East) and General Yeremenko, for Voroshilov, Budennyi, and Timoshenko, although for the last three as heroes of the civil war. And although Molotov recalled their "new achievements," in the stenographic report it was noted that they saluted Voroshilov, Budennyi and Timoshenko "particularly warmly." The toats for Malinovskii sounded as follows: "I raise my glass to the commander of the Second Ukrainian Front, Marshal Malinovskii, who liberated Budapest from the German aggressors! (those present salute Marshal Malinovskii, standing)."

By comparison, the toast for the marshal's neighbor and rival sounded thusly: "I raise my glass for the commander of the Third Ukrainian Front, Marshal Tolbukhin, who with his forces covered

---

59   Editor's note. Aleksandr Nikolaevich Tevchenkov (1902-75) joined the Red Army in 1919 and rose through the political apparatus. During the Great Patriotic War he sereved as a member of the military council in armies and *fronts* in Europe and the Far East. Following the war, Tevchenkov continued to serve in the political organs until his retirement in 1966.

60   Editor's note. Ivan Khristoforovich Bagramyan (1897-1982) served as a junior officer in the Russian imperial army during World War I. He joined the Red Army in 1920 and served in a number of command, staff and teaching posts during the interwar period. During the Great Patriotic War he served chiefly in staff positions at the *front* level, before making the jump to army commander. He later commanded the First Baltic Front and the Samland operational group in East Prussia at the end of the war. Following the war, Bagramyan commanded a military district and held a number of positions within the central military apparatus.

the south more than the others, and who liberated Bulgaria and its capital of Sofia. Marshal Tolbukhin's forces took the city of Vienna and are now masters of the situation in Austria. To Marshal Tolbukhin's health! (those present salute Marshal Tolbukhin standing)."

One is struck by the order in which the toasts for the marshals were proclaimed, which did not fully reflect their true hierarchy. Most likely, the hierarchical principle was combined with the geographical one. At first they drank to the marshals whose forces took part in the Berlin operation and who ended the war in the territory of the Soviet occupation zone in Germany. The first to be mentioned was Zhukov, as the former deputy Supreme Commander-in-Chief and the only one of the marshals who was a three-time Hero of the Soviet Union. This reflected his leading position in the military hierarchy at that moment. The mention of Konev secondly was due to the fact that his armies, along with Zhukov's, directly took Berlin. Konev was designated for the post of commander of Soviet forces in Austria, and Rokossovskii in Poland. However, it is likely that the post of commander in Poland was more significant in Stalin's eyes, insofar as the group of forces was larger than the one in Austria. Here Rokossovskii's Polish nationality played a role, as well as the fact that in the real military hierarchy Stalin placed him higher than Konev. However, at the same time, Konev received the rank of marshal earlier than Rokossovskii—20 February 1944, whereas Konstantin Konstantinovich got his only on 29 July of the same year. Konev and Rokossovskii were also distinguished by the fact that they were then the only marshals who were two-time heroes of the Soviet Union. Then came Marshal Govorov, whose forces fought in Courland. One cannot say that Stalin placed him in the military hierarchy after Rokossovskii and Konev. However, he received the rank of marshal only a few days before Rokossovskii—18 June 1944. However, in this case it was far more significant that Rokossovskii was twice awarded the Hero of the Soviet Union, while Govorov had only one gold star. Moreover, he received the Order of Victory only a week after the reception, on 31 May 1945. Moreover, Leonid Aleksandrovich's postwar career is none too impressive. He was appointed commadner of the Leningrad Military District, by no means the most powerful one, and as early as April 1946 was transferred to the honorific but insignificant post of chief inspector of the Ground Forces. In 1947 he became chief inspector of the armed forces, and in 1948 he was also made commander of National Air Defense. Although the latter post was important, it was by no means the most significant in the system of troop control. It's not excluded that Stalin did not fully trust Govorov, recalling his service with Kolchak, and so after the war did not give him command of large forces within the Ground Forces. On the other hand, he entrusted to him the doubtful honor (excuse the unintended pun) of heading in January 1948 the "court of honor", which convicted admirals N.G. Kuznetsov,[61] L.M. Galler,[62] V.A. Alafuzov,[63] and G.A. Stepanov,[64] who were rehabilitated following Stalin's death (Galler, unfortunately, posthumously).

---

61   Editor's note. Nikolai Gerasimovich Kuznetsov (1904-74) joined the Red Navy in 1919. He served as a naval advisor to the Spanish Republic during the civil war and was appointed people's commissar of the navy in 1939. During the Great Patriotic War he was a member of the *Stakva* and the State Defense Committee (GKO). Following the war he was convicted by a "court of honor" of passing naval designs to Great Britain and the US and reduced in rank. Kuznetsov returned to favor after Stalin's death, but ran afoul of Zhukov and was reduced in rank again.

62   Editor's note. Lev Mikhailovich Galler (1883-1950) joined the imperial navy in 1902 and the Red Navy in 1918. During the Great Patriotic War he was in charge of ship design and construction. Galler was convicted along with Kuznetsov and others in 1948 and died in prison.

63   Editor's note. Vladimir Antonovich Alafuzov (1901-66) joined the Red Navy in 1918 and fought in the civil war. During the Great Patriotic War he served in higher staff positions. He was convicted along with Kuznetsov and others and sentenced to prison in 1948. Alafuzov was freed and rehabilitated in 1953.

64   Editor's note. Georgii Andreevich Stepanov (1890-1957) joined the imperial navy in 1908 and the Red

Malinovskii and Tolbukhin followed behind Govorov. They were different from the other marshals in the fact that they were not heroes of the Soviet Union, although they carried the Order of Victory. By the way, Malinovskii, as opposed to Tolbukhin, was to receive the gold star very shortly—for the war with Japan. At the same time Malinovskii obviously stood higher in Stalin's eyes than Tolbukhin, which was emphasized, in particular, by the fact that Rodion Yakovlevich received the rank of marshal two days before Fedor Ivanovich. And in the toasts more of Malinovskii's services were recounted than Tolbukhin's. Those present well knew that there had been no war with Bulgaria and that he could not have liberated Sofia, where there was already a communist government by the time Soviet troops arrived. And his forces had actually taken Vienna together with Malinovskii's forces, although Molotov didn't mention that Malinovskii also took Vienna, in order that he not tower too much over Tolbukhin. Following the war, Tolbukhin headed the southern group of forces in Romania and Bulgaria, and was simultaneously chairman of the Allied Control Commission in Bulgaria, and from January 1947 he headed the Trans-Caucasus Military District. Taking into account the strained relations with Turkey, upon which the USSR made territorial demands after the war, this district was by no means the least important. In this case, Stalin obviously took into account the fact that before the war and at its beginning Tolbukhin had headed the Trans-Caucasus Military District staff.

There then followed a toast for Meretskov. He, as opposed to the two preceding marshals, was a Hero of the Soviet Union, although he was awarded the rank of marshal later—only on 26 October 1944. Moreover, Meretskov, just like Govorov, did not yet have an Order of Victory, although he had left for the Far East to earn one. At the end of the Great Patriotic War Kirill Afanas'evich commanded the second-tier Karelian Front and obviously occupied one of the last places in the hierarchy of marshals. It appears that Stalin did not completely trust him, although he had freed him following a brief arrest in 1941. Meretskov, following the Soviet-Japanese War, was appointed to command the Maritime Military District, which according to the number of troops was far inferior to the Trans-Baikal-Amur Military District, which Malinovskii began to head. To be sure, there was an unexpected rise in Meretskov's career, when in July 1947 he headed the Moscow Military District, the most important in all respects. It seems Stalin had resumed trusting him completely. By all appearances, Timoshenko, whose daughter Yekaterina married Stalin's son Vasilii in 1946, recommended Meretskov for this post to him. It's likely that Semyon Konstantinovich recalled his old comrade in arms, with whom he had broken through the Mannerheim Line.[65] Meretskov was then chief of the General Staff while Timoshenko was defense commissar. However, as early as June 1949 Meretskov was sent off to command the secondary White Sea Military District, which was hardly fitting for a marshal. Moreover, Meretskov could have quarreled with Stalin's son Vasilii, who commanded the air assets of the Moscow Military District from 1947 and who could have complained to his father and reported shortcomings in Meretskov's work. Or it could have been just the opposite: it's not excluded that his son's friendship with Meretskov put Stalin on his guard. Meretskov recommended that Vasilii Stalin be awarded the Order of Lenin for the successful conduct of the air parade on 1 May 1948, but obviously at the demand of his father, they lowered this to the Order of the Red Banner, which he was awarded on 22 June 1948. By the way, at his trial, Vasilii Stalin, who was accused of abusing his position and misappropriations, admitted that "Meretskov gave me two bear cubs."

Navy in 1918. During the Great Patriotic War he commanded a flotillaand headed the Main Naval Staff. He was convicted along with Kuznetsov and others and sentenced to prison in 1948. Stepanov was freed and rehabilitated in 1953.

65   Editor's note. The Mannerheim Line was the popular name for the system of defensive fortifications built along the Soviet-Finnish border between 1920 and 1939. During the Soviet-Finnish War of 1939-40 the Red Army was initially unable to penetrate the line, although it finally succeeded in early 1940.

After Meretskov, they drank for the marshal-heroes of the civil war, who had received their marshals' ranks before the beginning of the Great Patriotic War. Of these, upon the completion of the war, only Timoshenko was actively involved in the army. Voroshilov, as a member of the Presidium of the Central Committee, was now only involved in political affairs. In 1945-47 he was the chairman of the Allied Control Commission for Hungary and from 1946 deputy chairman of the Council of Ministers. One should note that in the last years of Stalin's life Kliment Yefremovich lost favor. As early as 1943 Budennyi had been in many ways transformed into a decorative figure, having become the commander-in-chief of the cavalry and in 1947 the deputy minister of agriculture for horse breeding. It's not accidental that Voroshilov and Budennyi were the only marshals of the Soviet Union in May 1945 who were not awarded the Order of Victory. Actually, this was only fair. Kliment Yefremovich and Semyon Mikhailovich did not conduct a single successful strategic operation during the Great Patriotic War, as the status for the order required.

Thanks to the fact that his daughter Yekaterina had become the wife of the leader's son, Timoshenko remained in Stalin's favor, although he did not occupy any important posts. After the war, Semyon Konstantinovich commanded the Belorussian (Baranovichi) and Southern Urals military districts, and then once again the Belorussian district. These districts were not the most important in the military hierarchy, but thanks to his closeness to Stalin Timoshenko's influence was obvious, and in the hierarchy of marshals he was among the top five.

Of the marshals, they drank last for Vasilevskii. However, in the hierarchy of Stalin's marshals, he occupied one of the tops spots in importance. At that moment Aleksandr Mikhailovich had only one gold star of a Hero of the Soviet Union, but the second was not far off. As early as the autumn of 1944 Stalin had decided upon his appointment as the commander-in-chief of the forces in the Far East in the future war with Japan. Vasilevskii became a twice Hero of the Soviet Union for the victory in this war and and became the equal of Konev and Rokossovskii according to this rating. And although he was inferior to Zhukov by one gold star, he shared the first or second place with him in the hierarchy. Only these two marshals had two Orders of Victory apiece. And very soon Vasilevskii undoubtedly occupied the first place, when in March 1946 he once again headed the General Staff and in 1949-53 was the military minister.

Thus one may picture the hierarchy of marshals in 1945 as follows:

1.-2.—Zhukov, Vasilevskii
3. Rokossovskii
4. Konev
5. Timoshenko
6. Malinovskii
7. Tolbukhin
8. Govorov
9. Meretskov

Malinovskii thus occupied a middle place—not in the first rank of marshals, but not in the last either. This would enable him under favorable circumstances, to count on further career advancement. And success in the war with Japan did much to assist this.

To a certain extent the marshals' military services depended upon what *fronts* they had commanded. On the Eastern Front the German army groups that bordered on the Baltic Sea fought the most successfully. Here the Germans never got into a "cauldron" and no significant groups of German forces were destroyed. Two factors worked in the Germans' favor. German troops operated almost exclusively on the northern flank of the Soviet-German front, and further north part of the Red Army's forces were occupied by Finnish troops, who were almost the equals of the Wehrmacht according to combat capability. What is even more important, the German fleet reigned in the Baltic and, if necessary, could evacuate German forces pinned against the sea, or could quite successfully supply them until the very end of the war. Soviet losses in men killed were very high. It's not surprising that the marshals who commanded Soviet forces along the northern flank ended up at the bottom of the hierarchical ladder.

The German army groups which operated in the center of the Eastern Front had the advantage in that they consisted almost entirely of German formations. However, there was a downside— they could be caught in pincers from both flanks in case of failures by the other army groups in the north and south. The most catastrophic situation for Army Group Center came about in Belorussia in the summer of 1944, when it was deeply outflanked from the south.

The southern German army groups, which operated in the far south, as a rule, had their right flank resting on the Sea of Azov or the Black Sea. This somewhat eased their task, insofar as a formal superiority on the Black Sea enabled them to carry out the naval evacuation of groups of forces that had gotten into a critical situation (the Soviet fleet conducted itself passively). However, a negative factor for the Germans was the presence along the southern wing of the Soviet-German front of a large number of Romanian, Hungarian and Italian formations, which were considerably inferior to the Wehrmacht according to combat capability. The catastrophe at Stalingrad came about when the Sixth Army penetrated deeply into the Eurasian continent, leaving its flanks open and defended only by allied troops. The catastrophe in Romania in August 1944 also occurred because it was impossible to evacuate their forces by sea. First of all, it was impossible to carry out an evacuation without the Romanian fleet. The main thing is that there was no place to evacuate them, insofar as there remained no countries in the basin of the Black Sea that were allied to or occupied by Germany.

The Red Army carried out several successful operations to encircle major enemy groups of forces along the central and southern sectors of the Soviet-German front. Thus Stalin's marshals who commanded fronts here ended up higher on the hierarchical ladder than the marshals on the front's northern flank.

In concluding the story of the Great Patriotic War, I would like to say a few words about the style of Malinovskii's leadership. This is what Rodion Yakovlevich's daughter recalls:

> Father never resorted to shouting and swearing—this is what literally everyone who knew him at the front or in the postwar years say. All are agreed that the contrast between the authoritarian and deliberately military style of Zhukov and papa's—who always addressed people by the formal "you" and by name and patronymic, without raising his voice (which did not of course, exclude being demanding)—was striking and not to everyone's liking. Some called papa's manner of treating people "civilian," but it's more likely that it was simply good breeding.
>
> But this was not just the consequence of self education. My father knew only too well what it's like to be a soldier, particularly during wartime, and never forgot that.
>
> Once V.S. Golubovich, the military historian, told me in passing, and quite calmly:
>
> "'Did you know that Rodion Yakovlevich never beat his soldiers?"
>
> He went on, but I was stuck on what he had said. If they say of a man that he walks on two legs, does that mean it's an everyday norm? Does this mean that others and they are not few, walk on four legs?
>
> "Do you mean to say that others beat people?"
>
> "Of course they did! So and so even carried around a special stick for that sort of thing. Anyone who fought there (there followed an exact description of where) knows that"

(according to the testimony of Chief Aviation Marshal A.Ye. Golovanov,[66] the marshal who used a stick to beat people was I.S. Konev, B.S.).

I remember once how a young lieutenant, who a little less than a year (naturally, in Alabino), upon calling on my mama on an errand from his mother, told us at lunch about how he "teaches his soldiers." And after he had repeated for the fifteenth time that "A soldier should be trained," papa interrupted him: "A soldier should be pitied. Until you see him as a human, he won't recognize you as a commander."

Here one should stipulate one thing. Soviet generals and officers beat their subordinates all the time. According to Khrushchev's testimony, Stalin supported this practice and sometimes even demanded that his commanders smash the face of some general or another. Of the marshals of the Soviet Union, it seems that only two were never seen using their fists. These were Rokossovskii and Malinovskii. The others beat people. But they chiefly beat generals and senior officers. For the majority of marshals it was simpler to shoot even a lieutenant or captain than to thrash them. According to Khrushchev again, only Marshal Budennyi, who recalled the prerevolutionary times when he was an NCO, allowed himself to beat up rank and file soldiers. The others were not so democratic in beating their subordinates. In this sense, Rodion Yakovlevich and Konstantin Konstantinovich, who, by the way, never employed a cursing style of command, were rare birds indeed. For this their subordinates, from soldier to general, sincerely respected and loved them. After all, not only did Malinovskii and Rokossovskii never beat anyone, but saw to it that their subordinate generals and officers did not do this either.

---

66 Editor's note. Aleksandr Yevgen'evich Golovanov (1904-75) joined the Red Army in 1918 and initially served in the secret police (GPU), receiving his pilot's wings in 1932. During the Great Patriotic War he commanded and air regiment and division and in 1942 was appointed commander of Long-Range Aviation. Golovanov was removed from his post after the war and given minor assignments, before being retired in 1953.

10

The War with Japan

Malinovskii met up with his family on the road to the war with Japan. His son Robert recalled: "… our next meeting took place only after a year, after the victory, when they transferred my father to Chita. I remember that he was traveling by train through Irkutsk, where we were living, and he told us to travel with him. He had a separate special rail car, with a compartment and large room for meetings."

Marshal Malinovskii traveled to the Far East wearing the shoulder boards of a colonel general and under the false surname of Morozov.

On 18 June 1945 Malinovskii presented to "the Supreme Commander-in-Chief, comrade Stalin," an operational plan for the Trans-Baikal Front in the war with Japan, marked "Top Secret. Very important. One copy only:"

> I'm reporting on the disposition of the Trans-Baikal Front's forces for the forthcoming operation.
>
> I.   An evaluation of the enemy's forces (see maps nos. 1 and 2 on the enemy).
>
> At present the Japanese have up to 17 infantry, two tank divisions (up to 900 tanks) and up to 400 planes in Manchuria and Korea.
>
> The Japanese used to have up to 1,000 planes; one must suppose that this number of planes will be transferred upon the commencement of operations.
>
> Of their 17 infantry divisions, the Japanese are holding 8-9 against the Far East, three infantry divisions in Korea, 2-3 infantry divisions in the central areas of Manchuria (Harbin, Mukden), and two infantry divisions against the Trans-Baikal Front. Aside from these two divisions (the 119th Infantry Division and another whose number is unknown), the Japanese have three fortified areas: the Manzhouli—Jalai Nur fortified area, which is occupied by units of the 8th Border Garrison, numbering 1,000-1,200 men and the Khingan Cavalry Regiment;
>
> Further in the depth is the Hailar fortified area, which is also occupied by units of the 8th Border Garrison, and also contains the headquarters of the 8th Border Garrison and the headquarters of the Japanese Sixth Army;
>
> > the Halun—Arkhan fortified area is occupied by a reinforced infantry regiment (90th Infantry Regiment).
>
> Aside from this, it is necessary to take into account that along the Kalgan axis, opposite the Mongolian People's Republic, the De Wang's Inner Mongolian cavalry, numbering up to 12,000 men, reinforced by one Janpanese infantry division and a Japanese infantry brigade.

It is also necessary to take account of up to 180,000 troops from Manchukuo,[1] of which up to 60,000 are deployed against the Trans-Baikal Front.

Conclusion:

1. In all, the Japanese can put up to ten infantry divisions and one tank division, consisting of 350 tanks, up to 1,000 planes, the forces of Manchukuo and Inner Mongolia—equal in strength to 6-7 Japanese divisions, against the Trans-Baikal Front at first.
2. Taking into account the extreme importance of the Trans-Baikal Front's operational axis, the Japanese will do everything they can to reinforce this axis; thus one must believe that they will transfer forces from northern China, equal to 7-8 infantry divisions, here. Thus in all, during the first 1½-2 months of the war the Trans-Baikal Front may encounter up to 17-18 Japanese divisions, 6-7 divisions from Manchukuo and Inner Mongolia, and two tank divisions, including up to 800-900 tanks.

II. The Trans-Baikal Front's forces by 1 August 1945.
28 rifle divisions.
2 motorized divisions.
1 tank corps.
2 mechanized corps.
2 tank divisions (old organization).
4 tank brigades.
1 motorized rifle brigade.
4 independent tank battalions.
1 cavalry division.
2 artillery divisions.
5 anti-tank artillery brigades.
3 High Command Reserve anti-aircraft divisions.
4 anti-aircraft artillery battalions.
2 M-31 mortar brigades.
8 M-13 mortar regiments.
3 assault engineer-sapper brigades.
1 engineer-bridge brigade.

These have been combined into four armies: the 17th, 36th, 39th, and 53rd armies, the 6th Guards Tank Army, and the 12th Air Army, consisting of two fighter, two assault and two bomber air divisions.

Conclusion:
These forces will be sufficient for the Trans-Baikal Front to overcome resistance and, under favorable conditions, to destroy 18-25 Japanese divisions, relying primarily on our superiority in tanks and artillery; that is, the rifle troops will barely suffice, taking into account the fact that a Japanese division contains an average of 13-15,000 men.

---

1   Editor's note. Manchukuo was that area of Manchuria and Inner Mongolia conquered by the Japanese in 1931 and held by them until 1945. Manchukuo was nominally ruled by the puppet Emperor Pu Yi, who had also been the last emperor of China.

III. An evaluation of the operational axes.
  1. The axis along the Chinese Eastern Railway: Hailar—Bugt—Qiqihar—Harbin will allow for the operations of a single army and is characterized by difficult conditions for overcoming the Great Khingan mountain range, with heights of up to 1,500 meters and the water barrier of the Nen River and the Argun River along the border. This axis is blocked by the Manzhouli—Jalai Nur and Hailar fortified areas.
  2. The Solun—Taonan—Szeping axis is characterized by more favorable conditions for overcoming the mountainous and forested Great Khingan range; it is less wild here and is being cleared of forests, with heights from 1,000-1,200 meters.
      The range runs closer to the Mongolian People's Republic's border with Manchuria: the network of dirt roads is more developed, which allows for the operations of large troop masses of two and more armies.
  3. The following axes: a) Ugodzir—Linxi—Chifeng; b) Olon Sume—Lake Artsakan—Dolonnor—Chengde; c) Dzamin Ude—Khuade—Kalgan—allow for the operations by a reinforced rifle corps along each of these, or by mobile formations of equal strength; they allow for maneuver along the steppe between each other and thus may be viewed as a single broad operational axis in the general direction of Beijing, Chengde and Kalgan. The downside of this axis is its great remove from the railroad.

Conclusion:
The most favorable operational axis is the one toward Solun—Taonan—Szeping, with the adjacent zone to the south of up to 200 kilometers in width.

IV. Disposition of forces, operational formation and the operation's deadlines.
  Proceeding from the Trans-Baikal Front's mission, to capture Manchuria and the Liaodong peninsula, together with the Maritime and Far Eastern fronts. The achievement of this goal is divided into two operations:
  The first is to capture central Manchuria, Qiqihar, Kailu, Szeping, Jilin, and Harbin, and a second operation to complete our arrival at the border of Manchuria with northern China and the capture of the Liaodong peninsula.
  For the first operation, it is necessary to have the following operational formation for the Trans-Baikal Front's forces:
  The 36th Army, consisting of two rifle corps—in all, seven rifle divisions, one cavalry division, two fortified areas, one tank brigade, two independent tank battalions, four High Command Reserve artillery regiments, one anti-tank artillery regiment, two mortar regiments, and one regiment of M-13 mortars.
  The main attack is to be launched north of Jalai Nur in the general direction of Hailar, and with part of its forces—1-2 rifle divisions—from Tsagaan launch an attack to the south to linke up with the forces that will be operating form the the Khamar Dobbe area to the north, to eliminate the salient west and south of Lake Dalai Nor.
  A supporting attack will be launched by one rifle division and one cavalry division from the Svetlyi Klyuch area toward Hailar.
  The army's immediate task is to capture the Hailar area by the fifteenth day of the operation. The subsequent task is to capture the Pokotu—Chalantun—Pusi area by the end of the month following the start of the operation. The operation's overall depth is 500 kilometers.

The 39th Army (Lyudnikov[2]), consisting of three rifle corps—nine rifle divisions—army reinforcement means, a breakthrough artillery division, two tank brigades, four High Command Reserve artillery regiments, two M-31 guards mortar brigades, three regiments of M-13 mortars, one anti-tank artillery brigade, and one assault engineer-sapper brigade.

The main attack is to be launched along the right flank in the general direction of Dzurkin-Harul, Hahsu-Nela and Vanemyao; the immediate task is to capture the Solun area by the twelfth or fifteenth day of the operation, and the subsequent task is to capture the Taonan—Talai—Kingsing area by the end of a month following the start of the operation.

A supporting attack is to be launched with the forces of 1-2 rifle divisions from the Khmar Dobbe area to the north in the direction of Ganchzhur and Solov'ev, to link up with the 36th Army's units attacking from the Tsagaan area and together with them to eliminate the salient west and south of Lake Dalai Nor.

The operation's overall depth is up to 500 kilometers.

The 53rd Army (Managarov), consisting of three rifle corps—nine rifle divisions—army reinforcement means, one breakthrough artillery division, one tank division, two High Command Reserve artillery regiments, two regiments of M-13 mortars, two anti-tank artillery brigades, and one engineer-sapper brigade.

The main attack will be launched along the left flank in the general direction of Dzun Uzemchin and Lubei. An attack will be made along the right flank by a single corps in the direction of Ergun Tala, Barun Su and Arukhorchin.

The army's immediate task is to capture the Ara Khundulun area by the fifteenth day from the start of the operation and cross the Great Khingan range.

The subsequent task is to capture the Tungliao—Kaitung—Chanyu area by the end of a month after the start of the operation.

The operation's overall depth is 500 kilometers.

The 17th Army, consisting of three rifle divisions, one tank brigade, one anti-tank artillery brigade, two High Command Reserve regiments, one anti-tank artillery regiment, one mortar regiment, two independent tank battalions, and one regiment of M-13 mortars.

The army is to launch an attack in the general direction of Ugodzir, Barun Khushi, Linxi, and Dobanshan.

The immediate task is to capture the Lindun—Dobanshan area by the 15th day of the operation, and to subsequently capture the Kailu—Chifeng area by the close of a month from the start of the operation.

The operation's overall depth is 550-600 kilometers.

A group from the Mongolian People's Republic Army, consisting of three cavalry divisions, an armored brigade, a tank regiement, one reinforced motorized rifle brigade from the Red Army, and one Red Army mechanized brigade is organized into the headquarters of the 85th Rifle Corps.

The group is to support the front's right flank and operate in the direction of Pankiang, Khuade and Kalgan, with the task of reaching the Pankiang—Khuade area.

---

2   Editor's note. Ivan Il'ich Lyudnikov (1902-76) joined the Red Army in 1918. During the Great Patriotic War he commanded a brigade, division, corps, and a number of armies in Europe and the Far East. Following the war, Lyudnikov held a number of command and administrative posts.

The group is to operate with a powerful detachment toward Kangpao and Kalgan and to capture Kalgan, under favorable conditions.

The 6th Guards Tank Army (Kravchenko), consisting of two mechanized and one tank corps, with army reinforcement means, two self-propelled artillery brigades, and one motorized infantry brigade is concentrating in the Matat Somon area for operations behind the front's shock group in the general direction of Dzun Uzemchin and Lubei and Siping, in order to capture the Kaiyuan—Szeping—Lishu—Liaoyuan area.

The army's forward detachments are to operate in the direction of Mukden and Changchun.

The front's reserve, consisting of two motorized divisions and one anti-tank artillery brigade, is in the Choybalsan (Bain-Tumen) area.

By 1 August the 12th Air Army will have 400 fighters, 240 assault aircraft and 128 bombers ready for action, for a total of 768 combat aircraft.

The air army's main forces will be directed toward covering and supporting the front's main group of forces.

The Mongolian People's Revolutionary Army will be supported by a Mongolian air division, which must be rearmed with 80 Il aircraft and 80 fighters by the start of the operation.

V. Materiel support.
   A) Munitions. Suppy, taking into account that being unloaded in July and arriving by August 15:
       4.5 combat loads for small arms.
       6.9 combat loads for 45mm guns.
       4 combat loads for 57mm guns.
       4 combat loads for 76mm regimental and divisional artillery.
       3.9 combat loads of 85mm tank ammunition (55 rounds in a combat load).
       6.7 combat loads of 100mm rounds (80 rounds each for 40 guns).
       Only 99 rounds each for SU-100 guns, or 3 combat loads.
       4.4 combat loads for 122mm howitzers.
       5.2 combat loads for 152mm guns/howitzers.
       5.4 combat loads for 203mm howitzers.
       6.4 combat loads for 82mm mortars.
       6.7 combat loads for 120mm mortars.
       6.4 combat loads for 47mm anti-aircraft guns.
       6 combat loads for 40mm "Bofors" anti-aircraft guns.
       9.1 combat loads for 76mm anti-aircraft guns.
       4.8 combat loads for 85mm anti-aircraft guns.
       21 salvoes for M-13 guards mortars.
       9.5 salvoes for M-31 guards mortars.
   B) An auto fuel reserve of 30 refills, or 21,540 tons, is being created in order to carry out the decree of the State Defense Committee.
       This is covered by available reserves.
       There are 20 refills of auto fuel, or 45,000 tons, of which 30,952 is available and 14,048 tons are being delivered in July, although taking into account the large expenditure of auto fuel due to the concentration and deployment of troops and with delivering munitions, it is necessary to deliver 12-15,000 tons to cover ongoing expenditures.

Diesel fuel is covered by available supplies of 3,485 tons, with another 2,765 tons being delivered in July, which will mean 6,250 tons, or ten refills.

It is necessary to deliver 2,000 tons to move the troops to their jumping-off areas.

C) The following are being delivered in July to cover ongoing needs and for 40 days' rations:

5,420 tons of rye flour, or 327 train cars

360 tons of various groats, or 20 train cars

1,700 tons of meat, or 170 train cars

296 tons of tobacco, or 37 train cars

The remaining products are covered by available stocks and their delivery in small amounts of 7-10 train cars.

VI. Reinforcements.

It is necessary to plan ahead for the delivery of the following to cover expected losses in the first month of operations:

120,000 men

500 tanks

100 SU-100s

200 SU-76s

100 fighter aircraft

100 assault aircraft

50 bombers

Aside from this, the front should be reinforced by 7-9 rifle divisions, with 2-3 corps headquarters and thre fighter air brigades.

The 12th Air Army should be reinforced with two fighter divisions, two assault air divisions, one bomber division and three air corps headquarters.

It is extremely necessary to provide each army as soon as possible with a reconnaissance squadron of 12 King Cobras each (this refers to the Bell P-63, which was usually employed as a fighter-bomber, B.S.) and a signals air regiment, with Po-2 aircraft and 50 percent amphibious and traing planes.

VII. Deadline for troop readiness.

Taking into account the completion of the troops' unloading on 1-5 August 1945 and their arrival in their deployment areas over dirt roads within 300-500 kilometers, and the necessary regrouping of forces, up to 20 days will be needed.Thus one may calculate the start of the operation at 20-25 August 1945.

Supplement:

1. A map of the enemy dispositions on a 3,000,000:1 map and another of 1,000,000:1.

2. A map of the operational decision on a 1,500,000:1 scale.

Marshal of the Soviet Union (Malinovskii).

One item is immediately worthy of attention. Malinovskii, assuming that the Soviet forces' real losses in the impending war with Japan would be at the same level as in the final battles along the Soviet-German front, requested reinforcements which obviously exceeded those losses which he was preparing to officially report. In the Great Patriotic War the Soviet forces' real irretrievable losses in the armies' and fronts' reports were lowered approximately three times, as a result of which overall losses were lowered by approximately two times. Moreover, the official losses were covered chiefly by centralized reinforcements, and irretrievable losses were not counted in reports by the higher headquarters and were mainly covered by those called up directly to the units. It's typical that in the Soviet-Japanese War, where combat operations took place in the territory of Inner Mongolia and Manchuria, where the call up of the local Chinese and Mongolian population into Soviet units was, of course, impossible, they planned to cover this additional and uncounted loss by getting additional rifle divisions. Malinovskii asked for nine of them, which approximately corresponds to the requested reinforcements in number. In four years of war the marshal had become convinced that the real losses in reports from the troops were significantly reduced. He calculated on preserving the previous strength of his shock groups with the aid of new divisions. Malinovskii undoubtedly was thinking of the actual level of monthly losses in the war against Germany. Otherwise, it's impossible to explain the demand for additional divisions. After all, as they moved to the south toward the Pacific Ocean ports, the Soviet forces' front did not expand, but in fact contracted.

Thus Rodion Yakovlevich assumed that the actual losses among his troops in the war with Japan would be in the realm of 240,000 men. They actually proved to be several times less.

One may say that the plan for the war with Japan was drawn up in an exemplary fashion, taking into account the experience of the war in Europe. And it was carried out well ahead of time, both as regards the time for the beginning of the operation, as well as the pace of its development, insofar as they had to operate in almost testing range conditions, when the enemy was only designated. Stalin was in a hurry and began the war not on 25 August, but on 9 August, because the state of the Kwantung Army was such that it could be boldly attacked without awaiting the arrival of all the supplies and units. Stalin was in a hurry, fearing that Japan would capitulate shortly to the western Allies and he would not be able to seize his portion of the spoils in time.

The strength of the Trans-Baikal Front on 9 August was 638,300 men, not counting 16,000 men from the Mongolian People's Revolutionary Army. Compare this to the strength of the First Far Eastern Front, at 586,500 men, and the Second Far Eastern Front, at 334,700 men.

On 5 July Malinovskii's proposals were formulated in a *Stavka* directive, signed by Stalin and Antonov. Only the readiness deadlines were more advanced. It was necessary to begin the operation as early as 25 July, without waiting for the complete arrival of the 53rd Army. Malinovskii also decided to commit the 6th Guards Tank Army in the first echelon, insofar as there were no signs that the Japanese would attempt to occupy the Great Khingan with any kind of significant forces. Two motorized rifle division, which were in the Far East before, as well as a number of other units, were added to the tank army.

Khrushchev recalled:

> They gave the most troops to Malinovskii. And we routed the Japanese Kwantung Army. To be sure, after Japan was already beaten, the Americans dropped two atomic bombs on the country. Japan was in its death throes and was looking for some way to get out of the war. We got into the war against her literally in the final month of events. I was present in Moscow during a conversation, when Stalin was hurrying his commanders to begin operations as soon as possible against Japan, otherwise she would surrender to the USA and we would be too late to join the war. Stalin had his doubts as to whether the Americans would keep the promise they had made earlier. He thought that they might not.

Malinovskii and other Soviet generals and marshals believed that the war with Japan would last no less than two months. Actually, combat operations lasted only a week. Following the declaration by the emperor about Japan's readiness to surrender, organized resistance ceased. Only those units and soldiers that had not received the order continued to resist.

The Soviet command overestimated the strength of the Japanese Kwantung Army. This was not only because the Japanese government, as a result of the atomic bombing of Hiroshima and

Nagasaki, surrendered only a week after the start of combat operations in Manchuria. By the time of the Soviet attack, almost all the combat-capable divisions and modern weapons had been transferred out of Manchuria to the Pacific theater of military operations. By August 1945 the overwhelming majority of the Kwantung Army's divisions had been formed that year, and had mainly been formed only in July. The Japanese command rated their combat capability at only 15-20 percent of the combat level of a typical full-blooded infantry division. Untrained conscripts of students and invalids predominated in the new divisions. The Japanese forces were catastrophically short of weapons and ammunition, and the fuel at their disposal in Manchuria was adequate for no more than 50 combat-ready planes. Anti-tank artillery was also absent, while the tanks were light models and out of date and, because of the absence of fuel and trained crews, they were unable to get into the fighting.

The assumed Soviet losses proved to colossally overestimated. According to official Soviet data, the Trans-Baikal Front's losses were 2,228 irretrievable (including 522 for non-combat reasons) and 6,155 medical losses, of which almost half—2,996 men—were due to sickness. This is even if one takes into account that the Japanese put Soviet irretrievable losses for the entire Soviet-Japanese war twice as high—20-25,000 men, as opposed to 12,031 according to official Russian data. However, if one assume that the Trans-Baikal Front's overall losses had been lowered by a factor of two, then you would still need another 103,000 losses to reach the assumed losses, which were 120,000 at a minimum.

In intelligence report no. 16 by the Trans-Baikal Front's intelligence section on 10 July 1945, it was noted:

> According to additional information, during March-May 1945 the Japanese have transferred our infantry divisions from Manchuria to other theaters: the 11th Infantry Division to the island of Shikoku, and the 71st Infantry Division to the island of Formosa.
>
> Thus in 1944 and the first half of 1945, 17 infantry divisions (1st, 8th, 9th, 10th, 11th, 12th, 14th, 19th, 23rd, 24th, 25th, 28th, 29th, 57th, 71st, and 304th) have left Manchuria and Korea for other theaters.
>
> It has been established that all the divisions that have left Manchuria for Korea have a strength of not more than 13-15,000 men each, while leaving up to 30-50 percent of their strength in their basing area, which later served as a base for forming new divisions.
>
> According to data that arrived in June of this year, nine infantry divisions (121st, 122nd, 123rd, 124th, 125th, 126th, 127th, 128th, and 160th) and two independent mixed brigades (41st and 42nd) have been identified in Manchuria. In all, by taking into account the previously identified (101st, 107th, 108th, 111th, 112th, 118th, 119th, and 120th divisions), the new numbers of 17 infantry divisions have been identified in Manchuria and Korea.
>
> All of the newly identified infantry divisions in Manchuria and Korea are those of the new organizational type (13-15,000 men).

Actually, the Japanese divisions in Manchuria were transferred wholly and did not leave any kind of cadre for new divisions. Strictly speaking, the intelligence of the Far Eastern Front, to which the troops along the Manchurian border were previously subordinated, exaggerated the Japanese forces and Malinovskii was not guilty. His units did not have time to carry out thorough intelligence and were forced to rely on the data of their predecessors.

By 9 August 1945 the Kwantung Army, under the command of General Otozo Yamada,[3] consisted of two fronts (army groups) and one independent army of mixed composition, supported

---

3   Editor's note. Ozoto Yamada (1881-1965) joined the army in 1903 and later commanded a division and

by an air army and the Sungari River Flotilla. General Seiichi Kita's First Front, which was defending eastern Manchuria, consisted of the Third and Fifth armies, each of which contained three infantry divisions. Aside from this, four infantry divisions and one mixed brigade were subordinated to the front. In all, the First Front numbered 222,157 men.

General Isoroku Jun's Third Front was defending central and western Manchuria, from the Amur River to the Liaodong peninsula. It included the Thirtieth Army (four infantry divisions, one independent mixed brigade and a tank brigade) and the Forty Fourth Army (three infantry divisions, one independent mixed brigade and a tank brigade). Besides this, an infantry division and two mixed independent brigades were subordinated directly to the front. In all, the Japanese Third Front numbered 180,971 men.

The Fourth Independent Army, under the command of Lieutenant General Uemura Mikio, with its headquarters in Qiqihar, was responsible for the defense of north-central and northwestern Manchuria. It consisted of three infantry divisions and four independent mixed brigades and numbered 95,464 men. Aside from this, the 125th Infantry Division in Tunghua was directly subordinated to the Kwantung Army command.

Following the beginning of combat operations on 9 August, the Imperial Supreme Command subordinated to the Kwantung Army the Thirty Fourth Army, which was in Korea, and the Seventeenth Front, whicn included the Fifty Eighth Army. The Seventeenth Front's forces, which consisted of seven infantry divisions and two independent mixed brigades, as well as the 3rd Tank Division's 11th Tank Regiment, were located in southern Korea, were not able to take part in combat operations. The Thirty Fourth Army, whose headquarters was in Hamhung (northern Korea), consisted of the 59th and 137th infantry divisions in Hamhung and Chonpyong and numbered 50,194 men.

There were four infantry divisions on the Kurile Islands and southern Sakhalin, and also the 2nd Tank Division's 11th Tank Regiment, which were subordinated to the Fifth Front.

Although a Japanese infantry division had an authorized strength of 20,000 men, in 1945 its strength varied from 9,000 to 18,000, and in the majority of cases was 14-16,000 men. The division had an authorized strength of 36 guns in an artillery regiment consisting of three battalions. By August 1945 the majority of combat-capable formations and practically all the modern heavy weaponry and combat equipment had been transferred from Manchuria and Korea to the Pacific theater of military activities. They were replaced by recently formed divisions and brigades from untrained conscripts and invalids of limited use. The Forty Fourth Army's 63rd and 117th infantry divisions were garrison formations; that is, they numbered only eight infantry battalions instead of nine and had no artillery whatsoever. The average strength of the independent mixed brigades did not exceed 5,300 men. Before January 1945 there existed only six divisions in the Kwantung Army—two garrison divisions, as well as the 39th, 107th, 108th and 119th. Of these, only the 108th Infantry Division, together with the two garrison divisions, was stationed opposite the Trans-Baikal Front. The Kwantung Army's remaining 16 divisions were formed only in 1945. All of these were catastrophically short of weapons, fuel and ammunition. This is why they could only launch no more than 50 planes into the air.

The Manchukuo army, which numbered 170,000 men, had been disbanded by the Japanese in July 1945, in order to arm the recently formed divisions. The Japanese well understood the unreliability of the Manchurian forces. The Manchukuo army's soldiers and officers understood that Japan's defeat was not far off and were not burning with desire to die for the Japanese emperor,

army in the 1937-45 war with China. He was appointed commander of the Kwantung Army in 1944. Following the war, Yamada was convicted of war crimes by the Soviets, but was released and repatriated in 1956.

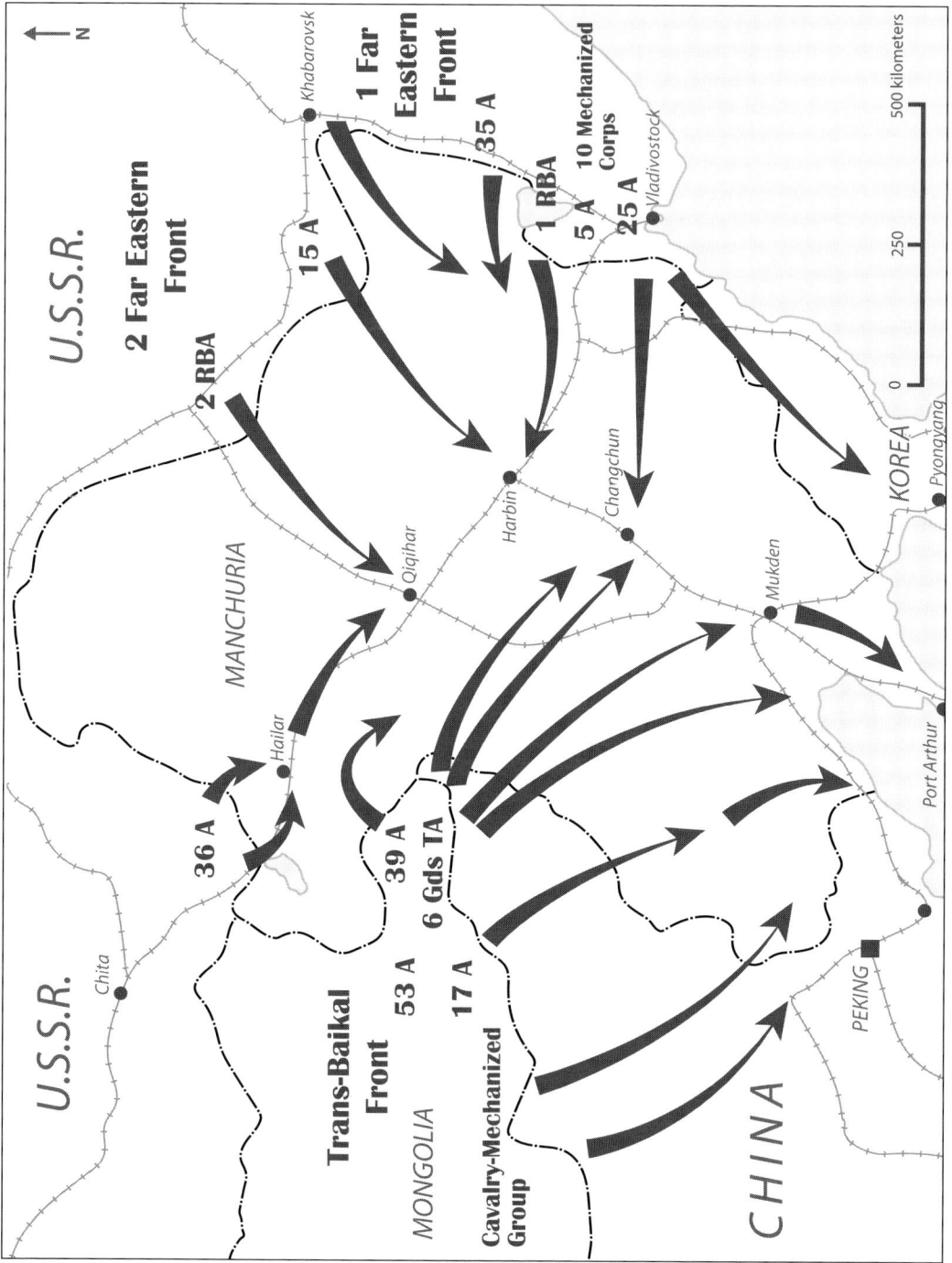

Map 5 Operations in Manchuria, 1945.

or for their own Manchurian one—Pu Yi.[4] In June 1945 the Kwantung Army command began to shift forces and construct fortifications in the depth of Manchuria. Only a third of the combat units were to remain along the border, while two-thirds were to concentrate in the country's depth, in order to wear out the Soviet units there through stubborn resistance. The Japanese were also counting on the broken terrain which was difficult for the passage of vehicles and tanks. However, by the start of the Soviet invasion of Manchuria, both the regroupings of forces and construction of fortificiations were far from complete. None the less, in the Trans-Baikal Front's combat journal for 22-31 August 1945, the following is noted:

> The enemy's frontier areas were covered by very weak border-police detachments, and along the most important axes: Hailar—by a single infantry brigade (80th) and units of the 119th Infantry Division; along the Solun axis)—the 107th Rifle Division. These units had the task of delaying and exhausting our forces, in order to give the Kwantung Army command time to evaluate the situation and deploy its main forces.

The Japanese command evaluated the combat-capability of its formations, deployed against the Trans-Baikal Front, in the following manner (the month they were formed is in parentheses):

119th Infantry Division (October, 1944)—70 percent;
80th Independent Mixed Brigade (January, 1945)—15 percent;
107th Infantry Division (May, 1944)—60 percent;
108th Infantry Division (September, 1944)—65 percent;
117th Infantry Division (July, 1944)—15 percent;
63rd Infantry Division (June, 1944)—15 percent;
133rd Independent Mixed Brigade (July, 1945)—15 percent;
9th Tank Brigade—no data;
125th Infantry Division (January, 1945)—20 percent;
138th Infantry Division (July, 1945)—15 percent;
39th Infantry Division (June, 1939)—80 percent;
1st Tank Brigade—no data;
130th Independent Mixed Brigade (July, 1945)– 15 percent;
136th Infantry Division (July, 1945)—15 percent;
79th Independent Mixed Brigade (January, 1945)—15 percent.

Thus the Japanese forces' combat capability was approximately equal to that of 3.55 infantry divisions and 0.6 of a mixed brigade, and if we count two independent brigades as an infantry division—approximately 3.85 infantry divisions. It was unlikely that the two tank brigades, which had just been formed, had a combat capability of more than 15 percent each and together were equivalent to 0.3 of a tank brigade. All of Malinovskii's formations had been brought up to authorized strength and had a combat capability close to 100 percent, and suffered no shortages in weapons, fuel and ammunition. Taking this into account, the Trans-Baikal Front disposed of 34 calculated rifle and mechanized divisions and approximately 12 calculated tank brigades, which yielded a superiority corresponding to 8.8:1 and 40:1.

---

4   Editor's note. Pu Yi (1906-67) was the last emperor of China until the revolution of 1912. The Japanese installed him as emperor of their puppet state of Manchukuo, where he nominally ruled from 1934 to 1945. The Soviets captured him in 1945 and turned him over to the Chinese Communists in 1949. He spent ten years in prison and was released in 1959.

Taking together, the 63rd and 117th divisions numbered no more than 18 antiquated mountain guns, the 148th Division had almost no light firearms for its infantry regiments, the 138th Division was in the process of mobilizing and numbered no more than 2,000 combat troops, and the 39th Division, which had been transferred from central China, was the most combat capable of all, but had less artillery than authorized. The two tank brigades had just been formed and armed with tanks taken from the Manchukuo army. Thus their combat capability was at a very low level. The troops from Inner Mongolia had been disarmed.

I should note that the Japanese situation facing the other Soviet *fronts* was even worse. They had two independent mixed brigades and two infantry divisions, each at 15 percent of combat capability, facing the Second Far Eastern Front. The single infantry division at 35 percent combat capability, the 149th, had, as opposed to the others, been formed not in July but in January 1945, and had almost no transport for its artillery. All of these formations were equivalent to 0.8 of an infantry division. The First Far Eastern Front had about 18 calculated divisions (11 rifle divisions, four rifle brigades, nine independent tank brigades, five fortified areas, and counting four independent tank brigades as a rifle division and five fortified areas as 2.5 rifle divisions), which yielded an advantage of 16.1:1.

The Japanese facing the First Far Eastern Front had only a few more troops (the month of formation is showed in parentheses):

15th Frontier Border Regiment (July 1945)—no data;
135th Infantry Division (July 1945)—15 percent;
126th Infantry Division (January 1945)—20 percent;
124th Infantry Division (January 1945)—35 percent;
132nd Independent Mixed Brigade (July 1945)—15 percent;
128th Independent Division (January 1945)—20 percent;
112th Infantry Division (July 1945)—35 percent;
1st Mobile Brigade—no data;
79th Infantry Division (February 1945)—15 percent;
127th Infantry Division (March 1945)—20 percent;
122nd Infantry Division (January 1945)—35 percent;
139th Infantry Division (July 1945)—15 percent;
134th Independent Mixed Brigade (July 1945)—15 percent;
59th Infantry Division (February 1945)—no data;
137th Infantry Division (July 1945)—15 percent.

We should note that in the 128th Division, instead of the authorized 23,000 men, there were only 14,000, but its combat capability was rated only at 20 percent, which speaks to a lack of weaponry, munitions and trained troops. We should note that the 15th Border Regiment, instead of the authorized 12 infantry companies and three artillery batteries, had only four companies and one battery, and its combat capability did not exceed 35 percent. The 59th Infantry Division was probably no more capable than the 79th Division, which was formed at the same time; that is, 15 percent. Also, the 1st Mobile Brigade, which was formed only in July 1945, probably had a combat capability of no more than 15 percent. Taking all of this into account, the overall combat capability of the Japanese forces facing the First Far Eastern Front may be rated at 2.8 infantry divisions. The forces of the First Far Eastern Front may be rated at no less than 41 calculated divisions (31 rifle divisions, one cavalry division, one mechanized corps, 11 independent brigades, and 14 fortified areas), which yields a superiority of 14.6:1.

This means that the Japanese had the most favorable correlation of forces for themselves in the sector of the Trans-Baikal Front, which was making the main attack. This is explained by the greater length of the Trans-Baikal Front's front (2,300 kilometers, including 1,700 kilometers of active military operations), compared with that of the First and Second Far Eastern Fronts (700 and 1,600 kilometers, accordingly, of which 500 kilometers involved active military operations). There were 638,000 men in the Trans-Baikal Front and 16,000 from the Mongolian People's Revolutionary Army, while there were 586,500 men I the First Far Eastern Front and 334,700 in the Second Far Eastern Front.

By August 1945 the Kwantung Army presented quite a pathetic sight. All of its cadre divisions had been long ago transferred to the area of the Southern Seas and for defending the homeland. The Red Army was faced by divisions that had been formed from either 17-or 18-year old recruits, or from older draft-age contingents, who had earlier been declared unfit for service. Not one of their planes—and there were only about 900 of them—could take off due to the absence of fuel and trained pilots, by the start of the Soviet offensive. The Kwantung Army only had about 600 tanks. Our forces captured almost all of these tanks and turned them over to Mao Zedong.[5] The only engagement involving Japanese tank troops was that of the 11th Independent Tank Regiment on 18 August on Shumushu (now Shumshu) Island in the Kuriles chain, where 21 tanks out of 64 were knocked out, although Soviet losses were 200 men killed. The Japanese suffered terribly from a shortage of fuel and munitions. The Kwantung Army's strength was about 900,000 men, of which half included non-combat units. Soviet forces numbered 1,747,000 men, of which 1,378,000 were in the ground forces. They disposed of 5,250 tanks and self-propelled guns and 5,171 combat aircraft. The Kwantung Army could not withstand such an overwhelming superiority. The Japanese command was not particularly worried about the fate of its forces in Manchuria, understanding that they were doomed. It still had the fleet and air force, in order to transfer the Kwantung Army to defend the Japanese home islands. For this reason, Manchuria's industrial potential could not be employed for the defense of Japan. Manchuria no longer had any kind of military significance for Japan, which is proven by the fact that Tokyo was ready to return to Moscow not only the southern part of Sakhalin Island and the Kurile Islands, but also Dal'nii and Port Arthur, and was also ready to agree to the demilitarization of southern Manchuria. All the USSR had to do for these concessions was to be a go-between between Japan and the Western Allies in putting an end to the war. However, this proposal went unanswered.

As early as 10 August, following the second atomic bomb, the Japanese government decided to accept the Allied powers' Potsdam Declaration,[6] with its demand of unconditional surrender. According to foreign minister Togo,[7] "Now, following the atomic bombing and the Russians' entry into the war against Japan, no one objected to, in principle, against accepting the declaration." The USSR's entrance into the war with Japan meant that all hopes of Soviet mediation in achieving peace had collapsed. The atomic bombings showed with what weapons the Americans would suppress the "total resistance" on the Japanese islands, which the Japanese leadership was threatening them with.

---

5   Editor's note. Mao Zedong (1893-1976) helped found the Chinese Communist Party in 1921 and gradually became its undisputed leader. He defeated the Nationalists and proclaimed the Chinese People's Republic in 1949. He sought to rapidly industrialize China and preserve the purity of the revolution, but his "Great Leap Forward" and "Great Proletarian Cultural Revolution" cost millions of lives.

6   Editor's note. The Potsdam Declaration was a statement issued by the governments of the US, Great Britain and China on 26 July 1945, during the Big Three conference in Potsdam, Germany. The statement called for Japan's immediate surrender. Japan agreed to the statement's terms on 15 August 1945.

7   Editor's note. Shigenori Togo (1882-1950) joined the Ministry of Foreign Affairs in 1912 and served in a number of posts abroad, including stints as ambassador to Germany and the Soviet Union. He served as foreign minister during 1941-42 and in 1945 urged Japanese acceptance of the Allied surrender terms. Following the war, Togo was convicted of war crimes and died in prison.

The main obstacle to the conduct of military operations was the difficult terrain. They had to widely employ aviation to ensure supply. On 12 August 35 tons of auto fuel, 32 tons of diesel fuel, and ten tons of oil, were shipped to Kravchenko's army. Auto transport delivered 158 tons of auto fuel, 102 tons of diesel fuel and 107 tons of oil to the 6th Guards Tank Army. From 16 August the units of Kravchenko's army, which had surged far ahead, had to be supplied exclusively by air. Malinovskii also agreed to Kravchenko's proposal to transfer auto fuel to the tanks, in order to move them as quickly as possible to the eastern slopes of the Great Khingan. The poor roads brought about an increased expenditure of fuel. So the infantry had to move on foot, insofar as there were very few roads passable for automobiles in these areas. Automobiles were left in the mountains under guard.

In the Trans-Baikal Front's combat journal for 13 August, it states:

> On 13.8.45 the *front's* forces continued their offensive and by the close of the day the infantry had advanced up to 45 kilometers along individual axes, while the mobile formations advanced up to 100 kilometers. The 39th Army's forces along the Solun axis, while overcoming the passes in the Great Khingan Range, reached with their forward units the valley of the Taoerh River and took the towns of Vanemyao and Solun in fighting, forced the Taoerh River and the Khalkhin-Gol River in the Solun area and were fighting to expand the bridgehead along the eastern bank of the Khalkhin-Gol River, while encountering the enemy's stubborn resistance from the heights east and southeast of Solun.
>
> As a result of the fighting on 13.8, 1,500 prisoners were captured, including three colonels. In the Vanemyao area a great number of large and small livestock were captured. On 12.8 units of the Mongolian People's Revolutionary Army captured a lama with a box of strychnine, and he testified that he was carrying out the orders of the Japanese command to poison the wells in the sector of the Red Army's offensive.
>
> Along the Kalgan and Chifeng axes, our aerial and ground reconnaissance did not turn up the enemy. Along the Solun axis the enemy is putting up resistance to our units with individual detachments, supported by artillery. The enemy is putting up insignificant resistance along the Hailar axis. Individual Japanese garrisons in pillboxes in the Hailar area are continuing their stubborn resistance…
>
> The 12th Air Army carried out 35 sorties.
>
> There were no air battles. There were no losses…
>
> Due to the shifting of the 6th Guards Tank Army's headquarters, wire communications with it have closed down. Wire communications with the city of Chita have closed down and wire communications set up with the 36th Army.

The fact that there were no communications with Kravchenko's army (due to the great distance and mountainous terrain, radio communications had been made more difficult) did not concern the *front* command very much. At the height of the war with Germany such an incident would have been considered extraordinary. But here, considering the weak Japanese resistance, the absence of communications for an entire day did not cause Malinovskii any alarm. The 6th Guards Tank Army would have the strength to repel any Japanese attack and to continue its headlong movement forward.

The 6th Guards Tank Army—the Trans-Baikal Front's main shock force—consisted of one tank and two mechanized corps, two motorized rifle divisions left over from 1941, a motorcycle regiment, two self-propelled artillery brigades, two brigades of light artillery, and other supporting units. The army disposed of 1,019 tanks and self-propelled guns and had 25 tank and 45 motorized rifle battalions.

Due to the absence of fuel and trained crews, the Japanese tank brigades did not enter the fighting against the Trans-Baikal Front's units.

On 19 August a Soviet airborne landing landed in Mukden (now Shenyang, and then Fentiang), the largest city in Manchukuo. The landing commander, Aleksandr Dorofeevich Pritula, reported the following to Malinovskii:

> To Marshal of the Soviet Union, comrade Malinovskii
> To Lieutenant General, comrade Tevchenkov
>
> I report.
> I have established personal contact with the commander of the Japanese Third Front. Everything is being carried out in accordance to instructions received from you.
> The railroad stations have been put under guard. I have halted movement along the railroad, forbidden work by the Mukden radio station and telegraph. I have closed the local newspapers. I have arrested the emperor of Manchukuo, Pu Yi, along with his retainers, numbering 13 people. Captain Tsygankov, a captain with the *front* staff's operational directorate, is accompanying the emperor. The commander of the C-47 is Senior Lieutenant Lyal'kin.
> P.S. There is order in the city. I urgently request you dispatch a commandant for the city of Mukden, with a staff.
> 19/VIII-45.
> 1715.
> Major General Pritula.

Pu Yi's arrest and his delivery to the Soviet Union had an unexpected continuation. Two planes were sent from Mukden to the headquarters of the Trans-Baikal Front. Pu Yi and his entourage, along with his valuables and some other property, flew on the first plane. The other "Douglas" carried Manchukuo's gold supply. The first plane, with Pu Yi, landed in Vanemyao in Manchuria to refuel (according to other data, at some airfield in Mongolia) and then landed safely in Chita. As to the second plane, which also made an intermediate landing in Vanemyao, it then disappeared without a trace, without making it to Chita. Marshal of Aviation Sergei Aleksandrovich Khudyakov, who commanded the Trans-Baikal Front's 12th Air Army, was in charge of evacuating Pu Yi and the gold supply. He and Malinovskii had been well acquainted since August 1944, when, as Air Force chief of staff, he coordinated the air operations of the Second and Third Ukrainian fronts in the Iasi—Kishinev operation. On 14 December 1945 Khudyakov was arrested in Chita and delivered to Moscow, where he was accused of treason and acquiring captured valuables; that is, the Manchukuo gold. It was soon revealed that Khudyakov was in no way Khudyakov, but rather Armenak Artemovich Khanferyants, from Nagornyi Karabakh and the son of the owner of fishing enterprises, who had changed his name, surname, nationality and biography in 1918, upon joining the Red Army. To all appearances, Khudyakov-Khanferyants himself told the investigators about changing his surname, hoping to distract the investigation from the more dangerous episodes of his case. In the same way the former people's commissar of internal affairs, N.I. Yezhov,[8] not long after his arrest in April 1939, made a written confession of homosexuality and drew up a list of his partners, in order to avoid a capital offense. Khudyakov-Khanferyants subsequently gave

---

8   Editor's note. Nikolai Ivanovich Yezhov (1895-1940) was drafted into the imperial army in 1915 and joined the Red Army in 1918. He rapidly made his way thorugh the party's administrative apparatus and in 1936 was appointed head of the NKVD, from which post he supervised the massive purge that still bears his name. Yezhov was himself arrested in 1939 and shot the following year.

testimony against Chief Marshal of Aviation A.A. Novikov,[9] the people's commissar of the aircraft industry, A.I. Shakhurin,[10] and others who figured in the aviation affair for accepting sub-standard equipment. But this did not help Khudyakov. He was executed on 18 April 1950—the only figure in the air affair, while the remainder got off with comparatively small prison sentences and were freed after Stalin's death. Stalin probably treated Khudyakov-Khanferyants so harshly because he was convinced that the marshal had nonetheless "made off" with a few tons of gold.

They also accused Sergei Armenak that while in Baku and still Khanferyants, he took part in convoying the famous 26 Baku commissars to their execution. It's still unclear from published documents what this accusation was based on. They further accused the marshal in spying for England. On orders from English intelligence, he supposedly joined the Red Army under someone else's name and made a brilliant career.

Khudyakov—Khanferyants was completely rehabilitated in August 1954. As early as 1952 they supposedly found the crashed remnants of the star-crossed plane in the Trans-Baikal taiga, but supposedly did not find any gold. However, no documents regarding the supposedly discovered plane have yet been published.

The secret of the Manchukuo gold has still not yet been solved. This is just like the secret of why Khudyakov—Khanferyants suddenly changed his name and biography and which facts from his previous life he was hiding. There could be two versions about the gold. It was either aboard the crashed plane and they transferred it to the preserve of the State Bank without any fuss, in order to avoid returning it to the Chinese authorities, who by this time were already communists. Or Khudyakov-Khanferyants really did steal the gold and Stalin's suspicions were not groundless. Naturally, Sergei Armenak could not confess to this, even under torture, because this would mean certain death. And if the marshal did nevertheless acquire the gold, he had to have accomplices, insofar as the gold had to be hidden in one of the innumerable Manchurian caves, and, secondly, it's possible that he carried out yet another crime by setting up the plane crash (if it was flying to Chita without the gold).

However, there could be yet another version. Khudyakov did not send any plane with gold to Moscow and passed off one of the planes that had crashed during combat operations in Machuria as the plane that disappeared without a trace. Then it would have been unnecessary to set up a plane crash, it being sufficient to order soldiers and airfield service units to store the gold in one of the caves.

Khudyakov-Khanferyants had reason to act this way. He was afraid that some secret of his youth might be uncovered. And what was more dangerous, a threat hung over the marshal in 1945. "For a series of mistakes committed while carrying out service-related negotiations on questions of external relations during the Yalta conference," Marshal of Aviation S.A. Khudyakov was relieved of his duties as deputy commander and chief of staff of the Red Army Air Force and appointed commander of the Trans-Baikal Front's 2nd Air Army. Stalin was probably not pleased that Roosevelt gave Khudyakov the latest sport plane, which he politely refused in favor of a youth air club. Thus the trip to the Far East was sort of an honorary exile for Sergei Armenak. However, accusations of mistakes in negotiations with foreigners could easily grow into an accusation

---

9   Editor's note. Aleksandr Aleksandrovich Novikov (1900-76) joined the Red Army in 1919 and moved to the air force in 1933. During the Great Patriotic War he commanded air forces in the northwestern part of the country and was chief of the Red Army Air Force during 1942-46. He was arrested in 1946 and forced to give testimony against Zhukov. Novikov was released in 1953, following Stalin's death, and retired in 1958.

10   Editor's note. Aleksei Ivanovich Shakhurin (1904-75) joined the Communist Party in 1925 and made his way through the party's industrial management ranks. He was people's commissar of the aviation industry during 1940-46. He was arrested in 1946 and released in 1953. Shakhurin retired in 1959.

of espionage, along with all the woeful consequences that flowed from that. It's possible that Khudyakov-Khanferyants got the idea of fleeing. He knew that within a few months Manchuria would come under Chiang-Kai-shek's administration and that Soviet forces would leave. Then the marshal could fly from Chita to China, hand over the gold to the Chinese authorities, having secured himself a sensible share, and then move on, to America, for example. After all, Roosevelt had presented him with the latest sport plane. The marshal could count on the American authorities being interested in him. And should he return to his Armenian roots, he could count on the assistance of the influential Armenian community in the USA. The complete publication of the marshal's investigation and trial materials could clear up to some degree the secret of Khudyakov-Khanferyants and the fate of the Manchukuo gold.

The Khudyakov-Khanferyants affair did not in any way reflect on Malinovskii's position. Stalin considered Sergei Armenak, who was responsible for the transport of the gold, responsible for its loss. One could say that Rodion Yakovlevich was lucky again.

In the Trans-Baikal Front's war diary for 22-31 August 1945, it was written:

> … as the course of the fighting showed, the Trans-Baikal Front operated along the main direction in the overall strategic plan for the Manchurian operation, and had enormous forces and played a decisive role in the rout of the Japanese forces.
>
> The axis of the main attack on Lubei and Changchun and the employment of the 6th Guards Tank Army, which had been reinforced with two motorized divisions and artillery, along this axis led the powerful mobile forces of the *front's* main group of forces into the rear and communications of the Kwantung Army as early as 11-13 August, putting it in a critical situation.
>
> There were no major battles during the Manchurian operation and the armies did not realize their entire fire and shock power.
>
> However, the troops had to operate in very difficult conditions of desert and mountains and during the rainiest time along the Khingan and in Manchuria. Heavy rains, which washed away the already-poor roads and made it difficult, and in some places impassable for all types of transportation, fell during 12-20 August along the Khingan and in Manchuria…
>
> The Japanese tanks were of outdated construction, had little power and could not even compare with our light tanks. There was no self-propelled artillery and automatic rifles in the Kwantung Army. There were also little artillery, mortars and machine guns. With such equipment, and in such an insignificant amount, the Kwantung Army could not only not count on success in a fight with the Red Army, but to also win any kind of serious modern engagement.
>
> The Kwantung Army actually proved to be significantly weaker than it was considered by our intelligence documents.
>
> The Japanese-Manchurian forces lost 8,000 killed and 222,000 captured, for a total of 230,000 men. We captured the following equipment: 9,400 machine guns, 87,000 rifles, 400 mortars, 860 guns, 480 tanks, 500 planes, and a large number of various depots with military and industrial goods and agricultural produce.
>
> Our losses were only 5,184 men, of which 1,750 were irretrievable.
>
> The 36th Army had the greatest losses.

As to the Manchurian operation, it was stated:

> The Japanese Third Front and Fourth Independent Army, which were operating against the Trans-Baikal Front, had ten infantry divisions, six infantry and mixed brigades, two tank brigades, and various reinforcements and support units—204,000 men in all.

Manchurian forces: seven infantry brigades, one cavalry division and nine independent cavalry regiments.

Mongolian forces: two cavalry divisions. In all, the Manchurian and Mongolian forces numbered 110,000 men (a large part of them ran away during the fighting and only 23,000 were captured).

In all, the Trans-Baikal Front was opposed by:

314,000 men
9,400 machine guns
1,000 guns and mortars
480 tanks
500 planes

The Kwantung Army also included tanks with the following tactical-technical specifications:

The 97 medium tank (1937): ten millimeters of forward armor and 19 millimeters of turret armor; it has one 57mm gun and two 7.7mm machine guns; it has a 170 horsepower diesel engine; it weighs 14.5 tons; it has a range of 100 kilometers; its combat load is 116 shells and 2,500 rounds.

The 95 light tank (1935): six millimeters of forward armor and nine millimeters of turret armor; it has a 37mmgun and two 7.7mm machine guns; it weighs 6.5 tons.

Needless to say, these tanks were inferior to the modernized Soviet T-34s.

There was simply no good strategy for the Japanese in Manchuria in August 1945. It was equally a losing hand to meet the Soviet forces at the border as to remove the main forces to central Manchuria. In any case, there was no chance of either repelling the Soviet attack or escaping pursuit, insofar as the Soviet mechanized forces would probably have caught up with the Japanese, who had been deprived of fuel and transportation equipment. But even an immediate withdrawal to the the seaports would not have saved the Kwantung Army, because it had neither the ships nor the planes for an evacuation. In all cases, only the area of capitulation would have been different.

Many Soviet soliders, however sad it is to say, besmirched themselves with war crimes during the Manchurian operation, although their scale was significantly smaller than in Germany. There remains testimony by western representatives, who spent time in the territories occupied by Soviet forces. They mainly killed, raped and robbed the Japanese civilian population that lived in north-eastern China. The Chinese, who had suffered so much during the years of Japanese occupation, also dealt with the Japanese colonists. However, the Red Army soldiers were crueler. One of the surviving Japanese recalled: "… if you ran into Manchurians (Chinese), they would take every-thing from you. However, the most horrible were the Red Army soldiers. They killed Japanese just for the sake of killing them. I saw many corpses that had been bayoneted. Mountains and moun-tains of bodies…" On 14 August, near Gegenmyao station in Manchuria, Red Army soldiers killed about 1,000 Japanese refugees from a train they had detained. According to Japanese estimates, the Soviets killed in all about 11,000 Japanese civilians in Manchuria.

Not only Japanese refugees became victims of the Red Army. The Chinese got it in the neck, too. The chief of the American mission, who had arrived in Shenyang (Mukden) for the repatria-tion of American prisoners of war, reported:

The Russians outdid the Chinese in robbing, marauding and rape. They rape women at bus stops, railroad stations and sometimes right on the street. There are rumors that the local authorities have been ordered to deliver a certain number of women to the Soviet command each night. As a result, women are shaving their heads, painting their faces with ink and applying bandages, in order to look less attractive… The Red Army soldiers are only interested in robbing and killing. And they rob not only the Japanese. Some soldiers wear ten wrist watches at a time… I had the opportunity of meeting decent people among the Soviet military, but these are one out of ten.

The American naval attaché with Chiang-Kai-shek's government, having been to Manchuria, recalled: "The Russian soliders broke into homes and took everything for themselves, except furniture. Soviet officers usually did not pay any attention to the robberies being carried out by their subordinates, and sometimes took part in them themselves." In the Chinese town of Pinchuan, according to accounts by local residents, "the Soviet soldiers steal wrist watches from people and shoot those who refuse to submit to robbery. The Red Army demands women from the peasants. The Red Army men shot two peasants who were unable to find them women to satisfy their lust." Even the Chinese communists protested that "the Red Army is doing things that are not fitting for a proletarian army, including rapes and the expropriation of food supplies from the peasants."

Of course, there could be no talk of revenge in relation to the Japanese, and all the more so in relation to the Chinese. The main reasons for the crimes were the same as in Europe: anger because the command used soldiers as cannon fodder and the necessity of taking out one's anger on someone defenseless, as well as hatred for the relatively well-to-do life that people led overseas.

On 8 September 1945 Malinovskii was awarded the title of Hero of the Soviet Union "for the exemplary carrying out of the Supreme High Command's combat tasks and conducting the combat operations of the Trans-Baikal Front's forces against the Japanese imperialists and the successes achieved as a result of these operations." On that same day the commander-in-chief of the Air Force, A.A. Novikov, the commander of the 6th Guards Tank Army, Colonel General A.G. Kravchenko, the commander of the 5th Army, Colonel Geneal N.I. Krylov, and the commander of the cavalry-mechanized group, Colonel General I.A. Pliev, became twice heroes of the Soviet Union. At first the name of K.A. Meretskov, the commander of the First Far Eastern Front, stood in Novikov's place in the text of the decree, but Stalin crossed it out. Instead of a second gold star for the war with Japan, Kirill Afanas'evich received the Order of Victory. The deputy commander-in-chief of Soviet Forces in the Far East, General I.I. Maslennikov, the chief of staff of the Trans-Baikal Front, General M.V. Zakharov, and the chief of staff of the High Command of Soviet Forces in the Far East, Colonel General S.P. Ivanov, received the gold stars of heroes of the Soviet Union for the war with Japan on 8 September.

On 10 September 1945 a *Stavka* directive appointed Malinovskii the commander of the Trans-Baikal-Amur Military District, which was formed out of the Trans-Baikal Front, with its headquarters in Khabarovsk. For him, the Second World War had ended.

11

In the Far East

In the unpublished manuscript of his memoirs, S.M. Shtemenko recalled: "In appointing Marshal Malinovskii commander-in-chief of Soviet Forces in the Far East after the war, Stalin characterized him as 'calm, collected and calculating and someone who makes mistake less than others'."

Rodion Yakovlevich spent the first months following the end of the war with Japan in Manchuria, which had been occupied by Soviet forces.

From 18 February through 9 March 1946 Malinovskii's forces carried out an operation against the local Honghuzi—bandits who were terrorizing the population, and who in November 1945 murdered the personnel of the Soviet district commandant's office in Changchun. More than 20 bands were destroyed, with up to 10,000 bandits killed and captured.

Soviet troops were withdrawn from Manchuria in the beginning of April 1946.

After this, Malinovskii's headquarters was removed from the Chinese city of Changchun to Khabarovsk. He now had to manage the affairs of a military district.

Only good recollections remain of Rodion Yakovlevich's activities in the Far East. Here they even drank to his health for several years following his death.

The writer Konstantin Simonov,[1] who spent a lot of time in the Far East after the war, declared at one of the memorial evenings for Malinovskii: "God grant that each of us leave behind, if only in a single village, the kind of memory which Rodion Yakovlevich left behind in the Far East."

In February 1946 Malinovskii was elected a deputy of the USSR Supreme Soviet from the Karym electoral district No. 319, and in December 1947 he became a deputy of the Khabarovsk Provincial Council.

On 17 July 1946 Malinovskii divorced his first wife and on 4 September of the same year he registered his marriage to Raisa Yakovlevna Kucherenko in the Red Fleet District registry office in Khabarovsk. On 6 September Rodion Yakovlevich adopted her ten-year old son, German, from her first marriage. This took place two months before the birth of Malinovskii's daughter. This is what the marshal's elder son from his first marriage, Robert, recalled about his parents' divorce:

> My parents became acquainted in Irkutsk, when my father was fighting against Kolchak during the civil war; they got married in 1925 and divorced in 1946. I was already suffi-ciently grown up then and did not condemn him. The fact of the matter is that he and mama grew apart during the war years. Father's new wife was younger, but she had a son from her first marriage, who later also joined the military. Mother and I lived in Irkutsk, where I became an engineer-metallurgist, after which I left for Noril'sk in the north, where father wrote me. Mama was a French teacher, which she had learned when they lived in Smolensk. She evidently wanted to speak with father in that language within the family, because he not only knew Spanish, but French as well. But field wives often shared all the difficulties of battle with the servicemen.

---

1   Editor's note. Konstantin Mikhailovich Simonov (1915-79) was a Soviet author, poet and wartime correspondent.

Rodion Yakovlevich wrote about the dramatic changes in his family situation in his 1948 autobiography:

> In 1925 I married Larisa Nikolaevna Sharabarova in Irkutsk and have two sons from this marriage: Robert Malinovskii, who was born in January 1929 and who is now a second-year student in the Mining Institute; the second son, Eduard Malinovskii, who was born in April 1934, is a high school student in Irkutsk, and both sons live with their mother, because I and L.N. Sharabarova (now Malinovskaya, as she kept my surname) were divorced by the Khabarovsk provincial court. I pay one third of my salary for their upkeep through their mother.
>
> In 1946 I married a second time to Raisa Yakovlevna Kucherenko, from the village of Bogorodichnoe, Slavyansk district, Stalin Oblast', Ukrainian SSR. I have a daughter, Natal'ya Malinovskaya, who was born on 7 November 1946 and adopted my wife's son—German Malinovskii—who was born in 1936 and who is now studying in the Kiev Suvorov Academy.

We should note that following the war, Malinovskii's mother, as he wrote in his 1946 autobiography, moved to Vinnitsa, where she lived at No. 6 9th of January St., apartment no. 9.

We should add a few words here about the fate of Malinovskii's sons from his first marriage. Robert Rodionovich finished school in 1946, in Khabarovsk, to where he had been evacuated, and enrolled in the ferrous metallurgy department of the Irkutsk Mining-Metallurgical Institute. Beginning in the 1960s, he was engaged in developing aluminum alloys for flying apparatuses, including spacecraft. He received the academic title of doctor of technical sciences and was awarded the USSR State Prize for developing parts for modern aircraft. He now lives in Moscow. He is married and has three children and seven grandchildren.

Eduard was a music teacher and for many years worked in a school in the town of Berezniki, in the present-day Perm' province, and died in 2004. He left a wife and daughter. As his elder brother Robert recalled, "Eduard began playing on a captured accordion, which father bought through a special commission, which was toting up captured goods. Everything was according to the law."

Natal'ya Rodionovna recalled: "Papa named me in honor of his aunt—Natal'ya Nikolaevna Malinovskaya, who took him in when he left home at the age of eleven. She perished together with her son Zhenya in occupied Kiev, about which papa found out the second day after the city's liberation, when he flew there to seek her out…" According to Natal'ya Rodionovna, "grandmother Varvara Nikolaevna expressed her dissatisfaction on the score of the granddaughter's name."

The marshal's daughter recalls:

> In all the twenty years I spent beside papa, I never witnessed family quarrels or scenes and did not even hear one of my parents raise their voice to the other. Was this due to papa's reserved character? In part. Was this due to mama's meekness? By no means—she had an explosive character with anyone else but papa. And this not the only reason she restrained herself—there was nothing in either of them that irritated the other. For example, it was winter and we were at the dacha, where it was a wonderful day, and mama felt like walking to Setun', where it was probably particularly pretty (we often walked to Setun', but only from the other side and not from Peredelkino). Meanwhile, papa had already opened his notebook and spread out a map, leaving no hope for a stroll. "You see, he doesn't want to," was the way mama summed it up, and smiled. (If I dared to not want to, I would hear, "No caprices from you!")
>
> Since papa was transferred to Moscow in 1956, I've never been back to Khabarovsk, but I know that no trace remains of my childhood world. Almost no one remembers the overgrown garden with the gazebo, intertwined with wild grapes, white lilacs by the steps to the terrace and a clover grove, where our setter played with a bear cub. Istomin Street, the governor's

house, in which, according to tradition, the military district commander always lived. And the dacha at the Red River, the slope down to the Ussuri River, which was violet from the Labrador tea, with the ancient stairs, where chipmunks set on the broken stairs and were not afraid. The deciduous path around the house, the peasant hut on the edge of the park, where they dumped the garden equipment in the fall, and the balcony on the roof, baked by the midday sun, which was called "asotea." Was it papa who gave it this Spanish name?

As far as I recall, we always had house pets, and in a respectable amount. When I was born there were a lot of babies in the house: five kittens and six puppies. There were another two large dogs, a tomcat and a cat. Papa's ceremonial horse, Orlik, with a star on his forehead, with white socks and an enormous brown eye, lived in the courtyard in the stable. And this is not even a complete listing of our menagerie. At various times we had a marsh bird with a broken wing, a lame, wild nanny goat, a bear cub who had lost his mother, and a tame squirrel. Fearing neither dogs nor cats, it would hop along the cupboards and curtains and would only go to its cage to sleep. Papa always had his cat with him (with its rightful place at his writing desk), and mama hers, and then I had one. The dogs were considered everyone's, but they recognized papa as the master. One was always a hunting dog, with long ears, while the other was usually a stray of unknown breed. When papa died, all of them, both dogs and two tomcats, could not take the sadness that invaded the home. Deprived of their master, they all died by the fortieth day from his death, which fell on 9 May.

Natal'ya Rodionovna further recalled: "Our family life included a lot of people in Khabarovsk; guest came often and then a large radio phonograph, the size of a trunk, would play. Towards the end, they would always sing papa's favorite "Shine, Shine, my Star," while before that we always heard Ukrainian folk songs (the entire selection of my bedtime songs), "Glorious Sea, Holy Baikal," and the waltzes "Amur Waves" and "On the Hills of Manchuria." The romance of that long-ago war at the start of the century still hung over the Far East."

However, according to the marshal's daughter, not everything was perfect for her father:

… a serious conflict arose with Goglidze,[2] who upon leaving for Moscow, promised to a friend, whose name he did not forget to mention, a great deal of unpleasantness for my father. An affair was soon trumped up and the clouds gathered, but Stalin supposedly said: "Don't take Malinovskii from the Far East. He's already sufficiently far from us." This phrase (spoken, according to the logic of things, *tete a tete*), was delivered a good distance, I believe, not without someone's sanction and not without an ulterior motive. Among those few whom they did not touch, there arose the impression that the supreme hand had removed the sword of Damocles.

Malinovskii displayed true paternal concern for Raisa Yakovlevna's son by her first marriage. On 13 May 1956, when already back in Moscow, the marshal wrote the head of the Kiev Suvorov Academy, where German was studying:

Hello, Ivan Petrovich!

---

2   Editor's note. Sergei Arsen'evich Goglidze (1901-53) served in the Red Army during the civil war, before making the transition to the security organs. He was a protégé of L.P. Beria and was responsible for the deportation of several thousands of people from recently-annexed Bessarabia in 1941. Goglidze was implicated in Beria's crimes in 1953 and executed with his former chief on the same day.

I received your letter of 4 May of this year. Thank you very much. All of German's grades, as before, range from three to five, although there are naturally more threes.

It's strange that you have some kind of misunderstandings with the examination schedule, aside from the fact that they transferred the mathematics teacher to the reserves right before the examinations; I have to talk with Kolpakchi[3] (Colonel General, later general, who at that time was a directorate chief in the chief directorate of combat training for the Ground Forces. Kolpakchi's directorate was probably in charge of educational institutions, B.S.) and find out what's wrong.

I understand that Gera has trouble with math, but he made his own difficulties, and no one else. If he is going to be lazy, then he'll have problems in any academy, even in a regular military academy. Why do I speak so confidently about this? I have some experience on this score. My education consisted of only three winters of village-church school when I decided to enroll in the Military Academy, nor had I any military education. This is the sort of base, as they say, upon which I began to prepare for the examinations—I simply worked a lot, 16-18 hours per day—and within four months I took the entrance examinations. 400 of us took the examination, and they accepted 90, and it was precisely in mathematics that I received a grade of five and was ranked sixteenth for all examinations to get into the Academy. German is in better condition and has a ten-year school as a base, and not a country school.

It seems to me that you are dampening his enthusiasm and looking to find an easy institute of higher education for him, while he should be fully mobilized for the difficult study which faces him. This is my opinion…

A hearty hello to you from myself and Raisa Yakovlevna. Say hello to Gera.

I warmly shake your hand.

Malinovskii.

I should add that on 30 December 2010 Colonel German Rodionovich Malinovskii passed away in Moscow at the age of 74.

Raisa Yakovlevna worked as a bibliographer and was not a bad amateur artist. She drew a lot after Rodion Yakovlevich's death. The pictures helped her forget her grief.

In May 1947 the directorate of the commander-in-chief of Soviet Forces in the Far East was established on the basis of the Trans-Baikal-Amur Military District and Malinovskii was appointed to that post. The Far Eastern and Maritime military districts were now subordinated to him.

In June 1953 all three military districts were combined into the Far Eastern Military District, which Malinovskii then began to command. The post of commander-in-chief of Soviet forces in the Far East was abolished, although this was not reflected in Rodion Yakovlevich's situation. They only removed the Pacific Fleet from his purview, about which he was not sorry at all. As before, Malinovskii commanded all the forces in the Far East.

Khrushchev recalled that when the Korean War began and the North Korean army got bogged down along the Pusan perimeter in the south and was unable to capture it, he advised Stalin: "We have Marshal Malinovskii. He commanded the Trans-Baikal Front's forces in the war. Why shouldn't we establish Malinovskii somewhere in order to draw up military operations incognito and issue the necessary orders, so as to help Kim Il-Sung?" However, Stalin rejected this proposal.

---

3   Editor's note. Vladimir Yakovlevich Kolpakchi (1899-1961) was drafted into the imperial army in 1916 and joined the Red Army in 1918. During the Great Patriotic War he was an army and *front* chief of staff and commanded several armies. After the war he commanded military districts and armies and served in the central military apparatus. Kolpakchi was killed in a helicopter crash.

On 2 June 1953, not long after Stalin's death, Malinovskii wrote his son Robert in Noril'sk, where the latter was working as an engineer in a mining-metallurgical plant.

> Hello Robik!
> I received your letter of 22 May of this year. From the letter it is clear that you have acclimated yourself in the north, as have all the members of your household. I have been to the Far North twice—both times in the summer, to be sure; that is, in June, although both times there was still a good deal of snow, particularly in the gullies and it was correspondingly brisk. It's good that you've begun working at an important task.
>
> Our Soviet people and its foundation—the Russian people, will never take offense at harshness and exacting conditions, as long as justice is observed. Therefore you should adopt as a principle the following: always be just and attentively hear out requests and manifest the care you can for your subordinates; never insult or degrade a person's dignity; nor should you show off or emphasize your superiority in front of lesser-ranking workmen, all the way down to an unskilled laborer and the cleaning woman and be for them a simple man, accessible and polite, although you should not be sickly sweet—people can't stand that—and don't seek out cheap authority by ingratiating yourself. Maybe you don't need my advice, but it won't cause you any harm and may be of use.
>
> That' all for now. Hello. Papa.

One feels that Malinovskii was a Russian patriot, although he wrote that he was a Ukrainian and never renounced his nationality. However, for him the Ukrainians remained an inalienable part of the Soviet-Russian empire.

In 1947 Gao Gang,[4] one of the leaders of the Chinese Communist Party, who was in opposition to Mao Zedong and considered in Moscow "a true internationalist," arrived for a secret visit in Khabarovsk, where Malinovskii's headquarters was located. Gao Gang sought to assure Rodion Yakovlevich that Mao Zedong and the majority of the leaders of the Chinese Communist Party adhered to nationalist and anti-Soviet positions. However, Stalin put his money on Mao Zedong, although he forced him to keep such a pro-Soviet politician as Gao Gang in the leadership. In 1954, not long after Stalin's death, Gao Gang was expelled from the party and, according to the official version, committed suicide on 17 August.

In the summer of 1948 Malinovskii, to whom the Pacific Fleet was subordinated as commander-in-chief of Soviet Forces in the Far East, undertook a several-day trip on the frigate EK-22 along the following route: Sovetskaya Gavan', Korsakov, the Kurile Islands, and Petropavlovsk-Kamchatskii, while carrying out a reconnaissance of the Far Eastern maritime theater. On 2 August the ship's commander, Captain Third Class Strel'tsov, issued the marshal a document, in which it stated:

> Issued to Marshal of the Soviet Union Malinovskii, Rodion Yakovlevich, that during 3 July through 2 August 1948 he sailed on the frigate EK-22 along the following route: Sovetskaya Gavan', Korsakov, the Kurile Islands, Petropavlovsk na Kamchatke, Anadyr', Providence Bay, Cape Chaplin, Ust'-Kamchatsk, Ust'-Bol'sheretsk, Magadan, and Nikolaevsk-na-Amure. 6,228 miles were covered in 398 hours of sailing, with 26 days spent sailing and five at anchor.

---

4   Editor's note. Gao Gang (1905-54) joined the Chinese Communist Party in 1926 and quickly rose to the highest ranks under the tutelage of Mao Zedong. He later became the semi-independent party boss of Manchuria and was considered closer to the Soviet Union than others in the party. Following a failed attempt to remove his rivals, Gao Gang committed suicide.

In May 1954, while speaking before the troops of the Khabarovsk garrison, Malinovskii declared that "If the imperialists, while putting their trust in atomic weaponry, embark upon insanity and want to test the power and might of the Soviet Union, then one should not doubt that the aggressor will be suppressed with the same weaponry…"

I don't know if Rodion Yakovlevich was informed that at that moment the American advantage in both the number of nuclear and hydrogen bombs, as well as in nuclear delivery systems, was overwhelming. The USSR did not actually have delivery systems for nuclear and thermonuclear weapons to US territory. Such systems appeared only upon the adoption of the first intercontinental ballistic missiles in 1957.

In the evenings Malinovskii often made notes in his notebook and their content often went far beyond the bounds of his service duties in commanding forces in the Far East. He became more interested in Germany, particularly after West Germany was admitted to NATO in 1955 and its rearmament, although limited, was allowed. In this regard, Malinovskii wrote:

> The Germans well remember the sayings of Grand Admiral Tirpitz,[5] which papered the walls of the assembly halls of the military academies under Hitler. Here they are: "I want to fix in the consciousness of our future generations that great peoples may be secure only through the aid of force. Since the time when the earth has been inhabited by people, force in the life of peoples has stood higher than the law." They are evidently conserved now in West Germany. I believe that in democratic Germany it is necessary to write in the Pioneer palaces and clubs for free German youth the words of the great German poet Goethe, from *Faust*:
>
> "Let the child, man and old man spend
> "Their entire life in a hard and unending struggle,
> "So that I may see in the sparkle of a wondrous strength
> "A free land, my free people!"
> (Translation by N.A. Kholodkovskii)
> This is far closer for the heart of a free German.

I think that Rodion Yakovlevich also dreamed that the Russian and Ukrainian peoples might also be free.

---

5   Editor's note. Alfred Peter Friedrich von Tirpitz (1849-1930) joined the Prussian navy in 1865 and continued to serve in the successor German navy. In 1897 he was appointed Secretary of State of the Imperial Naval Office, from where he conducted a lengthy campaign to make Germany a world-class naval power. The First World War found his navy unready to take on the British Fleet and Tirpitz resigned his post in 1916 as a result of disagreements over unrestricted submarine warfare.

12

How Zhukov was removed

On 16 February 1955 Marshal Zhukov, who had just become the new defense minister, presented a proposal for creating a high command and main staff for the Ground Forces, proposing for this position and simultaneously for the position of first deputy minister of defense Marshal Konev. His appointment was approved by Khrushchev, but within a year Nikita Sergeevich, while leaving Konev first deputy minister of defense, made him the commander-in-chief of the Warsaw Pact Forces, while he appointed Malinovskii the commander-in-chief of the Ground Forces and first deputy minister of defense in March 1956, right after the XX party congress. Rodion Yakovlevich was then elected a member of the CPSU[1] Central Committee (he had become a candidate member of the Central Committee in 1952, after the XIX party congress).

In the beginning of March 1956 Vasilevskii approached defense minister Zhukov with the following declaration: "I request you intercede with the Presidium of the CPSU Central Committee and the Council of Ministers about relieving me of the position of first deputy defense minister, due to the fact that lately I am very much troubled by headaches and a serious disruption of my sight and, from time to time, my memory. Those measures that the doctors are currently applying are not yielding an effective result."

This request was granted and Vasilevskii was appointed to the outwardly impressive position of deputy defense minister for problems of military science.

One should not doubt that this transfer was initiated by Khrushchev, who thus freed the place of the second first deputy defense minister for Malinovskii. Marshal of the Soviet Union Vasilii Danilovich Sokolovskii[2] was the third first deputy, although the post of chief of the General Staff had gradually lost its importance in the postwar years. Those positions occupied by Konev and Malinovskii were considered more significant. Besides, Sokolovskii became a marshal only in July 1946, in connection with his appointment as commander of the Group of Soviet Forces in Germany, and he was never viewed as an influential and independent figure in the military hierarchy. He was considered close to Zhukov, whom he served as chief of staff on the Western Front at the beginning of the war, and later as his deputy on the First Belorussian Front. It was believed that Konev was just as close to Zhukov.

Thus Malinovskii occupied the third place in the military hierarchy behind Zhukov and Konev. This took place thanks to the following circumstances.

Khrushchev already feared Zhukov's political ambitions. At the same time, Konev was known as Zhukov's friend and was supposed to be obliged to him for being promoted to the post of commander-in-chief of the Ground Forces and first deputy minister, although they had fallen out during the sadly famous race for Berlin. Malinovskii was completely Khrushchev's man and

---

1   Editor's note. Communist Party of the Soviet Union.
2   Editor's note. Vasilii Danilovich Sokolovskii (1897-1968) joined the Red Army in 1918. During the Great Patriotic War he served in a variety of *front* staff positions and also commanded a *front*. Following the war, Sokolovskii served as deputy commander and commander of the group of Soviet forces in Germany and the Soviet military administration in that country. He later served as chief of the General Staff.

had served under him in 1941-42. The main thing was that Nikita Sergeevich was well aware that Zhukov and Malinovskii barely tolerated each other. I should note that as opposed to the post of commander-in-chief of the Warsaw Pact Forces, the post of commander-in-chief of the Ground Forces was a key one for a military coup, insofar as all troop movements within the country were under its control.

As Malinovskii's daughter, Natal'ya Rodionovna, related from the words of her father's friend from the Frunze Military Academy, Major General Ivan Nikolaevich Burenin, during Zhukov's and Malinovskii's first meeting in Moscow in November 1929, to where Zhukov had been sent to the high command improvement courses at the military academy, and Malinovskii was a student at the same academy, Georgii Konstantinovich hailed Rodion Yakovlevich with a curse word and the latter answered in kind. Georgii Konstantinovich at first stepped back from this rebuff and then greeted him quite politely, by name and patronymic, without any kind of coarseness. Zhukov understood that Malinovskii would not tolerate any kind of loutishness and, if necessary, would give as good as he got, and that he was taller and no less broad in the shoulders. And everyone should be so strong! After all, during the First World War he had to carry a machine gun on his back! Thus during their joint service Georgii Konstantinovich did not only not punch him in the face, but didn't even utter a curse word. However, the two marshals sincerely could not stand each other, although they hid this outwardly.

Mikhail Smirtyukov,[3] the business manager for the USSR Council of Ministers recalled: "I once noticed that marshals Zhukov and Malinovskii had got into the habit of fishing from the Rublevskaya Dam. What's interesting is that they never fished together there. Zhukov would pull up and Malinovskii would pack up his poles. Or, just the opposite was the case. It's obvious they couldn't stand each other."

Khrushchev knew whom to appoint as Zhukov's first deputy. Nikita Sergeevich had no doubt that Zhukov and Malinovskii would never plot against him.

On 21 November 1956 Zhukov proposed relieving Marshal S.S. Biryuzov from his position as deputy defense minister, while leaving him as commander-in-chief of National Air Defense Forces. This was motivated by the necessity of reducing the number of deputy defense ministers. However, the Presidium of the Central Committee did not support Zhukov. Sergei Semyonovich was Khrushchev's and Malinovskii's man, and not Zhukov's, and Georgii Konstantinovich's attempt to lower Biryuzov's status in the central apparatus of the defense ministry could only put Nikita Sergeevich even more on his guard.

It's well known how they removed Zhukov from the post of defense minister. Khrushchev was concerned that Zhukov proposed replacing the chairman of the KGB, I.A. Serov,[4] and the minister of internal affairs, N.P. Dudorov,[5] with army generals and put forth Marshal Konev for the post of minister of internal affairs. This looked like the preparation of a military junta for a future coup. And when, during Zhukov's October visit to Yugoslavia and Albania, General Kh.U. Mamsurov informed Khrushchev and Malinovskii that he was the chief of a school for diversionists, which

---

3   Editor's note. Mikhail Sergeevich Smirtyukov (1909-2004) joined the Communist Party in 1940 and spent his entire career in the government apparatus until his retirement in 1989.

4   Editor's note. Ivan Aleksandrovich Serov (1905-90) joined the Communist Party in 1926 and later served in the army. During the Great Patriotic War he occupied high posts in the secret police (NKVD) and took an active part in organizing the deportation of suspect national groups from the north Caucasus. After the war he headed the Committee for State Security (KGB) and the Main Intelligence Directorate (GRU). Serov was removed from the latter position following the Pen'kovskii affair and was excluded from the Communist Party in 1965.

5   Editor's note. Nikolai Pavlovich Dudorov (1906-77) joined the Communist Party in 1927 and worked his way up the economic administration ladder. He served as USSR minister of internal affairs during 1956-60, before returning to the economic administration. Dudorov retired in 1972.

had been created in Tambov Oblast' without the knowledge of the party Central Committee, and which was supposed to be completely formed by 15 January 1958 (it was officially known as the Second Airborne School in Tambov and was subordinated to the General Staff's Main Intelligence Directorate), Khrushchev understood that Zhukov was creating a military unit loyal to him for a possible military coup and that it was time to remove him from the post of defense minister. This was all the more so as the future cadets were supposed to study for 6-8 years—more than in the other schools and academies. It appeared that Zhukov was training his own "Praetorian Guard," upon whose support he was counting on to seize and hold power.

When they removed Zhukov at the October plenary meeting of the Central Committee, Konev delivered the following note on the last day of the plenum's work, 29 October: "In his speech, comrade A.I. Mikoyan[6] called me comrade G.K. Zhukov's friend. This does not correspond to reality. My relations with comrade Zhukov were strictly work-related and nothing more. As far as friendship goes, you know the truth, Nikita Sergeevich." Konev also branded Zhukov in his address before the plenum, and then wrote (more likely, signed) an article in *Pravda* directed against Georgii Konstantinovich.

Ivan Stepanovich seriously feared that Khrushchev would recall his feats during the 1930s and arrange a trial on charges of a military plot. Then not only Zhukov would surely have been executed, but also Konev, as well as the chief of the GRU, S.M. Shtemenko, who also knew about the ill-starred school for diversionists, but did not inform Khrushchev about it and, during Zhukov's visit to the Balkans, warned Georgii Konstantinovich that his removal was being prepared. However, Khrushchev demonstrated humanity following Stalin's death. It was only in June 1957 that "the anti-party group of Malenkov, Kaganovich,[7] Molotov, and Shepilov,[8] who aligned himself with them," attempted to remove Khrushchev. However, Nikita Sergeevich not only did not shoot them, but did not even try them, and limited himself to removing the members of the group from the party leadership and transferring them to unimportant posts. To be sure and to be fair, we should note that the participants of the "anti-party group" did not attempt to arrest Nikita Sergeevich and, even more, were preparing to keep him in the Presidium of the Central Committee, while appointing him minister of agriculture. It is likely that this partially explains the softness displayed by Khrushchev in regard to the plotters. As regards Zhukov, this only concerned a possible future plot which was still only in the preparatory stage. If this had occurred under Stalin, one would have no doubt as to the said fate of the plotters. They would have put Zhukov, Konev, Shtemenko and, quite possibly, another half-dozen generals close to them up against the wall, having forced them beforehand under torture to confess that they were German-American-Japanese spies. All Khrushchev did was to send Zhukov into retirement, while Konev was left at his post, although

---

6   Editor's note. Anastas Ivanovich Mikoyan (1895-1978) joined the Communist Party in 1915 and for many years headed various economic ministries. During the Great Patriotic War he was a member of the GKO and in charge of supplying the armed forces with food and equipment. He fell out of favor after the war, but survived and recovered his positions following Stalin's death. Mikoyan was retired from public life in 1965.

7   Editor's note. Lazar' Moiseevich Kaganovich (1893-1991) joined the Communist Party in 1911 and rapidly worked his way through the party and government ranks and played a major role in Stalin's purges. During the Great Patriotic War he was a member of the GKO and responsible for evacuating industry from the war zone. Following the war he fell out of favor, but recovered his status following Stalin's death. Kaganovich was removed from his posts in 1957 and expelled from the party.

8   Editor's note. Dmitrii Trofimovich Shepilov (1905-95) joined the Communist Party in 1926 and became involved in academic affairs. During the Great Patriotic War he served as a private soldier and military commissar. After the war he became the editor of the party newspaper, *Pravda*, and in 1956 was appointed minister of foreign affairs. He was implicated in the plot to overthrow Khrushchev in 1957 and was deprived of all his posts.

this was insulting to Ivan Stepanovich. He had also dreamed of becoming defense minister and did not want to serve under Malinovskii and, so as not to have to deal with him, was sick almost all the time until he was sent into retirement in 1960—to be exact, to the group of general inspectors. And Shtemenko suffered a little more seriously. He was demoted from colonel general to lieutenant general for assisting Zhukov and appointed first deputy commander of the Volga Military District, far from the capital. However, as early as July 1962 Sergei Matveevich was appointed chief of the Ground Forces main staff—the first deputy commander-in-chief of the Ground Forces and restored to him the rank of colonel general. In February 1968, following Malinovskii's death, Shtemenko, who was then serving as deputy chief of the General Staff, was awarded the rank of general of the army.

Malinovskii's speech at the October 1957 plenum was one of the most denunciatory as regards Zhukov:

> Comrades, we military workers are very glad that the plenum of the Central Committee is discussing the question of strengthening party-political work in the Soviet Army and Navy. On the other hand, it is painful that we, the military workers and members of the party have come to such a pass… that the Central Committee was forced to interfere in this matter.
>
> We all unanimously greet the decision by the Presidium of the Central Committee of 19 October as absolutely correct and as absolutely timely, and which undoubtedly refreshes the entire situation in the Soviet Army and Navy and will be of assistance in strengthening our armed forces, so that they can more strongly and better defend the interests of our state and our party.
>
> There's no doubt, comrades that an abscess grew and grew on the healthy body of our army and navy. Sooner or later, according to the laws of biology, it was bound to burst, and perhaps with a greater stench that what we are now experiencing. And if the Presidium of the Central Committee has cut out and uncovered this ulcer, then this was a very timely and health-inducing surgical procedure.
>
> One might ask us, the deputy defense ministers, his assistants, just where were you?
>
> Voices. They can and must ask.
>
> MALINOVSKII: Where were you looking? A completely logical and correct question. I know Zhukov, although perhaps not as long as the other comrades who spoke before me; I've only known him since 1929…
>
> Voices. That's a lot.
>
> MALINOVSKII: Comrade Timoshenko knew him much earlier than I, as well as comrade Konev and Budennyi, etc.; but during that time I came to know him well.
>
> I must tell you forthrightly that I bear no ill will toward comrade Zhukov. I always was very well disposed to comrade Zhukov, man to man, but I always worked with him, I'll be straight with you, with very aggressive intentions. Knowing him and who he is, I approached him with the intention that if you are rude to me, then I'll be rude to you; if you are going to swear at me, then I will swear at you; and if, God forbid, you hit me, then I'll hit you back (laughter in the hall) and, by the way, it was as if he always guessed my intentions and throughout my lengthy service, no matter where we had to work together, I always saw in his conduct toward me the most courtesy and best regard, although I saw how he slighted others, how he literally reduced people to nothing. This outraged me, but why? I will tell you straightforward that I left the Far East with such intentions, where I worked for ten years in that glorious corner of our Motherland, for Moscow, to the defense ministry. I mulled over this question for a long time and decided: I always went to Zhukov with such intentions and I will go with just these intentions now.

And here, in the defense ministry, I didn't hear a single rude word directed at me. I saw, of course, how the defense minister, comrade Zhukov scoffed at Biryuzov and comrade Gerasimov,[9] and I was always troubled by the thought: what's going on here? This is a good man and I know him Biryuzov, very well, and also know his negative qualities, about which I spoke to him face to face in Moscow, when he was subordinated to me.

I would like to direct your attention to one incident.

The commanders of the military districts had gathered and we were acquainting ourselves with military equipment in order to find out what was new in the armed forces' arsenal. This was at the Ramenskoe airfield and there was a group of marshals under comrade Zhukov himself, examining the new combat weapons and systems. We approached one radar apparatus.

Well, Biryuzov, as the best informed man, who, as they say, had broken all his teeth on these radars, said that it would be nice to have an indicator light on these radars, which indicates a captured target and, upon the appearance of another target, would show another color; not white, but red, for example. Comrade Zhukov looked at him: "What a stupid observation. You don't understand a damn thing about this, so don't stick your nose where you ought not to."

I know comrade Biryuzov as a very obstinate man; however, he swallowed his pride and moved off.

Voice. There could be another color for the indicator light.

MALINOVSKII. He said that the designers are looking into this. Zhukov stated: "You don't understand anything about this," and that was that.

There was a second gathering. A new deputy defense minister had been appointed, Colonel General Gerasimov. This was his first major assignment. During this gathering our commanders were examining missile equipment, which is linked, as is known, to electronics. Comrade Gerasimov had been appointed deputy minister specifically for electronics. In this regard, he made a completely innocent remark about electronics. The minister looked at him: "You don't understand anything in these matters, so don't go sticking your nose into things." And I thought to myself, this is how he treats the deputy minister in front of all the troops! Gerasimov figured it wouldn't kill him, so he swallowed his pride and stepped away.

Why was this done? So that as soon as a deputy is appointed, he gets cracked over the head, and so that the cobbler should stick to his last and know how to behave himself in the minister's presence.

I've already been working two years with comrade Zhukov, have gone over a lot of questions and said that we've made mistakes in some areas, both in the corps and army. We eliminated the corps and created an army without the corps level. Overall, the organism of the armed forces is a complex one, and not simple, while sometimes it seems to people that there's nothing difficult about it—he got on his horse, raised his sword and said "after me," and that's all. I did not agree with the decision to eliminate the corps system and protested against this step even before my appointment to the ministry. Comrade Zhukov knew about this, because I defended the corps system in a conversation with him and he told me that it was stupid to defend it. I replied that nevertheless the corps system is a thing that should not be tossed aside, because in the beginning of the war we got rid of it and during the war we were forced to restore it. Zhukov said: "Let's conduct a war game; I'll command an army without

---

9   Editor's note. Anton Vasil'evich Gerasimov (1900-78) joined the Red Army in 1919 and fought in the civil war. During the Great Patriotic War he served in the National Air Defense apparatus in Europe and the Far East. Following the war, Gerasimov continued to serve in this branch in the central apparatus.

the corps system, and you'll command with the corps system against me. Let's see who beats whom." I replied: "Of course, you'll beat me in a war game, because the referees will be on your side (laughter), while in a war you won't beat me with an army lacking a corps system…" But it was nonetheless decided. The commanders spoke about this when they spoke from this lectern. I was still in the Far East when the Presidium of the Central Committee heard the commanders. That's the way it was.

It was nevertheless decided to eliminate the corps system. We retained it here and there, there where it was so obvious that one could not get along without it, and it was retained. This leads one to conclude that it was retained and could always be multiplied and expanded when it would be necessary for the army. This matter was nevertheless entrusted to the staff of the Ground Forces, and here we're speaking not about Zhukov's personality, but about the armed forces, and we worked hard and managed to create such an army that, one could say, is a large army corps which was fully ready and combat capable. If it proves necessary, we can increase the number of corps headquarters. So there is no great concern here. But how otherwise could we have done this? We experienced difficulties in our work and felt the leaden hand and personality of Zhukov hanging over us. Why did we not rise up and why did I personally, knowing Nikita Sergeevich, never approach him and speak about this? I knew that Nikita Sergeevich was very busy and I felt uncomfortable approaching him with my personal hurts. This is how I thought: when it becomes necessary, Nikita Sergeevich can always call and summon me.

However, comrades, this is not where the matter lies. Zhukov keeps on getting extolled and glorified: he's promoted from candidate member of the Central Committee to member, from member of the Central Committee to candidate member of the Presidium of our party's Central Committee, and then a member of the Central Committee Presidium. The Beria affair and the affair of the anti-party group all led to the glorification and strengthening of comrade Zhukov's role and influence. I will personally state that I thought that maybe that's necessary for high-level politics, but who's to say? Eisenhower's "friend," even if in quotes. Maybe this should be exploited. After all, politics is a very complex matter. (Commotion in the hall). This is how I thought: we'll put up with it. However, I believed, and believed very deeply that matters could not go on this way for long and that the Central Committee would take a hand in this matter and reveal this scab.

Zhukov, of course, is a very powerful man, a very gifted man. I will be blunt—he's not well educated, but his gifts outshine the shortcomings in his education. His is a powerful personality. A useful man. He achieved a lot during the war and I respect him for this and will respect him for what he has done for the Motherland. But we should all know, and you will forgive me this perhaps crude comparison, but that's the way it is; I did a lot of farm labor as a child and worked with horses. It happens that you have a good horse—once Stalin called Churchill England's good old horse—maybe not even a horse, but a good stallion, and if you put him in harness, then he can pull a very heavy load. But this is a very capricious stallion. If the reins are held tight, then he feels that a powerful driver is in charge and he is useful. But when this stallion begins to pull on the reins and charge ahead with dull eyes, then we may feel fear: just where will this stallion carry our state chariot? (Commotion in the hall).

That's why the Presidium of the Central Committee felt in time that the reins were breaking and that he could break free and where he would then carry us is unknown.

So, comrades, was it convincing for us to thus discuss comrade Zhukov's behavior? During the first break I heard snatches of conversation from some that there are no convincing facts; that things aren't clear and that this is a bolt from the blue, etc. There are convincing facts and there are facts that are very dangerous for our party and our state. I saw comrade Zhukov here for the first time in such an angelic pose as he was on the lectern, in which I saw him here.

He said that there were mistakes, but no one ever pointed these mistakes out to me. I did not feel these mistakes and did not notice these mistakes. If so, I would have corrected them.

Alright. Let's pursue this angle. What does it mean if an important leader in our party, which is what a member of the party's Central Committee Presidium is, doesn't feel or notice his mistakes? What kind of politician is that? Do we really need such politicians? Where can such a politician, who doesn't feel where he's going, take us?

This is an absolute lack of any kind of party and political maturity. Such a politician can move, not knowing where he's going.

However, I doubt that he didn't know where he was going.

Thus we have the very convincing fact that we don't need such politicians.

We, the party people, members of our great party, are obligated to be politicians and obliged to understand politics. We are obliged to build our entire work and behavior, proceeding from politics.

Politics is a very cruel thing. Politics never forgives political mistakes. You and I may forgive, but politics will not forgive this. And since we are members of the party, we are politicians, and we cannot forgive this.

There are other facts, of which I literally just became aware.

I sincerely worked and helped Zhukov, despite all the difficulties of my position.

However, there's the fact that in speaking before the Presidium of the Central Committee, he says in one place that we are weak and we will be defeated if we don't increase our budget, and afterwards in another place he says that we are stronger than everyone, that we will defeat everyone, and that why should we be afraid of opening our skies to the Americans? Let them fly over and see our country and we'll see, because we're stronger and will beat them.

That's not a policy!

This could only happen in the American congress, where everyone always takes a position based on opportunism.

And we in our Soviet state cannot blackmail our leadership by saying we're weak when we want money and, in another place that we are strong and should open our skies to the Americans, which is a dishonest policy. That's an important fact!

KHRUSHCHEV. That's right.

MALINOVSKII. The elimination of the military council within the Defense Council is, of course, a fact that fences off the leadership of our army and navy from the Central Committee. It's always very nice for the commanders of our military districts, armies and fleets when they feel a live contact with the Central Committee, when they can speak the truth to the Central Committee, and can speak about their needs and thoughts and receive instructions from the Central Committee, which they need like air in order to work profitably.

A third fact is the school for diversionists. He said that this was an innocent matter, that there were companies of diversionists in all the military districts and that they brought these 17 companies together. Nothing of the sort. The Ground Forces were ordered to find the necessary troops for this school beside those 17 companies that were in the military districts. And all of this was laid upon the Far Eastern Military District, whose commander can confirm this. I also found out about the school quite by accident, when Mamsurov raised this question in the Central Committee.

The belittling of the political organs and the disparagement of our party organizations in the army and navy—is this not a fact? Of course, I should say that this is a very complex tangle. Here one may say that Zhukov didn't investigate this tangle, because during the days of the chief of GlavPUR,[10] Lev Zakharovich Mekhlis, there were no military councils and there were no in the divisions and corps and that we only had sections for agitation and propaganda. He failed to clear this matter up and failed to understand this as minister of defense and set out on a false path, while fencing off the party from the army, while degrading the political organs and party organizations of our army. Without that, there can be no army.

And all of this was done under a good and plausible pretext.

It's like taking someone's home in order to improve his living conditions; take his clothes so that he's better dressed; to unify the academies under a single roof, so that they were better distributed. All of this was done under the pretext of improving things and acquired a complete different form.

Finally. What does "I will appeal to the people" mean? This was stated more than once. This was said at a meeting of party activists of the Moscow garrison, which was carried out in one day in accordance with the Central Committee's June plenum; this was said at a large meeting of communists at an exercise, where there were more than 1,000 people. Everyone applauded this declaration, insofar as people understood it as the unity of the army and its minister. However, I gave this matter some thought. I didn't like this declaration, as it sounded bad. However, I was not the only one at the meeting of party activists, or the only one at the meeting to note this. Nevertheless, during my first meeting with N.S. Khrushchev, I told him that it sounded bad. What is this—I will appeal to the people and army and it will understand and support me. This is dangerous. Who am I?

In general, in the defense ministry our alphabet's been in a muddle: the word I has been moved far from the tail end and we never heard the word "we," but only "I." I think, I instruct, I order, etc. This "I" has led to a terrible statement that is dangerous to the party: "I will appeal to the people and army." And where's the party Where's the Supreme Soviet of our country? Where are the trade unions? Does our people really not have organizations that can speak in the name of the peoples? What does that mean, "I'll appeal"? This is a rock that has been thrown far. He has decided to teach us: I'll say this here, I'll say this there, and people will get used to it, and then I'll do it Ukrainian style—I'll catch a strong and good stallion: here, here my dear, my good one, and then, giddy up, and I'll saddle you like I want.

All of these declarations force us to draw correct conclusions regarding comrade Zhukov: there's no place for such a politician in the Presidium and Central Committee of our party. We'll give him his due for his services and set him up to work and live as is necessary.

In his concluding remarks at the October plenum, Khrushchev characterized Zhukov thusly:

As a military man, and I believe this now, he should be retained. However, as a politician, he simply proved to be a bankrupt, and not only a bankrupt, but even proved to be a terrible person... Comrade Zhukov, dear Georgii Konstantinovich, you called me on Saturday and we talked for an hour over the phone. "You're depriving yourself of your best friend," he said to me. But, dear comrade, we're not speaking personally about me...

When you undo the chain, Zhukov's behavior and party activity is simply scary, and to top it off, there's his declaration: "I will appeal to the army and people and they will support me," and he said that meaning that he could at some time appeal, and he was applauded then and there. Rodion Yakovlevich Malinovskii said that this declaration struck him like a

---

10   Editor's note. The GlavPUR, which was one of the various names given to the main political administration, was the body entrusted with ensuring the allegiance of the armed forces to the Communist Party.

blow. When we told Zhukov about this on Saturday, he said: "That's right, I said it. What's the problem? I spoke correctly and fought the anti-party group. And now you would change and say that the anti-party group is condemning me." This is an appeal over the head of the Central Committee. I am the Lord, I am Zhukov, I said it, which means it's the truth. This is arbitrariness. This is a terrible thing, comrades…

Comrade Zhukov, you're not a party-minded man and you have no sense of party-mindedness. You are a dangerous and harmful man. Rodion Yakovlevich reminded me, when I spoke with him, what he thinks of Zhukov. I laid out my thoughts that Zhukov worries the members of the Presidium and even arouses fear. He heard me out and said I'll remind you of my opinion. When we were coming back from China, we were in Khabarovsk (this conversation took place in October 1954, when Khrushchev and Bulganin, following an official visit to the Chinese People's Republic, carried out a tour of the Far East, visiting the forces of the Far Eastern Military District and the Pacific Fleet, B.S.) and the three of us were sitting in headquarters or in an apartment. Comrade Malinovskii said that Zhukov is a terrible man. Bulganin confirmed this and I was silent. Comrade Malinovskii said that you were probably quiet for political reasons. Bulganin confirmed this then that such a conversation did take place. If I was silent, I don't want to be smart now, and I evidently did not agree with you then, because I believed too much in Zhukov. And now I want to say that you were right and that life has confirmed this and Zhukov actually was that way. This has been confirmed…

On 2 November 1957 Malinovskii conducted a meeting of party activists at the defense ministry, where he explained in greater detail his attitude toward Zhukov and for the first time publicly admitted, after Nikita Sergeevich himself had spoken about this at the plenum, that as early as 1954 he had warned Khrushchev and Bulganin regarding Zhukov's Bonapartism:

Zhukov is a gifted military man. Zhukov is stubborn and loves to work hard. He did the Soviet people a great service. He received the highest honors. We don't take back these services by Zhukov. However, alongside these qualities there are great sins.

You could say that now our tongues have been loosened, once the Central Committee took of this matter.

When Khrushchev, Bulganin and Mikoyan were leaving China, I told them in Khabarovsk that Zhukov is a dangerous and even terrible man. Bulganin said that we know his qualities. Khrushchev was silent.

I've worked with Zhukov for 30 years. He's an autocratic, despotic and ruthless man. I decided to go work with him. I decided: if he's going to be rude, then I'll be rude. If he's going to curse, then I will curse. If he's going to fight, then I'll do the same.

This is what was on my mind when I came to the ministry of defense.

He treated me with great respect, actually, politely.

Therefore I have nothing against him personally. However, I saw how Zhukov displayed incredible rudeness toward a number of people, including high-ranking military men (Biryuzov).

Zhukov's personality is such that if he wants to say something pleasant to someone, he can't do it.

Here's a fact. Someone was given the rank of marshal of the Soviet Union and Zhukov thanked him.

The recipient said that "I'm happy, I'm excited and will try to justify this." Zhukov replied: "I don't give a damn about your feelings and your excitement—it was my job to congratulate you."

Zhukov said that he didn't notice and didn't feel his mistakes.

Then why do we need such a leader, who is incapable of seeing his mistakes? Zhukov is not a mature politician, and an immature communist.

Under Zhukov discipline improved, although this was done through fear. Many commanders were punished for one illegality. Recklessness. A pain killer. The sailors have a saying about the three stages: Remove, demote and take off the ship…

Our cadre's condition was depressed.

Such discipline is unstable. At the first serious test, such discipline can fall apart like a house of cards. Discipline should be only on the basis of a high degree of conscientiousness and loyalty.

Now the question of the diversionists.

The airborne schools were for seven years (in that time you could teach a hare to light matches)…

There was a sailor's celebration in Leningrad and the sailors wanted to be in white tunics, but Zhukov ordered everyone to wear black ones, so that he could be in white against the overall dark background.

The glory of a commander turned Zhukov's head.

The glory of a commander gave him no rest…

Now he have wars that are different from what was earlier, when the commander played such a role.

Now the entire state and its potential wage war. A reflection… of overall glory may accidentally fall upon someone among us. This reflection of glory must be protected.

It turns out that Malinovskii was the first one who directly warned Khrushchev about Zhukov's Bonapartist ways, and Nikita Sergeevich admitted this publicly. Afterwards, after Konev wound up in semi-disfavor, due to his closeness to Zhukov, Malinovskii became the only candidate for the freed-up post of defense minister.

Khrushchev recalled:

Malinovskii's appointment as defense minister went through with difficulty. There were no objections to Malinovskii among the party leadership. Of course, Malinovskii's country-wide and worldwide reputation was lower than Zhukov's. On the other hand, Marshal Malinovskii had showed himself very well during the war and was not an unknown element in the military sphere. He was inferior to Zhukov personally, as concerns energy and being pushy, having a calm and somewhat slow character. However, he was not inferior in thoughtfulness. I preferred Malinovskii, compared to another glorified marshal, Konev, although I highly rated Konev's military capabilities. However, I believed that Konev was not capable of behaving in a straightforward manner with the party leadership and government.

When the question was being decided of whom to appoint defense minister in place of Zhukov, Zhukov put the question in soldierly fashion: "Whom are you appointing in my place?" I was forced to reply, although I didn't feel like discussing this question with him, and said: "We're appointing Malinovskii." "I would have proposed Konev," Zhukov snapped.

Konev was present at this conversation and I didn't want to offend him. Konev's virtues are no less than Malinovskii's. But Malinovskii was not inferior to him in knowledge and, maybe, he was even superior to Konev. These were people with different personalities.

13

USSR Minister of Defense

On 26 October 1957 Marshal Malinovskii was appointed minister of defense in a decree by the Presidium of the CPSU Central Committee. This is the way his daughter spoke about this appointment:

> On that October day, when they appointed papa minister, he arrived at the dacha darker than a cloud. He didn't bother to eat supper. We walked silently for a long time, until almost night. Mama well recognized situations that excluded questions. Finally, mama's brother appeared on the porch: "Rodion Yakovlevich, the radio reported that they have appointed you minister!" And here mama could not restrain herself:
>
> "Why didn't you refuse?
> "Go and turn them down."
> There were no more words.

> Papa accepted his new duties with a heavy heart. His adjutant, Aleksandr Ivanovich Mishin, told me that following the appointment, while concluding a party conference, at which, as was the tradition, the former lackeys did not miss the opportunity to insult Zhukov, father said clearly that the removal was not the equivalent of a civil execution and was not an excuse for whooping it up. "No one can take what Zhukov has done away from him." By the way, Zhukov's entire apparatus—the secretariat, the correspondence section and the typists—remained to work under papa. As they explained to me, this was a unique case, as they usually changed everyone and appointed their own people, as, for example, was done after papa.

Andrei Glebovich Baklanov, a diplomat and historian and the son of Colonel General Gleb Vladimirovich Baklanov,[1] who had the opportunity to serve with Malinovskii, characterized the army's reaction to the appointment of Rodion Yakovlevich as minister in the following way:

> Marshal Rodion Yakovlevich Malinovskii was appointed to replace G.K. Zhukov... He was loved and respected in the army and among the people as one of the front commanders during the Great Patriotic War. However, I must say frankly that Malinovskii was considered no more than "one of the galaxy of the marshals of victory." Thus they didn't place any great hopes on improving the situation in the army in connection with his arrival as the chief of the defense ministry. However, all the suppositions proved to be inexact or even incorrect. R.Ya. Malinovskii proved to be a truly amazing minister of defense. I believe that we never had a

---

1   Editor's note. Gleb Vladimirovich Baklanov (1910-76) joined the Red Army in 1932. During the Great Patriotic War he commanded a regiment, brigade, division, and corps. Following the war, Baklanov commanded corps, an army, a military district, and Soviet forces in Poland.

better minister since 1917 and his services in this regard have not been properly evaluated to this day. It was precisely during the time when Rodion Yakovlevich headed the defense ministry that unprecedented tasks were resolved—the nuclear missile rearmament of the army was completed and a historical parity of forces with the USA was achieved.

There was no self admiration in Malinovskii's manner of leadership and he conducted himself with the proper gravity, with dignity, but modestly, without any elements of lordliness. A characteristic feature was that the defense minister vacationed, as a rule, in sanitariums and rest homes together with his subordinates, although, of course, given the desire, he could have gotten a separate dacha without problems. I well remember how my parents and the Malinovskiis would vacation at the "Arkhangel'skoe" sanitarium. The minister occupied approximately the same first-class room as the other senior commanders.

Malinovskii decisively distinguished himself from Zhukov in his leadership style and in his relations toward his subordinates. At the same time, he really did in many ways reform the armed forces. If under his postwar predecessors, Bulganin, Vasilevskii and Zhukov, the Soviet army still remained an army of the Second World War, although it disposed of more powerful weapons, such as missiles, jet fighters and nuclear bombs, under Malinovskii the army became a truly modern and new one, not only in weaponry, but also in tactics and strategy. Stress was laid on nuclear missile weaponry and on atomic submarines in the navy. The new defense minister also gave priority attention to the development of radar and, which was new for the Soviet armed forces, to the development of command and supply systems. At the same time, one should note that Rodion Yakovlevich had no specialized education. His technical knowledge was limited to what he had mastered in the academy as early as the end of the 1920s. However, Malinovskii proved ready to be quite capable of correctly evaluating the prospects of employing new systems of weapons and communications and gave the green light for their introduction with the troops. The new minister paid a lot of attention to systems of troop control. He introduced automated control systems at the highest level and also employed new communications equipment at the tactical level.

During Malinovskii's tenure as defense minister a common organization of motorized rifle, tank and airborne divisions was introduced.

Formal parity with the USA in the number of delivery systems and warheads was not achieved at the time he was defense minister, but somewhat later, during the 1970s. But it was precisely under Malinovskii that Soviet strategic nuclear forces achieved such a potential that they could deliver guaranteed and unacceptable damage to any possible enemy.

During Malinovskii's tenure as minister of defense, the USA began a large-scale military intervention in Vietnam. The Soviet Union supported with weapons, combat equipment and advisers communist North Vietnam, which, in its turn, rendered assistance to the guerillas in South Vietnam. On 22 January 1966 General G.I. Obaturov[2] noted in his diary Malinovskii's speech before the Main Military Council, which became the marshal's last:

---

2   Editor's note. Gennadii Ivanovich Obaturov (1915-96) joined the Red Army in 1935. During the Great Patriotic War he held various command and staff positions with the armored forces. His tank division helped put down the Hungarian uprising in 1956. He later commanded a tank corps, a tank army and a military district. Obaturov also served as a military advisor during the Chinese-Vietnamese border conflict in 1979.

Yesterday was the first day of the meeting of the Main Military Council. Brezhnev, Kosygin,[3] Podgornyi,[4] Ustinov,[5] and Malinovskii were at the meeting, as well as the entire leadership of the defense ministry and from the provinces: Dmitriev, Yakubovskii,[6] and Golovnin.

Malinovskii delivered a speech on the condition of our combat readiness and our operational and combat training. In the three years since the last meeting of the Military Council, Vietnam has become a proving ground for testing various types of weapons, including chemical. There's no guarantee that they will not employ tactical nuclear weapons there. We believe that this will be North Vietnam. Europe is the main hotbed of danger. Here the USA, together with Germany, is playing the main role. Their bloc has 50 divisions, 1,100 guns capable of firing atomic shells, 3,500 aircraft, including 1,100 fighters. There are 12 West German divisions in NATO. West Germany is striving for a special role in NATO for revanchist purposes. The USA is devoting a great deal of attention to augmenting its strategic nuclear forces for a general nuclear war: it has 850 strategic missile launchers, aside from 350 "Polaris" missiles on submarines, and new strategic bombers are being introduced. They are preparing a surprise attack. Their missiles are at the highest state of readiness. The readiness and number of conventional forces is being increased. For example, the number of ground forces rose by 235,000 in 1965, particularly in army aviation and air-mobile formations. This enables them to unleash a war without major mobilization measures and at the same time wage limited wars. From this we draw conclusions to increase the Ground Forces' combat readiness for war, regardless of how it starts: with the employment of nuclear weapons or not. He then analyzed the condition of our combat readiness. During recent years our main efforts have been concentrated on developing the decisive service—the Strategic Rocket Forces. The development of the other services has continued simultaneously. Mistakes are being corrected and close relations and combat cooperation are being established with the armies of the Warsaw Pact countries. He pointed out the insufficient secrecy and how carelessness in maintaining secrecy is manifested. There is insufficient military-patriotic education. Many arrive at the army poorly prepared, both morally and physically, etc.

Genadii Ivanovich then briefly related what they spoke about on the second day of the Main Military Council's session:

Today is the second day. They spoke about problems of foreign policy and about relations with the socialist countries. Even relations with Romania have improved. The same with Korea.

---

3   Editor's note. Aleksei Nikolaevich Kosygin (1904-80) joined the Red Army in 1919 and the Communist Party in 1927. Kosygin's skills as an administrator enabled him to rise rapidly in the government apparatus, and during the Great Patriotic War he was in charge of evacuating the country's industry to the east. Kosygin's career suffered in Stalin's last years, but he came back under Khrushchev before replacing him as chairman of the Council of Ministers in 1964, where he served as the head of the government until his retirement shortly before his death.

4   Editor's note. Nikolai Vladimirovich Podgornyi (1903-83) joined the Communist Party in 1930 and advanced quickly through the government ranks, thanks to Khrushchev's patronage. In 1965 Podgornyi became head of state in the post-Khrushchev collective leadership. He was ousted from his position in 1977 and pensioned off.

5   Editor's note. Dmitrii Fedorovich Ustinov (1904-84) joined the Communist Party in 1927. During the Great Patriotic War he was people's commissar for armaments and later became a secretary of the CPSU Central Committee. In 1976 Ustinov was appointed minister of defense, from which post he continued his efforts to modernize the Soviet armed forces.

6   Editor's note. Ivan Ignat'evich Yakubovskii (1912-76) joined the Red Army in 1932 and fought in the Soviet-Finnish and Great Patriotic Wars as an armored officer. Following the war he commanded Soviet forces in Germany and a military district. Yakubovskii's last assignment was commander-in-chief of the Warsaw Pact forces.

Things haven't moved forward with China, and in fact we're going backwards. We need to isolate the Chinese leadership. Aid to Vietnam is very expensive, but necessary. It's difficult to say how this will end, but the USA will not achieve success. It's a mistake that the South Vietnamese comrades did not agree to negotiate. It will be difficult for the USA to withdraw, because who will believe them then?

It's clear from this notation that the Soviet leadership, as represented by Brezhnev, did not want to get closer to China, as opposed to Romania and even North Korea, but instead was only pursuing the aim of isolating the Chinese leadership in the international arena and, in particular, among the communist parties.

Mao Zedong's works on guerilla warfare came in handy for Malinovskii and his subordinates in Vietnam. South Vietnam, which is covered with jungles, represented nearly ideal territory for guerilla operations. And Soviet anti-aircraft missile systems forced the American air force to endure heavy losses in raids on North Vietnam. Unfortunately, the North Vietnamese forces and their South Vietnamese allies did not always strictly adhere to guerilla tactics. All too often, taking a page from the Red Army in the Great Patriotic War, they sought to seize American bases with the aid of large masses of infantry, taking advantage of their overwhelming advantage in men. However, the Americans had the same overwhelming superiority in weapons and combat equipment, and in the majority of cases such attacks ended catastrophically for the Vietnamese communists.

One of the largest such mass attacks took place on 21 March 1967, a few days before Rodion Yakovlevich's death. The North Vietnamese troops attempted to seize fire base "Gold" in South Vietnam's Tainan province, but were destroyed or forced to flee by American artillery, aviation and tanks. The Americans gathered up 647 Vietnamese corpses on the battle field. Another ten North Vietnamese soldiers were captured and two of them later died of their wounds. The Americans lost only 33 men killed, and one of them was a victim of "friendly fire." This yields a correlation of 20:1 killed in favor of the American army. This was approximately the same as the correlation of irreplaceable losses along the Soviet-German front in 1941-43. If the Vietnamese communists had strictly adhered to guerilla tactics, the correlation of losses for them would have been significantly more favorable. At the same time, the absolute number of American losses in men and materiel would obviously have decreased, while the main goal of the Vietnamese communists was, while not taking into account their own losses, to inflict maximum losses in men and materiel on the Americans, which would have produced a negative reaction in the USA.

On 23 November 1958, in connection with his sixtieth birthday, Malinovskii was awarded the title of Hero of the Soviet Union a second time for his services to the fatherland, and a bust of him was dedicated in his native Odessa.

In his diary entry of 22 March 1966, G.I. Obaturov cites a conversation with his friend, A.P. Dmitriev, who had just become a member of the military council for the North Caucasus Military District: He said: "Malinovskii is nevertheless a stubborn man. And I should know. You almost can't get anything with him if it doesn't coincide with his opinion."

Major General Mikhail Ivanovich Petrov, a former general for special assignments with the ministry of defense, recalled: "Rodion Yakovlevich's resolutions are still the stuff of legends. He wrote briefly and clearly—so that even someone who doesn't want to understand can understand. Often and unbelievably accurately, he would quote from his favorite *Woe From Wit*,[7] and in some of his resolutions one can feel the hand of an Odessa native in his sense of humor.

---

7   Editor's note. This was a satire in verse of the Russian aristocracy by the author and diplomat Aleksandr Sergeevich Griboedov (1795-1829).

"One colonel sent the minister a letter, in which he complained that in summer it was 'difficult to distinguish' the senior officers 'from the junior officers, while their Caucasian fur hats distinguish them in the winter, and I would like to get rid of this oversight in uniforms'. Rodion Yakovlevich drew up the following resolution: 'Comrade Bagramyan I.Kh. You may authorize this colonel to wear a Caucasian fur hat in the summer'."

While already minister of defense, Malinovskii wrote the following in his notebook in 1958:

We need military intellectuals now like air. Not just highly-educated officers, but people who have mastered the high culture of might and heart and a humanistic world view. Modern weaponry with enormous destructive power should not be entrusted to a man who only has skillful and firm hands. One needs a sober head, capable of foreseeing consequences and a heart capable of feeling; that is, a mighty moral instinct. These are the necessary and, I would like to think, sufficient conditions.

A year later Rodion Yakovlevich made the following entry:

A third world war will inevitably become a nuclear war and thus destructive for all mankind. There will be no victor in a nuclear war. Now, when we have, at the price of incredible, selfless and heroic efforts by the entire people, acquired military might, in its modern understanding, and have thus confirmed our right to a voice in the world community, we need to be aware of the enormous responsibility we carry in the new conditions and clearly realize what we are talking about. Mutual self-destruction is threatening mankind. And while it's still not too late, we must listen to the voice of reason and the voice of our heart. We must crush the ice of alienation between peoples and states. Man needs power only over himself.

Such judgments did not sound very Marxist. Only Rodion Yakovlevich probably never directly spoke like this to either Nikita Sergeevich or Leonid Il'ich, so that the leaders wouldn't think that the marshal was trying to appear smarter than they were. However, in his activity he certainly proceeded from a conviction about the unacceptability of global thermonuclear war in any case.

Malinovskii also wrote about the unpredictable nature of a future war:

Insofar as we have definite and unified tenets about the nature of a future war and its operations, it may appear to some that we've done everything, everything has been found and all that remains is to learn them. No, this is not the case! I admit that sometimes a future war appears to me as a cat in a bag, in that it will be so different from the one we went through. We all have to work a lot, study and learn, in order to profoundly and fully understand all of the aspects of military collisions, which, unfortunately for humanity, are still on the agenda.

Colonel Aleksandr Ivanovich Mishin, Malinovskii's adjutant during 1946-67, related the following:

When visiting the troops, Rodion Yakovlevich always looked into the barracks and the homes where the officers lived, took an interest in how supply had been set up, and talked with the military families. A new era altogether began with his visit to the garrison of Kushka. Malinovskii was the only minister of defense who visited Kushka, the Kurile Islands and the Northern Fleet. And there was not a single, even the most remote, place in the Far East which he did not reach.

I'll tell you about a characteristic case. Rodion Yakovlevich was inspecting the barracks. Everything was sparkly and shining and the local command was already ready to breathe more easily, when all of a sudden the minister made the following request: "Comrade colonel! Could I ask you for a cup of water?" The colonel ran to a dispenser with a cup attached to it, leaned over and filled the cup and tried to extend the cup and freezes in a semi-bending position: the chain is so short that it practically forces one to drink from it on all fours. Rodion Yakovlevich was quiet for a moment and then shook his head: "So you force a man to his knees for the sake of a cup of water?"

The former commander of a nuclear submarine, which carried out the first voyage to the North Pole under the ice in 1962, Hero of the Soviet Union Vice-Admiral Lev Mikhailovich Zhil'tsov, opined: "Malinovskii gave off the sensation of calm and colossal internal strength."

In 1959 Rodion Yakovlevich reported to the CPSU Central Committee:

The Ministry of Defense disposes of information that the state of affairs with finding employment and particularly with housing for officers released to the reserves remains unsatisfactory. As of 1 October 1958, of those officers listed by the military commissariats, 3,916 have not found jobs and 11,674 have not been provided with housing. Among those reserve officers who have not found jobs, 2,081 do not receive a pension. Taking into account those officers who have been discharged through other organizational measures, the number of those who have not found jobs is 4,736, with 47,674 without housing.

At the end of 1959, Khrushchev noted in a message to the Presidium of the Central Committee:

I think that we ought to move on further reducing the amount of armaments in our country, even without mutual agreement with other states and significantly reducing the rank and file of the armed forces. I believe that we could reduce this number, perhaps by a million or million and a half, but we should consult with and study the idea with the defense minister. I believe that such a significant reduction would not undermine our defensive capability. But to put forth and carry out such a decision would have a great and positive effect on the international situation and our prestige would increase greatly in the eyes of all the peoples. This would be an immense blow against the enemies of peace and proponents of the "Cold War"... Why do I believe this to be possible and safe right now? My opinion is based on the fact that, first of all, we have now achieved a good situation regarding the development of the Soviet Union's economy; secondly, we are in an excellent position as regards missile construction; we, speaking personally, possess an assortment of missiles for the resolution of any military problem, both over long and short distances, such as "ground to ground," "air to ground" and "air to air" missiles, atomic submarines, etc., as well as a good assortment regarding explosive power... I'm sure that this would be a very powerful and shocking step... I think that right now it doesn't make sense to have atomic and hydrogen bombs and missiles and at the same time maintain a large army.

In January 1960 the Presidium of the CPSU Central Committee adopted a resolution to reduce the size of the army by another 1,200,000 men.

Malinovskii had nothing against this. With the growth of the outfitting of the armed forces with more and more destructive and effective armaments and military equipment, the necessity of maintaining large infantry formations was lessening. However, the marshal protested that Khrushchev, while cutting the size of the army, did not concern himself with the fate of the discharged officers.

By the way, very soon the new missile equipment proved its effectiveness. This is how Khrushchev described the destruction of the American U-2[8] spy plane in May 1960:

> When early in the morning of 1 May 1960 (I recall that day very well) the telephone rang, I raised the receiver and defense minister Malinovskii reported: "An American U-2 is flying toward Sverdlovsk from the Afghanistan area, obviously from Pakistan."
>
> I replied: "We must distinguish ourselves and shoot this plane down. Take all measures!" "I've already given the order and everything will be done to shoot it down," Rodion Yakovlevich replied. I put the following question: "Is our anti-aircraft equipment located along the plane's route?" "Yes, it is and he will evidently come up against it. We have every opportunity to shoot him down if the air defense men don't slip up." He used the term "if they don't slip up" because in April, when the previous identical case occurred, our air defense men missed the U-2: they had not been prepared and did not open fire on time.
>
> In Moscow the 1 May troop parade began on Red Square. Then it ended and the workers' demonstration began. It was a beautiful and sunny day. The demonstration was very enthusiastic and everybody was in an excellent mood. Suddenly Marshal Biryuzov, who then commanded the National Air Defense Forces, appeared. They told me about his arrival and I told him to ascend the Lenin Mausoleum. Biryuzov whispered into my ear that the U-2 aircraft had been shot down and that the pilot had been captured and that he was now being interrogated. I congratulated the marshal on the occasion of the holiday and on his great success and I shook his hand warmly and he left.

On 30 May 1960 Malinovskii declared that if flights by the American U-2 spy plane over Soviet territory continue, then the Soviet Union would not only destroy them, but launch "a crushing attack against the bases from which they take off."

Boris Yevseevich Chertok,[9] one of the Soviet space scientists, described in his memoirs Malinovskii's visit to a testing range in the fall of 1961:

> During the most intensive period of preparing the "Zenith-2" for launch, we received a message at the testing range about the forthcoming inspection of our space missile achievements by the minister of defense, Marshal of the Soviet Union Rodion Yakovlevich Malinovskii, himself. During 1956-57 he had been the commander-in-chief of the Ground Forces. In military circles they said that he was not ambitious and in no way sought to become the defense minister of a nuclear superpower. Nevertheless, at the end of 1957, on Khrushchev's initiative, his candidacy for that high post was confirmed. Malinovskii now had to learn space missile technology.
>
> In the fall of 1961 there was a rumor at the testing range that Malinovskii would accompany Nikita Sergeevich, but it later transpired that Khrushchev would not be coming. Due to this high-ranking visit, almost all of the officers and soldiers were removed from their testing work and thrown into making things clean and putting things in order. At this time I was responsible for the timetable and quality of preparing the "Zenith" and sought to protest against pulling people off their job and made my indignation known to the chairman of the

---

8   Editor's note. The U-2 was a US high-altitude reconnaissance aircraft, capable of flying at 70,000 feet. The first model entered service in 1957 and follow-on models are still used.

9   Editor's note. Boris Yevseevich Chertok (1912-2011) began his career as an aircraft designer, before making the switch to missiles after the war. For many years he worked with S.P. Korolev in the Soviet space and military missile programs.

State Commission, Kerimov, and the chief of the testing range's first directorate, Colonel Kirillov.

Smiling, Kerimov replied that the testing range's command "knows what's best for it" and that they wouldn't listen to him anyway. Kirillov did not miss the opportunity to read me a lesson: "You civilians respect your ministers, but you're not afraid of them. One of them offends you and you go work for another, and in even more favorable conditions. Your ministers' power over people is primarily moral. The matter is quite different for us military men. In the army the minister's power manifests itself in a direct and open manner. They'll remove you for a mess on the road and a lack of order in the barracks, without any kind of advisement, and may even remove you from the base. We cannot respect the brass and despise him, but we are simply obligated to fear it."

Korolev[10] was getting ready to fly to the testing range, figuring that Khrushchev would be there. When it transpired that only Malinovskii was coming, he sent Mishin[11] there with the assignment to organize an exposition in the construction-testing complex of our achievements and the prospects for future projects. Sergei Pavlovich phoned and ordered me to help Mishin in any way in the organization and not to avoid a meeting with the marshal.

About three days before the high-level visit a personal chef and the help flew in to prepare the dining room at the tenth range, where the marshal's residence was, with our "first-class" dining hall for the chief constructors at the testing ground.

Malinovskii flew in on the evening of 27 November together with the commander-in-chief of the Strategic Rocket Forces, Marshal Moskalenko.[12] Zakharov, the testing range chief, and Smirnitskii, the chief of the Main Administration of Rocket Weaponry, who met him, tried to talk him into taking a rest. However, against expectations, the 60-year old marshal refused to rest and demanded that he be shown the launch of the R-7A[13] (8K74) intercontinental missile, that had been adopted. They had been preparing the launch for three days at the thirty-first range.[14] Everything was going well until a cavalcade of vehicles accompanying the marshal appeared at the 30-minute readiness time…

They explained to Malinovskii that the readiness time was 20 minutes. He did not approach the rocket at close range, but went to a specially dug and fortified trench on the summit of a hill that was buffeted by an icy wind. There immediately began the problems that manifest themselves when somebody visits. The "shoe" with valves for pumping in liquid oxygen had been set up at a slant and oxygen began to leak. They announced a delay of 30 minutes. When it came time to move the girders, they mistakenly broke the cable for registering how full the tanks were. They once again announced a delay, this time for an entire hour! When Korolev heard about this he asked me to relay the following message: "Drain the oxygen! Make note of the team's outrageous work! Change the cable!"

---

10   Editor's note. Sergei Pavlovich Korolev (1907-66) was a Soviet rocket designer and is considered the father of the Soviet space program.

11   Editor's note. Vasilii Pavlovich Mishin (1917-2001) was a noted Soviet rocket scientist who was blamed for the Soviet failure to send a man to the moon. His lack of administrative abilities led to his replacement by V.P. Glushko.

12   Editor's note. Kirill Semyonovich Moskalenko (1902-85) joined the Red Army in 1920 and fought in the civil war. During the Great Patriotic War he commanded a brigade, corps and armies. Following the war, Moskalenko commanded an army and military district and was also commander-in-chief of the Strategic Rocket Forces.

13   Editor's note. The R-7A was a Soviet intercontinental ballistic missile designed to carry a nuclear warhead. It first flew in 1959 and entered service the following year. It was retired in 1968.

14   Editor's note. This refers to the testing range at the Baikonur Cosmodrome in Kazakhstan.

The marshal had already been freezing in his trench for two hours. He became indignant and said: "You're supposed to be ready in 12 hours. You've already wasted three days on this. It's now 2300 hours. Be ready by 1100 tomorrow!"

On the way back they wanted to take him to our dining hall for a snack, where a dinner had been laid out which would do honor to the best big-city restaurants. Malinovskii turned down dinner at the testing ground and returned to his residence, warning us that he would be at pad no. 41 in the early morning, where Yangel's[15] R-16[16] was being prepared for launch. But bad luck also pursued Yangel's launch pad. The side battery ampoules were emitting reduced voltage and they had to be replaced. The launch was postponed for a few hours.

Malinovskii became angry and ordered the heads of the proving range and the chiefs of the administrations to remain at the forty-first and thirty-first pads to oversee the launch preparations. He promised to return before long and to check things out, and he and Moskalenko left to view our pad, the exhibition in the construction-testing complex and the launch of the R-9 rocket.[17]

At the first launch pad, Malinovskii went up to the edge of the gas dissemination trench. Leaning heavily against the railing, he asked Moskalenko:

"How far do the gases go?"

Marshal Moskalenko didn't know what to say. One of Barmin's people, who happened to be standing nearby, did not lose his presence of mind and answered:

"There, as far as that notch, Rodion Yakovlevich."

The defense minister looked around with dissatisfaction:

"Why did a chance civilian answer, and not an officer?"

They took him to watch the launch of the three-stage 8K72[18] rocket, with a "Vostok"[19] no. 5 and demonstrated its loading into the launch position. They wanted to show him one of the future cosmonauts in his space suit and had rehearsed this report for three days. But Malinovskii only said:

"Why is there so much ado in the cold?"

Without waiting any longer and not thanking anyone, he got into his car in order to go down to the R-9's launch pad. Mishin had only just managed to meet him there and begin his report explaining just what a great future intercontinental missile this was and what super cold oxygen was, when the marshal interrupted his report:

"Colonel General Ivanov has been here, looked into everything and reported to me. Don't waste time. Everything has been reported to me."

The launch of the R-9 was postponed and the defense minister left for the military construction site. When all of the soldiers had been gathered and lined up there, he asked an unexpected question:

"Soldiers! You are frontiersmen and volunteers. How's your work coming along?"

---

15   Editor's note. Mikhail Kuz'mich Yangel' (1911-71) was a Soviet missile designer whose bureau constructed several military models during the 1950s and 1960s.

16   Editor's note. The R-16 was the first successful Soviet intercontinental ballistic missile. Capable of carrying a nuclear warhead, it was phased out in 1976.

17   Editor's note. The R-9 (NATO designation SS-8) was a two-stage Soviet intercontinental ballistic missile designed to carry a nuclear warhead. It was first tested in 1961 and was in service during 1964-76.

18   Editor's note. This was a Soviet three-stage rocket for launching the "Vostok" spacecraft. This model was employed in 1960, before being replaced.

19   Editor's note. The "Vostok" ("East") was a Soviet spacecraft widely employed in the first manned flights during the early 1960s.

The soldiers broke ranks and surrounded the minister in a tight crowd and rained down complaints. The escorting personnel got the marshal out with difficulty and once again took him to Yangel's forty-first launch pad. There it transpired that the launch had been cancelled for the day. We needed another day for preparation and getting rid of problems.

"They've screwed up," Malinovskii said heavily. "If things are that way here, then what's going on in the launch units? Why aren't you following this, Kirill Semyonovich?"

This question was addressed to commander-in-chief Moskalenko. But what could an experienced ground forces marshal answer? They agreed that they would carry out two launches tomorrow: of the R-16 from launch pad forty-one, and the 8K74 from launch pad thirty-one an hour later.

On the cold and gray morning of 29 November there was once again a delay at launch pad forty-one. Malinovskii left for pad thirty-one. This time our R-7A and the combat crew did not let us down. Things went according to plan. The flight went as scheduled. The local command tried too hard to please the high-ranking visitor. They made the communications so loud during the flight that the surrounding locales could hear not only information about the course of the flight, but also top secret tactical-technical data.

"You should have invited foreigners to the show. You're only good for launching cosmonauts, and not combat missiles."

The combat crew was lined up at the launch pad following the successful launch of the "74." By tradition the results of the launch were to be briefly reported and the thanks of the command received, an order that had been laid down by Nedelin[20] and continued under Moskalenko.

The crew waited in anticipation of at least two or three words from the defense minister. However, Malinovskii, knitting his brows, began to walk not along the front, where a colonel, standing at attention, stood ready to report, but behind the crew. The command "About face!" sounded. Now Malinovskii was in front of the crew. However, he continued to slowly stride to the motor vehicle stop, without raising his lowered head. There was no command of "Dismissed!" but nevertheless the crew dispersed on its own. The insulted officers looked in bewilderment at the departed marshals…

Following this first successful launch, Malinovskii came to see us at the construction-testing complex. Of the military personnel meeting him, the most senior was Kirillov's assistant, Colonel Bobylev. Standing at attention, he began his report:

"Comrade Marshal of the Soviet Union! This is an assembly-experimental building. Here the preparation is carried out of…"

The marshal stopped the colonel's further eloquence with a wave of his hand:

"I can see what it is without you. You take me for a complete idiot. Better tell me where the toilet is"

The colonel drooped, but obediently led the marshal to the toilet, from which a lieutenant had been specially assigned to keep others away for three days.

Having relieved himself, the minister walked up to the hanging posters, evidently not wishing to see or listen. Mishin, not paying any attention to the high-ranking guest's behavior, went over to the attack and began to loudly and convincingly report on the global missile.

---

20   Editor's note. Mitrofan Ivanovich Nedelin (1902-60) joined the Red Army in 1920 and became an artillery officer. During the Great Patriotic War he commanded the artillery of several armies and fronts. Following the war, he served as chief of the army's artillery directorate and commander-in-chief of the Strategic Rocket Forces. Nedelin was killed in a rocket explosion.

"Ordinary rockets will not be effective within two or three years. Only our global missile, created on the basis of the R-9, will be capable of resolving any tasks. The Americans don't have such a design yet."

Upon hearing these words, it seemed as though Malinovskii came out of his depressed state, picked up his ears and began to listen. In observing him, I decided that he was either tired or sick and it was difficult for him to stand and listen to a report on the mechanics of the new missile's flight in his marshal's great coat and fur hat.

We had already put out tables and chairs by the stands with posters, figuring that both aged marshals would sit down for a rest and attentively listen to the reports, while quenching their thirst with mineral water. We had not even forgotten broad coat hangers for their greatcoats.

However, Malinovskii neither took off his coat nor sat down. This was a sort of demonstration of his dissatisfaction not only with the present state of missile technology, but with its prospects as well. However, during the report, he asked two questions: why do we need three stages, and where do the first two drop to? He then asked why we must slow down the third stage, where and how.

Mishin explained this in a very understandable manner, and it seemed as though Malinovskii understood. The "Desna" and "Valley" sites—future missile launch sites for the R-9 rocket—were also displayed on the posters. I had just begun to eloquently talk about the "Zenith" spy satellite, when an adjutant walked up and reported that an hour's readiness had just been announced at launch pad no. 41 and that it was time to leave for the launch of the R-16.

In reply, Malinovskii angrily stated:

"Don't bother, they'll still have a two-hour delay and then they'll call it off again."

I even managed to talk about the photo equipment and unexpectedly was asked:

"Do you change the focus in flight?"

The "Zenith" and the talk about its prospects evidently went over well. However, when I said that we are capable of uncovering the concentration and movement of armored formations, the minister noted with reason:

"While you're developing the film and figuring out where our forces are and where the enemy's are and reporting on this, the tanks will have moved far away."

He was right. Since then more than 30 years have passed. Our television technology enables us to transmit intelligence data directly from space in real time, without returning the cassette with the film to the Earth.

They once again returned the marshal from the "Zenith" to the R-9 lying on the transporter. Pointing to the engine nozzle, he asked:

"Is this where it burns?"

Mishin confirmed this, but did not miss the opportunity to say that it burns higher, in the chamber, and that the gases—the products of ignition—came out of these nozzles.

"Why did you use a new motor? Here's a tested one right here. Glushko[21] told me that this was a very reliable motor."

Here the marshal pointed for comparison the packet of document for the 8K74. Evidently, the morning launch of this missile had made an impression. Without waiting for the end of Mishin's lengthy answer, the marshal smiled for the first time, thanked us and shook everyone's hand.

---

21   Editor's note. Valentin Petrovich Glushko (1908-89) was a Soviet designer of rocket engines. He headed the Soviet missile program from 1974.

"You're staying here, after all. And what about you, the military intelligentsia? Or is there another chief engineer and this launch doesn't concern you?"

Finally, following much rechecking, the launch of the R-16 was also conducted normally. Taking into account the experience of the preceding launch at launch pad thirty-one and to avoid embarrassment, we decided not to line up the crew.

Having been informed of the successful launch of the R-16, we set out for the dining hall. After all, after two such difficult days, the marshal should check the work of the "marshal's" dining hall. We were warned in the morning during breakfast that lunch, should the marshal drop in, and would be special.

Despite such moral preparation, we were dumbfounded. A menu lay in a leather binding in front of each place setting. We read it as if a fairy tale: "Unpressed salmon caviar, sturgeon in aspic, cold smoked barbell, cured fillet of sturgeon, Siberian salmon back with lemon, sprats with lemon, crabs with peas under mayonnaise, roast beef, ham with horseradish, chicken salad, mushrooms with onions, radishes with sour cream, cottage cheese, sour cream, Moscow borscht, homemade noodles, soup with sturgeon, pikeperch Polish style, roast veal, boiled chicken, thin steak with baked potatoes and cucumbers, patties Kiev style, pancakes with jam, pancakes with sour cream, black coffee, coffee with milk, tea with lemon, and tea with jam." The fruits included oranges, apples and grapes, which lay heavily in crystal vases on the table. There were all sorts of mineral drinks, including the medicinal "Yessentuki" brand.

We began to compete to see who could try the most dishes. Someone expressed their disappointment that the menu did not include several components useful for our activity.

"No drinking in the marshal's presence!" warned the officer from the commissary. "We have a very strict dry law during these days."

Marshal Malinovskii nevertheless failed to grace our dining hall with his presence.

I tried to do my duty by the most attractive treats and dishes from the "reserve," but was unable spend more than three rubles on everything. Someone bragged that he had spent five rubles. The prices, for the times, were truly fantastic: the benchmark was the most expensive appetizer—unpressed caviar. A very decent portion only cost 47 kopecks.

Following such a luncheon, it was impossible to have dinner. We came back to the dining hall only on the next day, for breakfast. The fairy-tale magnificence had disappeared. We were not met by Moscow beauties, but by our long familiar waitresses. Nonetheless, we considered the fortified diet of the last two days a good compensation for the agitation due to the inspection.

Having quite objectively related the story about Malinovskii's visit to the proving ground, for some reason Chertok came to a conclusion not at all in keeping with his story. "Neither the commanders-in-chief nor defense minister Marshal Malinovskii wanted to understand our problems."

Actually, the story by Chertok, who was not too well disposed toward Malinovskii, actually yields quite a sympathetic portrait of the marshal. He does not tolerate effects and showiness and conducts himself modestly. Thus he refuses to take the parade of the missile crews, does not drop in to the dining hall, where a non-alcoholic banquet has been prepared for him. He does not attempt to throw dust in one's eyes, pretending that he knows everything and understands in this field that is new to him. He justifiably chews out the engineers and other specialists whose carelessness forced them to postpone the tests. He cuts off long-winded reports, full of specialized details which he doesn't understand in any event. On the other hand, he offers quite sensible advice in those matters which he understands immediately.

Chertok held it against Malinovskii that the latter regarded the Soviet moon program with skepticism and fought against the allotment of funds for its development. However, the Soviet lunar project during those years was an obvious adventure and would probably have led to a catastrophe and the death of people.

Aleksandr Shchelokov relates:

> At the Kubinka proving grounds the defense workers were showing Khrushchev the first serial anti-tank guided shells—PTURS.
>
> As is the practice, in order to earn the political leadership's blessing for technological breakthroughs, the demonstration's organizers sought to awe those who observed the firing with its effectiveness.
>
> For the most part, the firing took place under simplified conditions. The PTURS operators had been training on the same grounds where they later carried out their combat firing on targets. Here the lines and targets had already been registered, so that there were no unexpected surprises and could not be.
>
> The rockets' fiery streams flew over the field and crashed into the dark silhouettes of the tanks, which immediately flared up like fiery torches.
>
> Khrushchev nervously strode along the rostrum, where the leadership was situated, now and then took out his handkerchief and wiped his bald pate and oohed and aahed triumphantly when flame erupted over the latest tank.
>
> When the firing had ceased, the gaze of the military men turned to Khrushchev.
>
> The great strategist stuck out his belly. He understood: everyone was awaiting his evaluation. And any evaluation must be of historic importance. And here Khrushchev said:
>
> "The age of the tank is over," he pronounced in a solemn tone, most likely believing that his words would go down in history and that they would be called far-seeing and prophetic. "We won't build them anymore. Tanks will disappear from war forever."
>
> The stunned spectators were silent. The generals were brave on the battlefield. Not everyone is brave enough to object to the political leadership. Everyone understood that to object might cost one dearly.
>
> However, a brave man was found. He proved to the Chief Marshal of Tank Troops Pavel Alekseevich Rotmistrov. His mustache suddenly began to twitch and his eyes sparkled wrathfully and narrowed under his glasses. It was also evident that the marshal had sternly and angrily observed the battlefield at Prokhorovka,[22] where during the battle of Kursk his tank army had collided with the fascist *Das Reich*, *Totenkopf* and *Adolf Hitler* panzer divisions and the two steel forces began to smash one another.
>
> Rotmistrov advanced a pace and said in an agitated voice:
>
> "Comrade Khrushchev, to say that the age of the tank is over, is to…"
>
> Khrushchev's bald pate turned noticeably pink. The holders of power do not stand for someone doubting the accuracy of their opinions.
>
> "What's this?"
>
> Khrushchev, it should be admitted, was a smart politician. He grew up in a circle of refined intrigues and ruthless, secret struggle with his competitors and rivals. Had the conversation taken place in the office of the general secretary of the CPSU Central Committee, it is unknown how the chief marshal of tank troops would have emerged—a colonel or a corporal. But here everything took place in front of a number of other high-ranking generals, those

---

22 Editor's note. A small village in southern Russia, where on 12 July 1943 Soviet armored forces counterattacked the German spearheads during the battle of Kursk. The Soviets suffered very heavy losses, but succeeded in halting the German advance.

in whom Khrushchev saw his support and thus to give in to the syndrome of a merchant's behavior—"Don't dispute my will"—was dangerous.

Nonetheless, there was a note of poorly concealed irritation in the question, and particularly in the tone in which it was asked:

"What's *this*?"

However, Rotmistrov wasn't born yesterday. No matter how strong the tank's front armor, the designers did not forget to supply the vehicle with a reverse gear.

"It means, comrade Khrushchev, that they put a little something over you and me here. I would like to observe these rocket troops when the tanks are also leveling aimed fire at them. If you would like to check this, then I'm ready to personally get in a vehicle and then we'll see.

In the eyes of the generals who stood in a tight circle around, Khrushchev read that they were in agreement with the chief marshal. That meant that to insist on one's point of view was dangerous. Khrushchev's bald spot slowly took on its normal color and shine.

Malinovskii approached Rotmistrov.

"Pavel Alekseevich, don't get excited. You shouldn't take things so literally. The PTURS is a terrible weapon. This is what Nikita Sergeevich wanted to say. As to the tanks, we'll have to think about that…"

Leaving the testing ground, Malinovskii got into the same car as Khrushchev. No one knows what they spoke about on the road. However, when the cavalcade halted at the crossroads before Golitsyno (here Khrushchev turned to the left) he got out of the car to say goodbye. He smiled at Rotmistrov:

"Don't worry; we'll save your tanks…"

This is how Malinovskii managed to put out a number of Khrushchev's tangled ideas in the military sphere.

Khrushchev recalled:

> There were even echoes of the Maoist cult of personality in our country. In approximately 1962 I discovered that our military was publishing Mao Zedong's works on military problems. I immediately summoned the defense minister and said: "Comrade Malinovskii, as I understand it, your ministry is printing Mao's works. This is absurd! The Soviet army crushed the best forces of the German army at the same time that Mao's people were only stabbing each other in the ass with knives and bayonets for 20-25 years. And now you're printing Mao Zedong's works on war! What for? Is this in order to learn how to wage war in the future? Where was your head when you made this decision?" Malinovskii and the other military comrades were smart people, but the publication of the works of Mao Zedong on military questions was a stupid waste of time. I don't know what became of the printed copies. Maybe they're still lying somewhere on the shelves, or maybe they burned them.

One cannot but doubt that following this reprimand Rodion Yakovlevich began to relate even worse to Nikita Sergeevich. He was also sick and tired of Khrushchev's reductions in the size of the army, when officers who had given half their lives to the armed forces and who had no other profession besides a military one, were thrown out on the street with a miserly pension. According to his daughter's testimony, Malinovskii once blew up. Upon coming home from work, he said with indignation: "One shouldn't treat the army this way!" It's possible that this was said apropos of the unthinking reductions. And perhaps apropos of the Novocherkassk[23] shooting.

---

23   Editor's note. A small town in southern Russia, where striking workers were fired upon by units of the

Following the accusations of supporting Mao Zedong's cult of personality, Rodion Yakovlevich should have been even more indignant in the depths of his soul. After all, no one was preparing to take away the Red Army's victory over Hitler's Wehrmacht. However, Mao was truly considered a recognized classic in matters of conducting a guerilla war. His works on this subject had been translated into many languages and were studied in military academies around the world. Malinovskii did not want to fall behind, all the more so that the Soviet army had almost no experience in waging a guerilla war and this experience would come in very handy in creating special designation units. Is it possible that Khrushchev was not afraid of Mao's cult of personality, but of the content of his works? After the Zhukov affair, Nikita Sergeevich was afraid that the military might employ similar guerilla methods of struggle in order to seize the Kremlin and power.

Naturally, the defense ministry published Mao's works under the mark of "secret" or "for service use," as it had published the works of Churchill,[24] Manstein, Guderian and other figures from the Second World War. A special decision by the Presidium of the CPSU Central Committee would have been necessary for the open publication of Mao Zedong's works. As it was, Mao Zedong's books could only be circulated among officers and military libraries.

Malinovskii was entrusted with drawing up Operation "Anadyr'"—the transfer of Soviet troops with arms and missiles, armed with nuclear warheads, to Cuba. Rodion Yakovlevich proposed for the post of commander of the expeditionary corps General Issa Aleksandrovich Pliev, who only on 2 June 1962 crushed the riots in Novocherkassk. Khrushchev issued the order to crush the workers' demonstration with force to Pliev orally, having in turn received it from the other members of the Presidium of the Central Committee. I believe that Rodion Yakovlevich gave the order to shoot peaceful citizens and one's own countrymen with a heavy heart. Due to this, his feelings for Khrushchev suffered even further.

Lieutenant General and hero of the Soviet Union Matvei Kuz'mich Shaposhnikov, the first deputy commander of the North Caucasus Military District, refused to fire on the demonstrators. However, he was retired only in June 1966. Rodion Yakovlevich wrote the following on his letter: "Comrade Shaposhnikov, M.K. We were unable to find you a position, which is why you are being discharged. I can do no more. Malinovskii."

One has the feeling that the defense minister sympathized with the disgraced general and did not condemn his behavior. However, he could not act this way himself. Rodion Yakovlevich understood that should he refuse to transmit Khrushchev's order to Pliev, he would probably be retired himself. But the marshal believed that only he could bring the changes in the army to completion and oppose Khrushchev's destructive ideas for the armed forces.

At the same time, Malinovskii was convinced that General Pliev, who had served under his command more than once during the Great Patriotic War, would unswervingly carry out even the cruelest order, which is why he recommended him as the commander of the future missile expedition to Cuba. After all, it's quite possible that Pliev would have to issue the order to launch nuclear attacks on American cities.

Soviet army on 1-2 June 1962. More than two dozen strikers were reportedly killed and many more wounded. Some of the participants were later executed or sentenced to prison.

24   Editor's note. Winston Leonard Spencer Churchill joined the army in 1895 and served in various colonial conflicts. He entered Parliament in 1900 and remained at or near the top of British political life for over 50 years. He served as prime minister during 1940-45 and 1951-55, when he resigned due to ill health. He is considered the greatest British statesman.

Following the conclusion of the Cuban Missile Crisis, Khrushchev recalled:

> When our conversations became particularly friendly, I told Fidel[25] that at the height of the crisis I asked USSR defense minister Malinovskii: "What do you think? Knowing the armaments and number of the Cuban armed forces, if the invasion forces will have the same weapons that the US or we do, how much time will be necessary to rout the Cuban forces?" Malinovskii thought a bit and said: "Two days." When I told Fidel about this he became very excited and tried to prove that this was an incorrect estimate and that the Soviet Union would not allow this. I stopped him. "This is what you say. I agree with Malinovskii. He correctly evaluated the correlation of forces. Maybe not two days, but three or four instead. In any case, during this time the chief centers of resistance would have been suppressed and you would have gone into the hills and a guerilla war would have continued. It's possible that it could have continued for years, but the main thing would have been done: a bourgeois and counter-revolutionary government would have been created…"

Aleksandr Shchelokov, the journalist and writer, who worked for many years in the newspaper *Red Star*,[26] related this story about Malinovskii:

> During the famous Cuban Missile Crisis, which nearly placed the world before the possibility of the start of a nuclear war, one of the high-ranking military leaders, who was nervous because of the lack of clarity in the situation, asked defense minister Rodion Malinovskii:
> "What are we to do?"
> "Darn your gloves," answered the marshal, leaving those who heard the conversation in bewilderment.
> I later discovered what the marshal meant. During the First World War the calm exhibited by his company commander, which manifested itself particularly in a difficult situation, made an indelible impression on Malinovskii. When the Germans would open a hurricane of artillery fire on the Russian positions, the company commander would sit in his trench, take out his old gloves and scrupulously darn his gloves. When the bombardment would stop, the officer would put aside his work. He knew perfectly well what to do should the Germans attack.
> "Darn your gloves" is great advice for those who don't know how to get rid of their nervousness in a difficult situation.

Here he was undoubtedly speaking about an incident with Captain Prachek (Machek in the novel) in his novel *Soldiers of Russia*.

During the Cuban Missile Crisis Rodion Yakovlevich maintained complete composure, although as a military man he understood that the expedition undertaken by Khrushchev to Cuba was an adventure. The chances that the Americans would not discover traces of the Soviet rockets on Cuba before they could be brought to combat readiness were practically equal to zero. It was already a miracle that that during the movement of the armada of Soviet transport ships to Cuba the Americans had not guessed about its military significance. The marshal well understood that

---

25   Editor's note. Fidel Alejandro Castro Ruz (1926-2017) became involved in radical politics as a university student. He headed an anti-government guerilla struggle in the 1950s and overthrew the Cuban dictatorship in 1959, only to establish a totalitarian communist one in its place. Castro relinquished power to his brother in 2006, due to poor health.

26   Editor's note. *Red Star* (*Krasnaya Zvezda*) was the official daily newspaper of the Soviet armed forces since 1924 and plays the same role for the contemporary Russian armed forces.

the Americans had an overwhelming superiority both in the amount of thermonuclear warheads and also in the number of their delivery systems. The Soviet navy was significantly weaker than the American and was not in a condition to defend Soviet ships near Cuba.

Natal'ya Rodionovna testified that during the two weeks of the Cuban Missile Crisis her father never came home. He even slept at work.

B.Ye. Chertok recalled the Cuban Missile Crisis:

> In reply to the threat of an American invasion, on Castro's request, Khrushchev agreed to the creation of a group of Soviet armed forces on Cuba. However, you could not scare the Americans with conventional weapons. In order to parry a real military threat, Khrushchev made a truly bold decision: to move nuclear missiles directly to the American border. Neither the defense minister, the elderly Marshal Malinovskii (he was 63 at the time, only 12 years older than Boris Yevseevich, who was then 51. Malinovskii's successor, A.A. Grechko,[27] was 63 when he became defense minister, B.S.) nor any of the members of the Presidium of the CPSU Central Committee would have dared to take such a risky step. Following a reconnaissance-inspection trip to Cuba by the chief of the General Staff, Marshal Biryuzov, head of a group of military missile specialists, led by Smirnitskii, a final decision was taken.

There can be no doubt that the decision to station missiles and nuclear warheads in Cuba was taken alone by Nikita Sergeevich. To be sure, this was by no means done at Castro's request, but on the initiative of Khrushchev, who was searching for an answer to the American rockets stationed in Turkey. To be sure, one did not have to convince Castro for long. He decided immediately that a Soviet nuclear missile shield would securely cover him against a possible invasion by the US. However, the phrase about the "elderly" marshal Malinovskii sounds strange. After all, he was four years younger than Khrushchev.

This is the way Chertok described operation "Anadyr'," the transfer of missiles and other armaments and troops to Cuba:

> The Strategic Rocket Forces' 43rd Division was to comprise the heart of the combat composition of the group of Soviet armed forces in Cuba. The missile division consisted of three regiments, armed with R-12[28] missiles (24 launchers) and two regiments with R-14[29] missiles (16 launchers).
>
> A missile division, should it launch all of its missiles first (there could be no second launch), was capable of destroying at least 40 of the most important military-strategic targets in almost the entire territory of the USA (excluding Alaska, of course). The overall potential of the entire division in the first and only launch, should each missile was provided with a launcher and reach its target, would comprise, depending on the strength of the warhead, up to 70 megatons.

---

27   Editor's note. Andrei Antonovich Grechko (1903-76) joined the Red Army in 1919 and fought in the civil war. During the Great Patriotic War he commanded a cavalry division and cavalry corps, and armies, and was a deputy *front* commander. Following the war, he commanded military districts, Soviet occupation forces in Germany and was commander-in-chief of the Ground Forces and commander-in-chief of the Warsaw Pact forces. Grechko succeeded Malinovskii as defense minister and served at that post until his death.

28   Editor's note. The R-12 (NATO code name SS-4) was an intermediate-range Soviet ballistic missile, capable of carrying a nuclear warhead. It was first deployed in 1959 and phased out during the 1980s.

29   Editor's note. The R-14 (NATO code name SS-5) was an intermediate-range Soviet ballistic missile, capable of carrying a nuclear warhead. It was deployed in the early 1960s and phased out twenty years later.

Two anti-aircraft rocket divisions and a fighter air regiment covered the missiles against air strikes. Four motorized rifle regiments were to secure our missiles against an American land attack in the event of their invasion of the island. Besides this, cutters, equipped with rocket salvo systems (improved "Katyushas") were designated for combating an amphibious landing and Il-28[30] bombers.

The preparation of the equipment and troops, the transfer of all of this to Cuba by marine transport under the guise of delivering fuel and other peaceful cargoes, was truly a grandiose operation. The loading, disguising and positioning of the rockets, nuclear warheads and planes on the ships and then on the shore caused a great deal of concern. One must consider that all the military equipment required developed rear services, the supply with fuel, communications equipment, and the closed quartering of the entire rank and file. The first elements of Soviet troops, commanded by General I.A. Pliev, arrived in Cuba in July and the beginning of August. The scrupulously disguised transfer of nuclear warheads began in the middle of August…

R-12 missiles and Il-28 aircraft began to arrive in Cuba in September…

The first R-12 missile was prepared for fueling and fitted with a nuclear warhead on 4 October 1962. By 10 October another ten missiles were ready for mounting on their launch sites, and 20 missiles by 20 October. In some sources it is mentioned that the missiles stationed in Cuba were completely ready for launch. What do the historians of the Cuban Missile Crisis understand by this? I heard from Smirnitskii that the nuclear warheads had not been attached to a single missile. If this is true, then not a single missile was actually ready for launch.

If this is true, then Khrushchev was bluffing to the last in making John Kennedy go for a compromise. In the event of an American landing in Cuba, the Soviet forces would not have been in a condition to launch a nuclear strike against the United States from there. On the other hand, even knowing precisely that Soviet missiles would not fly toward American territory from Cuba, the US president would not likely have gone to war with the USSR. After all, Khrushchev would probably have launched intercontinental ballistic missiles against the Americans and against their allies and bases in Europe, with short-range missiles with thermonuclear warheads, as well as strategic bombers. It's likely that America would have won a nuclear war with the USSR, but afterwards would have been in a situation even worse than following its victory in 1945. Aside from significant destruction and losses on American territory, John Kennedy would have been faced with Europe and the Soviet Union lying in radioactive ruins, for which in all likelihood even 20 Marshall Plans[31] would have been insufficient.

At 2230 on 23 October Malinovskii, in a coded message addressed to I.A. Pliev, demanded that he take immediate steps to increase the combat readiness of the group of forces and to guard against, together with the Cuban army, a possible enemy attack. By this time, due to the establishment of a maritime blockade, two regiments of R-14s on ships in the ocean were turned back toward the USSR, but Rodion Yakovlevich feared that the Americans might attack Soviet positions in Cuba that remained without rocket protection.

---

30 Editor's note. The Il-28 was a Soviet jet bomber which first flew in 1948. The Il-28 carried a crew of three and had a maximum speed of 902 kilometers per hour. The aircraft could carry up to 3,000 kilograms of bombs and was armed with four 23mm cannons.

31 Editor's note. This is a reference to the European Recovery Program, commonly known as the Marshall Plan after George C. Marshall (1880-1959), who proposed the program in 1947 while secretary of state. The program funneled billions of dollars into Europe to help the continent overcome the destructive effects of the Second World War.

On 27 October two American planes were shot down over Cuba. An F-104[32] fighter was shot down by Cuban anti-aircraft gunners while flying at a low altitude. A U-2 plane, whose pilot died, was shot down on orders from Lieutenant General S.N. Grechko, the deputy commander of the group of Soviet forces in Cuba for anti-aircraft defense. The plane was flying at an altitude of 21 kilometers and was shot down by the first S-75[33] rocket (the anti-aircraft rocket system "Desna") by a battalion under the command of Major I. Gerchenov, which was on combat duty in the area of the city of Banos. Pliev was indignant; after all, the evening before he had forbade opening fire without his personal authorization. They had to report to Moscow. Malinovskii replied with a brief coded message: "You were in a hurry."

As is known, the crisis concluded and Khrushchev was forced to remove the missiles and other strategic systems from Cuba, as well as all nuclear warheads. On 22 December Malinovskii reported to Khrushchev: "By 20.12 all 42 Il-28 aircraft and all special warheads for missiles and air bombs have been delivered from Cuba to the Soviet Union."

The US, in its turn, promised not to attack Cuba. Besides this, in accordance with their gentleman's agreement, the Americans removed their medium-range "Jupiter"[34] missiles from Turkey within a year from the conclusion of the evacuation of Soviet missiles from Cuba. By this time they had acquired more modern "Polaris" missiles on submarines and the outdated missiles stationed in Turkey and Italy were deactivated.

Soviet and world public opinion didn't know anything about the agreement to remove American missiles from Turkey. But even if they had known, the conclusion of the Cuban Missile Crisis would nevertheless have been viewed as a defeat for Khrushchev. The very fact of evacuating the missiles and other equipment from Cuba under the observation of the Americans was humiliating. This is not to mention the fact that the trip of the commercial ships and a whole series of Soviet military vessels to Cuba and back cost a pretty penny, while a significant part of the combat equipment was put out of action following such a voyage. Cuba, where the USSR now had no right to station nuclear weapons, was transformed first of all into a burden requiring constant subsidies.

Following the Cuban Missile Crisis, Khrushchev's prestige in the country and in the world dropped sharply. The military and police elite was dissatisfied with Nikita Sergeevich. Added to this were Khrushchev's numerous experiments in the economy and the system of management and the beginning of grain imports, as well as the fact that no small amount of food was sent to Cuba and other allies. His removal was practically predetermined.

Khrushchev sought to justify the failure with the transport of the missiles to Cuba. On 8 February 1963, at a reception in honor of the participants of the Main Military Council, he, according to notes taken by General Obaturov, declared: "An idiot can start a war, but finding a smart man, who can finish it in the age of nuclear weapons (this is him returning to the question about delivering and returning the missiles from Cuba) is difficult." This is how Obaturov commented on Khrushchev's words that we had won in the area of Cuba: "God forbid such victories in the future, because no one needs a victory when nuclear war is possible. One must be able to win without extreme exacerbation—in this lies the skill of a true military diplomat." Khrushchev

---

32   Editor's note. The F-104 ("Starfighter") was a US single-engine supersonic interceptor, which first entered service in 1958. It had a maximum speed of 2,137 kilometers per hour and a range of 670 kilometers. It was armed with a 20mm cannon and could carry four missiles and up to 1,814 kilograms of ordnance.

33   Editor's note. The S-75 was a Soviet-built surface to air missile (SAM), which first entered service in 1957. This missile was widely used by North Vietnamese forces against American aircraft during the Vietnam War.

34   Editor's note. The Jupiter was a US medium-range ballistic missile capable of carrying a nuclear warhead. The missile was initially deployed in Italy and Turkey in 1961, but removed after the Cuban Missile Crisis.

was only trying to put a good face on things. The generals were not fooled as regards the so-called victory in Cuba.

Malinovskii's daughter characterized her father's relations with Nikita Sergeevich as follows:

> Father treated Khrushchev with respect and warmth, the roots of which dated back to the war. He said that Nikita Sergeevich was a wonderful member of the military council (this was what the job of a political worker in the army was called). First of all, because he did not interfere in purely military matters, and secondly because he did not sit around headquarters, but was with the troops. However, as a minister, father had to defend his opinion more than once. I know this, not from my father, naturally (he never spoke about work at home and, in general, was a man of few words), but from people who worked with him.

However, she felt that Rodion Yakovlevich did not have particularly close relations with Brezhnev. If the marshal's daughter knew Khrushchev's family well, she was not acquainted with anyone in Brezhnev's family.

Malinovskii's position had decisive importance during the plot against Khrushchev. According to legend, at the meeting of the Central Committee Presidium during Khrushchev's absence, the undecided members only took Brezhnev's side when Malinovskii, who was present, declared his support for the plot. Whether this was the case or not is not important. What is more important is that even the participation of the head of the KGB,[35] V.Ye. Semichastnyi[36] in the plot did not guarantee success. Had Malinovskii supported Khrushchev, the army could have dealt with the comparatively few units of KGB and internal security troops. However, Rodion Yakovlevich was not prepared to save him.

Strictly speaking, the October 1964 coup that removed Khrushchev was not even a coup from the formal point of view. In full accordance with the norms at the time, the Central Committee Presidium and then a plenum of the CPSU Central Committee relieved Khrushchev of all party and government posts and retired him with a personal pension. However, insofar as the government was a totalitarian one and was ruled by a single leader, all of the procedures of party and Soviet democracy were of a strictly formal character. The party and government organs obediently and unanimously approved the decisions by the leader. In order to force these organs to unanimously vote to remove the acting ruler, it was necessary to carry out a plot without stopping, in the event of necessity, before calling on armed intervention. In America Eisenhower realized his political ambitions without difficulty upon honestly winning the presidential election. For Zhukov the single possible path lay through a Bonapartist plot, for there were simply no other methods for him to come to power. Fortunately, Malinovskii never had any political ambitions.

Khrushchev's removal was greeted by the population, which had been forced to recall during the final years of his rule what ration cards were, calmly, and by the party-soviet *nomenklatura*[37] with undisguised glee. Nikita Sergeevich had made all the bureaucrats sick of him with his constant dashing about from one extreme to another and his reforms that were not well thought out, when they would first be sent to the boondocks and then returned to Moscow.

---

35   Editor's note. The KGB (*Komitet Gosudarstvennoi Bezopasnosti*), or Committee for State Security, was title of the Soviet secret police from 1954 until its dissolution in 1991. The KGB was chiefly known for its overseas espionage activities and struggle with internal dissent.

36   Editor's note. Vladimir Yefimovich Semichastnyi (1924-2001) joined the Communist Party in 1944 and rose to the top of its youth auxiliary. He later moved to party work and was chairman of the KGB from 1961 until his removal in 1967. He later served in the government apparatus in Ukraine.

37   Editor's note. Then *nomenklatura* were those people in the USSR and other Eastern European communist countries who could be appointed to government posts only with the permission of party authorities.

Shortly following Nikita Sergeevich's removal, Malinovskii made a denunciatory speech against Khrushchev at a meeting of the defense ministry's party activists. Lieutenant General of Tank Troops G.I. Obaturov, the commander of the 6th Tank Army in the Kiev Military District, wrote in this regard in his diary for 11 November 1964:

> Today Panin, the chief of the propaganda and agitation section, who was at the meeting in Moscow, related the bases of the content of Malinovskii's report to the party activists in the defense ministry following the October plenum:
>
> Khrushchev made a large number of mistakes in military construction because he was an ignoramus in military affairs. The sending of missiles to Cuba was an adventure that nearly ended in war. He placed the country on the brink of nuclear war. The reduction in force by 1,200,000 men in 1960 was inexcusable and caused harm. Great harm was done to aviation and combat ships. He interfered in a number of areas, not understanding them. He pushed through his son's bad missiles and got rid of good ones. It was only through cunning that we were able to get better missiles produced. In the summer of this year, having observed the latest anti-tank weapons, he ordered us to cease producing tanks, because "they are useless in modern war." He often raised the question of sharply cutting pay for the military and military pensions.

Following the October 1964 plenum Rodion Yakovlevich's position became extraordinarily strong. He never did become a member of the Central Committee Presidium, which was renamed the Politburo in 1966, but his real influence was greater than other members of the higher party leadership. Malinovskii personally decided everything that concerned the armed forces with Brezhnev and practically all of his petitions were satisfied. Leonid Il'ich, who was linked to the military-industrial complex for many years, was interested in strengthening the armed forces and completely trusted Malinovskii's opinion in military matters. Any kinds of reductions in armaments and manpower were halted.

Within a few days following Khrushchev's removal, Rodion Yakovlevich suffered a heavy loss. On 19 October 1964, when a plane crashed into Mount Avala near Belgrade, the chief of the general staff, Marshal Sergei Semyonovich Biryuzov, who was leading a delegation which was going to attend the celebrations on the occasion of the 20th anniversary of the Yugoslav capital, died. They became friends not long after they had first become acquainted at the end of 1942, in the 2nd Guards Army. Malinovskii probably had no closer friend than Biryuzov.

Not long after the "October coup," during a visit to Moscow by a Chinese party-governmental delegation, a characteristic episode took place that involved Malinovskii. On 8 November, before the official luncheon, the head of the delegation, the premier of the State Council of the Chinese People's Republic, Zhou Enlai,[38] complained to Brezhnev, Kosygin, Mikoyan, Andropov,[39] and Gromyko:[40]

---

38 Editor's note. Zhou Enlai (1898-1976) joined the Chinese Communist Party in 1921 and gradually rose through the party ranks in tandem with Mao Zedong. He became the first premier of the Chinese People's Republic in 1949 and held that position until his death. He also served as Chinese foreign minister in the 1950s. Zhou later tried to alleviate the excesses of the Cultural Revolution of the 1960s.

39 Editor's note. Yurii Vladimirovich Andropov (1914-84) joined the Communist Party in 1939 and rose through its youth organization in Karelia. He later worked in the Central Committee apparatus and was Soviet ambassador to Hungary during the uprising there. He later returned to Moscow and during 1967-82 was chairman of the KGB. Andropov succeeded Brezhnev as general secretary of the Communist Party in 1982 and held that position until his death.

40 Editor's note. Andrei Andreevich Gromyko (1909-89) joined the Communist Party in 1931 and had an academic career before being transferred to the diplomatic service. He served as Soviet ambassador to the US during the Second World War, was a delegate to the United Nations and ambassador to Great Britain.

As you know, our party and government sent a delegation, headed by me, to Moscow, in order to express our feelings of friendship and to take part in the celebrations on the occasion of the forty-seventh anniversary of the October Revolution. You also confirmed the opinion that our arrival is a friendly act.

Nevertheless, yesterday at a reception in the Kremlin Palace of Congresses, where, in particular, journalists from western countries were present, the USSR defense minister, comrade Malinovskii, publicly addressed me with insulting and provocative questions. At first he declared to me that we Chinese should not play tricks in politics. I understood what comrade Malinovskii wanted to say and decided to turn the conversation to another subject. I told him that these tricks are a simple matter and that one should move the curtains aside in order to see everything. However, comrade Malinovskii did not stop at this and went even further. He declared that we should not allow any devil to ruin our relations. I did not have time to ask comrade Malinovskii just what devil he had in mind, because he continued to say that the Soviet and Chinese peoples want happiness and that no Maos and Khrushchevs should interfere with that.

The question is clear: this was a provocation and insult. I did not fall for the provocation and, having turned to the other direction, wanted to leave, because American correspondents were literally standing beside us and were listening. At this time other Soviet marshals came up and comrade Malinovskii continued to speak. However, I wasn't listening to him and my translator did not translate. However, another translator heard what had been said by comrade Malinovskii. Comrade Malinovskii essentially said the following: we here in the Soviet Union overthrew Khrushchev, and now you overthrow Mao Zedong. Then comrade Malinovskii continued to speak with comrade He Long.[41] He told comrade He Long that he had a beautiful marshal's uniform. Comrade He Long noted that it was better to wear a service jacket. Comrade Malinovskii agreed with this and added that it's best to wear a body warmer, and then declared: "Stalin imposed this uniform on us and Mao imposed your uniform on you." Comrade He Long said that to speak in such a manner was incorrect and wrong.

I, continued Zhou Enlai, already told comrade Mikoyan that I personally heard only the first part of these statements by comrade Malinovskii, where he said that no kind of Maos or Khrushchevs should interfere with us. I could have acted otherwise: to answer comrade Malinovskii and continue our conversation, which probably would have shaken all those present. This is the way any honest communist would have acted in my place; all the more so, Zhou Enlai emphasized, that we're speaking about an insult to our delegation, our party, the leader of the Chinese people, as well as to me personally.

If I had made such a move, it would have been a normal, just and necessary step on my part. Of course, one could have undertaken another step—to appeal to the leading comrades of the CPSU and the Soviet government with a serious protest yesterday at the reception. In that case, an argument would have arisen, because the necessity would have arisen of clearing up all the circumstances on the spot. We, as communists, had the right to act in such a manner. However, we did not take these measures, insofar as the incident took place immediately after comrade Malinovskii's address and toast, in which he criticized American imperialism. Then comrade Malinovskii began to go around all those present, and I went up to the Soviet

---

He became foreign minister in 1957 and held that post until 1985. That year Gromyko was appointed chairman of the USSR Supreme Soviet.

41   Editor's note. He Long (1896-1969) became involved in revolutionary activities as a young man and joined the Chinese Communist Party in 1926. He commanded an army during the civil war and was promoted to the rank of marshal in 1955. He Long was purged during the Cultural Revolution and died under house arrest.

marshals in order to suggest we drink to the friendship of our two peoples and to the friendship between our armies. At that moment comrade Malinovskii came out with his insulting and provocative statement. Had we immediately offered a rebuff to him, then this would have been a good "story" for the correspondents of the western imperialist countries.

We constantly declared that one should carefully approach and think through actions that might give joy to our enemies and upset friends. What did comrade Malinovskii have in mind and how should one understand his offensive address to us immediately after he had spoken out harshly against American imperialism? It's quite clear that such an address directed at the party-governmental delegation of the People's Republic of China practically annulled his speech and toast. This is Khrushchevism. I myself saw how the American ambassador observed comrade Malinovskii's address with a smile. Then, as comrade Mikoyan told me, you exchanged opinions on the subject of comrade Malinovskii's toast and came to the conclusion that he expressed himself too harshly.

Comrade A.I. Mikoyan: I was telling you my point of view.

Comrade Zhou Enlai: Such addresses only show weakness before enemies. This is how Khrushchev behaved. We, as your allies, have felt the bitterness of this before. I remember how in 1954, when following the Geneva conference,[42] I was invited to the Soviet Union, Khrushchev's speeches displayed first weakness, then strength. But the American imperialists saw through him. This only served to harm the authority of the Soviet Union. Comrade Malinovskii's statements were insulting to the Chinese people, the Chinese Communist Party, and its leader.

This is the first reason why I did not offer a rebuff to comrade Malinovskii's statements right on the spot. If Khrushchev had been in his place, I would have done this immediately. However, this was comrade Malinovskii. We came to your country in order to express our congratulations and friendly feelings. If this had been an internal conversation or had occurred at a reception attended only by representatives of fraternal parties, then I would have immediately rebuffed him. However, this took place at a reception attended by a large number of invitees, so I decided to hold my tongue and tell you about this incident today. These are not tricks. This is precisely how communists should approach the resolution of such questions. The second reason why I didn't immediately reply to comrade Malinovskii's statements was that I wanted to clear up all the details. I didn't ask comrade He Long at the reception how the conversation with comrade Malinovskii ended, but found out later.

Comrade L.I. Brezhnev: This is news to us. We didn't know the details.

Comrade Zhou Enlai: Had I tried to clear up all the circumstances at the reception, this would have drawn everybody's attention. The second reason also is that this matter cannot be resolved with the aid of some kind of protest. The nature and significance of this question are more serious in order to react with only a protest. Upon returning from the reception and having studied all the circumstances, I came to the conclusion that the matter concerns not just comrade Malinovskii. He's not the only one with such thoughts. I mean the comrades in your Central Committee. Thus today I decided to officially place the matter before the three leaders of the CPSU and the Soviet government and hope that it will be resolved. How should this be understood—can it really be that one of the goals of your agreeing to the arrival of our delegation was to publicly insult and provoke us here? Further, can one believe that, as

---

42   Editor's note. The conference was held in Geneva Switzerland from 26 April to 20 July 1954 and was attended by delegates from the US, USSR, France, the United Kingdom, and the People's Republic of China, as well as other countries. The conference was called to discuss problems arising from the Korean War and the ongoing conflict in Indochina.

comrade Malinovskii said, that you are counting on us to treat Mao Zedong the same way you treated Khrushchev, by removing him from his posts? Another Soviet marshal spoke about that, who said that there's a time for everything.

Comrade A.I. Mikoyan: Which marshal?

Comrade Zhou Enlai: I personally did not hear this statement.

Comrade L.I. Brezhnev: Perhaps this did not relate to Mao Zedong?

Comrade Zhou Enlai: Two thoughts were moving in parallel in the conversation: about removing Khrushchev and about the desire to remove Mao Zedong. One could have understood these statements as an instigation to remove Mao Zedong. However, I'm not sure about this.

Comrade He Long: Two American correspondents were standing close behind our backs.

Comrade Zhou Enlai: If someone is putting together such plans, then these are vain attempts and illusions. This does not reduce comrade Mao Zedong's authority one iota, but this is the greatest insult and provocation for the Chinese people and the Chinese Communist Party. Can this really facilitate the improvement of relations between our two parties and two countries? This can only lead to a worsening of relations between them. Third, can one really understand that there is a point of view in the CPSU Central Committee, according to which principled disagreements and disputes between our two parties come down to personal arguments between two leaders—Mao Zedong and Khrushchev, as well as the personal character and personal qualities of these two leaders? This is what the imperialists maintain. This is precisely why I had to officially put the matter forward in conversation with the leaders of the CPSU and the Soviet government. It is necessary to resolve this matter; otherwise, what is there for us to talk about?

Comrade L.I. Brezhnev: First of all, I would like to say in the name of the Presidium and the CPSU Central Committee that we are satisfied that the Central Committee of the Chinese Communist Party has decided to dispatch such a representative delegation under comrade Zhou Enlai to Moscow. We viewed this as an extremely important fact and gave our consent to your proposal. In discussing this matter in the Presidium, and up to the present day, we had only a positive view of the matter of your delegation's arrival. We view this as an important step in the matter of establishing contacts for improving relations along party and governmental lines. Comrade Malinovskii did not take part in reviewing this matter in the Presidium, insofar as he is not a member or a candidate member of the Presidium…

We were guided by the interests of strengthening friendship between the Chinese Communist Party and the CPSU and are determined to be guided by this in the future. I want to emphasize once again that we view the decision of the Central Committee of the Chinese Communist Party to send a delegation to Moscow as a very important step, which will facilitate the normalization of the situation and to overcome existing differences. Late yesterday I found out from comrade Mikoyan about the first part of your conversation with comrade Malinovskii.

Comrade A.N. Kosygin: I also found out yesterday about this matter, which aroused indignation among us.

Comrade L.I. Brezhnev: Insofar as our conversation is taking place in the spirit of complete frankness, I can say that this fact made us indignant. Comrade Malinovskii's statement not only does not reflect the opinion of the CPSU Central Committee, but that overall he did not have the right to express a personal opinion in such a manner. We are grateful, comrade Zhou Enlai, for the tact which you manifested in connection with comrade Malinovskii's statement, and also for the frankness with which you expressed yourself on this matter.

Today I called comrade Malinovskii on the telephone and asked him about his conversation with comrade Zhou Enlai. Comrade Malinovskii explained that he did not want anything more than to express his concern about strengthening friendship between us, and at the same time said that a change in leadership facilitates an improvement in relations. He agreed that it's possible that he formulated his thoughts poorly and in connection with this is ready to make a personal apology. As to your statement that comrade Malinovskii's opinion reflects the opinion of the CPSU Central Committee, we want to declare to you that this is not the case. Naturally, if this in some degree reflected the opinion of our leadership, then you could view this as an insult for comrade Mao Zedong, the Central Committee of the Chinese Communist Party and for your delegation. But, I repeat that this is in no way the case. A man simply had something to drink and poorly said something while not sober.

We know the attitudes of our marshals and the leaders of the defense ministry. They highly regard the Chinese People's Liberation Army, the Chinese people and the Chinese Communist Party. Such is the opinion, for example, of comrades Chuikov, Sokolovskii, Zakharov, and others. And if comrade Zakharov dropped the phrase "there's a time for everything," then I can assure you that this referred only to comrade Khrushchev.

Comrade Zhou Enlai: I can't say exactly whose words these are. I know comrade Zakharov well. I worked with him more than a year in Peking.

Comrade L.I. Brezhnev: Comrade Malinovskii told me in conversation that he was misunderstood, but that he is nonetheless ready to offer an official apology. I believe he will offer an official apology. We express our regret that such an incident took place. I believe that you should believe us in this and that this should not interfere with the joint work we had in mind.

Comrade Zhou Enlai: This matter was especially serious, insofar as it arose at such a large reception which took place yesterday on the occasion of the forty-seventh anniversary of the October Revolution. Besides, this statement was made by none other than the minister of defense, particularly after his toast, in which he condemned American imperialism. This could not but arouse in me the considerations I have laid out. As concerns the statement that comrade Malinovskii had something to drink and that his statement does not reflect his feelings, then this only confirms my doubts.

We are Marxists and adherents of dialectical materialism. Being determines consciousness. If he did not have such thoughts in his head, then he would not have been able to express them. We have a saying: "A drunken man speaks the truth." I also like to have a drink now and then. Khrushchev once got me really drunk. You may want to ask Molotov about this, although, to be sure, he no longer works as your minister of foreign affairs, or comrade Fedorenko,[43] who was accompanying me. I was completely drunk then, but I said nothing like that. If a man didn't have such thoughts in his head, then he wouldn't have been able to express them, and comrade Malinovskii spoke yesterday logically and in an orderly manner. Why didn't this happen to me? Comrade Fedorenko is still alive and is working, so maybe you can check this through comrade Gromyko as to the truth of the matter.

Comrade A.I. Mikoyan: I drank with you and nothing like that happened.

Comrade Zhou Enlai: As minister of defense, he can't explain his actions thusly. Our former defense minister, Peng Dehuai[44] made a great-power and chauvinistic mistake in regard to our Korean comrades and we removed him for this. I don't interfere in your internal

---

43   Editor's note. This is probably Nikolai Trofimovich Fedorenko (1912-2000), a Soviet orientalist who also served as a deputy minister of foreign affairs, ambassador to Japan, and a permanent representative of the USSR at the UN.

44   Editor's note. Peng Dehuai (1898-1974) became a soldier in 1916 and joined Mao Zedong and the communists in 1928. He led armies during the Chinese civil war and commanded Chinese forces during the Korean War (1950-53). He was appointed defense minister in 1954, but was ousted in 1959 as the result of a policy dispute. Peng was arrested during the Cultural Revolution and died in prison.

affairs. As concerns Peng Dehuai, he really did adopt a great-power and chauvinistic approach and tried to interfere in the internal affairs of the People's Democratic Republic of Korea. As you recall, in 1956 our comrades, together with comrade Mikoyan traveled to Korea in connection with this matter.

Comrade A.I. Mikoyan: Peng Dehuai was trying to remove Kim Il-Sung.[45]

Comrade Zhou Enlai: We also reached the conclusion that Peng Dehuai should be removed from his position, but Khrushchev did not share our opinion.

Comrade A.I. Mikoyan: No, in this case he shared your point of view on Peng Dehuai. Khrushchev supported Peng Dehuai in connection with his letter to the Central Committee of the Chinese Communist Party.

Comrade Zhou Enlai: Let's not get into that. When we discovered that Peng Dehuai wanted to interfere in the internal affairs of the Korean comrades, we considered that one of his serious anti-party mistakes, and he had other serious mistakes. Thus more than once we explained to the Korean comrades that Peng Dehuai had committed a mistake and must be made responsible for it. I've put forward an example from our practice. As concerns how a fraternal party treats the mistakes of its comrades, that's your affair. I won't get into that.

Comrade Brezhnev has just stated: "First of all, the comrades in the Presidium have exchanged opinions about comrade Malinovskii's statement; that is, before I laid out all the circumstances, and you declared that in the Central Committee and the Presidium there were no thoughts like the ones that comrade Malinovskii expressed…"

Secondly, comrade Brezhnev said that according to comrade Malinovskii's own statement, the latter had expressed himself in an unfortunate way. I take into account comrade Brezhnev's statement on these two points. At the same time I retain the right that our delegation, upon discussing this question, will return to it another time.

Comrade L.I. Brezhnev: We want you to believe us, and this is not my personal opinion, but the opinion of the Presidium of the CPSU Central Committee.

Comrade Zhou Enlai: The delegation will discuss these circumstances and deliver its opinion.

Comrade A.I. Mikoyan: When comrade Zhou Enlai told me about the conversation with comrade Malinovskii, I, knowing the Presidium's opinion, immediately condemned comrade Malinovskii's statement.

Comrade L.I. Brezhnev: I found out about this conversation when I was already escorting the guests from the reception.

Comrade A.I. Mikoyan: If we had had such an opinion, then I would not have immediately condemned comrade Malinovskii's statements.

Comrade A.N. Kosygin: We're having an important conversation today. Insofar as you have put forward a serious matter, then we want to say that while discussing it in your delegation you should take into account the fact that what was said by comrade Malinovskii does not have any relation to us. We have officially communicated to you the opinion of our Central Committee. We completely and 100 percent adhere to what comrade Brezhnev said and that you can believe us. Of course, one could stir up a lot of fuss over this question. In no way are we justifying comrade Malinovskii and are indignant. I would like to cite one example, although not to justify comrade Malinovskii. Comrade Malinovskii and were standing on the

---

45   Editor's note. Kim-Il-sung (1912-94) joined the Chinese Communist Party in 1931 and fought several years as an anti-Japanese partisan. Kim arrived in northern Korea with the Red Army in 1945 and was declared leader of the Democratic People's Republic of Korea upon its founding in 1948. Kim unleashed the Korean War (1950-53) in an attempt to unify the Korean peninsula, but failed. Following the war, Kim tightened his control over the country and was able to pass the leadership to his son.

Lenin Mausoleum and talking about differences with the Chinese Communist Party; that is, about the matter which worries us. Comrade Malinovskii told me that he personally and all the Soviet marshals were glad of the arrival of the Chinese Communist Party delegation and the efforts being taken toward eliminating our differences. I was sure that that he agreed 100 percent with the opinion of our party on the development of contacts with the Chinese Communist Party. What he said in conversation to you came as a surprise to us. You probably noticed that he pronounced a toast in an excited state and blurted out something he should not have.

Comrade Zhou Enlai: One could do this in regard to enemies.

Comrade A.N. Kosygin: I'm laying out the subtleties and nuances for you. We ourselves are looking for an explanation, in order to weigh everything.

Comrade Zhou Enlai: Comrade Kosygin asks us to pay attention to the fact that the CPSU Central Committee officially rejects comrade Malinovskii's statement. But I want to state frankly that I'm sure that if I had gotten into a conversation with comrade Malinovskii, that he would have blurted out even more to me.

Comrade A.I. Mikoyan: He's blurted out enough already.

Comrade Zhou Enlai: I decided not to pay any attention to that.

Comrade L.I. Brezhnev: We appreciate that.

Comrade Kang Sheng:[46] I was not present at the conversation with comrade Malinovskii. Following the reception, when comrade Zhou Enlai told me about it, I was very surprised.

Comrade L.I. Brezhnev: We were also surprised.

Comrade Kang Sheng: It reminded me of the events that took place about five years ago, at a reception in honor of the participants of the meeting of the Warsaw Pact's[47] Political Consultative Committee, when Khrushchev insulted comrade Mao Zedong. I was not surprised at Khrushchev's words when he would insult our comrades, because I knew that he can talk nonsense. However, I was very put out by the fact that this has taken place in conditions when Khrushchev has been removed and that we have arrived to congratulate you on the holiday.

Of course, we have become accustomed to various insults directed at the Chinese Communist Party and comrade Mao Zedong by people of various types. This will not cause any harm to either the Chinese Communist Party or to comrade Mao Zedong. However, I was very upset by the fact that comrade Malinovskii made such a declaration directly to the head of our delegation. We are all striving to getting rid of differences and to unify in the face of the enemy. Can such a statement, made in the presence of American correspondents, really be of benefit to the cause of solidifying our ranks? We came with the intention of improving our party and governmental relations. A statement insulting our leader will not benefit this. I believe that the Soviet people warmly and approvingly relate to our delegation's arrival and that it would not allow anyone to make such statements. And if I repeated that which has been said here, then I

---

46   Editor's note. This is probably Kang Sheng (1898-1975), who joined the Chinese Communist Party in the early 1920s and soon became an ally of Mao Zedong, purging the party of the latter's enemies. He continued to support Mao during the Great Leap Forward and the Cultural Revolution. Sheng was posthumously expelled from the party in 1980.

47   Editor's note. The Warsaw Pace was established in 1955 as a counterweight to the North Atlantic Treaty Organization (NATO) and its decision to allow West German rearmament. The Warsaw Pact originally included Albania, Bulgaria, Czechoslovakia, East Germany, Hungary, Poland, Romania, and the USSR, although Albania withdrew from the organization in 1968. The Warsaw Pact was dissolved in 1991 in the wake of communism's collapse in Eastern Europe.

did it because I recall my conversation yesterday with comrade Kirilenko.[48] At the same time that comrade Malinovskii was talking to comrade Zhou Enlai, comrade Kirilenko was speaking with me. This is how comrade Kirilenko characterized me: "You, comrade Kang Sheng, used to be a good friend of the Soviet people and are now a bad friend." Of course, I didn't want to argue with comrade Kirilenko and answered him thusly: "I was, am and will be a good friend of the Soviet people." If we were not good friends of the Soviet people, we would not have come to see you. As regards insults directed at me, each time I came here I would hear this from Khrushchev. Each time I rebuffed these insults. However, yesterday comrade Kirilenko declared that I am not a good friend of the Soviet people, and this was very unpleasant for me. I didn't want to get into an argument. Comrade Andropov came up to us and we parted.

Comrade Zhou Enlai: We've decided to discuss this matter today.

Comrade L.I. Brezhnev: When we invited your delegation, we were guided by the best intentions. They reflect the opinion of our collective. There were no disagreements on that score between us.

We are deeply distressed by what comrade Malinovskii said and these new circumstances. Regarding comrade Kirilenko's conversation with comrade Kang Sheng, I can't say anything, insofar as I hadn't heard anything about it. We want you to trust and respect the opinion of the CPSU leadership.

Our decision to invite the Chinese delegation was sincere and straightforward. We communicated this to all the fraternal parties of the socialist countries even before your arrival in Moscow. This is also an expression of our friendship for the Chinese Communist Party.

Comrade Zhou Enlai: As to that matter, I can say this: I take account of comrade Brezhnev's opinion on two points and the comments by comrades Kosygin and Mikoyan, as well as what was just said by comrade Brezhnev. We should pay great attention to comrade Brezhnev's opinion as the first secretary of the CPSU Central Committee, and to the opinion of the Presidium of your party's Central Committee.

Comrade L.I. Brezhnev: We are grateful to comrade Zhou Enlai for such an approach to things and request that he inform the Central Committee of the Chinese Communist Party that we want to be sincere in our relations with you. No matter what bitter truths we may have to tell each other, we will be sincere and honest. I want to put a start to this in our conversation today.

And here is the official Chinese version of the incident with Malinovskii:

At an evening banquet, Zhou Enlai suggested to He Long that they walk up together to their old friends for a drink. Many marshals and generals of the Soviet Union were old friends of Zhou Enlai and He Long. Seeing that their Chinese friends were approaching them, many Soviet commanders became very animated and, one after another, went up to shake their hand or proposed a toast to traditional Chinese-Soviet friendship. At this time the USSR defense minister, Rodion Malinovskii, approached deputy premier He Long; insofar as He Long and the marshal of the Soviet Union had long been acquainted, and he raised his glass to

---

48   Editor's note. Andrei Pavlovich Kirilenko (1906-90) joined the Communist Party as a young man and made a career in provincial positions and was also a military commissar during the Great Patriotic War. During 1962-82 he was Central Committee secretary in charge of industry and was viewed as Brezhnev's successor. Kirilenko was sent into retirement in 1982 due to senility.

friendship between the soldiers of the two countries, while Malinovskii replied in a provocative way and said that "Stalin came up with the marshal's uniform in our country, and Mao in yours."

He Long condemned him indignantly, "What sort of nonsense are you talking? I don't understand you," and went to Zhou Enlai to tell him what had happened. Malinovskii followed behind him and shouted "We can't let Khrushchev and Mao (Mao Zedong) interfere with us." "What sort of nonsense are you speaking?" justly and sternly complained Zhou Enlai, who then, together with He Long went to Leonid Brezhnev. Like a madman, Malinovskii shouted after them: "We've already removed Khrushchev from the scene, and now it's your turn to remove Mao."

The departing premier didn't hear the second half of this phrase. Several marshals of the Soviet Union, who heard this, loudly proclaimed that "We don't agree with him." Since Chan Ganhua, our delegation's interpreter, wanted to translate this expression to the premier, but the other Chinese interpreter reminded him in time that there was an American journalist with a tape recorder. So Chan Ganhua refrained from translating it.

Zhou Enlai came up to Brezhnev and expressed a serious protest. Brezhnev explained that Malinovskii was drunk. Zhou Enlai said that "After taking alcohol people speak the truth," and demanded that Malinovskii apologize and then left the banquet hall with all the members of the delegation.

Upon returning to the Chinese People's Republic's embassy in the USSR, Zhou Enlai attentively heard out each member of the delegation, especially as regards the second and untranslated half of the phrase. Recalling the various circumstances before that, premier Zhou understood that this had not been an isolated incident, but an unbearable insult to our party, state and chairman Mao, and that it was necessary to treat this seriously. The delegation immediately drew up a text and informed the Central Committee of the Chinese Communist Party of what had taken place. When all of this had been done the clocks showed four o'clock in the morning.

The following day the leaders of the CPSU, Brezhnev, Kosygin and Mikoyan, came to call. Zhou Enlai once again made a sharp protest in connection with the previous evening's incident, asking "Did the CPSU invite us here to openly provoke us, or in the hope that China would remove Mao Zedong from his post? According to the western mass media, on 8 November the CPSU and the Chinese Communist Party had already reached an agreement to remove Mao Zedong from power and to replace him with Zhou Enlai, or was this really a coincidence? If the leaders of the CPSU had no had such thoughts in mind, would Malinovskii have dared to talk about it?"

Leonid Brezhnev hastened to explain that "Malinovskii spoke nonsense while drunk and cannot represent the CPSU Central Committee and that the CPSU has already criticized him, and we now officially apologize to the Chinese Communist Party in the name of the Central Committee of the CPSU and clearly distance ourselves from him."

Zhou Enlai noted that Malinovskii had not blurted this out while drunk, but had spoken the truth while drunk. This was not the action of some kind of chance individual, but rather proof of the fact that there continues to exist among the leaders of the CPSU a group of people who adhere to Khrushchev's position and engage in subversive activity against China.

The leaders of the CPSU hurriedly justified him, saying "Malinovskii was simply blabbing; he's already apologized, and we can consider the matter closed." "The matter remains open and we must still study it and report to the Central Committee," replied Zhou Enlai. Brezhnev only said "Of course, of course."

Malinovskii's open declaration about "overthrowing the leadership of Mao Zedong" created a serious obstacle to the official negotiations between China and the Soviet Union, which had not yet begun, and also dealt a hard-to-heal wound to Chinese-Soviet relations…

The Chinese premier, with his refined insight, drew a precise conclusion about the new leadership of the CPSU: although the new leadership of the Soviet Union had removed Khrushchev from his position, they continue to adhere to Khrushchev's course, believing they are stronger and above everyone else.

It would seem that on this point the incident was closed. The Chinese representatives openly hinted that Malinovskii should be sent into retirement for his stunt. However, the marshal remained comfortably at his post until his death and did not in any way lose Brezhnev's trust. This leads one to think that Rodion Yakovlevich acted on Brezhnev's orders (Zhou Enlai gave it to understand in his conversation that the Chinese side believed that it was precisely Brezhnev who was the real leader of the country, despite all the talk about collective leadership).

Dear readers, can you imagine, say, during the May 1st reception in the Kremlin in 1964, a drunk Brezhnev turns with a glass of vodka to a no less drunk Malinovskii and shouting throughout the hall: "What do you say Rodion! Let's get rid of that fool Nikita and live high on the hog." I can't imagine anything like it. Leonid Il'ich and Rodion Yakovlevich had only just successfully carried out a plot against Khrushchev, while only seven years earlier had just as successfully prevented Zhukov's plot. So, the general secretary and the marshal had a great deal of experience in this regard. And if they really did have the idea of trying to arrange a plot against Mao Zedong, with Zhou Enlai's participation, they would not have started to negotiate with the Chinese premier at a reception, but in a secluded spot and through third parties. This is all the more so as Rodion Yakovlevich drank moderately enough and never drank to the point of losing his memory.

I think that the mystery is solved quite simply. Following Khrushchev's removal, Mao Zedong hoped to normalize Soviet-Chinese relations, which had significantly worsened as a result of Khrushchev's unmasking of Stalin's crimes and his condemnation of the "cult of personality." However, Brezhnev, although he had foresworn public criticism of Stalin, was by no means preparing a return to the Stalinist order and to lionizing the former leader. However, even a partial public rehabilitation of Stalin was one of the necessary conditions for normalizing Soviet-Chinese relations. However, and what was more important, Brezhnev understood very well that the Chinese side expected most of all a resumption of fraternal Soviet assistance, both in the economic and military fields, particularly in the transfer of missile, nuclear and thermonuclear technology. However, Leonid Il'ich already regarded China as a geopolitical rival, including the area of influencing the world communist movement, and was not prepared to help her. Brezhnev didn't need the normalization of Soviet-Chinese relations, as opposed to some of the other members of the Central Committee, such as Shelepin.[49] However, the break had to be arranged in such a manner so that the initiative came from the Chinese and so that precisely the Chinese could be blamed for a worsening of Soviet-Chinese relations. Malinovskii's stunt at the reception was undoubtedly initiated by Brezhnev and had been precisely calculated. And the documents on the Chinese reaction, which are now open to researchers, show that Brezhnev and Malinovskii achieved their aim. They decided in Peking that no one in Moscow was preparing to reconcile with them or to help them. However, there was no way the Chinese leaders could make public the story of Malinovskii's

---

49   Editor's note. Aleksandr Nikolaevich Shelepin (1918-94) trained partisans during the Great Patriotic War and rose rapidly through the Komsomol, the Communist Party's youth auxiliary. He later served as chief of the KGB and was active in the plot against Khrushchev. Following Khrushchev's overthrow, however, Shelepin's influence declined and he was dismissed from his party and government posts in 1975.

proposal to Zhou Enlai to overthrow Mao Zedong. Thus worldwide communist public opinion, for the most part, placed the blame for the break between China and the Soviet Union on the Chinese side.

Of course, Brezhnev did not think of firing Rodion Yakovlevich from his job as minister of defense. Quite the opposite, his retention at this post was now necessary in view of the fact that Leonid Il'ich had no doubt as to his loyalty and was grateful for his support in overthrowing Khrushchev, and lest his removal be taken as a false signal by the Chinese.

Natal'ya Rodionovna recalled:

> In Moscow we mostly kept to ourselves. Papa's work was too intense. We spent the rare free days at the dacha with our house pets. After breakfast papa usually went immediately to his study. His relaxation was his work on his book…
>
> In Khabarovsk, where we lived until 1956, family life involved more people, guests came constantly, and a radio phonograph, as big as a trunk, would play. Toward the end of a gathering we always put on papa's favorite "Shine, Shine, my Star…," and before that we inevitably listened to Ukrainian songs and the waltzes "Amur Waves" and "On the Hills of Manchuria."
>
> Usually, in the evenings, when papa was home, mama and I would sit next to him in his study. We would sit quietly, so as not to disturb papa's chess game or reading. Our habits did not change in Moscow, but the books did. Papa's desk was taken up by university textbooks on physics and research in missile technology, and during the last three years they were pushed aside by history—everything that touched on the First World War and the Russian Expeditionary Corps in France was read with great attention to detail.

Natal'ya Rodionovna still recalls that in the library there were two books which beginning authors read: "… textbooks issued by the Leningrad *Red Newspaper* from the series 'What a Beginning Writer Should Know': 'Installment One. Choice and Combination of Words,' and 'Installment Two. The Construction of Tales and Poems.' Strange to say, these two booklets, with question marks and exclamation points along the edges, and notes along the edges are still here."

According to her, her father decisively influenced her choice of profession as a Spanish philologist.

> I had only just enrolled in the philological department's Spanish section and I told my parents about it, thus proving to myself my own maturation and independence. I won't say that I had dreamed of philology since I was a baby. It was only with the passage of time that I came to understand that my choice of Spain was not only correct, but had been predetermined by papa's fate. By the close of my first year, he presented me with an extremely rare book, which he had brought back from Spain in 1938, Federico Garcia Lorca's *Blood Wedding*, and printed in his lifetime, and it seemed to me that he was satisfied with my choice. Father was already sick when I started my third year. He sent my first published work—an article in *Nedelya*[50] about Lorca in the latest translations—to Dolores Ibarruri, signed in Spanish: "Look, Pasionara, about whom my daughter is writing." And he signed it in Spanish with his Spanish pseudonym—"Coronel Malino."

Another time Natal'ya Rodionovna related this episode in greater detail:

---

50   Editor's note. *Nedel'ya* ("The Week") was a weekly illustrated journal that appeared during 1960-95. It resumed publication in a different format in 2006.

When I brought papa my first article about the new translations of Garcia Lorca, papa was already in the hospital; he read the article, praised it a bit, criticized it a bit, and wrote in the upper corner of the newspaper page in Spanish: "Look, Pasionara, about whom my daughter is writing," and signed it Coronel Malino. He told me to put it in an envelope and send it to Dolores Ibarruri. After a month, when papa was no longer with us, a gift and a present arrived—a volume of Rafael Alberti,[51] with a touching message.

The daughter learned the same languages as her father: French and Spanish. This is how Natal'ya Rodionovna described her father's literary creativity:

The cause which papa served swallowed him up entirely, without leaving any time for reminiscences, which is generally a genre for a pensioner.

… I have the manuscript of the book—11 thick notebooks, written in a clear and handsome script, without excisions and corrections. The date of 4 December 1960 is on the first page, along with the preliminary title *The Illegitimate. Part One*, and above it the note "General plan (draft)." The eleventh and final notebook was completed in the autumn of 1966. Father's illness cut it short and one can only guess how father planned to work on the text further. However, one thing is clear: he considered what had been written a preliminary work, a rough draft. In this was manifested his natural demands on himself and his extremely responsible attitude toward any labor, including unfamiliar literary work. He considered that he was just starting to master it, so he never talked about the book. If he was asked, he kept quiet, but sometimes, as if apart from his work, he would relate some episode that had already been written or that had just occurred to him.

Nevertheless, why not memoirs? And why not about the main thing—the Second World War? These questions were asked by everyone who knew what papa was writing about, and they were few. A reserved man, he did not share his plans, did not ask for advice and did not go into explanations. If he had been able to finish the work, he probably would have explained himself why it was more natural for him to write about himself as if about another person. I think he needed distance between himself and his hero and the freedom and self-removal conditioned by it. However, besides this, it seems to me that such a view of his fate, as if it were another's, fitted his plan—to study how a person comes to be and becomes a person, to understand what is in him from time and other people, what is due to his own will and what is due to chance. And a book about the Second World War would have been written, had his life been extended. In the fall of 1966 father turned over to the printer an "approximate plan— rough draft," the first part was the manuscript of a book which they called *Soldiers of Russia* at the publisher's, but he was not able to work on it further or even to finish reading the proofs.

In another memoir Natal'ya Rodionovna relayed some additional details about the novel *Soldiers of Russia*:

His book… was written without corrections in a graceful and old fashioned handwriting, completely without markings, so thought-through and nurtured was each word… The variants of the preliminary title were "Baistryuk" and "Bastard"… The thrill of the book, which he had to work on in fits and starts, spoke of his calling, while the first rough draft spoke

---

51   Editor's note. Rafael Alberti (1902-99) was a Spanish poet and Marxist. Following the defeat of the Spanish Republic, he fled the country and later settled in Argentina. He returned to Spain in 1977 and resumed his political activity.

of undoubted literary talent. Each time, while examining the manuscript, which has not yet been touched by an editor's corrections, I am struck by the original style of the author's language.

The daughter is convinced that Rodion Yakovlevich was a well-rounded man: "It so happened that he became a military man, but I'm convinced that my father would have found himself in another profession, so lively was his curiosity of any trade and pursuit. He could have become a doctor, a literary man, a teacher, or a biologist—these professions attracted him in particular." By the way, it was likely that Vera Nikolaevna Malinovskaya was a biology teacher. And having closely associated with her, L.V. Rozhalin, Malinovskii's childhood friend, became a biologist on her recommendation—a specialist in the causes of potato diseases.

Natal'ya Rodionovna testifies:

Papa treated scientists with profound respect and even worshipfulness. If I had revealed a talent for the hard sciences, I think that papa would have been happy. He treated humanitarian talents more calmly, I think, because he himself felt words and had a talent for languages (he knew French and Spanish well). He bowed down before scientific geniuses. I remember that once father took me, as yet a schoolgirl, to some sort of celebration at the university and in the foyer he showed me a tall and thin man: "Look and remember—that's Landau."[52] A few years later, when father took me to Star City,[53] which as yet didn't have a name, I heard him pronounce with the same joyful respect: "Look, that's the chief engineer." Korolev's name was still unknown.

Once I asked: "What did you want to be?" That he had not wanted to be a soldier, I knew and had heard it before: "It's unnatural to want to be a soldier. One should not want war. It's natural for a man to want to become a scientist, an artist or a doctor. They create things. And you destroy, even while defending, and sacrifice. From this comes the internal burden of the military profession, which is difficult enough as it is."

As to the question of what to be, papa answered: "A forester." I think that's the truth, and namely the truth of that year, but not for his whole life. As a young man he might have (and even probably) answered otherwise, all the more so that the ambition in him would become aggravated by the memory of humiliations suffered in childhood. The job of a forester was a later utopia, which was deeply resonant with his nature. But history, as is known, does not know the subjunctive clause….

The marshal's daughter recalls:

Papa did not go hunting. We and the people close to him knew why. Not being afraid to appear sentimental, he said that having once killed a fallow deer (or a goat? during his first hunting trip. What is there on the Mongolian steppes?), he came up to it and saw its eyes. He never shot again. However, he went out hunting, while respecting the dog's right to any kind of work. The first was an English setter, Milord, as I recall, had no equals. He would bring every duck to papa and heard his approving: "Good boy, good boy" and the command, "Now take it to the one who killed it." The dog would unwillingly but without fail take it. Papa did

---

52   Editor's note. Lev Davidovich Landau (1908-68) was a Soviet physicist who won the Nobel Prize for Physics in 1962.

53   Editor's note. Star City (*Zvezdnyi Gorodok*) is the popular name for the Yurii Gagarin Cosmonaut Training Center outside of Moscow.

not go hunting while in Moscow (there was no free time compared to Khabarovsk), although it happened, when they called, that in Zavidovo they not only hunted but mainly resolved important matters. And there he did not change his habits and did not shoot; no matter how much they made fun of him.

This is what Natal'ya Rodionovna Malinovskaya recalled about her father's enthusiasms:

Most often in the evenings papa would solve chess problems or read Flaubert[54] in French, in order not to forget the language (and then, alongside the book, happily meowing, was our favorite—Lasik the Siberian cat). And when he got an off day or vacation arrived, papa would devote it to fishing. How many hours, no days, would I sit along the banks of all different kinds of rivers and lakes, watched by my parents, who would happily cast their lines in the cold or rain! Only now, while recalling this torture of my childhood and teen years do I understand that for papa these quiet hours were a spiritual necessity. An introverted and taciturn man (half a word in the evening and two sentences on Sunday), he needed to commune with the natural world, at least through fishing and house pets and thus restored his balance.

Altogether indifferent to things, no matter where papa was in the world he would buy fishing tackle and you should have seen with what taste and skill he did it! I remember once on the road to the Sacre Coeur (only three days in Paris!), papa and I came across a fishing shop and for an entire hour I suffered in silence while papa dug around the scatterings of sinkers and spoon bait, although then, upon acquiring some piece of iron with a feather, how he would speak about the *Comedie Francaise*,[55] about Montmarte,[56] and would recite:
"Violet Paris,
"Paris in aniline
"Arose behind the window of the Rotunda…"

As we see, Rodion Yakovlevich was no stranger to poetry and could recite from memory Vladimir Mayakovskii's[57] poem "Verlaine and Cezanne."

Natal'ya Rodionovna would stop in particular on her father's passionate love for chess:

… his youthful enthusiasm for chess grew over the years into a solid attachment. People in the know believe that papa played at a very professional level, and his chess library testifies that it was not compiled by a dilettante. By the way, there's a volume in it dedicated to Botvinnik's[58] mastery, with a gift inscription by the grand master.

As far as I can recall, a small, dark cherry-colored box, no bigger than your palm, lay on my father's desk. When opened, it would split into two squares—a chess board with holes in each square, where you could insert the pegs on the tiny pieces, and a space for the unused pieces, which was wrapped in strawberry-colored velvet. The chess box would be opened almost every evening; studying the games and solving problems became a habit, and only the big Siberian

---

54   Editor's note. Gustave Flaubert (1821-80) was a French novelist of the realist school. His most famous work was *Madame Bovary* (1857).

55   Editor's note. The Comedie-Francaise is a state theater in Paris founded by Louis XIV in 1680.

56   Editor's note. A hill in Paris containing the Basilica of the Sacre-Coeur. For many years the Montmarte area was a gathering place for artists.

57   Editor's note. Vladimir Vladimirovich Mayakovskii (1893-1930) was a Russian Futurist poet who later became a tribune of the Russian Revolution. He later grew disillusioned and committed suicide.

58   Editor's note. Mikhail Moiseevich Botvinnik (1911-95) was a Soviet chess grandmaster and several times world champion.

cat, Lasik, the brother of the legendary Noir, who considered the place on the desk under the lamp to be his, would allow himself to interfere with this taciturn dialog with the board, touching the pieces with his paw, or pulling at the yellow cut-glass pencil from the Faber firm.

Aleksandr Shchelokov, who for many years worked in the paper *Krasnaya Zvezda*, confirms Malinovskii's passion for chess:

> The editorial board of *Krasnaya Zvezda*, together with the Central House of the Soviet Army, conducted competitions for a long time in solving chess problems. The organization of such a competition is a difficult and labor-intensive task. It would be difficult for one man to do this, but with two we managed.
>
> Each time, following the publication of the latest group of problems, letters would arrive at the office, literally in sacks. We had to sort them out, review them, establish which ones contained the correct answers, and lay aside the incorrect ones. In these conditions the first rounds reminded one of a mass run over a long distance. A huge crowd would surge forward at the start and it was impossible to spot in it the future champions and outsiders, because it would be impossible to spot individuals and their expressions. Gradually, step by step, the group of competitors for the prize would shrink. And now the leaders were evident.
>
> By the end of the competition on the number of correctly solved problems, first place was occupied by a reader with the surname of Malinovskii, with the initials "R.Ya." In the physical culture and sport section, which was conducting the competition, we became thoughtful: did the defense minister himself solve the problems, or was it someone with the same last name. Maybe someone's trying to play a joke? We did not risk publishing the results without figuring out the circumstances.
>
> Nikolai Ivanovich Makeev, the chief editor, called the minister:
>
> "Rodion Yakovlevich, please don't be surprised at my question. A certain R.Ya. Malinovskii took part in solving chess problems. Is it really you?"
>
> "It is," the marshal answered, and explained: "I must admit that I love chess problems. But I have no time for them. That's why I prefer competitive ones. First of all, you have to give your answer by a designated time. This strongly disciplines one. Secondly, if you're a part of a competition, it wouldn't be right to drop the game. This is also a decisive factor. That's why I solved the problems to the end."
>
> "You solved them well," said Makeev. "I congratulate you on winning first place."
>
> "Thank you, Nikolai Ivanovich. It's nice to hear that. Only don't announce it in the paper that I won first place. You don't have to do that. Agreed?"
>
> Thus no one ever found out that the defense minister, Marshal of the Soviet Union R.Ya. Malinovskii was the winner of the competition.

Rodion Yakovlevich was a commander. And a game of chess, the same way as compiling chess problems and the solving of chess problems, which he engaged in, develops the same qualities that a commander needs: the ability to work out a strategy, the capability of subordinating the resolution of tactical tasks to strategic ones, and the ability to calculate the likely course of events.

Natal'ya Rodionovna described her father's library in detail:

> Papa was unbelievably thorough in everything, without a hint of dilettantism; theoretical equipping or the technology of a trade concerned him equally, no matter what the subject was—military affairs, chess or fishing. He gathered a magnificent library on military theory and history, which was later donated by mama to the Armored Forces Academy, which for more than 30 years, until last year, was named after father. I know that there are a number

of rare volumes among those books. Chess literature occupied an entire shelf in papa's library (which was donated within a year following papa's death to the Odessa Chess Club, and another to icthyological books in different languages (now they are in the library of the Moscow Zoological Museum). Next to it lay a notebook with a title on the binding: *A Fisherman's Diary*, with day by day entries for what, when and in what weather a fish was caught (of course on a lure, as papa did not fish with a net), in what channel of the Ussuri River one can better catch salmon trout or catfish. The lower shelf of the bookcase contained numerous fishing rods, hooks and sinkers, spinners and some kind of exotic baits, refined imitations of flies and dragon flies, and all other kinds of fishing tackle for any kind of fishing at any latitude!

I should add that in the marshal's library there was, in particular, a book by the German general Erich Ludendorff,[59] *Total War*. To all appearances, it had been printed on a duplicating machine in one of the military academies in a limited printing for students in the '50s or '60s. There are no markings in it. But there are a large number or markings and marginalia in two other books, Yu.G. Perel's *The Development of the Understanding of the Universe*, and R. Lepp's *Atoms and People*, which were published, respectively in 1958 and 1959. For example, in Perel's book, in the part where it tells about the execution of Giordano Bruno,[60] Malinovskii noted: "A mad crime." These books probably interested him due to the powerful development of astronautics and nuclear weapons, as well as the "peaceful atom."

Natal'ya Rodionovna noted:

Papa was pathologically indifferent to things and would have been satisfied, if he'd had his way, with a light blue flannel cowboy shirt (I have it now), an old pair of pants in "The Sea has Spread out Widely" style and a beret, which he learned to wear in Spain. In going through all his enthusiasms, I understood: he was indifferent to anything that you didn't need in a forester's hut. However, no matter what part of the Earth he was in, papa would buy fishing tackle and some kinds of small screwdrivers, screws and small hammers. He did have, however, one more passion—writing implements: Parker pens with a fine tip. "Omega" Swiss watches were a necessary luxury item. (I heard how once papa said over the phone, probably to the director of a watch factory about an army order: "'Commander' watches should be no worse than 'Omega'." A military man can't get by without an accurate and durable watch!) However, his main passion, of course, was books.

Not being a bibliophile in the full sense of the word, papa gradually put together a library which reflected all of his passions: the Russian 19th century, military history, chess, animals and voyages, dictionaries (bi-lingual, with definitions), and sayings from all ages and peoples. Thanks to mama's efforts (she completed the Leningrad Library Institute and before being evacuated in 1942 headed a district library), the library was in perfect order. However, there were books sitting on a special shelf, not according to library rules, but by love: Shevchenko[61] and

---

59   Editor's note. Erich Friedrich Wilhelm Ludendorff (1865-1937) joined the German army in 1883 and rose rapidly through its staff apparatus. During the First World War he served as an army chief of staff and was later appointed First Quartermaster, from which position he directed the country's war effort. Following the war, Ludendorff briefly allied himself with the Nazis.

60   Editor's note. Giordano Bruno (1548-1600) was an Italian monk who achieved fame as a philosopher, poet and mathematician. He was tried for heresy and burned at the stake.

61   Editor's note. Taras Grigor'evich Shevchenko (1814-61) was a Ukrainian poet, artist, writer, and political activist. His works were instrumental in forming the modern Ukrainian literary language.

Lesya Ukrainka[62] in Ukrainian, Yesenin[63] and *Woe from Wit*, Voltaire,[64] La Rochefoucauld,[65] and Pascal,[66] in French and in translation. And, of course, Marcus Aurelius,[67] a book that was bought at a used book shop, judging by the note on the dust cover, in the fall of 1936, on the eve of his trip to Spain. He had searched for it a long time and called it the "most necessary" book. More than once papa's favorite phrase from Marcus Aurelius would sum up all our conversations: "Each man is worth just as much as what he is busy doing." (And this sums things up for me even now). And de Exupery's[68] phrase that "We are responsible for those whom we have taught," which was adopted to our home circumstances by me, had besides a figurative, but also a literal meaning bearing on all the animals living in our house. As opposed to all the others, papa never forgot, in leaving, to give them something to eat, so they wouldn't get lonesome…

A number of other books also lay in his desk drawer. Not from caution—they had simply been rewritten on a typewriter, some with bindings and some without—they did not fit on the shelf: *The White Guard*,[69] *A Day in the Life of Ivan Denisovich*[70] (in 1962 a carefully bound separate edition came out), *Tyorkin in the Other World*,[71] and *For Whom the Bell Tolls*[72] (from the series "Distributed According to a Special List"), and a photocopy of *The Tale of an Unextinguished Moon*,[73] copied at his request in the National Library in Sofia. Papa gave all of these books to me, saying "Read them without fail," but unfortunately, without commenting. Only once did I ask about *The Tale of an Unextinguished Moon*."

"Is this the truth?"

"They wouldn't hide a lie so well."

Then, knowing that papa was writing a book about his childhood, I asked:

"Why not about the war?"

He replied in an unexpectedly sharp manner:

---

62   Editor's note. Lesya Ukrainka was the literary pseudonym of Larisa Petrovna Kosach-Kvitka (1871-1913), a Ukrainian poet, writer and political activist.

63   Editor's note. Sergei Aleksandrovich Yesenin (1895-1925) was a Russian poet who sang the praises of rural living. Although he at first supported the Bolshevik regime, he later became disillusioned and committed suicide.

64   Editor's note. This was the pen name of Francois-Marie Arouet (1694-1778), a noted writer and the leading figure of the French Enlightenment.

65   Editor's note. Francois de La Rochefoucauld (1613-80) was a French nobleman famous for his maxims.

66   Editor's note. Blaise Pascal (1623-62) was a French mathematician and physicist who in later life also became a Christian philosopher.

67   Editor's note. Marcus Aurelius (121-180 AD) was a Roman emperor who ruled from 161 to his death and expanded the empire to its greatest extent. He was also a prominent Stoic philosopher.

68   Editor's note. Antoine de Saint-Exupery (1900-44) was a French flier and writer. His most famous work is *The Little Prince* (1943).

69   Editor's note. This was a novel by Mikhail Afanas'evich Bulgakov (1891-1940), which was published in its entirety in the Soviet Union in 1966. Its more famous stage version is *The Days of the Turbins*.

70   Editor's note. This was a short novel by Aleksandr Isaevich Solzhenitsyn (1918-2008), first published in 1962. It details the hardships of life in Stalin's labor camps and at the time of its publication created a literary sensation.

71   Editor's note. This was a short poem by Aleksandr Trifonovich Tvardovskii (1910-71), written as a continuation of his earlier wartime epic *Vasilii Tyorkin*, about the adventures of a resourceful Soviet soldier during the Great Patriotic War.

72   Editor's note. A novel about the Spanish Civil War by Ernest Hemingway (1899-1961), which was published in 1940.

73   Editor's note. A short story published by Boris Andreevich Pil'nyak (1894-1938) in 1926, containing a thinly-disguised description of the supposed death of war commissar Mikhail Vasil'evich Frunze (1885-1925) and hinting at Stalin's complicity in the matter.

"Let them lie without me."

Many years later, coming across a memorial volume about the Battle of Stalingrad, covered with exclamation points and question marks, interspersed with cutting remarks, did I understand the sense of this phrase. Then I was only surprised at the unusual, as I now understand it, tone of his disagreement with the author and recalled the continuation of our conversation:

"No one will say or write the truth about this war for a long time."

"Is this because they won't print it?"

"Not only."

He proved to be right and is right to this day and, perhaps, for all time, although our conversation had a different ending.

"Sometime I'll try to write it. But one should begin at the beginning. Before this war there was war, war and war."

Three wars—the First World War, the Civil War and the war in Spain.

And now it is time to relate the saddest part—Rodion Yakovlevich's last illness. Natal'ya Rodionovna recalled:

7 November was my twentieth birthday. Papa was already ill, but neither mama or I, nor the doctors suspected the diagnosis. His leg hurt badly where he had his old wound, which he got as early as the First World War (and if papa said "badly," that means that it was unbearable). Following an unthinkingly prescribed mud bath treatment in Tskhaltubo,[74] he only got worse, but papa continued to work and on 7 November went to take the parade. Only mama and I knew what each step on the Mausoleum and each word of his speech cost him. Upon returning, he lay down and did not get up again (and he still had half a year to live). They took him to the hospital a week later—*on a Friday*, and this contempt for superstition frightened us…

Papa was a fatalist and stoic. Neither the doctors nor the nurses heard a groan or complaint from him and said later that he possessed *pathological patience*. He didn't have single question regarding the diagnosis or any instructions to mama as to "what to do later." He withstood the pain and the illness in silence, bravely and with dignity. On the evening of 30 March, as I was leaving the hospital, instead of the usual "Goodbye," papa said "Be happy" in a barely audible voice. I didn't understand that he was saying goodbye to me…

Papa was always taciturn…

Rodion Yakovlevich Malinovskii died at 3:15 p.m. on 31 March 1967. He had cancer of the pancreas, which metastasized into the bones and many internal organs. Raisa Yakovlevna outlived him by 30 years.

Not long before his death, Malinovskii seemed to be getting ready to write his memoirs about the Great Patriotic War. His daughter states:

A special folder with documents from the Great Patriotic War lay in the desk drawer awaiting its hour. He put them aside even then, and on each page under the "Secret" stamp was written "NB! For my special folder."

Not long ago papa's adjutant Vsevolod Nikolaevich Vasil'ev told me that he had seen and even read papa's notebook with notes on the first months of the war. The manuscript stunned

---

74   Editor's note. Tskhaltubo is a spa resort in the former Soviet republic of Georgia, famous for its mineral springs.

him: "I'm a front-line soldier and I can tell you that neither before nor after have I ever read anything so truthful. And in the beginning of 1966," Vsevolod Nikolaevich related, "Rodion Yakovlevich, as if continuing a conversation with himself, said: 'I'll stay another year and then leave—it's time for me to perform my duty as regards the war'." He was speaking about the Second World War.

I found out too late about the existence of these notebooks, when to ask why they didn't give them to us after papa's death and where they disappeared to from his office, was pointless, and there was no one to ask. And even if papa brought a notebook home, it likely would not have been preserved. Even before the funeral plainclothes people came to our home to remove the government communications apparatus—the direct telephone line and the Kremlin telephone. They took all his papers out of his desk and at the same time all the "Distributed According to a Special List" books from papa's safe. Two or three copies of Garaudy,[75] *For Whom the Bell Tolls*, which were in my room, remained, but who knew that they would come for papa's papers and that we should have just put them in another place…

They buried Rodion Yakovlevich Malinovskii on 3 April 1967. An urn with his ashes was placed in the Kremlin wall.

---

75   Editor's note. Roger Garaudy (1913-2012) served in the French army and Resistance during the Second World War. Following the war he joined the French Communist Party and later served as a deputy in the National Assembly. He was expelled from the party in 1968, following his criticism of the Soviet-led invasion of Czechoslovakia. Garaudy was successively a Protestant, Catholic and a Muslim. In his later years he was one of the foremost Holocaust deniers in Europe.

Appendix

The Main Dates in the Life and Work of Rodion Yakovlevich Malinovskii

10 (22) November 1898—in Odessa a son, Rodion, was born out of wedlock and given the patronymic of Yakovlevich, to Varvara Nikolaevna Malinovskaya, an Orthodox maiden and peasant from the Podol'sk province, Bratslavskii district, Shipkovskaya township. The assumed father was the Odessa chief of police, army colonel Yakim (Yakov) Ivanovich Bunin. Following the introduction of the Gregorian calendar in February 1918, his birthday was observed on 23 November.

1902—death of the assumed father, now Major General Ya.I. Bunin and the grandfather, Nikolai Antonovich Malinovskii. Rodion is turned over to be raised by his aunt, Vera Nikolaevna Malinovskaya, in Mariupol'.

1902-1903—lives in Mariupol' and spends the summer at the estate of Vera Nikolaevna Malinovskaya in the village of Staryi Belous, in the Chernigov district of Chernigov province. He studies in the grammar school or secondary school in Mariupol'.

1910 or 1911—Varvara Nikolaevna Malinovskaya's marriage to Sergei Isanurovich Zalesnoi.

spring 1913—arrives at his mother's in the village of Klishchev, Tyvrovskaya township, Vinnitsa district, Podol'sk province. Because of a quarrel with his stepfather, S.I. Zalesnoi, he leaves Klishchev no later than August.

September 1913—arrives in Odessa and works as a salesman M.P. Pripuskov's fancy good shop.

July 1914—leaves as a volunteer (hunter) for the front as part of the 256th Yelizavetgrad Infantry Regiment.

March 1915—awarded the St. George's Cross, fourth class, for the fighting near Kalwaria.

October 1915—wounded near Smorgon'.

April 1916—arrival in France as part of the 2nd Special Regiment, 1st Special Brigade of the Russian Expeditionary Corps.

April 1917—wounded in the hand near Fort Brimont.

December 1917 or January 1918—joins the Russian Legion of Honor as the commander of a machine gun platoon.

Spring 1919—the disbandment of the Russian Legion of Honor and his supposed promotion to warrant officer.

4 September 1919—awarded the St. George's Cross, third class, for the fighting on 14 September 1918, during the breakthrough of the Hindenburg Line.

August or September 1919—sailed from Marseilles to Vladivostok.

October 1919—arrival in Vladivostok.

November 1919—crosses the front line and joins the Red Army.

November 1919-February 1920—machine gun instructor with the 240th Rifle Regiment.

February-May 1920—sick with typhoid fever in military hospitals in Mariinsk and Tomsk.

May-June 1920—a rifleman with the 137th Independent Rifle Battalion, defending the Trans-Siberian Railroad, town of Kansk.

June-August 1920—a cadet in a school for training sergeants, 35th Independent Rifle Brigade guarding the Trans-Siberian Railroad, in Kansk. The play, *The Feat of a Life* was written about the Russian Expeditionary Corps' La Courtine uprising during June-September 1917.

August-December 1920—chief of a machine gun team with the 137th Independent Rifle Battalion, defending the Trans-Siberian Railroad, town of Kansk.

December 1920-January 1921—commander of a machine gun platoon in the 246th Rifle Regiment, town of Nizhneudinsk.

January-December 1921—chief of a machine gun team in the 246th Rifle Regiment, which was renamed the 3rd Siberian Rifle Regiment, Slyudyanka station, Trans-Baikal Railroad.

December 1921-August 1922—chief of a machine gun team with the 309th Rifle Regiment in the village of Pokrovskoe, Trans-Baikal area.

August 1922-August 1923—chief of a machine gun team with the 104th Rifle Regiment, Irkutsk.

August-November 1923—assistant to the battalion commander, 104th Rifle Regiment, Irkutsk.

November 1923-October 1927—battalion commander, 243rd Rifle Regiment, Irkutsk.

November 1923—candidate member of the VKP(b).

July-August 1925—on brief leave in Irkutsk, where he marries Larisa Nikolaevna Sharabarova, who was born on 30 October 1904 in Irkutsk.

October 1926—member of the VKP(b).

October-December 1926—on brief leave in the village of Klishchev, Vinnitsa Oblast'.

October 1927-May 1930—student at the Frunze Military Academy, Moscow.

1927—birth of son Gennadii.

19 January 1929—birth of son Robert.

May 1930-January 1931—chief of staff, 67th Cavalry Regiment, Kavkazskaya station.

December 1930 or January 1931—his son Gennadii dies from meningitis, Kavkazskaya.

January-March 1931—assistant to the chief of the first section of the staff of the North Caucasus Military District, Rostov-on-Don.

March 1931-January 1933—assistant to the chief of the third sector of the first section of the staff of the Belorussian Military District, Smolensk.

March 1933-January 1935—chief of the second sector of the first section of the staff of the Belorussian Military District, Smolensk.

November-December 1933—treatment in a sanatorium, Yalta.

29 April 1934—birth of son Eduard.

January 1935-June 1936—chief of staff, 3rd Cavalry Corps, Minsk.

June 1935-December 1936, and June 1938-September 1939—assistant to the army cavalry inspector for the operational section of the staff of the Belorussian Military District, Smolensk.

September 1935—promoted to colonel.

January 1937-May 1938—on duty in Spain.

17 July 1937—awarded the Order of Lenin.

22 October 1937—awarded the Order of the Red Banner.

1937—death of stepfather Sergei Isanurovich Zalesnoi.

15 July 1938—promoted to brigade commander.

September 1939-March 1941—senior instructor in the staff service department, Frunze Military Academy, Moscow.

June 1940—promoted to major general.

March-August 1941—commander of the 48th Rifle Corps.

August 1941—chief of staff, Reserve Army, Southern Front.

August-December 1941—commander of the 6th Army.

9 November 1941—promoted to lieutenant general.

December 1941-July 1942—commander of the Southern Front.

July-August 1942—deputy commander of the North Caucasus Front.

August-October 1942—commander of the 66th Army.

October-November 1942—deputy commander of the Voronezh Front.

November 1942-February 1943—commander of the 2nd Guards Army.

February-March 1943—commander of the Southern Front.

12 February 1943—promoted to colonel general.

March 1943-24 April 1944—commander of the Southwestern Front, which was renamed the Third Ukrainian Front in October 1943.

28 April 1944—promoted to general of the army.

24 April 1944-9 June 1945—commander of the Second Ukrainian Front (by order of 15 May 1944).

28 August 1944—slightly wounded in the back.

10 September 1944—promoted to Marshal of the Soviet Union.

26 April 1945—awarded the Order of Victory.

9 June 1945—left Moscow for the Trans-Baikal area.

9 June-10 September 1945—commander of the Trans-Baikal Front.

8 September 1945—awarded the Hero of the Soviet Union.

10 September 1945-May 1947—commander of the Trans-Baikal Military District, Khabarovsk.

February 1946—elected a deputy to the USSR Supreme Soviet from the Karym electoral district, no. 319.

17 July 1946—divorced L.N. Malinovskaya in Khabarovsk.

4 September 1946—married Raisa Yakovlevna Kucherenko in Khabarovsk.

6 September 1946—adopted R.Ya. Kucherenko's son, German, from her first marriage.

7 November 1946—birth of daughter Natal'ya.

May 1947-June 1953—commander-in-chief of Far Eastern forces.

October 1952—elected a deputy member of the CPSU Central Committee.

June 1953-March 1956—commander of the Far Eastern Military District.

1954—death of his mother, Varvara Nikolaevna Malinovskaya Zalesnaya (Malinovskaya).

March 1956-October 1957—commander-in-chief of the Ground Forces and first deputy minister of defense of the USSR.

26 October 1957-31 March 1967—USSR minister of defense.

23 November 1958—awarded Hero of the Soviet Union for the second time.

31 March 1967—died in the Kremlin hospital.

3 April 1967—ashes deposited in the Kremlin wall.

Bibliography

Andryushchenko, S.A. *Nachinali my na Slavutiche*. Moscow: Voennoe Izdatel'stvo, 1979.

Afanasenko, V.I. "K Voprosu o Poteryakh Voisk Yuzhnogo Fronta v Oktyabre-Dekabre 1941 Goda." *Bylye Gody. Chernomorskii Istoricheskii Zhurnal*. 2011, no. 2, pp. 55-61.

Afanasenko, V.I. "Proval Gross-Stalingrada." *Donskoi Vremennik*. 2009, pp. 87-92 (http://www.donvrem.dspl.ru/Files/article/m7/0/art.aspx?art_id=416).

Axworthy, M., Scafes, C., Craciunoiu. C. *Third Axis Fourth Ally. Romanian Armed Forces in the European War, 1941-1945*. London: Arms and Armour Press, 1995.

Baklanov, A.G. *Samyi Molodoi General (XX Vek-Strana, Lyudi, Sud'by)*. Moscow: TONChU, 2012.

Bashkeev, M. "Pis'ma Marshala." *Tribuna*. 2012, no. 27, 19 July (http://www.tribuna.ru/other_sections/history_club/pisma_marshala/).

Biryukova, L. "Otets Bereg Soldatskuyu Krov'." *Gazeta*. 2009, 7 May (http://www.gzt.ru/topnews/society/237474.html?from=copiedlink).

Biryuzov, S.S. *Kogda Gremeli Pushki*. Moscow: Voennoe Izdatel'stvo, 1961.

Bordyugov, G.A. *Prestupleniya Vermakhta protif Grazhdanskogo Naseleniya//Istrebitel'naya Voina na Vostoke. Prestupleniya Vermakhta v SSSR*. Moscow: AIRO, 2005.

Bunina, M.Ya. "Iz Tyurmyi na Marazlievskoi. Predislovie K.B. Ivanova//Uroki Gneva i Lyubvi": *Sbornik Vospominanii o Godakh Repressii (20-e-80-gg.). Vypusk 2*. Compiled and edited by T.V. Tigonen. Leningrad, 1991, pp. 80-91.

Butakov, Ya. "Russkie Legionery. Zabytye Soldaty Pervoi Mirovoi// *Stoletie.RU*. 2010, 24 September (http://www.stoletie.ru/territoriya_istorii/russkie_legionery_2010-09-24.htm).

Chertok, B.Ye. *Rakety i Lyudi*. Vols. 1-4. Moscow: Mashinostroenie, 1999 (http://militera.lib.ru/explo/chertok_be/index.html).

Cockfield, J.H. *With Snow on Their Boots: The Tragic Odyssey of the Russian Expeditionary Force in France During World War I*. London: Palgrave Macmillan, 1999.

Dugas, I.A., Cheron. F.Ya. *Vycherknutye iz Pamyati. Sovetskie Voennoplennye Mezhdu Gitlerom i Stalinym*. Paris: YMCA-PRESS, 1994.

Dzhuvaga, V. "Segodnya-69 Godovshchina Nachala Khar'kovskoi Katastrofy Sovetskikh Voisk." *Sait Goroda Khar'kova*. 2011, 12 May (http://www.057.ua/article/53735).

Fomin, V., Shchekochikhin. Yu. "Togda, v Novocherkasske." *Literaturnaya Gazeta*. 1989, no. 25, 21 June.

Gaiterova, A. "Buninskie Mesta pod Yel'tsom. (http://eletskraeved.ru/tag/anya-gaiterova).

Glantz, D. "August Storm: The Soviet 1945 Strategic Offensive in Manchuria." *Leavenworth Papers*, no 7. Combat Studies Institute, February 1983, Fort Leavenworth, Kansas.

Glantz, D. *Red Storm over the Balkans. The Failed Soviet Invasion of Romania, Spring 1944*. Lawrence: University Press of Kansas, 2004.

Gofman, I. *Stalinskaya Voina na Unichtozhenie. Planirovanie, Osushchestvlenie, Dokumenty*. Translated from the German. Moscow: AST-Astrel', 2006.

Golubovich, V.S. *Marshal Malinovskii*. Kiev: Politicheskoe Izdatel'stvo Ukrainy, 1988.

Goncharov, S.N., Lewis, J.W, Litai. X. *Uncertain Partners. Stalin, Mao, and the Korean War*. Stanford: Stanford University Press, 1993.

Gubar', O. "Ulitsa Politsmeistera Bunina. *Migdal' Times*. 2004, no. 48-49. (http://www. Odessitclub.org/reading_room/gubar/bunin.htm).

Isaev, A.V., Kolomiets. M.V. *Razgrom 6-i Tankovoi Armii SS. Mogila Pantservaffe*. Moscow: EKSMO, 2009.

Ivanov, V. *Literaturnye Zapiski*. Petrograd: 1922, no. 3.

Khazov, A.A. "Russkii Ekspeditionnyi Korpus vo Frantsii (1916-1918)." *Kadetskaya Pereklichka*, New York, 1989, no. 46 (http://www.xx13.ru/kadeti/rus_korpus.htm#hazov).

——*Khrushchev Remembers*. With an introduction commentary and notes by Edward Crankshaw. Translated and edited by Strobe Talbott. New York: Bantam Books, 1971.

Krivosheev, G.F. ed. *Velikaya Otechestvennaya bez Grifa Sekretnosti. Kniga Poter'*. Moscow: Veche, 2010.

Khrushchev, N.S. *Vremya. Lyudi. Vlast' (Vospominaniya)*. Books 1-4. Moscow: Moskovskie Novosti, 1999.

Lavrenov, S.Ya. Popov. I.M. *Sovetskii Soyuz v Lokal'nykh Voinakh i Konfliktakh*. Moscow: AST-Astrel', 2003.

Lister, E. *Nasha Voina*. Translated from the Spanish. Moscow: Politicheskoe Izdatel'stvo, 1969.

Malinovskaya, N.R. "Pamyat'-Sneg." *Druzhba Narodov*. 2005, no. 5.

Malinovskii, R.Ya. ed. *Yassko-Kishinevskie Kanny. Istoriko-Memuarnyi Ocherk*. Moscow: Nauka, 1964.

Malinovskii, R.Ya. ed. *Budapesht, Vena, Praga. Istoriko-Memuarnyi Ocherk*. Moscow: Nauka, 1965.

Malinovskii, R.Ya. *Gnevnye Vikhri Ispanii//Pod Znamenem Ispanskoi Respubliki*. Moscow: Nauka. 1965, pp. 139-190.

Malinovskii, R.Ya. ed. *Final. 3 Septembrya 1945. Istoriko-Memuarnyi Ocherk*. Moscow: Nauka, 1966.

Malinovskii, R.Ya. *Soldaty Rossii. Roman*. Moscow: Voennoe Izdatel'stvo, 1988.

Malyshko, Ye. "Chernigovskaya Khronika. Oleg Stefanov." (http://www.starybilouos.com.ua/index.php/publikacii/77-hronika).

Mal'tsev, Ye.Ye. *V Gody Ispytanii*. Moscow: Voennoe Izdatel'stvo, 1979.

Managarov, I.M. *V Srazhenii za Khar'kov*. 2nd ed. Khar'kov: Prapor, 1978.

Manstein, E. *Uteryannye Pobedy*. Translated from the German. Moscow: AST; St. Petersburg: Terra Fantastica, 1999.

Markevich, N. "Muzei Militsii: Sekrety Mishki Yaponchika i 'Korolya Shpionov'." Dumskaya.net 2014. 13 May. (http://dumskaya.net/news/sokrovischa-odesskikh-milicionerov-sredi-izvestny-029460).

Martel, Sir Giffard Le Quesne *Outspoken Soldier. His Views and Memoirs*. London: Sifton Praed & Co., 1949.

Martel, Sir Giffard Le Quesne *The Russian Outlook*. London: Michael Joseph, 1947.

Meyer, H. *The 12th SS. The History of the Hitler Youth Panzer Division*. Vols. 1-2. Mechanicsburg, PA: Stackpole Books, 2005.

Miller, T. *Agoniya 1-go Tankovogo Korpusa SS. Ot Ardenn do Budapeshta*. Moscow: Yauza-Press, 2009. (This book is a translation to Russian of the English-language edition of Michael Reynolds's *Men of Steel: 1st SS Panzer Corps. The Ardennes and Eastern Front, 1944-45*. London: Pen & Sword Books, 1999.

Mirzoyan, G. "Khudyakov, on zhe Khanferyants, Marshal Aviatsii… . *Noev Kovcheg*. 2011, no. 9 (168), 1-15 Maya (http://www.noev-kovcheg.ru/mag/2011-09/2570.html).

——*Na Preime u Stalina*. Moscow: Novyi Khronograf, 2008.

Nesterenko, A.I. *Ogon' Vedut Katyushi*. Moscow: Voennoe Izdatel'stvo, 1975.

—— *Nikita Khrushchev. 1964. Stenogrammy Plenuma TsK KPSS i Drugie Dokumenty*. Moscow: Materik, 2007.

Obaturov, G.I. "Dnevniki (1960-1993)//Sait, Posvyashchennyi Generau Obaturov G.I. (http://www.gereeralarmy.ru/diary/diary.pdf).

Obaturov, G.I. *Dorogi Ratnyi Krutye. Vospominaniya ob Uchastii v Velikoi Otechestvennoi Voine*. Moscow, 1995. (http://www.generalarmy.ru/book/).

Petrova, I. "Tam… Zhdala menya Otsovskaya Molodost'…" (http://iipetrova.narod.ru/rasskaz/bunin.html).

Pobol', N., Polyan. P. "Stalin i Khrushchev. Nikita ne Tol'ko Poteshal Tirana, no Pytalsya Spasti Sotni Tysyach Zhiznei." *Novaya Gazeta*. 2009, 9 February, no. 13 (http://old.novayagazeta.ru/data/2009/013/24.html).

Ponamarchuk, Ye. "Lyudskaya Volna//ArtOfWar. Tvorchestvo Veteranov Poslednykh Voin." Sait imeni Vladimira Grigor'eva (http://artofwar.ru/p/ponamarchuk_e/text_0220.shtml).

Ponomorenko, R.O. *12-ya Tankovaya Diviziya SS "Gitleryugend"*. Moscow: Veche, 2010.

Popova, S.S. "Boevye Nagrady Marshala Sovetskogo Soyuza R.Ya. Malinovskogo." *Voenno-Istoricheskii Zhurnal*. 2005, no. 5.

Raus, E., Newton. S.H. *The Eastern Front Memoir of General Raus, 1941-1945*. Cambridge, MA: Da Capo Press, 2003.

Rodimtsev, A.I. *Pod Nebom Ispanii*. Moscow: Sovetskaya Rossiya, 1985.

Rokossovskaya, A. "Marshal i Grafinya. O Marshale Sovetskogo Soyuza Malinovskom Vspominaet ego Doch'. "*Rossiiskaya Gazeta-Nedelya*. 2010, no. 97, 6 May.

Rokossovskii, K.K. *Soldatskii Dolg*. Moscow: Voennoe Izdatel'stvo, 1997.

—— *Russkii Arkhiv: Velikaya Otechestvennaya Voina. Stavka VGK: Dokumenty i Materialy*. Vol. 16 (5.1-5.4). Moscow: TERRA, 1996-1999.

Sarkis'yan, S.M. *51-ya Armiya. Boevoi Put' 51-i Armii*. Moscow: Voennoe Izdatel'stvo, 1983.

—— *Sevastopol'tsy. Uchastniki 11-Mesyachnoi Oborony Sevastopolya v 1854-1855 Godakh*. Compiled by P. Rerberg. Vypusk 1. St. Petersburg, 1903.

Shchelokov, A.A. *Ya Nachal'nik, Ty—Durak*. Moscow: EKSMO, 2004.

Shtemenko, S.M. *General'nyi Shtab v Gody Voiny*. Moscow: Voennoe Izdatel'stvo, 1989.

Skorzeny, O. *Neizvestnaya Voina*. Translated from the French. Minsk: Popurri, 2012.

Smolin, M.M. "Gosudarstvennoe Opolchenie 1855-1856 gg.: Opyt Prakticheskoi Realizatsii Ofitsial'nykh Ustanovok." *Problemy Rossiiskoi Istorii. Sbornik Statei*. Vypusk III. Magnitogorsk, 2004.

Sokolov, B.V. *Krasnaya Armiya Protiv SS*. Moscow: Yauza; EKSMO, 2008.

Sokolov, B.V. *Krasnyi Koloss. Pochemu Pobedila Krasnaya Armiya*. Moscow: Yauza, EKSMO, 2007.

Sokolov, B.V. *Rokossovskii*. Moscow: Molodaya Gvardiya, 2010.

Somov, L. "Orlinyi Priyut Yunogo Bunina." *Slava Sevastopolya*. 2009, 16 June (http://slava.sebas-topol.ua/2009.6.16/view.21883_orlinyi-priyut-yunogo-bunina.html).

—— *Stalingradskaya Epopeya*. Moscow: Lada IKTTs; Zvonnitsa-MG, 2000.

—— *Svyatogorskii Platsdarm 1941-1943. Dokumenty i Svidetel'stva Uchastnikov Boev*. Compiled by V.N. Dedov. Donetsk, 2008.

—— "Tove: Drevo Roda." (http://www.rgfond.ru/rod/rod_tree.php?idp=125291).

Tsentr Izucheniya Partiinoi Istorii pri Komitete KPK Provintsii Khebei. "Poslednii Vizit Chou-en-Lai v SSSR." *Zhen'min' Zhibao* (Russian-language version). 2009, 30 April (http://russian.people.com.cn/31521/6649117.html).

Ungvary, K. *Battle for Budapest. One Hundred Days in World War II*. Translated from the Hungarian. London-New York: I.B. Tauris & Co., Ltd., 2003. (A.V. Vasil'chenko's book, *100 Dnei v Krovavom Adu. Budapesht-"Dunaiskii Stalingrad"* (Moscow: Yauza-Press, 2008) is an abbreviated translation of the German edition of K. Ungvary's book, but without any kind of references to it. See K. Ungvary, A. Vasil'chenko, *100 Dnei v Krovavom Adu. Budapesht-"Dunaiskii Stalingrad"*. Moscow: Yauza-Press, 2008, 448 pages. *Zhurnal Rossiiskikh i Vostochnoevropeiskikh Istoricheskikh Issledovanii*, no. 1 (3), 2001, pp. 142-143. K. Ungvary's book has now been translated into Russian, but in an abbreviated form and without references. See K. Ungvary. *Osada Budapeshta. Sto Dnei Vtoroi Mirovoi Voiny*. Moscow: Tsentrpoligraf, 2013.

Vasil'ev, V.A. "Russkii Legion Chesti. *Chasovoi*, Brussels. 1981, no. 629. (http://www.xx13.ru/kadeti/rus_korpus.htm#vasiljev).

Vasilevskii, A.M. *Delo Vsei Zhizni*. Moscow: Politicheskoe Izdatel'stvo, 1978.

——"Vospominaniya o Professore L.L. Tove i ego Biografiya." *Izvestiya Tomskogo Tekhnologicheskogo Instituta*. 1918, vol. 39, no. 3, pp. 1-19.

Vvedenskaya, N.D. "Dmitrii Alekseevich Vvedenskii. Pis'ma o Tashkente." (http://mytashkent.uz/2011/07/13/dmitrij-alekseevich-vvedenskij-okonchanie/).

V'yunichenko, S. "Bitva za Slavyansk mogla by na God Priblizit' Pobedu." 8 September 2011. (http://tvplus.dn.ua/pg/news/8/full/id-7608).

Yakovlev, A.N. ed. *Georgii Zhukov. Stenogramma Oktyabr'skogo (1957 g.) Plenuma TsK KPSS i Drugie Dokumenty*. Moscow: Fond "Demokratiya," 2001.

Zakharov, M.V. "Marshal Sovetskogo Soyuza Rodion Malinovskii." *Polkovodtsy i Voenachal'niki Velokoi Otechestvennoi Voiny. Vypusk 1*. Moscow: Molodaya Gvardiya, 1971, pp. 221-256.

Zakharov, M.V. *General'nyi Shtab v Predvoennye Gody*. Moscow: Voennoe Izdatel'stvo, 1989.

Zavizion, G.T., P.A. Kornyushin. *I na Tikhom Okeane…* . Moscow: Voennoe Izdatel'stvo, 1967.

Zhirnov, Ye. "Sem'i Demobilizovannykh Prozhivayut v Zemlyankakh." *Vlast'*. 2006, no. 3, 26 January.

Zhirnov, Ye. "Proizoshel. Uvidel. Pobedil." *Vlast'*. 2006, no. 17-18, 8 May.

Zhirnov, Ye. "Gosudarstvo—eto on. Istoriya Zhizni Mikhaila Smirtyukova—Cheloveka, Prorabotavshevo 60 Let v Kremle, Raskazannaya im Samim." *Vlast'*. 2011, no. 33, 22 August.

Index

INDEX OF PEOPLE

INDEX OF PLACES

INDEX OF RUSSIAN & SOVIET MILITARY FORMATIONS

INDEX OF NON-RUSSIAN/SOVIET MILITARY FORMATIONS & UNITS

Other

Italian forces (in Spain) 112, 114-115, 120, 127, 134, 136-137, 142

Italian forces (eastern front) 173, 195, 207, 209, 333

Mongolian People's Revolutionary Army 339, 341, 347-348

People's Liberation Army of Yugoslavia 311, 321

Royal Armored Corps 240-241, 247

Austro-Hungarian army 42, 111, 268, 286

INDEX OF MISCELLANEOUS & GENERAL TERMS